Success Studybooks

Accounting and Costing
Accounting and Costing: Problems and Projects
Biology
Book-keeping and Accounts
British History 1760–1914
British History since 1914
Business Calculations
Chemistry
Commerce
Commerce: West African Edition
Economic Geography
Economics
Economics: West African Edition
Electronics
Elements of Banking
European History 1815–1941
Financial Accounting
Financial Accounting: Questions and Answers
Geography: Human and Regional
Geography: Physical and Mapwork
Insurance
Investment
Law
Management: Personnel
Mathematics
Nutrition
Office Practice
Organic Chemistry
Principles of Accounting
Principles of Accounting: Answer Book
Statistics
Twentieth Century World Affairs

Success in
TWENTIETH
CENTURY
WORLD AFFAIRS
from 1919 to the 1980s

Jack B. Watson, M.A.

John Murray

© Jack B. Watson 1974, 1977, 1979, 1981, 1984

First published 1974
Reprinted 1975
Reprinted (revised, and with an appendix) 1977
Reprinted (revised, and with a new appendix) 1979
Second edition 1981
Reprinted 1983
Third edition 1984
Reprinted 1985

Typeset by Inforum Ltd, Portsmouth
Printed and bound in Hong Kong by Wing King Tong Co. Ltd.

British Library Cataloguing in Publication Data

Watson, Jack B.
  Success in twentieth century world affairs from
  1919 to the 1980's.—3rd ed.—(Success studybooks)
  1. History, Modern—20th century
  2. World politics—20th century
  I. Title   II. Series
  909.82   D443

  ISBN 0–7195–4068–2

Foreword

This book attempts to outline and explain some of the major developments in contemporary history since the First World War. It is intended for the general reader who seeks understanding of how the problems of our day have come about; it also aims to provide a framework for students who wish to pursue a first course of study in preparation for examinations in schools and colleges.

The author of any book on contemporary history, especially one which rashly takes for its title *World Affairs*, must feel that his feet tread only through quicksand. Whenever he approaches the present day and tries to imprison it in the written pages of history, he is fully aware that the events of today can be perceived only dimly, and that the events of tomorrow may well overturn whatever judgment he has been reckless enough to venture. Yet he *must* make judgments and he *must* be selective, for no single volume can embrace more than a fragment of the history of a century when men and events move faster than ever before. Inevitably much must be omitted.

The historian's problem is to select events which seem, at the time of writing, to be of the greatest importance, and which will continue to be regarded as important in the future, when looked at again in retrospect. The perspective is always changing and this is one of the major hazards that confronts anyone who has the temerity to commit himself to paper on the subject of contemporary history.

In this book my selection of material has been governed by two aims: first, to throw light on events which have already happened, and second, to go some way towards explaining the problems which confront the world in the final quarter of the twentieth century. Thus the book moves steadily outwards from Europe, into the world of the superpowers and the world of the developing nations; from the problems of European frontiers, reparations and unemployment to the problems of under-development, minorities and race relations.

No historian can be totally objective; he is human and his own point of view is bound to show in anything he writes. However, he can try. Here I have tried to maintain as objective a view as possible not only in listing and describing important events, but also in offering comment and explanation which will help the reader towards a fuller understanding of these events. But understanding can only come from individual thought and inquiry and my aim throughout the book is to provoke thought. Students of contemporary history must always hesitate before making assertions too strongly; therefore this book may, at times, seem to be tentative, almost as if asking questions instead of answering them. Too many revolutions in attitudes have already occurred in our century for easy explanations always to lie at hand. On such ground a wise student will readily confess that he does not know all the answers, but he will do his best to arrive at some understanding of the problems we face and how these problems have emerged.

Students who are working for any of the sixteen-plus examinations for which this book is appropriate (including the present 'O' and 'A' levels), or who are studying at pre- or first-year university level, will find a number of aids to study incorporated in the text. The maps and tables are especially important, as is the detailed Index. The cross-references throughout each Unit help the reader to revise or look forward at will, to grasp connections and acquire confidence to move about in time and space. The exercises are designed to encourage not only thought and understanding, but further discovery; they also provide the opportunity to practise writing answers to questions which are typical of modern examination papers. This work requires a personal contribution which goes beyond mere feats of memorizing. Students need first to read the question with care, and then to think out an answer which is relevant. Public examinations today seek, above all, evidence from candidates of their understanding and of their ability to draw on factual information with which to illustrate their answers. In the early part of the book I have given some guidance on tackling questions; later the student should plot his own course, drawing where necessary on the Index and on the suggested further reading lists.

Contemporary history, of course, goes on. This book deals with the world since 1919. It is essentially a story without an end, but a story which every reader may update daily by referring to the news media, a good newspaper or a work of reference such as *Keesing's Archives*. In time, with the benefit of greater hindsight and the knowledge of events which have occurred after the writing of this book, the reader may wish to revise some of its judgments. If he is willing and able to do so, this book will have succeeded in one of its chief aims, that of encouraging the reader and student to develop his own informed opinions on the modern world.

Note to the Third Edition

In this third edition, while preserving the basic framework of the book which has stood the test of time, the coverage of *World Affairs* has been extended into the 1980s and the text substantially revised, in some cases to take advantage of lengthening perspectives. It has been necessary in this updating to take account not only of the many political upheavals in yet another decade of hectic change, but of the growing list of difficulties faced by the modern world. Not least of these has been the dislocation which has seriously afflicted the world economic order since this book first appeared. On the other hand, and in spite of the sluggishness of governments, there is also evidence of an increasingly healthy awareness of the need for radical change and co-operative action between peoples, expressed in documents such as the reports of the Brandt Commission – 'A Programme for Survival' in 1980 and 'Common Crisis: Co-operation for World Recovery' in 1983 – and in the Law-of-the-Sea Treaty in 1982.

The pace of change shows no signs of slackening. As was written in 1974, 'contemporary history . . . goes on' and, though this book is now longer and fuller than it was when first published, the challenge outlined in the final paragraph of the original Foreword remains undiminished. I hope that this new edition of the book may continue to fulfil the purposes for which it was first written, and that it will serve the interests of students and general readers alike who set out in search of some understanding of *Twentieth Century World Affairs*.

J.B.W.

Acknowledgments

Any author who can rely on the candid comment and constructive advice of well-informed colleagues is fortunate. In this respect I have been especially fortunate and I am happy to be able to acknowledge the debt I owe to those who have read this work in the course of its preparation and whose criticisms have undoubtedly done much to improve it. I must thank Sean Garrett who has given me invaluable assistance, not least in relation to the Far East where pitfalls abound to await the unwary westerner; and Edgar Rayner whose ability to take the broad view and at the same time to scrutinize the most minute detail commands the utmost respect of those who have the good fortune to work with him, and who has given me the benefit of his great experience both as a teacher and as a historian of the contemporary world. My thanks go also to Roger Moore who first thought that this work was possible and encouraged its beginning; and to my wife who endured its construction with patience and, with even more patient work on the Index, ensured its end.

I would particularly like to thank Irene Slade and Carolyn Nichols of John Murray who helped at all stages in the publication of the first edition.

But whatever the faults and omissions of the finished book, the responsibility is mine alone. All those mentioned above have undoubtedly done their best to exercise over me that 'restraining influence' upon a 'tendency to over-confident assertion' once referred to by L. C. B. Seaman. If this book provides but a fraction of the pleasure and benefit that I have received from the historical writings of others – not least Bernard Seaman's – the work will have been worth while.

J.B.W.

We are grateful to the following for their kind assistance in providing illustrations:

National Monuments Record (Fig. 1.1); BBC Hulton Picture Library (Figs. 2.1, 3.3, 3.5, 4.2, 5.4, 5.5, 7.3, 8.5, 12.4, 15.3); Barnaby's Picture Library (Figs. 2.5, 9.4, 11.4, 16.4, 18.1, 20.1, 22.1, 22.3); Library of Congress, Washington D.C. (Fig. 2.7); *Philadelphia Daily News* (Fig. 4.3); Keystone Press Agency (Figs. 4.4, 5.2, 10.1, 10.2, 12.2, 14.1, 15.1, 17.3, 20.3, 20.6); Cartoons by David Low by arrangement with Express Newspapers (Figs. 6.2, 8.2, 9.2); Associated Newspapers Group (Figs. 7.2, 11.3, 19.2); *Punch* (Fig. 8.3); Magnum Distribution (Fig. 12.5); Les Gibbard, cartoons from *The Guardian* (Figs. 13.3, 17.4, 19.4, 19.5, 23.1, 23.2); National Press and Information Office, Bonn, West Germany, cartoon from *Simplicissimus* (Fig. 14.2); *New Statesman* (Fig. 15.4); Camera Press (Fig. 15.5); Valtman–Rothco Cartoons (Fig. 21.1); Syndication International (Fig. 21.3); *The Guardian* (Fig. 21.5); Stanley Gibbons (All stamps).

The use of copyright material in the exercises at the end of Units is acknowledged with thanks from the following sources: Asa Briggs, *They Saw It Happen 1897–1940*, Blackwell, 1960 (Unit 3, Exercise 8); H.S. Commager, *Documents of American History*, Vol. 2, Prentice-Hall, 9th edn. 1974 (Unit 1, Exercise 5; Unit 9, Exercise 7); J.A.S. Grenville, *The Major International Treaties 1914–1973*, Methuen, 1974 (Unit 10, Exercise 8; Unit 14, Exercise 10); Sir Nevile Henderson, *Failure of a Mission*, Hodder & Stoughton, 1940 (Unit 5, Exercise 10); R. Morgan, *The Unsettled Peace*, BBC, 1974 (Unit 11, Exercise 8); J. Nyerere, *Ujamaa, Essays on Socialism*, Oxford University Press, Dar es Salaam, 1968 (Unit 22, Exercise 10); Times Newspapers Ltd, *The Times*, 1927 (Unit 7, Exercise 8).

Contents

List of Maps and Diagrams

List of Tables

Unit One
The World in 1919

1.1   1917–19

At two o'clock on the morning of 7 November 1917, the Bolshevik Revolution began in Russia. By daybreak the Bolsheviks (revolutionary communists) had a firm grip on Petrograd, the capital of Russia. Half-disguised in a wig and an old cap, Lenin, the Bolshevik leader, directed the remaining operations from the Smolny Institute, a fashionable girls' school. By nine that evening the Tsar's Winter Palace had fallen to the Bolsheviks, and the world's first communist government had come to power.

A year later, at the eleventh hour of 11 November 1918 an armistice ended the First World War. Germany admitted defeat after a conflict which had raged with devastating results for more than four years. On 18 January 1919, delegates from thirty-two states met in Paris for the Peace Conference which followed the war. They had high hopes of creating a settlement which would clear away Europe's outstanding problems and establish everlasting peace in a world sickened by war.

Of these three dates that of the armistice seemed at the time the most significant. For years afterwards, millions remembered 11 November 1918 with an annual two minutes' silence – remembering the precise moment when the terrible toll of human life had ended. Looking back, however, the date of the armistice was perhaps the least significant of the three, important though it was in ending a war which had taken over twelve million lives. Those who had expected the Bolshevik success to be temporary were proved mistaken, and 7 November 1917 turned out to be one of the outstanding dates in world history. Communist Russia made great strides after 1917, and developed within some thirty years into a superpower capable of challenging the United States of America. The Peace Conference too assumed a new significance in later years. Although its opening in January 1919 attracted plenty of attention, preliminary agreements seemed already to have paved the way for a settlement. It was generally believed that the First World War had been 'the war to end wars', 'the final war for human liberty'. A future war seemed unthinkable: the politicians were expected quickly to produce treaties which would solve Europe's problems and lay the foundations of future progress. Only later did men see January 1919 as the time when *new* problems began to take shape.

The First World War began in Europe in 1914, developing out of the quarrels of Europeans, and it remained predominantly European. Most of the fighting took place in Europe where the *Central Powers* (Germany, Austria–

Hungary and their allies) were locked in conflict with Britain, France, Russia and their allies. Many of the European states possessed great overseas empires and these too were inevitably caught up in the struggle. So too was Japan, bound to Britain by the alliance of 1902. The war thus sprawled like a plague across the world, reaching into Africa, the Middle East and the Far East and dragging in combatants from India and Australasia. The USA joined the war against Germany in 1917, angered by the activities of German submarines and German intrigue in Mexico. But Americans regarded it as a war to be settled 'Over There', that is in Europe.

Fig. 1.1 The Royal Artillery War Memorial, Hyde Park Corner, London. Thousands of war memorials in Britain and elsewhere provided evidence of the universal horror with which the First World War was remembered

When the war ended in 1918, the main problems certainly seemed to be European ones. The stability of Europe had been in doubt for some years before the war, yet Europeans still regarded their continent as the centre of importance in the world. Few nations existed outside Europe which could compete with European states in wealth. Although the United States possessed both wealth and power, Europeans consoled themselves that most Americans were of European descent. Elsewhere, it still seemed proper that

Europeans should control large overseas empires. Europeans (and even Americans) thought it reasonable to assume that the settlement of European problems would lead automatically to the settlement of world problems.

1.2   Europe

The search for solutions to Europe's problems at the end of the First World War began among the presumed reasons for the beginning of that war. It was soon fashionable to believe that all would be well in international relations if, in addition to setting up a *League of Nations* (an association of countries which settled problems by agreement), there could be yet another adjustment to the balance of power in Europe and an extension of nation states, republics and democracy.

The *balance of power* was an old problem. It meant that no power must remain strong enough to threaten another, and no alliance of powers should dominate other alliances. In practice, a satisfactory balance of power meant that one's enemies should not be strong enough to be dangerous. In 1918 it was assumed that the victorious powers would settle the problem of the balance of power by weakening their defeated enemies, because it was the Central Powers who had caused the First World War to occur.

People also believed war had been brought about by discontent among nationalities trapped in the empires of Austria–Hungary and Turkey. It followed that if each nationality was allowed to set up a *nation state* (one people, with a government of the people's choice), Europe would become more stable. It became fashionable to believe in self-determination although politicians used a variety of words to explain what this meant. Woodrow Wilson, President of the USA, laid down *Fourteen Points* as a basis for the negotiation of peace and referred to 'frontiers along clearly recognizable lines of nationality', 'autonomous development' and 'self-development'. He explained that his objective was 'justice to all peoples and nationalities'. David Lloyd George, Prime Minister of Britain, had earlier outlined his plan for a new Europe 'based on such grounds of reason and justice as will give some promise of stability'. Spelling out the details he too had spoken of 'self-government' and the 'recognition of separate national conditions'. Thus the Austrian and Turkish Empires were broken into fragments and many new states appeared on the map, among them Czechoslovakia and Jugoslavia. Some of the new nation states were also created from the empire which had once belonged to the Tsar of Russia, among them the Baltic states of Latvia and Lithuania. Although Russia had not been on the losing side in the recent war, the upheavals of 1917 had forced her to make an early peace with Germany, and had deprived the Russians of the power to resist major changes to their western boundaries.

The development of many new nation states made the map of Europe (and the Middle East) more complicated. Nevertheless, there was hope that, by removing the old European empires which had been the setting for so many

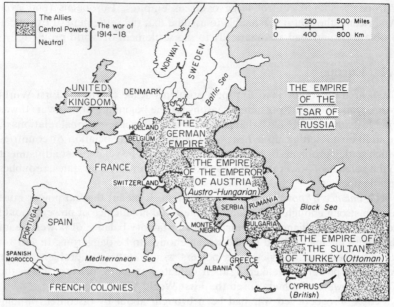

Fig. 1.2 Europe in 1914

crises before 1914, the nationalities of Europe would now rest content in their own nation states.

Many of the new nation states were *republics*. If greedy kings and emperors had contributed to bringing about the First World War, their removal from power seemed justified. Of the principal victorious powers in the war, France and the USA were already republics and the British would have argued that their monarchy, long since subdued by parliament, was not a greedy one.

The Russians had already deposed their Tsar in 1917. The defeated powers deposed their monarchies too. The Hohenzollerns ceased to rule Germany in 1918 and the Weimar Republic was established instead. About the same time, the Habsburgs, who had ruled the vast multi-racial Austro-Hungarian Empire, also went into exile, and the Sultan of Turkey survived only until 1922. Almost everywhere, the colourful pageantry of pre-war monarchy gave way to the humdrum gatherings of republicans and parliamentarians in sober suits and bowler hats. Where kings remained, in Britain and Belgium for example, they kept their thrones but had long since lost their powers. The lounge suit became the symbol of a Europe freed from the greedy ambitions of Hohenzollerns and Habsburgs, a Europe, it was hoped, 'made safe for democracy'.

The British, French and Americans had great faith in democracy. They could think of no more modern system of government than one in which the people elected their leaders and shared in determining their policies. The

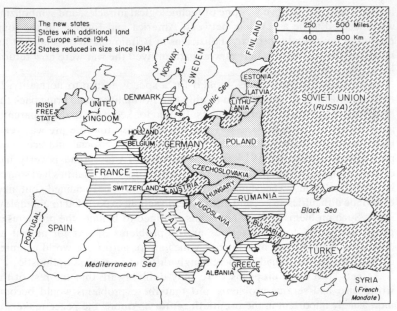

Fig. 1.3 Europe in 1923

soberly-dressed politicians whom the people elected might well lack glamour but they seemed to guarantee stability and decency. The defeated Central Powers and the new nation states were urged to follow the excellent example of the victors and establish democracies. Revolutionary Russia was an embarrassment, however: communism hardly fitted neatly into the new arrangements being made for Europe.

The Bolsheviks gained power in Russia under the leadership of Vladimir Lenin. Lenin believed that the bourgeois democracy of Western Europe was already outdated and that it was soon to be replaced by communism. He and his supporters confidently expected a wave of communist revolutions elsewhere, most probably in Britain and Germany. Industrial unrest had reached dangerous levels in pre-war Britain, and the war had imposed new strains on capitalist society and brought defeat and confusion to Germany. The Bolsheviks were wrong, however, in predicting that their own revolution would be followed immediately by other communist successes. Communists achieved power only in Hungary and even there, their leader, Bela Kun, was driven into exile after only four months. In Russia the Bolsheviks themselves had to struggle to remain in control, resorting to 'the dictatorship of the proletariat' (see Section 5.1).

Neither democracy nor communism in fact succeeded in making Europe stable in the years after the First World War. But in 1919 Europeans were optimistic. Alcock and Brown flew across the Atlantic in that year, confirming the view that the new age was one of technological miracles, and symbolizing what seemed to be a new link between America and Europe for the joint pursuit of peace and prosperity. Politicians in Britain talked of 'a land fit for heroes to live in', and the heroes who had survived the war were now returning to their families.

Europeans, like Americans, looked for a speedy return to normality. In their optimism, they assumed too readily that normality would bring back the best but not the worst of former times. Britain looked back to the apparently golden days of 1913. But she was quickly reminded that the pre-war years had not been golden and that the war had made her social and economic problems worse. In pre-1914 Britain, slums and widespread poverty had existed alongside apparent national prosperity. Grave inequalities had soured industrial relations. The slums, poverty and sourness remained, but new economic difficulties arose, and difficulties in selling exports led to unemployment. Such problems were by no means confined to Britain: the problems of peace threatened to be as serious as the problems of war for almost all countries. An epidemic of influenza which swept across the world claiming over six million lives made it increasingly difficult to remain optimistic.

As yet, however, Europeans were only dimly aware that the rest of the world also had serious problems and that these problems would become increasingly important in the twentieth century. Among the peace-makers in Europe in 1919 there were vague ideas of doing justice to these areas and peoples in the future, but the matter did not seem to be a particularly urgent one. The immediate problem for Europeans (and therefore for the world) was the settlement of Europe.

1.3   European Colonial Empires

A map of overseas colonial empires in 1914 shows instantly that few areas of the world had escaped European attention. The strength and prestige of the powers of Western Europe were sometimes judged by their overseas possessions. Austria–Hungary, Turkey and Russia sprawled across vast areas of Europe and Asia and their empires were huge blocks of land. For countries like Britain, France and Holland, empire had a different meaning. It meant possessions scattered across the whole world.

The British claimed a quarter of the world's territories and population. They had settled the almost uninhabited areas of Australia and Canada and imposed their authority on the crowded lands of India. In the last, almost frantic age of empire-building at the end of the nineteenth century, Europeans had carved up Africa and Britain had insisted on a major share. In 1914, therefore, subject peoples from almost every corner of the world joined her in the struggle against the Central Powers. To the British, as to all Europeans, the first duty of subjects in the colonies was to obey the instructions of the mother country.

By 1914, the only African states which remained free from European

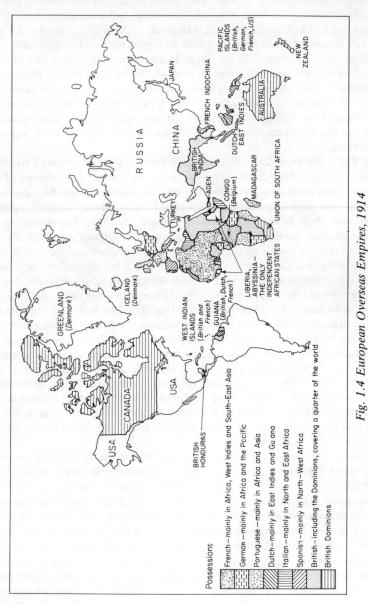

Fig. 1.4 European Overseas Empires, 1914

Possessions

French – mainly in Africa, West Indies and South-East Asia

German – mainly in Africa and the Pacific

Portuguese – mainly in Africa and Asia

Dutch – mainly in East Indies and Gu ana

Italian – mainly in North and East Africa

Spanish – mainly in North–West Africa

British – including the Dominions, covering a quarter of the world

British Dominions

control were Abyssinia and Liberia. The rest of the huge continent had fallen to the British, French, Germans, Italians, Belgians, Portuguese and Spaniards. South-East Asia had been seized earlier, by the British, French and Dutch, and earlier still, Western Europeans had monopolized the West Indies and much of South America. However, in these last areas the tide had already turned, and independent South American nations had emerged, such as Brazil and Argentina. In the West Indies, too, some states had already seized independence, Haiti from France and Cuba from Spain. Elsewhere, China had recently become a republic and had preserved some independence against European ambitions, though not without losing many of her ports, including Hong Kong. Nevertheless, at the beginning of the twentieth century, the European passion for empire-building showed little signs of weakening.

In 1919, the colonies of the defeated powers were transferred to other rulers, although this was not simply a device to enlarge the empires of the victors. Such colonies were known as *mandated territories* of the League of Nations (see page 40). The League would be responsible for their welfare; meanwhile their new masters would prepare them for independence. In almost all cases the new masters were Europeans. Although mandated territories were to be prepared for independence (and other colonies might also expect independence at some time in the future), hardly any of these territories were considered close to it in 1919. Europeans who were victorious in the First World War expected to rule their empires for many more years. Those who had lost in that war argued that they had been robbed, prematurely, of their colonies. Nevertheless, Montagu, the British Secretary of State for India, had cautiously declared that Britain's policy would be 'the gradual development of self-governing institutions, with a view to the progressive realization of responsible government in India as an integral part of the British Empire'. This was far from satisfactory for those Indian nationalists who wanted instant independence. It meant no more than that Indians would gradually be allowed to share in governing their country with a vague suggestion that they might eventually take control, although still within the British Empire.

Britain, however, had a special problem. Within the British Empire were four states into which there had been extensive European immigration. Australia and New Zealand were peopled mainly by the British and their descendants. The same was true of Canada, which also contained many of French descent. None of these states had a large native population. In South Africa, native Africans heavily outnumbered white settlers but the whites were numerous enough to dominate the country. Already, Australia, New Zealand, Canada and South Africa were known as the *Dominions*, and they possessed extensive rights of self-government. One of the most urgent problems for the British was to clarify the status of these Dominions. Soon after the war, their claims for independence were accepted, and a new name was adopted to replace the British Empire (although the old name continued to be used too). Britain and the Dominions were said to be linked in the *British Commonwealth of Nations*, suggesting a partnership of equals (see Sections 6.1 and 6.2). Thus Europeans were admitting the equality of *some* peoples outside Europe. These peoples, however, had close ties with Europe and they were white.

1.4   The United States of America

Europeans were uncomfortably aware that the USA was the richest country in the world in 1919. In spite of their involvement in the First World War, the Americans had increased their gold reserves by almost £300 million since 1914. Britain had borrowed £959 million and France £634 million from the United States; Europe was, therefore, in debt. Europe had also suffered far heavier casualties than the USA, and while American industries had expanded their production and were now well placed to achieve even greater success in world markets, European states were war-ravaged and their economies unhealthy.

No European country could now hope to exert the same influence in the world as the USA. The balance of industrial power was obviously shifting. Even by 1911, the USA's steel production was almost equal to the combined production of Germany, Britain and France. Her coal production was at that time over one-and-a-half times that of Britain, the world's leading industrial power in the nineteenth century. By 1920, American coal production was approximately twice that of Britain and Germany combined. In the twenty years before 1914, American exporters had increased their total sales almost six-fold. The USA, after 1918, seemed certain to be the most powerful economic force in the world.

In the years before 1914 Americans had shown a growing interest in the Pacific and the Caribbean, and in the affairs of China and of Latin America,

Table 1.1   **What governments spent on the First World War***

Allies	£m	Central Powers	£m
Britain	7 800	Germany	8 400
France	5 400	Austrian Empire	4 600
Russia	5 000	Bulgaria and Turkish	
USA	5 000	Empire	500
Italy	2 700		
British Empire	1 000		
Total	28 000	Total	13 500

* Figures adapted from Purnell's *History of the Twentieth Century*, Vol. 2, page 882.

but they were less involved with Europe. In 1914, they tried hard to keep out of Europe's war. Many Americans were of European origin, anxious to turn their backs on Europe and its problems. President Wilson saw the USA's role as that of mediator and peace-maker, not as that of a belligerent. Ties between the English-speaking peoples, however, and the USA's increasing financial and commercial interest in the victory of the Allies meant that neutrality failed to last: in 1917 the USA declared war on Germany.

Wilson led an American delegation to the Peace Conference in Paris in 1919 and seemed to bring with him for the first time a positive US willingness to be involved in Europe's peacetime affairs. That was Wilson's intention, since US involvement in Europe and the League of Nations might well help to guarantee peace. For many Americans, however, such involvement meant entanglement in European quarrels of which they wanted no part: they too wished to return to normality, and the USA's close relations with Europe ended when Wilson returned from the Peace Conference. Europe was thus deprived of the USA's powerful influence and, when new problems arose, they could only be referred to a League of Nations of which the United States refused to be a member. Britain and France were left as the League's major powers while, after 1920, the USA steadfastly steered clear of all political commitments. The Americans could not remain entirely aloof from Europe's economic problems, but US governments were determined that Europeans must solve their own political problems.

1.5   The Far East

Japan's part in the First World War involved little more than the occupation of German islands in the Pacific and German holdings in China. During the war, she increased her gold reserves by nearly £200 million, and her shipping losses were negligible. While European rivals threw their energies into production for the war, Japan made steady progress in developing her foreign trade and expanding industrial output. At the end of the war, her textile industry not only supplied domestic needs but was poised to make inroads into other British markets, including those in India. Europeans, in future, would face formidable competition from Japan. Moreover, Japan was without a serious Asiatic rival. Large areas of the Far East were still European colonial possessions. Russia had been routed by Japan in the Russo-Japanese War of 1904–5 and, in 1919, was quite unable to exert any influence in the Pacific. China was equally feeble.

Japan's involvement in the First World War, on the winning side, gave her a place at the Peace Conference. In spite of being allowed to keep many of the Pacific islands, the delegation was dissatisfied. Japan was quick to resent what seemed to be an indifference to non-European nations at the Conference, an indifference perhaps to those who were not white. On the other hand, Europeans and Americans were suspicious of what appeared to be Japan's aggressiveness, both in her attitude towards China and in her enthusiasm for intervening in the Russian civil war. After 1919 Japan was soon to establish herself as a major power, dominating the Pacific and making more demands on China.

Further Reading

Elliott, F.: *A Dictionary of Politics*, Penguin (Harmondsworth, 1970). This is a useful reference book from which to gain more detailed definitions of words such as *Communism, Democracy, Fascism*.

Gibbons, S.R. and Morican, P.: *World War One*. Longman (Harlow, 1965).

Remak, J.: *The First World War: Causes, Conduct, Consequences*. Wiley (Chichester, 1971).

Taylor, A.J.P.: *From Sarajevo to Potsdam*. Thames and Hudson (London, 1966). Chapter 1 provides another introduction to the period.

Watson, J.B.: *Success in European History 1815–1941*. John Murray (London, 1981). This book provides a European background to the First World War and its aftermath.

Watson, J.B.: *Success in British History since 1914*. John Murray (London, 1983). Unit 1 provides a British background to postwar problems and developments.

Watson, J.B.: *Empire to Commonwealth, 1919 to 1970*. Dent (London, 1971). Chapters 1 and 2 provide further information about the British Empire before and after the First World War.

Exercises

1. Using reference books (such as a dictionary or *A Dictionary of Politics* (above)) and the Index to this book, work out for yourself the meaning of the following terms: Democracy; Communism; Nationalist; Nation State; Empire; Overseas Empire; Republic; Balance of Power; Gold Reserves.
2. Compare the maps of Europe in 1914 and 1923 (Figs. 1.2 and 1.3). Write down the most important ways in which Europe had changed by 1923, compared with the map of the continent in 1914. Which of the terms listed in Question 1 may be used in accounting for the changes in European boundaries?
3. Show what support you can find in this Unit for *each* of the following arguments:
   (*a*) that Europeans in 1919 still thought Europe the most important area of the world;
   (*b*) that 1919 seemed likely to be the start of a more hopeful period in world affairs;
   (*c*) that the USA and Japan emerged from the First World War with increased strength.
4. Practise using the cross-references in this Unit, and the Index, to find out more about the Bolsheviks (page 5), mandated territories (page 8) and the British Commonwealth of Nations (page 9).
5. Using the references in this Unit to the USA and *each* of the following short extracts, write a brief account of US relations with Europe from 1914 to 1920.

> The United States must be neutral in fact as well as in name during these days that are to try men's souls. We must be impartial in thought as well as in action, must put a curb upon our sentiments as well as upon every transaction that might be construed as a preference of one party to the struggle before another.
> (*Woodrow Wilson, August 1914*)

With a profound sense of the solemn . . . step I am taking . . . , I advise that the Congress declare the recent course of the Imperial German Government to be in fact nothing less than war against the government and people of the United States; that it formally accept the status of belligerent which has been thrust upon it. (*Woodrow Wilson, April 1917*)

The United States assumes no obligation to preserve the territorial integrity or political independence of any other country by the employment of its military or naval forces, its resources, or any form of economic discrimination, or to interfere in any way in controversies between nations. (*Part of a Resolution debated in the US Congress, March 1920*)

Unit Two
The Peace Settlement of 1919–20

2.1 The Dead in the First World War

Those killed in the armed forces of the principal countries engaged in the war are shown in Table 2.1.

Table 2.1 The dead in the First World War

Allies	Dead	Central Powers	Dead
Russia	1 700 000	Germany	1 773 700
France	1 357 800	Austria–Hungary	1 200 000
British Empire	908 371	Turkey	325 000
Italy	650 000		
Rumania	335 706		
United States	116 516	*All belligerents*	8 528 831

These figures do not include those who survived to emerge from the war blind, maimed or mentally deranged. The First World War was the most bloody that the world had ever experienced. The horrors of the conflict, not least the terrible war of attrition on the Western Front, made such a profound impression that to most people a repetition of such barbarism seemed unthinkable. When the statesmen gathered for the Peace Conference the war was horribly fresh in their minds. Their basic aim was everlasting peace. The world, and especially Europe, had had its fill of misery: such a war must never occur again.

2.2 The Peace Conference, Paris, 1919

There was no disagreement about the basic aim when the Conference opened in January 1919. There had been much preliminary agreement among the victors, and even long before the armistice, war aims had been defined and points of detail agreed. Nevertheless, fundamental differences remained about the best ways to secure future peace and stability.

The Treaty of Versailles, which dealt with Germany, was presented to the German delegation in May. For four months the victorious powers had hammered out the details. It seemed proper to them that they should work out the terms of the Settlement and then present it to the defeated. The Germans said that they were dictating the terms, that it was hardly a peace agreement at all: it was a *Diktat*, an imposed treaty.

Behind this controversy lay the fundamental dilemma of the entire Settlement. The peace-makers genuinely wanted future peace, but they also wanted to punish the guilty. Europe's problems would be settled in a manner which seemed fitting to the victors, and the victors found it difficult to distinguish on occasions between that which would make future peace more likely and that which brought them revenge for their recent suffering. The French argued that the harsh treatment of Germany was itself essential to future peace. The balance of power must be adjusted so that Germany could never again threaten her western neighbours. The British and Americans disputed the degree of harshness which was necessary, but the principle was accepted. Thus the Settlement tried to combine idealistic solutions to old problems with an element of retribution. Self-determination, republicanism and democracy (see Unit One) would create a new Europe; the League of Nations would be a new world authority to bring about international harmony, but, at the same time, old scores against the defeated Central Powers would be paid off.

Paris was chosen to be the centre for the Settlement. The area around the city could offer a variety of convenient palaces, which gave their names to the separate treaties dealing with the defeated powers. Austria was dealt with at St Germain, Hungary at Trianon, Bulgaria at Neuilly and Turkey at Sèvres. Germany was dealt with at Versailles, the most glorious palace but also the scene of France's humiliation after the Franco-Prussian war of 1871, when the Germans had held there the ceremony at which the new German Empire was established.

Paris in 1919 was not the ideal place in which to make a fair-minded Settlement. All the delegates were under pressure. Lloyd George reported the difficulties under which they worked: 'Stones clattering on the roof and crashing through the windows, and sometimes wild men screaming through the keyholes.' Most of the advice which flooded over the peace-makers was 'to make Germany pay'. Even in Britain it was popular to affirm that Germany should be 'squeezed until the pips squeaked'.

Non-Europeans like Jan Smuts of South Africa found this passion for vengeance exasperating and difficult to reconcile with hopes of future goodwill. But the Settlement was firmly in the hands of Britain, France and the United States. Its course was directed by the Council of Ten, to which each of the five principal Allies (the USA, Britain, France, Italy and Japan) contributed two members. Neither Italy nor Japan, however, exerted much influence on the Council. Most of the decisions, in fact, emerged from agreements between the Prime Ministers of Britain and France and the President of the USA.

David Lloyd George was re-elected Prime Minister of Britain at the end of 1918. During the election campaign it became obvious that there was a widespread belief that Germany should be punished, and there was much talk of hanging the Kaiser, William II, who was held personally to blame for the war. As a wartime Prime Minister and as a politician seeking popularity and votes, Lloyd George had contributed to the hatred which many felt for the Germans. Wartime propaganda could not now easily be forgotten, but in so far as there was a voice of moderation among the Big Three at the Peace Conference, it was the voice of Lloyd George.

Lloyd George went to the Conference with many ideas for future peace. He had made known his war aims at least a year previously. 'We want peace,' he said. 'We want a peace which will be just but not vindictive. We want a stern peace. . . . The crime demands it. But its severity must be designed not to gratify vengeance but to vindicate justice.' Reparations were imposed upon Germany to make her pay for the war. Lloyd George wished to scale them down, but he got little assistance from the Americans and met downright hostility from the French. Here and there, in Silesia, for example, he was able to obtain slightly better terms for Germany, but on Germany's western frontiers Lloyd George could make little headway against the determination of the French. Once the principle of punishment had been accepted, it was difficult to be too pernickety about its extent.

Lloyd George certainly raised his voice for moderation in Paris, urging his colleagues to act as 'impartial arbiters, forgetful of the passions of war', and appealing to 'all reasonable opinion'. But the British Prime Minister was always a controversial figure with a capacity for attracting a bad press. Goodwill towards the defeated was not a popular cause and Lloyd George was attacked in both press and parliament for his lack of ruthlessness.

Woodrow Wilson, on the other hand, was regarded among European intellectuals as a high-minded idealist who came to Paris almost as a neutral. He had been first elected President of the USA in 1912, with an unprecedented majority, but when he arrived in Europe the Democrats had already suffered losses in the elections of 1918, and Wilson's support in the American Congress had been undermined. He was well placed, nevertheless, to stand aside from the revengeful passions which moved Europeans. He genuinely sought a just Settlement and contributed many constructive ideas, and the myth developed that Lloyd George was in some ways a go-between who tried to bridge the gap between the ferocity of the French and the idealism of the Americans. Wilson emerged from the Paris Conference with an enhanced reputation. In fact, the American President had agreed that there was a need to punish Germany and, though he came to be regarded as the founding-father of the League of Nations, he had taken up that idea rather late when others had prepared much of the ground. He also had a talent for making enemies, seeming self-righteous, obsessed with his own views and intolerant of others. The essential soundness of Wilson's aims was sometimes obscured by the manner in which he defended them, and he was not an easy man to work with. If Wilson and Lloyd George had been able to work in closer harmony a more moderate as well as a more coherent Settlement might have been produced.

Both, it turned out, had frequently to give way to Clemenceau, the veteran Prime Minister of France who presided over the Peace Conference. He had

Fig. 2.1 Clemenceau, Woodrow Wilson and Lloyd George at the Paris Peace Conference, 1919

thorough-going ideas for the humiliation of Germany. He had already earned the nickname 'the Tiger'. If Clemenceau had his way Germany would never again be strong enough to harm France. The Prime Minister was an old man, and twice in his lifetime he had seen German troops on French soil. He wanted immediate compensation for French losses in the recent war and guarantees that Germany could never strike again. Neither Britain nor America had been invaded by the Germans; it was difficult, therefore, to persuade the French to moderate their demands. Indeed, the lack of co-operation between Lloyd George and Clemenceau nearly caused a breakdown of the treaty negotiations at one point.

Not one of the Big Three survived long in office after the Peace Conference. Frenchmen thought that Clemenceau had not done enough, that Germany had been left alarmingly strong. In retirement, before his death in 1929, the old man brooded on the German problem and wrote his memoirs under the title *The Grandeur and Misery of Victory*. Lloyd George, after a troubled ministry from 1918 to 1922, lost the support of the electors and never again held office, although he continued to produce new ideas which lesser statesmen contrived to ignore. Wilson returned to America to campaign for active American involvement in world affairs, but by the end of 1919 he had collapsed and remained an invalid until his death in 1924.

Meanwhile, the American electorate rejected his party. Electors in all three countries had expressed their lack of confidence in their representatives at the Peace Conference.

Elsewhere, there was equal dissatisfaction. Neither Italy nor Japan thought that her rightful claims had been met. The defeated Central Powers saw the Settlement as one which added humiliation to defeat and hardship. The optimism which had followed the armistice found it difficult to survive the peace.

2.3   The Basis of the Settlement

In spite of the apparently harsh verdict of electors almost everywhere, the Peace Settlement contained much to recommend it, and many of its ideas were constructive. It aimed, ambitiously, to do far more than merely share out the spoils of the recent war. In spite of the pressures of the need to work quickly, appease public opinion and grapple with urgent domestic problems at the same time, the statesmen produced a remarkably comprehensive Settlement in view of the vastness of the problems. Undoubtedly, it could have been more coherent. The principles on which it was based were not always consistently applied; parts of the Settlement were vindictive, and above all, it failed to bring a period of stability and prosperity even to Europe. But amendments to the Settlement began almost as soon as it was written, and if organizations such as the League of Nations did not work as successfully as the peace-makers hoped they would, the fault lay less with the peace-makers than with the next generation of statesmen. Hitler's aggressive disregard of the Treaty of Versailles stemmed more from Hitler's aggressiveness than from the alleged faults in the Treaty.

Fig. 2.2 French suffering in the First World War had much to do with the outcome of the Peace Settlement. This French war widow stamp was issued in 1917 to assist relief work

Unit One has already mentioned some of the basic ideas on which the Settlement was founded. When the peace-makers arrived in Paris there was already general agreement on basic principles. In January 1918 both Lloyd George and Woodrow Wilson had made statements of their war aims. Lloyd George announced *Britain's War Aims* to trade unionists in London, and Wilson announced America's aims, the *Fourteen Points*, to the United States

Congress (see Sections 1.2 and 2.11). There was little disagreement about the aims in principle, though many of the Allies had reservations about precise meanings and detailed application. When they surrendered, the Germans agreed to accept a Settlement on the basis of the Fourteen Points. But the peace-makers also had other agreements to honour, and sometimes there was conflict. When Italy agreed to join the war against the Central Powers in 1915 a Treaty of London was signed which promised Italy territories such as Trieste and South Tyrol. Such promises had now to be matched with the later statements. Wilson had stated that Italy's frontiers should be 'along clearly recognizable lines of nationality', and he protested that the Treaty of London, previously secret, did not uphold this principle.

It remained clear, however, that much of the Settlement would be on the basis of nation states, created from the old European and Turkish Empires. Both Lloyd George and Wilson had stated this as part of their aims; both had insisted, for example, that an independent state of Poland should be established; both had marked the Austrian and Turkish Empires for breaking up.

There was also agreement that individual states such as Belgium and France should be restored completely. Lloyd George spoke of 'reparation' to Belgium, although Wilson used the words 'evacuated and restored'. Both agreed that Alsace-Lorraine, taken by Germany from France in 1871, must be returned to France.

Lloyd George and Wilson also agreed that the settlement of overseas colonial problems must be just. Both mentioned the interests of the inhabitants of these colonies as being of importance.

In some ways, Wilson went further than the British Prime Minister. Whereas Lloyd George spoke briefly of international law, the sanctity of treaties and an international organization, Wilson began his Fourteen Points by insisting on open diplomacy, freedom of navigation, freedom of trade and the reduction of armaments, and the last of the Points looked forward to an association of nations.

It remained, at Paris, to translate all these general statements into specific and detailed agreements. This difficult task must also be accomplished without the presence of representatives from Russia. In January 1918 Lloyd George had found it impossible to state precisely Britain's War Aims with regard to Russia. At that time the Bolshevik government was trying to get out of the war by making a separate peace with Germany. From its beginning Lenin had condemned the First World War as one in which 'hired slaves' in one country fought against 'hired slaves' in another. He argued that the working classes should fight not against each other but against capitalism and the bourgeoisie. If Russia now abandoned the war her western allies feared that Germany would be free to switch her troops to the Western Front, and Russia would be guilty of a sort of treachery. Lloyd George ended vaguely by remarking that 'Russia can only be saved by her own people'. Wilson was equally vague, although he looked forward to 'the evacuation of all Russian territory', to leaving the Russians to sort out their own affairs, and he recommended 'unselfish sympathy' towards them.

Russia had made a separate treaty with Germany, at Brest-Litovsk (see Section 2.8), where the Germans showed little of that charity which they later claimed should be extended to themselves. Civil war then developed in Russia. The Western powers forgot their intentions of leaving the Russians alone and tried to intervene, against the Bolsheviks (see Section 5.1(*b*)). They could hardly, at the same time, invite the Bolsheviks to the Peace Conference in Paris, and so the victors made the Settlement without their Russian ex-ally. Some discussions were eventually held with the Bolsheviks, well away from Paris, but little came of them. It was generally believed in the West that the Bolsheviks would not survive. There were protests against having dealings with them at all.

The Settlement, therefore, attempted to produce treaties based upon the Fourteen Points. This involved remaking the map of Europe and of other parts of the world and trying to create, through the League of Nations (see Section 2.9(*b*)), the machinery for more civilized behaviour in international affairs. Combined with the Fourteen Points, however, was an attempt to punish, although it was not one of the aims of the Settlement that the victors should simply collect booty. Lloyd George had argued that 'the destruction or disruption of Germany or the German people' was *not* a war aim. The Allies' aim was more constructive than that. By weakening Germany in Europe, they hoped to protect France and Belgium and to make the continent more stable; by imposing reparations, they hoped to compensate those to whom the war had been costly in lives and property; by dismantling the German overseas Empire, they intended to secure a better future for the peoples in the ex-German colonies. It was one of Hitler's delusions that Germany was robbed in 1919 by international pirates preying upon the defeated.

2.4   How Germany was Treated: the Treaty of Versailles

Lloyd George had asked for 'a stern peace'. The Treaty of Versailles, which the Germans were required to sign in June 1919, was certainly 'stern'. But it did not justify the frenzy of hatred and self-pity with which Hitler taught Germans to regard it. Article 231 of the Treaty rapidly became notorious:

> The Allied and Associated Governments affirm, and Germany accepts, the responsibility of Germany and her allies for causing all the loss and damage to which the Allied and Associated Governments and their nationals have been subjected as a consequence of the war imposed upon them by the aggression of Germany and her allies.

This was the 'War Guilt Clause'. It developed from the undertaking which Germany had accepted at the armistice to pay compensation to Allied civilians. In the Treaty it appeared to have become an over-simplified explanation of how the war began and an extension of Germany's obligation to pay compensation. Although in many ways the rest of the Treaty was often

Fig. 2.3 Germany: the Treaty of Versailles

remarkable for its moderation, Germans insisted on extracting from Article 231 the maximum humiliation. The Allies were guilty of slipshod wording. It was absurd to suggest that Germany alone had brought about the First World War. It was equally absurd of the Germans to take the 'War Guilt Clause' in isolation and pretend that on this alone the Settlement of Europe was based. Nevertheless, what Germany lost and what Germany was made to pay came to be regarded as the foundations on which the whole Peace Settlement was built.

The list of the provisions of the Treaty of Versailles (see page 38) and the map of Germany (Fig. 2.3) show the European territories which Germany lost. Two large areas, Alsace-Lorraine and the Polish Corridor, were seized outright. For the French, there could be no further argument about Alsace-Lorraine. The provinces must be restored to France which had mourned their loss to Germany since 1871. The city of Paris had sorrowfully veiled its monument to the city of Strasbourg (in Alsace) since that time and the French quickly pointed out that, by demonstrations, the people of Alsace had already frequently shown their hostility to German rule. French honour must now be satisfied.

Poland, it was decided, must have access to the sea and so most of Poznania and West Prussia were taken from Germany to provide Poland with a corridor of land to the Baltic. This corridor divided East Prussia from the rest of Germany. Germans bitterly resented its existence and it was this area which was in dispute when the Second World War began in Europe, in 1939.

Comparatively small areas of land were transferred to Belgium, Denmark and, eventually, Lithuania. Germany was deprived of the port of Danzig and, for the time being, of the Saar. The new state of Poland gained part of Silesia. In many of these areas, *plebiscites* were held, partly owing to the arguments of Lloyd George, so that the local people could determine where the boundaries should be drawn. Thus the principle of self-determination was upheld.

The plebiscites saved for Germany some two-thirds of Upper Silesia, a small area of southern Schleswig. the Allenstein and Marienwerder districts of East Prussia and, in due course, the Saar. Most of the plebiscites were held in 1920–1 but the Treaty stated that the Saar would be controlled by the League of Nations for fifteen years. Only then could its inhabitants vote upon their future. In the meantime, Saar coal mines would be in the hands of the French. (In 1935, the Saar plebiscite was held and 90 per cent of its people voted for reunion with Germany, which was promptly agreed.)

The plebiscites made it difficult to argue, unless one claimed, unconvincingly, that the votes were 'rigged', that the victors had gone all out to grab German land. Germany lost about 13 per cent of her European territory. These areas, however, contained some important economic resources. Lorraine was rich in iron ore, Upper Silesia and the Saar in coal. Alsace had a thriving textile industry. Danzig, of which the League of Nations took control, was an important port. Germans therefore pointed out that their true losses were:

Iron production	48%
Coal production	16%
Agricultural output	15%
Industrial output	10%

And to this list were to be added other grievous losses. The German overseas Empire was wiped out: Germany lost all her territories in Africa, China and the Pacific, most of them, such as German East Africa (Tanganyika), German South-West Africa, the Cameroons and Togoland, becoming mandates of the League of Nations (see page 40). German trade was handicapped by the loss of many treaty rights such as those which existed in China.

The German war machine was also crippled. West of the Rhine, and in some small areas east of the river, the Allies placed armies of occupation, to remain for fifteen years. Without time limit, Germany was to demilitarize all lands east of the Rhine for a distance of over thirty miles. This area was to be free from German troops and German fortifications, a safety buffer to protect France. The French would have liked to go further and make the whole area independent of Germany but that was totally unacceptable. The German army was limited to a force of 100 000, her air force abolished and her navy, with some limited exceptions, was to be handed over to the Allies. Never again should Germans build submarines. The naval fortifications on Heligoland were to be destroyed.

At the time, the disarmament of Germany was intended to be a step towards much wider disarmament and it was justified by referring to the tremendous damage which Germany's enemies had sustained in the war. Britain had lost nearly eight million tons of merchant shipping. France had seen great areas of her land ravaged to the point of almost total destruction. In the areas occupied by the Germans, over a quarter of a million houses had been destroyed, thousands of industrial plants wrecked and looted, mines devastated, agricultural land blasted and polluted to the point of uselessness and 500 000 cows and as many sheep carried off to Germany. Such evidence of devastation, much of it brought about by indiscriminate looting and vandalism as the Germans retreated, was used also to justify the sections of the Treaty of Versailles which dealt with economic matters and reparation.

Article 231 (see page 19) had asserted Germany's responsibility. The exact amount of compensation to be paid was left to be worked out by an Allied Reparation Commission. The Commission did not complete its calculations until April 1921. Meanwhile, the Allies had already taken steps to seize some of the more easily-removed German properties, such as railway engines, and the Treaty of Versailles gave them authority to seize the private property of Germans which lay outside Germany. The amount eventually fixed for Germany to pay was 136 000 million marks (£6 600 million) (see Fig. 4.1), plus interest. Much of the first instalment was paid in coal. The intention was that the Allies would take a regular share of the wealth Germany produced until the debt was paid. The Germans argued that this was a double punishment. The Treaty of Versailles deprived them of lands and resources making wealth more difficult to produce; it then required a share in that wealth for reparation.

In all, the Treaty of Versailles included 440 Articles. As with all the peace treaties the first twenty-six Articles set out the Covenant of the League of Nations (see page 40). It was another German grievance that they were not allowed immediately to join the League.

2.5 How Austria–Hungary was Treated

Two treaties were signed with what had formerly been the Austro-Hungarian Empire. Austria agreed to the Treaty of St Germain in September 1919. Hungary agreed to the Treaty of Trianon in June 1920.

(a) The Treaty of St Germain

The Austro-Hungarian Empire had broken up under the stresses of the last months of the war. Czechoslovakia already had a seat at the Paris Peace

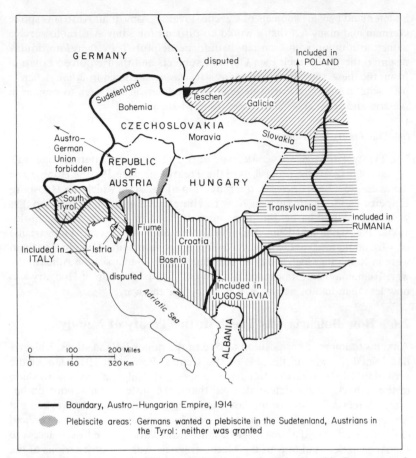

Fig. 2.4 The former Austro-Hungarian Empire: the Treaties of St Germain and Trianon

Conference. Republics had been set up in Austria and Hungary. By the Treaty of St Germain, the republic of Austria formally accepted the splitting up of the former Empire. The list of the provisions of the Treaty of St Germain (see page 38) and the map (Fig. 2.4) show what had become of this once-great Habsburg Empire.

Although the Austrian republic agreed in theory to make some reparation, no money was paid. Payments in kind were on a small scale because the new republic was obviously not wealthy. In March 1919, Austria sought to become a part of Germany but this was forbidden at St Germain. Austrians also complained that, although self-determination was used to justify the breaking up of the Habsburg Empire, the principle was ignored when Germans in the South Tyrol became subjects of Italy and those in the

Sudetenland became subjects of Czechoslovakia. Almost all Austrians spoke German and many felt that it would be difficult for a tiny Austria to survive alone; so a union with Germany would be helpful. They therefore doubly resented the loss of their own German subjects and their enforced isolation from the new republican Germany. It was a slight consolation when a plebiscite in southern Carinthia enabled Germans in that area to remain in Austria and resist the claims upon them of Jugoslavia.

(b) The Treaty of Trianon

The Treaty with Hungary was delayed until 1920 owing to internal upheavals in that country. By the provisions of the Treaty (see page 39), the Hungarians then accepted, under protest, the reduction of the state which the Habsburg Emperor had formerly ruled as King of Hungary. In vain, they protested that plebiscites should be held in areas now declared to be parts of Czechoslovakia, Jugoslavia and Rumania. Over three million Magyars (Hungarians) now found themselves the subjects of foreign governments. Over half of them were in Rumania which had been persuaded in 1916 to assist the Allies in the war; Rumania therefore expected a reward. The population of Hungary was now less than half of what it had been before the war.

2.6 How Bulgaria was Treated: the Treaty of Neuilly

Anxious to improve her position as one of the minor Balkan states, Bulgaria had joined the war on the side of the Central Powers in 1915. Under the provisions of the Treaty of Neuilly (see page 39), Bulgaria was now to share in the setbacks of the defeated. Like them, she suffered limitations on her armed forces and losses of territory and a figure was eventually worked out for reparation. The penalties imposed were by no means severe, however, and Bulgaria even gained a small area of land, from Turkey. The loss of access to the Aegean Sea, and thus to the Mediterranean, was the most serious of the injuries done to Bulgaria.

2.7 How Turkey was Treated

(a) The Treaty of Sèvres

There was no hope that the Turkish Empire, long-renowned for inefficiency and corruption, could escape the fate of the Austro-Hungarian Empire. The Allies had already made a variety of agreements about how they intended to deal with parts of this Empire. The principle of self-determination alone would be enough to ensure that it was broken up. By the provisions of the Treaty of Sèvres (see page 39) this came about. But the settlement of the Turkish problem was not a straightforward one.

Many of the Turkish possessions were populated by Arabs who hoped after the First World War to gain independence, but Europeans thought this would be premature and, in Palestine, Britain had already made conflicting promises to Arabs and Jews. Europeans were also worried about the effects of Arab nationalism on their economic interests at the eastern end of the Mediterranean. Among these was the Suez Canal, while Turkey herself bestrode the Dardanelles, an almost equally important international waterway. Moreover, both Greeks and Italians, successful though not decisive Allies in the First World War, hoped to profit at Turkey's expense.

The most striking feature of the settlement with Turkey in 1920 was the ending of all Turkish authority over North Africa and the Arab lands. A number of these Arab lands became mandates in the hands of Britain and France. Other parts of the former Turkish Empire became independent while Britain, Greece and Italy made good their claims to territories formerly Turkish. An international commission took charge of the Dardanelles and Bosporus to ensure free passage through the Straits.

The effect of this Treaty was to reduce Turkey to the barren and mountainous area of Anatolia (Asia Minor). She had been almost completely expelled from Europe; her capital city was separated from the rest of the country by Straits under international control and, even in Anatolia, the Greeks held the important city of Smyrna and the Italians held Adalia. The Treaty dealt the Sultan his death blow. Turkish nationalists, under the leadership of Mustapha Kemal, had been steadily undermining his authority. The Treaty was a surrender of which a nationalist, even one as realistic as Kemal who thoroughly understood his country's weakness, was forced to disapprove.

Kemal and the nationalists rejected the Treaty. The powers showed some readiness to give way. In summer 1921, the Italians left Anatolia and the French showed a willingness to negotiate. Lloyd George was in favour of standing firm but the Greeks made an already difficult situation worse. While the Turkish nationalists gathered their strength at new headquarters deep inside Anatolia, the Greeks set about extending their area of occupation around Smyrna. They invited defeat and when they tried to penetrate to the nationalist stronghold at Ankara, they were checked. The major powers offered concessions but Kemal saw no reason to stop now. When the hostilities began again, the Greeks were routed at Afyon and, in September 1922, chased out of Anatolia. Even Turkish citizens who had Greek connections felt that it was safer to flee from the vengeance of the Turkish nationalists.

There then developed the *Chanak Crisis* which proved to be a serious embarrassment to Lloyd George and the British government. Kemal was ready to extend nationalist authority to Constantinople and to depose the Sultan. From Constantinople, he could go on to chase the Greeks from East Thrace. But he would need to cross the Straits where international forces were stationed. The French and Italians promptly withdrew, and some of the forces from the Dominions, who shared the duties of the garrison with Britain, also left. Lloyd George felt that a stand should be made against Kemal. The Treaty of Sèvres could be renegotiated but it showed a dangerous lack of confidence in the postwar world to give in to the first violence which broke out. When the nationalists approached, the British garrison at Chanak was ordered not to give way. The danger passed only when the British commander, General Harington, reached agreement with the Turks at Mudania. This agreement, signed in October 1922, was the basis of a new treaty with the Turkish nationalists, to revise the Treaty of Sèvres.

A month later, the Sultan of Turkey was deposed and the Chanak Crisis helped to bring about the defeat of Lloyd George in a British general election. In July 1923, Kemal and his followers signed a new treaty with the Allies, the Treaty of Lausanne. The Turkish nationalists had been the first seriously to challenge the new order which had been created at the Paris Peace Conference. Britain had stood against them almost alone but even in Britain the Prime Minister had been condemned as reckless and irresponsible.

(b) The Treaty of Lausanne

At Lausanne, Kemal achieved most of his immediate ambitions. The Treaty (see page 39) returned East Thrace to Turkey and left to the Turks the control of the Straits. Anatolia remained free from foreign troops and the Turks were required neither to limit their armed forces nor to make reparation. The parts of the Treaty of Sèvres which dealt with the Arab states were confirmed and only minor changes were made concerning the ownership of islands. Greeks and Turks exchanged some populations to lessen the risks of Greek retaliation against Turks and vice versa, but old hatreds between them remained. These hatreds would find a stage on which to contend, in the second half of the twentieth century, in Cyprus (see Section 20.4).

2.8   How Russia was Treated: the Treaty of Brest-Litovsk

The Tsar of Russia lost his throne in March 1917. In November 1917, the Bolsheviks came to power (see Section 5.1(a)). The war against Germany was going badly and the Bolsheviks intended speedily to end it. 'The soldiers have voted against the war,' Lenin said, 'they have voted with their feet by running away.' The Germans had the upper hand and they drove such a hard bargain that Trotsky, the Russian negotiator, thought the terms unacceptable. Lenin persuaded the Bolshevik government to over-rule him and the Treaty of Brest-Litovsk was signed in March 1918. Within nine months, Germany herself was defeated and was therefore unable to profit much from the Treaty, but, not represented at the Peace Conference in Paris, Russia was unable to recover much of the land she had lost. Lenin later remarked, 'We gained a little time and sacrificed a great deal of space for it.' Not until the closing stages of the Second World War did Russia extend as far westwards again (see Section 9.5(b)). The map on page 95 (Fig. 5.1) shows the extent of Russia's losses.

By the Treaty of Brest-Litovsk (see page 39), Russia lost nearly 20 per cent of her territory and nearly 25 per cent (46 million) of her population. The losses included lands important for their coal and iron deposits. Germany also extracted from Russia a promise to pay 3 000 million roubles. Lenin had asked for a peace free of annexations and indemnities but he was over-optimistic in imagining that the Germans would agree to peace without annexing territory or imposing penalties. When the Germans lost lands at Versailles and were required to pay indemnities under their new name, reparations, they preferred not to remember their treatment of Russia.

When the Peace Conference at Paris began, many of the states which Russia had lost had already become new nation states. The peace-makers, therefore, upheld the principle of self-determination and welcomed the freedom which Finland, Estonia, Latvia, Lithuania and Poland had won. They also approved when Rumania seized Bessarabia from Russia.

Bukharin and three other members of the Bolshevik government had resigned when Lenin accepted the Treaty of Brest-Litovsk. Lenin had argued that peace was essential if communism was to survive in Russia: for the moment, Russia had no alternative but to pay the price of that peace. Her former Allies saw no reason, at Paris, to make reductions in that price, although the Bolsheviks renounced the Treaty of Brest-Litovsk when Germany was defeated and were able to withhold the indemnities which Germany had imposed and to recover much of the Ukraine.

2.9   The Constructive Work of the Settlement

A great deal of territory thus changed hands in the years 1918–23. Most of the changes involved the creation of new nation states. The essential purpose of these changes was to apply the principle of self-determination in the hope of satisfying old grievances. The Peace Conference at Paris also set up the League of Nations and carried the basic idea of self-determination into the non-European world by means of the system of mandated territories. In all of this, the Conference intended to be constructive, to improve the likelihood of lasting peace.

(a) New Nation States

Czechoslovakia and Jugoslavia may be taken as examples of the nation states created in Europe after the First World War.

(i) **Czechoslovakia** was created in 1918 to satisfy the demands of the Czecho-slovak National Council for a state free from Austrian control and an independent home for Czechs and Slovaks. It was made up of provinces formerly attached to Austria and Hungary within the Austro-Hungarian Empire. Eduard Beneš represented the new state at the Paris Peace Conference and from 1918 to 1935 was the Czechoslovak Foreign Minister. Together with Tómàŝ Masaryk, the country's first President, he secured the support of the victorious powers and, already possessing prosperous industry, the republic was regarded as an excellent example of how self-determination could bring a

Fig. 2.5 Tómàŝ Masaryk, the first President of Czechoslovakia, helped to give stability to the new nation state

new look and a new stability to Europe. The political system was democratic; the state had no aggressive ambitions against its neighbours; the resentment which had long smouldered, especially in Bohemia, against the rule of the Austrian Habsburgs could now be channelled into making the republic prosperous. Masaryk remained President until 1935 when he was succeeded by Beneš. Thus the state achieved political stability. Czechoslovakia also achieved a degree of international stability, developing close relations with Jugoslavia and Rumania in the Little Entente to preserve stability where once had been the Habsburg Empire. The Czechs who, from the outset, were popular with France, on whose system of government the Czechoslovak constitution was modelled, also made a new ally in the east when friendship was developed with Russia. Not everyone approved of ties with the communists but Czechoslovakia was in many ways a model of what the peace-makers had hoped to achieve in the new nation states.

The republic was not, however, free from handicaps. There was a week's fighting with Poland at the beginning of 1919 over a frontier problem. The squabble was settled by a Conference of Ambassadors when Poland gained the town of Teschen, but the quarrel left behind it some hostility between the two states so that co-operation when it was needed – against Hitler for example – was not forthcoming. Moreover, Czechoslovakia, with a population of only about 14 million people, seemed a fragile neighbour alongside Germany. In 1919, Germany was weak but in some ways the peace-makers built trouble into Czechoslovakia for the time when Germany grew strong again, by giving her difficult minorities problems. Of the 14 million, over

3 million were German, mainly inhabitants of the Sudetenland which ran along Czechoslovakia's boundary with Germany. Another group, nearly three-quarters of a million, were Magyars. The Sudetenland had never been part of Germany (it was formerly in the Austro-Hungarian Empire), but Germans argued that the logic of self-determination was to include it in Germany. Hungary argued similarly that the Magyars should be subjects of Hungary but, as defeated powers, Germany and Hungary received no satisfaction. It was Hitler who later made the Sudetenland the subject of a major international crisis (see Section 8.3(c)).

(ii) **Jugoslavia** was designed to satisfy the demands of South Slav peoples for a state of their own, uniting those who, before 1914, had been trapped in the Austro-Hungarian Empire with those who had already broken free from the Turkish Empire. In 1914, many of the latter were inhabitants of Serbia, at that time a free kingdom. In the war, Serbia had been on the side of the Allies and so could now properly be rewarded. During the war, the Serbian government had retreated to the island of Corfu and there, in 1917, the idea of a new state of Jugoslavia, in effect an enlarged Serbia, was worked out. Until 1929, the state bore the cumbersome title of the Kingdom of Serbs, Croats and Slovenes – Jugoslavia was its later name. The original name was, however, revealing for, like Czechoslovakia, Jugoslavia was not exactly a nation state and tensions developed between the various races who made up the South Slavs. The principle of national self-determination was an attractive one and had much to recommend it, but it was not by any means easy to define nationality, and to make sure that in every nation there was only one nationality was impossible. (Even in Britain, different nationalities exist in England, Scotland and Wales; but they have ceased to fight about it and limit their rivalry to football matches.)

In Jugoslavia, Croats and Slovenes complained that the state was too much dominated by Serbs. Democracy crumbled under the strain and in 1934 King Alexander was assassinated by Croatian extremists.

Meanwhile, Jugoslavia was less prosperous than Czechoslovakia and further disturbances were caused by religious differences. Disputes also developed with Italy about the boundary between the two, particularly about the port of Fiume, and with Hungary about the northern frontier of Jugoslavia. Jugoslavia was, in 1924, forced to abandon Fiume to Italy but the Italians then gave up their more ambitious claims to much more of Jugoslavia's coastline (see Fig. 7.1(a)).

Like the dispute over Teschen (see page 28), the dispute over Fiume developed from the loose ends left by the Paris Conference. It was enlivened by the exploits of Gabriele d'Annunzio, an Italian hothead, poet and airman. With three hundred volunteers, he determined to right some of the wrongs alleged to have been done to Italy and, in September 1919, he took possession of Fiume and held it for over a year. Many of the town's inhabitants were Italian but Jugoslavia claimed that the port was vitally important to her. On

Christmas Day, 1920, an apparently ungrateful Italian government bombarded d'Annunzio's headquarters and the poet surrendered. He had, nevertheless, whetted Italy's appetite. For a time, the League of Nations took over the town but what a poet could do, Mussolini could do. Fiume was taken over by the Italian Fascists and this time Jugoslavia gave up the struggle.

(b) The League of Nations

(i) **Origins.** When speaking of Britain's War Aims, Lloyd George referred to 'some international organization to limit the burden of armaments and diminish the probability of war'. The last of Wilson's Fourteen Points referred to 'a general association of nations' to guarantee independence and security to all states.

The idea was not new. After the Napoleonic Wars, which ended in 1815, Congresses had been held to try to secure international stability by agreements among the great powers. The Congresses failed to last but the idea was revived from time to time and was discussed when conferences were called to consider disarmament, at the Hague in 1899 and 1907. A few international organizations had been created in the nineteenth century for specific purposes, among them the International Red Cross and the Universal Postal Union. The First World War quickened the search for an organization to keep the peace.

There were plenty of plans. The British Foreign Office and Grey, who had been Foreign Secretary in 1914, Taft, ex-President of the USA, and Jan Smuts of South Africa, together with a host of others, put forward ideas. When the war was ending, they were taken up by Lloyd George and Wilson.

There was some difference of opinion, however, about the sort of association to be set up. Some favoured a narrow league, rather like the Congresses after 1815, which would simply deal with crises as they occurred and delay war until a settlement was reached. Others wanted a broad league which would do much more. A broad league could extend international co-operation and might deal with disarmament, colonies, even social and labour problems. Jan Smuts enthusiastically brought such ideas to Paris, and at the end of 1918 published *The League of Nations: A Practical Suggestion*.

Woodrow Wilson accepted the idea of a broad league and insisted that it should have priority in the peace talks. It was later argued that he then concentrated his attention on getting the credit for the idea instead of tackling the details of how it could be applied. Many of the details were worked out by the British whose first preference had been for a narrow league, although Lloyd George was prepared to go along with the broader one. From its beginning, the League suffered from some woolly thinking about the details of its machinery. These details were included in the *Covenant* (see page 40), hastily agreed among the victorious powers and written into all the Paris Treaties. They were careful to build into the system a predominant place for themselves. They also assumed that threats to peace would come from lesser powers and therefore glossed over the biggest problem of all: how could the League prevent war if a major power was determined to be aggressive?

(*ii*) **The League at work.** The League began its work with a membership of 42 states. By 1923, the membership had grown to 54 and the first of the defeated powers, Austria, Bulgaria and Hungary, had already become members. These first years were taken up mainly in expanding the League's machinery. The diagram (Fig. 2.6) and the summary of the Covenant at the end of this Unit show how this machinery fitted together and how the League was intended to work. The settlement of disputes would fall mainly to the Council and Assembly. The Permanent Court of Justice and Commissions for Disarmament, Mandates and Minorities would deal with problems of a special character. Other organizations would be responsible for social, economic and humanitarian matters. Servicing the entire structure was the Secretariat whose officials undertook to put loyalty to the League above their separate nationalities.

The *Assembly* worked on the basis of equality. All members had an equal vote. Almost all of the League's activities came under their review. They controlled the League's budget. Every state could express its opinion and, such was the goodwill, the right which every state had to veto a decision was seldom used. With an optimism which proved to be not unjustified, those who framed the Covenant ruled that decisions should be unanimous. In theory it was thus easy to obstruct them. In practice, matters were frequently thrashed out in committees and when the final votes were taken those in a minority preferred to abstain rather than block the will of the majority. Meeting annually, the Assembly made a real contribution to international goodwill.

The *Council* met more frequently, at least every three months and at all times of crisis. It was designed to be a smaller body than the Assembly and one which could quickly get to grips with a difficulty. The five major victorious powers were to have permanent seats (but the USA failed to join the League); four others were to be elected from time to time by the Assembly. The four became six in 1922 and nine in 1926 and so, if the great powers intended to dominate the Council, they were unable to do so. Most of the Council's decisions concerned political problems and those problems over which, through Commissions, the Council had a special control. Territories which the League looked after in the years following the Peace – Danzig and the Saar for example – and matters to do with the level of armaments and the mandates came under the Council's authority. Again, it was necessary for decisions to be unanimous. To obtain decisions, it was often necessary to compromise and thus the Council tended to be less decisive and to act more slowly than might have been hoped. Moreover, when real crises arose, the Council found itself without teeth. Over-optimistic and wary of setting up a machine which could be damaging to themselves, the peace-makers had made no real provisions for enforcing the will of the League. The Council could only with difficulty, and as a last resort, raise an army. Articles 10–17 of the

	MAIN ORGANS		STAFF OF CIVIL SERVANTS	PERMANENT ADVISORY ORGANS	COURT OF JUSTICE	AGENCIES	'AD HOC' COMMISSIONS For Special Duties
	(Consultative)	(In Crises)					
LEAGUE OF NATIONS (based on The Covenant)	THE ASSEMBLY (often worked through Committees) — *Central* →	THE COUNCIL	THE SECRETARIAT at Geneva	COMMISSIONS for DISARMAMENT, MANDATES, MILITARY AFFAIRS, MINORITIES	PERMANENT COURT OF JUSTICE at The Hague	*Auxiliary* COMMITTEES: Health Organization International Labour Organization Organization for Communications and Transit Intellectual Co-operation Organization Economic and Financial Organization SPECIAL COMMITTEES FOR: Drug Traffic, Women's Rights, Refugees, Child Welfare. Universal Postal Union Support for Red Cross	COMMISSIONS OF ADMINISTRATION: The Saar; Danzig COMMISSIONS OF INQUIRY: Manchuria (Lytton) 1931
	Original Membership: 42	Original Membership: 4 Permanent 4 Elected	First Secretary-General: DRUMMOND, 1919–33		Originally: 11 Judges 4 Deputy Judges		
UNITED NATIONS ORGANIZATION (based on The Charter)	THE GENERAL ASSEMBLY (often working through a complex structure of Committees)	THE SECURITY COUNCIL — *Principal Organs* →	THE SECRETARIAT at New York	TRUSTEESHIP COUNCIL ECONOMIC AND SOCIAL COUNCIL Social Commission Economic Commission Human Rights Commission (Universal Declaration of Human Rights 1948) Regional Commissions for Europe, Latin America, Asia, For East	INTERNATIONAL COURT OF JUSTICE at The Hague	*Auxiliary* SPECIALIZED AGENCIES: ILO – International Labour Organization FAO – Food and Agriculture Organization IRO – International Refugee Organization WHO – World Health Organization ITU – International Telecommunications Union WMO – World Meteorological Organization UNESCO – United Nations Educational, Scientific and Cultural Organization UNICEF – United Nations International Children's Emergency Fund IMF – International Monetary Fund INTERNATIONAL BANK UPU – Universal Postal Union Support for Red Cross	UN Peace-keeping Forces e.g. in Cyprus UNEF – United Nations Emergency Force UNCTAD – United Nations Conference on Trade and Development Korean Reconstruction Committee Technical Assistance Committee Commission on Narcotic Drugs
	Original Membership: 51	Original Membership: 5 Permanent 6 Elected	First Secretary-General: TRYGVE LIE, 1946–52		15 Judges		

Fig. 2.6 The machinery of the League of Nations and the United Nations Organization compared

Covenant barely faced up to the problem of major powers which refused to accept the League's rules. They were vague about non-members and too readily assumed that breaches of the peace could be dealt with by sanctions, a sort of economic boycott. Parties to a dispute were not allowed to vote on it in the Council but this was not enough to make sure that parties to a dispute would abide by a Council decision. In the 1930s, the League found itself helpless when states such as Japan simply ignored the League and walked out.

The *Secretariat* rapidly built up a large and dedicated staff of civil servants. They were soon to realize that a major handicap to the League was its poverty. Members of the Assembly co-operated most readily in cutting down the costs of the League's work and few nations contributed willingly to the organization's expenses. The world wanted peace. But it did not want to pay much for it.

In spite of this, however, many of the smaller bodies in the League did excellent work. The *Permanent Court of Justice* was set up at the Hague, in 1921. It had fifteen judges of various nationalities to deal with legal rather than political disputes and to advise the Council on judicial matters. As a safeguard against wasting time, cases were only accepted when disputing parties agreed in advance to accept the verdict. The *Mandates Commission* kept a watchful eye on the good government of the mandated territories and the *Minorities Committee*, though sometimes disappointing, performed some services in protecting minority groups against ill-treatment by majorities. The *Disarmament Commission* ran into difficulties. It was easy to accept the idea of disarmament. It was much more difficult to put the idea into practice (Section 7.4).

Other committees had many successes which frequently went almost unnoticed. Newspapermen were quick to report an international crisis and a storm in the Council. They found developments to improve world health (the Health Organization), communications (the Organization for Communications and Transit) and education (the Intellectual Co-operation Organization) rather boring, of little value as news. Among the many bodies which dealt with prisoners of war, white slaves, drugs and economic problems, only the ILO (*International Labour Organization*) achieved widespread publicity. This was partly due to Albert Thomas, the passionate French socialist who became the first director of the ILO, in 1919. Thomas threw his energies into a campaign to improve wages, working conditions, pensions and the status of trade unions, throughout the world. When he died in 1932, the ILO had influenced many backward governments towards more enlightened attitudes. Membership of the ILO was not limited to membership of the League of Nations so that even the USA joined it. Of the four representatives each member sent to the annual conference of the Organization, only two represented the government, the others representing employers and workmen. Millions of ordinary people had reason to be grateful to Thomas and the ILO.

(*iii*) **Keeping the peace.** The success of the League would be judged, however, not by the achievements of Albert Thomas but by its success in keeping the peace. In the 1930s, world war broke out again and it was said that the League had failed. Such a verdict was not entirely fair, but the League's record as a peace-keeping body was never very impressive. It began life with less than perfect machinery and, at birth, it was dealt a savage blow by the United States. Woodrow Wilson had foolishly refused to admit any Republicans to the delegation he took to Paris. Led by Cabot Lodge and his fellow Republicans, the Senate attacked the agreements that the President brought back from there. Wilson played his cards badly. He refused all concessions, asserting that it was 'better a thousand times to go down fighting than to dip your colours to dishonourable compromise'. The Senate therefore refused to ratify the Treaty of Versailles and, since the Covenant of the League was written into the Treaty, also refused to accept US membership of the League of Nations. Wilson hoped in vain for a massive victory for the Democrats in the presidential election of 1920 in order to turn the tide. His own health gave way, however, and the Democrats were routed by Warren Harding, the Republican candidate who won 16 million votes compared with the nine million cast for James Cox. It seemed that the American people had voted against the League. The USA therefore signed a separate treaty with Germany in 1921, distancing Americans from the Treaty of Versailles, and the League of Nations had now to try to keep the peace without US assistance.

Before the League was really functioning, squabbles developed in which it was to prove almost powerless, for example over Teschen (see page 28), and the Straits (see pages 25–6), over Memel, which Lithuania grabbed from the League's hands in 1923, and over Vilna which Poland had seized from Lithuania in 1920. Poland was a founder member of the League but showed little inclination to abide by its rules, launching a war against Russia in the same year that she seized Vilna. On the political problems which came before the Council in the League's opening years, and on those which passed it by, the Council could record few successes although it did assist Austria to survive grave economic difficulties by promoting a large loan. These were perhaps teething troubles. The history of the League as a peace-keeping body will be continued in Unit Seven.

(c) **The Non-European World**

A creditable and constructive step in the peace-making of 1919 – though a hesitant one – was the setting up of the mandates system (see Article 22 of the League Covenant on page 40). The system was based on 'a sacred trust', the recognition that Europeans had obligations to the peoples they ruled in other continents and an important new principle in international relations. The Treaties of Versailles and Sèvres placed former German and Turkish colonies under new administration (see pages 38 and 39), and the new administering powers under the supervision of the Mandates Commission (see page 33). But it was not until after the Second World War that Europeans firmly came

Fig 2.7 A cartoonist's comment on the refusal of Cabot Lodge and Senators Borah and Johnson to give up their seats for Peace. Republican obstructionism ensured that the USA did not join the League of Nations

to grips with the aspirations of their colonial subjects and their demands for independence. Though a useful reminder that non-Europeans too had rights and interests, the mandates system before 1939 was not always regarded by the colonizing powers as the 'sacred trust' that those who drafted the Covenant had envisaged. The Mandates Commission nevertheless worked hard to remind the powers of their duties.

Among the first members of the League, moreover, were former British possessions such as Australia and Canada, South American states such as Brazil and Uruguay, the African state of Liberia and the Asiatic state of Siam – each with a vote in the Assembly equal to that of Britain or France. Brazil was also one of the first members of the Council. The peace-makers inevitably thought mainly in terms of Europe and it was sometimes argued that the League of Nations was something of a European club. Nevertheless horizons were beginning to broaden. Non-Europeans were in a majority among the first members of the League, in number if not in wealth and influence. The failure of the USA to take up membership made the League less transcontinental than it might have been, however.

2.10   Assessments of the Work of the Peace of Paris

The Allies left Paris hopeful, but not confident. In a short space of time, they had attempted an enormous task of resettlement and construction. Their basic principles had been sound ones. The treaties and the League of Nations stood as monuments to their energy and hopes. But Wilson, the Democrat, returned to an America swinging to the Republicans and increasingly isolationist. Britain, too, seemed half to wish that it could be possible to ignore European affairs and to concentrate on domestic problems. France was uneasy. Germany had kept the Rhineland and the French seemed obsessed with fears of a German revival which the British thought tiresome. In truth, the French had depended on American membership of the League and American guarantees of the treaties for their security. When the USA renounced both the League and the treaties, France began a morbid brooding on her own weakness which seemed bound to end in disaster. Italy maintained that she had been cheated and before long Mussolini was compiling his shopping-list of what should have been, in his view, Italy's rightful property. China retired from the Conference dissatisfied with her own ineffectiveness and the apparent superiority of Japan. Japan retired dissatisfied with her apparent lack of superiority and brooding on the differences between white and yellow. Only Jan Smuts remained cheerful, returning to South Africa to become Prime Minister and to pursue his passion for international goodwill in the League of Nations and the British Commonwealth of Nations. But even he noticed that Europeans were already squabbling again, about places it was difficult to find on the map and about tiny frontiers which seemed absurd when measured against the vastness of Africa.

The Central Powers could at least disclaim responsibility for whatever mistakes had been made. They had been required only to sign the treaties, which they did under protest. They counted their losses, lamented that self-determination had not been wholeheartedly applied so that, for example, the Sudetenland Germans were locked inside Czechoslovakia, and convinced themselves that the treaties were vindictive. Only the Turks were able to do anything about it in the immediate future but in a Europe apparently full of dissatisfied nations, the Germans soon appointed themselves the most dissatisfied of all. They had particular grievances to the east of their country and, indeed, the further east one went from Paris the more unsatisfactory the Settlement seemed until, in Russia, it had nothing left to say. As they had no part in it, the Russians could regard the Settlement either as irrelevant or as a capitalist plot. It was sometimes argued that the peace-makers had reconstructed Europe with one eye on isolating Russia and creating barriers to prevent the westwards spread of communism. Certainly France and other Western powers were not unsympathetic to Poland when that country pushed its frontier further to the east in the Russo-Polish War which ended in 1921 in the Treaty of Riga (see Section 5.1(*b*)).

The Paris Settlement contained many good features (the more remarkable given the size of the task the peace-makers undertook), but even in 1919 the economist J.M. Keynes wrote his vigorous attack upon it in *The Economic Consequences of the Peace*. He concentrated his fire particularly on reparations; and it was on reparations, above all else, that future criticisms of the Settlement centred. Keynes argued that Germany would be unable to pay and that reparations would bedevil European economies for years to come. The latter claim certainly proved correct. When reparations ceased in the financial crisis of 1931, however, Germany had paid only about a quarter of the £6 600 million demanded and she had, in the meantime, received more than she paid in foreign loans, most of which were never repaid. The League of Nations had also arranged loans to aid Austria and Hungary, so that the defeated powers in the end received more aid than they paid in reparations. It may still be argued whether reparations were justifiable compensation for war damage or savage penalties to punish the defeated. It cannot be maintained that they crippled the defeated. Unfortunately, however, they prolonged the bitterness of the recent war, brought new controversy and made it more difficult to reconcile Germany to the new Europe which the peace-makers had toiled to construct. (The subject of reparations will be examined again in Unit Four.)

2.11   Appendix

British War Aims outlined by Lloyd George, January 1918:
 1. The restoration and independence of Belgium
 2. The restoration of Serbia and of the occupied lands of the Allies
 3. The restoration of Alsace-Lorraine to France
 4. 'Russia can only be saved by her own people'
 5. An independent Poland
 6. Self-government to nationalities in Austria–Hungary
 7. The union of all Italians in Italy
 8. Justice for Rumanians
 9. Separate national conditions for subjects of the Turkish Empire
10. Self-determination in German colonies
11. Reparation for injuries in violation of international law
12. The sanctity of treaties
13. Some international organization to limit armaments and reduce the risk of war.

Wilson's Fourteen Points outlined in January 1918:
 1. Diplomacy shall be open
 2. Freedom of navigation on the seas
 3. The removal of economic barriers
 4. The reduction of armaments
 5. The settlement of colonial problems with reference to the interests of colonial peoples
 6. The evacuation of Russia. Goodwill towards her
 7. The restoration of Belgium
 8. The restoration of France and her recovery of Alsace-Lorraine
 9. Italian frontiers along lines of nationality

10. Autonomous development for the peoples of Austria–Hungary
11. Territorial integrity for the Balkan states
12. Free passage through the Dardanelles and autonomous development for the peoples of the Turkish Empire
13. An independent Poland
14. An association of nations.

Summary of the Treaty of Versailles, 28 June 1919:
1. The Covenant of the League of Nations
2. German losses of territory:
   to France: Alsace-Lorraine
   to Belgium: Eupen-Malmedy (after plebiscite, 1920)
   to Denmark: Northern Schleswig (after plebiscite, 1920)
   to Poland: Poznania and West Prussia. Also part of Upper Silesia (after plebiscite, 1921)
   to direct League of Nations control: the Saar, Danzig
   to Allied control and then Lithuania: Memel
   to Allied Powers as mandated territories of the League of Nations: East Africa (Britain); South-West Africa (South Africa); Cameroons and Togoland (divided between Britain and France); Samoan Islands (New Zealand); New Guinea (Australia); Marshall Islands and Pacific Islands north of the Equator (Japan)
3. The loss of German concessions and trading rights in China, Egypt and elsewhere
4. The reduction of German military power. The Rhineland and Heligoland demilitarized. Restrictions on armed forces
5. An army of occupation west of the Rhine and in bridgeheads east of the Rhine at Cologne, Coblenz and Mainz
6. Germany undertook to make reparation and accepted responsibility for certain war damage
7. The Treaty of Brest-Litovsk became void. Germans were required to withdraw from the Baltic provinces as from all other occupied territory.

Summary of the Treaty of St Germain, 10 September 1919:
1. The Covenant of the League of Nations
2. The former Austro-Hungarian Empire was broken up:
   (a) the new state of Czechoslovakia was recognized
   (b) Austria and Hungary became separate states with no control over other lands which had formerly belonged to the Austro-Hungarian Empire
   (c) the new state of Jugoslavia was created, partly from lands formerly in the Austro-Hungarian Empire
   (d) parts of the former Empire were given to Poland (which gained Galicia), Rumania (Transylvania), Italy (South Tyrol, Trentino and Istria)
3. Boundaries of Austria defined with a plebiscite in southern Carinthia
4. Austria was forbidden to unite with any other country without League of Nations approval
5. Limitations on Austrian armed forces
6. Austria accepted responsibility for certain war damage.

Summary of the Treaty of Trianon, 4 June 1920:
1. The Covenant of the League of Nations
2. Hungary accepted the break-up of the Austro-Hungarian Empire (see St Germain above)
3. Hungary was reduced in size
4. Limitations on Hungarian armed forces
5. Hungary accepted responsibility for certain war damage.

Summary of the Treaty of Neuilly, 27 November 1919:
1. The Covenant of the League of Nations
2. Bulgarian losses:
   to Jugoslavia: areas along Bulgaria's western boundary
   to Greece: West Thrace including Bulgaria's only access to the Mediterranean Sea at Dedeagach
3. Bulgarian gains:
   from Turkey: land on Bulgaria's south-eastern boundary
4. Limitations on Bulgarian armed forces
5. Bulgaria agreed to make some financial reparation.

Summary of the Treaty of Sèvres, 10 August 1920:
1. The Covenant of the League of Nations
2. Turkey's losses:
   as mandates: Syria (France); Palestine, Iraq and Transjordan (Britain)
   several states gained independence, e.g. Hedjaz and Arabia
   to Greece: East Thrace. Greek claims to many islands such as Chios were recognized. Greece would occupy Smyrna and a surrounding area for five years when a plebiscite would be held
   to Bulgaria: land on Bulgaria's south-eastern boundary
   to Italy: Rhodes and the Dodecanese islands, and Adalia
   to Britain: Cyprus (which Britain had occupied since 1878)
3. The Straits (Dardanelles and Bosporus) placed under an international commission
4. Britain, France and Italy retained troops in Turkey.

Summary of the Treaty of Lausanne, 24 July 1923:
1. Hardly any changes were made in the Treaty of Sèvres concerning the Arab countries and Mediterranean islands
2. Turkey regained East Thrace from Greece. Both sides of the new Greek-Turkish frontier were demilitarized
3. Turkey was left free from foreign troops (the Greeks had already left Smyrna and the Italians had already left Adalia)
4. The Straits would be demilitarized but under Turkish control
5. No restrictions were imposed on Turkey's forces and no reparations were required.

Summary of the Treaty of Brest-Litovsk, 3 March 1918:
1. Russia was to pay 3 000 million roubles to Germany
2. Russian losses:
   Estonia, Latvia, Lithuania and Poland (independent), Kars and Batoum (to Turkey)

influence over Finland (independent)
the Ukraine (independent of Russia but under German domination).

Summary of the Covenant of the League of Nations:
1 (Article): Membership – originally the Allies who signed the Paris Treaties and thirteen states neutral in the First World War; new admissions to be approved by two-thirds of the Assembly
2–6: Basic machinery:
  (a) The Assembly of all member states with one vote each
  (b) The Council composed of the USA, Britain, France, Italy and Japan (permanently) with four additional members elected by the Assembly; one vote each
  (c) Unanimous agreement of all members present in Assembly or Council required for decisions except where otherwise agreed
  (d) The Secretariat led by a Secretary-General, financed by members of the League
7: League headquarters at Geneva
8–9: Members undertook to reduce armaments. A Disarmament Commission would advise the Council
10–12: Members undertook to preserve all members against aggression, to refer disputes to the Council and not to go to war for three months after a Council decision
13–15: Members agreed to submit disputes to arbitration and accepted various methods of arbitration including a Permanent Court of International Justice
16: Members undertook to take action against a member who resorted to war and broke the Covenant. This action would take the form of economic sanctions (i.e. boycott). If further action was needed, the Council could request contributions from members for military action. Offending members could be expelled.
17: Non-members involved in disputes could be invited to accept the above rules of the League
18–21: All treaties should be made public and should be consistent with the principles of the League
22: The colonies of the defeated countries became mandated territories (mandates) where 'the well-being and development of (the) peoples form a sacred trust of civilization'. Selected powers undertook to look after these territories, reporting to the Council which would be advised by a Mandates Commission
23–25: Members undertook to co-operate for the common good (e.g. concerning conditions of labour, colonial subjects, traffic in drugs and the control of disease), to bring existing organizations in these fields under the League and to encourage the Red Cross
26: The ways in which the Covenant could be amended.

Further Reading
Ayling, S.E.: *Portraits of Power*. Harrap (London, 1965) – Lloyd George.
Barker, B.: *Versailles: The Peace and After* (History Replay). Blackwell (Oxford, 1979).
Gibbons, S.R. and Morican, P.: *The League of Nations and UNO*. Longman (Harlow, 1970).

Lederer, I.J.: *The Versailles Settlement: Was It Foredoomed to Failure?* Heath-Harrap (Boston, 1960).

Longford, Lord, and Wheeler-Bennett, J.: *The History Makers*. Sidgwick & Jackson (London, 1973) – Clemenceau, Wilson, Lloyd George.

Raffo, P.: *The League of Nations*. Historical Association (London, 1974).

Seaman, L.C.B.: *From Vienna to Versailles*. Methuen (London, 1955) – Chapter XV.

Documentary

Bettey, J.H.: *English Historical Documents, 1906–1939*. Routledge & Kegan Paul (London, 1967). Includes Lloyd George's War Aims, Wilson's Fourteen Points and the Covenant of the League of Nations.

Henig, R.: *The League of Nations*. Oliver & Boyd (Edinburgh, 1973).

Exercises

1. Explain how Fig. 2.4 shows that the Austro-Hungarian Empire was fragmented by the Treaties of St Germain and Trianon.

2. What reasons are suggested in Units One and Two for the breaking-up after the First World War of both the Austro-Hungarian and Turkish Empires?

3. How far does the evidence in this Unit support the argument that the Treaty of Versailles dealt harshly with Germany?

4. Divide a piece of paper into two columns, the first headed 'Satisfactory Points', the second headed 'Unsatisfactory Points'. Making use of the text, maps and appendices to this Unit, make entries in these columns concerning the Treaty of Versailles from the point of view of a Frenchman.
   Repeat the exercise from the point of view of a German.

5. Making use of the details of all the treaties of the Paris Settlement (Sections 2.4, 2.5, 2.6, 2.7 and 2.11), consider which of Lloyd George's War Aims and Wilson's Fourteen Points were included in the Settlement.

6. How did Germany punish Russia in the Treaty of Brest-Litovsk?
   Using the references to pages 1 to 40 listed in the Index under Russia, explain why Russia came not to be represented at the Paris Peace Conference. How far does it seem likely that the peace-makers nevertheless had 'one eye on isolating Russia' (page 36)?

7. How would the statesmen of 1919 have explained their eagerness to set up the League of Nations? Why did the USA not become a member of the League and in what ways was this important?

8. Which Articles in the Covenant of the League of Nations would you consider best served the interests of the League's members? What criticisms would you make of the other Articles in the Covenant?

9. 'The Paris Settlement contained many good features' (page 36). Select *three* features of the Settlement you consider it justified to describe as 'good', in *each* case writing a brief argument in support of your opinion. Select *three* features you consider less easy to defend, again adding brief supporting argument in *each* case.

Unit Three

A World Safe for Democracy?

3.1 Enthusiasm for Democracy

The powers that were victorious in 1918 assumed that democracy was the best form of government. But definitions of democracy have not always been the same. In 1918 it was still a novel idea that women should be allowed to vote and take part in politics. New Zealand and Australia were the first to give women political rights, in 1893 and 1902 respectively, but many countries were slow to follow them. Women over thirty who were deemed to be 'responsible' were given the vote in Britain in 1918. In 1920 votes for women

Fig. 3.1 UK stamp commemorating the campaign of Mrs Pankhurst and the Act of 1918

became general in the USA, but in France, Italy and Japan women had to go on fighting for the right to take part in politics and did not win the vote until after the Second World War. Equality between the sexes was an essential feature of communism, however, and Russia gave women the vote in 1917. Germany, moreover, was more enlightened than France, for universal suffrage (the right of all adults to vote) was a central feature of the German Weimar Republic in 1919.

However, there was general agreement in 1919 that democracy required governments to be based on elections and that governments should be answerable to the people (that is, people would be able to vote at regular elections to remove unpopular governments from power and to keep some control over what governments did with their power). Democracy, it was argued, offered a stable form of government. The system had worked effectively in the USA for over a century. Democratic Britain was remarkably stable in comparison with other countries in Europe. France pursued democracy with enthusiasm if not always with success and Italy, since the creation of a united state in 1861, had persevered similarly. In 1919 there was a widespread respect for democracy, even among the defeated powers. Demo-

Table 3.1 Votes for women achieved

Country	Year	Country	Year
New Zealand	1893	Sweden	1921
Australia	1902	Turkey	1934
Finland	1906	Hungary	1945
Norway	1913	Italy	1945
Denmark	1915	Jugoslavia	1945
Russia	1917	France	1946
Britain	1918 and 1928	Japan	1946
Austria	1919	Rumania	1946
Germany	1919	China	1947
Holland	1919	India	1949
Poland	1919	Pakistan	1956
Czechoslovakia	1920	Switzerland	1971

cracy had apparently enabled the Allies to win the war, and the Allies were now eager to encourage it. Democratic constitutions were rapidly worked out in new nation states and in states where old monarchies, like those of the Habsburgs and Hohenzollerns, had fallen.

In 1917 Wilson had told the American Congress, 'The world must be made safe for democracy'. In 1919, democracy seemed to have the power to make the world safe. Basing governments upon the wishes of the people was thought to be a foolproof recipe for the future welfare of the world. Hereditary monarchies and systems based on privilege were swept away. 'One man, one vote' became a popular twentieth-century slogan, and the League of Nations was founded on the principle, 'One nation, one vote'.

3.2   Successful Democracies

(a) The United States of America in the 1920s

No country talked more about the virtues of democracy than the United States. But between 1920 and 1939, the USA did very little to preserve democracy outside America. The presidential election of 1920 brought to power the first of a succession of Republicans. Top of their list of priorities was the vigorous encouragement of ever-growing riches in the USA, *not* international co-operation to assist infant democracies. Warren Harding (1921–3)* won the first postwar election on the policy of 'Back to Normalcy'. The word was newly invented, but the idea behind it was an old one. Life for

---

* American presidential elections occur in the November of leap year (e.g. 1920). The President takes office at the beginning of the following year (e.g. 1921). See Table 13.1.

Americans would not be complicated by foreign involvement: they would concentrate on growing more prosperous. Wilson lamented, 'We had a chance to gain the leadership of the world. We have lost it.'

Harding died in office and was succeeded by Calvin Coolidge, who then won the election of 1924, persuading the voters that business was booming, that this was 'permanent' and that Republicans were good for them. He retired in 1928 and Hoover became President. There was not another Republican President until 1952.

Herbert Hoover thought the strength of the American system lay in 'rugged individualism'. Throughout the 1920s Americans, individually and ruggedly, pursued material comforts, a rising standard of living and a larger income per head than was to be found anywhere outside the USA. Their success owed little to the positive actions of their government, for Republicans interfered as little as possible. Such a policy seemed to be highly effective, at least up to 1928.

(*i*) **Legislation and government policy.** Central to what little legislation was introduced were laws which dealt with tariffs and immigration. In 1922 the Fordney-McCumber Act imposed higher tariffs (customs duties) than ever before on foreign goods coming into America; and in 1930 they were raised even higher. Sheltered by high tariffs from European competition, already prosperous American industry became more prosperous, and other nations found it difficult to sell their exports to what, potentially, was the world's richest customer. A series of Immigration Acts cut down the rights of foreigners to enter the USA and limited the numbers of those who could share in America's booming prosperity.

The Republicans conducted the government in a businesslike way, encouraged technological improvements in industry, and fed vital information to American businessmen so that they could sell their goods abroad and increase their profits. Taxation was reduced, for the Republicans had no desire to undertake ambitious schemes which would require public money. Occasionally they were pushed into passing laws designed to bring about social and economic improvements, for example assisting poor farmers with loans, but such activity was unusual. Many Republicans were extremely conservative and believed that it was quite wrong to handicap private enterprise by state regulations, or build welfare schemes* on the basis of government action. They despised socialism and communism which interfered with personal freedom. They disliked trade unions which interfered with a businessman's freedom to make profits. In the early 1920s the courts were used to smash strikes in coalmines and in transport, and troops were called in to disperse those who protested.

* A later Republican President, Richard Nixon (in 1972), still associated the 'welfare ethic' with weakness and dependence, the 'work ethic' with strength and independence.

'The business of America is business,' Coolidge declared in 1925. There was little room for sympathy with the weak, whether they were American citizens who found it difficult to keep up in the rat-race or luckless foreign states struggling to pay their debts to the USA. 'They hired the money, didn't they?' Coolidge asked. They must therefore pay it back at a proper business-man's rate of interest.

(*ii*) **Economic prosperity.** For those able to prosper in this system of 'rugged individualism', life in America in the 1920s was exciting. Henry Ford brought mass production to the car industry, flooding the country with fifteen million Model 'T' Fords by 1927. One came hurtling off the assembly line every twenty seconds. They could be bought on hire purchase, as could almost everything else: it was a matter of 'hiring money' and paying it back later. Never before had there been so many things to be bought: motor cars and radio sets, household gadgets, hats and clothes and cigarettes, tickets to travel

Fig. 3.2 Ford and the Model T – symbols of American prosperity in the 1920s, commemorated on a stamp of 1965

and tickets for cinemas and even shares on the stock exchange. Frenzied and syncopated music, skirts which became steadily shorter, the fashionable use of make-up, the tango and the Charleston all heightened the illusion that people had never before been so free and so rich, and that never again could they ever be poor. Few had much time to spare for those who contrived to remain poor amidst the plenty.

(*iii*) **Prohibition and violence.** One thing, in theory, money could not buy. In 1919, legislation was introduced in the USA to prohibit the manufacture and sale of alcoholic drinks, and in 1920 the whole of the country became 'dry'. During the war a long-powerful temperance movement had taken the oppor-tunity to argue that alcohol was unpatriotic, apparently because it was frequently sold by Americans of German descent. *Prohibition* lasted from 1920 to 1933 and involved the authorities in an endless struggle with the numerous people who sought to break the law. Since Prohibition agents were comparatively few, evasion of the law was widespread.

Illegal 'booze' was seldom difficult to obtain. Illegal places mushroomed in which to drink it and Chicago alone had ten thousand of these 'speakeasies'. Businessmen who had no objection to gaining their profits by breaking the law set up criminal gangs to obtain and distribute alcoholic drinks, to bribe the police and to keep rival gangs from getting a share of their profits. Gangs had private 'armies', well-equipped with firearms, including portable machine-guns, and found the motor car ideal for conducting mobile warfare. Supplying the drinks trade ('bootlegging') thus became a major factor in spreading crime. Gang leaders such as Al Capone became as notorious as Jesse James and the wild men of previous American generations. Capone's annual earnings were an estimated 60 million dollars: when the law finally sent him to prison it was not for murder, violence or 'bootlegging' but for evading income tax – and that was not until 1931. It was not a matter on which the government wished to spend much money: the staff of the Bureau of Prohibition never exceeded 4 500. They were poorly paid, quite likely to be shot and it did little for their morale when they were required, in 1927, to take civil service examinations. In the end, the only way to deal with the problem was to abolish Prohibition.

It was not only Prohibition which made America violent in the 1920s: there was widespread intolerance. The *Ku Klux Klan*, a Southern white supremacist society, was active in the 1920s in support of 'pure Americanism'. This theoretically secret organization had a membership of well over four million, who hunted down and terrorized those who seemed to threaten the purity of the USA. Those who were black attracted their vicious attention, and Jews and Roman Catholics were also attacked, as were those who tried to introduce un-American ideas. To members of the Klan, it was un-American to believe in international co-operation, the theories of Darwin, communism or racial equality. And the Klan was not without influence over the government.

Americans as a whole, however, were little interested in the ideas of the outside world. Many regarded socialism, the League of Nations and even trade unions as un-American and undesirable. The Ku Klux Klan and the frequently violent denunciation of suspected communists merely carried to more extreme lengths the views which many Americans held during the Republican domination of the 1920s.

The American bubble burst in 1929. Prosperity gave way to the Depression. The Republicans gave way, shortly afterwards, to the Democrats. Democracy survived but many other American attitudes had to be changed (see Unit Four).

(b) Great Britain in the 1920s

Before 1914 it had become a feature of democracy in Britain that the electors would choose to be ruled either by the Conservatives or by the Liberals. In 1906, they chose the Liberals and, at the same time, elected to the House of Commons twenty-nine members of the Labour Party. The Liberals continued to rule until the First World War brought about first a coalition government and then a change of Prime Minister. The new Prime Minister, at the end of 1916, was David Lloyd George. He was a Liberal but, when he became Prime Minister, he displaced Asquith, the leader of the party. Many Liberals considered that this was an act of disloyalty. Thus when Britain held a general election in December 1918, party politics were in a state of some confusion.

Lloyd George had gained a reputation as 'the man who won the war', through his energy and capacity for producing new ideas. He wanted to remain Prime Minister. The act which extended the right to vote (see Section 3.1) prepared the way. An armistice ended the war on 11 November and three days later the date of the general election was announced. Some people thought that it was too soon to hold a general election and that Lloyd George was rushing things simply to make the most of his current popularity.

(*i*) **The election of 1918.** The Labour Party withdrew from the Coalition at once and prepared to offer itself as an alternative government. Britain had never had a Labour government and the party had only a few MPs in the House of Commons. In 1918 it provided itself with a new constitution, with some commitment to socialist policies ('a new social order' and 'planned co-operation in production and distribution'). But few considered that the Labour Party could win the election. The traditional choice between Liberals and Conservatives was of more immediate interest.

Lloyd George could not rely on wholehearted Liberal support. He was not willing to give way to the section of the party which thought he should now step down in favour of Asquith. The war had been won and Lloyd George was now full of enthusiasm to win the peace. The Liberal Party was thus divided between Lloyd George supporters and Asquith supporters (the Squiffites).

Bonar Law led the Conservatives and on 22 November he and Lloyd George issued a joint manifesto. They argued that it would be sensible to continue the Coalition to tackle the formidable problems of postwar reconstruction. Lloyd George was thus assured of substantial backing, adding the Conservatives to those Liberals who preferred him to Asquith. The Conservatives gained too: they could cash in on the Prime Minister's popularity and benefit from the even more embittered divisions among the Liberals. The election of 1918 was therefore a three-cornered contest between the Labour Party, the Squiffites and the Lloyd George–Bonar Law combination.

Coalition supporters received a letter from Lloyd George and Bonar Law recommending their election. Asquith called the letter a 'coupon', meaning the term to be disparaging, and the election came to be called 'the coupon election'. Lloyd George remained Prime Minister. But the election was a disaster for Asquith's Liberals: they won only 28 seats. The Labour Party won 59; the rest were Coalition supporters, the bulk of them Conservatives. It was a massive victory for Lloyd George but it was a dangerous victory which left him almost a prisoner of the Conservatives, who provided 389 of his 526 supporters in the new House of Commons. Lloyd George would now have to keep the Conservatives happy in spite of his strong anti-Tory inclinations. When it suited them, they could abandon him.

(*ii*) **Lloyd George's government 1918–22.** Baldwin later referred to Lloyd George as 'a dynamic force'. The government was often vigorous but fewer major reforms were passed than might have been expected. The housing problem was an urgent one and, in 1919, Addison's Act laid down the new principle that the government would help local authorities to build 'council houses'. About 200 000 were built while Lloyd George was in power. The scheme was not perfect but it went some way towards the 'homes fit for heroes' which the Prime Minister had promised. The Unemployment Insurance Act of 1920 extended to many more of the working classes the scheme of insurance against unemployment which Lloyd George himself had introduced in 1911. In the following year, the 'dole' was introduced. This allowed those who had been unemployed for so long that they did not qualify for unemployment benefit to get 'extended' benefits, paid for by the government. The government might have done better service to tackle the causes of unemployment (see also Section 4.2(*b*)).

An immediate postwar boom gave way to a slump, and serious economic problems led to economies and the shelving of ambitious schemes. The government was plagued by industrial troubles. It avoided taking decisive action such as nationalizing the coal mines, which would have been of benefit in the years to come. But Lloyd George could not afford to annoy his Conservative supporters. Like American Republicans, they were unwilling to spend public money and, in 1922, government spending was actually cut when the business world became obsessed with the idea that it was leading to bankruptcy. (Economic problems are considered, together with industrial problems, in Section 4.2(*b*)).

Problems in other parts of the world also clamoured for the attention of Lloyd George's government. Almost as soon as the election results were published the Prime Minister had to attend the Peace Conference in Paris (see Unit Two). New foreign problems quickly followed the Peace Settlement, among them the Chanak Crisis (see Section 2.7 and Unit Seven). There were problems too in the Empire, particularly acute in Ireland, and pressing in India and Egypt (see Section 6.2). Lloyd George bubbled with ideas, many of them constructive, but his government from 1918 to 1922 seemed caught up in 'a journey through chaos'. The magic of the Prime Minister's name faded, and he had outlived his usefulness to the Conservatives. Prodded by Stanley Baldwin in a famous meeting at the Carlton Club, the Conservatives voted to withdraw their support. Lloyd George had no alternative but to resign immediately. He never again held political office.

(*iii*) **Bonar Law's and Baldwin's governments 1922–3.** A general election was held in November 1922. Bonar Law had already replaced Lloyd George as

Prime Minister, and the Conservatives had no difficulty in winning the election against a still-divided Liberal Party and a still-young Labour Party. In May 1923, however, on the point of death, Bonar Law was forced to retire, leaving behind him a scramble for the Conservative leadership.

The choice fell on Baldwin who was a loyal party man and who, unlike Austen Chamberlain and Lord Curzon, had not made personal enemies. He was also very different from Lloyd George, unlikely to get involved in crises like that at Chanak, a man who might be expected to usher in a quiet time. He was quickly able to create his own legend as 'Honest Stan'; with the coming of radio, indeed, he was able to present himself as the nation's uncle, calmly unfolding his policies to the people through their wirelesses and inspiring every confidence. In a man of such virtue, ability seemed to be of secondary importance.

At the start, however, Baldwin's behaviour was hardly predictable. His party had a substantial majority and seemed likely to hold office for another four years. But at the end of 1923, Baldwin decided to hold another election. Economic problems were grave: to solve them, Britain needed to abandon free trade and follow the example of the USA and other countries in putting tariffs on foreign goods. This had not been part of the Conservatives' policy at

Fig. 3.3 Ramsay MacDonald (Margaret Bondfield and J.H. Thomas to his left), Britain's first Labour Prime Minister, 1924

the 1922 election so it would be honest to hold another election and put the issue before the people. This was democracy at its finest. Of course, there were suggestions that Baldwin had other motives, perhaps to declare support for tariffs before Lloyd George could do so, lest Lloyd George work some miracle and once more become a popular hero.

The Liberals scrambled to re-unite their party and managed to win 159 seats. Labour did even better and raised their total to 191. The Conservatives lost substantially and secured only 260 seats. No party had an overall majority. Baldwin's gamble had failed. Since the Liberals would not support a Conservative government, George V invited Ramsay MacDonald to take office. For the first time, Britain had a Labour Prime Minister.

(*iv*) **MacDonald's government 1924.** The minority Labour government lasted only from January to October 1924. It could only remain in office with Liberal support – so it could pursue only those policies of which the Liberals approved. It was impossible to bring about the 'new social order' which the Labour Party had been advocating since 1918, and the country's economic problems were too deep-rooted to be dealt with quickly (see Section 4.2(*b*)). The Labour government treated the trade union movement with near-indifference and industrial unrest remained acute. As Foreign Secretary as well as Prime Minister, however, MacDonald worked hard for international goodwill (see Section 7.2(*c*)).

MacDonald's government passed only one outstanding Act. The Wheatley Housing Act allocated £9 million a year to be paid by the government to help local authorities build more 'council houses' (which expanded the building industry). When the Act was scrapped in 1933, 500 000 houses had been built under its provisions.

MacDonald then doomed his government to commit suicide like Baldwin in 1923. He stubbornly refused to accept a Liberal demand for an inquiry into why the prosecution of the editor of the *Workers' Weekly* had been dropped. The editor, J.R. Campbell, had written an article which, some said, was an incitement to mutiny. The *Workers' Weekly* was a communist paper and the government was already suspected of being too friendly to communist Russia (see Section 5.1, page 94). The Campbell affair was no more than a storm in a teacup, but MacDonald's refusal to accept an inquiry was fatal. The government was defeated and resigned. Britain held yet another general election, the third in less than two years.

(*v*) **Baldwin's second government 1924–9.** What was needed was a clear electoral verdict and a period of stable government, preferably by a government which would tackle basic social and economic problems. Partly due to the *Zinoviev Letter*, the electoral result was clear and until 1929 Britain secured the stable government of Baldwin. The Letter was said to have come from Zinoviev, acting for the *Comintern* (a Russian-based organization for the spreading of communism). Its purpose was to encourage communist revolution in Britain but it may well have been a forgery. In any case, it said nothing new, though it said it at an inconvenient moment. Conservative newspapers did their best to promote a 'red scare', to daub MacDonald and the Labour Party with unsavoury connections with the Bolsheviks.

When the votes were counted, Labour had actually collected over a million votes more than in the previous election, but such were the oddities of the British electoral system that they managed at the same time to lose 40 seats. The Conservatives won 419 seats, ensuring a stable Conservative government. The Liberals, on the other hand, lost both votes and seats and had only 40 MPs in the new House of Commons.

Opinion had apparently polarized and the majority of the voters now looked on elections as involving a choice mainly between Conservatives and Labour. Voters now put the Liberals as a sort of middle-of-the-road party, somewhere between Conservatives and Labour. On issues such as the Zinoviev Letter, they tended to choose one of the main parties, either to demonstrate their own loyalties or to try to keep those they disliked from power. It was often claimed that British democracy rested on a two-party system. The Liberals had now ceased to be one of the two major parties, apparently the real victims of the Red Letter scare.

Baldwin's government did almost nothing to solve basic economic problems. Probably the most spectacular event in these five years was the General Strike of 1926 (see Section 4.2(b)). The Strike passed with remarkably little violence. It was undoubtedly one of Baldwin's achievements that he gave the country 'tranquillity'. Even the class war, so active elsewhere after the Bolshevik revolution of 1917, was lulled almost to sleep. When the next election occurred, in 1929, the Conservatives put their faith in posters of Stanley Baldwin and the slogan 'Safety First'; they even produced a song in his honour for grateful and musical electors to sing. Unfortunately posters, slogans and songs were unavailing. Baldwin was defeated.

His government left on the statute book a variety of useful Acts. The most outstanding was the Local Government Act of 1929. The most unexpected was the Franchise Act of 1928. The Franchise Act gave the vote to women on the same terms as men and enfranchised the 'flappers', the young women aged from twenty-one to thirty. It was almost the first occasion on which the Conservatives had seized such an initiative in extending democracy in Britain.

Neville Chamberlain, a highly successful Minister of Health, put a great deal of thought and work into the Local Government Act. It was one of the outstanding Acts of the interwar years. The poor law unions, which dated from the previous century, were abolished. County and borough councils took over their responsibilities for the poor. Sweeping changes were made in local government, the powers of county councils enlarged and new arrangements introduced to assist local government with money from government funds. The Act was the government's and perhaps Neville Chamberlain's most impressive achievement.

Earlier Chamberlain, working with Winston Churchill, the Chancellor of the Exchequer, produced a Pensions Act in 1925. It further extended the insurance schemes of Lloyd George, now making provision for widows and orphans and for old age pensions for workers and their wives. The first old age pensions dated from 1908 but they had been little more than a form of meagre state charity. The new pensions were to be part of the insurance scheme. Workers contributed to the insurance fund and secured pensions as a right when they reached sixty-five.

The Conservatives also set up the Central Electricity Board to control the generation of power and to distribute it throughout the country on a national grid, a measure of considerable importance. In the same year, 1926, the BBC (British Broadcasting Corporation) was established, putting broadcasting firmly under the control of a public corporation – a type of body later much favoured by the Labour Party.

These were among the solid achievements of Baldwin's government. Some other accomplishments were more open to question. In 1925, Churchill returned Britain to the gold standard (see Section 4.2(b)) with results that were damaging to Britain's exports. Unemployment did not fall below the million mark and the government seemed to have few ideas for dealing with the problem. The government had every intention of keeping down public spending and, although generally unsuccessful in this, it added to its unpopularity by holding down the payments of unemployment benefit.

Baldwin's government also showed hostility to trade unionism. The General Strike was followed by the Trades Disputes Act, in 1927. This Act made both general strikes and strikes in sympathy illegal, forbade civil servants' unions to link with the Trades Union Congress and the Labour Party, and struck a damaging blow at unions which used funds for political purposes. The working classes, especially the miners, had already suffered a major defeat in the General Strike. This Act could easily be made to look petty. Labour supporters continued to grieve about it and Attlee's government repealed it after the Second World War.

(vi) **MacDonald's second government 1929–31.** The election of 1929 again produced an indecisive result, and once again MacDonald became Prime Minister without a majority in the House of Commons.

This second Labour government lasted only until 1931. Margaret Bondfield became the first woman to hold Cabinet rank when she was appointed Minister of Labour. Arthur Henderson became Foreign Secretary and showed the concern for international co-operation which had been a feature of MacDonald's first government (see Section 7.2(c)). The government also showed an interest in the Empire and especially in trying to improve the situation in India by holding Round Table Conferences (see Section 6.2(c)). But like all governments between the wars, this one had no convincing policies to deal with economic problems. It was also unfortunate in coming to power when the problems were worsening; only a few months after MacDonald took office, the world made a steep dive into the Depression.

The need to rely on Liberal votes in the Commons was once again a severe handicap. The government made a study of the unemployment problem, which produced hardly any results at all. Public works were undertaken to provide a few jobs, but unemployment had risen sharply since 1929. Snowden was the Chancellor of the Exchequer and he had a deep dislike of spending public money. The crisis deepened and the government was reduced to a state of near-paralysis.

Its death blow was struck in August 1931. A deep division developed within the Cabinet. Unemployment was nearing three million. A variety of committees of 'experts' produced gloomy reports. All the 'respectable' organizations such as those of financiers, employers and newspaper-owners maintained that the only salvation lay in cutting public spending. There was now a financial crisis as well as the basic economic crisis with its high level of unemployment. Cutting public spending would restore confidence among financiers. But it would not help the unemployed; trade unions and most of the Labour Party recoiled in horror at the suggestion that rates of benefit to the unemployed should be cut, along with the salaries of public servants, in order to help the confidence of financiers. In fact, benefits to the unemployed were in 1931 a third higher than they had been ten years earlier and the cost of living had fallen, but the issue was an emotional one. To most Labour supporters, it seemed indecent to kick the unemployed to help the Bank of England. But MacDonald, Snowden and Jimmy Thomas, the Lord Privy Seal, all had great respect for authority and insisted on making the cuts. The rest of the Cabinet protested. MacDonald resigned. Thus the economic crisis and the financial crisis combined to produce a political crisis (see Sections 4.2(*b*) and 4.3).

(*vii*) **National government 1931–5.** MacDonald in fact performed a somersault. He handed in his resignation as Prime Minister of the Labour government but instantly accepted reappointment as Prime Minister of the National (Coalition) government. For the next four years, like Lloyd George before him, he led a government supported mainly by the Conservatives. The electors obviously approved. In October 1931 they returned 554 supporters of MacDonald's National administration compared with only 52 Labour MPs and 37 Liberals of various allegiances. The Labour Party licked its wounds in Opposition and waited for better times.

It was a remarkable tribute to British democracy that, in its gravest economic crisis in history and when other states were turning desperately to imagined saviours such as Adolf Hitler, Britain sought salvation in a quietly unimaginative government which was a sort of double-act between MacDonald and Baldwin. MacDonald remained Prime Minister while Baldwin looked over his shoulder as Lord President of the Council. In 1935, for want of any better idea, they changed places (see Section 4.4(*b*)).

(c) **France to 1939**

The Third Republic, established in France in 1870, lasted until 1940. The head of state was an elected president. Government was carried on by a prime minister supported in and responsible to parliament. It was a democratic but not always an efficient system. Unlike Britain, France had no tradition of a choice between two major parties. There were so many parties that governments could only be formed by grouping several of them together in coalitions. With the first heated controversy, such coalitions then tended to fall apart. As a result, French democracy from 1917 to 1940 produced 44 different governments, and called on over 20 different prime ministers. But France did not abandon her democratic system until she was invaded by Germany in 1940.

After the Peace Conference of Paris Clemenceau was Prime Minister only until January 1920. At this time, the dominant groups in French politics were right wing. They were known as the *Bloc National* and their main aim was to ensure the weakness of Germany. Poincaré was Prime Minister from 1922 to 1924 and gave expression to the Bloc's anti-German feelings by occupying the Ruhr (see pages 61, 126 and 129).

A swing of opinion against the Bloc brought in a series of governments in which Aristide Briand was influential. He controlled French foreign policy from 1925 to 1932, and was Prime Minister in 1925–6 and again in 1929. In all, between 1909 and 1929, Briand was Prime Minister of eleven governments and yet his total time in office was less than that of Baldwin from 1924 to 1929. French foreign policy under Briand's influence became more constructive with the making of international agreements, some of them involving Germany.

France, being less dependent on foreign trade than other major European nations, suffered fewer economic problems than did Britain during the 1920s. The war left tremendous problems of reconstruction but by 1924 much progress had been made. Agriculture regained a degree of prosperity. An influx of foreign workers helped to repair losses in manpower. Heavy industry developed rapidly: the need to replace devastated industrial plant enabled France to equip herself with the most up-to-date and efficient machines. Tariffs were used to protect both agriculture and industry. After the immediate period of postwar reconstruction, the main problems were the stability of the franc and the balancing of successive governments' budgets. France also faced industrial unrest.

Poincaré was again Prime Minister from 1926 to 1929 and while Briand pursued better relations with foreign governments, Poincaré took measures to stabilize the value of the franc and encouraged a measure of prosperity based partly on cheap money (loans, that is, at low rates of interest).

Major reforms were few in this period. In 1928 and 1930, social insurance schemes were introduced. In 1932, family allowances were added. But by this time, the world was in the grip of the Depression (see Section 4.3). Although the effects on France were less severe than elsewhere the Depression did coincide with another period of serious instability in French politics. Briand and Poincaré were elderly and with their retirement a new generation of politicians took control. Few of them showed outstanding qualities.

French politics became so unstable in the 1930s that there even seemed to be a possibility that France would abandon democracy. Particularly serious were the riots in 1934 which resulted from the *Stavisky Affair*. When Stavisky, a shady financier, was found to have committed 'suicide', rumours circulated that he had been murdered to cover up corruption among politicians and the police. Political and financial scandals were not new in France, but the Depression was beginning to take effect; unemployment figures were rising; discontent was widespread and a succession of weak governments, under Daladier, Sarraut and Chautemps, produced only despair. The Stavisky Affair led to street rioting. The extreme right demonstrated in favour of strong government. The extreme left demonstrated in favour of a communist system. A government led by Daladier lasted for only nine days. Paris rioters tried to break into parliament.

A new government under Doumergue with sweeping emergency powers managed to restore stability. It was a broad coalition, almost an all-party government whose powers, in effect, temporarily suspended French democracy in order to weather the storm. New elections followed in 1936, however, and brought a new experiment. The parties of the left drew together in a Popular Front with policies of reform and a determination to preserve France against fascism. Blum became the first Popular-Front Prime Minister and the government busied itself with social reform and with dissolving antidemocratic fascist groups. But the Front fell apart in 1938. Daladier now led a radical government and had to deal with a general strike. He was still in office when the Second World War began and France was still clinging stubbornly to her democratic system. But economic problems and political instability had weakened the country during the 1930s, playing into the hands of Hitler and Mussolini (see Unit Eight).

3.3 Unsuccessful Democracies

Except in France, Scandinavia, the north-western corner of Europe and Czechoslovakia, democracy enjoyed little success on the continent of Europe in the 1920s and 1930s. A democratic experiment in Russia in 1917 lasted for less than a year (see Section 5.1). Similar experiments in Hungary, Poland and Austria quickly ran into difficulties. Italy's pursuit of democracy ended soon after Mussolini became Prime Minister in 1922. Spain hovered between democracy and dictatorship and arrived at a Popular Front only to plunge into civil war and a new dictatorship towards the end of the 1930s (see Section 3.3(c)). Section 2.9(a) has already mentioned the collapse of democracy in Jugoslavia. When Hitler came to power in Germany in 1933, the Weimar Republic too was quickly destroyed though it had lasted longer, and

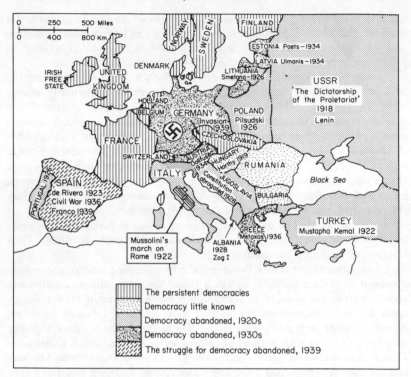

Fig. 3.4 The eclipse of democracy in Europe, 1918–39

been more successful, than many other democratic systems. For supporters of democracy the many political upheavals were disheartening, even bewildering. They weakened the League of Nations and quickly destroyed whatever confidence had remained after the Peace Settlement of 1919–20.

(a) Italy to 1923

(*i*) **Instability after the war.** Italy had combined a monarchy with a system of parliamentary government since 1861. The right to vote was given only to a minority of the population and political life was handicapped by the opposition of the Pope who instructed Catholics not to take part in Italy's government. As in France, numerous political parties gave rise to weak coalition governments. Frequently, politicians seemed to be concerned more with manoeuvring for power (and bribery was not uncommon) than with the solution of Italy's many serious problems.

When the First World War ended, the Pope withdrew his ban on political life and a Sicilian priest formed a Catholic Popular Party. This party (like the Socialists) gained considerable support in the postwar years. But parliament became even more fragmented than before, and it was even more difficult for stable coalitions to be formed. Ministries continued to be short-lived and unstable, just when Italy needed a period of lengthy and stable government. The country was discontented and frustrated. The war had caused many casualties. The economy was disrupted and exports, mainly luxury goods, could not be sold. There were few tourists to boost Italy's income and it was difficult to pay for vital imports. Unemployment increased the industrial unrest which had already been serious before the war (with a general strike and a near-revolutionary situation in 1914). There was a deep-rooted problem of poverty, especially in the south of Italy and bandits plagued the country, their numbers swelled by deserters from the war.

From 1917 to 1919, Orlando was Prime Minister but he lost favour during the Paris Peace Conference, and after him nobody could establish effective government. The parliamentary system and professional politicians were discredited. Italians began to look elsewhere for effective action to deal with unemployment, high prices, lawlessness and what appeared to be a weak foreign policy.

The left wing took their inspiration from the Bolshevik Revolution in Russia and conflict between right and left grew fiercer towards the end of 1920. Strikes were common; factory-owners replied with lock-outs and some workers then seized control of factories, only surrendering when minor concessions were made. A few soviets were also established, on the Russian pattern, and early in 1921 the Communist Party separated from the Socialists, apparently committed to the violent revolution being preached from Moscow.

Giolitti, the Prime Minister, wavered uncertainly and then decided to hold a general election in April 1921. The Communists won only 13 seats (out of 535). A new, right-wing party, the Fascists, whom Giolitti had foolishly regarded as allies in the election, won 35 seats and at once turned against his government. Unable any longer to cope Giolitti resigned, but his successor, Bonomi, was equally helpless in a country becoming increasingly violent. When he resigned, the divisions in parliament were such that it took weeks to find a new Prime Minister. When one was found, Facta, he led an even weaker coalition, almost powerless to act at all. It was only a matter of time before the manoeuvres in parliament became altogether irrelevant. Such an unstable political situation was ready-made for a seizure of power by some unscrupulous and ruthless man of action.

(*ii*) **Mussolini and the Fascist Party.** Benito Mussolini led the 35 Fascists in the Italian parliament. He had been born in 1883, the son of a socialist blacksmith. At first his career was totally undistinguished. He narrowly avoided expulsion from school but qualified as a teacher. After a year's teaching, he left Italy for Switzerland, thus avoiding military service. Manual labourer and vagrant, he was expelled from Switzerland for his violent socialist opinions, spent some time in France and returned to Italy to do his military service. A breach of the peace brought a short spell in prison, in 1908, after which he went to Austria from where he was deported.

When the war began in 1914, Mussolini had made a certain mark as a violent socialist agitator and editor of *Avanti*, a left-wing journal. But his career was littered with quarrels to which he was soon to add another. Italy was at first neutral in the war but it was Mussolini's opinion that she should join it. He set up his own paper, *Il Popolo d'Italia*, and tried to combine socialist and nationalist views. The Socialists disapproved and he was expelled from the party.

Mussolini persisted. His paper preached violent nationalism and he set up action groups to demonstrate, mainly in Milan. They were known as *Fasci di Combattimento*. When Italy joined the war, in 1915, against the Central Powers, Mussolini was conscripted into the army but discharged in 1917, having been wounded in an accidental explosion. He returned to Milan and his paper.

At the end of the war, Mussolini was able to continue to express violently nationalist views, to spread them through his paper and through the Fasci which were now revived. He had a contempt for democracy and for pacifism and at this point he developed a new mission: to save Italy from communism and to bring her strong government. Industrialists and landowners provided funds – to destroy the 'Reds' and protect their own property – and the movement grew. Mussolini's supporters were dressed in black shirts. They adopted the Roman salute and carried daggers, taking as their symbol the *fasces* of Ancient Rome, a bundle of rods bound round an axe. They organized a national party, the Fascist Party – but, in 1919, they could not win a single parliamentary seat.

The Fasci, however, developed, with practice, into highly successful thugs. They broke up communist meetings and beat up their opponents. Early in 1921, they claimed to have a quarter of a million members although they could still win only 6 per cent of the seats in parliament and had little in the way of a coherent programme. They did much to break up the socialist organizations which Mussolini had previously supported and to smash trade unions, to the delight of many employers. All over Italy, walls were decorated with Mussolini's portrait and the new Fascist slogan, 'Believe. Obey. Fight.'

In July 1922, the left tried to fight back with a general strike. It was a disastrous failure but it was Mussolini's opportunity. While Mussolini pointed to the weakness and inadequacy of the government, his Fascists kept the public services running and launched new attacks on left-wing organizations. They burned the printing presses of *Avanti* and their lawlessness went unpunished.

(*iii*) **The March on Rome.** Mussolini thought it important to act quickly, to make the most use of the discontent and chaos. He intended that Fascists would at least share in the government, in spite of being so few in parliament. Showman that he was, however, he felt that this needed a grand gesture.

Already Mussolini had helped to make himself more respectable, declaring that he had no hostile intentions toward the monarchy or the Church, thus reversing previous declarations. Now the Fascists planned a march on Rome: 50 000 Fascists, armed and drilled like soldiers, would occupy the capital. Mussolini had powerful friends among the propertied classes but the loyalties of the army were uncertain – he could, however, slip into exile again if the plans misfired.

In the event, no march was needed. The King, Victor Emmanuel III, refused Facta's demand for emergency powers. He, too, lacked confidence in the government and was unsure of the army. It was simpler to give in to the Fascist leader. Facta resigned. A telegram was sent to Mussolini and he came to Rome to be Prime Minister, arriving in borrowed morning suit, top hat and spats. The Fascist Blackshirts followed, in time to hold a victory parade. Mussolini had succeeded with the mere threat of a march.

In spite of the bluster, Mussolini had come to power almost legally. His first government was yet another coalition, with only four Fascists in the cabinet. But within a month, parliament granted him full powers until the end of 1923. In 1923, it was agreed that the party with the most votes in an election would have two-thirds of the seats in parliament. In 1924, a general election, in any case, gave the Fascists two-thirds of the votes. A few months later the forceful Socialist parliamentarian, Matteotti, was found murdered, a victim of the Fascists who resented his outspoken book, *The Fascists Exposed*. Italy was clearly on the road to dictatorship, especially when Mussolini resorted to censorship and repression, as well as filling local appointments with Fascists. (The history of Italy under Mussolini continues in Section 5.2(*a*).)

(*b*) Germany to 1933

William II, the German Kaiser (Emperor) was forced to abdicate two days before the armistice in November 1918. In February 1919, a Constituent Assembly met at Weimar to work out a new German constitution. The details were agreed within six months and the *Weimar Republic* created. The government moved from Weimar to the capital, Berlin, in 1920.

On paper at least, the new constitution provided Germany with an almost perfect democracy. There would be elections every four years, to elect (by universal suffrage, secret ballot and proportional representation) the Reichstag (lower house of parliament). Every seven years, the people would elect a President, as head of state. It would be one of the President's duties to appoint a Chancellor who, with his ministers, would be responsible to the Reichstag and would therefore need the support of the majority of that House. According to their size, the German states such as Prussia and Bavaria would send representatives to the Reichsrat, an upper house with a delaying power similar to that of the British House of Lords. The constitution contained guarantees of basic human rights. It even provided for plebiscites, to register the wishes of the people on matters of grave importance.

The Chancellor was more important than the President. The success of the system depended on whether a Chancellor could command a clear majority in the Reichstag. If not, Germany, like France and Italy, would be plagued by short-lived and weak coalition governments. Success also depended on the readiness of Germans to turn almost overnight from the authoritarian system of the former Kaiser to the liberal and democratic system of the Weimar constitution. From the beginning, some Germans showed a preference for different systems and a willingness to back their opinions with violence.

(*i*) **Opposition to the system.** Communists wanted a revolution similar to that of the Russian Bolsheviks. Nationalists and militarists hated the communists and despised republican democracy. They associated democracy with surrender and with the allegedly unfair treatment of Germany in the Treaty of Versailles (see Section 2.4). The new constitution was soon under attack from both left and right.

The left struck first. The German Spartacus League (*Spartacists*, who took their name from a rebel-gladiator and slave-leader of Ancient Rome) aimed to establish communism. Soviets were set up in Berlin and the Baltic ports. Revolutionary sailors briefly took prisoner Ebert, the first President of the Weimar Republic. Eisner proclaimed an independent socialist state in Bavaria. But Karl Liebknecht and Rosa Luxemburg, the leaders of the Spartacists, were murdered. Eisner met the same fate and, after a bitter struggle, the authorities regained control of Berlin. For the moment, victory lay with the moderates. In the first postwar elections, German communists won no seats whereas nearly 40 per cent of the Reichstag consisted of moderate socialists, the Social Democrats. On the right, however, nationalists won 10 per cent of the seats.

The nationalists wanted a Germany which was strong. They condemned those who had accepted Germany's surrender and forced the Kaiser to abdicate as 'November Criminals' (a term used at various times to denounce democrats, republicans, communists, socialists and Jews). Many who supported the nationalists volunteered for service in the *Frei Korps*, a sort of vigilante army with a passion for order and a hatred of communism. In 1920 there were further attempts to destroy the new republic. A communist-led rising in the Ruhr was put down by the army and the Frei Korps, but when, about the same time, other army units and members of the Frei Korps tried to seize Berlin they were defeated by the city's workers who paralysed the capital with a general strike after the government had fled to Dresden. This attempt came to be known as the *Kapp Putsch*. The government was too weak to punish many of the conspirators. Only the luckless Dr Kapp was singled out and imprisoned. He died in prison.

The courts showed a reluctance to punish right-wing law-breakers throughout the violent period of the early 1920s. There were further communist-led risings of workers. Munich and Bavaria became a breeding-ground for nationalist (often anti-Jewish) agitation, and a base from which to plot the overthrow of the republic. The nationalists showed open hostility to democracy in the Reichstag. Political assassinations were not uncommon. With a series of weak coalition governments from the outset and with a variety of Chancellors, the Weimar Republic struggled for its life.

(*ii*) **The crises of 1923.** Matters came to a head in 1923. Coalition governments had been no more successful in managing the economy than in dealing with lawlessness. Germany's balance of payments position had been precarious since the war. Exports were difficult to sell. Reparations had to be paid. The mark was weak and its value fell steadily. In a short-sighted effort to solve immediate difficulties, governments simply issued more money and inflation resulted. Prices galloped ahead more quickly in Germany than elsewhere in Europe and in 1922 the situation was already grave.

In January 1923 French troops, assisted by the Belgians, occupied the Ruhr. Germany was unstable, economically weak, unable to keep up her payments of reparations, and the French decided to help themselves by seizing the rich Ruhr industrial area. On the advice of their government and Chancellor Cuno, the Ruhr workers refused to co-operate with the French: they were punished by mass arrests and France imposed an economic blockade of the whole area, including much of the Rhineland.

The occupation of the Ruhr created even more havoc in Germany. The French gained little but their invasion disrupted the German economy and dealt a death blow to the mark. In 1914, it took just over 4 marks to purchase an American dollar. At the end of 1922, it already took over 7 000. In July 1923, the figure was 160 000. The German currency was out of control and in November one needed 4 200 000 000 000 marks to equal a dollar. Printing-presses could not keep up with the changes. Bank notes and stamps were printed and overprinted with ever more crazy figures. It was easier to resort to barter than to try to keep up with the useless flood of paper money. Bank balances became valueless, wiping out savings. A suit-case became more useful than a purse for carrying one's money.

Not unnaturally, there was a wave of anger which agitators were quick to exploit. There was a communist rising in Hamburg which was routed by the police. Left-wing and right-wing plots multiplied. But the army remained loyal. Chancellor Cuno resigned and Ebert called on Gustav Stresemann to form a new government.

Stresemann took office in August 1923, with a widely-based coalition to save the republic. In November, the *Munich Putsch* occurred. It was already too late and was also badly planned. Supported by the veteran soldier General Ludendorff, who had already backed the Kapp Putsch, it was organized by Adolf Hitler who intended to take control of Bavaria and then lead a nationalist attack on Berlin. The Bavarian police killed sixteen of Hitler's supporters but Hitler, sufficiently insignificant for the authorities to risk punishing him, was sent to prison for five years. Ludendorff was acquitted.

The Weimar Republic had at last produced an able politician in Stresemann. He quickly overcame the threat of civil war, ordered a return to work

Fig. 3.5 Stresemann, leader of the People's Party, brought new hope both to Germany and to Europe in the mid-1920s

in the Ruhr, pacified the French with a resumption of reparations payments and set about restoring the currency. It was impossible to recover lost savings and it was not until well into 1924 that an entirely new currency was devised, based on the Reichsmark and an independent Reichsbank. But from the appointment of Stresemann, the outlook brightened. Although he remained Chancellor for only three months, he did much to restore confidence. He was in charge of German foreign policy from the end of 1923 to his death in 1929, and he provided an element of stability in the Weimar Republic. One of his first achievements in foreign policy was to persuade the French to leave the Ruhr.

(*iii*) **Prosperity and optimism.** The crises of 1923 which had threatened to destroy the Weimar Republic proved, in fact, to be the beginning of a more hopeful period. The Dawes Plan and the Young Plan (see Section 4.2(*c*)) helped Germany to keep up with reparations payments. Foreign investment in the country provided capital for expansion. Unemployment was reduced, although as in Britain it obstinately refused to fall below a million. From 1925, Germans began to enjoy a degree of prosperity. There was more confidence in the republic. International relations were also improving, for the Locarno Treaties heralded a more co-operative period, to which Stresemann and Briand of France made considerable contributions (see Section 7.2), and Germany was admitted to the League of Nations in 1926.

Ebert's death made it necessary to elect a new President and in 1925 Field Marshal Hindenburg took office. He was already nearly eighty, but his aristocratic and military background pleased the nationalists: portly and nearly immobile, he seemed to personify stability.

Governments also seemed slightly more stable. Wilhelm Marx held office as Chancellor for much of the period from 1923 to 1928, with a coalition of moderate parties. Meanwhile, the Social Democrats played the part of a normal democratic opposition and although the nationalists did well in the 1924 elections they lost ground in 1928. The communists throughout kept about 10 per cent of the seats. The Reichstag was thus not free from extremist parties, but the moderates were making the system work satisfactorily. In addition, they passed useful reforms. In 1927, for instance, Marx introduced an extensive scheme for unemployment insurance and created machinery for the settlement of labour disputes.

Prosperity and optimism were short-lived, however. By the end of 1928, trading prospects were less hopeful. October 1929 brought a double disaster. The death of Stresemann in Germany and the Wall Street Crash in America again put the Weimar Republic in danger. Germany depended on foreign loans. When these suddenly ceased and when export sales rapidly dwindled, there was an almost immediate rise in unemployment. Germany plunged into the Depression (see Section 4.3).

Confidence in democracy was again shaken. Unemployment now seemed to be the first problem, but the Reichsbank was soon in trouble and the Reichsmark came under pressure. Though deflation rather than inflation was the problem, troubles in the banking world naturally revived memories of the hyper-inflation of 1923. Like MacDonald's Cabinet in Britain, German politicians argued about how to get out of their difficulties and about the need for reducing public spending and cutting unemployment benefit. German voters meanwhile showed an ominous shift away from the moderates and democrats, giving more support in 1930 to both left- and right-wing extremists.

(*iv*) **Hitler and the Nazi Party.** At last, the climate was right for Adolf Hitler to emerge from insignificance. Hitler had been born in Austria in 1889 but he joined the German army in 1914, attracted by what seemed to him the greater efficiency of the Kaiser's Germany. In any case, he had been outstandingly unsuccessful in Austria, unsuccessful at school, denied admission to art college and for years a near down-and-out on the streets of Vienna. His military career earned him two Iron Crosses and Germany's defeat filled him with shame. When the war ended, he remained in Germany and, in 1919, joined the German Workers' Party in Munich. He was not attracted by the socialism of some members of the party, but by their extreme nationalist and anti-Jewish opinions.

Hitler became one of its most fanatical members and soon rose to the party's leadership. The name was changed to National Socialist German Workers' Party, then abbreviated to National Socialists, the first four letters in the German producing *Nazi*. They developed their organization further afield than Bavaria but did not win seats in the Reichstag until after the Munich Putsch of 1923.

The Putsch and the trial which followed brought Hitler notoriety. In prison he began work on *Mein Kampf (My Struggle)*, dictating much of it to Rudolf Hess, a fellow-prisoner later to become the Nazis' deputy leader. Like Mussolini's Fascists, the Nazis by the mid-1920s had already developed many of their theatrical trappings (the Swastika, raised-arm salute and uniforms) and equipped themselves with an incoherent programme rooted in hatred – hatred of the 'November Criminals', the Treaty of Versailles, France, Russia and communism, Jews and, above all, pacifists. They won seven per cent of the seats in the Reichstag in 1924 though quickly lost most of them again. More important, they spread their party organization and recruited new fanatics. The Nazis were waiting when the crises of 1929 began.

(*v*) **The Nazi rise to power.** Hitler had already gathered his principal henchmen, among them Hess and Goering. His Brownshirts (the SA, *Sturmabteilung*) had some skill in thuggery. Hitler himself had skill in oratory, a master of abuse but also a master of promises. Others had 'betrayed' Germany, 'knifed her in the back'. Hitler and the Nazis would make Germany great again, purify the country from inferior races, such as Jews, and traitors, such as communists, solve outstanding problems, such as unemployment, and end the nonsense of reparations. In the election of 1930, they won nearly a fifth of the seats in the Reichstag although the communists also achieved their best results so far. It was a turbulent election with open violence especially by Nazis and communists.

The economic situation also grew worse. In the summer of 1931, unemployment rose to about 4 million, early in 1932 to above 6 million. The presidential election was then due. The aged Hindenburg got over $18\frac{1}{2}$ million votes and kept his office but Adolf Hitler polled a remarkable 11 million, increasing this to nearly $13\frac{1}{2}$ million in a second ballot which was necessary for Hindenburg to establish an absolute majority according to the rules of the constitution. Hitler was at last a major national politician.

The President was now senile, befuddled by the intrigues of army officers, landowners and industrialists, dismayed by the economic problems but still possessing as President the deadly power to make and un-make governments in a Reichstag where no one had a clear mandate to rule. Hindenburg appointed the aristocratic von Papen who tried in vain to gain more substantial support in two elections in 1932. The only significant result of the elections was that the Nazi Party became the largest single group in the Reichstag with 37 per cent of the seats in July 1932, falling back to 33 per cent in November. The Social Democrats were the next largest party with the communists close on their heels. Von Papen represented none of these. For a time he kept office by using emergency powers but at the end of the year Hindenburg replaced him and called on von Schleicher.

The Weimar Republic was now in its death agony. Even the ending of reparations could not save it. The President floundered ineffectively. Only the Nazis, who despised the system, could rely on substantial support in the Reichstag. The Depression was acute and Hindenburg grabbed at what seemed to be the only workable compromise, appointing Hitler Chancellor on 30 January 1933. This was the result of the latest deal among the politicians. Von Papen had thrown in his lot with Hitler in return for the office of Vice-Chancellor.

Hitler promptly arranged another election for March 1933. The campaign was a vicious one: rival parties were handicapped, their meetings broken up, members battered and newspapers muzzled. The Reichstag went up in flames, evidence, Hitler claimed, of a communist plot. The result, for the Nazis, was hardly satisfactory. They won only 44 per cent of the seats and had to rely on the Nationalists to secure a majority in the new parliament. That, however, was enough. The opposition was quickly weakened by arresting or expelling communist members and the *Enabling Law* was passed. This Act, 'For the Removal of the Distress of the People and Reich', destroyed the Weimar Republic. It gave the government full powers for four years, including the right to make new laws. Like Mussolini, Hitler achieved power by means which were almost legal; and having got power, he proceeded to destroy German democracy. (The history of Germany under Hitler continues in Section 5.2(*b*).)

(*c*) Elsewhere

Fig. 3.4 shows that supporters of democracy found little comfort elsewhere in Europe. Only *Czechoslovakia* among the new states after 1918 was able to make the system work smoothly, and Hitler destroyed Czechoslovakian democracy in 1939 (see Sections 2.9(*a*) and 8.3(*d*)).

Hungary got no further than the provisional stage in setting up a democratic republic. The system was overthrown by Bela Kun's communist revolution, and Kun himself was overthrown in August 1919 when Admiral Horthy came to power. Horthy proclaimed himself Regent for life in 1920, deputizing for the Habsburg King Charles who was not even allowed into the country. Horthy's regime carefully safeguarded the privileges of the nobility, presiding over a system which was near to being a dictatorship in spite of maintaining a few trappings of democracy. In the 1930s, Julius Gömbös was a Prime Minister who combined many of the fascist views of Mussolini with the anti-Jewish prejudices of Hitler. Hungary joined Nazi Germany in the Second World War to crusade against Communist Russia, and Horthy retained his grip on the country until the war's closing stages.

Austria persevered longer with democracy but was bound to face problems in the wake of the Treaty of St Germain (see Section 2.5). There was always tension between the city of Vienna, with its Social-Democrat sympathies and enthusiasm for ambitious socialist reforms, and the rest of Austria, conservative, suspicious of socialism and devoted to the Church. In the 1920s, Social Democrats and Christian Socialists worked together with some success to overcome economic difficulties, and international aid helped to establish the democratic system. It was little more than a veneer, however. Austrian reactionaries came under the patronage of Mussolini, creating the *Heimwehr*, which had similarities to the German Frei Korps, and a fascist political machine. In 1927 they fought in Vienna with the socialist *Schutzbund*.

The Depression brought new strains, with rising unemployment and a financial crisis in which Austria's leading bank collapsed. The Republic began to totter. Engelbert Dollfuss became Chancellor in 1932, an admirer of Mussolini and of Horthy. He regarded the democratic system as a legacy of defeat in 1918, and in 1934 suspended the constitution and gave himself emergency powers. The Social Democrats and the workers resisted but were routed in a brief civil war by the army and the Heimwehr. Dollfuss did not live to enjoy his success, however. There were Austrian nationalists who looked not to Italy but to Germany, rejoicing in the rise of Hitler and resentful that the peace-makers of 1919 had forbidden union with Germany. These Austrian Nazis murdered Dollfuss in July 1934, though their attempt to unite with Hitler's Germany proved premature (see Section 8.2). Austrian independence was nevertheless coming to an end and in 1938 the *Anschluss* occurred when Hitler incorporated the Republic in the German Reich (see Section 8.3(*b*)).

Poland experimented with a parliamentary republic which was represented at the Paris Peace Conference by the pianist-Prime Minister, Paderewski. The constitution, however, worked badly. There were too many parties for stable government, partly owing to an elaborate system of proportional representation. In 1926 the veteran Polish nationalist, Pilsudski, returned from retirement to seize Warsaw with three regiments of soldiers. From that time until his death in 1935, Pulsudski was a dictator in all but name. His regime was not entirely illiberal and elections continued to be held. After his death, army officers continued to rule, but with a viciousness that nearly provoked civil war. They admired the other dictatorships in Europe which seemed to function with an efficiency they could not achieve. And they fell victim to the efficiency of the German army in 1939.

Bulgaria, alone among the Central Powers, retained a monarchy after 1918. Until 1923 King Boris combined his monarchy with a curious peasant dictatorship led by Stamboliisky. Stamboliisky, himself of peasant origin, so organized the state that peasants got the maximum benefit at the expense of the rest of the community. He was murdered. His successors were usually nominated by the King. The country continued to be turbulent, frequently torn by the violent activities of the IMRO (Internal Macedonian Revolutionary Organization) which had a passion for assassinations. Not surprisingly, in 1934, a dictatorship of military officers came to power, with strongly fascist sympathies. The regime was further modified before the Second World War but such parliaments as were allowed had little power. Only the throne of King Boris was stable.

Albania became a monarchy. An attempt was made to set up a democratic republic in the years immediately after 1918 but the country had only existed since 1913 and there were serious economic problems. The first President of the Republic proclaimed himself King Zog I in 1928. His regime was close to dictatorship and, in any case, Italian Fascists were already preparing to take over Albania, but it was not until 1939 that Mussolini felt confident enough to chase Zog into exile.

In *Rumania* democracy might have succeeded, but the monarchy offered poor leadership, politicians were corrupt and in the 1930s the governments were often right wing and anti-Jewish. King Carol II paid little regard to popular wishes in choosing his ministers, swung from one group to another and only in 1938 arrived at the decision to devise a new constitution and to exercise more effective control through a Party of National Rebirth. It was too late. The country was soon under the control of Hitler.

Portugal had driven out her king in favour of a democratic republic in 1910 but democracy in the Iberian Peninsula, when it existed at all, existed only precariously. The army remained a force in Portuguese affairs and continuing economic backwardness, corruption and inefficiency led in 1926 to a military dictatorship. Antonio Salazar became Prime Minister in 1932 at a time of further economic confusion and was confirmed in power with a new fascist constitution a year later. His *Estado Novo* (New State) brought stability and some economic and social progress, but there was little evidence in Salazar's Portugal of democracy and liberty. The country remained apart from the mainstream of developments in Europe, almost standing still until ill-health forced Salazar's retirement in 1968.

Spain in 1918 still retained her monarchy, combining with it the Cortes, a parliament representative mainly of the propertied classes. Neither King Alfonso XIII nor his governments provided the reforming leadership the country needed. Spanish politics were often unstable, and, to economic backwardness, was added a nationalist revolt in Spanish Morocco led by Abd-el-Krim. Primo de Rivera, like Pilsudski in Poland, a military man exasperated by democratic inefficiency, seized power in Spain in 1923 to set up a fascist-type regime which had the approval of Alfonso and the powerful Catholic Church. Primo dismissed the Cortes, curtailed Spanish liberties and curbed the separatist movements, for example of the Catalans, which regularly threatened Spanish unity. He injected new life into the economy, and developments in industry and communications improved employment prospects. Abd-el-Krim was defeated and placed in custody for the next twenty years. But ill-health forced Primo's retirement in 1930, and Spaniards made a spirited attempt to restore democracy. The King had not been forgiven for supporting dictatorship and he was driven into exile when a republic was proclaimed under President Zamora. Zamora and Manuel Azaña, his Prime Minister, launched a vigorous attack on the old enemies of Spanish demo-cracy – the Catholic Church, the army and the landowners. The liberal phase and the assault on privilege did not last, however. The vote for all adults brought disappointments for the republicans with a swing to the right in the elections of 1934 and a new government, which proceeded to undo much of Azaña's work. When the workers went on strike in protest, they were routed by the army with heavy casualties.

Elections in 1936 showed some return of support to the left-wing parties which united in a Popular Front, much influenced by Azaña, now President. On the right wing, fascists, influenced by the successes of Mussolini and Hitler, prepared to resist by force. On the left wing, communists, hopeful of support from Russia, were prepared to defend the government. Thus, the stage was set for the Spanish Civil War (see Section 5.2(c)).

3.4   Why Did Democracy Not Succeed?

Economic problems partly answer this question. A democratic system must rest upon agreement. Poverty, unemployment and insecurity produce little incentive to agree. In post-1918 Europe, poverty and unemployment afflicted almost every country (see Unit Four), providing a powerful stimulus to dis-content in countries such as Italy, Germany and Austria.

Democracy is also a sophisticated form of government. In Britain and the USA, democratic systems developed over a long period of time. In many European countries after 1918, the system had no roots, the people little experience of such a system. Germans, for example, were used to an authori-tarian regime. Democracies which appeared perfect on paper, such as that of the Weimar Republic, often produced so many parties in parliament that stable government was impossible, and it was necessary to form coalitions. To get agreement within a coalition government usually meant avoiding contro-versial questions altogether; yet controversial questions demanded solutions. It was all too easy to believe a Mussolini or a Hitler who promised the action which was obviously lacking.

For several powers, moreover, democracy was associated with defeat in the recent war. Dollfuss in Austria, like Hitler, thought of the system as part of an Allied plot to impose an ineffective system of government and thus prevent any radical reversal of the Peace Settlement. Nationalists, such as Mussolini, had no patience with democratic systems which were ineffective in foreign policy and did not impose their will by force.

Force, indeed, had more appeal in the post-1918 world than the Allied statesmen at Paris thought possible. Unit Eight will show how force was often applied in foreign policy, to the dismay of the League of Nations. The violence of the First World War left not only horror behind it but even some admiration; and it divided Europe's statesmen into two camps, those, like MacDonald and Neville Chamberlain, who had a horror of war, and those, like Mustapha Kemal and Mussolini, to whom war could be a means to an end. The difference was often that between democracy and dictatorship.

Unit Five will take a closer look at the dictatorships which sprang up after 1918. Meanwhile Unit Four will examine some of the economic problems which faced the world between the wars, the rocks on which democracy often foundered.

Further Reading

Brooks, J.R.: *The United States of America 1919–80*. Harrap (London, 1982).
Hiden, J.W.: *The Weimar Republic*. Longman (Harlow, 1974).
Holland, P.: *Twentieth-Century France*. Oxford University Press (London, 1965).
McKenzie, J.R.P.: *Weimar Germany, 1918–33*. Blandford (Poole, 1971).
Musman, R.: *Hitler and Mussolini*. Chatto & Windus (London, 1968).
Seaman, L.C.B.: *Post-Victorian Britain*. Methuen (London, 1966).
Snowman, D.: *America since 1920*. Heinemann (London, 1978).
Tint, H.: *France since 1918*. Batsford (London, 1970).
Watson, J.B.: *Success in British History since 1914*. John Murray (London, 1983).
Watson, J.B.: *Success in European History 1815–1941*. John Murray (London, 1981).

Documentary

Corkery, J.F. and Stone, R.C.J.: *Weimar Germany*. Heinemann (London, 1982).
Phillips, D.M.: *Hitler and the Rise of the Nazis*. Arnold (London, 1968).
Snyder, L.L.: *The Weimar Republic*. Anvil (Dublin, 1966).

Exercises

1. What do you understand by the adjective 'democratic'? How does this Unit show that the USA and Britain were democratic states in the 1920s?
2. What does Section 3.2(*a*) show were the main characteristics of life in the USA in the 1920s?
3. List the various governments which ruled Britain from 1918 to 1931. Which of these governments do you consider was the most useful to the British people in its domestic policy?
4. 'The world must be made safe for democracy' (page 43). How does this Unit show that democracy was not 'safe' in Europe after 1918?
5. What reasons are suggested in this Unit for the survival of democracy in the USA, Britain and France?
6. Set down in two columns the reasons why democracy did not survive (*a*) in Italy and (*b*) in Germany. Use what you have written to write a further paragraph to explain what *common* reasons there were why democracy came to an end in both Italy and Germany.
7. Using the text of this Unit and Fig. 3.4, make a list of European dictators in the 1920s and 1930s. Arrange them in the order in which they came to power. Write brief paragraphs about the intentions when they came to power of (*a*) Mussolini, (*b*) Hitler and (*c*) any two other dictators.

8. The following extracts are taken from a memorandum by Asquith. Write *three* paragraphs to explain in your own words what Asquith was referring to in *each* of the extracts. In *each* case add your own comment as to the accuracy of what Asquith wrote.

(*a*) The disintegration of the Liberal Party began with the Coupon election of December 1918. . . . I myself was turned out of a seat which I had held against the Tories for thirty-two years. . . . The Liberal members in the new House were reduced to a handful of little more than thirty. The bulk of the old Liberal parliamentary party deserted to the Coalition.

(*b*) After we had been brought to the verge of war by the adventure at Chanak, a section of the Conservatives . . . became mutinous, and, under the leadership of Mr Bonar Law and Mr Baldwin, brought about the downfall of the Coalition, and the formation of a Bonar Law Government.

(*c*) The folly of Mr Baldwin, after Mr Bonar Law's death, in hoisting the Protectionist flag brought about a strong movement for 'Liberal Reunion'. . . . For the purposes of the election of 1923 we joined forces with Mr Lloyd George and the bulk of his Coalition or National Liberals. In the Parliament then elected, the 'reunited' Liberals were a respectable, if not a formidable, minority.

Unit Four
Economic Rocks, 1919–39

4.1 General Problems

Before 1914, an enormous expansion of industry had taken place which made the USA and some European countries richer than any others in the world. Individuals and nations pursued profits, and technological advances in production processes and communications held out the hope of ever-increasing wealth. The prosperous nations expected to grow more prosperous. Others envied them and struggled to catch up. Vigorous competition was the basis of the system. Nations competed with each other to obtain more raw materials from which to make manufactured goods, and to find new markets in which to sell them.

Production continued to expand after 1918; the world's output of manufactured goods almost doubled between 1918 and 1939. In this period, however, economic problems which had seemed of limited importance before the war became acute.

(a) Trade

Nations such as America and Russia had the advantage of size. They were big enough to be almost self-sufficient (able to supply the food and raw materials their populations needed). Other countries had to buy such supplies, paying for them with exported goods. For Britain, this had not been difficult in the nineteenth century although, even before 1914, increasing competition had caused problems about finding markets. After 1918 competition was even fiercer. The situation was worsened because countries defeated in the war were struggling to pay their debts and repair the devastation, and could not afford to import many manufactured goods.

Protection worsened the position further. Developing nations were accustomed to protecting their own infant industries with *tariffs* (imposing duties on foreign goods to make them more expensive). Widespread tariffs made the sale of exports more difficult. Britain was heavily dependent on international trade; she rejected tariffs as a hindrance and steadfastly refused to agree with the Dominions who wanted her to impose tariffs on goods from outside the Empire. After 1918 most countries preferred to protect their own industries while resenting the tariffs which other countries imposed. Britain persevered with free trade almost alone.

It was disastrous for Europeans that the USA also adopted protection (see Section 3.2(*a*)). The USA was a wealthy customer, desperately needed by the rest of the world. But Republican America in the 1920s was concerned more with the prosperity of the USA than with the prosperity of Europe.

Faced with serious obstacles in selling their goods, producers hesitated to manufacture more. As a result, unemployment became a problem in many countries. Unit Three has already shown that high unemployment persisted in Britain, Italy and Germany after the First World War.

(b) Rich and Poor

Industrialization produced wealth, but it did not share out that wealth evenly. The result was resentment. Even before 1914 the conflict between rich and poor, between capital and labour, was producing violence in many countries, among them Britain, Russia and France. Industrial relations grew increasingly bitter. The workers wanted a fairer share of the wealth their work produced. They pressed their employers and governments for concessions, through trade unions (where they were permitted), through strikes and sometimes through demonstrations and rebellion. Frequently the workers turned to socialism and communism which held out the promise of a more equal distribution of wealth. The propertied classes almost invariably resisted, not infrequently turning to fascism with its seemingly attractive belief in discipline, law and order.

Vast differences in wealth existed between nations as well. In Europe envy and jealousy often embittered international relations. Mussolini and Hitler developed aggressive ambitions, partly as a means to increase national wealth. France resented and feared a return of German prosperity. In Asia, Japan was determined to grow rich like the white nations. And communist Russia worked with back-breaking fury to catch up with the capitalist powers.

Commissions of the League of Nations did their best, but before the Second World War little thought was given to the development of the world's wealth by co-operation. Attitudes were determined by economic nationalism: national prosperity almost invariably came first. Debtors were expected to pay what they owed. The rich intended to become richer.

(c) Confidence

Confidence was essential for the stable growth of prosperity. Unfortunately the world between 1918 and 1939 was far from stable. There was ideological conflict between capitalism and communism. International relations, especially in Europe, were often stormy (see Units Seven and Eight). Governments were frequently unstable. Even currencies wobbled, undermining confidence in money. The German and Austrian inflations of 1922–3 created near-panic: in the financial crisis of 1931 Ramsay MacDonald carried an inflated German bank-note as a dreadful warning of what, so he argued, might happen in Britain. The uncertainty discouraged financiers and businessmen from investing in industry. Expansion did continue but it was at a slower rate than before 1914. Thus, in the interwar period, nations were trapped in a vicious circle: selfishness and economic nationalism, protective tariffs, unemployment and inequalities of wealth created tensions; tensions undermined confidence; and without confidence, the basic problems remained unsolved.

4.2   The Particular Problems of Individual Countries

(a) The United States of America

The USA's prosperity in the 1920s was the envy of the world (see Section 3.2(a)). But it was not based on solid foundations. Industry and agriculture produced more goods than could be sold. America had much money invested overseas in countries which found repayment difficult since they were handicapped by American tariffs. Even within America the prosperity was denied to millions. President Hoover looked forward to an America with 'a chicken in every pot and two cars in every garage', but Republican governments did almost nothing to spread purchasing power evenly. Chickens and cars were produced. Neither in America nor in the rest of the world could enough people afford to buy them.

Over-production led to a slowing down of trade in the late 1920s. As goods remained unsold, production was cut back and men became unemployed. Accustomed by the boom years of the 1920s and the complacent speeches of politicians to an ever-expanding economy, Americans suddenly became less confident. Many of them were deeply in debt. They owed for goods bought on hire-purchase, for houses bought on mortgage. Five per cent of the population earned one-third of personal incomes in the USA and the majority of people had only limited resources or none at all. They now became unwilling to spend. Even so, enthusiastic speculation on the stock exchange continued well into 1929.

Many Americans had discovered what seemed to be a key to untold wealth: buying shares, often on borrowed money, and reselling them at a profit. While industry boomed and share prices rose, quick profits could be made. In September 1929, share prices ceased to rise. Confidence wavered. Some of those who held shares began to suspect that the prices were artificially high. Instead of a rush to buy shares (which forced up their price), there was a desire to sell them (which forced their price down). Many shareholders, having gambled with their savings and even borrowed to get the shares, panicked. The rush to sell forced prices still lower until, on 24 October, 13 million shares were sold.

Prices continued to plunge for two years. Thousands of shareholders were ruined. This collapse of the New York Stock Exchange (the Wall Street Crash) was a disaster not only for America but for the world. Debt and bankruptcy spread in all directions but most damaging of all was loss of confidence. The value of the shares had little direct relation to the industries they represented. They were no more than a claim to a share in the profits of those industries. But those who were ruined in the Wall Street Crash could not repay their debts and mortgages. They had to withdraw their savings from the banks. Banks and financial houses then felt the effects. Even fewer goods were sold in the shops, leading to more closures of factories and more unemployment. By the end of 1931 the USA had almost eight million unemployed and the figure was still rising. The trade recession of the late 1920s, prodded by the Wall Street Crash, became the Great Depression.

(b) Great Britain

From 1920 until the Second World War the level of unemployment in Britain never fell below one million. Exports in 1920 were valued at nearly £1 350 million. After that, they dropped dramatically. From 1919 until 1927 there were frequent and bitter industrial disputes which culminated in the General Strike. While, in 1939, the USA produced a third of the world's manufactured goods, Britain in that year produced less than 10 per cent and trailed behind both Russia and Germany. The decline was, however, only comparative. Britain as a whole remained a wealthy nation, although the wealth was unequally shared out, and the smallness of Britain made it inevitable that she would fall behind America and Russia. The complacency of successive governments, which did little in the period 1919–39 to tackle basic economic and social problems, stored up trouble for the future rather than producing an immediate decline in Britain's economic status.

(i) **Basic industries.** Britain's nineteenth-century superiority was based mainly on textiles, coal, iron, steel and heavy industries such as shipbuilding. It was these industries which suffered most in the highly-competitive world after 1918. In the coalfields, in the Lancashire textile towns, in shipbuilding areas such as the Clyde and Jarrow, the workers felt the full force of the difficulties, and the interwar years were years of hardship.

Markets lost during the war were not won back in many cases. British production costs were often too high to compete successfully. Countries which industrialized later than Britain or re-equipped their war-damaged industries with new machines after 1918, had an advantage over Britain, with its old-fashioned machinery and out-of-date plant. In new industries such as chemicals and motor-car manufacturing, Britain did better and areas such as the Midlands and the South East escaped many of the problems of the basic industries.

Coal-mining suffered most from the changes. Production fell from 287 million tons in 1913 to 220 million tons in 1934. In the same period, exports fell from 94 million to 53 million tons. There was strong competition from Germany and Poland. Russia also began to supply her own needs. There was competition, too, from oil. The percentage of coal-burning ships gradually declined in favour of oil-burning vessels.

Many British mines were small and uneconomic. The owners usually thought of producing coal more cheaply by paying lower wages. During the war, the mines had been under government control. The miners wished this to continue, and called for the nationalization of the pits. By the chairman's casting-vote, the Sankey Commission of 1919 recommended this, but Lloyd George rejected the idea because he knew it would be unpopular with his Conservative supporters (see page 48). For the next twenty years the industry was in depression. Industrial relations were bitter. Modernization proceeded slowly and, by 1937, still only about half of Britain's coal was cut by machine. The whole industry was generally demoralized by the low wages, unemployment and inefficiency. Other basic industries were not much better off.

(*ii*) **Exports and balance of payments.** Coal was one of the few raw materials Britain produced. It was essential to export to pay for other raw materials which were needed, like grain, cotton, iron, timber and rubber. Until 1932, however, Britain persisted with a policy of free trade. This made it easier for foreign countries to sell to Britain than for Britain to sell abroad.

Interwar governments hardly reacted to this unhealthy situation, except during the crisis of the Great Depression. In 1925, Baldwin's government even made the situation worse. Having lost the election of 1923 on the issue of protection (see Section 3.2(*b*)), Baldwin abandoned his idea of departing from free trade but joined other European countries in linking the nation's currency to the price of gold. Others devalued their currencies but Winston Churchill, Baldwin's Chancellor of the Exchequer, fixed the value of the pound in relation to gold at only a fraction below the 1914 level. Other countries considered the pound was too expensive and, consequently, British exports were too expensive. In terms of Britain's trade, it was a costly attempt to gain prestige. Exports slumped after 1925 and, during the Great Depression, it was necessary to allow the pound to depreciate (float downwards) to a lower, less ambitious level.

The weakness of Britain's position was partially disguised by her invisible exports. These earnings from investments, services such as insurance and banking and the carrying trade continued to augment the earnings from the sales of exports. In the 1920s, Britain continued to enjoy a surplus on her balance of payments and in the 1930s went only occasionally into the red. Both the First and Second World Wars badly damaged her 'invisible exports', however, and it was a sign of trouble to come that, in 1938, Britain's overall balance of payments showed a deficit of £70 million.

(*iii*) **Industrial relations and the General Strike.** The Triple Industrial Alliance (an alliance of unions representing miners, railwaymen and transport workers) had been set up shortly before the war at a time of much bitterness in industrial relations. It was thought that such an alliance was powerful enough to force the authorities to pay attention to the grievances of the working classes. Before 1914, its strength remained untested. After the war, the miners soon called upon it to help them in their troubles.

In March 1921, the government ended the wartime control of the mines. The private owners promptly cut the pitmen's wages. When the miners resisted they were locked out. Unemployment had already soared well over the million mark and there was general unrest throughout industry. The miners called for a general strike and the government prepared a middle-class Defence Force. On *Black Friday*, 15 April, the Triple Alliance backed down.

By the end of June, the pitmen accepted defeat. A general strike had been avoided but nearly 90 million working days were lost that year in industrial disputes. This was even worse than the turbulent pre-1914 period.

The workers felt cheated. The savage war had brought them few benefits. Politicians' promises were unfulfilled. Unemployment topped the two million mark and wages were generally low. The Bolshevik Revolution in Russia inflamed the class war. But the crisis passed, for the moment, and in the years 1923–5 the unemployment figures dropped slightly.

The coal industry, however, ran into new difficulties with vigorous competition from the German Ruhr coalfield. As usual, the owners saw salvation in a wage cut, coupled this time with lengthening the working day. Baldwin appointed a Commission of Inquiry under Samuel, which found no case for longer hours since the owners could not sell existing coal supplies. It recommended modernization of the industry and, for the time being, a rather less severe cut in wages than the owners wanted.

The coal-owners instantly seized on the recommendation that wages be cut. They had little interest in costly modernization. But the pitmen were determined: 'Not a Penny off the Pay, not a Minute on the Day'. The Trades Union Congress felt unable to desert the miners on this occasion but had made few preparations, resting on the woolly hope that a showdown could be avoided. Coal-owners and miners reached deadlock. The miners would not work for lower wages and the owners locked them out at the end of April 1926.

Without much enthusiasm, the TUC called a General Strike on 3 May. A visit to the Prime Minister at the last moment failed to save them: Baldwin had gone to bed.

The General Strike lasted for nine days. The miners' stoppage lasted for seven months. Middle-class volunteers worked with enthusiasm but not much efficiency to operate essential services, such as buses and trains. The TUC helped them, being reluctant to cause too much suffering. Churchill edited the *British Gazette* which, in the absence of the usual newspapers, tried to frighten the workers with charges of treason or something near it. Baldwin branded the strike as a challenge to 'the existing Constitution of the country' and as an attempt to 'substitute the reign of force' for the existing authority. The TUC defended itself in the *British Worker*: 'The General Council does not challenge the Constitution' but 'is engaged in an Industrial Dispute'. The strike, it argued, was to defend 'the mine-workers against the mine-owners'.

But the TUC defended the mine-workers poorly for on 12 May it deserted them. Much influenced by J.H. Thomas, a leader of the railwaymen who had a great respect for authority, the TUC leadership called off the strike without any concessions from Baldwin. The miners' leaders were not consulted but neither Herbert Smith, the President, nor Arthur Cook, the Secretary of the Miners' Federation, would have agreed to surrender. The Federation continued the strike alone but had to accept defeat at the end of the year when the pitmen returned, on the owners' terms.

The General Strike was remarkably free of violence. No one was killed. When it was called off, there was bitterness against the TUC leaders and for a time some workers (in addition to the miners) refused to go back to work. Some were victimized, in spite of promises to the contrary, and forced to join the unemployed. Ringleaders among the miners were similarly singled out. The working classes had been defeated and, for a time, trade union membership fell dramatically, from $5\frac{1}{2}$ million in 1925 to $4\frac{1}{2}$ million in 1932. Some argued that Baldwin had won a great victory for quiet and peaceable leadership. Certainly the class war seemed to die down after the strike. Over 162 million working days were lost in 1926 but the figure did not rise again above 10 million in any year before the Second World War. Many left-wingers turned from industrial action to political action, working to strengthen the Labour Party in parliament. The strike had little effect on the country's economy as a whole. Equally, it failed to prod complacent governments into action. The ever-present fear of unemployment continued to demoralize the working classes and within a few years the Great Depression caused unemployment figures to soar.

(c) Germany

Germany's main economic problems after 1918 were the same as those of other European countries: the transition from war to peace, finding markets for exports and jobs for her workers. In addition, Germany was required by the Treaty of Versailles to pay reparations (see Section 2.4 and Fig. 4.1). The figure finally agreed (136 000 million marks) seemed enormous. In fact, it was only a fraction of Germany's wealth. Reparations payments produced heated arguments but they did not produce economic disaster.

Reparations did however contribute to the lack of confidence in the German mark and thus to the inflation of 1923. Default in the payment of reparations also gave the French an excuse to invade the Ruhr in that year, creating turmoil, delaying Germany's economic recovery and quickening the inflation (see Section 3.3(b)). Moreover, politicians generally could make use of reparations – blaming them, in order to explain away economic and financial weaknesses which already existed, or attacking them as Hitler did, to whip up discontent. From 1924, however, Germany made her reparation payments with borrowed money and in the process became entangled in debts to the USA. The Dawes Plan of 1924 provided Germany with American help and loans, and laid down a new scale for reparations payments. Thus Stresemann had US support for a new start after the hyper-inflation of 1923 and Germany was able to make reparation payments regularly for the next five years. In 1929 the Young Plan was devised to cut drastically the total reparations still to be paid and to spread them over the years to 1988. But the Young Plan was stillborn. With the beginning of the Depression, the world faced financial confusion, in the course of which reparations were suspended. A new low figure, no more than a mere token, was fixed in 1932 at the

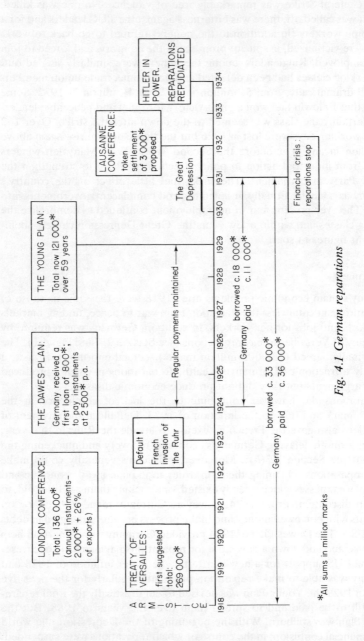

Fig. 4.1 German reparations

Lausanne Conference; but even this comparatively small sum of 3 000 million marks was never paid. Hitler became the German Chancellor and repudiated entirely the reparations he had always condemned.

Between 1924 and the end of reparations, Germany had borrowed 18 000 million marks and paid back 11 000 million. Not until 1952 did Germany even agree to repay this profit on her reparations dealings. Meanwhile the loans had helped Germany to recover a measure of economic stability. They also pumped dollars into Europe, which helped to stimulate trade.

4.3   The Great Depression

The trade depression at the end of the 1920s shattered whatever confidence was beginning to grow in Europe. In 1929, there was a trade recession in America and it spread rapidly to the rest of the world. Unsold goods accumulated. Production slowed down and stopped. Producers of coffee in Brazil could find no better use for their beans than as fuel for railway engines. Tons of grain rotted in America and other farming areas. With factories falling silent, unemployment figures began to rise. There was even less money in the pockets of the unemployed, so even fewer goods were sold.

A financial crisis quickly developed from the trade depression. Just as individuals had to draw on their savings, so creditor nations looked for the repayment of outstanding debts. Feeding on the panic produced by the Wall Street Crash, Americans tried to recover money they had loaned to Europe. There was an all-round demand for money, often in the form of gold. Banks began to totter as their reserves drained away and in May 1931 Credit Anstalt, Austria's leading bank, had to close. Driven to further panic by their losses in Austria, financiers put pressure on other banks. There was a swift loss of confidence in Germany. The German Reichsbank was seriously weakened and within weeks the crisis spread to London, with a run on the reserves of the Bank of England. Stirred by almost irrelevant memories of the German inflation of 1922–3 (irrelevant since the problem was now one of deflation, not inflation: prices were very low, not high), Europeans had a general distrust of paper money. In this crisis of confidence, they wanted gold and few countries outside America had large gold reserves.

Banks such as the Bank of England and the German Reichsbank were so closely linked with government that their weakness inevitably led to political crises. Governments and political systems were sorely tested. The first instinct of those in power was to practise thrift, which financial experts alleged was essential. In the summer of 1931 the Bank of England desperately needed support to check the drain on its reserves, and most of that support could come only from the USA. American financiers insisted, however, that the British government must first reduce its spending. A series of committees painted gloomy pictures of the British economy and, at the end of July, the May Report advised increases in taxation and sharp cuts in expenditure. Otherwise, it was suggested, the British government might go bankrupt. The strain was too much for MacDonald's Labour government and it resigned in August 1931 (see Section 3.2(*b*)). The cuts were made, including the cut in unemployment benefit, and American loans helped to save the Bank of England. The financial crisis gradually subsided, but reduced government spending had the effect of further reducing purchasing power and demand. It did nothing to lift the Depression and the general result was to make unemployment worse.

In the USA, meanwhile, President Hoover pursued a somewhat erratic course. The Hoover Moratorium of June 1931, imposing a standstill on the settlement of debts between governments, helped to restore stability. But the Hawley-Smoot Tariff Act of the previous year had further depressed international trade by sharply raising the duties on goods imported into the USA. The Act did little to help American workers. Even the Ford works in Detroit closed in 1931, with the loss of 75 000 jobs. Hoover's name was linked with *Hoovervilles*, the squalid shelters built by unemployed ex-servicemen who flocked to Washington in 1932 to demand government action. Demonstrators produced placards with the slogan, 'In Hoover we trusted. Now we are busted.' Hoover was not indifferent to their plight and much of his thinking

Fig. 4.2 The search for work: men queue anxiously for jobs at a Birmingham labour exchange during the Depression in 1930

showed an enlightened awareness of the need for public works, tax reductions and government aid to stimulate demand. But his faith in 'rugged individualism' remained, and he had a Republican's reluctance to use federal power for any vigorous interference with the economy. He preferred gentle persuasion to government directives, and the measures he took were slow to bring noticeable results. The Republicans paid the price in the presidential election of 1932 when Hoover could win only six states and there was a massive swing to Roosevelt and the Democrats (see Table 13.1). Soon after Hoover's defeat, Hitler became Chancellor in Germany, where the Depression contributed to the downfall of the Weimar Republic (see Sections 3.3(*b*) and 5.2(*b*)). About the same time, Dollfuss in Austria began to undermine what was left of democracy in that country (see Section 3.3(*c*)).

Unemployment figures in 1932 reached some 14 million in the USA, 6 million in Germany and 3 million in Britain. Production in the USA and Germany had almost halved since 1929, though the fall in Britain was rather less. When the financial crises had passed and the political upheavals were over, it still remained to try to bring about economic recovery – and that was bound to take many years, casting a shadow over the rest of the 1930s.

4.4   The Effects of the Great Depression and Recovery

(*a*) The United States of America

Franklin Delano Roosevelt romped home as the new President, with the largest majority ever known. He was the first Democrat to become President since Woodrow Wilson. He remained in office until his death in 1945, being re-elected in 1936, 1940 and 1944. His immediate aim was to restore confidence in banks, in business and in spending. 'The only thing we have to fear is fear itself,' he said. He pledged his party, as he pledged himself, 'to a new deal for the American people'. 'Action, and action now' became his government's motto.

Roosevelt took office at the beginning of 1933. He began with a vigorous period of a *Hundred Days* to tackle immediate problems, programmed a *First New Deal* from 1933 to 1935 to set the country on the road to recovery and a *Second New Deal* from 1935 to 1939, mainly to expand the welfare services. This vigorous government was popular but not with some industrialists and Republicans, who were bitterly hostile to such governmental activity, accused Roosevelt of socialism and tried to use the Supreme Court to block some of the new laws by declaring them 'unconstitutional'.

(*i*) **The Hundred Days** did much to restore confidence in the banks, which were closed while experts examined their accounts. The Emergency Banking Act then forced weak banks out of business and gave government backing to sound ones so that when the banks reopened, they were again trusted. A Federal Emergency Relief Administration was set up to help the unemployed

Fig. 4.3 'FINIS' – Roosevelt bustles into office and Hoover departs, leaving his slogans to the trashcan. Philadelphia Daily News, *3 March 1933*

and the poor; it did not distribute charity but provided work. At the same time, Roosevelt aimed to win the confidence of businessmen by cutting some of the government's spending. The Economy Act reduced pensions and the salaries of state employees. Americans were impressed most of all by the new bustle in government offices. Lights burned late. Prohibition was swept aside and an attack made on corruption.

(*ii*) **The First New Deal** kept up the pace. The Civilian Conservation Corps (CCC) found work for the young in reforestation projects, planting trees and strengthening river banks. The Civil Works Administration (CWA), later the Works Progress Administration (WPA), combined relief for the unemployed with work of public value. At first, money was often paid out for very little work, to increase purchasing power, but later the WPA built roads and schools, and even organized painters and actors into activities which enabled them to earn. The National Industrial Recovery Act regulated conditions of work, forbade child labour, encouraged trade unions and created the Public Works Administration for major projects. The WPA built the Hoover Dam on the Colorado River. Even more ambitious was the Tennessee Valley Authority (TVA) to tame the Tennessee River and use its waters for irriga-

Fig. 4.4   The end of Prohibition: the queue outside the Board of Health offices in New York for licences to sell beer

tion, shipping and hydro-electric power. The TVA cut into the authority of seven state governments and there was some resentment of this federal interference from Washington, but Roosevelt was concerned with national well-being, not sectional interests. Through the activities of all these various bodies, the 'alphabet agencies', the Depression began to lift. There was money to buy goods and factories returned to a higher level of production. More than 10 per cent of the US labour force remained unemployed, however, throughout the 1930s (see Fig. 4.5).

Meanwhile, the First New Deal gave special assistance to farmers. The Agricultural Adjustment Administration (AAA) set out to increase their earnings. With the help of government subsidies, farmers were encouraged to reduce their output. A smaller output of grain, cotton and other produce would make prices rise and farming would become profitable. The scheme was drastic, but it worked. Farmers were also encouraged to use more modern methods and machinery. The hungry found it hard to see the logic of destroying food but Roosevelt's work strengthened American agriculture.

Most of the new organizations dated from 1933 and in that year Roosevelt also introduced the Home Owners' Loan Corporation which helped the poor to overcome their difficulties in repaying mortgages.

(*iii*) **The Second New Deal** placed more emphasis on helping the poor. The government's efforts to provide work continued, especially through the WPA. The Social Security Act of 1935 was passed, introducing insurance against unemployment for millions of workers. It also provided pensions for the old, widowed and maimed. The USA still lagged behind the most advanced nations in welfare services but the Social Security Act was a major breakthrough.

In the election of 1936, Roosevelt won support in every state but two. Shortly afterwards, the President tackled the problem of the Supreme Court which had several times proved hostile to parts of the New Deal. Congress refused to agree to his proposal to create additional members of the Court to outvote his opponents there. Some things even Roosevelt could not do, but the Court learned its lesson and gave him little further trouble.

The Second New Deal therefore went on. At the same time, Roosevelt strengthened American democracy. 'People who are hungry and out of a job,' he said, 'are the stuff of which dictatorships are made.' He believed that trade unions should be strong enough to protect their members and the Wagner Act of 1935 gave them protection. Hours of work and wages were regulated by the Fair Labour Standards Act of 1938. The National Housing Act of 1937 set aside government money for homes and attacked rents which were too high. Monopolies were investigated to protect the consumer and small businesses which found it difficult to compete with the giants. In 1940, Roosevelt was re-elected as President, defeating Wendell Wilkie, although his victory was less decisive than in former years.

Roosevelt had not intended to seek further office, for it was a tradition that Presidents did not serve a third term. But in 1940 there was war in Europe and in Asia. America was not yet involved but at this moment the country needed Roosevelt's leadership. The Democrats had not done well in the Congressional elections of 1938 but the country still had faith in Roosevelt as President.

Roosevelt's foreign policy before 1940 differed little from that of the Republicans in the 1920s. He made some limited changes, recognizing the USSR and then launching a 'Good Neighbour Policy' with Latin America in 1935. He himself visited South America, spreading goodwill and promoting trade and defence agreements. But towards Europe, the USA remained cool. A series of Neutrality Laws in 1935 and 1937 aimed to sever connexions with countries which might go to war although Roosevelt himself was not indifferent to the aggression taking place in the Pacific and in Europe (see Unit Eight). He was eventually to lead the USA into war against the dictators and the aggressors (see Unit Nine).

(b) Great Britain

Britain was ruled by National governments from August 1931. MacDonald's acceptance of office as Prime Minister of a National government (see Section 3.2(b)) began a period of conservatism, for although governments were coalitions in theory, they were Conservative in practice. MacDonald remained Prime Minister until June 1935; Baldwin succeeded him until his retirement in 1937 and then Neville Chamberlain led the government until 1940. Britain had no New Deal so recovery was slow and painful. Unemployment did not fall below two million until 1936 and it remained obstinately high until the war. Exports were similarly slow to recover and were always lower than in the 1920s.

(*i*) **Economic policies.** Much that the National government did was accidental. It abandoned the gold standard in September 1931 to stop the drain on gold reserves, although MacDonald had intended to preserve it as an aid to confidence. Again almost accidentally, the government introduced a policy of cheap money. Interest rates on government stock were cut to $3\frac{1}{2}$ per cent to reduce the government's interest payments. This set a new low level of borrowing rates and did a little to stimulate business activity. At the same time, the government was intent on reducing spending. Almost nothing was done to follow Roosevelt's lead, his ambitious schemes to provide work. The National government wished to please the financiers, balance its budget and avoid all accusations of recklessness and extravagance (see Fig. 4.5).

USA UNEMPLOYED (Millions)	USA GOVERNMENT INCOME*	USA GOVERNMENT EXPENDITURE*	(Party)	YEAR	YEAR	BRITAIN GOVERNMENT INCOME⊖	BRITAIN GOVERNMENT EXPENDITURE⊖	BRITAIN UNEMPLOYED (Millions)
1·5	4·0	3·1	R	1928	1928–9	836	818	1·2
1·5	4·0	3·3	E	1929	1929–30	734●	749	1·2
4·3	4·2	3·4	P/U	1930	1930–1	776●	799	1·9
8·0	3·1●	3·5	B/L	1931	1931–2	770	770	2·7
12·0	1·9●●	4·6	N	1932	1932–3	745●	777	2·7
12·8	2·0●●	4·6	D	1933	1933–4	699	697	2·5
11·3	3·0●●	6·7	E	1934	1934–5	716	689	2·2
10·6	3·7●●	6·5	M	1935	1935–6	753	750	2·0
9·0	4·0●●	8·2	O	1936	1936–7	797●	803	1·8
7·7	4·8●●	7·6	C	1937	1937–8	876	847	1·5
10·4	5·5●●	6·8	R	1938	1938–9	945	944	1·8
9·5	4·9●●	8·7	A	1939	1939–40	WAR		
8·1	5·1●●	8·8	T	1940	1940–1	WAR		
WAR				1941	1941–2	WAR		

(USA vertical labels: REPUBLICAN, DEMOCRAT; Britain vertical labels: ...NATIONAL LABOUR)

*Thousand million dollars   ⊖ £s million

USA: Government spending in   ●Budget deficit   BRITAIN: The financial
the New Deals   ●●Major budget deficit   orthodoxy of
balanced
budgets

Fig. 4.5 The USA and Britain: unemployment and government spending, 1928–40. British governments remained reluctant to spend to cure the Depression

In 1932, Britain abandoned free trade. A 10 per cent duty was placed on most foreign goods. It was soon raised to 20 per cent, but it was not applied to food, raw materials and Commonwealth produce. An attempt was made to promote trade agreements within the Commonwealth (see Section 6.2(*a*)), but with limited success. Britain had at last come into line with the rest of the world but the tariffs were too low to be very effective, and the Depression still hung over her basic industries.

Government money to promote industrial activity was issued with the utmost caution. In 1936, there were subsidies to tramp-shipping and Cunard was helped to build the luxury liner, *Queen Mary*. Special Areas Acts, the first in 1934, made a feeble effort to encourage production in the depressed areas but provided very little money for the purpose. In 1938, mining royalties were nationalized to relieve some of the difficulties of the coal industry and the thousand mining companies were encouraged to join together in larger units. A year later, Chamberlain's government set up the British Overseas Airways Corporation (BOAC), showing a willingness to consider the sort of economic planning and control which Keynes and other economists considered essential. Their advice was welcomed by the Labour Party but, on the whole, it found little favour with the government.

A revival in house-building did something to break the grip of the Depression but that owed almost nothing to the government. Wheatley's Housing Act of 1924 (see Section 3.2(*b*)) was scrapped in 1933 although new legislation in that year and in 1935 encouraged some slum clearance work. Fortunately builders found a market for private houses, which could be bought through building societies, and their activities helped to provide work for some of the unemployed.

(*ii*) **Social policies.** The most-detested measure introduced by the National government was the Means Test. On top of the cuts in unemployment benefit imposed in 1931 (but restored in 1934), the unemployed were required to reveal the income of the entire family. If the family's means were sufficient, the dole could be cut or stopped. This enabled the government to pursue its passion for saving money, but at the expense of the pride of those jobless who now found themselves supported by wives and children. The system of the dole and the means test became a little less harsh in the later 1930s but for the long-term unemployed these were bitter years.

The 1930s were not unprosperous for those with a steady income. Prices remained low. The new consumer industries, making such goods as wirelesses and gramophones, and exciting new entertainments such as the cinema, coupled with expanding home ownership, left many unaware of the hardships of distressed areas. From the latter, in the Jarrow Crusade of 1936 for example, the jobless marched to London to seek assistance. Such Hunger Marches brought charity from the middle classes, but the government was less responsive.

The years before the Second World War were remarkable mainly for governmental inactivity. Only occasionally did the National government rouse itself to significant action: in 1938 the Holidays with Pay Act made it legal to have a week's paid holiday each year. But the lengthy and unpaid holidays of a million-and-a-half unemployed continued.

(*iii*) **Retirements, Democracy and Fascism.** MacDonald resigned as Prime Minister shortly before the general election of 1935. An outcast from the Labour Party since his somersault of 1931, he was abused and defeated in the election campaign; and though he re-entered the Commons a year later he died in 1937. He continued to believe that his National government of 1931 had saved the country but the Labour Party could not forgive him for the blow he had dealt his former supporters. Labour's recovery was slow and the Party won only 158 seats in 1935. Baldwin on the other hand was riding high, though he too retired in 1937, considering it his final triumph and a fitting seal on his years in politics that he had managed a peaceful change of the monarchy at a time of new crisis. The latter arose when, after the death of George V, Edward VIII came into conflict with the Archbishop of Canterbury and the establishment over his proposed marriage which they thought unsuitable. Edward was persuaded to abdicate and the quiet accession of George VI was Baldwin's last act of political manipulation. Baldwin himself was quietly succeeded by Neville Chamberlain.

Outside parliament Britain had a glimpse of less orderly politics. Oswald Mosley left the Labour Party in 1931, having earlier left the Conservatives. Soon afterwards, he founded the British Union of Fascists (BUF), confirming his growing admiration for Mussolini during a visit to Italy in 1932, returning with a passion for black shirts. The BUF showed some enthusiasm for the Commonwealth but its other enthusiasms were more sinister. Its members had little use for free speech and for democracy. They picked up something of Hitler's anti-Semitism and caused disturbances, especially in the East End of London. In a book *The Greater Britain* Mosley argued for the strong government the British showed little signs of wanting.

Violence and extremism had little appeal in Britain. Neither the Communist Party nor the BUF attracted much popular support. Extremists clashed in Hyde Park but the British Communist Party never won more than two seats in parliament and the BUF won none at all. By the late 1930s, support for the BUF was declining. The British seemed content on the whole with the tranquil administrations of MacDonald, Baldwin and Chamberlain, at least until they were shaken by the outbreak of war.

(*iv*) **The Empire and Foreign Policy.** British governments in the 1930s divided their attention abroad between the British Empire and the ominous activities of the growing band of aggressive powers. In 1931 the Statute of Westminster went a long way towards satisfying the Dominions (see Section 6.2(*a*)). The India Act of 1935 went some way towards meeting the demands of Indian nationalists (see Section 6.2(*c*)). There were also problems to be faced concerning Britain's relations with the Irish Free State (see Section 6.2(*b*)) and with Palestine (see Section 19.1(*b*)).

At the same time Britain remained one of the leading members of the League of Nations with a responsibility not only for the security of the Empire but for world peace. Throughout the 1930s British governments responded only cautiously to the growing international lawlessness. Pacifism was strong in the Labour Party and National governments were reluctant to spend money or to become entangled either in Europe or further afield. MacDonald accepted the need for some rearmament as early as 1935 but it began, very slowly, under Baldwin. Chamberlain stepped up the programme with few marked results either in terms of jobs or of military strength. The aggressor-nations were not deterred and it seemed the final failure of National government that Britain ended the 1930s at war with Nazi Germany (see Unit Eight).

(*c*) The Totalitarian Powers

The effect of the Depression on Germany and Austria was to hasten the abandonment of democracy. Its effect on Japan was to strengthen the influence of the military and to encourage aggression in Manchuria (see Section 8.1(*a*)). Italy had already turned to totalitarianism and Mussolini's response to the Depression was typically theatrical: he launched a Battle for the Lira, a Battle for Grain and even a Battle for Births. The Italian economy remained weak and by the mid-1930s Mussolini was looking for a dramatic victory in Ethiopia to distract Italian attention from the shortcomings of his government (see Section 8.2(*a*)). The Depression had little effect on the Soviet Union, however, since the Soviet economy had been largely detached from the capitalist system during the years which followed the Bolshevik Revolution of 1917.

The history of the major totalitarian powers is treated in the next Unit.

Further Reading

Ayling, S.E.: *Portraits of Power.* Harrap (London, 1965) – Roosevelt.
Cootes, R.J.: *The General Strike, 1926.* Longman (Harlow, 1964).
Hill, C.P.: *Franklin Roosevelt.* Oxford University Press (London, 1966).
O'Callaghan, D.B.: *Roosevelt and the United States.* Longman (Harlow, 1966).
Renshaw, P.: *The General Strike.* Methuen (London, 1975).
Seaman, L.C.B.: *Life in Britain Between the Wars.* Batsford (London, 1970).
Stevenson, J. and Cook, C.: *The Slump.* Quartet (London, 1979).

See also **Further Reading**, Unit Three.

Documentary

Bettey, J.H.: *English Historical Documents 1906–1939.* Routledge & Kegan Paul (London, 1967).
Hill, C.P.: *Franklin Roosevelt and the New Deal.* Arnold (London, 1975).

Lane, P.: *Documents on British Economic and Social History 1870–1939*. Macmillan (London, 1968).

Mountfield, A.: *The General Strike*. Wayland (Hove, 1980).

Yass, M.: *The Great Depression*. Wayland (London, 1970).

Exercises

1. Make use of a reference book (such as S.E. Stiegeler and G. Thomas, *A Dictionary of Economics and Commerce* (Pan, 1976)) to ensure that you understand economic terms used in this Unit such as free trade, tariffs, balance of payments, inflation, deflation, depression.

2. Explain how troubles in the mining industry led to the General Strike in Britain.

3. Making use of Fig. 4.1 and the Index to this book, outline the history of German reparations. Compare what you have written with the entry on Reparations in A.W. Palmer's *Dictionary of Modern History 1789–1945* (Penguin, 1964).

4. 'The American bubble burst in 1929' (page 46). How do Units Three and Four illustrate the truth of this statement?

5. Examining much of the detail used in Fig. 4.3, explain what the cartoon refers to and state, with evidence, whether you think the cartoonist sympathetic either to FDR or to HH.

6. Explain how the following came to be combined in Britain in 1931: the trade depression; a financial crisis; a political crisis.

7. What points about government policies are illustrated by Fig. 4.5? Use this Figure and the text of this Unit to explain how Roosevelt's policies for dealing with the Depression differed from those of National governments in Britain.

8. Find out more about the lives of the unemployed in Britain in the 1930s. (See for example L.C.B. Seaman's book listed above and George Orwell's *The Road to Wigan Pier* (Penguin, 1970).)

9. The following extract is taken from Roosevelt's inaugural address on becoming the US President, March 1933. Write brief paragraphs to show how (*a*) a Democrat and (*b*) a Republican would have felt about the views Roosevelt expressed.

This nation asks for action and action now. Our greatest task is to put people to work. . . . It can be accomplished in part by direct recruiting by the government itself . . . accomplishing greatly needed projects to stimulate and reorganize the use of our natural resources. Hand in hand with this, we must . . . provide a better use of the land for those best fitted for the land. This task can be helped by definite efforts to raise the values of agricultural products. . . . It can be helped by national planning for and supervision of all forms of transportation and of communications and other utilities which have a definitely public character. . . . There must be strict supervision of all banking and credits and investments; there must be an end to speculation with other people's money, and there must be provision for an adequate and sound currency. . . . Our international trade relations, though vastly important, are . . . secondary to the establishment of a sound national economy. . . . I shall ask the Congress for . . . broad executive power to wage a war against the emergency as great as the power that would be given me if we were in fact invaded by a foreign foe.

The Totalitarian States: the Alternatives to Democracy

5.1 Communism

Two firmly-held beliefs gave strength to communists. They were convinced that communist systems would one day succeed everywhere; and they believed that a co-operative communist society offered the highest form of civilization. They drew inspiration from the writings of Karl Marx who, in the *Communist Manifesto* of 1848, wrote: 'What the bourgeoisie produces above all is its own gravediggers'. He argued that history was a series of conflicts out of which new societies developed. In Marx's time, industrial development was producing bourgeois (middle-class) capitalism which he saw as a greedy, competitive free-for-all in which the workers were exploited for the profit of the bourgeoisie. The workers (the proletariat) would eventually be the gravediggers of this system, overthrowing it in violent revolution and putting in its place a communist society. The new society would be based on co-operation and equality, free from exploitation, in such harmony that eventually government itself would wither away, being no longer needed. When all states became communist, there would be world harmony and no more wars.

The greater the advance of industrialism and capitalism, Marx believed, the greater the class strife and the nearer the proletarian revolution. When Marx died in 1883, he expected the revolution to come first in Britain or Germany, the two most industrialized nations. But the first successful communist revolution occurred in Russia, in 1917.

(a) Russia: the Revolutions

Russia under Tsar Nicholas II was corrupt, inefficient and lagging behind Western Europe in almost every form of development. During the First World War the country suffered heavy military defeats by the Germans. Russia was accustomed to hunger, poverty and savage repression, but in 1917 discontent reached a new peak.

Only the Tsar really mattered in the system of government. He had reigned since 1894, a period littered with disasters and stupidities. He had ignored all advice and refused any real partnership with the *Duma* (a toothless parliament which he had been forced to accept in 1906). When he left his capital in March 1917, vague as ever about whether to inject energy into the war effort or merely to rest and play dominoes, there was sudden agreement in St Petersburg (Petrograd) and other towns that his rule must end. Railway workers halted his train at Pskov. In Petrograd the army, diluted with discontented conscripts, sided with the rioters. Nicholas abdicated on 15 March.

The Revolution was unplanned. It was simply an explosion of deep anger with Tsarism. A scramble for power was now inevitable. First in line were the mainly middle-class members of the Duma. A Duma Committee was set up under Prince Lvov to act as a provisional government. They had hoped to set up a democratic monarchy like that in Britain but the Grand Duke Michael Alexandrovitch, Nicholas's brother, refused to be a puppet king. Russia then became a republic. The Provisional Government intended to hold a constituent assembly to draw up a new constitution but it was frequently postponed.

The Petrograd Soviet, a Council of Workers', Peasants' and Soldiers' Deputies, was another important body. There was an uneasy relationship between the Soviet and the Provisional Government, although a few men were members of both, Kerensky outstanding amongst them. His influence grew and, in July 1917, he became Prime Minister and Lvov retired.

Kerensky was a socialist but also a democrat. His aim was a democratic republic, an aim supported by the middle classes mainly through the party known as Kadets (KDs, constitutional democrats). Stronger in the Petrograd Soviet and in Soviets elsewhere were the Socialist Revolutionaries (SRs), a party long given to violence, close to the peasants, but often incoherent in their aims. Marxists were also numerous and influential in the Soviets. Although known as Socialist Democrats (SDs), they had little faith in Western democracy. One group of SDs, the Bolsheviks, was dedicated to communist revolution. The other SDs, the Mensheviks, were less fanatical but Marxists nevertheless. SRs and SDs were critical of the Provisional Government but uncertain as to their own roles.

Vladimir Lenin, leader of the Bolsheviks, was not uncertain. He had been surprised by the suddenness of the March Revolution. He could not get back to Russia from exile in Switzerland until April 1917, but promptly produced his *April Theses*. At first they astounded even the Bolsheviks. The time had come, Lenin argued, for the proletariat to take control, to destroy bourgeois capitalism in Russia. (Compared with the West, Russia had so far seen little bourgeois capitalism: Tsarist Russia was mainly agricultural and peasant, a more primitive form of society.) But Lenin convinced the Bolsheviks and even some of the Mensheviks such as Leon Trotsky. While Lenin adapted Marxism to Russia (*Marxism–Leninism*), he also planned the Bolshevik strategy, seizing on two slogans: 'Peace, Bread and Land' and 'All Power to the Soviets'. The first had a wide appeal especially to poverty-stricken peasants.

The Provisional Government had continued the war, hoping vainly for a victory to restore Russian morale. They also postponed settlement of the land problem until the Constituent Assembly could meet. The Revolution therefore brought little immediate relief, and discontent continued. Lenin whipped up the hope that the Soviets could do better, although the Bolsheviks were not yet strong enough to dominate the Petrograd Soviet or the congresses of

Soviets which met from time to time. They must wait until their own strength grew.

For most of 1917 Russia remained unstable and sometimes violent. There were army mutinies, strikes and riots, especially in Petrograd. The Bolsheviks were blamed for an outbreak of violence in July (the July Days), their leaders arrested and Lenin forced to flee. Kerensky's government, however, was weak and unconvincing, taking too long to establish democracy and produce results. In August, forces on the right wing under General Kornilov made a bid for power, intent on bringing discipline to Russia, hanging Bolsheviks and troublemakers, stamping out strikes, strengthening the army and preserving the authority of landlords. They failed, but Kerensky had to rely on the left to help him and left-wing extremism began to flourish again.

Support for the Bolsheviks grew and, in November, Lenin felt they were ready. He returned secretly from exile. On the eve of a meeting of the All-Russian Congress of Soviets, Bolsheviks seized control of Petrograd. They had a tiny majority in the Congress and won support from some of the SRs. The Congress became a law-making body and the right to govern was conferred on a Council of People's Commissars (Sovnarcom) of which Lenin was Chairman. With very little bloodshed, power had passed to the Soviets and to the Bolsheviks. A week later their rule was accepted in Moscow.

(b) Lenin's Government 1917–24

(i) **1917–18.** The Bolsheviks at once produced a flood of decrees. The Decree on Land seized 540 million acres, without compensation, from private landlords and the Church, to be shared out among poor peasants. A Supreme Council of National Economy was created to plan the economy. Banking and foreign trade were nationalized. Comprehensive social insurance was planned. Wages were fixed, an eight-hour day introduced, foreign debts repudiated. Such activity was in marked contrast to Kerensky's government.

Priority was also given to making peace with Germany and the Treaty of Brest-Litovsk was signed (see Section 2.8).

The Constituent Assembly met in January 1918, but Bolsheviks got less than a quarter of the votes. The majority of Russians had voted for democratic socialism or for the SRs. KDs had already been outlawed and the Assembly met with armed revolutionary sailors in the gallery and surrounded by troops. A Sovnarcom decree abolished it on its second day. To transform Russian society into a communist one, the Bolsheviks intended to rule with a dictatorship, 'the dictatorship of the proletariat', through Sovnarcom and the Congress.

But 1918 brought further chaos. The economy was already in ruins. There was inflation: like Kerensky the Bolsheviks paid their way by printing banknotes. There were food shortages: the peasants had bourgeois ambitions and wanted to make profits, not simply to feed the towns out of a duty to society. The Bolsheviks had to requisition grain and direct labour and, with workers seizing control, there was anarchy in many factories.

The Bolsheviks were too ambitious. With a flood of decrees, they hoped to make Russia communist. Private inheritance was abolished in April 1918, all major industries nationalized in June, mortgages cancelled in August. By that time, however, there was civil war. For a time, Lenin's government tried to impose War Communism. They nationalized smaller industries at the end of 1918, put the peasants under state control, seized their surplus crops and fixed official prices. They also created the *Cheka* (a committee for fighting counter-revolution) under Dzerzhinsky. It came to employ a staff of 30 000 and its own army. As a political police force, its main purpose was to keep the Bolsheviks in power. Some Bolshevik leaders were assassinated and Lenin himself was wounded in August 1918; the Cheka struck back with 'a mass red terror' to deal with 'the bourgeoisie and its agents'.

A new constitution in July 1918 consolidated the system the Bolsheviks had created. Russia became the Russian Soviet Federal Socialist Republic (RSFSR). The constitution made no mention of the Communist Party nor of the Cheka. But like the KDs, other parties were gradually eliminated, first the Mensheviks and finally even the left-wing SRs who had helped the Bolsheviks in November 1917. Thus Russia became a one-party state. Moscow was its new capital.

(*ii*) **Civil war: the wars of intervention, 1918–21.** Resistance to the Bolsheviks began in Russia as early as December 1917. By the following summer the Whites (counter-revolutionaries) had set up alternative Russian governments at Samara, Omsk and Archangel (see Fig. 5.1). The Whites included supporters of the Tsar, of landlords and of democracy, and a mixed collection of anti-Bolsheviks. Foreign powers intervened too. At first the Allies had vague ideas of persuading Russia to carry on the war against Germany to draw German troops away from the Western Front; or Allied forces could at least try to make sure that supply dumps did not fall into German hands. But the First World War ended in November 1918 and the aims of the interventionists changed. They now wanted to strike a blow at communism, whose spread they feared and Lenin confidently expected. Britain, the USA and Japan were the first to land troops in Russia. The Japanese had an eye on possible territorial and economic gains, and the Americans wanted to keep an eye on Japan. Before long, French and Germans joined in. By now there was fury that the Bolsheviks had repudiated the Tsar's foreign debts and confiscated foreign assets in the shape of property and businesses, which especially hit the French.

It seemed that the Bolsheviks could not survive. At one time they held little but Petrograd, Moscow and an area west of the Urals. Trotsky, however, expanded the Red Guards into the Red Army, which he personally led with energy and skill, while the Bolsheviks defended their Revolution with fierce determination. But the armies involved in the struggle were never large and major battles were few. The intervention of the capitalist powers was half-hearted and the Whites lacked unity. Their popularity with landlords made them unpopular with peasants, and their association with capitalist interventionists was regarded as treacherous, part of a plot perhaps to exploit Russia's resources during her troubles. There was great cruelty on both sides, with White atrocities at least as great as the ruthlessness of the Cheka. By the end of 1920, the civil war faded out leaving Russia in even greater economic ruin. Meanwhile Nicholas II and the royal family vanished, presumably murdered by Bolsheviks in Ekaterinburg.

The Bolsheviks were still denied peace, for Poland launched an attack and, in May 1920, advanced as far as Kiev. The Red Army rallied again, chased the Poles almost to Warsaw and were stopped only when the French sent General Weygand to assist Pilsudski. By the Treaty of Riga, Russia surrendered extensive parts of White Russia and the Ukraine to Poland, lands which Stalin recovered through a deal with Hitler in 1939.

(*iii*) **1921–4.** In March 1921, the Kronstadt sailors, previously loyal Bolsheviks, raised a new cry: 'Soviets without Communists'. They were routed in ten days of bloodshed but for Lenin it was 'the flash that lit up reality'. Faced with economic chaos, seething discontent and a cry for a Third Revolution even among those once loyal, Lenin had to compromise to save communism in Russia. He had to water down Russian Marxism and allow time for the Russian people to be educated to understand and accept true communism. At no time had the Bolsheviks had the mass support of Russians. Peasant support for 'Peace, Bread and Land' was support for peasant ownership, not the nationalization of land. By the New Economic Policy (NEP), Lenin accepted some return to private enterprise. Peasants were allowed, after tax, to sell surplus crops; some private trading was allowed; small factories were denationalized together with some banks. Incentives and bonuses were introduced. Individuals were able to prosper again, and some peasants built up large and profitable farms. These men were the *kulaks*, who were hostile to communism. NEP did a lot to restore stability to Russia but it was a marked retreat from the full-blooded War Communism of 1918–21.

Lenin also sought contacts with foreign powers. By the end of 1921 he had made trade pacts with fourteen countries including Britain, Finland and Turkey. In 1922, a treaty of friendship was made with Germany, the Treaty of Rapallo. In 1924 the Communist government was recognized by many European countries, the Labour government in Britain giving a lead (see Section 3.2(*b*)). US recognition, however, had to wait until 1933 when Roosevelt became President.

In 1923 Russia adopted a new constitution whose drafting owed much to Stalin. The state became known as the Union of Soviet Socialist Republics (USSR) or the Soviet Union. All adults had the right to vote for a local Soviet. Elections to higher levels were indirect and the system of 1918 remained basically unaltered. The Congress of Soviets remained the law-making body. The People's Commissars, invariably communist, continued to rule. Although the Cheka had in theory been wound up, there was still a political police

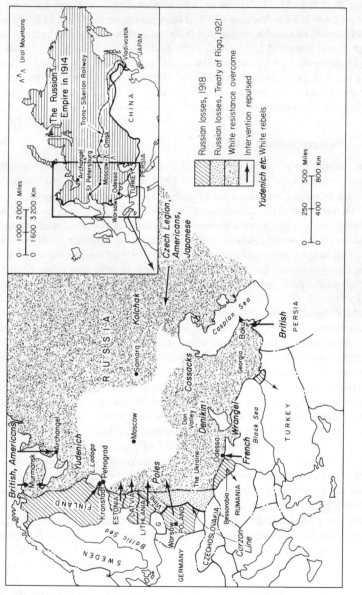

Fig. 5.1 Civil war and the wars of intervention in Russia, 1918–21

force, known now as OGPU. It gave Russia effective government although, in western eyes, an undemocratic one.

Lenin died in 1924. He had been a professional revolutionary for most of his life and was in exile for almost all of the years from 1900 to 1917. He was remembered with near-devotion by millions: his body was embalmed and Petrograd was renamed Leningrad. With Marx, he shares a place of honour among communists everywhere. Above all, Lenin gave Russia hope in the stormy years of 1917–24. There would be no return to Tsarism but the task of establishing real communism still remained to be tackled. One communist historian has suggested that that could take two hundred years.

(c) Stalin's Government 1924–53

(i) **The struggle for power.** Unlike Lenin, Josef Stalin was of peasant birth. He returned from exile in Siberia in March 1917, to edit *Pravda*, the Bolshevik paper. He became Commissar for Nationalities in Lenin's government, then Secretary-General of the Communist Party in 1922. As Commissar, he had much success in holding together the union of Russian states, using force in his native Georgia and elsewhere. As Secretary, he built up great personal power within the party, adding to the prestige he had won in the Civil War. Lenin, always modest and personally unambitious, had distrusted Stalin as 'the crafty Georgian' and hoped to be succeeded as ruler of Russia by Leon Trotsky.

Trotsky shared many of Lenin's ideas. He believed in world revolution to spread communism and had a similar dislike of personal advancement. Under Lenin, he served as Commissar for Foreign Affairs, then Commissar for War to organize the Red Army in the Civil War. Trotsky himself might have been Chairman of the People's Commissars in 1918 but he was Jewish and he preferred to accept the leadership of Lenin lest anti-Semitism should rise against the Bolsheviks. When Lenin died, a coalition of Stalin, Kamenev and Zinoviev made sure that Trotsky did not succeed him.

Stalin had no time for the intellectual arguments on which Trotsky thrived. It was his aim to rid the Communist Party of argument and to pursue the policy of 'Socialism in One Country' (to make Russia strong and self-sufficient, to avoid becoming entangled in international revolutions and to enforce obedience in Russia). Full communism could later grow out of that obedience. Stalin's first aim was to smash the influence of Trotsky and, in 1929, Trotsky was exiled to Turkey. (He later went to France and wrote a lengthy *History of the Revolution*, underwriting his own part in it which in November 1917 had been more active than Lenin's; but his continued hostility to Stalinism was fatal. In 1940 in Mexico, Trotsky was killed by a Stalinist agent with an ice-pick.)

Meanwhile Stalin consolidated his own position within the USSR. Kamenev and Zinoviev were expelled from the Communist Party in 1927 for urging rapid industrialization and an attack on the kulaks – policies Stalin

Fig. 5.2 Lenin and Stalin: Lenin had grave misgivings about allowing Stalin to come to power

himself was soon to adopt. For a time he found new allies such as Bukharin, but then turned on them too. From about 1928, Stalin's authority was supreme. He ruled as a dictator having inherited from Lenin the 'dictatorship of the proletariat', the dictatorship of the Communist Party over which Stalin himself now had absolute control. It was a dictatorship which Stalin was about to transform into a tyranny.

(*ii*) **Purges and the Constitution of 1936.** Stalin continued to insist on total obedience and to strike down all rivals both by purges and by a general terror. The great purges of 1936–8 followed an earlier purge in 1933, and further purges occurred after the Second World War. Yet another was being planned when Stalin died in 1953. Those purges that began in 1936 destroyed almost all that remained of the Bolshevik Party of Lenin's day. In a series of dramatic trials the accused often 'confessed' their guilt, even asking for death in order to purify the communist system. Kamenev and Zinoviev were among the victims and it seems likely that Bela Kun perished too in the general blood-letting. Purges of the armed forces accompanied those of politicians. Marshal

Tukhachevsky and seven other army leaders were shot, calling into question the continued effectiveness of the Red Army. Thousands of lesser men were also executed: even a hostile peasant was not unimportant enough to escape Stalin's savagery. His terrorism was similar to Hitler's in the same period; at times, it was even anti-Jewish.

Stalin's verdict was final in everything. He dictated to scientists, writers and composers, pronounced official verdicts on works such as Shostakovich's Fourth Symphony, and imposed his own version of Soviet culture. No freedom of expression remained in the USSR, and a new constitution in 1936 gave no more than a hollow appearance of democracy. This constitution preserved much of the earlier communist constitutions. All adults over eighteen could vote, by secret ballot. There were written guarantees of human liberties. Candidates could be nominated by bodies such as trade unions but local soviets then pruned the list, offering only one to the voters. Russia's parliament, the Supreme Soviet, was divided into two houses: the Soviet of the Union represented the people in proportion to population, the Soviet of Nationalities represented the many states which made up the united states of Russia. Power remained with the Communist Party, for all the candidates were communists, and the Council of Ministers was much the same as the Party's Central Committee. Real power lay with an inner group of that Committee, the *Politburo*, and since Stalin controlled the whole party, with Stalin.

(*iii*) **Economic planning.** Stalin carried the control of the economy begun by Lenin much further. NEP was abandoned in 1928, and from then on Russia's economy was driven forward with ruthless fury. The Five-Year Plans, introduced in 1928, 1933, 1937, 1946 and 1951, laid down production targets and penalties for failure. Russians worked with tremendous energy and not only from fear. There were incentives and rewards, called 'socialist competition'. Outstanding workers were called Stakhanovites in honour of a miner who, in 1935, cut over a hundred tons of coal in a single shift. By the outbreak of war in 1939, nearly half the industrial work force were Stakhanovites.

Stalin based the First Plan on rapid industrialization and the collectivization of agriculture, adopting policies he had previously rejected. In industry, the emphasis was on development to produce the means for further expansion – machinery, tractors and power stations. Hydro-electric power was essential to fulfil Stalin's intention of doing in a decade what other countries had done in a century. The Second Plan continued with this emphasis. The Third envisaged a great production of consumer goods to reward the people for their efforts but it was interrupted by the war with Nazi Germany.

By the end of the 1930s, Russia was a major industrial power, second in production only to the USA. There were huge new power stations on rivers such as the Dnieper, vast steel plants such as that at Magnitogorsk and new railway links, such as the Turkestan-Siberian. The output of chemicals, steel and coal soared as workers were diverted from agriculture into industry. In spite of a heavy price paid in freedom and blood for Stalin's rule, there was a new pride in Russia. Russians continued to endure shortages of consumer goods but they thought it an honour to be classed as a 'Hero of Socialist Labour' and there were other rewards in the form of educational opportunities and welfare services.

The First Five-Year Plan had also set out to transform Russian agriculture. Much of the country's farming was still inefficient, most of its farms small and outdated in their techniques. The USSR needed not only to feed its people but to grow surplus grain for export in order to buy machinery and foreign technology. But the peasants showed little concern for anything except self-interest: the more prosperous and efficient among them, the kulaks, were not supporters of communism. In 1927 the peasants were again withholding their produce as a protest against the lack of consumer goods on which to spend their profits under the NEP. Stalin's intention therefore was to reorganize Russian farms into larger units, to increase production by mechanization and more modern techniques and 'to destroy the kulaks as a class'.

The larger farming units were basically of two sorts. One was the government-owned state farm (*sovkhoz*) which Stalin would have preferred. The other was a co-operative (*kolkhoz*) where the peasants pooled their resources and shared the profits on what was sold to the state. The *kolkhozy* became the more common, groups of them being serviced by Machine Tractor Stations (MTS) which made equipment available. The transition was painful. In quick succession Stalin tried cajolery, brutality and then a mixture of incentives and penalties, dragging the peasantry into the new units. Violence reached a peak in 1930 with the ruthless extermination of the kulaks, and perhaps some ten million peasants died during the 1930s as a whole. Some were murdered, others died in labour camps and yet more died of starvation, since the agricultural system came near to collapse. There was a mass killing of livestock by kulaks who would not yield their animals to the collective farms and, in 1932, the USSR was reduced to importing grain urgently. In that year Stalin's wife committed suicide, sickened by the ruthlessness of her husband's government.

The future of collectivization was assured by 1935 but at heavy cost. In fact, Stalin had had to make concessions. Not only were there comparatively few state farms but the commonest form of kolkhoz came to be the *artel*. Here the peasants were allowed private homes, plots and livestock. They shared in the profits of the collective, 90 per cent of whose output was sold to the state at fixed prices, and they also sold at market for private profit the produce of their plots. The principles of NEP were therefore not entirely dead.

Stalin nevertheless achieved many of his objectives. The kulaks were eliminated. Some 25 million peasants were moved to the towns to work in industry, while those who remained trebled the output of grain and doubled that of meat and milk by 1939, compared with 1914. When Stalin died, the 25 million smallholdings of 1928 had given way to 100 000 large collectivized units. Even so, Russian agriculture produced less than was expected of it for generations to come.

(*iv*) **Welfare services.** The brutality of Stalin's rule must be set alongside improvements in the quality of life for Russians. Trade unions, with a membership of nearly 20 million in the 1930s, had important functions in supervising a Labour Code for the welfare of workers. State health services and social security schemes were expanded. The Constitution of 1936 laid down the right to pensions in old age and benefits during sickness, although there was not always sufficient money to pay them. There was emphasis, too, on education, especially in science and for workers' children. Illiteracy was cut from about 50 per cent in 1924 to 19 per cent in 1939. In 1934, four years' elementary education for all children was made a priority with seven years' secondary education to follow, although a new effort was needed in 1949 completely to implement the latter. Stalin had said that Russia was about a hundred years behind the advanced countries. In many ways, the gap had been closed when he died.

(*v*) **Foreign policy.** Stalin's policies remained isolationist even when Russia joined the League of Nations in 1934. The *Comintern* (the Communist Third International, set up in 1919) was still pledged to international revolution but its voice was subdued and the policies of the Russian Foreign Office were less aggressive. In the 1920s, Russia had a limited alliance with Germany (the Treaty of Rapallo) and gave some limited assistance to the communists in China. For the rest, Russia was content simply to seek recognition. In the 1930s, Stalin attempted to co-operate with the West against Nazi Germany (see Unit Eight), but there was distrust on both sides. Stalin made his own pact with the Germans in 1939, claiming to see evidence of a capitalist plot to turn Hitler against Russia (see Section 8.3(*f*)). But two years later Hitler launched *Operation Barbarossa* and attacked the USSR. Russian victories enabled Stalin greatly to expand the power of Russia and the appeal of communism. After 1945, most of Eastern Europe became communist (see Unit Twelve). 'Socialism in One Country' thus kept the communists in power in Russia in the interwar years and provided a base for massive advances in the years to come.

5.2 Fascism

Fascism was a fiercely anti-communist, intensely nationalistic creed which began in Italy and was developed by Mussolini. Although the word 'Fascist' has since been widely applied to many regimes based on the admiration of force, national prestige, theories of racial superiority and hero-worship, Fascist systems were strictly a feature of the interwar years. Their aims were often woolly but they claimed to support neither capitalism nor communism and to oppose the class war. Sometimes, as in the Italian Corporate State, they sought to create a partnership between classes in the interests of national greatness. They had a belief in active government and in radical measures to deal with problems such as unemployment. Their policies could sometimes be vaguely socialist and Hitler called his movement National Socialism. It was

*Fig. 5.3 Fascism in the German Reich: 'One People. One Nation. One Leader'
– a stamp issued at the time of the plebiscite which followed the union of
Germany and Austria*

more nationalist than socialist and, in the end, Fascists usually rested their
confidence in slogans of obedience. The essence of Italian Fascism lay in the
slogan, 'Mussolini is always right'. Germans expressed it more briefly: 'Heil
Hitler'.

(*a*) Fascist Italy

(*i*) **Fascist government.** 'The Leader' in Italy, *Il Duce*, was Mussolini. It took
him some time to establish all the trappings of a Fascist dictatorship after the
March on Rome (see Section 3.3(*a*)). By the time Matteotti was murdered,
there was a Fascist Grand Council to run the Party and the Fasci now existed
as a sort of private army to keep Mussolini in power. In 1925 Mussolini began
to make certain that his Fascist supporters had complete control of the
country. The Italian parliament offered little opposition. At the end of 1926
all political opposition was outlawed and, by this time, Mussolini had secured
for himself the right to rule, legislate, and even direct the course of justice.
Fascists occupied all positions of authority and parliament itself could now be
filled with Mussolini's stooges. After 1928 the Fascist Grand Council simply
drew up a list of approved candidates, which the voters could only accept or
reject in its entirety.

The system was geared to keeping Mussolini in power. Endless publicity
and propaganda proclaimed the Duce's brilliance until Mussolini believed it
himself. Censorship and persecution stifled all criticism. In fact, Fascist Italy
was corrupt and inefficient and Mussolini himself was a windbag who
achieved little except to remain in power for some twenty years. But the
Fascists gave the appearance of bustling energy with a constant display of
parades, speeches, salutes and posters. Their black shirts suggested a dedica-
tion to duty, the uniforms of politicians and even of schoolteachers a disciplined commitment to the common good. Organization was the keynote.
Even sport was mobilized and regimented for the glory of Fascism. Football
had a chief referee in Rome, his symbol of office a gold whistle. There was

national as well as Fascist delight when Italy won the World Cup in 1934 and 1938.

Italian Fascism was a theatrical and, for a time, successful confidence trick. But although there was thuggery and some opponents of the system were murdered, Mussolini's regime was less vicious than Hitler's and less systematically brutal than Stalin's. The price that most Italians paid was to lose their sense of reality and eventually their dignity under a leader whom others dubbed a 'Sawdust Caesar'.

(*ii*) **The Church and the corporate state.** Mussolini had one important success. In 1929 he managed to settle the long quarrel between the Italian government and the Papacy (see Section 3.3(*a*)). By the Lateran Treaties, Pope Pius XI agreed to recognize Mussolini's authority and the Italian state. In return, Mussolini paid compensation for lands the Pope had lost to Italy in 1870, accepted Catholic authority over Italian morals, and gave official recognition to the Catholic religion in Italy. Although the monarchy continued to exist in Italy, the King had long since been overawed by Mussolini. Now the Duce had weakened another source of possible opposition to his government by coming to terms with the Catholic Church.

In their early years the Fascists had strongly supported private enterprise. Later they showed more interest in governmental economic controls, though never very consistently. But in the 1930s Corporations lay at the heart of the Fascist system. Under Fascism, it was claimed, class warfare was outdated and Corporations were intended to provide a blueprint for co-operative effort between employers and workers. They also provided yet another device for extending Fascist authority. The Corporations were based on occupations and brought together employers, managers and workers subject to a Fascist Minister of Corporations. Trade unions were similarly brought within the fold and, since disputes would be settled by officials of the Corporations, strikes and lock-outs were forbidden. On paper the system looked attractive, with a promise of harmony and progress. In practice the Fascists used the Corporations to muzzle opposition. Inefficiency and corruption remained commonplace. The Fascists were nevertheless satisfied enough to abolish the Italian parliament in 1939, replacing it with a Chamber of Fasces and Corporations, representing the Party and the Party-dominated Corporations.

(*iii*) **The economy.** Mussolini's aim was to make Italy self-sufficient, but the winning of prestige was frequently confused with projects of real value. When the currency was in difficulties in 1925, Volpi revalued the lira, but fixed the value too high.* It became even more difficult to sell Italy's exports and unemployment rose. The Great Depression made the situation even worse. Wages fell, the jobless increased and the government ceased to issue statistics. Mussolini resorted to propaganda.

* Compare Churchill, page 75.

Fig. 5.4 Dutiful Fascist salutes in 1923: cyclists organized for the greater glory of Mussolini

There was a dramatic *Battle for Grain*. More was produced, often on land better suited to fruit-growing, but the Battle distorted the economy. Impressive public works were launched. Land was reclaimed and the Pontine Marshes successfully drained. Railways were electrified, impressive motorways (*autostrada*) built. Progress was made in developing hydro-electric power. Imposing new public buildings such as railway stations and sports stadiums as well as blocks of flats were erected. But the effects on unemployment were small, although propaganda made the most of every Fascist achievement.

The Fascists made little impression on poverty in the south. Their record showed an improvement on the work of previous governments but welfare schemes were low on the list of Fascist priorities. There was economic assistance for large families but the motive was not humanitarian. Mussolini wished to increase Italy's population. He ordered a *Battle for Births*. Bachelors were taxed to encourage them to do their duty to the state – marry and father children; but the birth rate remained disappointing.

(*iv*) **Foreign policy**. 'I adore war,' declared Mussolini. 'War is to men what childbirth is to women.' But here too Mussolini's ambitions outran his capacity to achieve them. He had visions of a great Italian empire, dominating the Mediterranean (*Mare Nostrum*, Our Sea) and extending Italy's possessions in

Africa. At first he chose his victims with care and had some early successes against the weak states in the Balkans and in Africa – there were Fascist triumphs over Jugoslavia (see Section 2.9(*a*)), Greece (see Section 7.1(*a*)), Ethiopia and Albania (see Section 8.2). But in 1940 Mussolini felt confident enough to attack France, then on the point of being defeated by Nazi Germany, and the results were disastrous (see Sections 9.1 and 9.4).

Nothing was more typical of Fascism than its intense nationalism and aggressiveness. Yet Mussolini was, at times, a responsible statesman until he finally threw in his lot with Hitler in the late 1930s. Britain and France long continued to hope that Fascist Italy could be a force for international stability and for the effectiveness of the League of Nations. It was one of the illusions from which well-meaning politicians suffered between the wars. Mussolini was carried away by his own propaganda. 'The twentieth century will be the century of Fascism,' he once proclaimed. He became fascinated with the power of '8 million bayonets'. For the peace of Europe it was a tragedy that the weakness of democracy in Italy produced only Mussolini, weakening still further the Alliance on which the League of Nations was founded (see Units Seven and Eight).

(*b*) Nazi Germany

(*i*) **Nazi ideology.** The roots of the German National Socialist Party lay in an arrogant belief in the superiority of the *Herrenvolk*, a master-race of Aryans (in effect, Germans) whom the Nazis themselves intended to lead. For the Herrenvolk to achieve its rightful place it was alleged to be necessary to purify it: to purge it of those elements, such as the Jews, who polluted it. Anti-Semitism carried to extremes was therefore another feature of Nazi gobble-degook. 'No Jew,' the Party programme asserted, 'may be a member of the nation'. It was always easier to identify what the Nazis opposed than what they themselves intended to build (see Section 3.3(*b*)), but Hitler and his followers had expansionist ideas for the glory of Germany and the Herrenvolk. Insofar as they had any clear plan it seemed to fall into two stages: first, the Peace Settlement of 1919–20 must be overturned to restore Germany to greatness and to bring within the Reich all German-speaking peoples and, secondly, Germany should expand eastwards. This eastwards expansion would secure *Lebensraum* (see Glossary) for the Herrenvolk at the expense of such lesser breeds as Slavs, and it might also lead to a conflict with the USSR in which communism – which the Nazis also pledged themselves to destroy – might finally be wiped out in Europe.

The first requirement, however, was to ensure that the Nazis had total control within Germany itself. Official policy had at first included some socialist ideals about equality and welfare and plans for nationalization. Such policy had been useful in the 1920s in attracting recruits and winning support. But Hitler himself had too much contempt for his fellow-men to be a socialist. During the Depression the socialist ambitions were played down in order to make greater appeal to anti-socialists and anti-communists, and the socialists within the Nazi Party were eventually purged. What was left was a ruthless determination to dominate and control the German people, to reduce them to a robot-like obedience to Hitler himself, the *Führer* (Leader). Having become Chancellor (see Section 3.3(*b*)), Hitler's first objective was *Gleichschaltung*, the 'co-ordination' of all German institutions under Nazi control. He was then able to carry to extremes the Fascist readiness to obey the Leader and the Fascist yearning for national glory; and he could add a new dimension to Fascism by extending hatred of the Jews into the Holocaust (see Glossary).

(*ii*) **Nazi government.** The Enabling Law which followed Hitler's appointment as Chancellor suspended the Weimar constitution until 1937. Long before 1937 the Nazis had completed Gleichschaltung and the destruction of Weimar democracy. In 1934 Hitler abolished the separate parliaments of the states (e.g. Prussia) and then all parties except the Nazi Party. In the 'Night of the Long Knives', 30 June 1934, he destroyed many former supporters including Strasser who deplored Hitler's ruthlessness, Röhm and others in the SA who had socialist ideals, and General von Schleicher, an ally no longer needed. The SA (Brownshirts) were less reliable than the Blackshirts (*Schutzstaffel*, SS), fanatically led by Heinrich Himmler, a sadistic ex-schoolteacher. Hitler intended to have no rivals, only devoted followers. When Hindenburg died in August 1934, Hitler combined the offices of President and Chancellor, called himself *Führer* and, in a plebiscite, won the approval of nearly 90 per cent of those who voted. Hitler also took charge of the army, and soldiers took oaths of personal loyalty to him.

The Reichstag was packed with Hitler's supporters, ready to agree on every issue. Trade unions were abolished. All free expression was muzzled. In the hands of Goebbels, the Ministry of Propaganda distorted all truth in the service of the Führer. The young were indoctrinated in schools and youth organizations. Himmler set up the *Gestapo*, a vicious political police force. From 1934, all power lay with the Nazis and above all with the Führer.

(*iii*) **Opposition.** A Concordat (agreement) with the Pope in 1933 gave Hitler some support from the Roman Catholic Church but his racialist theories and persecution of the Jews led to a quarrel. In 1937, Pius XI condemned Hitler's doctrines in the Encyclical, '*Mit Brennender Sorge*' (With Burning Anxiety). The German Lutheran Church was equally uneasy and a section led by Pastor Niemöller expressed opposition. Those who protested were sent to concentration camps (bestial prison camps which reinforced the activities of the Gestapo and the SS to stifle all opposition).

On the other hand, many Germans approved of Hitler's regime and the majority expressed no opposition. In 1935, the Nuremberg Law deprived Jews of their rights as citizens, required them to wear a distinguishing patch and imposed many humiliations; in 1938, vicious persecution followed humiliation. Germany only had about half a million Jews but when Poland was

Fig. 5.5 Two of the faces of Nazi Germany:
(a) Hitler addressing some of the Hitler Youth at Nuremberg, 1938, the
stadium a cauldron of Führer-worship and disciplined obedience

invaded in 1939 many more Jews fell into Hitler's hands and he eventually embarked on 'The Final Solution', a policy of genocide to destroy their race.

Hitler exercised hypnotic control over the young, turning many of them into state spies, ready to denounce even their own families. One could join the Little Fellows at six, the *Jungvolk* at ten and the Hitler Youth at fourteen. Boys swore to devote their lives to the Führer, 'the saviour of our country'. Girls were trained, in the League of German Maidens, to regard the mothering of Hitler's soldiers as their highest aim. Mussolini and communist Russia had dedicated youth organizations but nowhere was more attention paid to regimenting children than in Hitler's Germany. Not all of them took readily to Nazi training but the youth movements gave Hitler a deadly weapon both against opposition within Germany and later in war.

(*iv*) **The economy.** Hitler's promise to reduce unemployment was to some extent fulfilled; it fell from 6 million to 1 million by 1936. Public works such as the building of motorways (*Autobahnen*) provided some jobs, but many of the jobs which the Nazis provided were in unproductive organizations such as the Gestapo. Vacancies were also created by dismissing Jews and enemies of the state, and rearmament and the expansion of the armed forces helped to provide work. Like so much in Hitler's Germany, the solving of the unemployment problem was less successful than it seemed at first sight.

(b) Victim of the Herrenvolk – a Jew exposed to public humiliation. His placard reads: 'I am a Jew but I don't wish to complain about the Nazis'

Nevertheless, many had grounds for satisfaction. Prices and rents were controlled. Slums were cleared. State health services were expanded. Attention was paid to the welfare of workers. The 'Strength Through Joy' movement (*Kraft durch Freude*) made cheap holidays and sports facilities available to them. Nazi parades and torchlight processions brought colour to drab lives and even attracted tourists to help the economy. For those to whom politics and the right to think and speak were unimportant, Nazi Germany seemed, in the 1930s, to offer more than did democracy.

Hitler aimed at self-sufficiency. Frantic efforts were made to cut down imports by producing substitutes for materials such as rubber. But by 1939 Germany was faced with serious difficulties in paying for imports, and stealing vital supplies from other countries by an aggressive foreign policy became increasingly attractive to the Nazis. Hitler's Germany had a major balance of payments problem, and by 1939 the Nazi economy, geared to military might, was an unhealthy one.

(*v*) **Foreign policy.** Germany's power produced instability in international affairs. It is unlikely that Hitler had deliberate plans for European war, but his was the major responsibility for the Second World War (see Unit Eight).

(*c*) **Falangist Spain**

(*i*) **The Civil War.** The Spanish Civil War began in July 1936 with a rising of the armed forces in Morocco which quickly spread to Spain itself. The aim of the rebels was to overthrow the government of the Popular Front (see Section 3.3(c)). Their leader was General Franco, Chief of the Army General Staff. Among the various right-wing groups which rallied to Franco was the Falange, a fascist party founded in 1933 by the son of Primo de Rivera. Franco was declared Chief of the Spanish State in October 1936, and by the end of the year the rebels had won control of much of the north and west of Spain and laid siege to Madrid. Mussolini and Hitler recognized a kindred spirit in Franco and gave support. In 1937, Franco became *El Caudillo*, yet another 'Leader' whose supporters, especially the Falangists, enthusiastically imitated the raised-arm salutes of Fascists and Nazis.

Britain and France decided not to interfere, and a non-intervention committee met in London in the autumn of 1936 carefully to study how not to aid the Spanish government against the rebels. Spain nevertheless became a battleground for ideologies. The USSR sent advisers, food and military aid to fight the rebellion. Volunteers, eager to halt the spread of Fascism, formed International Brigades. Communists, socialists, liberals and democrats rallied to the Popular Front and for three years a vicious and costly struggle raged.* The aims of the supporters of the Popular Front were varied and imprecise. They quarrelled amongst themselves and in the end were no match for Franco, some 50 000 Italians and the German air force which perfected its new technique of dive-bombing, notably at Guernica.

In 1936, the rebels won about half of Spain. In 1937, their progress was checked although they were successful against the Basques in the far north. In 1938, they cut through the middle of Spain and reached the Mediterranean coast. Madrid was besieged again and with the capture of Barcelona, at the beginning of 1939, the hopes of the Popular Front crumbled. Russia withdrew support.† The International Brigades broke up and in March 1939, Madrid surrendered. The Civil War had taken three-quarters of a million lives, given Germany and Italy a dress rehearsal for the Second World War and resulted in yet another defeat for democracy. Britain and France recognized the government of Franco but he failed to repay his debt to Hitler and Mussolini by joining them in the Second World War. He preferred 'benevolent neutrality' which enabled him to concentrate on Spain's problems.

(*ii*) **Franco's government.** Franco's regime was usually regarded as fascist because of his association with Hitler and Mussolini and because of the nature of the Civil War. It was fiercely anti-communist and had some trappings of

---

* Among the volunteers was George Orwell, the British journalist and novelist, who recorded his experiences in *Homage to Catalonia*, as he had previously recorded the sufferings of the English working-classes in *The Road to Wigan Pier*. But Orwell was disillusioned by the cruelty and intrigue.

† Stalin had probably wished only to prolong the war. He did not wish to antagonize the West by achieving a communist victory.

fascism, including a violent, political police force. At the same time, it was peculiarly Spanish – a Catholic dictatorship based on a right-wing, nationalist coalition which included the Falangists. It ruled for the benefit of the privileged – the army, the Church, financiers and industrialists. The Cortes, Spain's parliament, was restored in 1942 but the system remained a dictatorship and, in 1947, Franco was declared Chief of State for life with the power to appoint his successor.

After 1945, when Hitler and Mussolini were dead, the survival of Franco was an unhappy reminder of pre-war Fascism. But no rebel body was strong enough to topple him. Many states preferred to ignore him but he remained the Caudillo until his death in 1975. Neither Franco nor Salazar, his Portuguese neighbour, played much part in the affairs of the outside world, other than to delay for as long as possible the independence of the Spanish and Portuguese overseas empires and to keep alive there some of the fascist theories of racial superiority (see Section 6.5).

5.3   Nationalism

Parallel to European fascism between the wars there developed a variety of intensely nationalist regimes in other parts of the world.

(a) Turkey

(i) **The government of Mustapha Kemal.** The opposition of Turkish nationalists to the Treaty of Sèvres resulted in the new Treaty of Lausanne and the downfall of the Sultan at the hands of Mustapha Kemal (see Section 2.7). From then until he died in 1938, Kemal ruled the Turkish Republic. He was elected President of the Republic in October 1923, and he created and dominated the Republican People's Party. Rivals were purged in 1924 and, some years later, Turkey became a one-party state. Kemal was a dictator but he seldom resorted to the brutalities of the fascists and he kept alive the hope of a return to democracy; he was also progressive and determined to modernize his country. He earned the gratitude of the Turkish people and there was general agreement when, in 1934, he took the surname Atatürk ('Father of Turks').

One obstacle to modernization was the power of the Mohammedan Church and, in 1928, Islam ceased to be the state religion. Politics were divorced from religion and Turkey became a secular state.

(ii) **Reforms.** In the nineteenth century, Turkey was referred to as 'the sick man of Europe'. Kemal Atatürk was determined to use strong government to make Turkey well. Central to his policies was Westernization. By reducing the influence of religion, he was able to introduce new codes of law, to raise women's status in society and to attack the traditions which held Turkey back. The Western weekend, Western dress and the Western alphabet were introduced. Education was expanded and modernized. Women gained social and political rights. Polygamy was abolished, divorce and civil marriage legalized, and Turkey's health services and social insurance schemes were developed.

(*iii*) **The economy.** Kemal built up economic strength through state management. The state took control of railways and industries such as sugar, and the government set aside money for industrial development, protecting the Turkish economy with tariffs. Some farming co-operatives were set up and scientific farming methods encouraged.

Kemal's management did not make Turkey a wealthy, industrial state but he gave the nation stability in a critical period. By 1938, the Turks had come to terms with the twentieth century and regained their self-respect.

(*iv*) **Foreign policy.** After negotiating the Peace Treaty at Lausanne in 1923, Kemal was prepared to live in peace. He made trade pacts with his neighbours and favoured international stability. In 1926, he accepted League of Nations arbitration in a frontier dispute over Mosul, which Britain claimed as part of the mandate of Iraq. Turkey joined the League six years later. Kemal disliked Russian communism and Turks continued to dislike Greeks but relations with both remained amicable. Kemal also supported Britain and France in trying to ensure stability in Europe: his nationalism was concentrated on the internal development of Turkey. In foreign policy, he sought only Turkey's security.

(*b*) Japan

(*i*) **Imperial government.** Japan adopted the principle of a vote for all adult males in the mid-1920s, but the Prime Minister, Kato Takaaki, could do little to alter the fundamental weakness of the Japanese constitution. The power of governments rested on placating vested interests and not on elected members of parliament. The army had a traditional grip on Japanese politics; the emperor was surrounded by influential conservatives, and the influence of businessmen was growing. All these groups combined to resist the development of real democracy, and left-wing ideas were frequently suppressed by a powerful police force. The creation of a small Japanese Communist Party in 1922 led the police to be even more watchful, alert for 'dangerous thought'.

Hirohito, the Emperor from 1926, had some progressive attitudes but any hopes that the Japanese system of government could grow into a truly democratic one were shattered by the Great Depression. There was already dissatisfaction with the weakness, corruption and inconsistencies of the parliamentary system. The administration of Kato, for example (1924–6), maintained close connections with the Mitsubishi industrial empire. As a result governments were short-lived and charges of self-interest common.

In 1931, disregarding the civilian government, the Japanese army launched an attack on Manchuria (see Section 8.1). Army leaders were far from united, but for the rest of the 1930s the militarists were the dominant force in Japan. They tried to solve by aggression Japan's social and economic problems –

overpopulation, a shortage of raw materials and of markets. Hirohito was little more than a figurehead, appointing a bewildering number of prime ministers, some civilian, some military. But, although elections were still held, the system was even less democratic than in the 1920s. Japan had turned to fierce nationalism and militarism, not to democracy.

(*ii*) **The economy.** Private enterprise, in which the big industrial combines (*zaibatsu*) played a leading part, was the basis of Japan's industrial expansion after 1918. At first, textiles dominated Japanese industry but there was expansion into other fields such as chemicals. Not until about 1937, however, was great emphasis placed upon engineering and heavy industry; by that time, the aggressive foreign policy required the country to be geared to war. The output of steel was expanded and new industries developed, such as the production of motor vehicles. The government, which had previously interfered little beyond providing protective tariffs, began to exercise more control over industry for military reasons.

Agriculture was generally efficient. In the early twentieth century Japan became the world's greatest producer of silk and silk made up over a third of the country's exports. The Great Depression, therefore, hit Japan hard, for silk was a luxury which the world could do without. Japan's trade in other goods made new progress in the later 1930s, however. Her goods were often cheap, and she won extensive markets in Asia and Africa. But without the help of 'invisible exports' Japan would seldom have been able to pay for her imports.

Japan provided formidable competition to European producers, especially of textiles, but she was also a customer with many needs to be supplied. The militarists intended to improve Japan's trading position by getting a stranglehold on China. Later in the 1930s, they were attracted by fascist theories of self-sufficiency. Expansion became as essential to Japan as it was for Hitler. The Japanese consequently developed the idea of a 'Co-Prosperity Sphere' in East Asia (an area from Manchuria to Indonesia, self-supporting and dominated by Japan), a sort of Japanese *Lebensraum*.

(*iii*) **Foreign policy.** The nature of Japan's political system thus combined with greed to produce a foreign policy which became increasingly aggressive. It was based upon rampant nationalism and encouraged by the weakness of Japan's neighbours. China seemed likely to be an easy victim but aggression in the years after 1931 led eventually to conflict on a much larger scale. Japanese ambition resulted in the Second World War in the Pacific (see Unit Eight).

Further Reading
Ayling, S.E.: *Portraits of Power.* Harrap (London, 1965) – Lenin, Stalin, Mussolini, Hitler, Franco, Kemal.
Cash, A.: *The Russian Revolution.* Benn (London, 1967).

Elliott, B.J.: *Hitler and Germany*. Longman (Harlow, 1966).
Footman, D.: *The Russian Revolutions*. Faber (London, 1966).
Jackson, N.C.: *Russia in the Twentieth Century*. Pergamon (London, 1977).
Jamieson, A.: *Leaders of the Twentieth Century*. Bell (London, 1970) – Lenin, Stalin, Mussolini, Hitler, Franco, Kemal.
Jardine, C. Bayne: *Mussolini and Italy*. Longman (Harlow, 1966).
McCauley, M.: *The Soviet Union since 1917*. Longman (Harlow, 1981).
Pearson, R.: *Revolution in Russia*. Harrap (London, 1975).
Procktor, R.: *Nazi Germany*. Bodley Head (London, 1970).
Robottom, J.: *Modern Russia*. Longman (Harlow, 1969).
Snellgrove, L.E.: *Franco and the Spanish Civil War*. Longman (Harlow, 1965).
Williams, B.: *Modern Japan*. Longman (Harlow, 1969).

Documentary

Berwick, M.: *The Third Reich*. Wayland (London, 1971).
Gregory, D.: *Mussolini and the Fascist Era*. Arnold (London, 1968).
Smith, D.: *Left and Right in Twentieth-Century Europe*. Longman (Harlow, 1970).
Stacey, F.W.: *Lenin and the Russian Revolution*. Arnold (London, 1968).

Exercises

1. How would you define and illustrate *Communist government* from the history of Russia under Lenin and Stalin?
2. 'It was a dictatorship which Stalin was about to transform into a tyranny' (page 97). Explain what the author means by this statement and illustrate the truth of it.
3. How would you define and illustrate *Fascist government* from the history of Italy under Mussolini?
4. Referring to the entry under *Nationalism* in the Glossary at the end of this book, write down the points you could make in arguing that *each* of the following had a strong belief in nationalism: Stalin; Mussolini; Hitler; Kemal.
5. Using this Unit and Unit Four, (a) show how Mussolini and Hitler tried to deal with the Depression; and (b) explain why the USSR was not much affected by the Depression.
6. Divide a large sheet of paper into columns, one for each of the countries USSR, Italy, Germany, Turkey and Japan. Enter briefly in *each* column for the period dealt with in this Unit: (a) the basic system of government; (b) how opposition was dealt with; (c) how the economy was organized; (d) the main aims of the government in power.
7. Using the material you have assembled in Exercise 6, write paragraphs to explain (a) what similarities there were between Fascist Italy and Nazi Germany; (b) what similarities and differences there were between Nazi Germany and the USSR; (c) why it would not be fitting to describe either Turkey or Japan as 'fascist' states.
8. Why should 'Mussolini and Hitler' recognize in Franco 'a kindred spirit' (page 108)?
9. Show how the lives of ordinary citizens were affected by the governments of any *two* of Stalin; Mussolini; Hitler.
10. Use the following extract from a description by the British ambassador and Fig. 5.5(a) to describe the annual Nazi ceremonies at Nuremberg in the later 1930s. How far would you agree with the ambassador's comments on these ceremonies?

Nobody who has not witnessed the various displays given at Nuremberg . . . can be fully acquainted with the Nazi movement in Germany. It was an extremely necessary . . . experience. . . . In addition to attending the review of the party leaders, 140 000 in number, and representing at that time (1937) over two million members of the Party (a year later . . . Hitler was to tell me himself that there were well over three million Party officials); a rally of the Hitler youth, 48 000 strong with 5 000 girls; and a supper party in Herr Himmler's SS camp of 25 000 blackshirts, I had talks with Hitler himself. . . .

The displays themselves were most impressive . . . the massed formations of brownshirts . . . indescribably picturesque. I had spent six years in St Petersburg before the war in the best days of the old Russian ballet, but for grandiose beauty I have never seen a ballet to compare with it. The German, who has a highly developed herd instinct, is perfectly happy when he is wearing a uniform, marching in step, and singing in chorus, and the Nazi revolution has certainly known how to appeal to these instincts in his nature. As a display of aggregate strength it was ominous; as a triumph of mass organization combined with beauty it was superb.

Unit Six

Restless Empires

6.1 Nationalism

The huge overseas empires of the Europeans (see Fig. 1.4) survived almost intact until after the Second World War. Under the mandate system (see Section 1.3), the German and Turkish Empires had been broken up among the victorious powers. In the 1930s, Italy and Japan endeavoured to expand their empires. But, in the interwar years, the most significant developments were the growth of nationalism among subject peoples and the beginning of the British attempt to transform the British Empire into a Commonwealth.

Nationalism took the form of a demand for independence, a demand which was to grow to a clamour after 1945. The Paris Settlement had encouraged the growth of nationalism; President Wilson had proclaimed the need for colonies to be ruled in the interests of the inhabitants. The Commonwealth grew in time to become a novel twentieth-century experiment, a multiracial partnership of equals. Before 1939, however, few people had clear ideas about where these developments were leading.

6.2 The British Empire

(a) The British Commonwealth of Nations

The White Dominions (see Section 1.3) were a unique feature of the British Empire. By 1914 they had won rights of self-government in almost everything except foreign policy. Canada was the first to achieve this, in 1867. Australia, New Zealand and South Africa followed. A government 'like Canada's' gradually became the aim of many states within the British Empire, but after 1918 Canada and other White Dominions wanted independence in foreign policy too. They began to agitate for a definition of *Dominion Status*.

Britain placed few obstacles in their path. The Dominions were represented at the Peace Conference in Paris. They joined the League of Nations, and some took charge of mandates. In 1926, Balfour, a former Conservative Prime Minister, found words to define Dominion Status and, in 1931, MacDonald gave this definition the force of law in the Statute of Westminster. Britain confirmed that her laws no longer bound the Dominions. They were completely free. They 'freely associated' with Britain and one another as members of the British Commonwealth of Nations. The British King remained Head of State of each Dominion, but the Commonwealth was a partnership of equals. By 1931, the number of Dominions had already increased with the granting of Dominion Status to the Irish Free State and Newfoundland.

There was talk before 1939 of making India a Dominion as well but the deed itself was delayed. The Irish Free State was a reluctant Dominion, too anti-British to wish to remain in the Commonwealth and, in 1934, Newfoundland reacted to economic difficulties by returning to colonial status as a prelude to joining Canada in 1949. Nevertheless, the foundations of the Commonwealth had been laid. Eventually it became multi-racial, but until 1939 it was a white man's club.

The partnership of the Commonwealth helped to preserve democratic governments and human liberties. The members had a common language, English. Most of them played cricket and they established many ties for mutual assistance. All except Ireland freely chose to join Britain in the war against Germany in 1939, recognizing the value of what Britain sought to preserve against fascism. On the other hand, the results of the partnership were sometimes disappointing. The Commonwealth had almost no machinery for co-operation. Prime Ministers, and such people as defence experts, met fairly regularly, but co-operation was often haphazard.

Trade may serve as an example. In 1924, Britain staged the Empire Exhibition at Wembley to encourage the buying of 'Empire' goods. In 1926 the Empire Marketing Board was set up, only to be abandoned six years later. In the Dominions, it was argued that Commonwealth countries could help one another with a system of imperial preference such as that practised by Canada: tariffs were imposed on foreign goods but lower duties, or none at all, on Commonwealth goods. In the 1920s, Britain clung to free trade; the system of imperial preference did not appeal to her.

When Britain abandoned free trade in 1932, Baldwin, Neville Chamberlain and Thomas represented the country at the Ottawa Conference where members of the Commonwealth tried to work out a trading system to help one another in the Depression. There was no general plan but some partial agreements were reached. Britain gave preferences to the Commonwealth under the Import Duties Act (see Section 4.4(b)). Even within the Commonwealth, however, countries were reluctant to put the welfare of others above self-interest. All wanted to sell rather than to buy, and all now wanted to protect their own agriculture and industry against competition. Quarrels were not unusual. Australia put duties on British cloth and Lancashire cotton workers retaliated by trying to boycott Australian produce. Even so, members of the Commonwealth, in 1938, sold almost 50 per cent of their exports within the association.

(b) Irish Nationalism

In 1918, Irish nationalists wanted a complete break from Britain. Ireland had long been denied self-government and when, in 1916, Britain savagely repressed the Easter Rising of Irish republicans, opinion swung behind *Sinn Fein* (the Irish Republican party). Sinn Fein won most of the Irish seats in the general election of 1918. The party was in favour of a free Ireland and its MPs boycotted Westminster, setting up an illegal Irish parliament in Dublin.

In the Government of Ireland Act of 1920 Lloyd George offered only Home Rule. The Act offered Ireland less than Canada had gained in 1867 – self-government in only a limited number of matters and the right to continue electing MPs to Westminster. Moreover, it divided Ireland, with Home Rule for the north at Belfast and for the south at Dublin. In a strongly Conservative House of Commons, Lloyd George felt obliged to satisfy the Protestants of Northern Ireland, and they refused to be ruled by the Catholics who made up 75 per cent of Ireland's total population. This problem of the Protestant minority had delayed the settlement of Ireland's future before 1914 and it has embittered the history of Ireland ever since.

Sinn Fein rejected the Act. They wanted more than Home Rule and they angrily rejected the division of Ireland. A fighting wing, the Irish Republican Army (IRA), was too strong for the Royal Irish Constabulary and Lloyd George had already recruited extra help for the police (whose emergency uniforms gave rise to their nickname, 'Black and Tans'). A bloody conflict developed. The Black and Tans and the IRA, led by Michael Collins, were both guilty of barbaric atrocities. When elections were held in the south, however, it was obvious that the Catholics were solid in their support for Sinn Fein and De Valera who led the party, so Lloyd George had to negotiate.

It was impossible for him to abandon the Protestants. They were numerous enough in the six counties of Northern Ireland to accept the Act of 1920 for that part of the country. Southern Ireland, on the other hand, agreed to Dominion Status in 1921. Britain hastily passed the Irish Free State Agreement Act of 1922. Ireland was thus divided after all, but in the Irish Free State (the south) parliament accepted the settlement by only the narrowest of margins. De Valera rejected it as a betrayal. Michael Collins, who had been one of the Irishmen who signed the Agreement, was murdered. The Irish Free State was a Dominion but it had still to accept the British monarchy.

For a time, during 'The Troubles', there was civil war in the Free State. The IRA fought a bloody campaign against the Irish government which had agreed to partition. Stability did not return until De Valera resumed his place in parliament in 1926 with a new party, *Fianna Fail.*

In 1932, De Valera became Prime Minister, an office he held until 1948 and to which he returned in the 1950s before becoming eventually the President of Ireland. He could not reunite Ireland but he won some successes against the British in the 1930s. The Irish language was revived, the name of the Free State changed to Eire and links with the British monarchy were steadily undermined. Neville Chamberlain was persuaded to write off most of the debt the Irish still owed to Britain and to abandon certain ports which Britain had retained since 1922. In spite of these efforts to appease her, however, Eire played little part in Commonwealth affairs.

In 1939, De Valera chose neutrality and it was not much more than a formality when Eire was declared a republic in 1949 and left the Commonwealth. The actual break was made by John Costello but it was De Valera

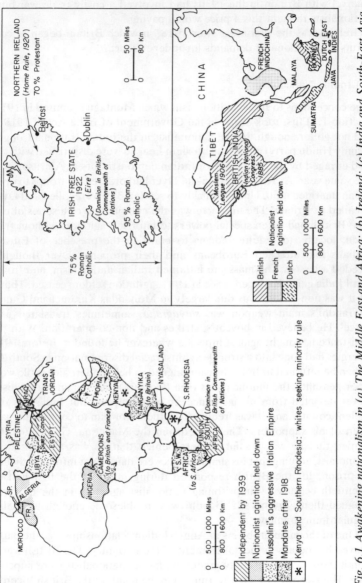

Fig. 6.1 Awakening nationalism in (a) The Middle East and Africa; (b) Ireland; (c) India and South-East Asia

who had prepared the way, building a successful democracy in the Free State after uncertain beginnings and making a start on economic development. The quarrel with Britain in the 1930s had involved a costly trade war but Irish nationalists thought this a price worth paying.

Ireland was the first area, after 1918, in which Britain began to come to terms with nationalist demands for independence.

(c) Indian Nationalism

The concessions to Indian nationalism which Montagu promised in 1917 (see Section 1.3) first took shape in the Government of India Act of 1919. They did not go far enough. Indian nationalists in the Indian National Congress (a mainly Hindu party) and in the Moslem League were dissatisfied with the Act and enraged by the 'massacre' of Indian demonstrators at Amritsar in April, the same year. At Amritsar, General Dyer had ordered his troops to open fire on an unarmed mob. Unable quickly to scatter, 379 were killed and Dyer was recalled to Britain. The massacre was the culmination of a series of clashes. The British had taken special powers to imprison agitators without trial and even, locally, to require Indians to crawl in the presence of Europeans. Indians had attacked Europeans and their property. Dyer thought they needed a lesson. The massacre inflamed Indian nationalism, and from then until India gained independence in 1947, agitation seldom ceased. That much of it was non-violent was due largely to Mohandas Karamchand Gandhi.

Gandhi's main weapon was *satyagraha*, sometimes translated as 'soul force'. He believed in boycotts, strikes and non-co-operation. With passive resistance he fought against injustice wherever he found it. Before 1914, his energies had gone into a struggle against racial discrimination in South Africa. When he returned to India, he campaigned to help underpaid textile workers, poor peasants, the untouchables (see Glossary) and Indian nationalism. He never deviated from his insistence on non-violence, but India was often a violent country and it was frequently difficult for him to control the passions even of his supporters. They called him the Mahatma, Great Soul, but he denied that he was a saint. Others denied that he was a politician or an economist, arguing that his simple ideas were naïve. Not infrequently he went to prison, for the British responded during much of the first half of the twentieth century by imprisoning nationalist agitators in the Empire who plagued them. From 1922 Gandhi was troublesome enough to qualify for regular imprisonment.

One of the main problems in Anglo-Indian relationships was the part to be played by Indians in the government of their country. The British wanted to admit them to responsibility gradually. Indian nationalists were impatient to rule. The Act of 1919 left government in the hands of the British Viceroy, but allowed Indians some control of minor areas of government in the provinces, such as Bengal. Gandhi led the chorus of protest. Indians boycotted the Prince of Wales's visit to India in 1921. When Baldwin sent the Simon

Commission to investigate Indian problems, they boycotted that.

In 1931 Gandhi visited England, where MacDonald hoped to secure agreements on India's future in the Round Table Conferences. The scraggy frame of Gandhi, his eastern peasant dress and apparent sincerity won him many friends, among them the Lancashire mill-workers to whom he explained India's poverty and his boycott of British textiles. But his lack of formality disturbed King George V and infuriated Winston Churchill. Many Indian politicans boycotted the Conferences and little was achieved. Nevertheless, the Government of India Act of 1935 was passed.

This went a long way to giving Indians control of the provincial governments. The Indian National Congress, in 1937, gained power in eight of the provinces in which elections were held. India as a whole remained subject to the Viceroy but, in certain matters, he shared power with the Indians. This was still not enough for them – Indians had no say in foreign policy, for example.

Fig. 6.2   Cartoon in the Evening Standard, *28 July 1931. Gandhi was a constant source of exasperation to the British*

When, in 1939, the Viceroy, then Lord Linlithgow, foolishly declared war on Germany without consulting them at all, he showed an arrogance which could only anger the nationalists.

Meanwhile, Gandhi gave up the leadership of the Indian National Congress, leaving it in the hands of more professional politicians, among them

Nehru and the more conservative Patel. Gandhi himself continued to advocate Indian independence. His message to Britain was simple: 'Quit India'.
But he underestimated a basic difficulty which became more important the
nearer India came to independence. As in Ireland, it was the problem of a
minority. Moslems were unwilling to be ruled by Hindus. They feared that the
Indian National Congress would rule India after independence and most of its
leaders were Hindu. The Moslem League, led by Mohammad Ali Jinnah,
favoured the division of India, with Pakistan as a separate state for Moslems.
Congress and Gandhi wanted a united India and Gandhi worked tirelessly to
encourage brotherhood and goodwill between the religions.

The Second World War gave Britain an excuse to delay the final settlement. India was encouraged by the promise that Dominion Status would
follow the war. Those who disrupted the war effort were sent to prison.
Gandhi was, of course, among them, and his wife, Kasturba, died in prison
before the war ended. In 1942, the British Government sent the Cripps
Mission to India and confirmed the promise of Dominion Status. When the
war ended, in 1945, India was high on the list of problems that had to be
settled quickly (see Section 16.6(*a*)).

(*d*) Nationalism in Other Parts of the British Empire

Nationalists in the *Arab states* also put pressure on Britain before 1939. Lloyd
George agreed to the near-independence of Egypt in 1922 but British troops
and influence remained there nevertheless. There was a new agreement in
1936 by which the troops would be withdrawn, but not all had left when the
Second World War began and Egypt became involved in it (see Section 9.2).
In any case, the British had insisted on keeping troops in the Canal Zone to
protect European interests in the Suez Canal; and from this developed
further controversy in the 1950s (see Section 19.1). Of Britain's mandates in
the Middle East two moved to independence comparatively smoothly – Iraq
in 1932 and Transjordan in 1946. The third, Palestine, involved Britain in a
struggle, partly of Britain's own making, between Arabs and Jews. The
British withheld independence but in the end, in 1948, handed the Palestinian
mandate back to the United Nations Organization, with the problem not only
unsolved but far more difficult than it had been when the mandate began in
1920 (see Section 19.1(*b*)). British government had no deep roots in the
Arab states and they had virtually no permanent British inhabitants. No Arab
state chose to join the Commonwealth after independence.

Nationalism in other parts of the British Empire developed more slowly.
Africa before 1939 was comparatively quiet: as yet there was little popular
support for ideas of independence. Like the Indians, however, nationalist
leaders organized Congress Parties and made preparations. A generation of
future leaders like Jomo Kenyatta, Kwame Nkrumah and Hastings Banda
pursued their studies in Britain and the USA, and Africa waited for political
consciousness to become more widespread. In the mid-1920s Ormsby-Gore

at the British Colonial Office announced Britain's intention of ruling her African possessions for the welfare of their inhabitants but there seemed less urgency about preparing Africans to rule themselves than about preparing Indians. For the moment there was no serious threat to continuing British rule.

Some Africans welcomed British rule not only for the stability it provided but as a protection against white settlers. Since giving South Africa Dominion Status in 1909, Britain had begun to have second thoughts about white minority rule. Whites in Southern Rhodesia had a large measure of self-government, although they were a small minority in the country. The constitution of 1923 gave most of the power in Southern Rhodesia to those wealthy enough to qualify for the right to vote. They were nearly all white. But Dominion Status was withheld and Southern Rhodesia remained a British dependency. In Kenya, whites were an even smaller minority in the population but they, like the settlers in Southern Rhodesia, hoped to gain the same privileges as the whites in South Africa. Black Africans realized that Dominion Status, before 1939, could only mean the rule of white settlers and were, therefore, content to defer independence until African nationalism developed. But they were dissatisfied with the rate of economic progress. Britain passed a Colonial Development Act in 1929 which expanded some of the benefits of European rule – schools, hospitals and meagre social services – but the pace was slow.

In the *West Indies*, dissatisfaction with British rule was mainly a protest against low wages and unemployment. Nationalists were also dissatisfied with the slow progress towards self-government but much of the rioting in the 1930s, in Trinidad, Guiana, Jamaica and elsewhere, sprang from poverty. A Commission of Inquiry revealed an alarming picture of squalor, illiteracy, sickness and juvenile delinquency. Britain passed a new Colonial Development Act in 1940. Up to that time, however, little thought had been given to the political future of the British West Indies.

The same was true of other parts of the Empire. Neither in tiny colonies such as *Mauritius* nor in larger areas such as *Malaya* did Dominion Status seem a matter of urgency. It was the Second World War which quickened the rate of nationalist development and made essential new thinking about the future of the British Empire and Commonwealth (see Section 16.6).

6.3   The French Empire

Unlike Britain, France allowed her colonial possessions to be represented in the French parliament. On the other hand, French rule of her dependencies was quite undemocratic. The Arabs who made up the bulk of the population of *Algeria* were denied political rights. Arab nationalism and nationalism elsewhere in the Empire was discouraged. In French *Indochina*, the economy was ruthlessly exploited for the benefit of the Europeans. Almost all power lay with the French, and nationalism inevitably took revolutionary forms, often influenced by communist ideas which thrived where there was poverty and unemployment. France resorted to repression, adding strength to the argument of Russian Bolsheviks that imperialism, the exploitation of empires, was 'the last stage of monopoly capitalism' which needed to be eliminated. French Indochina became the scene of one of the most long-drawn-out struggles between capitalism and communism after the Second World War (see Section 16.3). Before 1939, however, the French Empire continued and nationalism was held down.

Nationalism was also held down in *Syria* which France received as a mandate. The French were so vigorous that, after savage repression in 1925 and 1926, they were censured by the League of Nations Mandates Commission. Syria was broken into two states, Syria and the Lebanon. Republics were established but France refused to grant them independence, and discontent was never far below the surface. French control was not removed until the Lebanon was liberated by the British in 1941, when the French there declared support for fascism, and until Syria, in the same year, was occupied by the Allies and the Free French, who agreed to its independence. Even then, France made a half-hearted attempt to recover Syria in 1945.

By the end of the Second World War, the French Empire was doomed. By the end of the 1950s it had collapsed in an explosion of dammed-up nationalist feeling.

6.4   The Italian Empire

Italy had cherished the idea of a Mediterranean Empire from her early days as a united state. The foundations for such an empire were laid before 1914 when Italy secured Eritrea, Somaliland and Libya. It was Mussolini's ambition to expand it. Between the wars, Italy was almost alone among Europeans in producing grandiose schemes for imperial expansion overseas. Mussolini's most impressive success was the conquest of backward *Ethiopia* (see Section 8.2). As yet Africans were no match for Europeans, their spears hardly effective against aeroplanes, tanks and flamethrowers. With such instruments, Mussolini intended to 'civilize' them. His Empire was short-lived, however, overthrown not by nationalist organization but by Italy's defeat in war. When Mussolini committed himself to the support of Hitler in 1940, he doomed Italy's African Empire to premature collapse. It was quickly occupied by other powers and at the end of the Second World War remained to be disposed of like Germany's Empire in 1918.

Libya became independent in 1951 as the result of a decision in the United Nations General Assembly. Italian *Somaliland* was merged into Somalia which became an independent republic in 1960. *Eritrea* became part of Ethiopia which had been liberated from the Italians in 1941. Italy also lost islands in the Mediterranean to Greece and Jugoslavia and was expelled from the other areas at which Mussolini had nibbled, among them Albania.

6.5   Other Empires

The *Netherlands* government was already fighting a rearguard action against nationalism in Indonesia (the Dutch East Indies) when the islands were invaded by Japan at the beginning of 1942. The Dutch, like the British, had developed ideas about the welfare of their colonial subjects and about preparing them for self-rule. For Indonesian nationalists, however, the pace was too slow. There were communists among the nationalists and there were serious revolts in 1926 in Java. The Dutch suppressed them and preserved their Empire, but the Indonesian Nationalist Party was founded on the lines of the Indian National Congress. The Party discovered a leader in Ahmed Sukarno who practised the policies of non-co-operation advocated by Gandhi. In 1942 Sukarno was waiting, like nationalist leaders elsewhere, for an opportune moment at which to seize independence from the Dutch (see Section 16.2).

Other European countries had empires in Africa. The possessions of *Spain* were now small, the once-vast Spanish Empire in South America and the West Indies having already broken free – Cuba, for example, in 1898 with the help of the USA. Spain's most important colony was now Spanish Morocco and in 1921 even that was in revolt. The first rebels, the Riffs led by Abd-el-Krim, represented tribal interests but a more broadly-based Moroccan nationalism grew during the 1930s. Spanish authority survived, however, until the 1950s and Spain remained in the Spanish Sahara longer still (see Section 16.3(*c*)).

Portugal had larger African territories, though Portugal too had already lost much of her Empire elsewhere. Angola, Mozambique and Portuguese Guinea gave Portugal little trouble before 1939 since it was not in the nature of Portuguese colonial rule to do much to develop the country's overseas territories. Portugal's African Empire was later to be remarkable for its survival at a time when other empires crumbled, but nationalism eventually triumphed in the 1970s when change also came to Portugal herself (see Section 16.5).

Belgium too had a large African Empire – the Belgian Congo some eighty times the size of Belgium herself. The Belgians ruled the Congo with an almost total disregard for African nationalism and for the future. Nowhere was the aftermath of European rule to be more tragic, since, when the Belgians withdrew in 1960, hardly anything had been done to prepare the country for independence and the Congo plunged into savage civil war (see Sections 16.4 and 20.2).

Further Reading

Ayling, S.E.: *Portraits of Power*. Harrap (London, 1965) – Gandhi.
Johnson, D.: *The World of Empires*. Benn (London, 1973).
Murphy, J.A.: *Ireland in the Twentieth Century*. Gill & Macmillan (Dublin, 1975).
Nanda, B.R.: *Gokhale, Gandhi and the Nehrus*. Allen & Unwin (London, 1974).

Oliver, R. and Atmore, A.: *Africa since 1800*. Cambridge University Press (Cambridge, 1972) – Chapters 13–15.

Pandey, B.N.: *The Rise of Modern India*. Hamish Hamilton (London, 1967) – Chapters 4 and 5.

Watson, F.: *Gandhi*. Oxford University Press (London, 1967).

Watson, J.B.: *Empire to Commonwealth, 1919 to 1970*. Dent (London, 1971) – Pages 34–74, Ireland, India, nationalism in other parts of the British Empire.

Watson, J.B.: *Success in British History since 1914*. John Murray (London, 1983) – Units 4 and 8.

Watson, J.B.: *The West Indian Heritage*. John Murray (London, 2nd edn. 1982) – Chapter 13.

Younger, C.: *Ireland's Civil War*. Fontana (London, 1979).

Documentary

Breach, R.W.: *Documents and Descriptions, the World since 1914*. Oxford University Press (London, 1966) – Sections 26 and 38.

Briggs, A.: *They Saw It Happen, 1897–1940*. Blackwell (Oxford, 1960) – Part III.

Cumpston, I.M.: *The Growth of the British Commonwealth, 1880–1932*. Arnold (London, 1973).

Exercises

1. What do you understand by *Nationalism* in the sense in which it is used in this Unit? What other forms have you seen nationalism take in earlier Units in this book?

2. Write a paragraph such as would have been suitable for including in a reference book in 1939 to describe the British Commonwealth of Nations as it then was.

3. How did nationalists after the First World War try to gain independence for their country (*a*) in Ireland and (*b*) in India?

4. What can you learn from this Unit about the aims of Mohandas Gandhi and the ways in which he tried to achieve them? Making use of the Index to this book, write a summary of Gandhi's career, and then compare what you have written with a reference-book summary such as that in *The Penguin Dictionary of Twentieth Century History* by Alan Palmer.

5. Study the cartoon at Fig. 6.2. To what particular issue does the cartoon refer? In what more general sense does the cartoon suggest that Gandhi was a '*source of exasperation to the British*' (page 119)?

6. What similar minority and religious problems did Ireland and India face in the years to which this Unit refers?

7. What evidence can you find in this Unit to suggest that Mussolini's 'grandiose schemes' (Section 6.4) were already out of date?

8. Refer to J.H. Bettey, *English Historical Documents 1906–1939* (Routledge & Kegan Paul, London, 1967) for (*a*) Montagu's ideas on the future of India (pages 130–5), (*b*) British legislation on Ireland in 1920 and 1922 (pages 151–6), and (*c*) definitions of Dominion Status in 1926 and 1931 (pages 164–6). Making use of this documentary material, briefly explain the importance of *each* of (*a*), (*b*) and (*c*).

Unit Seven
International Relations to 1931

7.1 The Crises of Readjustment, Early 1920s

Almost as soon as the Settlement of Paris was made (see Unit Two), discontented states began to amend it. Alterations were made to the treaties throughout Europe and sometimes outside it. Many were made by force of arms and, although most of the changes were small ones, involving squabbles between minor powers, precedents were established. The use of force brought rewards.

(a) Major Crises

The most extensive upheavals concerned Turkey (see Section 2.7) and Russia (see Section 5.1). But there were other trouble spots.

(i) **Poland.** In 1918 Poland was reconstituted as an independent state after more than a century of foreign control. At once, the Poles looked for opportunities to make their new state as large as possible. Because of the confused condition of Russia, Poland's eastern frontier was ill-defined and, in 1920, Lloyd George suggested a boundary which came to be known as the Curzon Line. It was unsatisfactory to the Poles who wished to free their fellow-countrymen to the east of the line. War against Russia and the Treaty of Riga (see Section 5.1(b)) added over 50 000 square miles of land to Poland. At about the same time Polish troops occupied Vilna, a district claimed both by Lithuania and Poland. Vilna had formerly been a part of the Empire of the Russian Tsar and during the Russo-Polish war it was, for a time, over-run by the Red Army. The Russians gave it to Lithuania but it was reoccupied by a Polish general. The League of Nations showed little interest. Vilna was eventually incorporated into Poland, in 1922, and the settlement was confirmed by the Conference of Ambassadors a year later (see Fig. 7.1(b)).

Polish troops had already been in action in other areas. Having put pressure on the Paris Conference in 1919 and gained Lvov, the Poles pushed further in Eastern Galicia in spite of opposition from some of the Ukrainians there. As the result of a plebiscite they gained parts of Silesia including rich coal and iron deposits and a steel industry. Then they tried to expand further at the expense of Czechoslovakia in a dispute which centred on Teschen (see Section 2.9(a)). Here they were only partly successful and 100 000 Poles remained under Czech rule until 1938 (see Fig. 8.4(a)).

(ii) **Italy.** Fig. 7.1(a) shows some of the ambitions of Italy. The first crisis involved Fiume (see Section 2.9(a)). Albania also attracted the Italians, their nearest Balkan neighbour across the Adriatic Sea, and this led to another crisis. In August 1923, an Italian general and four of his staff were ambushed and shot on Greek territory while mapping the Greek-Albanian frontier on behalf of the Conference of Ambassadors. Within days, Mussolini resorted to force to avenge this insult to Italian honour. He demanded 50 million lire from the Greek government and demonstrated Italian power by bombarding and occupying the Greek island of Corfu. The League of Nations had no answer to irresponsibility such as this on the part of a major power, and left it to the Conference of Ambassadors to persuade the Greeks to apologize and pay. Within a month, Mussolini withdrew from Corfu, boasting of his triumph. The successful outcome of the dispute over Fiume with Jugoslavia in the following year was another triumph for Mussolini, and he was now prepared to behave less aggressively for a time.

(*iii*) **France.** The Italian occupation of Corfu lasted only a few weeks. The French occupation of the Ruhr lasted for over two years (see Section 3.3(*b*)). Unlike Mussolini, however, France gained little from her invasion. For a time, under the new provisions of the Dawes Plan, Germany kept up steady payments of reparations after the occupation (so France could claim some success) but the invasion was hardly a legal action. It demonstrated once again the readiness of even major powers to use force in pursuit of self-interest.

(*b*) **Minor Crises**

Smaller nations were involved in a bewildering number of disputes in the years after the Settlement of Paris. At first, the League of Nations was unable to cope with the problems which mushroomed in the wake of the Settlement. It was even unable to defend its own property for Lithuania, robbed of Vilna by Poland, seized the port of Memel from the Allies. Detailed settlements at Vilna, Corfu and elsewhere were often left to the *Conference of Ambassadors*, which met in Paris under the chairmanship of Cambon and included the representatives of Britain, France, Italy and Japan. In 1924, MacDonald ruled that the Conference was concerned only with matters arising from the Peace Settlement but the Conference was not dissolved until 1931.

Meanwhile, the League of Nations began to win respect. In 1921, it successfully settled a dispute between Sweden and Finland about the Aaland Islands. Sweden's acceptance of the League's ruling was in contrast to the selfishness of other nations. Arbitration was also successful between Colombia and Venezuela in 1922, Chile and Peru in 1925 and Guatemala and Honduras in 1938. The League mediated over Mosul in 1926 (see Section 5.3(*a*)).

The attack by Greece on Bulgaria in 1925 may serve as an example of the League's intervention. The Greeks had learned from Mussolini and after a series of border incidents they sought satisfaction by force. They were

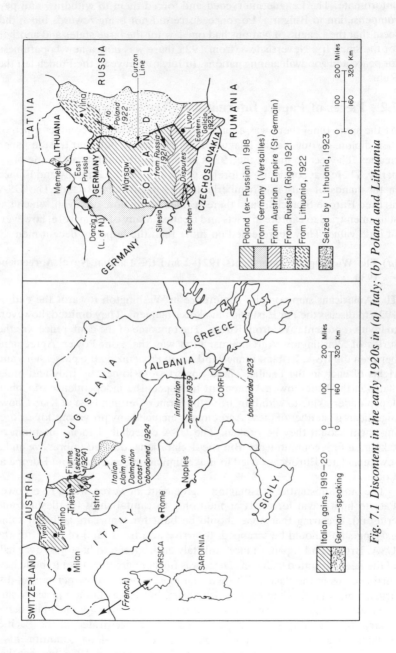

Fig. 7.1 Discontent in the early 1920s in (a) Italy; (b) Poland and Lithuania

unfortunate. The League intervened and forced them to withdraw and pay compensation to Bulgaria. For once, force did not bring rewards but it did seem that the League of Nations had one law for the large states and another for the small fry. Nevertheless, from 1925 there was now a new hopefulness for peace and goodwill among nations. In July of that year, the French left the Ruhr.

7.2   Pieces of Paper, International Treaties

At the same time, there was a tendency for the nations to conduct much of their diplomacy outside the League of Nations and to put their trust in paper treaties. The second half of the 1920s brought more stability and some prosperity. There was continuity in foreign policy in Britain, Germany and France in the hands of Austen Chamberlain, Stresemann and Briand. The USA assisted Europe financially and there seemed to be more goodwill, which the statesmen tried to capture in pacts and treaties. Many of them were, however, of little value. They represented no more than the hopes of decent men.

(a)   The Washington Agreements 1921–2 and the London Naval Agreement 1930

The Americans summoned a conference in Washington towards the end of 1921 to discuss the Far East and naval disarmament. They omitted, however, to invite representatives from Russia. The outcome of the conference was the series of Washington Agreements. One was the Four-Power Agreement between the USA, Britain, France and Japan recognizing the possessions and rights of each in the Pacific. These powers were joined by Italy and other states in the Nine-Power Agreement to respect the independence of China, Japan undertaking to withdraw from the former German base at Kiao Chow. Significantly, neither of these Agreements included any provisions for enforcing them should they be broken. The USA especially had no intention of taking on firm commitments. But the declarations sounded impressive and a few years later Europeans tried to make similar agreements about Europe at Locarno.

The most substantial Washington Agreement, however, was a Five-Power Pact to limit naval forces. It applied only to capital ships (battleships and cruisers), declaring that none should be built for ten years and that some existing ships should be scrapped, to arrive at a fixed ratio of 5:5:3 for the USA, Britain and Japan. France and Italy each agreed to have just over half of the fleet permitted to Japan. There was further agreement not to build new fortifications in the Pacific. This was the most substantial agreement on disarmament to be reached between the wars, but it was limited in scope and some alleged that the scrapped ships were obsolete anyway. The main beneficiary was probably Japan: Japan's fleet was concentrated in the Pacific, while the fleets of the other powers were stretched by global commitments.

Nothing came of further proposals to limit navies in 1926 but another

REMOVING THE TREASURES.

Exclusive picture from the "Valley of the Tomb of the Kings."

Fig. 7.2 A cartoonist's comment on French and Belgian enterprise in the Ruhr (Daily Mail, 19 January 1923). But Poincaré and his supporters found helping themselves to Ruhr coal and other reparations less profitable than expected. Poy's idea for the cartoon came from the discovery of King Tutankhamen's tomb in 1922, popularizing Egyptology

conference met in London in 1930, encouraged by Henderson, Britain's Labour Foreign Secretary. This time they considered non-capital ships, that is smaller warships, including submarines. The USA, Britain and Japan agreed a ratio of 10:10:7, but France and Italy declined to be party to these new limitations.

(b) The Treaty of Rapallo, 1922

At about the time that the Washington Conference met, Lloyd George, ever fertile in new ideas, proposed a world economic conference. He wanted discussion of economic problems and co-operation for reconstruction. He also wanted to include the defeated Central Powers and Soviet Russia. Briand was interested and the powers met in Genoa. Britain was prepared to offer more concrete promises of help to France in the event of any attack from Germany but required, in return, evidence of French goodwill to Germany and Russia. Briand could not obtain the necessary support in the French parliament and was forced to resign. The French doomed the meeting to failure and nothing was achieved.

An unexpected consequence was a treaty between Germany and Soviet Russia, signed at Rapallo in April 1922. Both were treated as outcasts, especially by France. They therefore drew together. In fact, the Treaty said little. They renounced financial claims, the one against the other, undertook to co-operate in economic matters and, most important, Germany recognized the Communist government. Secretly, Russia undertook to allow Germany to build and test weapons on Soviet soil, in defiance of the Treaty of Versailles. Russia was now able to enjoy normal diplomatic relations with a major power and other states followed suit in recognizing the Soviet government, especially after Britain did so in 1924. The USA dragged behind but Roosevelt recognized Russia in 1933.

(c) The Treaties of Locarno, 1925

During his brief period as Prime Minister in 1924 and with the co-operation of Herriot of France, MacDonald set in motion a series of events which were designed, first, to strengthen the League of Nations. The Geneva Protocol was drafted: members were required to recognize as compulsory the authority of the Permanent Court of International Justice and more thought was given to sanctions against aggressors. MacDonald's government fell before the Protocol was ratified. For Baldwin, Austen Chamberlain and the Conservatives, the Protocol went too far and so the project was abandoned.

Chamberlain was, however, prepared to undertake some further commitments in Europe and it seemed to be time to reconsider Germany's part in world affairs. France, now again influenced by Briand, was ready to co-operate. Stresemann was eager to obtain German admission to the League of Nations. The result was the signing of a series of complicated agreements at Locarno in December 1925.

One of the Treaties of Locarno was a Rhineland Pact. France, Germany and Belgium confirmed the sanctity of their boundaries as laid down in the Treaty of Versailles and of the Rhineland as a demilitarized zone. Britain and Italy joined in guaranteeing these frontiers and the demilitarization. Another Treaty, of Arbitration, bound Germany and France to accept mediation in disputes. Germany made similar agreements on arbitration with Belgium, Poland and Czechoslovakia. France, in separate treaties with Poland and Czechoslovakia, guaranteed to protect them in the event of German aggression.

A few months later, to satisfy Russian fears, Germany renewed the Treaty of Rapallo with the USSR. And later in 1926, the League of Nations admitted Germany to membership with a seat in the Council.

Fig. 7.3 The men of Locarno, optimists all: Baldwin and Austen Chamberlain seated at the end of the table on the right; Briand of France, moustached, end right; Stresemann of Germany, diagonally opposite Briand, end left

It was too readily assumed that all this treaty-making meant the end of Europe's problems. The Rhineland Pact was broken by Hitler in 1936 when he remilitarized the Rhineland, and no country moved to honour the Locarno obligations. Similarly, France deserted Czechoslovakia in 1938 and 1939 (see Unit Eight). The Treaties of Locarno, overlapping the Treaty of Versailles as they did, cast doubt on how far the earlier treaty was now valid. Britain had undertaken only very limited commitments, as had Italy. For the moment all seemed well, however, since Chamberlain, Briand and Stresemann were genuine in their hopes for international goodwill. Locarno was greeted with enthusiasm in Britain. There was general satisfaction in Germany. But France had reservations and Italy was almost indifferent. In Eastern Europe, Germany's failure to confirm her Polish and Czechoslovak frontiers was noted and, even after the renewal of the Treaty of Rapallo, the USSR continued to suspect that Locarno was part of some capitalist plot against the Soviet system.

(d) The Kellogg–Briand Pact, 1928

Two years after Locarno, Briand produced a new plan. He proposed that France and the USA should sign a pact to renounce war. Kellogg, the

American Secretary of State, was enthusiastic. He suggested extending the declaration to more countries and, in 1928, 65 states signed the Pact. They included Soviet Russia as well as the USA and, at first sight, it seemed an important, world-wide agreement, helpful to future peace. In fact, nations retained the right to fight in defence of national interests, and the Pact said nothing about punishing aggressors. One of the signatories was Japan who only three years later resorted to war in Manchuria, carrying out naked aggression in alleged defence of national interests.

(e) Ententes

Meanwhile, the lesser powers tried to protect themselves in a confusion of alliances and treaties of friendship. One of the most significant was the 'Little Entente' between Czechoslovakia, Rumania and Jugoslavia. It developed from a series of separate treaties between these states which were consolidated into one alliance in 1929. Their first concern was to protect themselves against the possibility of a war of revenge by Hungary and their aim was to guarantee the frontiers laid down in the Treaties of St Germain and Trianon. In 1933, the Entente developed into an economic community with a common secretariat, but the community and the alliance collapsed at the end of the 1930s.

The pieces of paper multiplied but it became apparent in the 1930s how little they were worth. The fate of Czechoslovakia in 1938 and 1939 revealed the emptiness of paper guarantees.

7.3   The League of Nations

The League of Nations had a respectable record in the 1920s. Its Commissions and Committees achieved a great deal and the League began to cope with international disputes (see Sections 2.9(b) and 7.1(b)). It overcame some of the Central Powers' hostility towards it though not yet that of Soviet Russia. It functioned smoothly as the international climate improved in the later 1920s.

There was, however, awareness that the League lacked teeth. The Locarno Treaties and other alliances also showed some lack of confidence in the League, for they represented a search for additional security. The League would not really be tested until it was confronted with a major international crisis. Such a crisis did not occur until 1931.

Germany was the only great power to be admitted to the League in the period from 1923 to 1931. At Locarno, she had been promised a permanent seat on the Council but this created difficulties. Poland was apprehensive about Germany's new friendships and demanded a similar concession. Quarrels between Poland and Germany became frequent at League meetings after 1926, for, after some hesitation, the League gave a permanent seat on the Council only to Germany. As a compromise, they increased the elected members from six to nine and made re-election possible. This did not satisfy

Poland, and Brazil and Spain also resented the privileges Germany obtained. Brazil withdrew from the League in protest. To smaller powers and non-Europeans, the League now seemed to be too much dominated by the Locarno powers.

7.4   Disarmament

There was hope, however, that the Treaties of Locarno would at last make possible some real progress towards disarmament as envisaged in the Covenant of the League of Nations. In 1919, the reduction of German armed forces was held to be the first step towards 'a general limitation'. At Washington, in 1921, some progress was made in reducing navies (see Section 7.2(*a*)). Other steps added up to nothing but running on the spot.

There was general agreement that disarmament was desirable but no state wished to be the first to reduce its own security. The Disarmament Commission of the League therefore proposed, in 1923, a Treaty of Mutual Assistance, a system of collective security under which countries would help to protect each other. It was accepted by France, Czechoslovakia and others, criticized by Poland and some Balkan states as inadequate and rejected by Britain as too binding. The Disarmament Commission, therefore, began in 1926 to prepare the ground for an international Disarmament Conference at which problems could be tackled by governments, but the Commission had little on which to work except the woolly hope that the Locarno Treaties had somehow strengthened the will to disarm.

The Commission laboured for five years without results. Germany constantly reminded the powers that she had been disarmed and that it was time for others to follow suit. Litvinov, who became Russia's Foreign Minister in 1930, made a vigorous attack on capitalism and proposed immediate and total disarmament. Such a startling idea was rejected, after a decent interval in which to consider it. The Russian composer, Shostakovich, wrote a new ballet, *The Age of Gold*, bitingly satirical about capitalist society and scathing on the subject of disarmament diplomats. When, at the end of 1930, the Commission finally agreed on a draft convention, the USSR and Germany voted against it. The League decided to shift the action to a wider stage and, in February 1932, sixty nations met in the Disarmament Conference.

The Disarmament Conference met under the chairmanship of Henderson, Britain's former Foreign Secretary devoting himself now to working for the League of Nations. It largely ignored the previous work of the Disarmament Commission and it was handicapped by Russian opposition and the instability of German politics. France still wanted guarantees of mutual security before disarmament. Germany wanted equality, which appeared to mean rearmament. The delegates were also perplexed about how to enforce an agreement, assuming they reached one. In 1933, MacDonald produced a new plan for a reduction of armaments, partly designed to meet Germany's demand for equality, but by that time Hitler had become Chancellor. The French raised difficulties about the weapons to be allowed to Germany and, in October 1933, the Germans walked out. Hitler also withdrew from the League of Nations. With Germany now openly rearming there was no hope for disarmament and the Conference held its last session in 1934. In that year, France completed the building of the Maginot Line which fortified her eastern frontier.

7.5   Collective Insecurity

There was, therefore, little progress at all towards disarmament and, in spite of the creation of the League of Nations and the busy signing of agreements, many states continued to feel insecure at the end of the 1920s. The agreements brought nothing more than collective insecurity and persisting uncertainty as to how they would be enforced in time of crisis. France and Poland seemed particularly uneasy. The French still fretted that the USA had neither guaranteed the Peace Settlement of 1919–20 nor joined the League of Nations. Though the USA had signed pieces of paper during the 1920s none included any sure commitment. The French also lacked confidence in Britain, since the British also preferred to avoid commitments in Europe, having accepted at Locarno no more than an obligation limited to the west of the continent. Most of Britain's occupation forces in Germany were withdrawn in 1926, nine years earlier than had been laid down in the Treaty of Versailles. The French remained longer, but they too were withdrawn in 1930 when Britain pressed for the total evacuation of all occupying troops. The rise of Hitler only strengthened French anxiety, yet German nationalism and rearmament were natural consequences of the failure of others, including the French themselves, to disarm.

Like the USA, the USSR played little part in European politics in the 1920s. Soviet communism nevertheless also disturbed European governments: this too was seen as a threat. The Soviet government in fact, especially when Stalin came to power, was fully occupied with internal development – with 'Socialism in One Country' (see Section 5.1(c)). With or without the approval of the Soviet Foreign Ministry, the Comintern occasionally encouraged communist agitation in European societies, but never to the point at which it might involve the USSR in conflict. From time to time the Soviet government itself claimed to detect hostile capitalist plots but was not sufficiently concerned about any new anti-communist crusade to want to be much involved with the outside world. The Treaty of Rapallo was enough, and the USSR was far from dismayed by the distrust and fears which divided Europeans. The Russians blamed such distrust, like the failure of disarmament talks and the West's economic problems, on the weaknesses of capitalism. A wide gulf therefore separated the Soviet Union from the rest of Europe. Neither side made much effort to bridge it before the Nazis came to power in Germany and destroyed the Treaty of Rapallo. Only then did Soviet interest in collective security begin to quicken, the USSR joining the League of Nations in 1934.

Events in 1929, meanwhile, began to bring to an end the most hopeful period in international relations between the wars. 1929 was the year the Depression began (see Section 4.3). It was also the year in which the partnership between Stresemann, Briand and Austen Chamberlain was broken. Stresemann died unexpectedly. Briand resigned for the last time as French Prime Minister, dying three years later in 1932. Chamberlain lost office when the Conservatives lost the British general election. Moreover, a more disturbed period opened in 1931 with Japanese aggression in Manchuria. The initiative was about to pass from the democracies and supporters of the League of Nations to the nationalist and totalitarian regimes which held the League in contempt.

Further Reading

Bloncourt, P.: *The Embattled Peace 1919–1939*. Faber (London, 1968).
Bruce, M.G.: *From Peace to War, Europe 1918–1939*. Thames & Hudson (London, 1967).
Hastings, P.: *Between the Wars*. Benn (London, 1968).
Marks, S.: *The Illusion of Peace, 1918–1933*. Macmillan (London, 1977).
Scott, G.: *The Rise and Fall of the League of Nations*. Hutchinson (London, 1974).
Taylor, A.J.P.: *The Origins of the Second World War*. Penguin (Harmondsworth, 1964).

Documentary and Maps

Adamthwaite, A.P.: *The Lost Peace, 1918–1939*. Arnold (London, 1980).
Richards, I., Goodson, J.B. and Morris, J.A.: *A Sketch Map History of the Great Wars and After*. Harrap (London, 1965).

Exercises

1. What made the 1920s a period of hopefulness in international affairs? Why did many states nevertheless still 'feel insecure at the end of the 1920s' (page 134)?
2. Use Sections 7.2(a) and 7.4 to show what attempts were made between the wars to bring about disarmament and to explain why they had only limited success.
3. Explain how Figs. 7.2 and 7.3 illustrate different phases in French foreign policy during the 1920s.
4. Refer to *Fifty Major Documents of the Twentieth Century* by L.L. Snyder (Anvil, 1955) to find out some detail of what was agreed in (a) the Locarno Treaties and (b) the Kellogg–Briand Pact. Explain why *each* of these agreements was thought to be important at the time of signing. After reading Unit Eight, explain whether you think they had any lasting importance.
5. Making use of the Index to this book, draw up a balance sheet of the successes and failures of the League of Nations during the 1920s.
6. Explain what this Unit, together with the cross-references included in it, shows of the foreign policy and ambitions of *three* of the following powers in the 1920s: Britain; France; Italy; Poland; the USA; the USSR.
7. Compare the progress made towards disarmament shown in this Unit with progress

made towards disarmament after 1945 outlined in Unit 17.2(*b*). Were there similar reasons why the progress made was in each case only limited?

8. Study this extract from an editorial in *The Times* in 1927, and then (*a*) explain how this editorial illustrates both the hopes and uncertainties of the 1920s; and (*b*) show why you think this view of the League of Nations in 1927 was *either* justified *or* unjustified.

> The League of Nations . . . is steadily developing into a most useful centre for the transaction of international business. The mists of the early years are clearing away. . . . A great deal of patient work has been done in building up machinery. . . . The League is worth while. . . . Delegates come and go continually, representing nearly every country in the world – and how many wishes, hopes, and plans? No dispute is now possible about the value of certain departments of the League. . . . The services of the humanitarian departments are illustrated in the report on the White Slave Traffic issued last week. The admirable Health Department is quietly extending its range and efficiency. . . . Yet it is not by any of these services, valuable as they are, that the League will finally be judged. Its humanitarian and economic activities are subordinated to a much more ambitious aim – the prevention of war. No one on earth knows whether war can ever be made altogether impossible. . . .

International Relations, 1931–41

8.1 Japanese Aggression

Various factors made Japan an aggressive nation. One was the prestige and influence enjoyed by the armed forces, all the greater when set alongside the weakness of civilian governments (see Section 5.3(*b*)). Others were economic: Japan looked for space for her expanding population, food to feed the people and raw materials. She also sought racial equality and brooded on the refusal of the statesmen at Paris, in 1919, to insert a declaration of support for that principle into the Covenant of the League of Nations. The suspicion that white nations regarded Japan as inferior grew in the 1920s, feeding on the immigration laws of such countries as the USA and Australia. The 'White Australia' policy closed that country's doors to Asians and was resented by them. The suspicion also fed on the Washington and London Naval Agreements (see Section 7.2(*a*)) which denied Japan equality with the USA and Britain. After the Agreement of 1930, a Japanese naval officer made his protest by committing suicide although the minister who signed the treaty declined an invitation to do likewise.

Japan was also tempted to aggression by China's weakness, and hoped to exploit the split in China between the communists and nationalists (see Section 15.2(*c*)). One outcome of the Washington Conference of 1921–2 was the Nine-Power Treaty, binding Japan, with others, to claim no special rights in China. It did not prevent Japan from meddling intermittently in Chinese affairs in the later 1920s.

(*a*) Manchuria

Japan first leased the territory of Kwantung around Port Arthur in Manchuria as a result of the Russo-Japanese war of 1904–5. Manchuria was part of China but the Japanese made vast investments in the area and gained a stranglehold on the South Manchurian Railway and other economic enterprises. Power in Manchuria, however, was exercised by the Japanese army, which demonstrated its independence of the government by bombing the train of the warlord ruler of Manchuria in 1928. The Prime Minister, Tanaka, was not consulted. In 1931, the army took a more ambitious decision, to occupy the whole of Manchuria (Fig. 8.1).

To avenge alleged sabotage of the railway by the Chinese, the Japanese army seized the city of Mukden and went on to over-run all of Manchuria by early 1932, an area five times the size of Great Britain. China appealed to the League of Nations.

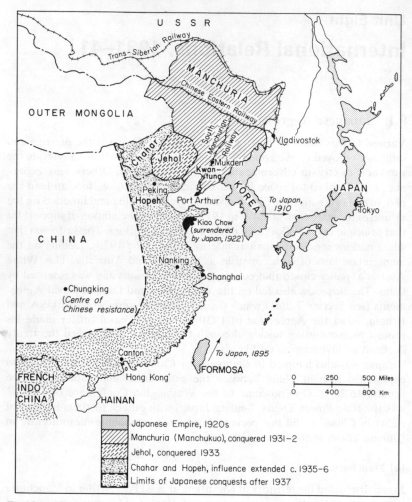

Fig. 8.1 The origins of the Second World War: Japanese expansionism in the 1930s

The League sent a commission under Lord Lytton, which eventually made a leisurely journey by sea, produced a report in October 1932 and stated the obvious. Japanese aggression was condemned. It was recognized that Manchuria belonged to China but that Japan had special interests there. A large measure of self-government was recommended for the state but the Japanese must give up their conquests and withdraw their troops. Instead, Japan gave notice of withdrawal from the League of Nations, in March 1933, and extended her conquests into Jehol.

The Lytton Commission was much too late. Before it arrived in Manchuria, the Japanese had declared the state to be *Manchukuo*, nominally independent under Pu Yi, China's last Manchu Emperor who had been overthrown in 1912. Pu Yi was no more than a Japanese puppet and Manchukuo was developed as an economic appendage to Japan.

THE DOORMAT.

Fig. 8.2 Sir John Simon, Britain's Foreign Secretary, repairs the face of the League of Nations while Japan tramples on the League in Manchuria. Evening Standard, *19 January 1933*

The League of Nations was powerless. Outside it, Stimson, the American Secretary of State, recommended a policy of moral force, designed in some way to shame Japan into more lawful actions. The policy was called the 'Doctrine of Non-Recognition' which meant a refusal to accept the fact that Japan had over-run Manchuria. The USA applied it with an equal lack of effect towards the government of Mao Tse-tung when China became communist in 1949. Only Italy and Germany recognized Manchukuo but Japan was unperturbed. The state was remote from Europe, Europeans were hampered by the Depression and Britain could expect no support for a policy of resistance to Japan. So Japan went on to penetrate further into northern China and by the mid-1930s had taken the provinces of Hopeh and Chahar. She also renounced her obligations under the Naval Agreements.

The League rescued only one shred of prestige. Inspired by the example of their army in Manchuria, the Japanese navy tried, at the end of 1931, to seize Shanghai in central China. With some prodding by Britain, the League persuaded Japan to withdraw in May 1932. Shanghai was thus saved for the moment.

(b) **The 'China Incident'**

In July 1937, the Japanese army claimed to have been provoked again, this time in an incident at the Marco Polo Bridge, near Peking. They alleged that the Chinese had fired on a Japanese night patrol. Japan struck back with a full-scale war against China which went on until 1945 and which in the first year alone uprooted sixty million Chinese from their homes. The Japanese absurdly referred to this war as the 'China Incident'.

Shanghai was taken after months of fierce struggle. The Japanese then drove quickly southwards, capturing Nanking and then Canton. The Chinese government retreated inland and set up headquarters at Chungking. It was forced to leave almost the whole of the Chinese coast in Japanese hands and, when it refused to surrender, the Japanese set up another puppet ruler in Nanking in 1940. But stubborn Chinese resistance and the sheer size of the country prevented the Japanese from winning total victory. Half their forces were still tied down in China when the more widespread war in the Pacific began in 1941.

Again China appealed to the League of Nations but the Council merely recommended individual members to apply sanctions against Japan, a recommendation they ignored. Europeans were now preoccupied with the aggressions of Hitler and Mussolini. Before embarking on the 'China Incident', Japan had signed an Anti-Comintern Pact with Hitler to which Mussolini attached himself a year later. Britain wanted the USA to take the lead in defending China but even when the Japanese sank an American gunboat on the Yangtse River at the end of 1937, the USA accepted their apology.

The USSR took more positive action. Russia and China signed a non-aggression pact in 1937. The Red Army moved troops to the Manchurian border and, when Japanese anti-communists challenged them, they were quick to inflict heavy casualties on the Japanese. In 1939 Russo-Japanese fighting began again, and for the first time Japan suffered a major defeat. By that time, however, war had broken out in Europe and Japan signed an armistice with Russia, ready to turn her attention elsewhere.

(c) **Expansion Southwards**

The outbreak of the Second World War in Europe quickened Japanese interest in extending the 'Co-Prosperity Sphere' southwards (see Section 5.3(b)). The rapid defeat of France and Holland left Indochina and Indonesia exposed to a Japanese invasion but, at first, Japan proceeded cautiously. Britain's weakness in the summer of 1940 was exploited by persuading the British to close the Burma Road and cut off supplies to the Chinese. Britain was anxious to avoid involvement with another enemy. But within months Japan signed a new treaty with Germany and Italy, turning the Anti-Comintern Pacts into the Tripartite Axis Pact for joint defence against any power 'not already engaged in war'. Japanese troops moved into the north of Indochina and Britain reopened the Burma Road. A year later, Hitler's puppets in the Vichy government in France agreed to a joint protectorate with Japan over the whole of Indochina and Japanese troops landed in the south.

Compromised by his pact with Germany in August 1939 (see Section 8.3(*f*)), Stalin accepted a non-aggression pact between Russia and Japan in April 1941. The USA, on the other hand, viewed Japanese activities with increasing displeasure. When Japanese troops landed in the south of Indochina, the USA stopped the sale of oil to Japan, having already cancelled trading agreements between the two nations. Britain and Holland took similar steps. Japan was still dependent on the West for oil and certain metals such as copper. But America's terms were too high for the Japanese militarists: the USA had insisted that Japan must evacuate both Indochina and China. The Prime Minister was replaced by General Tojo whose policy was to take what Japan needed by force, particularly Indonesian oil. The USA would not tolerate this and so Tojo decided to strike first.

Japanese negotiators continued to discuss a settlement with the Americans while preparations were made. Japanese aircraft carriers put to sea towards the end of November 1941. On 7 December they launched their attack on Pearl Harbor, Hawaii, where they crippled the American Pacific fleet. At the same time, they attacked American airfields in the Philippines and British bases in Malaya, Singapore and Hong Kong. Japan had achieved surprise and success. The USA and Britain instantly declared war; and Germany and Italy honoured their obligations to Japan under the Axis Pact and declared war on America.

Thus the wars of the late 1930s truly became the Second World War, exploding from Japan's war against China, which began in 1937 (or, it may be argued, in Manchuria in 1931), the war in Europe which began in 1939 and the war between Germany and Russia which began in June 1941.

8.2 Italian Aggression

In the late 1920s, Mussolini was in a mood for signing pieces of paper. He arrived at Locarno by speedboat, on the last lap of an appropriately dramatic journey which also included a special train and a racing car. He signed the Kellogg–Briand Pact in 1928 and, in the same year, a pact of friendship with Ethiopia. In 1933, he wanted to sign a pact to preserve peace between Italy, Germany, Britain and France but that ended with only the signatures of Mussolini and Hitler. Mussolini's foreign policy seemed to be a peaceful one and his aggression in Corfu was long past.

Mussolini, however, was easily impressed – impressed by Japanese vigour in Manchuria and by German rearmament, by the weakness with which other states responded, and above all, by the apparent defencelessness of Ethiopia which lay between the Italian colonies of Eritrea and Somaliland. He was also impressed by his own show of strength, when he sent four Italian divisions to the Brenner Pass in 1934.

The occasion was a disturbance in Austria in the course of which Austrian Nazis murdered Dollfuss, the Chancellor (see Section 3.3(c)). Hitler hoped to use the occasion to incorporate Austria into Germany, but there was a general outcry which deterred him. At the time, Mussolini had no wish to see Germany expand to his frontiers and the movement of Italian troops contributed to preserving the peace. In 1935 Mussolini met the Prime Ministers of Britain and France at Stresa to declare solemn disapproval of Hitler's intrigues and rearmament. They undertook 'close and cordial collaboration' to maintain treaties. Britain and France hoped that the *Stresa Front* would guarantee peace in Europe; but Mussolini was turning to aggressive policies again, looking for victories abroad to compensate for economic disappointments and repression at home.

(a) Ethiopia

At the time of the Stresa Conference, Italy and Ethiopia were already in dispute about the obscure oasis of Walwal on the border of Italian Somaliland. Following a skirmish there in December 1934, Mussolini demanded both the oasis and compensation for the deaths of thirty Italian soldiers. Haile Selassie, Emperor of Ethiopia, appealed to the League of Nations, who recommended him to negotiate with Italy. Mussolini was massing troops but it seemed more tactful at Stresa not to raise the matter, lest the Duce should be less firm against Hitler. Throughout the summer Italian troops streamed through the British-controlled Suez Canal on their way to East Africa.

A quarter of a million Italians launched their attack on Ethiopia in October 1935. The League of Nations reacted swiftly. Within a week, first the Council and then the Assembly declared Italy an aggressor and *economic sanctions* (prohibitions on trade) were applied to deprive her of supplies. It took a month for them to take effect and Austria and Hungary, as well as Germany, refused to apply them. In any case, the League excluded oil, coal and steel from the sanctions, the very commodities Mussolini needed most desperately. The USSR, Rumania and other oil-producing countries were ready to impose sanctions. Britain and France gave them no encouragement and even declined to interfere with the Suez Canal Company, so that the Canal remained open, preserving Italy's supply-lines.

Samuel Hoare, Britain's Foreign Secretary, and Laval, the French Prime Minister, went further, conjuring up the *Hoare–Laval Plan* in December. The Plan proposed giving Italy about two-thirds of Ethiopia (adjoining lands, to enlarge Italian Somaliland and Eritrea, and much of the south of Ethiopia for 'economic expansion and settlement'). In return, Britain offered Haile Selassie a strip of British Somaliland with access to the sea. The Plan was rejected by everybody and Hoare had to resign. His successor was Anthony Eden, who had more enthusiasm for sanctions but not to the extent of making them work by including oil. The conquest of Ethiopia went on unchecked and in May 1936, Marshal Badoglio made a triumphant entry into the capital, Addis Ababa. Haile Selassie went into exile and Victor Emmanuel III of Italy

THE AWFUL WARNING.

FRANCE AND ENGLAND
(*together?*).
{ "WE DON'T WANT YOU TO FIGHT,
BUT, BY JINGO, IF YOU DO,
WE SHALL PROBABLY ISSUE A JOINT MEMORANDUM
SUGGESTING A MILD DISAPPROVAL OF YOU."

Fig. 8.3 A Punch *comment on how France and Britain responded to Mussolini's aggression in Ethiopia (Abyssinia). Hardly surprisingly Mussolini was unmoved*

was proclaimed the new Emperor of Ethiopia. Mussolini reconstructed all his possessions in the area into one huge colony, *Italian East Africa* (see Fig. 8.4(*b*)). Shortly afterwards the League abandoned sanctions.

The Ethiopian war was a disaster for collective security through the League of Nations. The League had failed miserably, undermined by the feebleness of Britain and France, although the absence from the League of important states such as Germany and the USA was a contributory factor. Sanctions were discredited and force had once again succeeded. Worst of all, for Britain

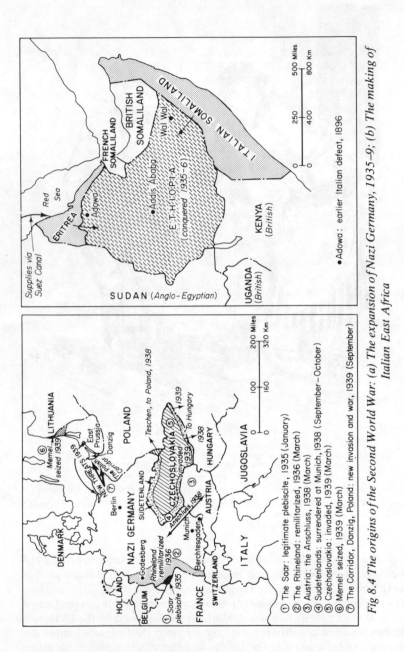

Fig 8.4 The origins of the Second World War: (a) The expansion of Nazi Germany, 1935–9; (b) The making of Italian East Africa

① The Saar: legitimate plebiscite, 1935 (January)
② The Rhineland: remilitarized, 1936 (March)
③ Austria: the Anschluss, 1938 (March)
④ Sudetenlands: surrendered at Munich, 1938 (September–October)
⑤ Czechoslovakia: invaded, 1939 (March)
⑥ Memel: seized, 1939 (March)
⑦ The Corridor, Danzig, Poland: new invasion and war, 1939 (September)

and France, the Stresa Front collapsed: though tolerating Mussolini's aggression they had still failed to retain his support against Germany.

For Mussolini, too, the Ethiopian War was a disaster in spite of his apparent triumph, because it brought him closer to Hitler. Hitler had taken the opportunity of the Ethiopian crisis to remilitarize the Rhineland (see Section 8.3(a)) and he and Mussolini now found themselves in partnership in intervening in the Spanish Civil War (see Section 5.2(c)). Mussolini's fancy was captured by a line from Rome to Berlin which he called an *Axis*. In 1937, he joined Germany and Japan in the Anti-Comintern Pacts and left the League of Nations. In May 1939, he strengthened his understanding with Hitler in an alliance, dubbed 'The Pact of Steel', which was extended, in 1940, to the Tripartite Axis Pact with Japan. Misled by the glory of his soldiers in Ethiopia, Mussolini thus sank ever more deeply into the fatal alliances which were to destroy Fascist Italy in the Second World War. Italian East Africa was a short-lived empire.

(b) Albania

From 1936 to 1939 the centre of European attention shifted steadily from Rome to Berlin; Mussolini was increasingly overshadowed by Hitler. He won some minor victories, however. The activities of Italian submarines which preyed on supplies to the Popular Front in the Spanish Civil War caused anger in Britain and France. They made an agreement at Nyon to patrol the Mediterranean and to take action against such submarines, although they stopped short of identifying them as Italian vessels. Mussolini demanded an equal share in the patrol duties and was given a zone of the Mediterranean to police, a curious arrangement which made his meddling in Spain all the easier. The Duce was also a leading figure at the Munich Conference in 1938 (see Section 8.3(c)) and he basked in the glory of visits exchanged with Hitler, martial displays and the photographs which recorded their friendship.

Above all, he was inspired to demonstrate yet again the strength of a fascist army. He turned to Albania. There seemed little chance of effective resistance since that country was already economically dependent on Italy, its army Italian-trained. Mussolini struck in April 1939: King Zog fled and Victor Emmanuel was given a new crown. Mussolini celebrated by signing the Pact of Steel with Hitler. But when Hitler became involved in war over Poland in September (see Section 8.3(f)), Mussolini at last showed wisdom in remaining neutral.

By June 1940, however, Mussolini was convinced that Germany would win. He hoped for new gains, especially at the expense of France. He even dreamed of an Italian Mediterranean Empire stretching from Gibraltar to the Suez Canal. So on 10 June 1940, Italy declared war on Britain and France.

8.3 German Aggression

In the years before 1936, Hitler watched the progress of the Japanese and

Italians with interest. He made no secret of his hostility to the Treaty of Versailles and to communism. After leaving the League of Nations (see Section 7.4), he went ahead with rearmament, especially of the navy, and missed no opportunity to remind Europe of Germany's grievances over such matters as the Saar and the Polish Corridor.

The Nazi accession to power produced a flurry of diplomatic activity among Germany's neighbours. Stalin felt there would be advantages in seeking better relations with Russia's neighbours and had signed a non-aggression pact with Poland in 1932. In September 1934, the USSR was admitted to the League of Nations, with a permanent seat on the Council. In 1935, Litvinov, Russia's Foreign Minister, secured mutual assistance treaties with France and Czechoslovakia. The French Foreign Minister, Barthou, worked tirelessly to bring about for Eastern Europe the sort of guarantees given to Western Europe at Locarno. European countries continued to sign a bewildering collection of pieces of paper in their search for collective security. When the leaders of Britain, France and Italy met and reached agreement at Stresa in April 1935 (see Section 8.2) security seemed to have been reached. It was almost instantly destroyed by Mussolini's invasion of Ethiopia.

(a) Hitler's First Moves

At the beginning of 1935, the plebiscite provided for in the Treaty of Versailles was held in the Saar. Nine votes in every ten were cast in favour of reunion with Germany, which was quickly arranged. The Saar was added to Hitler's state quite legally but Hitler hailed it as a victory for the Nazis. He followed up this alleged triumph by announcing conscription in Germany and a massive new programme of rearmament, in public defiance of the Versailles settlement. The programme was instantly condemned at Stresa. Checked in Austria in 1934 (see Section 8.2) and apparently surrounded by hostile powers, Hitler's scope for more assertive action was limited.

But in June 1935 Hoare, the British Foreign Secretary, still anxious to pacify potential enemies, agreed to sign a Naval Agreement with Germany. It was a triumph for von Ribbentrop who served Hitler as a roving ambassador. The *Anglo-German Naval Agreement* allowed Germany to build a navy up to 35 per cent of the tonnage of that of Britain. This could include as many submarines as there were in the Commonwealth, although both powers looked forward to the abolition of submarine warfare, at some suitably vague time. Hitler was jubilant. The Agreement accepted a revision of the Treaty of Versailles and it antagonized the French, who regarded the Agreement as an act of betrayal. Within two months of the Stresa Conference, Britain was thus beginning to practise towards Hitler too what came to be known as *Appeasement* (see Glossary).

In March 1936, Hitler had another success. While Italian troops were over-running Ethiopia, German troops marched into the Rhineland, a demilitarized zone in the Treaty of Versailles to which Germany had given additional agreement in the Rhineland Pact at Locarno (see Section 7.2(c)). The

League of Nations condemned the German action, but France hesitated and Britain gave her no encouragement to act. For months, the Locarno powers negotiated with Hitler about the matter and in the end they did nothing.

(b) Austria, the Anschluss

By the end of 1937, Hitler had made the Anti-Comintern Pacts and further advanced the cause of fascism in the Spanish Civil War. Purges in Russia, the disarray of the League of Nations and the shift of Mussolini's allegiance from Britain and France to Germany combined to increase Hitler's confidence. German military power was growing and, like the Japanese militarists, Hitler looked for further conquests. An interview with Lord Halifax in November 1937 convinced him that Britain would not oppose expansion in Austria, and perhaps not in the Sudetenland.

   In February 1938, therefore, Hitler summoned the Austrian Chancellor Schuschnigg to pour on him a torrent of abuse for the alleged ill-treatment of Austrian Nazis. An ultimatum was issued which Schuschnigg accepted, agreeing among other things to appoint Seyss-Inquart, an Austrian Nazi, as Minister of the Interior. Schuschnigg then tried to seize the initiative by ordering a plebiscite in Austria to test opinion for an *Anschluss* (a total union with Germany). Hitler demanded that Seyss-Inquart should be appointed Chancellor and Schuschnigg reluctantly resigned. Seyss-Inquart at once claimed the discovery of a communist plot, and requested German assistance. It arrived promptly and in two days Austria ceased to be independent, with Seyss-Inquart ruling the state as a province of Germany. Over 99 per cent of those who voted in a plebiscite approved the *Anschluss*. All possible resistance to the Nazis was eliminated by arrests, which filled the concentration camps, and by murder.

   Neither Britain nor France had the will to resist the *Anschluss*, although it was forbidden in the Peace Settlement of 1919. Austria appeared to want it. Austrians and Germans were racially similar and so the matter rested. It remained to be seen whether Britain and France would defend Czechoslovakia, for Hitler now pressed on that country from three sides and he had a grievance about the Sudetenland.

(c) The Sudetenland

There was Nazi agitation from time to time after 1933 among the Germans in the Sudetenland (see Section 2.9(a)). Led by Konrad Henlein, they claimed they were ill-treated. They seemed to be demanding self-government. But Henlein by 1938 was little more than Hitler's puppet whose antics combined with the Führer's rumblings to persuade Britain and France that the question of the Sudetenland was now urgent. It was Neville Chamberlain, Britain's Prime Minister since 1937, who took it upon himself to solve the question. Hitler ordered the German army to make ready, but expressed no specific objectives. In August 1938 Chamberlain sent Lord Runciman to Prague.

Runciman seemed eager to persuade the Czechs to grant whatever Henlein wanted, and President Beneš went a long way towards meeting Britain's wishes. There seemed to be no obstacle to self-government for the Sudeten Germans, but Hitler wanted no such easy end to the crisis. Further disturbances were whipped up in the Sudetenland, while Hitler poured verbal abuse on Czechoslovakia, deriding it as an 'artificial state' of mixed nationalities and as an ally of the USSR.

On 15 September Chamberlain made a personal visit to Hitler at Berchtesgaden and another, a week later, to talk with him again at Godesberg. Between the meetings, Chamberlain and Daladier, the French Prime Minister, produced a plan to transfer to the German Reich those parts of Czechoslovakia where the population was more than 50 per cent German. Beneš was not consulted: he was simply required to agree, which he did under protest. At Godesberg, however, Hitler raised the stakes. He now wanted the immediate evacuation of the Sudeten areas which would be occupied by the German army. Chamberlain was taken aback. He passed Hitler's new demands to the Czechs who promptly rejected them.

Fig. 8.5 Neville Chamberlain and Mussolini, two of the men of Munich photographed the following year in Rome. Lord Halifax, Chamberlain's Foreign Secretary, behind them (centre)

War seemed imminent. Czechoslovakia was prepared to fight. The French mobilized reservists and sadly accepted the need to honour their treaty to defend Czechoslovakia. The USSR was also bound to help the Czechs, but only if the French did so first. On the other hand, Poland and Hungary, encouraged by Hitler, were also making claims on Czechoslovakia. In a radio broadcast, Chamberlain solemnly observed, 'How horrible, fantastic, incredible it is that we should be digging trenches and trying on gas masks here because of a quarrel in a faraway country between people of whom we know nothing.' Britain had no treaty obligations to Czechoslovakia but felt obliged to assist France.

Chamberlain made a final effort and proposed a third meeting with Hitler. He sent a telegram to Mussolini too and the Duce was partly instrumental in persuading Hitler to meet Chamberlain at Munich, together with Daladier and himself. They met on 29 September. No invitation was sent to Russia and Czech delegates were left in a hotel while the Big Four decided the fate of their country. The Big Four simply agreed to Hitler's terms: the Sudetenland was to be handed over to Germany; an international commission would later hold plebiscites where necessary and draw up final boundaries. On the following day, Hitler signed another piece of paper expressing with Chamberlain his confidence in 'consultation' as a means of avoiding war. Chamberlain returned home to a warm welcome. He waved Hitler's paper. 'I believe it is peace for our time,' he said.

In the House of Commons Churchill summed up Chamberlain's achievements at Munich: '£1 was demanded at the pistol's point. When it was given, £2 was demanded at the pistol's point. Finally the Dictator consented to take £1.17.6 and the rest in promises of goodwill for the future.'

(d) The Rest of Czechoslovakia

After Munich, Czechoslovakia could now fight alone or submit. Beneš resigned and the country submitted. The loss of the Sudetenland robbed her of vital industries and the only defendable frontiers. Poland claimed and took the town of Teschen. Hungary made claims, on which Germany and Italy sat in arbitration. She too got her way. As Churchill put it, 'Czechoslovakia recedes into the darkness'.

The state began to break up. Slovakia and Ruthenia questioned the authority of government from Prague and the new President, Hacha, had to accept a federal constitution. This was of little importance for, in March 1939, Hitler demanded special rights for any Germans still left under Czech rule. The demand was followed by invasion and Czechoslovakia came under German rule, except for Ruthenia which Hungary made haste to occupy.

(e) Memel – and Guarantees

A week later, Hitler persuaded Lithuania to surrender Memel (see Section 7.1(b) and Fig. 8.4(a)). Before the month was out Britain and France embarked on a change of policy. Since Hitler's mounting collection of trophies suggested that appeasement led only to new crises, Chamberlain resorted to guarantees, pledging Britain to defend Polish independence. France at the same time strengthened her existing alliance with Poland and in April, the month that Mussolini invaded Albania, Anglo-French guarantees were extended to Rumania and Greece. Chamberlain had argued in 1938 that geography made the defence of Czechoslovakia impossible, but geography now seemed less important. Chamberlain's pride had been injured and Halifax, his Foreign Secretary after the resignation of Eden, now put his trust in a strong policy statement, hoping to deter the Nazis from further aggression. The outcome, six months later, was involvement in war – which in fact did nothing to keep the Germans out of Poland.

(f) Danzig and Poland

Already in March 1939 Hitler was discussing the future of Danzig and demanding German rights to a route to East Prussia across the Polish Corridor (see Fig. 8.4(a)). As yet he expressed no intention of breaking the non-aggression pact he had made with Poland in 1934, but the Poles were already worried enough to soften their attitude towards the USSR. At the time of the Sudetenland crisis, Poland, like Rumania, had opposed any idea that Soviet troops should cross her territories to go to Czechoslovakia's defence, though the Russians sent a few troops to Czechoslovakia by air. Poland now signed a treaty of friendship with the USSR at the end of 1938.

The role of the USSR was now a vital one. Hitler would hesitate to commit further aggression if it would lead Germany into a war on two fronts, east and west. Britain and France therefore followed the Polish lead, exploring with the Soviet government how they could work together to deter Hitler. But neither the West nor the USSR showed much sense of urgency. The Russians had bitter memories of their exclusion from the Munich Conference, and Stalin suspected that the capitalist powers would have no regrets if the Nazis were to launch an anti-communist war against the Soviet Union. Molotov replaced Litvinov as the Soviet Foreign Minister in May 1939. He seemed less anxious than Litvinov to reach agreement with the West and did not have his Jewish predecessor's emotional hatred of the Nazis. By July Molotov was negotiating with Germany as well as with Britain and France. The talks with Germany made the greater progress and on 23 August, in the presence of Stalin, Ribbentrop and Molotov signed the Nazi–Soviet Pact. On the surface, this was a ten-year non-aggression pact. But it included secret clauses: if Eastern European frontiers were disturbed, the USSR would share with Germany in the division of Poland and the Baltic states. The Pact was a triumph for Hitler. The threat from Britain and France seemed irrelevant. They were remote from Poland, even if they were to honour their treaties with that country. For Stalin, the Pact held out the prospect of recovering much that Russia had lost in the years after 1917 and of neutrality in any European war which Germany might fight with the West. He could thus preserve communism while the capitalists fought among themselves. Nevertheless, it was a bizarre agreement, a marriage of convenience between fascism and communism.

Hitler seized Danzig and attacked Poland on 1 September 1939. On 3 September Britain and France declared war on Germany. 'Everything that I have worked for,' Chamberlain lamented, 'has crashed into ruins.' The long struggle for peace in Europe had failed. The League of Nations had become almost irrelevant as a peace-keeping body although it lived on until 1946. Negotiations outside the League and Britain's policy of appeasement had also become irrelevant. From 1939 until the defeat of the Axis powers, war spread relentlessly to almost every corner of Europe and across the whole world.

8.4 Russian Aggression

The Red Army entered Poland from the east two weeks after Hitler attacked in the west. Russians and Germans met in the middle of the country and consolidated their conquests. The Russians also moved troops into the Baltic states and met significant resistance only in Finland.

The Russian demands were not extravagant. They required bases as a future safeguard against German expansion into Finland. The Finns protested and Russia attacked at the end of November 1939. The difficulties of the terrain and Russia's casual preparations for the campaign resulted in setbacks to the Red Army and the war lasted for over three months. Newsreel pictures of this strange conflict in the snow, where soldiers often moved on skis, produced a considerable effect in Britain and France. Plans were made to send assistance to the gallant Finns but nothing came of them. In a last expression of vigour, the League of Nations expelled the USSR from membership. But in March 1940 Finland had to submit, and the USSR demanded additional territories as the price of defeat.

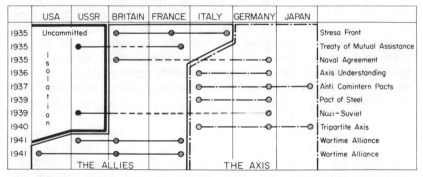

Fig. 8.6 The origins of the Second World War: some treaties and alliances, 1935–41

8.5   Why Did the Second World War Come About?

'War sets the seal of nobility on those peoples who have courage to face it.'
Such was the opinion of Mussolini. The Second World War had its roots in
the willingness of Japanese militarists, German Nazis and Italian Fascists to
go to war to get their own way. Their countries had grievances, which militarists, Nazis and Fascists strenuously encouraged. There were flaws to be found
in the Peace Settlement after the end of the First World War. But the flaws
were exploited to serve the purposes of unscrupulous leaders bent on power.
By 1931, the faults were widely acknowledged. In Britain and France, there
were even feelings of guilt which led to a willingness to admit, for example,
that the union of Germany and Austria was legitimate. In the end, the Second
World War occurred because Japan and Germany were prepared to use force
for illegitimate purposes. Their reasons were partly economic, the quest for
supplies which could only be obtained by plundering.

To place the blame for the Second World War on others is to do no more
than criticize a man for defending his property. It can, of course, be argued
that the weakness of their neighbours tempted the aggressors to strike. The
League of Nations showed many weaknesses and from its birth was severely
handicapped by the non-membership of the USA. It lacked an effective
weapon with which to resist aggression and when attempts were made to
strengthen it, they failed. Baldwin would not accept the Geneva Protocol.
Instead, the search for collective security (joint defence against aggression)
led to the signing of almost endless pieces of paper which undermined the
authority of the League (see Unit Seven). Even worse, the pieces of paper
were not honoured in times of crisis, for example when Hitler remilitarized
the Rhineland and raped Czechoslovakia. But the only way to honour them
was to go to war or at least to be prepared to go to war.

There were occasions when the aggressors might have been deterred by a
firmer show of resistance. The sanctions imposed on Italy after Mussolini's
attack on Ethiopia might have been effective if extended to oil and passage
through the Suez Canal. Hitler might have been persuaded to retreat from the
Rhineland. It is legitimate to blame both Britain and France on these occasions. On the other hand, Britain and France bore an unfair burden. They
were not free from pressing internal problems; they were unassisted by the
USA, they were bewildered by the rise of fanatical totalitarian regimes and
they had a naïve belief that the dictators could be appeased. Hitler constantly
declared that each claim was his last and that the settlement of an illegitimate
demand would be a guarantee of peace. In their eagerness to preserve peace,
the democracies were hoodwinked.

At the same time, Britain and France were guilty of sluggishness. Throughout the 1930s, the National governments in Britain showed a talent for ignoring problems rather than solving them, while France staggered from one
political crisis to another (see Unit Three). At times they blundered. Too
often, there was a lack of trust between Britain and France and both failed

utterly to tackle the problem of involving the USSR in a policy of collective security.

Under Stalin's ruthless rule (see Section 5.1(c)), Russia seemed as unattractive to the democratic powers as Hitler's Germany. But Stalin's foreign policy was not aggressive until 1939. The USSR often expressed a willingness to play a part in defending the weak and demonstrated against Japan, in 1938 and 1939, a capacity to act effectively. How far Russia's expressed willingness was genuine remained untested. In 1939, Britain and France went to war with Hitler in defence of Poland, a cause already lost. Stalin made a sordid deal with Hitler and remained neutral. Anti-communists would argue that such lack of scruple was only to be expected. Russians argued that, in excluding the USSR from the Munich Conference, the West showed its contempt and perhaps something more sinister, a readiness to gang up with Hitler against communism. It was the final tragedy which made war in Europe inevitable in 1939 that Britain and France reached no agreement with Russia but Germany did – and that removed the fear of a war on two fronts for Hitler. He was able to attack Poland, safe in the knowledge that the USSR would not interfere. Britain and France alone no longer alarmed him. 'Our enemies are little worms,' he had said, 'I saw them at Munich.'

But Poland was only one among many victims. The Second World War really began when Japan attacked China. China was the first victim. Ethiopia, Austria, Czechoslovakia and Albania followed. General war was only avoided until 1939 because no country went to the rescue of these victims. In attempting to rescue Poland, albeit in vain, Britain and France only enlarged a conflict which had already begun. The blame for starting it can lie nowhere but with Japan and Germany, supported by Italy. It was in the nature of fascism to be aggressive and expansionist. 'I want to make Italy great, respected and feared,' Mussolini said. Japan and Germany shared his ambitions and, in the end, all three chose war as their instrument.

Further Reading
See **Further Reading** for Units Five and Seven.

Adamthwaite, A.P.: *The Making of the Second World War.* Allen & Unwin (London, 1977).

Carr, W.: *Arms, Autarky and Aggression.* Arnold (London, 1972).

Gilbert, M.: *The Holocaust.* Board of Deputies of British Jews (London, 1978).

Rock, W.R.: *British Appeasement in the 1930s.* Arnold (London, 1977).

Stone, R.: *The Drift to War.* Heinemann (London, 1975).

Watson, J.B.: *Success in British History since 1914.* John Murray (London, 1983) – Unit 8.

Watson, J.B.: *Success in European History 1815–1941.* John Murray (London, 1981) – Units 23–24.

Documentary
Adamthwaite, A.P.: *The Lost Peace, 1918–1939.* Arnold (London, 1980).

Bettey, J.H.: *English Historical Documents, 1906–1939*. Routledge & Kegan Paul (London, 1967) – Pages 167–98.

Henig, R.: *The League of Nations*. Oliver & Boyd (Edinburgh, 1973).

Parkinson, R.: *The Origins of World War Two*. Wayland (London, 1970).

Exercises

1. Write short definitions to show what you understand by *each* of the following terms: aggression; non-aggression pact; appeasement; collective security.

2. Account for the aggressiveness in the 1930s of (*a*) Japan and (*b*) Italy.

3. Explain why it may be said that the Second World War began in the Far East.

4. How does this Unit show that Mussolini, having opposed Hitler, became his ally? How do you explain this change in Mussolini's policy?

5. Referring to Units Two and Eight including the relevant maps, identify Hitler's grievances in international affairs. How would you summarize Hitler's aims in foreign policy after he had come to power in Germany?

6. Study Figs. 8.3 and 8.6. Explain the point being made by the cartoonist in Fig. 8.3 and state, with reasons, whether you think it was a valid one. Write an explanatory account of what Fig. 8.6 shows of international relations in the years 1935 to 1941.

7. 'The League of Nations had one law for the large states and another for the small fry' (page 128). How far does the evidence in Units Seven and Eight support this statement?

8. Explain what Churchill meant by the statement quoted at the end of Section 8.3(*c*) on page 149. Why did so few of the British people support Churchill's view of the Munich Agreement at the time that Chamberlain returned from Munich?

9. 'All three (Italy, Japan, Germany) chose war as their instrument' (page 153). List the states which were the victims of these powers in the years up to 1939, and show which of these victims you would use to illustrate the truth of this statement.

10. Explain what Hitler meant by *each* of the following statements in *Mein Kampf. In each case*, write a paragraph to show how Hitler later put his ideas into practice.

> (We) must bear in mind the fact that we are members of the highest species of humanity on this earth, that we have a correspondingly high duty and that we shall fulfil this duty only if we inspire the German people with the racial idea, so that they will . . . care for the purity of their own blood.

> Our people will not obtain territory . . . as a favour from any other people, but will have to win it by the power of a triumphant sword.

> When we speak of new territory in Europe today we must principally think of Russia and the border States subject to her. . . . This colossal Empire in the East is ripe for dissolution. And the end of Jewish domination in Russia will also be the end of Russia as a State.

> France is and will remain the implacable enemy of Germany. . . . We must stop at no sacrifice in our efforts to destroy the French striving towards hegemony over Europe.

Unit Nine

The Second World War: an Outline of Events

9.1 The Nazi Conquest of Europe

(a) Poland

The declaration of war on Germany by Britain and France could do nothing to save Poland. German *blitzkrieg* (lightning war) tactics proved too successful; and Poland faced overwhelming odds. By 1939, six German *Panzer* divisions (heavily-armed, mobile forces) had torn into Poland while the *Luftwaffe* pounded the country from the air. Polish soldiers and civilians made a heroic effort to hold Warsaw but the city was battered into submission on 27 September. Poland capitulated a week later, and the Nazis began to herd Polish Jews into ghettos.

No country experienced the savagery of Nazi rule more than Poland. Two-and-a-half million Poles were taken to Germany for forced labour. Two hundred thousand young children were taken to be 'Germanized'. From 1941, Polish Jews were shipped steadily to concentration camps and a final attempt to resist in the Warsaw Ghetto, in 1943, brought terrible retribution. The Nazis killed over 3 million Polish Jews before the war ended. The Russians also deported thousands of politically suspect Poles from the areas of Poland they occupied.

(b) The 'Phoney War'

The war subsided with the conquest of Poland. German generals were reluctant to launch an immediate attack on France, and Britain and France wanted more time to gear their countries to war. There was even hope that the war would be called off or that Germany could be blockaded and starved into submission without fighting. The *Maginot Line* defended the French frontier from Luxemburg to Switzerland. Hitler had built the *Siegfried Line* facing it, but extending further north to cover the Belgian frontier. With absurd optimism, a British popular song declared the intention of hanging out 'the washing on the Siegfried Line'. But few hostilities occurred in the winter of 1939–40. Rearmament and training went on but the terrible events the democracies had feared were confined to Poland. In the West, the war was dubbed 'phoney'.

(c) Scandinavia and Britain's Change of Government

Many plans were made on paper during the 'Phoney War' to achieve some

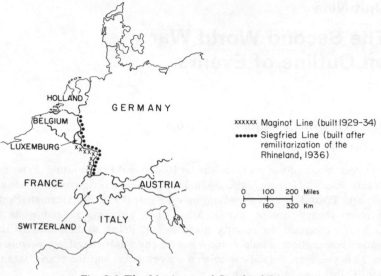

xxxxxx Maginot Line (built 1929-34)
•••••• Siegfried Line (built after remilitarization of the Rhineland, 1936)

| 0 | 100 | 200 | Miles |
| 0 | 160 | 320 | Km |

Fig. 9.1 The Maginot and Siegfried Lines

dramatic master-stroke. The attention of all three belligerents, Britain, France and Germany, came, curiously, to centre on Norway. During the winter, Britain and France thought of sending help to Finland against Russia (see Section 8.4). Norway lay along the route. The idea of a British landing there appealed first to Churchill, then to Chamberlain. Quisling, a Norwegian fascist, went to warn Hitler. In February 1940, a German ship, the *Altmark*, was chased into a Norwegian fjord and boarded by the British. Both sides were now interested in control of the Norwegian coast but Germany struck first. On 9 April both Denmark and Norway were attacked by the Nazis. Denmark was in no position to resist. Norwegian resistance was handicapped by Quisling and his supporters. A British landing near Trondheim did nothing to save southern and central Norway, and Germany soon completed the conquest of the rest of the country. Norway's neighbour, Sweden, managed to remain neutral throughout the war.

In Britain, Chamberlain was made a scapegoat for the failure to keep Norway out of German hands. The failure of appeasement before the war, the inactivity of the 'Phoney War', and Chamberlain's rash prophecy that Hitler had 'missed the bus' combined with the Norwegian setback to convince even many Conservatives that there must be a change of Prime Minister. Chamberlain was replaced by a Coalition government under Churchill, an outspoken critic of British foreign policy in the later 1930s. Churchill made no optimistic promises, offering only 'blood and toil and tears and sweat' to put the country on the road to victory. He took office on 10 May 1940. It was too late to save Norway. Within a few months, Britain was being fully tested to save herself.

(d) The Low Countries and Dunkirk

On the day that Churchill became Prime Minister, Germany attacked Holland, Belgium and Luxemburg. Holland surrendered almost at once. Belgium resisted for less than three weeks. This was a grave situation for France, for the Maginot Line did not extend along the Belgian border. Even worse, German Panzer troops driving through Luxemburg struck across the northern edge of France to reach the Channel coast south of Calais, cutting off British and French troops in Belgium. Total disaster seemed inevitable.

As the Germans closed in, nearly 200 000 British and 140 000 Allied troops were rescued from beaches pulverized by shells and bombs. The evacuation went on until 4 June and was remembered as the 'Miracle of Dunkirk'. It was a magnificent achievement even though almost all the military equipment had to be left behind. Hundreds of vessels, many of them small craft able to get close inshore, and almost anything capable of floating, were organized by the British navy. The RAF provided the best air cover possible. A gallant holding action at Calais helped to delay the Germans and the operation was aided by a calm sea and soft sand which lessened the blast of bombs. But the main factor which made it possible was that Hitler meddled with the plans of his generals and slowed down the German advance. This provided time for the miracle to be performed.

(e) The Fall of France

The collapse of Belgium made the Maginot Line irrelevant. A week after the evacuation from Dunkirk ended, General Weygand informed the French Prime Minister, Reynaud, that the Germans could not be stopped. The Germans entered Paris on 14 June. Reynaud resigned; his place was taken by Marshal Pétain, a veteran of the First World War, who signed an armistice on 22 June. Hitler insisted that the armistice should be signed in the same railway coach and at the same place as the armistice in 1918 at which Germany had surrendered.

Meanwhile, on 10 June Mussolini felt sufficiently confident of a German victory to declare war on France and Britain. He was just in time to make a separate armistice with France, taking a small strip of French territory.

Pétain's government felt that there was no alternative but to collaborate with the Nazis. By the terms of the armistice, Germany occupied the western coast and northern France, including Paris, and France agreed to bear the costs of this occupation. Pétain took the title 'Head of the French State' and his government made its headquarters at Vichy. The Vichy government agreed to return German refugees to the Nazis and to leave French prisoners of war in German hands. They were allowed to keep control of the French fleet but much of it was destroyed by the British navy to keep it from use by the Nazis. Pétain then broke off relations with Britain. The Vichy government shared with the fascists a belief in authority, law and order but it was not until its final year, 1944, that it became wholly fascist. It collaborated with the Germans but Hitler felt sufficient distrust to order the German occupation of the whole of France in 1942. The Vichy politicians were, in fact, distrusted by both sides, and were regarded as traitors after the war.

The *Free French* set up an alternative to Vichy collaboration in 1940. General Charles de Gaulle escaped to London and called on Frenchmen to continue the struggle. In exile and in the *maquis* (an underground resistance movement), the Free French rejected both Nazi domination and Vichy peace-making.

ON TO GLORY—AND WHATEVER
WE CAN GRAB

Fig. 9.2 A British propagandist comment on Mussolini's declaration of war in June 1940. But the image was one Mussolini himself had created and Low's gun, suggesting a reluctant Italian rank-and-file, proved prophetic

(f) The Battle of Britain

Hitler's next objective was Britain. Churchill refused to abandon the struggle and so the Germans prepared Operation Sealion, the launching of a new invasion. In July 1940, the Luftwaffe began a preliminary bombardment of

Britain's shipping and airfields. Goering was confident that the RAF could be destroyed, and then the invasion could take place. His confidence was misplaced, for the Luftwaffe suffered heavy losses at the hands of Fighter Command. British *Spitfires* and *Hurricanes* piloted by the 'few' airmen to whom Churchill paid tribute,* destroyed over half of Goering's aircraft. By mid-September, the Luftwaffe had lost the Battle of Britain. Operation Sealion was postponed indefinitely and German bombers changed their tactics. British cities became their main targets. The Nazis intended to punish and terrorize British civilians for stubbornly continuing to resist.

This was Hitler's first major setback. His armies were supreme on the continent but they could not reach Britain because of the strength of the British navy and the apparent strength of the RAF. But in September 1940 Britain was equally powerless to invade Europe.

(g) The Balkans

London provided a rallying-point for exiles from the lands Hitler had conquered; but his complete mastery of continental Europe was demonstrated again before the middle of 1941. His attention turned to the Balkans where an Italian attempt to invade Greece met disaster in the autumn of 1940. The Greeks replied by invading Albania and Mussolini needed German assistance. Hitler needed supplies: agreements with Hungary and Rumania, in November 1940, provided food, oil and stepping-stones to the south. In March 1941, Bulgaria also decided to collaborate with Germany and, in April, Hitler attacked Jugoslavia and Greece. Sixty thousand British troops went to Greece's defence but they were quickly driven from the mainland and then from the island of Crete. By the end of May, the whole of the Balkans was under Axis control although the independence of Turkey was guaranteed by the USSR.

9.2 The Extension of the Conflicts

(a) The Position in June 1941

Spain, Portugal, Switzerland, Eire and Sweden still clung to neutrality. The Soviet Union followed her own policy and only Britain and the Commonwealth continued to resist Axis aggression in Europe. In the Far East, Japan continued her own war against China and expanded into Indochina (see Section 8.1(*c*)). Of the Axis powers, only Italy suffered defeats. By June 1941, the Italians had been driven from their Empire in East Africa and Haile Selassie had returned to his throne in Ethiopia. The Italians had also failed in an attack on Egypt, and now relied upon German troops to hold on to Libya. It was at this point that Hitler made a decision which was ultimately to prove disastrous. On 22 June, a hundred German divisions marched against Russia, setting into motion Operation Barbarossa.

* 'Never in the field of human conflict was so much owed by so many to so few.'

(b) Operation Barbarossa

Hitler felt confident that he could now at last destroy communism. He also expected to seize Soviet resources and looked forward, perhaps, to linking up with the militarists of Japan, assuming the USSR would surrender when Nazi forces reached Moscow or, if not Moscow, the Urals. At first Germany's advance was rapid, but Hitler badly misjudged the size, strength and determination of the Soviet Union. Operation Barbarossa was also delayed for six weeks while German troops went to the help of Mussolini in the Balkans, since the Duce was now proving to be more of a liability to Germany than an asset. The delay was disastrous: the Russian winter was now six weeks nearer. Supported by Hungary, Rumania and Finland, the Nazis nevertheless reached the outskirts of Leningrad and Moscow by the winter of 1941 but at heavy cost. Stalin rallied the Russian people to the 'Great Patriotic War' to defend Mother Russia rather than communist ideology, and the war was savage from the outset. The Germans saw it as a 'war of annihilation' against Slavs, Jews and communists. The Russians were not willing to yield. They devastated their country by 'scorched-earth' tactics rather than leave food, supplies and shelter to the invaders; and, as German supply-lines grew longer, they were a constant target for guerillas (see Glossary). The Russian winters took a heavy toll of both sides and casualties on the Russian Front were enormous (see Table 9.2). Britain and the USA sent supplies to help the Russians resist, and the Führer found himself trapped in a war the Nazis could not win. His 'war in the east' eventually undermined the very foundations of Nazi Germany.

(c) South-East Asia

In December 1941, the Japanese attack on Pearl Harbor (see Section 8.1(c)) extended the conflict still further and directly involved the USA in war against the Axis powers. Like the Nazis in Europe, Japan was at first highly successful. In only three months, Japanese armies seized Hong Kong, overran Thailand, Malaya and Singapore, wrested Indonesia from the Dutch and the Philippine Islands from the USA and made inroads into Burma and New Guinea. They cut the Burma Road, the main road for supplies to China, and so threatened India and Australia that the latter recalled troops from North Africa.

The advance was stemmed in May 1942, when the USA won a naval action in the Coral Sea to the south of New Guinea. American and Australian troops prevented the total conquest of New Guinea itself. East of Japan, aggression was halted when the Japanese were defeated at Midway Island. Burma proved the limit of their advance towards India. The position stabilized in the second half of 1942. For a time, Japan was able to reap immense profits from her new conquests but her Empire was surrounded by enemies against whom further advances were now impossible.

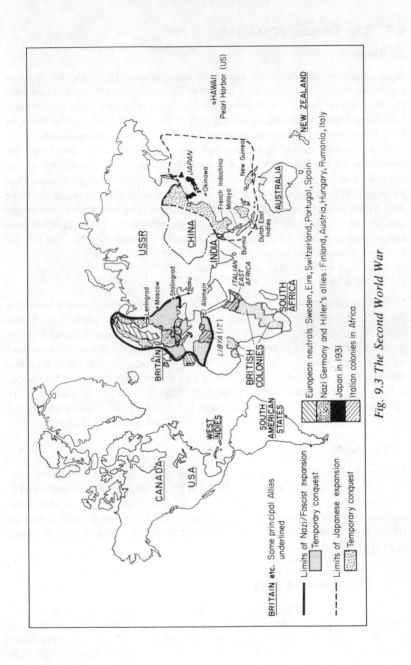

Fig. 9.3 The Second World War

9.3   The Turning of the Tide

(a) Russia

In the summer of 1942, the Germans were unable to break the Russian resistance at either Leningrad or Moscow. They desperately needed to defeat the Red Army. So far the Russians had resisted, destroyed the countryside (including many hard-won achievements of the 1930s, such as the Dnieper Dam), and retreated. Now the Russian forces fell back to Stalingrad and once again the winter closed in on the fighting. A terrible battle developed for possession of the city, and 21 German divisions were committed to the struggle. On 31 January 1943, 90 000 Germans were forced to surrender; thousands more were already dead. Leningrad was also under relentless siege until 1944, with the Russians suffering casualties on a vast scale: over three-quarters of a million died, most of them from starvation. (Shostakovich later commemorated their sufferings in his 'Leningrad' Symphony (No. 7).) But the German advance had been halted.

(b) North Africa

In 1942 General Rommel and the German Afrika Korps succeeded in driving the Allies from their last foothold in Libya. They were pushed back into Egypt as far as El Alamein. In October, British and Commonwealth forces took the offensive. They were led by General Montgomery and after another struggle at El Alamein, the Germans began to retreat. In little more than two months, they were driven right across Libya and into Tunisia. Meanwhile, British and American forces landed in Algeria and drove eastwards to squeeze the Axis forces from two sides. On 7 May 1943, Tunis was entered and a week later the Axis troops in North Africa admitted defeat.

(c) The Pacific

For Japan, too, 1943 was an ominous year. The USA, 'leap-frogging' over strongly-held Japanese positions, began to retake islands in the Pacific and to turn them into bases for future air-strikes. The war output of American industry steadily increased. For the moment, the Japanese Empire remained almost intact but Japan was rapidly losing the initiative that had been seized at Pearl Harbor.

9.4   The Defeat of Italy

The American General, Dwight Eisenhower, launched the invasion of Sicily only two months after defeating the Axis powers in North Africa. The island was captured by the end of August 1943, and the following month Allied forces landed in the 'toe' of Italy and at Salerno, south of Naples. This blow into 'the soft under-belly of the Axis' by the forces of the USA, Britain, members of the Commonwealth and countries such as Poland, created consternation among Italians.

The landings in Sicily led to the instant downfall of Mussolini: he was overthrown, arrested and imprisoned by the Fascist Grand Council, and Badoglio took over Italy's government. Though Badoglio thought of continuing the war, he promptly agreed to unconditional surrender when Allied troops crossed to the Italian mainland. The surrender did not spare Italy from becoming a battlefield. The Germans determined to hold Italy from a line slightly north of Naples, so that Badoglio now persuaded King Victor Emmanuel to declare war on Germany. The struggle to free Italy from the Nazis lasted until the spring of 1945 by which time Badoglio had gone into retirement. Rome fell to the Allies in June 1944 but the Germans built new defences further north, delaying the Allies until the following year. By that time, however, Germany was under severe pressure both from east and west.

Mussolini, in the meantime, was rescued from imprisonment in September 1943 by German parachutists. Hitler established him as a puppet-ruler of a new *Fascist Republic of Salò*, in the north of Italy behind the German lines. But the Republic grew ever smaller and, when at last German resistance in Italy was broken, Mussolini scrambled to join the Nazis in the retreat into Austria. His luck was out: he was captured by Italian guerillas.

9.5   The Defeat of Germany

(*a*) Western Europe

On 6 June 1944 the Allies made landings on the Normandy beaches, with Eisenhower as the Supreme Commander. Stalin had long demanded the opening of a 'Second Front', always ready to argue that the Russians were bearing the brunt of the war. But the landings were not made until thorough preparations had been undertaken. Apart from special landing craft, the Allies had PLUTO (a fuel pipeline under the ocean) and prefabricated harbours ready to tow into position. Highly-trained troops stood ready. A hundred and thirty thousand men were landed on the first day, a million by the end of the first month. There was fierce resistance but the bridgehead was held. The Germans had thought their defences in the Atlantic Wall were strong enough to make invasion impossible. But Hitler had expected the invasion to be attempted near Calais and, once the foothold was secured in Normandy, the Germans were driven back. Paris was liberated and on 25 August, de Gaulle and the Free French were able to enter the city. In September, the whole of France was free.

The total defeat of Germany took longer. The Rhine was still a formidable obstacle, and a premature attempt to win a bridgehead at Arnhem in Holland with parachute troops proved costly. The Allied advance was further delayed when the Germans launched a vigorous counter-attack in the wooded hills of the Ardennes in the winter of 1944. The Allies did not cross the Rhine until March 1945 and only then was Germany finally opened up to invasion from

Fig. 9.4 Allied reinforcements landing in Normandy in 1944 after the Second Front had been opened

the west. At about the same time, the Allies at last broke German resistance in Italy.

(b) Eastern Europe

The Russians began their advance in the summer of 1943, driving the Germans back in the Ukraine. At about the time of the opening of the Second Front in Normandy, the Germans were driven from Russian soil. Before the end of 1944, Rumania and Finland surrendered. Hungary surrendered in January 1945. Guerillas under Marshal Tito produced an uprising against the Germans in Jugoslavia. The Russians pressed on through Poland and entered Germany from the east in February 1945. In late April, Berlin was besieged and Hitler was trapped. Rather than face capture by the Russians, Hitler chose to commit suicide on 30 April among the ruins of his capital. At almost the same time Mussolini too was shot by Italian anti-fascists.

Admiral Doenitz, Commander-in-Chief of what was left of the German Grand Fleet, briefly took responsibility for the German government – long enough to make an unconditional surrender to the Allies on 7 May. On 8 May, VE Day was celebrated: Victory in Europe was achieved. It was a Europe in ruins, however, pounded and trampled by armies. Most of Germany's cities and towns were devastated, shattered by the massive bombing which accompanied the final defeat of Nazism. Dresden, hardly a significant military target, was reduced to ruins in February 1945, with the loss of over 100 000 lives. Almost every nation emerged from the war with dreadful scars, although none suffered more than Poland, Germany and Russia. On both sides, the wounds would take many years to heal.

9.6   The Defeat of Japan

(a) The Japanese Retreat

In 1944, American forces were 'island-hopping' northwards towards Japan. A decisive naval victory at Leyte made possible the reconquest of the Philippines by General MacArthur. At the same time, British and Commonwealth troops pushed into Burma.

Fig. 9.5   'Island-hopping'. The Americans were forced to pay a heavy price for the liberation of Iwo Jima and similar Pacific islands

Early in 1945 with the fall of Rangoon, Burma was liberated. Supplies to China could again be sent along the Burma Road. In June 1945, MacArthur took Okinawa: he was now within 400 miles of the southern tip of Japan. But the campaigns were costly in lives and the Allies still faced daunting problems. The Japanese continued to hold most of South-East Asia and large areas of China; to invade Japan itself could be even more costly. As in Europe, the Allies insisted on unconditional surrender and the Japanese seemed to show no signs of yielding.

(b) Atomic Bombs

Scientists in all countries had experimented with new and more terrible weapons throughout the war. In 1944 Germany produced the V1 flying-bomb, pilotless and jet-propelled, refining it in the V2, a higher-flying rocket bomb. For a time they caused extensive damage but they came too late and the Allied troops, advancing in Western Europe, over-ran their launching sites. A far more deadly weapon was developed in the USA, the first nuclear weapon, the atomic bomb. The bomb became available in July 1945. The decision whether it should be used fell to Harry Truman, who had become President of the USA three months earlier on the death of Roosevelt.

The first atomic bomb was dropped on the Japanese industrial town of Hiroshima early on the morning of 6 August. A third of the population of nearly a quarter of a million were killed instantly and the whole town was devastated. Another 100 000 were injured, many of them condemned to intense suffering and lingering death from the effects of radiation. The USSR declared war on Japan two days later. Still the Japanese hesitated and a second atomic bomb was dropped on Nagasaki on 9 August. Again the results were devastating. Hastily, Japan agreed to unconditional surrender although the final capitulation was not signed until 2 September. By that time, American troops had already landed in Japan.

The atomic bombs undoubtedly shortened the war in the Pacific and thus saved the lives of many Allied soldiers but arguments soon raged about the morality of their use. Nuclear weapons heralded a new era in human destructiveness and the effects of the radiation they created are still incalculable. American possession of such weapons created fear in the USSR. Indeed, it has been argued that Truman had this in mind, that their use against Japan was simultaneously a warning to the Soviets of the strength of the USA. The United States refused to share nuclear expertise with the Russians, but the USSR nevertheless showed determination to catch up, developing a Soviet atomic bomb in 1949. By then even more destructive nuclear weapons were being invented in the USA. The Soviet Union rushed on to match America with a hydrogen bomb which both had perfected by 1953. A new, more terrible arms race was under way in which America and Russia were soon joined by Britain, France and China.

Meanwhile, peace was restored in the Pacific, and Japanese armies were withdrawn from China and South-East Asia.

9.7   Why Did the Axis Powers Lose the War?

The early successes of Japan and Germany were the result of ruthlessly efficient war machines. Of the Axis powers, only Italy proved incompetent in war. But the aggressors over-reached themselves and by their greed built up such a hostile coalition of powers that disaster became inevitable. Hitler's failure to defeat Britain seemed unimportant at the end of 1940, as did Japan's failure totally to defeat China. But by keeping the struggle alive, Britain and China denied complete success to the aggressors and with the involvement of the USSR and the USA in 1941, Allied strength grew steadily.

All the Axis powers underestimated their enemies. Hitler failed to understand that war against Britain involved war against almost the whole of the Commonwealth. He expected communist Russia to collapse and Japan imagined that victory at Pearl Harbor would paralyse the USA indefinitely. They underestimated not only the strength of their enemies but also their will to resist.

The British navy played havoc with German shipping, but there were heavy casualties on both sides. German raiders and submarines, especially, took a severe toll of Allied shipping though Germany never won control of the seas. By the summer of 1943 the Nazis were penned in their European fortress and German submarines too were being contained. While the Allies could draw on supplies from almost the whole of the world, the Axis powers had increasingly to rely simply on what they had already conquered. In spite of early successes, the Japanese navy was similarly battered in the Pacific, especially by the USA. Thus Allied operations everywhere were supported from the sea with a power that even Japanese *kamikaze* pilots, directing their aircraft to destruction as piloted bombs, could not break.

The Allies also achieved superiority in the air. At first it was a massive achievement for the RAF to prevent a German invasion in the Battle of Britain. London, Liverpool, Coventry, Plymouth and many other British cities and towns had to endure ferocious bombing by the Germans but the pendulum swung in the opposite direction. Agents and supplies were dropped behind the Axis lines to encourage sabotage, Axis ships were tracked and often destroyed and, from about 1942, Nazi Germany was steadily pounded with bombs. The Americans could not reach Japan with land-based aircraft until Iwo Jima fell, but air superiority also came to play an important part in the Allied victory in the Pacific. Accurate bombing, however, was only perfected in the later stages of the war. In 1943, precision bombing was demonstrated by the Dambusters on Germany's Möhne Dam and, in the invasion of Western Europe in 1944, it played an important part in disorganizing German communications. Moreover, the sheer weight of bombs also

Table 9.1   What governments spent on the Second World War*

Allies	£m	Axis Powers	£m
USA	84 500	Germany	68 000
USSR	48 000	Italy	23 500
Britain	28 000	Japan	14 000
Canada	4 000		
France	3 750		
Total	171 250	Total	105 500

* Adapted from Purnell's *History of the Twentieth Century*, Vol. 5, pages 2 048–9.
Compare spending in the First World War, Table 1.1, page 9.

increased until thousand-bomber raids on German cities produced almost unimaginable destruction.

Germany and Japan fought desperately to the end. They were required to surrender unconditionally: there would be no argument about the terms of an armistice such as there was in 1918. Devastation throughout Germany, Italy and the Pacific, in Hiroshima and Nagasaki, bore witness to the total collapse of the Axis powers. Devastation elsewhere showed something of the price which had been paid to secure that collapse.

Table 9.2   The dead in the Second World War

Allies	millions	Axis Powers	millions
USSR	20.0	Germany	4.2
Poland	4.3	Japan	1.2
China	2.2	Rumania	0.5
Jugoslavia	1.7	Hungary	0.4
France	0.6	Italy	0.4
USA	0.4	Austria	0.3
Britain	0.4		

Compare total dead in First World War, Table 2.1.

Further Reading

Ayling, S.E.: *Portraits of Power*. Harrap (London, 1965) – Churchill.

Calvocoressi, P. and Wint, G.: *Total War: Causes and Courses of the Second World War*. Allen Lane (London, 1972).

Jardine, C. Bayne: *World War Two*. Longman (Harlow, 1968).

Liddell Hart, B.H.: *History of the Second World War*. Cassell (London, 1970).

Savage, K.: *The Story of the Second World War*. Oxford University Press (London, 1957).

Sellman, R.R.: *The Second World War*. Methuen (London, 1964).

Taylor, A.J.P.: *The Second World War, An Illustrated History*. Hamish Hamilton (London, 1975).

Documentary

Breach, R.W.: *Documents and Descriptions, the World since 1914*. Oxford University Press (London, 1966) – Sections 14 and 23.

Peacock, R.: *The Second World War*. Arnold (London, 1970).

Ray, J.: *The Second World War*. Heinemann (London, 1977).

Yass, M.: *Hiroshima*. Wayland (London, 1971).

Yass, M.: *The Home Front*. Wayland (London, 1971).

Exercises

1. 'The aggressors' . . . 'built up such a hostile coalition of powers that disaster became inevitable' (page 166). Explain and illustrate the truth of this statement.

2. Making use of Units Eight and Nine, trace the rise and fall of German armed might under Hitler. Select and explain what you think were Hitler's *two* most important mistakes in the years 1939 to 1945.

3. What is meant by calling Fig. 9.2 *propagandist*? How far do you consider this cartoon is, nevertheless, fair comment on Mussolini's record in foreign policy? How true is it that, in the Second World War, Italy was 'more of a liability to Germany than an asset' (page 160)?

4. Show what parts were played by *each* of the following in the defeat of the Axis powers: Britain and the Commonwealth; the USSR; the USA. Do you consider that each of these Allies was of equal importance in achieving victory?

5. What do Tables 9.1 and 9.2 show of the nature of the various campaigns in the Second World War and of the contributions made to the outcome of the War by various powers? Account for the high numbers of dead in Poland and the USSR, shown in Tables 9.2 and 10.2.

6. Referring to some of the Further Reading listed above, write more detailed accounts of *two* of the following campaigns with the reasons for their outcomes: Britain's struggle for survival in 1940; Operation Barbarossa; the war in North Africa; the war in Western Europe, 1944–5; the war in the Pacific, 1944–5.

7. Study the following extract from a report issued on 1 December 1943 after the summit meeting at Teheran (see Section 10.2(*a*)), and then answer the questions which follow:

> We – the President of the United States, the Prime Minister of Great Britain, and the Premier of the Soviet Union – have met these past four days . . . and have shaped and confirmed our common policy. . . .
>
> As to war – our military staffs have joined in our round table discussions, and we have concerted our plans for the destruction of the German forces. We have reached complete agreement as to the scope and timing of the operations to be undertaken from the east, west and south.
>
> The common understanding which we have reached guarantees that victory will be ours. . . . No power on earth can prevent our destroying German armies by land, their U Boats by sea, and their war plants from the air.

(*a*) Name the three leaders who met at this Conference in the order in which they are referred to in the first sentence of this extract.

(*b*) What *operations* were there between the time of this report and the surrender of Germany in *each* of the areas referred to in the second paragraph: *east*; *west*; *south*?

(*c*) Explain the term *U Boats*. Why did this report make special mention of them?

(*d*) Bearing in mind the date of this report, what reasons were there at this time for the confidence in *victory* shown in the final paragraph?

(*e*) What was the importance of *air* power in the Second World War?

Unit Ten
Aspects of the Second World War

10.1 The Atlantic Alliance

(a) The Arsenal of Democracy

Towards the end of the 1930s, President Roosevelt began to show increasing sympathy for the victims of the aggressors. At the same time, the USA was anxious to remain uninvolved, although she did try to deter Japan with words and then with an embargo on trade (see Section 8.1). Her first response to the outbreak of war in Europe was to supply Britain and France on the 'Cash and Carry Plan': they could buy the goods they needed for cash but must carry them from America in their own ships. But that, for the moment, was as far as Roosevelt could go, restricted as he was by Neutrality Laws and isolationist opinion in the American Congress (see Section 4.4(a)).

The ruthless expansion of German power in 1940 caused alarm in the USA. But Roosevelt had only contempt for Mussolini's attack on France. 'The hand that held the dagger,' he said, 'has struck it into the back of its neighbour.' Defence spending was stepped up and Congress agreed to give Britain fifty destroyers which were left from the First World War in exchange for the use of bases on certain British-owned islands. Roosevelt's success in the presidential election at the end of 1940 strengthened his hand and on 29 December he told the American people, 'We must be the great arsenal of democracy.'

(b) The Atlantic Charter

More supplies were soon made available to fight the Nazis. In March 1941, the Lend-Lease Act was passed, to lend war supplies which, if they still existed, could be returned to the USA at an indefinite future date. At first the supplies were intended mainly for Britain and the Commonwealth, but they were extended to Russia after the launching of Operation Barbarossa (see Section 9.2(b)) and, by the end of 1941, to nearly forty other countries including China. Meanwhile, in August 1941, Roosevelt and Churchill drew up the Atlantic Charter, looking forward to the destruction of Nazi tyranny and to some form of future international co-operation for peace and the spread of prosperity.

The USA had now clearly declared her interests in the war. The Atlantic Charter also encouraged the hope that, when it ended, America would not return to isolationism. Her troops took over the defence of Greenland and Iceland (which Britain had occupied to try to prevent a possible German attack). The USA was still waging economic war against Japan, but America only formally entered the struggle against the Axis when the Japanese attacked Pearl Harbor.

10.2   International Co-operation

(a) Summit Conferences

The signing of the Atlantic Charter marked the beginning of a close personal relationship between Roosevelt and Churchill. They met again in December 1941, when Churchill went to Washington. They agreed to give priority to the defeat of Germany and set up machinery for united action. But America and Britain were not always in complete agreement: the USA wanted an early attempt to invade Europe but Churchill persuaded Roosevelt to accept Operation Torch instead (the invasion of North Africa from the west, see Section 9.3(b)). Churchill also went to Moscow to explain the strategy to Stalin and then met Roosevelt again at Casablanca, Morocco, in January 1943. This time they agreed on the invasion of Italy and that the Axis powers must make an unconditional surrender.

Stalin was impatient for them to begin a Second Front in Western Europe. Others fretted because they felt they were not always fully consulted, including Commonwealth leaders and leaders in exile, such as de Gaulle and the Free French. It was not practicable, however, to bring them all into the decision-making and most of them continued to be consulted, separately, mainly in London. Some, like the Australians with their special interests in the Pacific, reached particular agreements with the USA. But the USSR was powerful enough to demand more equal consultation and, in November 1943, Stalin, Roosevelt and Churchill met together for the first time in Teheran, Persia (now Iran). They agreed to co-ordinate Russian attacks in the east with the Second Front in Western Europe, to a postwar organization to preserve peace, and to a Russian declaration of war against Japan at some suitable moment. The war had produced a strange alliance between the leaders of world capitalism and world communism.

The Big Three met again in February 1945, at Yalta in the Crimea. They agreed to the temporary division of Germany into four zones (one of them French) after Germany's surrender, to the punishment of war criminals, reparations for war damage and the paralysing of German military power. They also agreed to a conference at San Francisco to launch a United Nations Organization. They reaffirmed the principles of the Atlantic Charter, to liberate conquered nations and Axis satellite states and to prepare the way for free and democratic elections. But they often disagreed on matters of detail. The boundaries of Poland, the size of reparations and the precise moment for Russia to join the war against Japan could not be settled, although Stalin undertook to declare war on the Japanese within a few months of the defeat of Germany.

Roosevelt died in April 1945. Churchill lost the general election in Britain

Fig. 10.1 The new 'Big Three' at the Potsdam Conference, July 1945 – Attlee, Truman and Stalin

in July and when the Big Three next met, at Potsdam, Berlin, in July 1945, Stalin faced new Western leaders, President Truman and Clement Attlee (see Section 11.1).

(b) The United Nations

Agreement on a new international organization had been reached at all the summit conferences since 1941. In November 1943, the principle was accepted by a meeting of Russian, American, British and Chinese representatives in Moscow. In August 1944 the same powers agreed on many details of the new organization's structure, although the right of the great powers to have a veto was not decided until the summit meeting at Yalta. In April 1945, fifty nations attended a conference at San Francisco to draft the Charter of the United Nations and the Statute of the International Court of Justice. The United Nations Organization came into formal existence in October 1945 and permanent headquarters were established in New York at the end of 1946 (see Section 11.3).

(c) The Superpowers

Nothing did more to determine the outcome of the Second World War than the might of the USA. Before the war ended, the USA built nearly 300 000 aircraft, 86 000 tanks and 12 000 ships. Every Allied country relied on the

Table 10.1 Some important conferences during the Second World War

Date of opening	Place	Those taking part	Purpose/Business	Page reference
August 1941	Off Newfoundland	Roosevelt, Churchill	Atlantic Charter drafted	170
December 1941	Washington	Roosevelt, Churchill	Planning joint strategy	171
August 1942	Moscow	Churchill, Stalin, Harriman (USA)	Planning joint strategy	171
January 1943	Casablanca	Roosevelt, Churchill	Planning joint strategy – invasion of Italy	171
August 1943	Quebec	Roosevelt, Churchill, Mackenzie King (Canada)	Planning joint strategy – Far East	—
November 1943	Moscow	Representatives of USA, USSR, Britain, China	A new international organization	172
November 1943	Teheran	Roosevelt, Churchill, Stalin	Co-ordination of strategy	169 and 171
May 1944	London	Imperial Conference: Churchill, Prime Ministers of Dominions*	Commonwealth strategy	177
July 1944	Bretton Woods	44 nations represented	Trade and reconstruction	179
August 1944	Dumbarton Oaks, Washington	Representatives of USA, USSR, Britain, China	A new international organization	—
September 1944	Quebec	Roosevelt, Churchill	Co-ordination of strategy	—
February 1945	Yalta	Roosevelt, Churchill, Stalin	Co-ordination; final objectives	171 and 181
April 1945	San Francisco	50 nations represented	United Nations Charter drafted	171 and 190
August 1945	Potsdam	Stalin, Truman, Attlee	German problems; peace settlement	172 and 182

* Representatives of the Dominions also paid individual visits to London at various times.

United States for supplies, and it was inevitable that the USA would dominate much of the postwar world.

Others paid a higher price for victory in blood. Estimates of the total dead in the war are sometimes put as high as 60 million (see Table 9.2) of whom only 400 000 were American (compared with 390 000 British, 100 000 in the rest of the Commonwealth and over half a million French). The USSR had some 20 million dead, almost half of them civilians. Poland too suffered enormous casualties, many of them Jewish victims of the Nazis. Even Jugoslavia had over a million-and-a-half dead. The war had thus taken a tremendous toll in Eastern Europe which was over-run by the USSR in the final stages of the conflict. The war had resulted in a tremendous shift in the balance of power. The League of Nations and world affairs before 1939 had been dominated by Britain, France and the rising Axis powers. After 1945, no country could match the USA. The only country which could even begin to challenge her was the Soviet Union. The postwar world was thus one in which two so-called 'superpowers' had emerged, neither of whom was concerned solely with Europe.

10.3   The Effects of the War in Europe

(a) The Nazi Tyranny

The Nazis had a variety of administrative systems for dominating Europe. Some conquests were incorporated directly into the Great German Reich. Such was the fate of Austria and of Alsace-Lorraine. Elsewhere, for example in the Netherlands, there were separate Nazi regimes. Yet other states, such as Vichy France and Quisling's Norway, were under the puppet regimes of men considered traitors by many of their own countrymen. Hitler's allies, such as Hungary and Rumania, managed to preserve only a small measure of independence. The Nazis were always ruthless but they demanded ever-increasing obedience as the threat to their European fortress grew. In the end, even Mussolini had to obey their orders. All conquests were organized for the benefit of Germany. European economies were controlled, and more than seven million foreign workers were conscripted for German armaments production.

The most savage Nazi policies were directed against the Jews and the peoples of Eastern Europe whom Hitler regarded as inferior to the Herrenvolk. The 'Final Solution' to the so-called Jewish problem began in 1941. In death camps such as those at Auschwitz and Treblinka, the Nazis attempted the total annihilation of their Jewish prisoners – genocide known as the Holocaust. Not all of the Nazi collaborators gave full co-operation: the Vichy government made some effort to protect French Jews, and both Italy and Hungary resisted German pressures to deport their Jewish subjects. In 1944, however, the Germans were themselves in occupation of northern Italy and Hungary, and Jews there could no longer be shielded. In all, about six million Jews perished at the hands of the Nazis.

Hitler had almost equally vicious plans for the peoples of Eastern Europe generally, though his inability to defeat the USSR frustrated their complete fulfilment. Czechs, Poles, Russians and other Slavs were to be enslaved for the benefit of the Herrenvolk, many to be banished from the German Lebensraum to Siberia, beyond the Urals. But the Nazi armies never reached the Urals. Resistance was often suppressed with savage cruelty in the regions they did reach. The SS and the Gestapo hunted down countless victims and countered protest and sabotage with brutal reprisals. In 1942, for example, the Nazis took revenge for the shooting of Reinhard Heydrich, a close associate of Himmler: they shot the entire male population of the mining community of Lidice in what had been Czechoslovakia, and burned the whole village.

Table 10.2   The Nazi slaughter of the Jews

Poland	2 900 000
USSR	1 000 000
Rumania	400 000
Czechoslovakia	300 000
Germany	200 000
Others	1 100 000
Total	almost 6 000 000

(b) The Resistance

Resistance movements existed throughout Europe in spite of such reprisals. None was more active than the *maquis* in France and there too the Nazis struck back. In 1944 the male population of Oradour-sur-Glane was killed, the women and children herded into the village church and burned to death. But resistance movements constantly harassed the conquerors by sabotage and espionage, by massive strikes in the Netherlands and by guerilla warfare carried out wherever possible by partisans. The Allies and free governments in exile encouraged them by radio, by operations from the air and sometimes by commando raids on occupied Europe.

(c) Capitalism or Communism?

Resistance fighters agreed on the urgent need to harass the Nazis. But they were far from united about the future government of their countries. Some, like Tito's partisans in Jugoslavia, were communists. Communism won converts during the war, both in Europe and elsewhere. In China, Malaya and Indonesia, communists resisted the Japanese. In Europe and especially Eastern Europe they resisted the Germans. When Germany and Japan collapsed, there were often struggles to determine the new systems of government. The Western powers resisted concessions to communism. The coun-

Fig. 10.2 Wartime devastation: Allied tanks move through the ruins of Munster, Germany, in 1945

tries they liberated were encouraged to set up systems based on Western democracy and capitalism. Where the Red Army advanced, however, communist systems developed. Where neither gained much of a foothold there was sometimes civil war to determine the outcome, as in China.

10.4   The Commonwealth at War

(a) Co-operation

Commonwealth troops fought with distinction in the war, even though in its early stages it threatened none of the Dominions. There was some hesitation in South Africa about joining the conflict. Australia and New Zealand did not hesitate and Canada waited only a week in order to make it clear that her declaration of war was a voluntary one. India could make no voluntary choice and like the rest of the British Empire became involved in the war when Britain did.

The Commonwealth too, in its own way, was an arsenal of democracy. Malaya stepped up her production of rubber; the West Indies supplied sugar and other foodstuffs, and all Britain's colonies provided what they could. In spite of disputes about independence, India provided soldiers to fight in North Africa, Europe and the Far East. Dominion forces were active on all fronts, though South Africa restricted her forces to the African continent. In

Europe, Malta found herself in the front line. In Asia, some British colonies were over-run by the Japanese and the Pacific War came near to both India and Australia (see Fig. 9.3). Commonwealth dead in the war included nearly 40 000 Indians, about 30 000 Canadians and a similar number of Australians, and the Commonwealth's contribution to victory was an important one. Commonwealth support was especially valuable when Britain stood alone against Germany in 1940. Almost all members of the Commonwealth made sacrifices in the cause of resisting fascism but, at the same time, the war inevitably brought changes in attitudes − it would prove necessary to pay attention to these in the postwar world.

(b) The Effects of the War

Many Dominion Prime Ministers visited London during the war, and an Imperial Conference was held in 1944. The increasing importance of American power, especially in the Pacific, persuaded Australia and New Zealand that they should look beyond the Commonwealth for future allies. Eventually the ANZUS Pact of 1951, an agreement for the joint defence of their interests, was drawn up by the two Dominions and the USA.

The shifting balance of power inevitably weakened some of the ties which bound Britain to the Dominions and her colonies, in spite of their close co-operation in the war. The authority of Europe in general was weakened by the war. Japan had conquered many of Britain's possessions in Asia: when these areas were restored, there were some who did not welcome the return of the British. Communists in Malaya claimed independence and resorted to civil war in an effort to obtain it. In fact there was a quickening of interest in independence everywhere. Dominion Status had already been promised to India, partly to secure wartime co-operation (see Section 6.2(c)). Even in Africa and the West Indies there was greater awareness that British rule was unlikely to last for ever and that Europeans were not invincible. During the war small and poor states like Nyasaland had built up credit balances in London by supplying Britain's needs. This gave them new confidence in themselves. The Empire and Commonwealth could not revert to their pre-war positions: new relationships would have to be worked out (see Section 16.6).

10.5   The Effects of the War on Other Empires

Italy's Empire fell in ruins during the early stages of the war. Japan over-ran the Asiatic possessions of France and Holland. Changes were also to be expected both in Africa and South-East Asia when the war ended. The myth of European superiority was now exploded and neither continent was likely meekly to return to a situation similar to that of 1939. Nor were European mother countries in 1945 well placed to begin vigorously to reimpose their authority on reluctant colonies. It was soon to become clear that overseas empires had become time bombs and that explosions were unavoidable. The first occurred only two days after the surrender of the Japanese, when Dr Sukarno declared the Dutch East Indies the independent republic of Indonesia (see Sections 6.5 and 16.2). The end of the great colonial empires was at hand.

10.6   Social and Economic Consequences of the War

(a) Refugees

In Europe alone, there were an estimated 21 million people who had been 'displaced' from their homes or were simply refugees from the conflict. Some were survivors of the Nazi concentration camps. There were over five million Russians, a million-and-a-half Poles and almost as many French. A vast resettlement operation was required. Some preparations had been made with the founding, in 1943, of UNRRA (the United Nations Relief and Rehabilitation Administration), to which the USA, Britain and Canada contributed funds for relief work. When the war ended, the Allies made an enormous co-operative effort to bring relief and repatriation to those in need. But it was impossible to do more than make a start on solving the problem. When UNRRA was wound up in 1947 new international agencies had been established by the United Nations, but huge problems still remained both in Europe and China.

(b) Devastation

Wreckage and devastation on a scale previously unknown also bore witness to the colossal disruption brought about by the war. In continental Europe and China, the destruction of homes, farms, factories, schools, hospitals and transport systems was on an immense scale. In Poland, a third of all buildings had been destroyed and in those parts of Russia invaded by the Germans the devastation was even greater. France, Belgium and the Netherlands suffered devastation equivalent to about three years' total production, reckoned in pre-war terms; and the damage to factories and communications meant that it would take many years to return to pre-war levels of production. Even in Britain, which had escaped invasion, a third of the houses had been destroyed or damaged by bombing and both industrial plant and people were worn out with the strains of total war.

(c) Disrupted Economies

Without massive aid to repair their economies, most countries faced a grim future. Apart from the devastation, many were deep in debt. Countries like Britain had used up many of their overseas assets to help to pay for the war. This reduced their income from 'invisible exports' and left them in difficulties over the balance of payments; it would be vital to sell exports in order to pay for imports.

Again, there had been some preparations to meet these problems. At the Bretton Woods Conference in 1944, an International Monetary Fund (IMF) was set up to make gold and currency available to facilitate trading and a Development Bank was to provide loans for reconstruction. Efforts were made to reduce tariffs which had handicapped trade between the wars and 1947 saw the General Agreement on Tariffs and Trade (GATT). Inevitably, such attempts at international co-operation had to lean heavily on the wealth of the USA. This led to fear and resentment among the communist states and contributed to the development of the Cold War soon after 1945 (see Section 17.1). In spite of the fact that the war had wiped out much of the progress Russia had made in the 1930s, the Soviet Union preferred to recover by her own efforts. Stalin called upon the Russian people to make new sacrifices in the years after 1945.

(d) The Will for Change

Sacrifices were necessary almost everywhere. The end of the war brought a new struggle to re-establish at least the old standards of life. The old standards in themselves, however, were not good enough. The war accelerated the demand for social change. The Beveridge Report of 1942 had already provided a massive plan for the development of welfare services in Britain. The (Butler) Education Act of 1944 provided free secondary education for all and looked forward to raising the school leaving age to fifteen, and sixteen when possible. The Family Allowances Act of 1945 provided state payments to assist larger families. In the general election of 1945, the British people showed a clear intention to move away from the pre-war complacency which accepted squalor and a high level of unemployment as inevitable. For the first time the Labour Party was returned with an absolute majority: the party programme contained a commitment to economic planning (the active intervention of the government in economic affairs to achieve certain fundamental objectives such as the reduction of unemployment). British electors seemed to show ingratitude in rejecting Churchill after his inspired wartime leadership, but Churchill and the Conservatives offered few ideas for the future. In 1945, Britain wanted real social improvements.

Some thought, wrongly in the case of Britain, that this shift in attitudes meant that there was now a desire for complete social equality and the end of class divisions. In some countries, such as China, there was certainly increased support for communism. But what was more widespread was the unwillingness of the underprivileged to endure further hardships. A new militancy developed after 1945 among the under-dogs. Colonies clamoured for independence and small nations for equal rights. Workers and trade unions, Jews, minority groups and the underprivileged non-whites became keenly aware of injustices. In the 1950s and 1960s the world seemed to grow increasingly turbulent. At the same time, the war which ended in 1945 left violence in its wake, as did the First World War. The barbaric savagery of allegedly-civilized governments had made violence a way of life for millions.

10.7   War Crimes

In 1945, however, shock and horror were the main feelings about the war. Hitler and Mussolini were dead and Himmler also committed suicide. Other Nazi leaders were tried at Nuremberg, by representatives from the USA, the USSR, Britain and France. The offences with which they were charged were various but many fell within the category of 'crimes against humanity'. Twelve were sentenced to be hanged, among them von Ribbentrop, Seyss-Inquart, Goering and Bormann. Bormann was not found and was tried in his absence, though later evidence suggested that he had already died with Hitler. Goering committed suicide. Seven others received sentences of imprisonment, among them Doenitz and Rudolf Hess, once the Führer's deputy. Doenitz was freed in 1956, but Hess was still in custody in 1983, the last surviving prisoner. Three Nazis were acquitted at Nuremberg in spite of Russian protests. Others guilty of atrocities had already covered their tracks and disappeared, to be hunted down with painstaking care by Jewish and other organizations in future years. One such was the Austrian Adolf Eichmann, executed in Israel in 1962. Meanwhile, similar war-crimes trials were held in the Far East in 1946. Seven Japanese leaders were sentenced to death by a tribunal representing eleven nations. Tojo was one of those executed.

Trials in national and local courts continued for several years after the war. Thousands were charged for their parts in atrocities committed by the aggressors and about 2 000 were put to death. There were legal and moral arguments about whether the trials should have taken place at all. Controversy also raged about whether one could successfully argue that crimes were committed on the orders of a superior. The courts ruled that one could not, and many paid dearly for their obedience to the Nazis and the Japanese militarists.

Further Reading

Ayling, S.E.: *Portraits of Power*. Harrap (London, 1965) – Churchill, Roosevelt, Stalin and de Gaulle.
Clemens, D.S.: *Yalta*. Oxford University Press (London, 1970).
Gilbert, M.: *Winston Churchill*. Oxford University Press (London, 1966).
Gilbert, M.: *The Holocaust*. Board of Deputies of British Jews (London, 1978).
Smith, N.D.: *Winston Churchill*. Methuen (London, 1960).
Watson, J.B.: *Empire to Commonwealth, 1919 to 1970*. Dent (London, 1971) – Chapter 5.

Documentary

Morgan, R.: *The Unsettled Peace*. British Broadcasting Corporation (London, 1974).
Snyder, L.L.: *Fifty Major Documents of the Twentieth Century*. Anvil (London, 1955).

Exercises

1. How did the Second World War influence attitudes? Note the changes in American policies towards the outside world; in colonies towards European mother countries; among the underprivileged towards injustice.

2. Why did it seem likely that a struggle would occur after 1945 between capitalism and communism?

3. Using Table 10.1 and documentary sources, show how, in international conferences, Allied war strategy was planned and preparations were made to deal with postwar problems.

4. Identify and explain *four* major international problems which existed in 1945 as a result of the Second World War.

5. Roosevelt called Stalin 'Uncle Joe'. How did each of Roosevelt, Churchill and Stalin regard his allies?

6. Show what you understand by resistance movements in Nazi-occupied Europe. Give some account of them and of how the Germans responded to them.

7. Argue for and against the decision to hold trials after the Second World War for war crimes.

8. Study this extract from the Report of the Allied Conference at Yalta in February 1945, and then answer the questions which follow:

> Nazi Germany is doomed. . . . We have agreed on common policies and plans for enforcing the unconditional surrender terms which we shall impose on Nazi Germany. . . . These terms will not be made known until the final defeat of Germany has been accomplished. Under the agreed plan, the forces of the Three Powers will each occupy a separate zone of Germany. . . .
>
> It is our inflexible purpose to destroy German militarism and Nazism and to ensure that Germany will never again be able to disturb the peace of the world. We are determined to disarm and disband all German armed forces . . . bring all war criminals to just and swift punishment and exact reparation in kind for the destruction wrought by the Germans; wipe out the Nazi party, Nazi laws, organizations and institutions. . . . A Commission for the Compensation of Damage will be established. . . . The Commission will work in Moscow.

(*a*) Name the representatives of the *Three Powers* who made this agreement.

(*b*) Why did these powers insist on *unconditional surrender terms*?

(*c*) Which power, not party to this agreement, also obtained a *zone of Germany*?

(*d*) Why could it be said at the time of this Conference that *Nazi Germany* was *doomed*?

(*e*) What was meant in this report by *war criminals*? Explain how the intention to deal with war criminals in the way described in this report was fulfilled.

(*f*) What was meant in this report by *reparation*? Why should the Commission, referred to in the final sentence of the report, *work* in the place named?

(*g*) How far do you think the *Three Powers* were justified in their attitudes towards Nazism shown in this report?

Unit Eleven
Peace After the Second World War

11.1 Peace-making

(a) The Conferences

There was no attempt to make an instant and comprehensive peace settlement. In August 1945, the Big Three (the USA, the USSR and Britain) followed up their Conference at Yalta with one at Potsdam (see Section 10.2). They agreed that the Oder–Neisse line would mark the new boundary between Germany and Poland. The division of Germany into zones of occupation was confirmed and, while it was agreed that for the time being there would be no central government for all Germany, the powers accepted that the country should be treated as a single economic unit. They also decided to send those Germans who were living in Poland, Hungary and Czechoslovakia to Germany, in the hope of avoiding another minority problem such as that in the Sudetenland. But already it seemed difficult for the USSR and the Western powers to reach agreement on the future of Germany, although they did agree to work out some details of the peace treaties in a Council of Foreign Ministers on which France and China would also be represented.

The Foreign Ministers held their first meeting in London a few weeks later. Agreements were not reached easily but on 29 July 1946, a Peace Conference of 21 nations assembled in Paris to consider their proposals. By February 1947, it was possible to sign treaties with the European allies of Nazi Germany, leaving the problems of Germany and Austria unsettled. The Council of Foreign Ministers paid further attention to these but it soon became clear that they could not bridge the fundamental differences which existed between Russia and the West.

A peace settlement with Japan was also delayed. After Japan's surrender, General MacArthur kept that country tightly under American control. The USA decided that the Council of Foreign Ministers was unsuitable for working out a Far Eastern settlement and the treaty was eventually drawn up by the Americans in separate consultations with interested governments. Like the other defeated powers, Japan was not consulted in the making of the treaty. In 1951, a Conference of 49 nations met in San Francisco to approve it.

(b) The Treaties

The decisions of the Council of Foreign Ministers were mainly those of the representatives of the USA, the USSR and Britain. There had been many differences of opinion, and disputes were often lengthy and bitter but compromises were eventually reached and treaties were therefore signed at Paris.

(*i*) **The Treaties of Paris (1947)** were imposed on Italy, Hungary, Bulgaria, Rumania and Finland. They were all required to disband their fascist organizations and to limit their armed forces. All had to make reparations payments, mainly to Russia, Jugoslavia and Greece although Italy had to make repayment to Ethiopia.

Territorial changes were comparatively modest but the defeated powers had to give up their ambitions. Thus Italy had to abandon her claims to Albania and Ethiopia, and she also lost her overseas empire. Libya became an independent state; Eritrea was in due course merged into Ethiopia; Italian Somaliland eventually became part of the independent republic of Somalia in 1960. Fig. 11.1 shows the most important territorial changes made in Europe by the treaties.

(*ii*) **Separate treaties (1945)** were made by the Soviet Union with several of her neighbours. Poland agreed to an eastern boundary with Russia roughly along

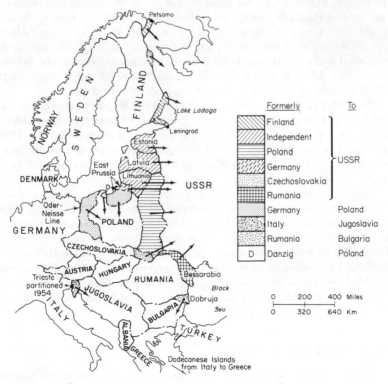

Fig. 11.1 Central and Eastern Europe after 1945

the old Curzon Line. Czechoslovakia transferred what had formerly been the eastern tip of the Czech state to Russia. The Soviet Union also pronounced a verdict in a long-standing dispute between Czechoslovakia and Poland over Teschen, deciding in favour of the former. A treaty with China went some way to establishing a joint Chinese-Russian influence in Manchuria to replace that of Japan.

(*iii*) **The Treaty of San Francisco (1951)** removed the Japanese from the Chinese mainland and from the island of Formosa. Japan also surrendered the Pacific islands she had held as mandates since the First World War and gave certain other islands to the USA to hold as *trusteeship territories* of the United Nations. Reparations were not fixed but Japan undertook to negotiate with the states she had injured. On the other hand, by 1951, the USA was disturbed by the successes of the communists in China: the Treaty, therefore, gave Japan the right to make defensive alliances, a provision which the Soviet Union found objectionable.

(*iv*) **The Austrian State Treaty (1955)** completed the peace-making, except for the settlement of the German problem. Hitler had incorporated Austria into the German Reich. It was agreed at Potsdam that, like Germany, the state would be divided into four occupation zones. But unlike Germany, Austria was allowed to elect her own civilian government in 1945. The occupation continued and a treaty was delayed until 1955, partly because the Western powers (the USA, Britain and France) could not reach agreement with the USSR on Austria's boundaries or on the scale of reparations.

The Treaty pledged Austria to neutrality in the disputes between Western and Eastern Europe. She was restored to her 1937 frontiers and forbidden to unite with Germany. Her military strength was restricted and the USSR secured rights to Austrian oil and to reparations. Austria thus became a neutralized state with some similarities to Switzerland, her western neighbour.

Austria also agreed to hold free and democratic elections and, in spite of the frequent need for coalitions in government, she succeeded in establishing a stable democracy. Industrial development brought a measure of prosperity and, in foreign policy, Austria's only major anxiety concerned the South Tyrol. This area had been transferred to Italy in 1919 and the Italians were confirmed in possession by the Treaty of Paris of 1947. It included German-speaking peoples whose loss Austria resented (see Fig. 7.1(*a*)). It was an international problem which added spice to Austro-Italian football matches but posed no threat to world peace.

11.2   The German Problem

Even in 1955 the powers could not agree on a solution to the German problem. Far from being settled, the problem continued to produce a great

Fig. 11.2 The divisions of Germany and Austria in 1945

deal of friction between the West and the Soviet Union in the years after 1945.

(a) The Division

The Allies began by dividing Germany into four zones of occupation in accordance with their agreements at Yalta and Potsdam. All former German lands east of the Oder–Neisse Line were incorporated into either Poland or the USSR. Fig. 11.2 shows how the zones were proportioned and also that

Berlin lay deep inside the Russian zone. Special arrangements were, there-fore, made for the city which was divided into four sectors, reproducing in miniature the divisions of Germany as a whole.

These divisions were meant to destroy militarism and Nazism in Germany, to persuade Germans of the enormities of the Nazi regime and to prepare the way for democracy and reconstruction. It was expected that a peace settle-ment would follow and Germany would then be left to herself as Austria was in 1955. Meanwhile, an Allied Control Council representing the four occupy-ing powers directed German affairs. Early co-operation between them to bring relief to suffering people and to deal with refugees quickly turned into recriminations and distrust.

The Russians felt fully justified in seeking recompense for the huge losses they had suffered in the recent war. They proceeded to take what they could from their zone, to press Germans to forced labour and to demand a share in the spoils of other zones. It was an attitude with which France had some sympathy but of which the USA and Britain disapproved. Each side accused the other of breaking faith over the Potsdam agreement to treat Germany as a single economic unit (see Section 11.1(a)).

(b) Suspicion

Ideological differences inevitably became involved in the disputes. The USSR fostered communism in the Russian zone. The others discouraged it in their areas, the USA in particular arguing that communism would be less likely to make an appeal if economic recovery was rapid. The Council of Foreign Ministers reached deadlock on the question of Germany's future. Both sides paid lip service to the idea of reuniting the country but they could not agree on reparations and on the future political structure of Germany.

As early as March 1946 Churchill declared, 'From Stettin* in the Baltic to Trieste in the Adriatic, an Iron Curtain has descended upon the Continent.' To the east of this Iron Curtain lay the Russian zone of Germany and states such as Poland where communism took root. To the west lay the other zones of Germany and states which remained capitalist. Suspicion between the two sides hardened into a Cold War with an almost total lack of co-operation between them. Germany was trapped in the conflict and by 1947, it became clear that the German problem would not be solved for many years to come.

(c) Economic Conflict

Towards the end of 1946, the USA and Britain decided to merge their zones, forming one economic unit, known as the BiZone. In this area, Germans were encouraged to participate in local and regional government and to assume economic responsibilities, although recovery rested firmly on American assis-tance. The USSR protested, but in June 1948, the western zones adopted a

---

* Churchill was not accurate. He should have said Lübeck, not Stettin.

PEEP UNDER THE IRON CURTAIN

Fig. 11.3 The Daily Mail *cartoonist was quick to comment on Churchill's 'Iron Curtain' speech, 6 March 1946*

new currency, to re-establish stability. Since the end of the war, Germany had suffered from inflation. Shortages and demoralization had produced a flourishing Black Market and extensive corruption. A new start with a new currency was essential, but no agreement could be reached on a single currency for the whole of Germany. When the West German mark was introduced, the Russians replied with an East German mark for their zone.

The Cold War was by this time no longer confined merely to Germany. Political and economic divisions between the West and the communist states hardened in 1947 when the Truman Doctrine and the Marshall Plan gave clear indication that the USA intended to remain involved in Europe – a major departure from the USA's traditional isolationism. The USA was now bent on the containment of communism and of Soviet influence (see Sections 14.5 and 17.1(*a*)). The coup in Czechoslovakia in 1948 completed the consolidation of the communist bloc in Eastern Europe (see Section 12.1). The USSR too was determined to limit US influence and would not yield the areas to which communism and Soviet authority had already spread.

(*d*) Confrontation over Berlin

The new currency for the western zones produced an immediate confrontation over Berlin. In March 1948, the Russians began harassing the communications of the Western powers with their sectors of Berlin. They insisted on inspecting trains and, when an American troop-train refused to accept inspection, it was shunted into a siding, left for several days and forced to make an undignified withdrawal. On 24 June all land communications with Berlin were cut. Two million citizens in the western sectors of Berlin seemed likely to starve unless the city was handed over to the Russians.

France refused to use force. The West considered withdrawal, but that had the smell of appeasement. It was decided to ferry supplies by air, and for almost a year this was West Berlin's only source of supply. A procession of aircraft, sometimes at intervals of only twenty seconds, carried over two million tons of food, coal and all kinds of essentials into Berlin. Lives and aircraft were lost in accidents, but day and night the air-lift went on and, in May 1949, Stalin agreed to raise the blockade.

The Berlin Air-Lift was a considerable achievement but neither side gained anything from the confrontation. The USSR had not gained control of Berlin. The West had no guarantees that land communications with Berlin would not be cut again. Above all, the confrontation made both sides even more stubborn.

(*e*) Consolidation

One way that their stubbornness was shown was in the establishment of separate and independent states in Germany. In the West, a constituent assembly began work in 1948 on a new constitution for a state of Western Germany, and the Federal Republic of Germany came into existence in May 1949. It was not given complete independence until 1955 but from the beginning its independence was almost complete. Preparations in the Russian zone ran parallel to those in the West. The Democratic Republic of Germany came into existence in October 1949; that, too, gained independence in 1955 in a treaty with the Soviet Union. The Federal Republic (West Germany) had a democratic system on the Western pattern and an economy based on capitalism. The Democratic Republic (East Germany) had a system of government based on the Russian interpretation of democracy and an economy based on Marxism. Although discussions between West and East about a peace treaty for Germany continued to take place from time to time, neither side would abandon its own German state in order to bring about one, united

Fig. 11.4 The division of Berlin: 'Checkpoint Charlie' in the US Sector of West Berlin, gateway to East Berlin

German nation. (The history of East Germany is continued in Unit Twelve and the history of West Germany in Unit Fourteen.)

(f) Berlin

West Berlin continued to be occupied by the Western powers after 1949. It was given a new constitution in 1950 and in effect was self-governing. At the same time, the Federal Republic regarded it as a part of West Germany, although it was impossible to make it the capital city. With assistance from both West Germany and the Western Allies, reconstruction went on rapidly after 1949. The West was eager to make West Berlin a shop window in which to display capitalist prosperity to unsettle the communists, but it was also well-governed by a succession of mayors, among them Reuter who died in 1953 and Willy Brandt, both of them Social Democrats. Brandt later became Chancellor of West Germany.

East Berlin in the 1950s, was under a Social Unity administration, backed by the communists. In 1953, Russian tanks were needed to suppress disorders but in the 1960s extensive reconstruction was carried out and life improved for East Berlin's citizens. The area was incorporated into the German Democratic Republic in 1966.

West Berlin, in the meantime, was often used as an escape route to the West by those eager to flee from the East. After 1952, the German Democratic Republic made it almost impossible simply to cross the border which divided Germany. At the end of the 1950s, escapes by way of West Berlin were at the rate of about 200 000 a year. The numbers going in the opposite direction were a great deal smaller. In August 1961, therefore, an Iron Curtain in the shape of a concrete wall was built across Berlin. The Berlin Wall did not stop the movement but it did much to reduce it, for communist guards seldom hesitated to fire on those who attempted an illegal crossing. Thus the division of Berlin became as rigid as the division of Germany.

For thousands of individuals, such divisions were tragic but as the world moved into the second half of the twentieth century, the divisions brought a strange stability to international relations in Europe. Many, like President Kennedy of the USA, went to Berlin to peer over the Wall but ideas of using force became increasingly unpopular. For at least a generation the 'temporary' division of Germany brought a sort of peace by steering away from actually making a peace (see Section 17.2(c)).

11.3   The United Nations Organization

(a) Foundations

A succession of wartime conferences agreed that a new organization was needed to maintain international peace (see Section 10.2 and Table 10.1). In 1945, fifty nations signed the Charter of the United Nations Organization at San Francisco. With 111 articles it was a more substantial document than the Covenant of the League of Nations. Unlike the Covenant, it was independent of the peace treaties, so that UNO was not regarded by the defeated as an instrument for their punishment, although the great powers took care to preserve their own interests and influence.

The original membership of 50 states grew to double that number by 1960 and to over 150 when the island of Dominica, formerly a British colony in the West Indies, was admitted in 1978. Every state had a vote in the General Assembly regardless of its wealth and size. New states emerging from old colonial empires almost invariably hastened to seek admission to the United Nations Organization, regarding membership as a badge of independence as well as offering security and the chance to gain respect. Many, like India and the Republic of Ireland, played a significant part in UN peace-keeping operations, serving the world community. Others were less prominent but prized the right to be represented. Although Indonesia resigned in 1965 during her clash with Malaysia, she found it useful to resume membership a year later.

In its early years, the United Nations inevitably became a forum for conflict between the great powers and for the propaganda of the Cold War. The great powers sometimes blocked the admission of new members who might support their rivals. Of 31 applications submitted between 1945 and 1950 only nine were accepted. The most spectacular obstruction was that organized by the

USA to prevent the admission of communist China to the Organization. This obstruction lasted until 1971 so that China's Security-Council seat was until then occupied by Taiwan, the refuge of Chiang Kai-shek (see Section 15.2(*e*)), and communist China was not accepted into UNO until the communists had been in power for more than twenty years.

Great-power rivalries often seemed irrelevant, however, to many of their fellow-members of UNO. Taking their lead from Nehru, Prime Minister of India, and others like Tito and Nasser, many of the lesser states tried to stand aside from the East-West power blocs, and there was an attempt at Bandung in 1955 to launch a non-aligned movement (see Section 19.2(*a*)). With a flood of new admissions to the United Nations in the 1960s and 1970s, an Afro-Asian and non-aligned view began to make itself heard. The USA and other major powers were often disconcerted by this new development. The Afro-Asian countries were especially hostile to South Africa and to Israel. In 1974 the UN General Assembly voted temporarily to suspend South Africa's membership in condemnation of apartheid and of South Africa's continued hold on South-West Africa (see Section 21.2). Meanwhile a UN resolution was passed which equated Zionism with racism and the USA often found itself embarrassed by fierce Afro-Asian criticism of its Israeli ally. The great powers had thus begun to find that they could no longer easily get their own way in an association where Americans and Europeans could now be outnumbered.

On the other hand the emergent nations were by no means themselves always united. Non-alignment was never an easy path and in the late 1970s the non-aligned movement found itself in difficulties. A deep split developed between members such as Cuba who argued that non-alignment actually meant alignment with the socialist countries, chiefly the USSR, and others such as Jugoslavia who aimed to keep an equal distance from both the Soviet bloc and the US capitalist bloc. But the emergent nations shared many common economic and social problems – the problems of the Third World (see Glossary) – and in spite of their lack of unity could combine at times in criticism of the richer nations who often seemed unsympathetic to the plight of the poor. Here too the United Nations provided a forum for debate and, by the 1980s, many new interests, which had been envisaged only dimly when the Charter was approved in 1945, were represented in the General Assembly.

The Charter began with a statement of UNO's ideals. The Organization aimed 'to save succeeding generations from the scourge of war', 'to reaffirm faith in fundamental human rights', to establish respect for international law and to promote 'better standards of life in larger freedom'. These aims were similar to those of the League of Nations and the two organizations had much in common. But in framing the Charter, the founder-members of UNO hoped to avoid some of the faults of the League and to learn from past mistakes.

(*b*) UNO at Work

Fig. 2.6 and the summary of the Charter (see Section 11.5) show at first sight many similarities between UNO and the League of Nations. The General Assembly, Security Council, Secretariat and International Court of Justice gave UNO the same basic framework as the League. The UN Trusteeship Council performed a similar function to that of the earlier Mandates Commission. The work of other League committees was drawn together under a UN Economic and Social Council, although in this field the work of the United Nations was more comprehensive. Those who framed the Charter, however, made important changes in the rules under which many of these bodies worked, mainly to try to secure more effective action in times of crisis.

The *General Assembly* still operates on the basis of equality, with one vote allowed to each member. It meets annually, in September, and additional sessions can be called in times of need. The UN's budget, admissions and all matters within the scope of the Charter, indeed almost all the work of the United Nations, come under the scrutiny of the General Assembly. Much of its work is done through committees and is carried on in the five official languages of the Organization – English, Russian, French, Chinese and Spanish. The League's requirement that all decisions must be unanimous has been dropped. In some matters, a simple majority is sufficient but major decisions require a two-thirds majority.

The *Security Council* follows in the footsteps of the Council of the League of Nations. In moments of crisis, it can meet almost immediately. Apart from carrying out decisions made by the General Assembly, the Security Council's principal role is to deal with all threats to peace. Beginning with eleven members, from 1965 it has had fifteen. Since its foundation, five of these have been the victorious powers of 1945 – the USA, the USSR, Britain, France and China. (China, in 1945, was the China ruled by Chiang Kai-shek. He preserved his seat in the Security Council even when he was driven from the Chinese mainland by the communists in 1949, and kept it until 1971.) Preserving the principle of the League of Nations Council that there should be permanent seats and elected seats, the five great powers were careful to make their places in the Security Council permanent ones. The other members are elected for two-year terms by the General Assembly.

Two problems were fundamental in setting up the Security Council. The first concerned the rights of the great powers. At first, a decision required seven votes. It now requires nine. But, in all matters of importance, the great powers must be among those giving approval. This means that the USA, the USSR, Britain, France and China keep, in effect, the right of veto. This right they have used not infrequently, particularly the Soviet Union.

The second problem concerned the powers of the Security Council to act effectively. It has been given the right to call on members to apply *sanctions* (usually economic) against offending states and also, when necessary, to request them to provide armed forces. These operate as the forces of the United Nations. Until the Security Council takes action, states retain the right to act singly or together in their own self-defence. The Security Council's authority has not been greatly extended compared with the powers of the

Council of the League of Nations. Forces have been assembled by the United Nations to deal with a number of crises, in the Middle East (see Section 19.1), Korea (see Section 17.1(c)), the Congo (see Section 20.2) and Cyprus (see Section 20.4) for example. But there is still no standing army; and it is often difficult to collect a United Nations force. The Big Five may also use their right of veto to prevent any attempt to raise a force if they so wish.

But it is sometimes suggested this right of veto may no longer exist. In 1950, the General Assembly passed a 'Uniting for Peace' resolution, which claimed that if the Security Council, through lack of agreement among its permanent members, failed to act effectively to maintain peace, the General Assembly could do so even to the extent of recommending the use of armed forces. The Charter was not amended and it remains open to dispute whether a two-thirds majority in the General Assembly could over-rule a veto in the Security Council.

The *Secretariat* operates in a similar way to that of the League. The Secretary-General is recommended by the Security Council and appointed by the General Assembly for a term of five years, during which time he controls the Secretariat and may bring before the Security Council matters which threaten peace. Differences among the great powers have sometimes led to difficulties in choosing a Secretary-General. But all the Secretaries-General have been chosen from the lesser powers. They have been men of ability, dedicated to the Organization. Trygve Lie, a Norwegian, served from 1946 until his resignation in 1952. His successor, Dag Hammarskjöld, who served until killed in an aeroplane crash in 1961 while seeking a solution to the crisis in the Congo, came from Sweden. U Thant of Burma then gave ten years of dedicated service but refused to continue in the office after 1971 and was replaced by Kurt Waldheim of Austria. Waldheim's influence, Austria's geographical position and the country's neutral role after the State Treaty of 1955 combined to make Vienna increasingly important as a centre for UN activities and international negotiation. At the end of 1981, however, with China persistently vetoing the reappointment of Waldheim (a European), Javier Perez de Cuellar (a Peruvian) was elected the new UN Secretary-General.

The *International Court of Justice* sits at the Hague, its traditional home, and not at the UN headquarters in New York. Its fifteen judges are chosen jointly by the Security Council and the General Assembly, a third of them retiring every three years. Its functions are similar to those of the Permanent Court it replaced, and nations agree in advance to accept its findings. Some nations have expressed reservations about this. Britain, for example, excludes from the Court's jurisdiction disputes with members of the Commonwealth.

The *Trusteeship Council* continues the work of the Mandates Commission in preparing colonial states for independence. But so usefully did the Council carry out its work that little remained to be done in the 1980s. When it began its work, the Council made new trusteeship arrangements with the states which still had charge of mandates, and with the USA, which took charge of the mandates that had been held by Japan. Most of the trust territories moved smoothly to independence, among them Papua New Guinea which received independence from Australia in 1975.

One mandated territory was less fortunate. South Africa refused to enter into a trusteeship agreement for what had once been German South-West Africa, refusing at the same time to concede South-West Africa's independence. When the International Court of Justice in 1950 ruled that she was still accountable for the territory to the UN, South Africa took no notice. The United Nations recognized the African name, Namibia, for South-West Africa, and considered it a just cause in 1971 for SWAPO (South-West African People's Organization) to struggle for Namibia's liberation. But it was more difficult to wrest Namibia from South Africa's grip. Inside Namibia, resentment led to strikes and extensive disorders, especially among the Ovambo people. At the United Nations, however, major powers such as Britain obstructed effective action against South Africa and so the problem dragged on. It seemed to Africans that the whites made a point of sticking together, and it was not until the later 1970s that South Africa began even to consider making concessions (see Section 21.2(c)).

The *Economic and Social Council* whose twenty-seven members are elected by the General Assembly, a third of them retiring each year, supervises the Organization's work in economic, social, educational and similar fields. The Council has established Commissions to deal with matters as varied as trade, drugs, population and the status of women. It has set up regional Economic Commissions in areas such as Africa and Latin America. It also co-ordinates the work of the *Specialized Agencies* of the United Nations whose activities and names, frequently reduced to initials, combine into a bewildering but vitally important pattern of effort to improve the lot of mankind. The International Labour Organization continues to be one of these Specialized Agencies, operating along the same lines as at the time of the League of Nations (see page 33). Its headquarters remain in Geneva. Other Specialized Agencies were also inherited by UNO from the League but many more were newly created after 1945. Among the new bodies was WHO (the World Health Organization), set up in 1948, to combat disease and to promote co-operation and knowledge in matters of health. WHO spends some 40 million dollars a year in this work.

There are Specialized Agencies for various types of communication. These include the Universal Postal Union, the International Telecommunication Union and the International Civil Aviation Organization (UPU, ITU and ICAO). Economic co-operation is encouraged by the International Trade Organization (ITO) and the Food and Agricultural Organization (FAO). Financial matters may be dealt with by the International Bank and the International Monetary Fund (IMF) (see Section 10.6(c)) and, since 1956, by the International Finance Corporation (IFC) which was established by the International Bank to encourage investment and development. The United Nations Educational, Scientific and Cultural Organization (UNESCO) came into existence in 1946 to wage war against illiteracy and to further the projects which are associated with its name. In the same year, the United Nations International Children's Emergency Fund (UNICEF) began. It is now concerned mainly with the welfare of children in underdeveloped countries although its first duties were to assist children in countries torn by war. In 1965, UNICEF won the Nobel Peace Prize. But even this catalogue by no means completes the list of UN Specialized Agencies, to which thousands devote their services and which draw support from scores of nations. In recent years newly emerging needs have increased UN activities. The United Nations Conference on Trade and Development (UNCTAD) was set up in 1964 chiefly to promote trade which would be helpful to developing nations. The World Food Council was a new Specialized Agency set up in the late 1970s to tackle the problem of feeding the world's rapidly growing population, especially in the poorer areas.

Fig. 11.5 A United Nations stamp of 1955 with the symbol of UNESCO and the Organization's five official languages

(c) Keeping the Peace

The United Nations Organization has undoubtedly accomplished much in its non-political work. It has also been more active than the League of Nations in dealing with international crises. Yet its achievements have often been disappointing. Like the League, UNO has made little headway in trying to bring about disarmament; and, like the League, it has been caught up in the rivalries of the powers and sometimes prevented from taking effective action. It has often proved unable to solve even comparatively minor problems such as the Indo-Pakistani dispute over Kashmir or Britain's conflict with Argentina in 1982 over the Falkland Islands. What must be remembered, however, is that the success or failure of the United Nations is the success or failure of its members. The UN seeks to create and represent the collective will of the world's nations; but it cannot be effective when that collective will does not exist. When the UN may be said to 'fail', therefore, the 'failure' is that of the nations themselves, lacking the determination, unity and collective strength to achieve 'success'.

All powers, great and small, resent interference in their interests, jealously excluding UNO from affairs they consider 'domestic'. Thus Britain argues that the affairs of Northern Ireland are of no concern to the United Nations and the outside world, and at times took a similar stance on issues in Rhodesia. Nigeria maintained that the struggle over Biafra was a civil war and a purely domestic matter. The USA takes a similar view of racial conflicts within her boundaries. But the great powers also tend to regard their spheres of influence as 'domestic', the problems there of no concern to UNO. The USSR asserted this view when suppressing the uprising in Hungary in 1956 and that in Czechoslovakia in 1968, and when intervening in Afghanistan at the end of the 1970s. The USA keeps its own watch on the affairs of the American continent, denouncing all outside interference. Although the UN asserts an international concern for human rights which should in theory over-ride the sovereign rights of individual members, in practice international concern is often thwarted. Only occasionally is UNO allowed a role in internal crises as it was in the Congo in 1960. Like the League of Nations, the UN has also sometimes been only a mere bystander in times of international crisis, its members preferring to settle their affairs away from the Security Council. One example of this was the Cuban Missiles Crisis (see Section 17.1(e)). Moreover, over a longer period of time, the United Nations could find little to contribute to settling the conflict in Vietnam (see Section 17.1(d)).

As long as self-interest continues to govern the policies of the nations, the struggle for world peace and for the authority of UNO must be long and arduous, wearing down those who, like U Thant, become exhausted in the service of international co-operation. UNO has, however, already survived longer than the League of Nations, and although it may often achieve less than optimists expect, it is by no means totally ineffective. Its headquarters in New York provides a permanent forum for the exchange of ideas among almost all the nations in the world.

11.4   No Peace After the Second World War

The end of the Second World War opened a new phase in world history of which the peace-making and the reconstruction of Europe and Japan were only parts. Upheavals had not been uncommon after the First World War and upheavals were to be expected after the Second. The world of the twentieth century was one of rapid and often startling change which accelerated as the century went on. It was no longer a world dominated by Europeans, and the Munich Conference of 1938 was one of the last where European statesmen sought to solve major international crises in isolation. The postwar world seemed for a time to be dominated by the superpowers whose conflicts were certainly dramatic. But the Units which follow will show that, alongside the manoeuvrings of the superpowers, new issues were already in the making and turbulence was worldwide. The USA and the USSR found their relations complicated by the emergence of communist China. And to the East–West struggle between capitalism and communism was added a new and potentially more significant problem – that of the relationships between North and South, between the rich and mainly white areas of the world and the non-white and mainly poor countries of the southern hemisphere.

11.5   Appendix

Summary of the Charter of the United Nations Organization, 26 June 1945

Chapter 1 (Articles 1–2): A statement of purposes and principles

Chapter 2 (Articles 3–6): Membership and expulsion

Chapters 3–5 (Articles 7–32): The machinery of UNO. The composition and duties of the General Assembly and Security Council

Chapters 6–7 (Articles 33–51): Procedure for the peaceful settlement of disputes by arbitration or for action against aggression. Articles 43 to 49 concern the procedure for raising armed forces when the Security Council considers it necessary, acting with the advice of a Military Staff Committee

Chapter 8 (Articles 52–4): Regional arrangements permitted if consistent with the aims of UNO

Chapters 9–10 (Articles 55–72): The organization of UNO's work in economic and social co-operation: the Economic and Social Council

Chapters 11–13 (Articles 73–91): Members undertaking the administration of territories not yet self-governing agree to regard as paramount 'the interests of the inhabitants of these territories' and to recognize the well-being of these peoples as 'a sacred trust'. In certain cases, 'trust territories' may be set up under the supervision of the Trusteeship Council

Chapter 14 (Articles 92–6): The International Court of Justice as 'the principal judicial organ of the United Nations'

Chapter 15 (Articles 97–101): The Secretariat in which the aim is to secure 'the highest standards of efficiency, competence and integrity'

Chapter 16 (Articles 102–5): Miscellaneous Provisions, amongst them an undertaking to make all agreements public

Chapters 17–19 (Articles 106–11): Transitional Arrangements until the Charter came into force and procedure for amending the Charter.

Further Reading

Childs, D.: *Germany since 1918*. Batsford (London, 1980) – Chapter 6.

Cowie, L.W.: *The Super Powers*. Nelson (London, 1971).

Dukes, P.: *The Emergence of the Super Powers*. Macmillan (London, 1970).

Gibbons, S.R. and Morican, P.: *The League of Nations and UNO*. Longman (Harlow, 1970).

Morgan, R.: *Modern Germany*. Hamish Hamilton (London, 1966).

Nicholas, H.G.: *The U.N. as a Political Institution*. Oxford University Press (London, 1967).

Documentary

Breach, R.W.: *Documents and Descriptions, the World since 1914*. Oxford University Press (London, 1966) – Sections 8a, 15c and 46.

Challener, R.D.: *From Isolation to Containment, 1921–1952*. Arnold (London, 1970).

Morgan, R.: *The Unsettled Peace*. British Broadcasting Corporation (London, 1974).

Exercises

1. Using Figs. 11.1 and 11.2, explain the territorial changes in Europe which resulted from the Second World War.

2. Use the text of the Potsdam Declaration (L.L. Snyder, *Fifty Major Documents of the Twentieth Century* (Anvil, 1955) pages 111–18) to write a more detailed account of what Stalin, Truman and Attlee agreed at Potsdam in 1945.
3. What was the *German Problem* after 1945? Why had it not been solved by 1955?
4. Show how the United Nations Organization (*a*) resembled and (*b*) differed from the League of Nations according to Fig. 2.6. To what further similarities and differences is it possible to refer?
5. In what ways did four-power occupation affect the lives of the people of Berlin? What is meant on page 189 by the phrase 'a shop window in which to display capitalist prosperity'?
6. How did the aims and methods of the peace-makers after the Second World War differ from those of the peace-makers after the First World War?
7. Use the Index to this book (*United Nations Organization*) to write accounts of (*a*) UN peace-keeping operations, and (*b*) other UN mediation.
8. Study this extract from a speech in September 1946 by the US Secretary of State, James Byrnes, and then answer the questions which follow:

> More than a year has passed since hostilities ceased. The millions of German people should not be forced to live in doubt as to their fate. It is the view of the American Government that the Allies should, without delay, make clear to the German people the essential terms of the peace settlement which they expect the German people to accept and observe. It is our view that the German people should now be permitted and helped to make the necessary preparations for the setting up of a democratic German government. . . .
>
> Security forces will probably have to remain in Germany for a long period. I want no misunderstanding. We will not shirk our duty. We are not withdrawing. We are staying here.

(*a*) What *hostilities* did Byrnes refer to in the first sentence of this extract? Why should there be *doubt* about the German people's *fate*?
(*b*) Name the head of the *American Government* at this time and the political party to which he and Byrne belonged.
(*c*) Which of the *Allies* most strongly supported the views expressed in this extract?
(*d*) Explain the likely attitudes of France to (i) the proposal Byrnes made about *German government*, and (ii) the declaration Byrnes made in the second paragraph.
(*e*) By what US economic device were Germans *helped* in the year after Byrnes made this speech? What *democratic German government* of which Byrnes would have approved was then set up in 1949?
(*f*) What importance do you attach to the final sentence in this extract?

Unit Twelve
Soviet Russia and the European Communist Bloc

12.1 The Communist Bloc

The Russian Red Army advanced over 1 500 miles from Stalingrad to the centre of Germany in the closing years of the war. It also penetrated deep into the Balkans. Stalin intended to establish regimes sympathetic to the Soviet Union in the countries of defeated enemies (Rumania, Bulgaria, Hungary and East Germany) and of liberated Allies (Poland, Czechoslovakia, Jugoslavia and Albania). Communists were already strong in many of these countries, where they were respected for their resistance to Nazism and popular among those accustomed to poverty. Stalin set out to create communist governments obedient to the wishes of Moscow from left-wing coalitions and Popular Fronts. The West called these countries 'Russian satellites', and Churchill called the division between them and the West an 'Iron Curtain' (see Fig. 11.2).

In return for political obedience, the satellites got Russian aid (although in the early stages the USSR was intent on collecting reparations from her former enemies). Some states, such as *Albania*, turned readily to communism because they had little to gain by a return to the old form of government. In *Bulgaria*, a left-wing coalition of the Fatherland Front deposed the monarchy and won a general election. The communists then turned on their allies within the Front, hanged the Agrarian leader and, a year later, purged the Social Democrats. The Fatherland Front thus followed in the footsteps of Lenin, allowing almost no opposition.

A similar left-wing coalition abolished the monarchy in *Rumania* in 1947. Within the Popular Democratic Front, the communists took longer to establish total supremacy than in Bulgaria but they were always dominant in the country after 1945 when their leader became Prime Minister.

Hungary, too, put up some opposition to total communist domination. The communists became the largest single party in the elections of 1947 although they ruled in a coalition People's Independence Front. This had followed the Russian example of 1918 in giving land to the peasants and nationalizing major industries. Gradually, opposition was eliminated. Agriculture was collectivized and an attack launched against the powerful Roman Catholic Church.

In *Poland*, the communists were handicapped at first because rival governments had developed during the war. There was a communist one and one in exile in the West under Mikolajczyk. A provisional arrangement merged the two together in 1945 but, in 1947, Mikolajczyk fled, fearing arrest. Poland was then ruled by a coalition of Workers' and Peasants' parties, effectively under communist control and led by Gomulka until his dismissal at the end of 1948.

In *East Germany* where the German Democratic Republic was created in 1949 (see Section 11.2(*e*)), there was a similar communist-controlled coalition under Grotewohl. Postwar hardships, shortages, the division of Germany and the suppression of opposition led to rioting in 1953. This affected both the Democratic Republic and East Berlin, but was put down by Russian troops. The regime then remained loyal to the Soviet Union under the influence of Grotewohl and Ulbricht, Secretary of the Socialist Unity Party and Deputy Prime Minister. Many citizens still tried to escape to the West, however, and in near desperation it was thought necessary to build the Berlin Wall in 1961 (see Section 11.2(*f*)).

Although the USSR abandoned eastern Austria in 1955 and made no attempt to impose communism on Finland, similar concessions were not made to *Czechoslovakia*. President Beneš returned from exile in 1945 hoping for a democratic system of government. The first postwar government was a coalition of left-wing parties and, in 1946, the communists won the largest number of parliamentary seats with 38 per cent of the votes. They set up a National Front government under Gottwald. But 1947 was a year of shortages and there were protests when, on Soviet instructions, Gottwald rejected Marshall Aid (see Section 14.5(*a*)). A constitutional crisis resulted but the communists found sufficient allies to stage a coup, and to remain in power with a communist-dominated National Front. Opposition candidates were not allowed to stand in the election of 1948 and President Beneš resigned. Jan Masaryk, the Czech Foreign Minister and son of Tómaš Masaryk, President before Beneš, was found dead in strange circumstances, having apparently fallen from an open window.

At the end of the war, Russia had incorporated the Baltic provinces of Estonia, Latvia, and Lithuania into the Soviet Union. Except in Scandinavia, Austria and Greece, the communists were in control in every state in Eastern Europe by about 1950. But one communist state refused to accept dictation from Moscow. In *Jugoslavia*, Marshal Tito was elected President of the new republic by a large majority in 1945. Tito had won prestige as Jugoslavia's wartime resistance leader. He was a convinced communist but he was also determined to apply Marxist principles in Jugoslavia in his own way. He was unwilling to collectivize agriculture, preferring peasant smallholdings, and would not tolerate Russian agents within the Jugoslav Communist Party although he did make economic and military agreements with the Soviet Union. Such independence was not encouraged in Moscow and, in 1948, Jugoslavia was expelled from the *Cominform* (the Communist Information Bureau through which Stalin exercised Russian influence over communists in many countries). Tito was not intimidated. He stuck to his independent path and, while not deviating from his communist principles, made contacts with

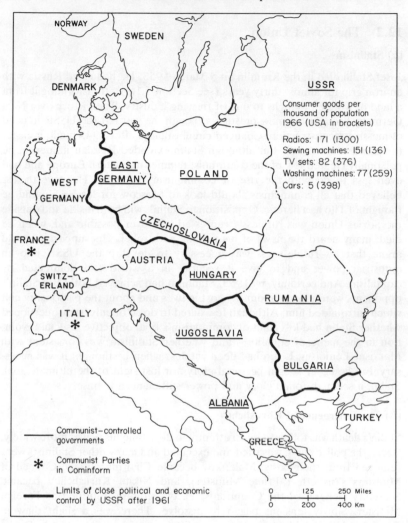

Fig. 12.1 The European communist bloc

non-communist powers which would be beneficial to Jugoslavia. He received loans from the International Monetary Fund and later showed considerable interest in associating Jugoslavia with the Afro-Asian bloc in the United Nations. After Stalin's death the Soviet Union became reconciled to Tito's independent attitude.

12.2   The Soviet Union

(a) Stalinism

Josef Stalin died in the Kremlin on 5 March 1953. He had ruled Russia with an iron grip for almost thirty years (see Section 5.1(c)), transforming it from a land of wooden ploughs to one of thriving industry. The victory over Nazi Germany brought him new prestige although the war left the USSR in need of massive reconstruction. Changed circumstances after 1945 made it easier to spread communism: but although Stalin extended Russian influence, he personally created few of the communist regimes in Eastern Europe and had even less to do with the rise of communism in China. He nevertheless believed that all communists should look to Moscow for leadership and he thought of Tito as a heretic. Opposition to Stalin's will both inside and outside the Soviet Union was ruthlessly repressed wherever possible and, when he died, many heard the news of his passing with relief. His supporters could argue that his ruthlessness was necessary to develop the USSR into an industrial power and to give it security in a world still dominated by capitalism. And certainly, by 1953, Stalinism had achieved both. But Stalin's opponents were uneasy about the cost in lives and about the personality cult which surrounded him. Although few dared to do so openly, they questioned whether Stalin had lost sight of communism's final objective – social revolution in the name of equality – and whether Stalinism was consistent with Marxism–Leninism. Lenin had been ruthless when he thought it was necessary, but he never sought personal glory nor lost sight of the ultimate goal. Stalin, it seemed, found glory and power sufficient in themselves.

(b) The Emergence of Khrushchev

Stalin's death was followed by an attempt to distribute his power more widely. Beria, the police chief, was tried and executed and many other Stalinists were removed from their posts. Malenkov became Chairman of the Council of Ministers* (in effect Prime Minister), and Nikita Khrushchev became Secretary-General of the Communist Party. Molotov returned as Foreign Minister. Slowly tensions began to dissolve. There was a slight thaw in Russia's relations with foreign powers, a little more freedom within the Soviet Union and some attention to the production of consumer goods to improve living standards.

But intrigue within the party was already tilting the system towards Khrushchev. In 1955, Malenkov was replaced by Bulganin, who was perhaps more agreeable to Khrushchev. Russia's leaders continued to show a greater interest than Stalin in the non-communist world but, internally, the emphasis shifted back to heavy industry and conformity. Russia's basic policies did not

---

* Council of People's Commissars until 1946.

change much even though Bulganin and Khrushchev visited Britain in 1956 and received both the French and Tito in Moscow.

Yet one event in 1956 was remarkable. At the Twentieth Russian Communist Party Congress, Khrushchev felt sufficient confidence in his own position to make a spirited attack on Stalin's reputation. The attack had three effects. First, it blackened Stalin's name and caused confusion over what to teach Russian children about the Stalinist period. Stalin now stood accused of abusing his powers, persecuting loyal communists, failing to prepare for the war and making strategical blunders. Second, it created confusion in the satellite states and helped to produce risings in Poland and Hungary. Third, it contributed to Khrushchev's growing influence within the Soviet system.

Khrushchev was criticized by Malenkov and Molotov but Zhukov and the army leaders rallied to the Secretary-General's defence. Malenkov and Molotov were expelled from the party leadership. Zhukov, however, was discredited shortly afterwards and replaced as Minister of Defence by Marshal Malinovsky. Although disgrace now served as a substitute for execution, Khrushchev was nevertheless steadily pursuing Stalinist tactics by removing rivals from power. He pushed aside Bulganin, relegating him to the office of Chairman of the State Bank and, in 1958, added to his own appointment of Secretary-General of the party that of Prime Minister. Stalin's body had meanwhile been reburied in a less honoured spot, outside the Kremlin. Even the risings in Poland and Hungary did little, in the short term, to check the progress of the man who threatened to become Russia's new Stalin having, at the Twentieth Party Congress, so dramatically denounced the old.

(c) The Khrushchev Era

Tubby Nikita Khrushchev seemed almost jovial in comparison with other Russian leaders. He was the son of a mine-worker and had a long record of service to the party. He was 64 when he became Prime Minister. He had fought in the Red Army during the Civil War, worked for the party organization in the Moscow area, won the Order of Lenin for his services to the building of Moscow's underground railway and advanced slowly throughout the Stalinist period. He did not secure a major appointment until 1949, when he took charge of Russian agriculture. When he denounced Stalin, seven years later, he carefully exonerated himself and others like him from responsibility for the purges and the blunders. He won a certain admiration in the West, although he was unpredictable and once startled the United Nations by banging the table with his shoe. He kept a firm grip on the Soviet Union until deprived of his offices in 1964.

In 1956, Khrushchev could inform the Russian people that the Soviet Union was at last 'in a position to promote rapidly the production of both the means of production and of consumer goods'. This was the base which Stalin had achieved while paying attention at the same time to progress in such fundamentals as education and health services. After all their sacrifices, it now seemed possible that the Russian people could begin to enjoy the luxuries of shorter hours, more consumer goods and improved housing, although output was still carefully regulated by Plans. In 1961, longer-term objectives were laid down, declaring that socialism had now been achieved in Russia and that economic progress by 1980 would mean the country was closer to the full achievement of communism.

Russian achievements continued to be impressive: in 1957, the Soviet Union launched Sputnik 1, the first man-made satellite to orbit the earth in space. Two years later, a Russian space vehicle took photographs of the far side of the moon and, in 1961, Yuri Gagarin was the first man to travel round the earth in space in Vostok 1. Such space ventures were expensive but Khrushchev could rightly boast that they put Russia's technological mastery beyond dispute.

Khrushchev tried to achieve greater efficiency in industrial organization by dismantling much of the centralized management of Stalin's days in favour of regional authorities, the People's Economic Councils. But difficulties still remained.

Khrushchev also wished to achieve better returns from Soviet agriculture which still lagged behind the most advanced farming in the world. Again, he favoured regional control rather than centralized direction from Moscow. Stalin had achieved total collectivization originally in some 250 000 units, which Khrushchev had by 1953 reduced to about 100 000 larger units (see Section 5.1(c)). Some of these larger units were now merged and Khrushchev toyed with the idea of *agrogoroda*, agricultural cities where the workers on the *kolkhozy* might live. In the meantime he abolished the Machine Tractor Stations, too readily assuming that the enlarged collective farms would have enough machinery of their own. Alongside the collectives, official encouragement was still given to state farms, *sovkhozy*, but with limited results. The peasants still preferred collectives where they could also cultivate private plots and were not direct employees of the state. They welcomed Khrushchev's relaxations of restrictions on private plots as well as his reduction of tax burdens on the peasantry.

Khrushchev's most ambitious agricultural exercise was the *Virgin Lands Project*. In 1954 he started the ploughing of many of the infertile lands of central Russia, particularly areas of Siberia. By 1962, 145 million acres had been reclaimed and hundreds of thousands of Russians were recruited to work on them, mainly in sovkhozy, encouraged by tax concessions. But increased production could do no more than keep pace with the expansion of Russia's population. Results were disappointing, for the climate and the nature of the soil made progress difficult, and agriculture in general continued to be handicapped by peasant hostility to the communist system. Khrushchev's successors tried to place the blame for the disappointing results on him but his principal fault was no more than over-optimism.

Russian society during Khrushchev's years in power began to change. Writers like Pasternak and Solzhenitsyn and composers like Shostakovich became increasingly fretful about censorship and restrictions. Western influences were more difficult to keep out. Modern art began to find a place alongside the People's Art, which glorified the people's struggle for socialism. Russians began to show an interest in Western fashion and pop music. There was more lawlessness and even hooliganism. Khrushchev travelled extensively and Russians inevitably became more interested in the outside world. Tourists were now cautiously admitted to Russia. The Government continued to practise censorship and to defend the system with propaganda and a rigorous code of law, supported by capital punishment which was extended in 1962 to cover bribery, but the brutality of Stalinist tyranny in the USSR was now much reduced.

Khrushchev also made changes in Soviet foreign policy. He advocated a policy of 'peaceful coexistence' with the West (see Section 17.2). That helped to sharpen the developing conflict between the USSR and communist China, and relations became strained between Khrushchev and Mao Tse-tung (see Section 15.3(c)). But, although the Soviet leader encouraged a thaw in the East–West Cold War, there were still clashes, the USSR coming near to military confrontation with the USA over Cuba before Khrushchev showed the good sense to back down (see Section 17.1(e)). Like all Soviet leaders since 1945, however, Khrushchev would permit no weakening of the communist bloc in Eastern Europe and no Western interference there. He was criticized by colleagues for an external policy which overall seemed to hover between caution and recklessness, compromise and ruthlessness. Khrushchev could be a Dove and a Hawk almost simultaneously.

Fig. 12.2 Khrushchev and Mao Tse-tung, apparently communist allies. But relations were already strained when this photograph was taken in 1959

(d) The Fall of Khrushchev

In 1964 the Conservatives lost the British general election and Alec Douglas-Home ceased to be Prime Minister. At almost the same instant, Khrushchev ceased to be the leader of the Soviet Union. Khrushchev fell not as the result of a general election but through the censure of the Communist Party's Central Committee. Age and ill-health were at first put forward to explain his sudden dismissal. Later, the charges were stated more precisely and Khrushchev was accused of reviving the Stalinist personality cult and making blunders. His quarrels with China and humiliation over Cuba, his mistakes in economic management and over-concentration on consumer goods were held to be sufficient for his forced retirement, both from the office of Prime Minister and from that of Secretary-General of the party. His retirement was quietly obscure and he died in 1971.

(e) The Triumvirate

When Khrushchev fell there was another attempt, like that at Stalin's death, to distribute power more widely. Again, however, the office of Secretary-General of the Communist Party was the key one. It passed to Leonid Brezhnev, comparatively young at 58 but a zealous servant of the Party for the last twenty years. Kosygin, the new Prime Minister, and Podgorny, Chairman of the Presidium of the Supreme Soviet, had given similar long service. Their Triumvirate lasted until Podgorny resigned in 1977 and Kosygin died three years later. Brezhnev survived them and it had already become clear that it was he who had inherited the mantle of Lenin, Stalin and Khrushchev. A new Soviet constitution was drafted in 1977 to replace that of 1936 but it made no fundamental changes in the country's system of government. Unlike earlier constitutions it did, however, identify the key role of the Communist Party; and it defined the USSR as a 'socialist state of the whole people'.

(f) The Brezhnev Era

The Triumvirate made no dramatic changes in the policies pursued by Khrushchev, though the People's Economic Councils were wound up in 1965 in favour of a return to centralized management. The problem still was how best to manage a planned economy. There were adjustments to the balance between the manufacture of consumer goods and other forms of production, with the former continuing to expand only slowly. A disastrous grain harvest in 1975 again underlined the weaknesses of Soviet agriculture, leading to a new Plan for increased investment and more effective organization. During the 1970s, the USSR and Eastern Europe generally increased their trade with the West, and imports of grain helped the Soviet Union through its difficulties. Although isolated to some extent from the world's economic problems in the 1970s and 1980s, the USSR was not entirely unaffected. International problems in obtaining oil, for example, led to Soviet efforts to increase production in Russia to supply both domestic needs and those of the USSR's allies, some of whom, like Cuba, continued to receive Soviet oil at reduced prices. It was still vigorously asserted that economic management was a superior system to that of free enterprise, but 'socialist competition' continued to be a feature of the Soviet economy, with new incentives introduced in 1977 to encourage higher levels of production.

In Brezhnev's later years, outside attention began to focus sharply on the question of civil liberties in the Soviet Union. There had been fewer denunciations of Stalin in the USSR after the fall of Khrushchev. There had been no return to Stalinist tyranny but, equally, Brezhnev seemed to have no enthusiasm for further liberalization. The USSR nevertheless signed an agreement in 1975 at the Conference on Security and Co-operation in Europe, promising 'respect for human rights and fundamental freedoms' (see Section 17.2(c)). President Carter of the USA then appointed himself spokesman for those in the Soviet bloc termed Dissidents, whose human rights were not respected. One result was a check to developing East–West trade links, the Americans sometimes withholding grain in protest at the Soviet repression of liberties. Another was a running commentary, inside and outside the communist bloc, on the heavy-handedness of Brezhnev's government. The Dissidents criticized communist authorities. Many were harassed and some were tried and imprisoned for activities the authorities considered seditious. Western interest made it possible for the Soviet authorities to dub the Dissidents as capitalist lackeys, and Carter's apparent concern perhaps did more to embitter than to ease the situation. The West could nevertheless sometimes give some help to the Dissidents – for example, in 1976, securing for Vladimir Bukovsky the right to leave the Soviet Union. Other Dissidents stayed to continue their fight for greater freedom, among them the noted Soviet physicist Andrei Sakharov and, in Czechoslovakia, members of the civil-rights group founded in 1977, known as Charter '77.

Like Khrushchev, Brezhnev could be both a Dove and a Hawk in foreign policy. Soviet leaders continued to travel and to make peaceful agreements. In 1967 Kosygin visited Britain and the USA. In 1968 and subsequent years, efforts were made to limit the arms race (see Section 17.2(b)). More Western visitors were welcomed in Moscow, among them President Nixon in 1972. By 1976, Brezhnev was seeking further improvement in the USSR's relations with Yugoslavia. There were also spasmodic attempts to bridge the gulf between the USSR and China but with little success. At the same time, however, Soviet policy bore traces of the adventurism Khrushchev had shown in placing missiles in Cuba. Brezhnev much increased Soviet influence in Africa, especially in Angola (see Section 16.5) and Ethiopia (see Section 19.3). In December 1979 Soviet troops also invaded Afghanistan, triggering a new international crisis (see Section 17.2(d)). US–Soviet relations steadily deteriorated during the later 1970s, giving rise to fears that a new Cold War was beginning.

There were fewer uncertainties about Soviet policy in Eastern Europe. Soviet forces were used by Brezhnev to suppress dissent in Czechoslovakia in 1968, much as they had been used by Khrushchev in Hungary in 1956 (see Section 12.4). In the Brezhnev Doctrine, the Soviet leader proclaimed the right of socialist states to intervene where an established socialist system was in danger of being overthrown. Changes were taking place in Eastern Europe, but Brezhnev was as determined as his predecessors that the Eastern European bloc should remain intact.

(g) The End of the Brezhnev Era

The rule of Leonid Brezhnev came to an end when he died in November 1982, after several years of failing health. Almost at once, Yuri Andropov replaced him as the leader of the Soviet Communist Party, seemingly an indication of the movement of power within the Kremlin. Andropov had been head of the KGB from 1967 to early 1982 and thus, for most of the Brezhnev era, responsible for internal security in the Soviet Union. At 68 years of age, however, it seemed unlikely that Andropov would match Brezhnev's eighteen years in power. On the other hand, he was a comparatively 'new' man, having joined the Central Committee in 1951 only a short time before the death of Stalin. The Soviet Union was now beginning to pass to a new generation of leaders.

(h) Is the Soviet Union a Communist Country?

Nearly 70 years after the Bolshevik Revolution of 1917, the Soviet Union is still trying to apply the principles laid down in the writings of Marx and Lenin and to achieve 'communism' (see Section 5.1). The West has long used the phrase 'communist Russia', but the Soviet constitution of 1977 described the USSR as a *socialist* state. The Marxist historian Isaac Deutscher had often argued that the Revolution of 1917 was only the beginning of the journey to communism. Lenin too had accepted that a transitional phase was needed before communism was achieved. But neither *socialist* nor *communist* is a word for which it is possible to arrive at an agreed definition. To call the USSR a 'communist' country may be convenient but its exact meaning can be debated.

The Soviet Union is certainly a one-party state. Political activity takes place only within the Communist Party, where long service brings rewards, as it did for Khrushchev, Brezhnev and Kosygin. Russians argue that this is a democratic system: there is room for discussion within the Party. But the Party also has a tradition of obedience to decisions once they have been made, and argument, of course, can only be about the interpretation of Marxism–Leninism. There is no room for alternatives, and the gap between a loyal Soviet citizen and a Dissident may well be determined merely by adherence to whatever happens for the time being to be the party-line, the government's official policy.

A central feature of the system is the devotion to economic planning. Nothing important is left to private enterprise. All economic activities, through state-owned agencies and agricultural collectives, are carried on for the benefit of the nation. This requires a considerable bureaucracy (civil service) and decisions on priorities inevitably curtail the individual's freedom of choice. But this system also eliminates unemployment and it is possible to give priority to welfare services, especially the health service, to public transport, power stations and education. Differential payments, privileges and incentives remain – part of the difference, it is argued, between socialism and communism.

Outside the communist states, it is sometimes thought that communism means only repression, censorship, propaganda and the state control of work in schools. Communists think these devices are necessary to complete the transformation of their society. The Communist Party has brought enormous improvements to the Russian people but it also brought them much grief, especially in the days of Stalin. Cynics may argue that it can never bring the free and equal society at which Marxism–Leninism aims. The Russians themselves earlier named the 1980s as their goal for this achievement.

Meanwhile, priorities are often different from those in the West. In Volgograd (formerly Stalingrad) state apartments were being built in the early 1970s at the rate of 10 000 a year to be let at a very low rent. Few private houses existed, private building being forbidden. As in other towns the citizens of Volgograd received free medical services almost without parallel in other countries. Through their trade unions, the workers received benefits ranging from cheap holidays and day-nurseries for their children to pensions at the ages of 50, 55 or 60 according to the rigours of their work. Minimum wages were laid down by law and as early as 1922 workers had been protected and their rights guaranteed by a comprehensive Labour Code. Education was free, all fees having been abolished in the flood of reforms introduced by Khrushchev. There was education for all to the age of 15 and a wide range of opportunities for further education beyond that point. In addition to television, Russians enjoyed and supported a wide range of cultural entertainments. In the shops, the number of consumer goods increased steadily and the ownership of washing machines, refrigerators, television sets and even cars was growing slowly. There were still, however, formidable waiting lists, especially for cars.

These were the state's priorities with which the majority of Russians seemed content. The aim was to raise the living standards of the *whole* population. Russians were free to grumble about poor workmanship, shortages and queues but they were not free to try to undermine the basic system. Only within the Communist Party was it possible to work for change and even there many decisions could not be questioned. The Committee of State Security (the KGB), the latest of a long line of special police forces which began with the Cheka, kept open a watchful eye for sedition. But the days of Stalinist terror had passed. Many restrictions remained and seemed likely to remain for some time longer but the Marxist experiment, begun in 1917, was continuing.

The outcome of the experiment still remained in doubt. In some, it roused hatred and fear. Among communists, there was controversy about the best means by which to arrive at their goal. By the 1980s, other nations had followed the example of Tito in arguing that there could be different paths to communism. While the Soviet Union travelled along one road, other states like China, Jugoslavia, Cuba and Angola, developed their own routes and, even in the communist bloc in Europe where uniformity seemed most apparent, there were variations on the Russian pattern.

12.3   Co-operation in the European Communist Bloc

The Communist Information Bureau (*Cominform*) was established in 1947. Its purpose was to co-ordinate communist activities, which was interpreted by Stalin to mean that it would be the instrument for imposing Russia's will on all the communist parties in Eastern Europe and on those in France and Italy which were also represented. Its first headquarters were in Belgrade but, after Jugoslavia's expulsion in 1948, they were moved to Bucharest in Rumania. Rumania at this time toed the Russian line with enthusiasm. The Cominform played a major part in establishing a considerable degree of uniformity in the communist bloc. It was wound up by Khrushchev, in 1956.

The Council for Mutual Economic Assistance (*Comecon*) was set up in 1949 to organize economic co-operation in Eastern Europe. By 1950 Comecon included all the communist states in Europe except Jugoslavia. In 1962, it also admitted the Mongolian People's Republic (Outer Mongolia) and about the same time associate membership was allowed to other communist states including China and Cuba. Ten years later, Cuba was admitted to full membership. In 1964, Comecon set up a Bank for Socialist Countries. The basic aim of the Council was economic development and co-operation along lines similar to those being pursued in Western Europe through organizations such as OEEC (see Section 14.5). Some conflict developed about whether members should specialize in production for the benefit of all or whether each member should aim at self-sufficiency. Other conflicts were ideological. In 1961 Albania withdrew in protest against the Soviet Union's quarrels with China. But, leaning on credits supplied by the USSR (as Western Europe often leaned on the USA), Comecon did much to bring recovery and some growth of prosperity among members of the communist bloc.

A military alliance was not signed until 1955 when the Eastern European Mutual Assistance Treaty (the *Warsaw Pact*) made provision for joint defence for twenty years. It was signed by all the communist states in Europe except Jugoslavia. Albania was excluded in 1961. The Warsaw Pact was a response to similar movements in the West, especially the creation of NATO in 1949 (see Section 14.5) and the granting of full independence to the German

COUNTRY	COMINFORM (dissolved 1956)	COMECON	WARSAW PACT	POPULATION (est. millions) 1960	1979	MAIN EXPORT (% of whole) (1969)	EXPORTS MAINLY TO (% of whole) (1969)	IMPORTS MAINLY FROM (% of whole) (1969)
USSR	✓	✓	✓	208·9	262·4	Machinery 23%	East Germany 15% (Communist States, 66%)	East Germany 16% (Communist States, 65%)
POLAND	✓	✓	✓	29·7	35·0	Machinery 36%	USSR 35%	USSR 38%
EAST GERMANY		✓	✓	17·2	16·7	Machinery 38%	USSR 38%	USSR 40%
CZECHOSLOVAKIA	✓	✓	✓	13·7	15·2	Machinery 51%	USSR 34%	USSR 34%
HUNGARY	✓	✓	✓	10·0	10·7	Machinery 26%	USSR 35%	USSR 37%
RUMANIA	✓	✓	✓	18·4	22·0	Machinery 22%	USSR 28%	USSR 27%
JUGOSLAVIA	Expelled 1948	Associate		18·5	22·1	Machinery 11% Metals 11%	Italy 15% USSR 14%	West Germany 20% Italy 13% USSR 13%
BULGARIA	✓	✓	✓	7·9	8·9	Machinery 27%	USSR 55%	USSR 56%
ALBANIA	✓	Left 1961	Excluded 1961	1·6	2·8	Fuel and minerals 54%	China 40%	China 63%

EXPORTS OF MEMBERS OF COMECON:

1970 31·2 billion dollars (about 10% of world total)

about $\frac{1}{3}$ sold to USSR

about $\frac{1}{3}$ sold to other COMECON members

about $\frac{1}{3}$ sold elsewhere

Fig. 12.3 The European communist bloc

Federal Republic (West Germany) in 1955. Like NATO, it set up united military forces. These were under the command of Marshal Konev of the Soviet Union. The Pact also allowed Russia to continue to keep troops in the satellite states. The Treaty spoke only of peaceful intentions and defence.

In 1955 the USSR put forward a proposal for the abolition of both the Warsaw Pact and NATO, in return for an all-European security system. But the West feared the size of the Warsaw Pact armies and both alliances remained. Neither would West Germany agree to the Rapacki Plan, put forward by Russia in 1957, for a nuclear-free zone in central Europe to include the two Germanies, Poland and Czechoslovakia, because she feared such an arrangement would expose her to the danger of communism.

12.4   Dissent Among the Satellites

Stalin had to tolerate Tito's defiance and the independent course steered by Jugoslavia. But he was not prepared to accept similar independence elsewhere in Eastern Europe. Gomulka, therefore, was removed from power at the end of 1948 and was later held in custody until after Stalin's death. His offence was to show signs of following in Tito's footsteps and seeming to advocate a measure of independence for Poland. He returned to power in Poland in 1956, however, when, after the death of Stalin, there was some reassessment of relations between Eastern Europe and the USSR.

(a) 1953

In the summer following Stalin's death in March 1953, the first signs of protest against the tight grip of the USSR were seen in East Berlin and East Germany (see Sections 11.2(f) and 12.1). Soviet troops put down the disturbances without difficulty but the new Russian leaders for a time adopted a softer policy and made a start on winding up the collection of reparations.

(b) 1956, Hungary

Changes within the USSR and Khrushchev's attack on Stalin at the beginning of 1956 raised hopes in Eastern Europe of further concessions. There were strikes and rebellions in Poland during the summer against high prices and Soviet supervision, but the return to power of Gomulka was enough to restore calm. Soviet troops withdrew to Poland's frontiers, leaving the Poles themselves to re-establish the authority of communist government.

Events in Poland encouraged dissent in Hungary, where there were also economic difficulties and anti-Soviet discontents. The government of Rákosi had long been unpopular for its Stalinist methods, and Rákosi resigned in July 1956. The hardliners looked to Hegedüs who made a short-lived attempt to reassert Stalinism. Others looked to Imre Nagy, a former Prime Minister whose liberalism had brought expulsion from the Hungarian Communist Party in 1955. When Hegedüs sparked off an anti-Soviet rebellion, Nagy

Fig. 12.4 Russian tanks in Budapest, Hungary, November 1956

again became Prime Minister in October 1956. Khrushchev seemed at first to be willing to leave the Hungarians, like the Poles, to sort out their own problems, and Soviet troops retired. But Nagy could not control the disorders in Budapest and elsewhere in the country. He took an increasingly hostile attitude to the USSR, formed a new government which included non-communists and declared that Hungary would leave the Warsaw Pact. Nagy seemed to have been influenced by the Austrian State Treaty, aspiring to achieve a neutrality for Hungary like that of Austria, his western neighbour. This was something the Soviet Union was not prepared to tolerate. Early in November, Soviet troops occupied Budapest and the rebellion was crushed. Nagy and his associates were executed and the authority of the Hungarian Communist Party was restored under the leadership of János Kádár. Kádár had once been imprisoned by Rákosi and he combined the necessary qualifications to restore stability in Hungary. He cautiously introduced many of the liberal reforms which Hungarians had demanded but strongly defended the country's membership of the Warsaw Pact, satisfying the Soviet Union. He therefore remained in power into the 1980s.

The West loudly lamented the suppression of the Hungarian revolt but made no attempt to interfere. The lines had been drawn in Europe by 1956 and, though not admitting it, the West was not prepared to challenge Soviet authority in the Eastern bloc. In any case, the Anglo-French invasion of Egypt during the Suez Crisis in November 1956 did much to divert international opinion (see Section 19.1(*d*)).

(c) **1968, Czechoslovakia**

The communist bloc experienced no further major disturbance until 1968. When Gottwald died in 1953, Antonin Novotný became the leader of Czechoslovakia, Secretary of the Communist Party and, from 1957, President of the Republic. Novotný preferred Stalin to Khrushchev and he ruled with an iron hand. At the same time, however, Czechoslovakia followed her own line in economic development. She was more industrialized than other countries in the communist bloc (see Exports, Fig. 12.3), and Novotný concentrated his attention on further industrialization. Competition was encouraged and planning was more localized than in the Soviet Union, even under Khrushchev. Like Stalin, however, Novotný showed little patience with the peasants. He faced difficulties arising from tension between Czechs and Slovaks, each jealous of the other, and from general dissatisfaction with Soviet influence and uneven economic progress. Demonstrations led to Novotný's downfall early in 1968 when he could no longer assert his authority.

A Triumvirate took charge of Czechoslovakia with Dubček the Party Secretary, Černík the Prime Minister and Svoboda the President. The aim of the new government was 'Socialism with a Human Face', a more liberal organization of society than Novotný had allowed. Černík would have gone as far as totally to abandon censorship but the members of the Triumvirate were not in complete agreement. Dubček did not envisage weakening the political control of the Communist Party and, unlike the Hungarians in 1956, there was no intention to leave the Warsaw Pact. But more contacts with the West and fewer economic controls were recommended while maintaining a socialist framework. Brezhnev determined to call a halt. Warsaw Pact forces, except those of Rumania, now herself more independently-minded, entered Czechoslovakia in August 1968, occupying Prague and forcing the Czech government to come to heel. The USSR vetoed a motion of censure at the UN and the West again, though critical, showed no signs of interfering.

Political reorganization in Czechoslovakia followed. A new federal constitution was adopted to try to resolve Czech–Slovak differences, but what the Soviet Union chiefly insisted on was a change in personnel among the country's leaders. Dubček was removed and replaced as Party Secretary by Husák who, like Kádár in Hungary, had once been a victim of Stalinism but was now approved of by the rulers in Moscow. Further reconstruction followed when a Czech ice-hockey victory over the Soviet Union led to riotous jubilation in Prague in March 1969. Dubček was steadily downgraded, sent as ambassador to Turkey and finally expelled from the Communist Party. It was not a total victory for the hard-liners, however. General Svoboda remained President until 1975, popular in Czechoslovakia as a Free Czech leader against the Nazis on the Russian Front during the Second World War and as a force for moderation. Husák too avoided the excesses of Novotný. A series of political trials of 'right-wing opportunists' in 1972 never-

Fig. 12.5 A street cartoon in Prague 1968: the Soviet Liberator has turned Oppressor

theless showed the extent to which the liberalism of 1968 had been curbed. Husák combined the Presidency with his Secretaryship when Svoboda retired, and the Dissidents of Charter '77 were dealt with sternly.

(d) Poland

Poland preserved her allegiance to the communist bloc into the 1980s but the restlessness of 1956 (see (b) above) returned from time to time. Although geographically vitally important to the USSR as a barrier against the West, Poland retained distinctive national characteristics. One was the popularity among Poles of the Roman Catholic Church; another was the extent to which agriculture remained in the hands of private producers. The Poles were reluctant to accept Soviet direction, and they seemed regularly to wish somehow to combine socialist and capitalist economic systems. During the 1960s Gomulka grew more repressive, until serious rioting broke out in Poland in 1970. The protest was mainly against rising prices and the lack of civil liberties, and it was particularly strong in the Baltic areas which had once been German, in the cities of Gdansk (Danzig) and Szczecin (Stettin). Blood was shed among Polish workers and, unable to control them, Gomulka was forced to resign.

Edward Gierek replaced Gomulka as Party Secretary, remaining in power throughout the 1970s. With Soviet help he was able for a time to manage the economy without raising prices; discontent was contained and in the early 1970s Poland's economy grew impressively. When Gierek planned price rises in 1976, however, at a time of inflation in many Western countries, there were more riots and peace was restored only when prices were again frozen. Growth slowed and, in 1979, there was a downturn, when Poland's national income, capital investment and agricultural production all fell. Poland's economy was now in serious trouble. The recent expansion of trade with the West had led to massive debts to the capitalist world, and the export of food to earn Western currencies had led to serious shortages within Poland.

Discontent flared again, the workers demanding increased civil liberties, especially for trade unions free of state control, and an economic package which aimed to achieve the impossible – the workers wanted the capitalist advantages of higher wages and improved conditions but the simultaneous socialist advantages of pegged prices and full employment. Polish farmers joined the protests, demanding higher payments for their crops. This time Gierek could not survive: he resigned in 1980 and for a time Stanislaw Kania became Party Secretary.

Poland's problems defied ready solution and such was the unrest, especially in Gdansk, Szczecin and other industrial areas, that there were fears that the Soviet government might intervene. The Poles in 1980 set up a free trade-union movement, *Solidarity*, resembling unions in the West rather than the official administrative unions of the communist bloc. They found a folk-hero in Lech Walesa, whose devotion to the Polish masses and the Catholic Church, combined with defiance of the authorities, won widespread support. *Rural Solidarity* was set up to represent the interests of about half a million private farmers. Solidarity itself went on to recruit around ten million members. Kania struggled with Poland's problems without much success, and resigned in favour of General Jaruzelski in October 1981. By the end of the year, martial law was enforced and Walesa was among those in detention.

Great as Poland's debts were, there were countries in the West, such as Mexico, even deeper in debt. But it was clear that the world's economic troubles were now affecting 'communist' states as well as others. Rumania and even East Germany began to report difficulties arising from debts, and the meetings of Comecon members in 1982 were over-shadowed by the association's problems. Poland had meanwhile not yet seriously threatened to leave the Warsaw Pact or to abandon her one-party state, though military rule was something of a new phenomenon in the affairs of the Communist bloc. Andropov hoped that the Poles might still sort out their own problems, stabilize the country's society and repair the Polish economy. He had no wish to invoke the Brezhnev Doctrine and send in foreign troops, but events in Poland continued to cause anxiety in Moscow.

12.5   Communist Variations

Although *Jugoslavia* undertook no military alliances with the Soviet Union, diplomatic relations between the two countries improved after 1955. Inside Jugoslavia, Tito became President for life although prime ministers and other members of the government were limited to four years in power under the constitution of 1963. At that time, about half of the population was still engaged in agriculture but industrialization was proceeding steadily and the encouragement of tourism brought Jugoslavia further links with the outside world. Tito was able to rule with less repressive methods than were used elsewhere in Eastern Europe, though Jugoslavia's mixed nationalities and religions made her a difficult country to govern. Croatian nationalists created a succession of disturbances. Jugoslavia's economy also had weaknesses and help was needed from the IMF in the 1970s. For many years economic controls were less centralized and workers were encouraged to play a part in their own management but, towards the end of his life, Tito began to favour increased central planning. He died in 1980, having provided a large measure of stability and leadership which was progressive in many ways. The impressive attendance at his funeral showed the extent of the feeling that an international statesman and not merely a nation's leader had died.

(a) Trade and Economies

Tito clearly established the point that there could be differences among communist states in Europe. Geography, and the individual problems which the satellites faced, reinforced it. Czechoslovakia was nearer to the West and more industrialized than the others. Bulgaria was more remote and, with Albania, the most underdeveloped. Rumania had important oil fields. Thus the communist states pursued economic development within Comecon but by varying methods. East Germany introduced Five-Year Plans, beginning in 1958, and concentrated on engineering, chemicals and optical equipment, devising new methods for the production of iron and steel using brown coal as fuel. Hungary concentrated on engineering and electrical equipment and Rumania led the way in promoting tourism. Most East European enterprises were under state control though East Germany was slower than her neighbours to complete her programme of nationalization. Fig. 12.3 also shows that most of Eastern Europe's trade in 1970 was within Comecon. The basic trade patterns continued into the 1980s though oil and petroleum products became increasingly important among the exports of the Soviet Union. In 1978, some 5 per cent of Russian exports also went to each of West Germany, Japan and the USA. East Europeans similarly, to varying extents, increased their trade with the capitalist world, especially with West Germany. One result of such increasing contacts was that world economic problems began to make themselves felt in Eastern Europe. Hungary began to feel the effects of inflation. Rumania, once an oil producer, had to ration petrol for tourists in 1979. Here and there unemployment began to become a problem. Most East Europeans, especially East Germans, had nevertheless grown more prosperous, demanding more consumer goods, whether from members of Comecon or from the West. For example, almost 10 per cent of Rumania's trade was with West Germany in the late 1970s.

Differences, meanwhile, continued in the ways in which East Europeans organized their agriculture. While almost 90 per cent of agricultural land in Poland remained in private hands, hardly any in Bulgaria was not collectivized and Rumania completed collectivization in 1962.

(b) The Catholic Church

The Catholic Church continued to command support in several countries of the communist bloc, especially in Poland and Hungary. In Poland, Cardinal Wyszinski was a stubborn critic of Gomulka's regime in the 1940s though they arrived at a compromise when Gomulka returned to power in 1956. Polish governments could never entirely ignore the Church, and, when the Archbishop of Cracow became Pope John-Paul II in 1978, the confidence of the Catholic Church in Poland was greatly strengthened. John-Paul's visit to his native land produced scenes of jubilation with which the communist authorities thought it wise not to interfere. Wyszinski remained a source of inspiration to many Poles until his death in a Warsaw hospital in 1981.

Some Catholic opposition to communism in Hungary rallied behind Cardinal Mindszenty, once arrested for his opposition to Bela Kun and arrested again on a charge of treason in 1948. He was released in 1955 and took up residence in the US Legation in Budapest a year later, remaining there until 1971 as a symbol of defiance of Kádár's government. He then left Hungary to spend his last years in exile.

(c) Constitutions and Politics

All of the communist-bloc countries were dominated by their communist parties but there were many variations in constitutional details. It was the experience of most, however, that party secretaries played the key role and that such officials often held power for many years. Walter Ulbricht dominated East Germany until his death in 1973, ruling with a Stalinist insistence on discipline. Otto Grotewohl was Prime Minister of the German Democratic Republic from 1952 to his death in 1964, working in close partnership with Ulbricht. A similar partnership developed in the 1970s between Honecker, who succeeded Ulbricht as Secretary of the Socialist Unity Party in 1971, and Stoph who became Prime Minister. In Albania, Enver Hoxha came to power at the end of the Second World War like Tito, as a hero of the resistance to the Nazis. But Hoxha admired Stalin far more than did Tito, and he outlived his Jugoslav neighbour. In Bulgaria, Dimitrov died in 1949 and there was a succession of communist leaders before Zhivkov began a long period of authority, having become Secretary of the Bulgarian Communist Party in the mid-1950s. Rumania rid herself of her monarchy at the end of 1947 and Gheorghiu-Dej eventually became President of the Republic. He had held power in Rumania as Secretary of the Communist Party since the end of the war and, when he died in 1965, had already groomed Nicolae Ceausescu as his successor. Gheorghiu-Dej and Ceausescu both maintained a measure of independence from Moscow, and during the 1970s Rumania several times distanced herself from Soviet foreign policy.

Changes came to all the countries of Eastern Europe, and only in Albania, geographically isolated from other Warsaw Pact members and economically backward, did communist rule continue as inflexibly as under Stalin in the USSR. Hoxha maintained a rigorous police state. At first, Soviet economic aid was extensive and Albania gave the USSR a footing on the Adriatic Sea.

Some industrial development took place in textiles and oil products. But Hoxha disliked the changes which occurred in the Soviet Union after Stalin's death and, in 1961, he seized on the USSR's quarrels with China to break off diplomatic relations with Moscow. Albania built a strange new alliance with communist China and in 1968 resigned from the Warsaw Pact, having been only a nominal member and virtually excluded since 1961. At loggerheads with neighbouring Jugoslavia as well as with Eastern Europe generally, Albania's isolation was almost complete. In 1978, Hoxha became disenchanted with China too, finding lesser men in power there after the death of Mao Tse-tung; and here too ties were broken. Moscow showed only lukewarm interest in wooing Albania back to the East European bloc. Albania was of little importance in international affairs and Hoxha himself seemed little concerned about his isolation.

By the 1980s, the European communist bloc remained intact save for the independence achieved by Jugoslavia and Albania (see Fig. 12.1). It had at first been held together by poverty and firm police action. But economic development brought rising living standards and most of the regimes became less rigid. The Brezhnev Doctrine seemed to define what the Soviet Union regarded as two basic essentials – membership of the Warsaw Pact and the continuation of one-party systems of government. In other respects there was room in Eastern Europe for differing ideas about the road to communism, and the Soviet Union tolerated national diversities. Rumania joined the World Bank and the IMF. Poland permitted a good deal of freedom to the Catholic Church, and, even before 1980, Gierek had encouraged trade unions to be responsive to the wishes of their members and not merely instruments for state policy. Hungary imported foreign books and, both in the capital, Budapest, and in the countryside, preserved much of the atmosphere of a Central European rather than of an 'Iron Curtain' country. Everywhere in Eastern Europe there were increasing contacts with the outside world. It seemed impossible that the tight uniformity of Stalin's days could return, though the West was perhaps premature in speculating as to whether the European communist bloc might eventually fall apart.

Further Reading

Ayling, S.E.: *Portraits of Power*. Harrap (London, 1965) – Tito, Khrushchev.
Franchere, R.: *Tito of Yugoslavia*. Macmillan (London, 1971).
Fry, D.G.: *Russia, Lenin and Stalin*. Hamish Hamilton (London, 1966).
Johnson, A.R.: *Yugoslavia in the Twilight of Tito*. Sage (London, 1974).
McCauley, M.: *The Soviet Union since 1917*. Longman (Harlow, 1981).
Mooney, P.J.: *The Soviet Superpower, 1945–1980*. Heinemann (London, 1982).
Nove, A.: *Stalinism and After*. Allen & Unwin (London, 1975).
Pryce-Jones, D.: *The Hungarian Revolution*. Benn (London, 1969).
Westwood, J.N.: *Russia since 1917*. Batsford (London, 1980).
York, B.: *The Soviet Union 1917–1980*. Harrap (London, 1983).

Documentary

Breach, R.W.: *Documents and Descriptions, the World since 1914*. Oxford University Press (London, 1966) – Sections 24–5.

Exercises

1. How did the USSR establish influence over the countries of Eastern Europe after the Second World War? In what ways and to what extent has this influence since been (*a*) maintained and (*b*) weakened?

2. Identify and explain *four* distinctive features of the rule of Stalin which help towards a definition of *Stalinism*.

3. Write an account of the career of Khrushchev from 1949 to 1964 dividing your work into four sections: his rise to power; his main achievements; his weaknesses; his fall from power.

4. Consider *each* of the following terms as suitable adjectives with which to describe the Soviet Union in recent years: authoritarian; democratic; communist; socialist; wealthy.

5. How does life in the Soviet Union differ from life in your own country?

6. How in the 1970s did the states of Eastern Europe, compared one with another, show (*a*) similarities and (*b*) differences?

7. 'It was the experience of most . . . that party secretaries played the key role and that such officials often held power for many years' (page 218). Explain this statement with reference to the states of the East European communist bloc, and illustrate the truth of it by reference to the history since 1945 of the USSR and *two* other states.

8. Using the Index to this book, construct outline histories of *each* of the following states since 1919: Czechoslovakia; Hungary; Jugoslavia.

9. Using Figs. 11.1, 11.2 and 12.1, explain what changes were made to the boundaries of Poland after the Second World War. What was the importance of Poland to the USSR and how has the USSR ensured that, since 1945, Poland has been 'friendly'?

10. Use the text of this Unit and Fig. 12.3 to write paragraphs suitable for inclusion in a historical dictionary on *each* of the following: the *Cominform*; the Warsaw Pact; *Comecon* and trading patterns in Eastern Europe.

The USA and the European Capitalist Bloc – 1 The USA and Britain

13.1 Democracy and Capitalism

It could be argued – indeed, many Americans argued it noisily – that the West held liberty to be the first essential and, in general, preferred liberty to equality. The democracies rejected the restrictions which were common in the communist bloc. Freedom of speech and of the press, free elections in the sense that voters had a choice of parties and a completely secret vote, and freedom from political police forces such as Hitler's Gestapo and the KGB were regarded as fundamental. Similarly private enterprise continued to play the major part in the economies of the democracies, with an emphasis on private ownership, private profit, competition and such consumer goods as the public, prodded by advertising, could be persuaded to buy.

But, after 1945, it was difficult to maintain that there should be no economic planning by governments and no interference in the management of the economy and in the making of social improvements. Governments in general were expected to interfere sufficiently to steer developments in desired directions, away from unemployment, poverty and squalor and towards greater efficiency, at least in public services such as the supply of electricity. Most governments in the democracies leaned a little towards socialism although less so in the USA than in Europe. They all faced the problem of finding a balance in a mixed economy between private enterprise and state control.

The Labour Party in Britain and its counterparts in Europe, the Social Democrats, usually preferred a greater emphasis on state ownership (nationalization) than did private enterprise parties such as Conservatives and Liberals. But when, during the British election of 1945, Churchill suggested that the Labour Party would 'have to fall back on some form of Gestapo', his remarks were received with derision. The Labour Party and Social Democrats had little in common with communists except a general willingness to pay more attention to economic planning, put some limitations on the worst features of capitalism, and to move vaguely in the direction of equality. They were not ruthless and they were not prepared to sacrifice liberty. They had no rigid long-term plan for the complete transformation of society.

In the USA, however, social democracy had little appeal. The traditional American parties, Democrats and Republicans, maintained their grip and their devotion to private enterprise. In presidential elections from 1948 to

1980, winning candidates got popular votes ranging from about 24 to 43 million votes but the highest vote for a socialist candidate was only 140 000, registered in 1948.

13.2   The United States of America

(a) Attitude to Communism

Many Americans regarded socialism and communism as a sort of treason and their hysteria reached fever pitch in the *McCarthyism* of the early 1950s. While a Commission on Employee Loyalty combed carefully through the records of state employees, and known communists were restricted under the Internal Security Act of 1950, Senator Joseph McCarthy began a more bizarre witch hunt for communist sympathisers. He made an exuberant claim to have detected 57 (quoted as 205 by some of his audience) in the State Department. A Senate committee failed to find any, but from 1950 to 1954 McCarthy conducted much-publicized inquiries into the communist sympathies of prominent citizens with all the enthusiasm of a medieval witchfinder. He imported into the USA something of the definition of communism current in South Africa, where the Suppression of Communism Act tried to outlaw almost anything which threatened the existing order. In 1954, McCarthy himself was censured in the Senate for conduct 'contrary to Senate traditions'. Nevertheless, a thorough determination to hold down communism in the USA survived McCarthy.

Less flamboyant methods did uncover Russian spies, though not as often as suggested in television serials. In 1953, Julius and Ethel Rosenberg were executed for passing atomic secrets to the Russians. But long before then, anti-communism had become a central policy of American politicians, both at home and in foreign relations. One way in which it found expression was in the remorseless pursuit of communists by J. Edgar Hoover, Director of the FBI (Federal Bureau of Investigation) from 1924 until his death in 1972. Before the Second World War, his G-Men hunted America's Public Enemies (mainly gangsters) and waged war against the Ku Klux Klan. After 1945, their energies were devoted to seeking out communists and everyone suspected of 'Un-American' activities.

(b) Social and Economic Problems

Every President from Truman to Reagan was also aware of the need to do something about America's two most serious internal problems. These problems were often inter-related: there was a great gulf in the USA between white and non-white citizens and between the rich and the poor. In 1960, nearly 12 per cent of the population were non-white and many of these were desperately poor. There were also a good many poor whites. Non-whites grew increasingly resentful of poverty, of the slums in which millions lived in the decaying city centres and of the continued discrimination against them by an arrogant section of the white population.

In the South, this arrogance was often rooted in the past, when plantation owners had kept slaves. It found some expression in the politics of George Wallace who became Governor of Alabama in 1963. He set himself up as the champion of property-owners, and the defender of the rights of individual states against federal interference. Above all, he took upon himself the defence of America against all 'Un-American' activities, whether negro, liberal, socialist or communist. As such he was the scourge of the Civil Rights Movement. In the presidential election of 1968, he got nearly 10 million popular votes, almost a third of the total given to Nixon who was elected. There could be no doubt that he represented a strong current of opinion which was not entirely confined to the South.

Presidential policies usually brought changes at a slower pace than in Europe. A 'war on poverty' was launched in the 1960s, further expanding welfare provisions in the USA, but about 20 per cent of America's families continued to be officially classified as 'poor'. The Civil Rights Movement campaigned to help them to get a more equal share in America's great wealth and also to free the non-whites and other under-privileged people from discrimination and squalor. In the North, non-whites often lived in ghettos in the large towns, such as Harlem in New York, too poor to follow the whites who moved out to the suburbs, away from the decaying slum property. Low wages, unemployment and atrocious housing conditions combined to turn such ghettos into breeding-grounds of angry discontent and, in the later 1960s, many American cities were rocked by violent riots in which racial antagonisms played a considerable part.

The USA had traditions of violence from the days of the sordid if not necessarily 'Wild' West, through the Civil War to gangsterism and the persistent vicious activities of the Ku Klux Klan. Americans cherished their right to possess guns and it seemed to some that the American population was armed to the teeth. Combined with the deep social divisions, festering slums and general turbulence of the twentieth century, this tradition encouraged new crime waves in the USA after 1945, which were complicated by the rapid expansion of drug-taking. In spite of this, however, the USA followed the example of more liberal countries in moving away from capital punishment.

Great wealth did not, however, bring great tranquillity to the USA. There were explosive labour disputes, bitter social conflicts and violent confrontations which in the 1960s frequently involved students. Even the stars of the American film industry became involved in the arguments. John Wayne stood forth for law and order like a latter-day Western Marshal. Ronald Reagan became an authoritarian Governor of California, in 1966. Marlon Brando inclined to the side of the under-dog and Charlie Chaplin left the USA, under suspicion of left-wing leanings. There seemed to be no real danger to the American Constitution but there was plenty of furious argument about the nature of society.

Involvement in the struggle over Vietnam (see Section 17.1(d)) deepened the divisions within the USA and became an explosive issue in American politics, especially in the 1968 presidential election. This war also imposed heavy burdens on the American economy until, from 1971, even the dollar was involved in international currency crises (see Table 13.2).

(c) Truman's Presidency, 1945–53

Truman steered the USA through the last months of the Second World War, took the decision to use atomic weapons against Japan and then set America on her postwar course in foreign policy. He gave his name to the *Truman Doctrine* for the containment of communism and deeply involved the USA in the defence of Western Europe (see Section 17.1(*a*)). He committed America to the active support of UNO. He presided over the rehabilitation of Japan and the framing of the Treaty of San Francisco and, in 1950, he took a leading part in the Korean War (to preserve South Korea from communism). Probably no previous President of the USA had taken such an active and far-reaching part in world affairs.

At the same time, Truman was charting America's course in domestic affairs. There were problems to be faced in the transition from war to peace, in extending the reforms begun by Roosevelt and in dealing with new issues such as the peaceful application of atomic power. There was also the question of internal security, from which arose McCarthyism (see page 222). In 1946, Truman created an Atomic Energy Commission and, in 1949, a new Department of Defence. Atomic power was to remain under government control but the USA was willing to share its knowledge with other countries for peaceful purposes. Where security was concerned, however, Truman kept a tight grip. He avoided the hysteria of McCarthy but diligently searched out potential traitors, and preserved American military might. The army was run down and servicemen returned to civilian life smoothly and quickly, aided by training schemes and financial help. But the USA placed reliance on air power and nuclear weapons and, in due course, the Department of Defence in the Pentagon became strongly influential in American affairs.

Like Attlee in Britain, Truman gave the appearance of being modest and unassuming, but his policies were often firm and decisive. He was prepared to take control although he ran into difficulties in social and economic affairs, clashing with those forces in the USA which were quick to resent government interference.

In September 1945, Truman outlined his plans for continuing Roosevelt's domestic work with *Twenty-One Points*, hopeful of expanding social security and house-building and of improving working conditions. But labour unrest, linked with soaring prices, helped to swing American opinion to the Republicans in the mid-term elections of 1946 and for two years after that Truman was handicapped by a Republican majority in Congress. Although he had secured the passage of an Employment Act in 1946, economic planning and controls soon became unpopular. Truman abandoned most of them and was further embarrassed when the Republican Congress insisted on a new Labour Management Relations Act (Taft–Hartley Act) in 1947, to free employers from certain legal restrictions but to impose others on trade unions. Congress also insisted on cuts in taxation which undermined the extension of welfare schemes.

Table 13.1   Elections in the USA, 1916–80

Year of presidential election	President	State votes For	State votes Against	House of Representatives
1916	Wilson (D)	277	254	D (Mid-term: R)
1920	Harding (R)*	404	127	R
1924	Coolidge (R)	382	136	R
1928	Hoover (R)	444	87	R (Mid-term: D)
1932	Roosevelt (D)	472	59	D
1936	Roosevelt (D)	523	8	D
1940	Roosevelt (D)	449	82	D
1944	Roosevelt (D)*	432	99	D (Mid-term: R)
1948	Truman (D)	303	189	D
1952	Eisenhower (R)	442	89	R (Mid-term: D)
1956	Eisenhower (R)	457	73	D
1960	Kennedy (D)*	303	219	D
1964	Johnson (D)	486	52	D
1968	Nixon (R)	301	191†	D
1972	Nixon (R)	521	17	D
1976	Carter (D)	297	241	D
1980	Reagan (R)	489	49	D

D: Democrat   * Died while in office
R: Republican   † Wallace (Ind.) 46

Note on American Elections

Presidents are elected by the votes of states' representatives in an electoral college. These representatives (usually) mandated to the support of a particular presidential candidate, are elected by the voters who are thus voting for presidential candidates indirectly. Each state elects as many members of the electoral college as it has representatives in Congress. For example, in 1964, there were 538 members in the electoral college and, of these, 43 represented New York, 29 Pennsylvania, 3 Nevada. The presidential candidate who obtains a majority in the electoral college takes office as President in the January following the election.

Congress is made up of two Houses: the House of Representatives (in proportion to population); the Senate (two senators from each state). Mid-term elections to Congress (in 1918, 1922 and so on) may alter party representation there and thus handicap or help the President in carrying out his programme. For example, in 1946, the Republicans won a majority in the House of Representatives and thus handicapped the President who was a Democrat. N.B. Eisenhower (in 1956) and Nixon (in 1968 and 1972) were elected without a Republican majority in the House of Representatives.

Rather unexpectedly, Truman won a narrow victory in the presidential election of 1948 and the Democrats regained control of Congress. He now put forward his programme for a *Fair Deal*, expanding the Twenty-One Points of 1945. It stopped short of any thorough economic planning but aimed to make improvements to assist the poor, for example with a building programme, to obtain more social justice (extending old age pensions) and to move towards more secure civil rights. Like Roosevelt, Truman pushed ahead with public works schemes and assistance to small farmers, always trying to raise the level of those with small incomes. Much of the Fair Deal programme could not be made law, however, in the face of the combined opposition of Republicans and Southern Democrats.

(d) Eisenhower's Presidency, 1953–61

Fig. 13.1 An American commemorative stamp of 1969. Personal popularity brought Eisenhower to the Presidency on the slogan 'I like Ike'. His non-interventionist policies bore many traces of traditional Republicanism

In 1952, Eisenhower retired from the army and the command of the forces of NATO to stand for the Presidency as a Republican candidate. He served two terms in office. In foreign affairs, Eisenhower's first task was to wind up the Korean War in 1953 but the Cold War continued. Until his resignation and death in 1959, Dulles was mainly responsible for the foreign policy of the Eisenhower administration. These years saw few fundamental changes in international relations (see Unit Seventeen). A new alliance, SEATO, was set up in 1954 to contain communism in Asia. The *Eisenhower Doctrine* of 1957 announced America's willingness to contain it in the Middle East, and when it grew in Cuba under Castro, the USA broke off diplomatic relations in 1961. It was in this period too that America first undertook commitments in Vietnam (see Section 17.1(*d*)) but, essentially, the foreign policy of the Republicans was not much different from that of the Democrats. After 1959, Eisenhower expressed a belief in personal diplomacy, but his summit meeting with

Khrushchev in 1960 collapsed in recriminations over the U-2 affair (see Section 17.2(*a*)).

In domestic matters, Eisenhower himself was a moderate. He had few ambitious plans and envisaged no Deals, New or Fair. He was usually content to leave matters to experts, especially businessmen, and for most of his years in power the economy prospered. After 1956 he vetoed Democrat attempts to push him into greater spending on housing and welfare measures, but he made no attempt to dismantle what had already been achieved by Roosevelt and Truman. Most Americans enjoyed a rising standard of living but the problem of unemployment persisted and there were brief recessions in 1953 and 1957. There were also labour disputes including a serious steel strike in 1959. Congress hit back with a measure to attack the union bosses and make America's trade unions more democratic.

Even more controversial than the status of trade unions was the question of *desegregation.* In 1954, the Supreme Court ruled that white and non-white children should be educated together and not in separate schools. Eisenhower supported the ruling but it was resisted in the South. Southern states claimed that it was an interference with state rights and Eisenhower had to send federal troops to Little Rock, Arkansas, to enforce the law. The troops had to protect non-white students at Little Rock's Central High School against the bigotry and prejudice of the whites. Even then, other states such as Alabama refused to accept desegregation.

In 1955, negroes in Montgomery, Alabama, began to protest against racial segregation on buses and, by 1960, such protests were challenging 'whites-only' drug-stores, hotels and libraries. This Civil Rights Movement found a dedicated and moderate leader in Martin Luther King and, by 1960, most Democrats and Republicans had accepted the principle of equality. Eisenhower meanwhile, accepted a Civil Rights Act in 1957, to protect the rights of minorities and especially the negro's right to vote. When Eisenhower retired in 1961, Civil Rights had become a burning issue.

(*e*) Kennedy's Presidency, 1961–3

John Kennedy was the youngest of all American Presidents. His father had been an American ambassador in Britain and Kennedy was a Roman Catholic, of Irish descent. The fact that he was the first Roman Catholic president seemed to many at the time to indicate a growing spirit of tolerance in the USA. He brought to the Presidency a certain youthful vigour and a more outward-looking attitude than was usually associated with the office. This found expression in the *Peace Corps*, which was founded in 1961 to enable skilled volunteers to give active and constructive assistance to the developing nations. By 1966, the Corps had 12 000 Americans at work in over fifty countries, mainly in Africa, Asia and Latin America.

In the same spirit, Kennedy signed the Alliance for Progress with Latin America, for economic co-operation and to raise the standard of living. A year later, in 1962, he persuaded Congress to make sweeping tariff cuts in the Trade Expansion Act, giving encouragement to international trade. The Kennedy Round, whereby GATT made progressive reductions in the tariffs of many countries, developed from the Act. All this was in keeping with Kennedy's stated aims of moving towards a *New Frontier* with a world-wide attack on poverty, war and tyranny. In the Nuclear Test Ban Treaty of 1963, he was able to reach a constructive agreement with the USSR but he relaxed none of America's vigilance against communism. It was during Kennedy's Presidency that the USA became more deeply involved in Vietnam and confronted the communist world over Cuba (see Sections 17.1(*d*) and (*e*)).

Within the USA, Kennedy's plans for the New Frontier included progress in Civil Rights and Medicare (a health and welfare service for the aged). Federal troops were used, as at Little Rock, to protect the rights of negro students in the universities of Mississippi and Alabama. But Republicans and Southern Democrats in Congress blocked further legislation on the subject. Before the deadlock could be resolved, the President was assassinated in the streets of Dallas, Texas, in November 1963. Kennedy had brought a certain liberalism to the American Presidency but he was able to do little more than point the way before his violent death.

Fig. 13.2 An American commemorative stamp of 1964. There was a long history of attempts to assassinate US Presidents and Kennedy was the fourth President to be killed while in office

Violence continued to disfigure US society in the years after Kennedy's death. Luther King was murdered in 1968 in Memphis, Tennessee. Two months later Robert Kennedy, younger brother of the former President, and Attorney-General in 1961, was killed while himself campaigning for the Presidency. During the election campaign of 1972, Governor Wallace was shot and left paralysed. Two attempts were made to kill President Ford, and President Reagan was wounded by a gunman almost as soon as he became President in 1981. Murders and attempted murders were only one aspect of the violence which plagued American life. Rioting, violent protest and violent retribution were all too common, evidence of the American's attachment to the gun. There were those who argued that there were too many freedoms in the USA, and the continued freedom with which organizations such as the Ku Klux Klan went on spreading their messages of hatred and intolerance remained as an ugly blemish on the record of one of the world's foremost democracies.

(f) Johnson's Presidency, 1963–9

Kennedy died in Texas. The Vice-President, Lyndon Johnson, his successor, was, by chance, a Texan. The Johnson administration became deeply enmeshed in the struggle in Vietnam (see Section 17.1(d)), which came to overshadow almost everything. In other American-communist relationships, the USA seemed to have settled for coexistence. No attempt was made to interfere in Czechoslovakia in 1968 (see Section 12.4) nor to change the balance of power which had developed between West and East.

But within America Johnson's administration was an active one. In 1964 he succeeded in manoeuvring Kennedy's Civil Rights Act through Congress, outlawing discrimination on racial grounds in matters such as education and employment. The Voting Rights Act a year later abolished the various tests, for example of literacy, which had often been used to disqualify black voters. In 1964 Johnson aimed to help other under-privileged groups too by means of the Economic Opportunity Act which extended vocational training for the young, set up a Jobs Corps and provided financial help for small farmers and businessmen in areas of poverty. When re-elected at the end of 1964, Johnson put forward a new programme for the *Great Society*. The Democrats were now stronger in Congress and further substantial legislation followed.

Johnson conducted a 'war on poverty', spending federal money and promoting community action schemes. Some progress was made in attacking the USA's hideous slums. Aid for rebuilding decaying city areas was made available in the Development Act of 1966. Legislation allocated federal money for sewage disposal and educational expansion. A Social Security Act introduced medicare for those over 65. Administrative reorganization was undertaken to deal more effectively with problems of slums and transport. Minimum wages were raised and extended to cover more workers and some attempt was made to deal with unemployment. But a more liberal trade union law was blocked in Congress. Congress also passed a new Immigration Act to make the admission of immigrants more selective.

Mid-term elections in 1966 strengthened the Republicans and Southern Democrats who were reluctant to move too quickly, especially regarding Civil Rights. An inquiry into the extensive rioting which occurred in negro ghettos, especially in 1967, nevertheless placed much of the blame on persistent 'white racism', and the murder of the non-violent Luther King prodded Congress into further action. More Civil Rights legislation was passed in 1968, outlawing discrimination in the letting of accommodation and the sale of properties.

There was now little more Johnson could do. His involvement in Vietnam had lost him the support of many liberals but in any case the campaign for the complete equality of all America's citizens, white and non-white, could not be won quickly in the teeth of prejudice. Johnson himself was not a candidate in the election of 1968, faced, he admitted in his memoirs, by 'divisions' he 'felt powerless to correct'. The country moved to the right in electing the Republican Richard Nixon and even further to the right in giving a substantial vote to George Wallace. The Democrats, however, retained a majority in Congress.

(g) Nixon's Presidency, 1969–74, and Ford's Presidency, 1974–7

Nixon had been Eisenhower's Vice-President after 1956 but had failed to defeat Kennedy for the Presidency in 1960. Many people felt his chances of political power had vanished for ever. But over the next few years Nixon steadily built up support in the grass roots of the Republican Party.

Opinion in the USA was now deeply divided about the conflict in Vietnam and Nixon worked towards the withdrawal of American troops through a policy of Vietnamization. He hoped that South Vietnam would be able to resist communism without the American army, if not without the American air force. The *Nixon Doctrine* of 1969 continued to oppose communist expansion but expressed the hope that Asian nations would be able to defend themselves against it. The collapse of the South Vietnamese before a communist offensive in 1972, when America's withdrawal was well advanced, put Nixon in a dilemma, but he persevered to negotiate a face-saving peace-treaty in 1973 and the withdrawal continued (see Section 17.1(*d*)).

He made other important changes in American foreign policy, agreeing at last to the admission of communist China to UNO and making a personal visit to Mao Tse-tung (see Section 15.3(*e*)), followed by another to Moscow. He was prepared to travel extensively both in the communist and non-communist worlds and to follow the example of Kennedy in seeking agreements on armaments with the USSR. In 1969, he and Podgorny signed the Nuclear Non-Proliferation Treaty to try to limit the spread of nuclear weapons, and entered into the Strategic Arms Limitation Talks (SALT) (see Section 17.2(*b*)).

Nixon also worked to settle problems within America. On taking office, he appointed a Council for Urban Affairs to tackle the problems of the cities and for much of his first term as President, the USA was generally quieter than in the late 1960s. On the other hand, there were economic difficulties in the early 1970s. Unemployment rose to more than 4 million but, at the same time (quite differently from the Depression of the 1930s), it was accompanied by rapidly-rising prices. Nixon tackled the problems with further administrative reorganization and attempts to freeze wages and prices. The USA then ran into balance of payments difficulties which resulted in a 10 per cent surcharge on imports, to secure time in which to reconsider the levels of the world's currencies. After a prolonged currency crisis, adjustments were made and the surcharge removed but, at the end of 1971, the dollar had been devalued, particularly in relation to the West German mark and the Japanese yen. In 1973 the dollar was in trouble again. The strain of financing so many operations throughout the world was beginning to affect even the richest of all nations.

Economic problems multiplied in the mid-1970s. Increases in the price of oil stoked up inflation in many countries of the world. Unemployment rose higher (see Section 18.1). The USA suffered along with other countries, but for the moment political scandals attracted attention and Nixon became ever more deeply involved. At the heart of the scandals was the Watergate Affair. Evidence came to light that Republicans had broken into Democrat headquarters in the Watergate buildings to plant microphones and rifle files, part of the operations, it seemed, of CREEP – the Campaign to Re-Elect the President in 1972. Investigations brought to light a variety of irregularities among Nixon's associates. Spiro Agnew, the Vice-President, resigned during 1973 amid scandals about tax evasion and bribery. Meanwhile doubts arose about Nixon's denials of his own connections with Watergate. The President was pressed relentlessly to release the tapes of conversations in the White House which might help to clear up the affair. Arguments about the tapes led on to questions about a 'cover-up', and further murky details about Nixon's private life began to emerge. He too was suspected of tax irregularities. There was much talk of impeachment and such tapes as were produced only led to more controversies about Nixon's fitness to remain President. To avoid impeachment Nixon resigned in August 1974. Gerald R. Ford, having only recently replaced Agnew as Vice-President, now found himself replacing Nixon as President. He too began controversially, promptly granting Nixon a full pardon.

The Watergate Affair and the other scandals discredited Washington politicians generally. Rumours abounded. Even Henry Kissinger, the energetic Republican Secretary of State (for Foreign Affairs) only narrowly escaped involvement. Ford and he had only two years before the next presidential election in which to try to rebuild the party's reputation. Moreover, they were difficult years. Although there was general relief that the USA was no longer involved in Vietnam, the communist success there caused unease. At home, Ford inherited difficult economic problems which sometimes seemed to leave him at a loss. He made only limited progress in trying to curb rising prices and rising unemployment.

The Republicans nevertheless confirmed their faith in Ford as their candidate in the presidential election of 1976. The Democrats had already won sweeping victories in the mid-term elections in 1974, and few political observers gave Ford much hope of remaining in office. The Democrats made James (Jimmy) Carter their candidate. Carter made a good deal of his earlier remoteness from Washington and its scandals, being a southern peanut-grower and a former Governor of Georgia. Carter had plenty of targets to attack, but Ford did remarkably well in the election, winning 48 per cent of the popular vote. Table 13.1 shows that Carter's victory was the narrowest since Wilson's in 1916, but the Democrats had won back the Presidency and they remained dominant in the House of Representatives.

(h) Carter's Presidency, 1977–81

Continuing economic difficulties dogged Carter's presidency. In common with the rest of the world, the USA experienced some small improvement in 1977–8 but this failed to last. Americans watched with dismay the decline in the value of the dollar and a similar decline in the USA's economic pre-eminence. West Germany and other countries overtook the United States in terms of income per head of population, though all now had their problems. Carter had some success in creating jobs, but unemployment began to rise again as the 1980 election neared. Carter struggled at the same time with inflation and high interest rates, and met considerable resistance in attempting to reduce the US consumption of energy in a world where oil became ever more costly and oil resources were dwindling. The events of the 1970s had damaged the prestige of the Presidency and Carter was handicapped by the lessened respect for the wishes of the White House. At the same time, however, the suspicion grew that Carter himself was no more competent than Ford. He certainly seemed accident-prone.

The President was ambitious to make his mark in international affairs and to solve outstanding problems. With Cyrus Vance replacing Kissinger as Secretary of State, and with Andrew Young as the US Ambassador to the United Nations, the new administration had a liberal image. Carter himself sought improved relations with the USA's southern neighbours and negotiated a treaty for the eventual withdrawal of US authority from the Panama Canal Zone. Young, a black American whose appointment was very popular among those of his race, showed a lively sympathy for the under-privileged and countries of the Third World, contributing to the search for solutions to the problems of southern Africa. The administration continued to improve US relations with China, but perhaps Carter's chief success was in the vigorous encouragement he gave to peace-making between Egypt and Israel (see Section 19.1(g)). Even here, however, progress slowed down, disappointing the President's hopes for further triumphs.

Relations with the USSR deteriorated. Carter's concern for civil liberties in the USSR and Eastern Europe highlighted differences between the super-powers (see Section 12.2(f)). Anti-Soviet feeling grew stronger in the late 1970s. Though Carter negotiated a new SALT agreement with Brezhnev, he could not persuade Congress to ratify it. Suspicion of the USSR intensified when the Russians invaded Afghanistan in 1979 (see Section 17.2(d)). With vociferous support from Margaret Thatcher, the British Prime Minister, an angry Carter tried to organize a boycott of the Olympic Games held in Moscow in 1980. The boycott was only partly successful but itself produced almost as much wrangling as the Soviet Afghan adventure.

Most humiliating of all for Carter, however, was the rebuff he suffered at the hands of Iran. The Shah of Iran had long been a close ally of the USA but he was deposed in 1979 by a Moslem uprising. An Islamic religious leader, the Ayatollah Khomeini, returned to Iran from exile and the Shah took refuge in the USA. The Iranian uprising was strongly anti-Western and particularly anti-American. Radical students seized the US Embassy in Teheran and took US citizens prisoner, eventually holding some 50 Americans as hostages. Khomeini demanded the return of the Shah to stand trial for crimes against his people, and the return to Iran of assets in US banks which Iranians claimed were rightfully theirs. The Shah soon went to Egypt where he died, but the US-Iranian quarrel went on. In the meantime, Carter had resorted to economic sanctions. When they failed, he authorized a commando raid to rescue the hostages in April 1980. The result was tragedy. Eight of the rescuers were killed in a helicopter collision and the attempt was abandoned. The USA seemed no more able to influence Iran than she had been able to win the war in Vietnam. Vance resigned after the unsuccessful commando raid, claiming that he had not been adequately consulted by the President. Carter had earlier dismissed Young for various indiscretions and, though Young's successor was also black, the administration was rapidly losing popular confidence, not least among the American negroes who had helped to elect it.

It was a demoralized administration which approached the presidential election of 1980. Fig. 13.3 is a cartoonist's comment during the summer of that year on Carter's record. The Democrats confirmed Carter as their candidate but even many of his supporters lost heart. The President desperately needed some success. Instead, he suffered a further setback when his brother Billy became involved in a minor scandal concerning financial dealings with Libya (*Billygate*).

Ronald Reagan was the Republican candidate. Former film star, ex-Governor of California and a right-wing conservative, Reagan at first seemed an unlikely future President. He was already 69 and opinion polls suggested that neither he nor Carter roused much enthusiasm. Reagan shared many of the views of Mrs Thatcher in Britain. Both were deeply suspicious of the Soviet Union and eager to increase national spending on defence. Both admired the economic doctrines of Milton Friedman, and were keen to reduce other forms of national spending, to cut the part played by government in national economic affairs and to return to free enterprise and 'rugged individualism'. Economic problems, it was boldly asserted, were made worse by over-active government. Inflation could be cured by control of the money supply. There were many like Edward Kennedy, younger brother of the former President, who argued that in 1980 such thinking was naïve. But the American voters were in the mood to welcome simplicity in the face of their many baffling difficulties, and Table 13.1 shows the extent of the massive defeat Reagan inflicted on Carter.

Carter spent his last weeks in office still negotiating desperately to free the US hostages in Iran. The Shah's death had removed one major obstacle and

Fig. 13.3 A British cartoon (The Guardian, *August 1980) on President Carter's track record and approach to the presidential election which was to deny him a second term in office*

the negotiations made progress. They nevertheless dragged on: as if in spite, Khomeini and his associates delayed the release of the hostages into 1981, until the very moment when Carter had handed over the Presidency to Reagan and had left the White House.

13.3   Britain

(a) Party Politics

The general election of 1945 (see Section 10.6(*d*)) signalled Britain's return to party politics after the wartime coalition government. The Labour Party was in power from 1945 to 1951 and from 1964 to 1970, the Conservative Party from 1951 to 1964. By the end of this period, it was the Conservatives' view that Labour was the party of big spending and heavy taxation, and Labour's view that the Conservatives were the party of big business and missed opportunity. Conservatives taunted Labour over devaluation and low growth rates. Labour taunted Conservatives over 'thirteen wasted years' from 1951, and over the balance of payments deficit. Some who adhered to neither party alleged that there was little to choose between them anyway, an opinion to some extent encouraged by *Butskellism.*

This piece of jargon to describe the common ground between the parties took its name from the Conservative R.A. (Rab) Butler and Labour's Hugh Gaitskell. The common ground on which it was assumed they were in some agreement was that governments should be moderate and liberal, accepting great responsibilities for economic management and public welfare, but avoiding the extremes of doctrinaire policies. Yet 'Butskellism' was always misleading, for there were still many differences between the parties and although each leaned towards the centre, Labour remained a party of the left, the Conservatives a party of the right. They were often deeply divided in areas as varied as education, race relations, taxation and labour problems.

Such divisions became clearer in some ways during the 1970s. Heath's Conservative government, elected in 1970, showed every intention of moving further to the right, with a stronger emphasis on free enterprise, less government support for economic 'lame ducks' and firmer resistance to the trade unions. But Heath's government ended disastrously. The policy of confrontation with the unions combined with an energy crisis to produce a state of emergency and a hurried election in February 1974 which the Conservatives lost. Labour returned to power, first as a minority government and then after a second election, in October, with a tiny overall majority. 1974 was the first year since 1910 in which Britain had two general elections. Wilson was Prime Minister from 1974 to 1976, when he retired from office, leaving leadership of the Labour government to James Callaghan. Electoral defeat had meanwhile sealed the fate of Edward Heath, and the Conservatives replaced him as leader with Margaret Thatcher. The battle lines were now drawn for the next general election. The Labour government grappled with a confusion of economic problems and held on until 1979 when the voters were offered a clear choice. Callaghan and Labour recommended perseverance in the economic struggles they claimed to be winning. Thatcher and the Conservatives demanded a fresh start. Their policies were even further to the right than those of Heath in 1970. At the heart of them was a strong belief in monetarism (see Glossary). Around this they built demands for reduced government spending, reduced government support for uncompetitive businesses, reduced government efforts to control prices and wages, but stronger laws to curb the activities of trade unions. They also wanted strengthened defence forces, mainly to warn the Soviet Union, and firmer support at home for law and order. This was a path similar to that later chosen by Reagan in the US presidential election of 1980 (see Section 13.2(h)). It produced electoral support both in Britain and the USA, and the Conservatives came to power in 1979 with a comfortable majority.

Events had already shown, however, that theory alone was no answer to Britain's many problems. Like Heath before her, Thatcher quickly found that urgent difficulties produced their own shifts in government policy. Like Britain's voters, governments too seemed to flounder in the seemingly never-ending struggle to overcome economic problems.

(b) The British Economy

In 1945, Britain stood £3 000 million in debt. Many overseas assets no longer existed. Britain's ability to pay her way and to retain a favourable trading balance of payments depended now, more than ever, on selling her exports

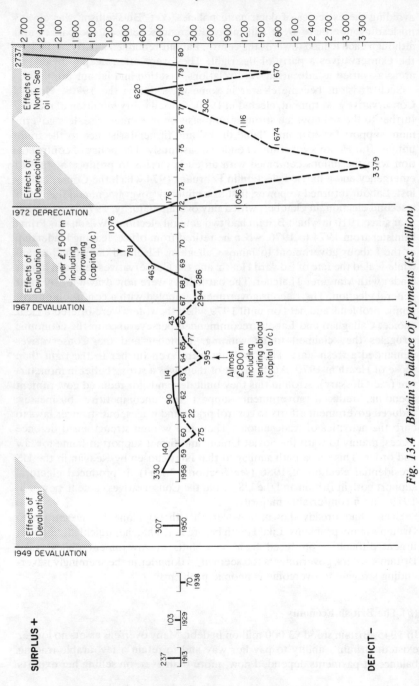

Fig. 13.4 Britain's balance of payments (£s million)

(see Section 10.6(c)). Inevitably this problem was linked with the value of the pound in terms of other currencies, so that exports and the strength of the pound soon became almost an obsession in Britain (see Fig. 13.4). There was no easy solution to the problem, for after 1945 there was even fiercer competition for markets. Britain, moreover, faced the urgent need to modernize machinery, management, marketing and labour relations, matters which had been seriously neglected before the war.

Governments were also expected after 1945 to avoid a high level of unemployment and to secure rising living standards. There were expectations of affluence, particularly after 1950. The fundamental balancing act which was required of governments was to provide increased wealth together with a healthy balance of payments. But increased wealth often led to increased imports which had to be paid for in exports. Britain had constantly to try to produce goods which could be exported and these were no longer the earlier basic exports such as textiles, coal and ships.

The revolution in technology also created rapid change. In old industries such as textiles, coal and shipbuilding the number of jobs steadily declined. Heavy investment was needed to finance new industries, such as aircraft-construction, in which the costs were enormous, and to modernize old ones. The competition was so fierce that it was essential to keep down costs and everywhere the emphasis was on productivity (the maximum and most efficient production for the lowest cost). Machinery, although initially expensive, often provided the key to productivity. But this raised old fears of machines putting men out of work.

Governments thus became trapped in a new dilemma. Expectations of wealth drove up prices and wages. Expensive exports were difficult to sell. This led to balance of payments problems. At the same time, efforts to reduce costs and increase productivity placed great strains on workers or even made them unemployed, angering trade unions. And the costliness of new machinery and of wage increases helped to drive prices still higher.

Governments, not infrequently, solved part of this jigsaw puzzle. In the late 1960s, Harold Wilson's Labour government produced a healthy balance of payments position but when it fell from power, in 1970, both prices and unemployment were beginning to rise sharply. Early in 1972, under Heath, unemployment had again topped the million mark yet the inflationary price rise went on, particularly in the prices of houses. In many respects, the problem was similar to that in the USA, but Britain had an even more desperate need than America to sell exports. Fig. 13.4 shows that Britain again plunged into balance of payments problems after 1971. Part of the problem was the old one of Britain's eagerness to buy more from abroad than exports could pay for, but it now grew worse because of the energy crisis and escalating price of oil.

The oil producers began to raise the price of oil partly to secure for themselves a fairer share in the profits from its sale and partly because it was becoming clear that supplies were being used up at an alarming rate, especially by the USA and other wealthy countries. Producers of other commodities such as copper also began to try to raise their prices. The old world economic order was breaking down and the result was a confusing mixture of inflation and recession for all countries which depended on international trade (see Section 18.1). Britain seemed at first to suffer more than most. In 1971, the annual rate of inflation topped 10 per cent. It topped 20 per cent at the end of 1974, then briefly rose beyond 25 per cent. By 1978, it had been reduced to single figures but rose in 1980 above 20 per cent again before another cutback to around 7 per cent in autumn 1982. Unemployment showed a more persistent upwards trend, reaching 1.4 million in 1977–8, falling back only slightly in 1979 and then hurtling beyond 3 million at the start of 1982. The pound fell in 1976 to buy only about 1.60 dollars (see Table 13.2). Two things helped the pound to recover, however. One was the increasing weakness of the dollar itself as the US economy ran into difficulties. The other was Britain's good fortune in securing supplies of oil from the North Sea. Britain was therefore able to reduce her oil imports and to produce a dramatic improvement in her balance of payments in the early 1980s. Britain seemed likely to be self-sufficient in oil during the 1980s, though that was likely to be only until the supplies were exhausted. In the meantime, North Sea oil created artificial confidence in the pound, leading to a high exchange rate which put up the cost of British exports, thus creating new problems and adding to the unemployment of British workers.

There was always widespread agreement that increased productivity would help to lessen Britain's difficulties. There was less agreement on how increased productivity could be achieved. Britain invested less than other countries in new machinery, but new machinery itself tended to create problems, seeming often to go hand-in-hand with unemployment. Britain in the 1970s was richer than ever before but the wealth was still very unevenly distributed and, as in the 1930s, unemployment hit hardest at the country's older industrial regions. The welfare state had not got rid of poverty. Unlike the USA, Britain had no fixed minimum wage and the plight of the poor was worsened by inflation.

Inequality bred discontent. The British system remained something of a free-for-all struggle between vested interests in which greed played its part. Before 1939 many had preferred to argue about the level of unemployment benefit rather than about cures for unemployment itself. In the 1970s, many preferred to look for scapegoats rather than attempting the more difficult task of finding solutions to the nation's problems. The right wing blamed trade unions and obstructionist and lazy workers. The left wing blamed financiers, speculators and weak management. The political parties blamed one another. Though government often seemed busy, the underlying problems changed little and, indeed, new problems were allowed to take root. Early in 1980 the British were shocked by a sudden outbreak of violence in Bristol, and shocked again by another outbreak in Brixton, London, in 1981. Both had a good deal to do with the deprivation and resentment building up in Britain's non-white communities (see Section 21.4(c)). There were those who thought that strengthening the police force was an inadequate substitute for social and economic policy of a more constructive sort.

(c) Labour Government, 1945–51

Attlee's government, elected in 1945, was the first Labour administration to have an overall majority. It threw its energies into postwar reconstruction and social advances. It was already committed to implementing the Beveridge Report (see Section 10.6(d)) and measures for social welfare were given a high priority. The National Insurance Act of 1946 extended existing schemes for insurance against sickness, retirement and unemployment. The principle was the same as that in the first such Act in 1911, that all workers would contribute to the insurance fund and in return would have the right to benefit in times of need. Contributions from employers and, out of taxes, from the government swelled the fund. The National Assistance Act of 1948 provided additional help for those in special need, this money supplied by government out of national taxation. The National Health Service was also financed mainly from taxation. Promoted enthusiastically by Aneurin Bevan, the Minister of Health, the National Health Service Act of 1946 made medical, dental and optical treatment available without charge and brought hospitals under national control. Until 1979 this welfare-state framework remained unchallenged by any government, though numerous amendments were made to the detail of it.

Attlee's government undertook extensive nationalization partly for more effective economic control and partly to provide better conditions for the workers. The major coal-mines were transferred to the National Coal Board in 1946, with compensation to their former owners. In 1947, railways, inland waterways and long-distance road-haulage were placed under the British Transport Commission. The Electricity Act of 1947 organized supply under the British Electricity Authority and 14 regional boards, generation continuing under the Central Electricity Generating Board. At the same time, the Gas Council (replaced by the British Gas Corporation in 1972) took over the gas industry, working like the Electricity Authority through regional (area) boards. Meanwhile, in 1946, the Bank of England was nationalized, and British European Airways (BEA) was set up as a second public corporation for air travel alongside BOAC (see Section 4.4(b)(i)). (BEA and BOAC were merged into British Airways in 1972.) Cable and Wireless was nationalized in January 1947. The fiercest opposition to nationalization and public ownership centred on the iron and steel industry, and it was not until 1950 that the 107 major companies in the industry were taken over by the state. The Conservatives then returned many of them to private hands after 1951 though retaining some oversight through the Iron and Steel Board. Re-nationalization followed under Wilson's government in 1967, when the Steel Corporation was set up.

Attlee's government made various other reforms. The delaying power of the House of Lords was reduced to one year. The right of electors to vote in more than one constituency was abolished – university seats and the vote attached to business premises being removed. In local elections, voters no longer had to be ratepayers. A Town Planning Act was passed, and an Act to create new towns. The government repealed Baldwin's Trade Disputes Act of 1927, something the Labour Party had long wanted to do. The Local Government Act of 1948 gave help to the poorer local authorities, and the poor were helped a year later with free legal aid. The government also granted independence to India and made changes in the Commonwealth (see Section 16.6).

This legislation was passed against a background of international readjustment and economic struggle. The government wished to move carefully from war to peace and to establish a firm economic base for the future. Priority was given to exports. Wartime controls and rationing were retained. Loans from America and Canada, however, were not enough to stave off a crisis. In 1947, a bitter winter with an acute shortage of fuel held up production and handicapped exports. Confidence in the pound fell and Cripps, the Chancellor of the Exchequer, had to place severe restrictions on spending, cut imports and try to freeze wages, hoping to divert Britain's energies into exports. Large food subsidies were used to hold down the price of food and thus demands for higher wages. But there was new uncertainty about the pound in 1949 and the devaluation of Britain's currency became inevitable. In September, the value of the pound was reduced from 4.03 to 2.80 American dollars. This made British exports cheaper and relieved the pressure on the balance of payments. But Attlee's government continued to be cautious. Many restrictions remained, especially on wages, and the government itself made cuts in its spending, even trying to reduce its spending on the Health Service by making charges for certain prescriptions.

These cuts infuriated Bevan, especially when the government embarked on heavy expenditure on arms in connection with the Korean War. Attlee made Gaitskell Chancellor of the Exchequer in 1950, clearly refusing to follow the more left-wing path of Bevan and Wilson, both of whom resigned in protest against health charges. This move was significant, for when Attlee retired in 1955, Gaitskell succeeded him as leader of the party. But, in the meantime, Attlee called another general election in 1951, after winning the election of 1950 with only a small majority. This time, the Conservatives under Churchill were returned with a small majority.

(d) Conservative Government, 1951–64

The Conservatives further increased their majority in elections in 1955 and 1959. Churchill retired in 1955 and Eden became Prime Minister. In 1957, Eden gave way to Macmillan and he, in turn, retired in 1963 to leave Douglas-Home to lead the party in the 1964 election.

The Conservatives believed in some movement away from controls and towards freedom. They had promised to return the iron and steel industry to private enterprise and, in the Steel Act of 1953, plants were restored to private owners but the Iron and Steel Board remained as a supervisory body. Long-distance road-haulage was also returned to private hands. The renewed fragmentation of control made the planning of a national transport system almost impossible. Commercial television, financed by advertising rather than licence fees, was set up in 1954, to compete with the BBC. By that year too, Churchill was able to announce the end of food rationing. The government's most constructive work was probably in the drive for more home-building, led by Macmillan as Minister of Housing.

Churchill retired shortly before the election of 1955. Eden was successful in that election but his short administration was overshadowed by the Suez Crisis (see Section 19.1(*d*)). The Clean Air Act of 1956, which did much to reduce smoke and fog in Britain's towns, was one of the most important measures passed by this government. A private member's bill to abolish capital punishment was rejected by the House of Lords, but Eden put through a Homicide Act, in 1957, to abolish the death penalty for all but a few types of murder.

Macmillan continued to build on earlier developments in town planning and hospital expansion. He introduced the system of life peerages in the House of Lords in 1958 and, in 1963, it became possible for peers such as Lord Hailsham (Quintin Hogg), to surrender inherited peerages in order to stay in the House of Commons. The Rent Act of 1957 removed rents from official control, leading to the charge that the Conservatives favoured landlords rather than tenants. Conservatives argued that profits were necessary if property was to be repaired. When Douglas-Home became Prime Minister, in 1963, he too had to surrender his peerage in order to secure election to the Commons. His Government was not long in office but Heath got through the Resale Prices Act, preventing manufacturers from denying supplies to those who wished to cut prices. In effect, 'recommended' prices replaced 'fixed' prices.

The years 1951–64 were an age of inquiries and reports. The Robbins and Newsom Reports were major studies of higher and secondary education. New towns and motorways began to change the face of Britain; the Buchanan Report studied traffic in towns and the Beeching Report the problems of the railways. These were controversial subjects, and there was also much controversy about Britain's continued production of nuclear weapons (first begun by Attlee's government), and about whether Britain should join the European Economic Community (EEC) (see Section 14.5(*c*)). Decisions about the future of the Empire and Commonwealth also needed to be made (see Section 16.6).

1951 to 1964 came to be called the *Age of Affluence*, and Macmillan's remark about the financial situation in 1957, 'You've never had it so good', came to be applied both to the prosperity of the times and to alleged Conservative complacency. In fact governments faced continuing problems with

Britain's economy. In Macmillan's last years they set up a National Incomes Commission (Nicky) and a more long-lasting National Economic Development Council (Neddy). Even for Conservatives, at least some planning and control seemed now to be essential.

Butler was Chancellor of the Exchequer under Churchill. Building on the foundations of Cripps and Gaitskell, he was able to reduce income tax and to encourage spending. But by 1956, labour disputes and a worsening balance of payments led to a reversal. Macmillan was now Chancellor and he raised taxes and tried to divert money from spending into savings with the introduction of Premium Bonds, a sort of state lottery. Thorneycroft, Chancellor in 1957–8, tried to reduce taxes while collecting money from increased charges for welfare services. Spending again threatened the balance of payments and now prices were rising quickly, leading to wage demands and further industrial troubles. Heathcote Amory, Chancellor from 1958 to 1960, stamped on wage increases but at the expense of a halt in the growth of output, an increase in unemployment and a squeeze on credit in 1960, to reduce spending. His successor, Selwyn Lloyd, found it necessary to fight a worsening balance of payments position. He introduced higher interest rates, new taxes, and a pay-pause to hold down increases in income. But he was replaced by Maudling, who again reversed the direction, perhaps with an eye on the coming general election. His aim was to stimulate the economy and let the people demonstrate their affluence by spending. The result was a record deficit on

Table 13.2 The pound and the US dollar
Some of the principal adjustments reflecting the trading difficulties of the democracies

Year	Dollars to the £
1914	4.86
1925	4.80 (Britain returned to the Gold Standard)
1931	c. 3.30 (pound allowed to depreciate; off Gold Standard)
1933	c. 5.00 (dollar allowed to depreciate)
post-1945	4.03
1949	2.80 (pound devalued)
1967	2.40 (pound devalued)
1971	2.60 (dollar devalued)
1972	2.35 (pound allowed to depreciate)
1973	c. 2.40 (dollar allowed to depreciate)
1976	c. 1.60
1981	c. 2.20 (dollar weak; confidence in British North Sea oil; exchange controls abolished from 1979)
1982	c. 1.80 (high US interest rates under Reagan, strengthening the dollar)

the balance of payments, approximately £400 million in one year and new worries about the strength of the pound.

In this 'Age of Affluence', the progress of Britain's economy was obviously erratic, moving on a stop-go pattern. The 'stops' cut back the rate of growth and led to jealous comparisons with other nations who seemed to grow richer, faster. Credit squeezes and efforts to hold down wages caused frustration and worsened industrial relations. On the other hand, 'go' periods led to problems with the balance of payments and some movement towards inflation. Moreover, unemployment still continued to fluctuate. In 1964, the electors were not sufficiently convinced that 'Life is Better under the Conservatives' to return them to power again. The Labour Party, led since Gaitskell's death by Harold Wilson, put forward a policy of 'getting things done' and won a tiny overall majority of four. In another election, in 1966, Wilson got a larger majority.

(e) Labour Government, 1964–70

Although there were differences in detail, Labour policies were in broad agreement with those of the Conservatives on a number of issues, among which were Commonwealth affairs (see Section 16.6) and especially the Rhodesian problem (see Section 21.3), the EEC (see Section 14.5(c)), the need to raise benefits such as old age pensions, but also the need to control immigration (see Section 21.4). In other respects, Labour sought changes. The Rent Act was repealed in 1965 with tribunals set up to decide fair rents. Health charges were dropped, although Wilson found it necessary to reimpose them in 1968. After a lengthy struggle, the iron and steel industry was renationalized. In education, the Government tried to step up the movement towards comprehensive schools and finally fixed a date (the early 1970s) for raising the school leaving age to 16.

Wilson's government also placed emphasis on the development of policies for those regions of Britain which lagged behind the general affluence, and on schemes for compensating and retraining those who became redundant. The Plowden Report of 1967 produced a study of primary schools, emphasizing the needs of the under-privileged. The Open University, in 1969, provided more opportunities in higher education. Concern for the less-privileged led to rate rebates in 1966, to allow the poor to escape the payment of local rates, and to option mortgages in 1968 to allow them to borrow money to buy houses at lower rates of interest. National Assistance benefits were replaced by Social Security supplements and the Health Service was extended to include family planning.

Many other changes were made. The Road Safety Act of 1967 tried to discourage driving under the influence of drink. The Transport Act in the following year amalgamated local transport authorities in certain congested areas. The age of majority was lowered from 21 to 18. The Post Office ceased to be a government department and became instead a public corporation, similar to the National Coal Board. An Ombudsman was introduced, to investigate bad administration. A start was made on the Anglo-French development of *Concorde*, a supersonic airliner. The government also began to tackle some of Britain's developing social problems, planning for the environment, investigating the role of trade unions and introducing a Race Relations Act to overcome some of the problems faced by coloured people. In 1965, the death penalty was completely abolished for a trial period which was later renewed.

The government also faced grave new problems in Northern Ireland (see Section 20.6) but it was the management of the economy which still provided its chief anxiety. The Labour Party confirmed its belief in planning by setting up a Department of Economic Affairs under George Brown. A National Board for Prices and Incomes was established and other bodies like Neddy continued. But the immediate problem which confronted Callaghan as Chancellor of the Exchequer was the balance of payments. To deal with the immediate crisis in 1964, the government borrowed heavily from IMF, imposing a surcharge on imports, cuts in spending and heavier taxation. Incentives were given to exporters and an attempt made first to freeze wages and then to restrain them and link them to productivity. In 1965, new taxes were imposed on corporations and capital gains. Even so, 1966 brought further troubles and a serious loss of confidence in the pound. As in 1931, a Labour government found it difficult to win the confidence and support of financiers. In 1967, the government decided that the pound had to be devalued, from 2.80 to 2.40 dollars. Further borrowing and another fierce attack on spending, which was continued by Jenkins who replaced Callaghan as Chancellor, finally brought improvement in 1969. The balance of payments began to appear more healthy, but there was an unpleasant upsurge in prices and unemployment.

It was at this point that Wilson called for a general election. It was won by the Conservatives under Heath, who had taken over leadership from Douglas-Home in 1965.

(f) Conservative Government, 1970–4

Heath became Prime Minister with some intention of moving away from 'Butskellism' towards a greater emphasis on private enterprise, competition, profits and efficiency. Comprehensive legislation was planned to deal with industrial relations, housing and rents and other outstanding problems. There were vigorous plans to restructure the tax system and many aspects of the welfare state, with lower taxes to encourage enterprise and more charges for services which had been subsidized out of taxation for many years. But results were not encouraging. Unemployment rose to its highest level since 1940, industrial relations were embittered, prices soared as never before and there was considerable outcry on behalf of the poor who were increasingly required to submit to means tests in order to obtain help. It seemed that there were now fundamental differences between the Conservative and Labour parties in matters of principles and priorities.

Heath's government nevertheless made some changes of direction. Economic problems led to some support being given to firms in difficulties and to a Price Commission and a Pay Board, none of which Heath had appeared to want. At the same time, efforts were made to protect the poor with a Family Income Supplement and a variety of rebate schemes. Local government reform brought sweeping organizational changes of a sort the public did not seem to want. In 1972 the pound was allowed to float downwards on the foreign exchanges, a form of devaluation (see Table 13.2), but that did little immediately to check a worsening problem with the balance of payments. Before long the government was in even deeper trouble.

As promised in the election of 1970, and in an effort to curb strikes and subdue the trade unions, the government had brought in an Industrial Relations Act. It was opposed bitterly. Heath got little co-operation from the unions when he found it necessary to resort to wage controls and in 1973 tried to use the Pay Board to hold down earned incomes. On top of industrial unrest came the energy crisis with higher fuel costs and alarm about oil supplies. The National Union of Mineworkers intended to use the sudden new importance of coal to improve wages in the industry, but the government sought to impose pay limits. In November 1973, Heath declared a state of emergency. 1974 began with fuel supplies so precarious that much of industry went on a three-day working week. The miners banned overtime and there were troubles in the electricity industry and other industries as well. When the NUM threatened an all-out coal stoppage, Heath called a general election for the end of February 1974.

Labour was returned as the largest single party and, when Heath failed to obtain Liberal support to remain in office, Wilson formed a minority government. The Labour Party argued that Conservative policies of confrontation had been a disastrous failure and had been rejected by the voters, but Labour too had lost votes compared with 1970. Labour lost more votes when Wilson held a second election in October 1974, but this time Wilson won an overall majority of three seats because the Conservative vote slumped by almost a million and a half. The Labour government remained in office with slightly less than 40 per cent of the total votes cast. Britain, it seemed, was becoming disenchanted with the two main political parties, with unending economic crises and even with the EEC which the country had only recently joined (see Section 14.5(c)).

(g) Labour Government, 1974–9

But economic crises were the background now to all that governments did. Much of Labour's programme was concerned with economic reorganization, including the nationalization of the aircraft and ship-building industries and the creation of the British National Oil Corporation (BNOC). A National

Enterprise Board (NEB) was set up to promote technological change and to help industries in difficulty. Changes were made in the docks. There was extensive social reform too. The Sex Discrimination Act of 1975 aimed to promote equal opportunities for women, and another Race Relations Act in 1976 the more equal treatment of Britain's ethnic minorities. The government encouraged faster movement towards comprehensive schools and there were further developments of the social-security system, with a more elaborate arrangement for earnings-related pensions, and child benefits to take the place of the earlier family allowances. Legislation was carried to tighten up on safety standards in workplaces and to protect workers from arbitrary dismissal. In response to the rise of Scottish and Welsh Nationalist parties, legislation was prepared to set up regional parliaments in Scotland and Wales but, for the time being, these changes were not put into effect.

Heath's Industrial Relations Act was repealed soon after Labour came to power. In its place, the government made a 'social contract' with the labour movement, seeking voluntary co-operation in the control of incomes and the improvement of industrial relations. The contract worked imperfectly. Unemployment stood at well over a million, and at the same time inflation created pressures for wage increases. When Wilson came to office in 1974, he quickly made a deal with the miners and got the country back to a normal working week. When he handed over to Callaghan in 1976, however, there was still no sure machinery for settling wage claims in the national interest. Continuity was provided throughout the years 1974 to 1979 by Denis Healey, Chancellor of the Exchequer, who became convinced that there must be another pay policy until the social contract became more effective. For some years, Healey had successes. The rise in unemployment was at least checked. Inflation was brought down. The balance of payments improved. In 1978 it seemed that the government was once more bringing Britain's wayward economy under control, considerably helped by the goodwill of the trade-union movement and ceilings on increases in incomes. At the same time, North Sea oil, the first of which had been brought ashore in 1975, was beginning to help the economy generally.

Healey demanded another year of incomes restraint, partly under pressure from the IMF from which Britain had had to borrow during the crisis of the mid-1970s. But the winter of 1978–9 turned out to be 'a winter of discontent'. The unions argued that in relation to inflation Healey had set the limits for pay increases too low, and there was a series of industrial conflicts involving, in particular, workers who were among the low-paid. Labour's claim to some special expertise in handling industrial relations took a hard knock. There was new enthusiasm for legislation which might somehow conjure up better industrial relations, in spite of both the Donovan Report of 1968, which had decided that such legislation would not be helpful, and the failure of Heath's Industrial Relations Act. It was against this background that Callaghan fixed the date of the next general election for May 1979.

The Labour Party defended its record during the previous five years and held on to its vote of 1974. Mrs Thatcher and the Conservatives attacked this record for its continued attachment to Keynesian economic theories of government intervention and as the continuation of postwar policies which failed to solve underlying problems. New jargon was thrown into the debate: the Conservatives wanted an emphasis on 'privatization' and movement away from government intervention, so that individuals and private businesses might prosper because of their own initiative. Milton Friedman, not Keynes, was the *guru* of these new doctrines. They had echoes of Heath's arguments of 1970 but they included a vital new ingredient – monetarism (see Glossary). The central policy of a new government should be a tight control of the money supply to 'squeeze inflation out of the economy'. One result would be the cutting down of government spending. Another would be – so it was hoped – an upsurge of enterprise and competitiveness. The argument that the state had come to interfere too much in the lives of the people had some popularity. So too had Conservative promises of lower taxation. There was also hope, if not confidence, that Friedmanism and Thatcherism might at last solve Britain's stubborn economic problems, though opponents of the Conservatives argued that the proposed solutions were far too simple. What undoubtedly counted, however, was the disillusionment of the voters with Labour's management of industrial relations and the Conservative promise to legislate on the subject of trade unions. The Conservatives gained over 3 million votes more than in October 1974 together with a healthy majority in the House of Commons. Margaret Thatcher took office as Britain's first woman Prime Minister.

(h) British Politics in the 1980s

The Thatcher government had no quick successes. Inflation quickly soared to an annual rate of over 20 per cent in the summer of 1980, and the money supply proved less easy to control than the Chancellor, Geoffrey Howe, had seemed to anticipate. A new battle had to be fought to bring inflation down again, with some success by 1982. The balance of payments plunged to a staggering new deficit, though North Sea oil and recession, which cut imports, then brought a large surplus in 1980. Cuts in government spending helped to deepen the recession, which grew worse in 1980 and 1981, while unemployment leapt upwards to surpass 3 million early in 1982. In 1981, it also turned out that, far from cutting taxes, the government had increased them, though by indirect methods. Whether Thatcherism would eventually produce the results prophesied for it remained open to argument. In the meantime, new industrial relations law was milder than had been expected and the government found itself helping economic 'lame ducks' even more vigorously than did Heath. It also whistled valiantly to keep up its courage, claiming in 1981 to see light at the end of the tunnel. Thatcher announced that the results of her policies would be 'a new realism' in a Britain which for too long had enjoyed higher living standards than the country's output could sustain. Economic observers forecast that the recession might begin to lift during 1983 but there was little or no agreement on what might be the long-term consequences of the monetarist experiment.

The Labour Party meanwhile, having lost the election of 1979, plunged into confusion much as in the 1950s. Callaghan retired and Michael Foot was elected Labour's leader, inheriting the task of wrestling with a tug-of-war between the right and left of the Party. Right-wingers alleged that extremists were trying to take over. Left-wingers alleged that the right had dominated the Party for far too long, ignoring the decisions of the annual conference and thus losing elections by failing to inspire the voters with visions of a more equal society. A group of MPs and former MPs such as Jenkins, Brown (now Lord George-Brown) and David Owen, recently Callaghan's Foreign Secretary, left the Labour Party to found a new group calling themselves the Social Democrats. They claimed that their aim was to break the traditional mould of British politics, allying with the Liberals to free British elections from the grip of Conservatives and Labour. It was their contention that Thatcher had carried the Conservative Party to the extreme right, while the Labour Party was being taken over by the extreme and Marxist left. Such terms were relative and, by outside standards, British parties remained generally moderate. There was nevertheless considerable disquiet among Conservatives about their new leadership and unease within the Labour Party about an apparent struggle for power between staid men like Healey and radicals like Tony Benn. After a rush of initial support, however, the Social Democrats appeared to falter in spite of the election of Roy Jenkins as their leader. British politics were further complicated in 1982 when a crisis over the Falkland Islands and confrontation with Argentina seemed to restore some of the prestige of the Prime Minister and her government, at least in the short term.

Outside parliament, social disorder increasingly worried the authorities. British society grew more unpredictable. The 1960s and 1970s had seen a general escalation of violence by both criminals and hooligans. High unemployment and the bleak outlook for many young people at the beginning of the 1980s seemed to make the problem worse. Many of the unemployed were non-white and it was particularly difficult for non-white school-leavers to find work. West Indian youngsters, especially, grew resentful of a society which seemed to condemn many of them to sub-standard housing in the inner cities and dismal prospects for advancement (see Section 21.4(c)). Extremist groups like the National Front inflamed the situation, preaching racial hatred with a bigoted frenzy many found reminiscent of pre-war fascism. Indeed an Anti-Nazi League came into being to resist the activities of the National Front. Disastrous election results showed that the National Front held little appeal for the mass of British voters, all its candidates failing dismally in the general election of 1979. On the other hand, the level of lawlessness in Britain and the tensions in British society were now such that the Thatcher government specifically exempted the police from the widespread cuts in public spending that were part of its policy.

(i) British Foreign Policy since 1945

Attlee's selection of Ernest Bevin to be Foreign Secretary in 1945 was somewhat unexpected. Bevin had been a Chairman of the TUC and wartime Minister of Labour; but the appointment was in many ways a successful one. Bevin wore himself out in this gruelling office and retired in 1951 only a few weeks before his death. During this period, he committed Britain to the side of the USA in the Cold War and readily joined both in the defence of Western Europe and in the war in Korea against communist expansion. He also disentangled Britain from the developing crisis in Palestine (see Section 19.1(b)). He took little part in the moves which produced the European Coal and Steel Community in 1951 and prepared the way for the EEC, for his health was failing and, in any case, Britain's ties with the Commonwealth seemed to exclude closer economic involvement in Europe. When Bevin retired, therefore, Britain had a major role in NATO but was already being left behind in the movement towards European unity (see Section 14.5).

Churchill's Foreign Secretary, Eden, made no substantial changes in Bevin's policies. Britain joined SEATO but refused to adopt the USA's hard line towards communist China. Eden negotiated the Geneva agreement of 1954 over Indochina but the summit meeting with Khrushchev and Eisenhower in 1955 achieved little. Eden was now Prime Minister and, in 1956, he became disastrously involved in the Suez Crisis and a short-lived war with Egypt (see Section 19.1(d)). British forces were withdrawn amid a storm of criticism and in January 1957 Eden resigned.

Although Selwyn Lloyd was Macmillan's first Foreign Secretary and Douglas-Home took the office in 1960, Macmillan had ideas of playing an important part in world peace-making himself, but nothing could disguise the fact that Britain now had only limited influence on the USA and the Soviet Union. The 1960 summit meeting proved unproductive. Britain avoided involvement in America's growing commitments in Vietnam, and remained on the side-lines when the Berlin Wall was built in 1961 and a crisis developed over Russian missiles in Cuba in 1962. Iain Macleod as Colonial Secretary, however, managed to give a liberal appearance to his government's handling of Commonwealth problems. Macmillan also brought a new approach to Europe when, in 1961, he decided to explore the question of entry into the EEC, although long negotiations proved unproductive in the face of French opposition. Meanwhile Britain was a founder-member of the European Free Trade Association (EFTA) in 1959. Support was also given to the Test Ban Treaty of 1963.

Wilson ran into difficulties similar to those which defeated Macmillan. The French blocked Britain's entry into the EEC though Wilson and Brown toured the member-countries of the Community in 1967. Nor was it possible to make a dramatic breakthrough in improving relations with the Soviet Union although Wilson and Kosygin exchanged friendly visits. Britain supported the Nuclear Non-Proliferation Treaty in 1968 and joined in the discussions of SALT, but her principal problem in the late 1960s was Rhodesia, which Wilson was quite unable to bring to a successful conclusion. Wilson, however, showed a more sensitive regard for the feelings of the non-white world over the problems of southern Africa than did Heath who, upon taking office, promptly reversed a Labour decision not to sell arms to South Africa and aroused the anger of the Afro-Asian bloc in the United Nations.

Heath's main aim in foreign affairs was to attach Britain to the EEC. This was achieved in 1973, taking advantage of the changes in French policy which followed the retirement of de Gaulle (see Section 14.5(c)). But neither Heath nor his Labour successors could solve Britain's Rhodesian problem. It was growing African pressures on Smith's Rhodesian government that finally opened the way for a settlement, and this was achieved by Lord Carrington, Foreign Secretary in Britain from 1979 to 1982 (see Section 21.3(d)).

Before 1979, British governments had played their part in the improvement of relations between the major powers, both in developing links with China and in promoting agreements with the Soviet Union (see Section 17.2(c)). The change of government in Britain in 1979, however, coincided with less cordial relations between the USA and the Russians. Mrs Thatcher had already been dubbed 'the Iron Lady' by the Soviet authorities, critical of her uncompromising speeches in support of President Carter and in opposition to what she regarded as expansionist ambitions in the Kremlin. When she became Prime Minister, with Carrington at the Foreign Office, British foreign policy hardened, and the movement towards detente seemed to grind to a halt (see Section 17.2(d)). But it was in conflict with Argentina, not the USSR, that the Thatcher government was tested. The Argentines seized possession of the Falkland Islands, a British dependency in the South Atlantic, early in 1982. Carrington resigned from the government, accepting responsibility for the inadequate defence of the Islands about which there had long been a dispute. A huge task force was prepared and despatched, however, and Britain regained possession of the Falklands – an action which had the effect of raising the popularity of the Thatcher government at a time of considerable economic gloom (see Section 19.5).

Further Reading

Buchan, A.: *The U.S.A.* Oxford University Press (London, 1971).
Cootes, R.J.: *The Making of the Welfare State*. Longman (Harlow, 1966).
James, R.: *Towards the Welfare State*. Nelson (London, 1971).
Jamieson, A.: *Leaders of the Twentieth Century*. Bell (London, 1970) – Kennedy.
Mooney, P.J. and Bown, C.: *Truman to Carter*. Arnold (London, 1979).
Seaman, L.C.B.: *A New History of England, 410–1975*. Harvester (Brighton, 1981) – Pages 483–525.
Sloman, D.: *America since 1920*. Heinemann (London, 1978).
Watson, J.B.: *Success in British History since 1914*. John Murray (London, 1983).

Documentary

Breach, R.W.: *Documents and Descriptions, the World since 1914*. Oxford University Press (London, 1966) – Section 16.

Chambers, W.N.: *The Democrats 1789–1964*. Anvil (London, 1964).

Lane, P.: *Documents and Questions, British History 1914–1980*. John Murray (London, 1981).

Lane, P.: *Documents on British Economic and Social History, 1945–67*. Macmillan (London, 1968).

Wroughton, J.: *Documents on British Political History, 1914–70*. Macmillan (London, 1972).

Exercises

1. What does Table 13.1 show of American presidential elections since 1916 in terms of the contest between US political parties? What does the Table reveal of the problems which arise from the constitution of the USA?

2. Explain what is meant in Sections 13.2(*a*) and (*b*) by (*i*) 'Un-American activities' and (*ii*) 'traditions of violence'. What general reasons have there been in the USA since 1945 for 'furious argument about the nature of society' (page 223)?

3. Using cross-references in this Unit and the Index to this book, write assessments of the achievement of *two* US presidents since 1945.

4. Why has dissatisfaction been widespread in the USA since the end of the 1950s? Identify *two* groups in American society with particular reasons for being dissatisfied and explain their grievances.

5. Why has the USA had so many different presidents since the retirement of Eisenhower?

6. Making use of the Index to this book, trace the record in office of President Carter and explain why he was unable to win re-election in 1980. In the light of what you have written, how far do you consider that the cartoon at Fig. 13.3 offers a fair summary of Carter's presidential record?

7. What do you understand by a *welfare state*? What were the main features of such a state in Britain at the beginning of the 1950s?

8. For what major developments were the Labour governments of 1945 to 1951 responsible? How do you account for the Labour Party's defeat in the general election of 1951?

9. Explain what Fig. 13.4 shows of Britain's economic problems since 1945, and what you understand by (*a*) *devaluation* and (*b*) *depreciation*. How does Table 13.2 illustrate your definitions of devaluation and depreciation?

10. Which, in your opinion, better deserves the description of 'wasted years' – the period of Conservative government, 1951–64 *or* the period of Labour government, 1964–70?

11. 'Economic crises were the background now to all that governments did' (page 245). Explain and illustrate the truth of this statement with reference to Britain in the 1970s.

12.   I am going to build the kind of nation that President Roosevelt hoped for, President Truman worked for and President Kennedy died for. (*President Johnson, December 1964*)

    Write five paragraphs to show:

    (*a*) what *kind of nation* Johnson was trying *to build*;

    (*b*) in what ways Johnson's policy was similar to that of Roosevelt;

(c) how Truman *worked for* a similar policy;
(d) in what circumstances Kennedy *died*;
(e) why Johnson decided to abandon his struggle in 1968.

The USA and the European Capitalist Bloc – 2 Western Europe

14.1 France

(a) The Mixture as Before

With the liberation of France in 1944, General de Gaulle became head of a French provisional government, assuming the office of President a year later. There was general agreement that the Third Republic, which had collapsed in 1940 after years of instability, should be replaced by a Fourth Republic with a new constitution. The latter was drafted by a constituent assembly and formally adopted in October 1946. Before then, however, de Gaulle had resigned his office, angered by the demands for reduced military spending but, above all, infuriated by what he suspected would be a return to instability and government by coalition. Under the new constitution, the powers of the President were less than de Gaulle thought essential. For some years, he campaigned, but with little success, for a stronger system of government, organizing right-wing opinion in the Rally of the People of France (RPF). In 1951, he retired from politics in frustration.

The constitution of the Fourth Republic gave women the right to vote and adopted proportional representation. The Senate was replaced by a Council of the Republic, with reduced powers, but the lower house of the French parliament, the National Assembly, continued to be the heart of the system. Unfortunately, divisions in this Assembly continued to produce only a procession of unstable coalition governments.

The early governments were dominated by Socialists, Radicals and the Mouvement Républicain Populaire (MRP), especially after the exclusion from office of the strong postwar Communist Party in 1947. Governments were too weak to deal effectively with France's basic problems of inflation and industrial unrest, although the French economy was propped up with American aid. In its first five years, the Fourth Republic produced twelve governments under seven prime ministers. Only one government, Blum's in 1946, was not a coalition: it lasted for six weeks. A government under Queuille, in 1950, lasted for only four days. The politicians pursued moderate policies and, for a time, resisted both the left-wing challenge of the communists and the right-wing challenge of the RPF. French democracy survived, though unconvincingly, as it had before 1939.

The 1950s brought little improvement. From 1952 to 1958, there were ten more governments, almost all of them conservative in their policies. There were now new frustrations. Defeat in Indochina in 1954 (see Section 16.3(*a*)) was accompanied by a fresh rebellion in Algeria (see Section 16.3(*b*)); intervention in the Suez Crisis in 1956 brought only humiliation (see Section 19.1(*d*)). Pressing economic problems combined with the political instability to bring new waves of protest. Opinion generally tended to shift towards the right in a search for stable government. In 1953, the RPF was disbanded as a political force, freeing Gaullists in the National Assembly to exert pressure within the governments (although they could do little to strengthen the parliamentary system). Outside parliament, the RPF continued its campaign for a more effective constitution. A more violent attack on the system was made by the Poujadists, the followers of Henri Poujade who appealed in particular to the prejudices of the lower middle classes and aroused some echoes of Mussolini.

The French economy developed better than might have been expected in the 1950s, and the Fourth Republic made an effective contribution to European unity (see Section 14.5). But political instability led to exasperation and French failures overseas to despair.

(*b*) **The End of the Fourth Republic**

A crisis which had long been in the making came to a head in 1958. French settlers and right-wing forces in Algeria rejected the authority of the French government. France seemed to face a situation not dissimilar to that in Spain in 1936, when Franco, launching his campaign from North Africa, challenged the republican government and produced civil war. President Coty and Pflimlin, the Prime Minister, now surrendered power rather than risk a French civil war. There was only one sufficiently heroic Frenchman to whom it was possible to turn and, in June 1958, de Gaulle came out of retirement. He was given full powers to rule and the authority to produce a new constitution. France would have a *Fifth Republic*, in which the President's powers would be greatly strengthened (although not to the extent of adopting the USA's presidential system). France continued to have prime ministers who relied on support in the Assembly but the President was no longer merely a figurehead. De Gaulle himself was President until 1969.

(*c*) **The Years of de Gaulle**

From 1958 to 1969, de Gaulle was largely able to impose his own will on France. He appointed sympathetic prime ministers, first Michel Debré and from 1962 Georges Pompidou, and there was strong Gaullist support in the Assembly. De Gaulle himself was elected to the Presidency in 1958 and re-elected in 1965 and he also made use of referenda (to obtain popular votes of confidence over specific issues). During this period, there was a steep decline in support for communism and, at least for a time, considerable satisfaction with a system of government which could produce results.

Fig. 14.1 A warm welcome for General de Gaulle in Algeria in October 1958, but the white settlers were soon to be shocked when de Gaulle conceded Algerian independence to an Arab government

(*i*) **Foreign policy.** De Gaulle was a man of strong opinions, with a belief in French greatness. He intended to restore France's individual importance in the world and her independence of the USA. France developed her own nuclear weapons and refused to sign the Test Ban Treaty of 1963. In 1964, she recognized communist China and began to cultivate direct and cordial relations with the USSR. In 1966 de Gaulle withdrew from military commitments to NATO, forcing the Alliance to move its headquarters from Paris to Brussels. Though de Gaulle supported the development of the EEC, he denied Britain admission to it, perhaps resentful of Britain's English-speaking ties with the USA, mindful of his strained relations with the Allies when he led the Free French during the war but, above all, reluctant to have another rival for the leadership of Western Europe. One of de Gaulle's main achievements was to build a new friendship between France and West Germany, where he found a leader in his own image in the authoritarian Adenauer (see Section 14.3(*a*)). This was an association the French President preferred to any closer links with Britain, whose involvement with the Commonwealth was a further complication from which he wished the EEC to remain free. In de Gaulle's eyes, the EEC was a continental club and France was its rightful leader. Even West Germany was expected to fall in with French designs: de Gaulle would not support any German ambitions to recover lands to the east. In this and other policies the French President was a realist. He refused to prop up the narrow interests of white settlers in Algeria though they had welcomed him to power as their saviour (see Section 16.3(*b*)). Nor did he intend to get involved in old-fashioned attempts to preserve what was left elsewhere of the French overseas empire, though the constitution of the Fifth Republic brought into being the French Community (see Section 16.3(*d*)). But de Gaulle could also be a romantic, sometimes unrealistic. One of his strangest exploits was to meddle in Canadian affairs, even to the point of seeming to encourage a separatist movement of Canadian extremists of French descent.

(*ii*) **Domestic affairs.** Within France, his main achievement was political stability but he also pursued efficiency and reform. He aimed to build up substantial gold reserves, and vigorous economic policies brought an impressive rate of growth in the early 1960s. Progress was made in education, the social services and town-planning and France had a minimum wage, related to the cost of living. But de Gaulle's regime was authoritarian. It tended to antagonize students and trade unions and, by 1968, it was being criticized for currency troubles and a high level of unemployment. In May 1968, there were violent strikes, student demonstrations and bloody clashes. De Gaulle made concessions to the working classes by promising better wages, shorter hours and some consultation of their representatives by management. But in the autumn, the franc was under pressure and confidence in de Gaulle fell. It seemed to him an intolerable blow to French prestige to allow the franc to be devalued. He decided to make another grand appeal to the French people to confirm him in authority, linking a vote of confidence in himself to a referendum on a minor constitutional reform. The vote in April 1969 showed 10½ million in support of de Gaulle but almost 12 million against him. He promptly resigned and retired for the last time, to die in 1970 at the age of 79.

(*d*) The Fifth Republic after de Gaulle

De Gaulle had designed the Fifth Republic with care, and left-wing parties complained that it had a built-in bias towards the right. Gaullism certainly lived on after de Gaulle's resignation. The new President was the Gaullist, Georges Pompidou, who held office to his death in 1974. Pompidou had been a supporter of the General since 1944 and a Prime Minister of the Fifth Republic for six years. He agreed to devalue the franc and imposed restrictions to deal with the economic problems left by de Gaulle. He also adopted a more open-minded attitude to new admissions to the EEC but, in other respects, Gaullist policies continued – it was a strong Presidency with generally conservative attitudes. There was an emphasis on French independence, though rather less weight was given to de Gaulle's own vision of France's destiny.

Giscard d'Estaing also had a Gaullist background. Giscard was elected to succeed Pompidou but by only a narrow majority over François Mitterrand, candidate of the left. Giscard had become Minister of Finance in 1962 and served as a financial expert in a succession of governments before becoming President. He now inherited the economic problems which were common in the mid- and late-1970s (see Section 18.1). France coped rather better than Britain and Italy with inflation and unemployment, but there were difficulties in exporting enough to pay for imports, and industrial relations were often stormy. Against the background of economic struggles, political changes occurred. Giscard's support came mainly from Republicans, both moderates and conservatives. The Gaullists found him too flexible, and Chirac founded a new Gaullist group to stick more closely to Gaullist principles. Giscard therefore came under fire from both left and right. The Fifth Republic had nevertheless provided a good deal of stability in France and, for many Frenchmen, a good deal of prosperity, and it withstood the political and economic uncertainties of the late 1970s.

In spite of Gaullist discontent, Giscard was the clearly-preferred candidate of the right when he stood for re-election in 1981. His re-election was nevertheless in doubt since neither his personality nor his policies aroused real enthusiasm. As had often been the case in the past, however, the left was handicapped by its own divisions, especially between socialists and communists. Mitterrand stood again and, as in 1974, the final choice before the electors was between Giscard and Mitterrand. The outcome – Mitterrand's election – gave the Fifth Republic its first left-wing President. Some weeks later the Socialists also did well in elections to the Assembly, though the Communist Party seemed already to be beginning to regret the support it had given to Mitterrand. The political balance in France had nevertheless shifted significantly. Mitterrand had plans for far-reaching reforms of French society and of the economy, and at last it seemed that France was making a break with the age of de Gaulle.

14.2 Italy

By a narrow margin, in a referendum in 1946, Italy agreed to abolish the monarchy and thus set up a republic. From the outset, the Christian Democrats, a moderate conservative party, were the dominant political force. Their strength was matched, however, by the Socialist and Communist parties. Communism was more firmly established in Italy than in other western capitalist states but, under the leadership of Togliatti, Italian communists reserved a Tito-like right to follow a different path from that of Moscow. Italian communists, therefore, took an active part in trying to advance the welfare of Italians by working within the republican constitution.

Italian politics were fairly stable until 1953. De Gasperi was unable to win outright majorities for the Christian Democrats, but he proved an able Prime Minister as the leader of coalitions, with a talent for survival which might have been envied in France. From 1953 onwards the strength of the moderates began to decline and, after de Gasperi's death in 1954, the Christian Democrats themselves showed a tendency to split into factions. Christian

Democrat-dominated coalitions continued to govern but they were based on constantly-shifting alliances and frequent changes of prime minister. At times government came near to total paralysis, but Italy had no de Gaulle to carry through political reorganization. Instead, the Christian Democrats benefited from the divisions of the left and went on stitching together coalitions. In 1963, for example, the Socialists joined the Christian Democrats in government rather than the Communists in opposition, and there were five years of comparative stability while Aldo Moro was Prime Minister. But political confusion was never far away and it increased during the 1970s. Andreotti formed a government in 1972 without the Socialists but including Social Democrats. A year later Rumor formed a government of Christian Democrats, Social Democrats, Socialists and Republicans. Both Moro and Andreotti returned to form new governments and in 1980 Cossiga formed Italy's forty-third government since 1943, having just lost control of the forty-second. In 1981, Giovanni Spadolini took office as Italy's first postwar Prime Minister who was not a Christian Democrat.

In the 1970s the Christian Democrats regularly won just under 40 per cent of Italian votes. The Italian Communist Party won something between 30 and 35 per cent. These two parties were the main choices of Italian electors, but the Christian Democrats managed to keep the Communists out of power into the 1980s. The Italian Communist Party nevertheless had successes in local government, and in 1976 won control of Rome, Bologna, Florence and Naples. In spite of the Italian Communists' independence of Moscow, continued under Berlinguer after Togliatti's death in 1964, Italy's NATO allies worried that Italy was the one state in the Organization where government including communists seemed always to be at least a possibility. Communists in Western Europe generally asserted their independence from the USSR, developing a *Eurocommunism* they believed more appropriate for the economic and social problems of the capitalist states. In Italian cities and regional governments, such as that of Tuscany, Eurocommunists were able to begin to put some of their reforming ideas into practice.

There was need in Italy for economic and social reform. The Marshall Plan helped Italy towards postwar recovery, and Italy gained some advantages from being a founder-member of the European Communities (see Section 14.5(c)). But in the 1970s, Italy remained the poorest continental member of the EEC and the new economic crises of that decade brought widespread unemployment, rampant inflation and many other difficulties. Italy had shared in the general development of prosperity in postwar Western Europe but never to the extent of the countries further north. Governments were too weak to make any sustained attack on the deep-rooted problems of an Italy still markedly divided between north and south. Southern Italy remained poor, backward in industrial development, under-productive in agriculture, plagued by the criminal activities of the *Mafia* which Mussolini had tried in vain to destroy, and weakened by the regular migration northwards of those with the enterprise to search for higher standards of living. The north, too, had its problems, especially areas of poor living conditions and industry prone to periods of unemployment. Like poor countries everywhere, Italy tended to put an unhealthy reliance on tourism as a means of earning foreign currency.

Violence in Italian society caused even more concern. Impatience with weak central government helped to make industrial relations turbulent, with confrontations which were often fierce. There was a violent strand in politics too. The general election of 1972, for example, was stormy. It was ominous that the toyshops in Rome did a brisk trade in plastic figures recalling Mussolini's March on Rome of 1922, and that neo-fascists led by Almirante made significant gains. After that, the neo-fascists slipped back again, but violence by the extreme right and extreme left increased rather than abated. The Communist Party was a respectable institution in Italy's democratic political system, but there were those to the left of the Communists in organizations, such as the Red Brigades, which were at war with society. Kidnappings and murders were all too common. In 1978 the Red Brigades gloried in the kidnapping and murder of Moro, now the country's veteran statesman. In 1980, an explosion at Bologna railway station killed more than 75 people, perhaps in protest at the city's Communist government which had launched a vigorous hunt for terrorists. But much of the violence had little to do with politics. There was a high crime-rate generally, and the island of Sardinia won special renown for kidnapping and holding to ransom. There was violence too in Corsica, to the north of Sardinia, which was part of France and where an explosion at the airport in 1981 was part of an unsuccessful attempt to kill President Giscard. Corsican nationalists wanted independence, though some argued, rather like Mussolini, that Corsica ought rightfully to be part of Italy. Western Europe grew increasingly violent in the 1960s and 1970s but Italians had particular reason for concern at the scale of the outrages they endured.

Italy was hardly equipped to play a major role in international affairs after 1945. Her admission to UNO was delayed until 1955 by Soviet opposition, but Italy joined NATO and remained firm in her commitment to the West. Deprived of overseas empire as the result of Mussolini's activities and with her frontiers adjusted in the peace settlement of 1947 (see Section 11.1(b)), Italy's claws had been clipped and there was a new realism among Italian politicians about the country's limitations in foreign policy.

14.3 The German Federal Republic (West Germany)

(a) The Adenauer Years

The birth of the German Federal Republic in 1949 was the beginning of a success story (see Section 11.2). The Federal Republic had a similar constitution to that of the Weimar Republic, but it was stable and it was also soon prosperous. Konrad Adenauer, the first Chancellor, ruled from 1949 until 1963 when he retired at the ripe age of 87. He was a former mayor of Cologne who had been dismissed by Goering for opposition to the Nazis. After the war, he founded the Christian Democrat Party (CDU) which in coalition with the Christian Socialists (CSU), a similar party based in Bavaria, and smaller groups with a similarly conservative outlook, formed the first government of the new republic. The CDU–CSU alliance provided stable government for many years, with the Social Democrats developing as the principal Opposition.

Adenauer's governments took vigorous action to avoid many of the difficulties of the Weimar Republic. Extremist parties, such as the Socialist Reich Party, with similarities to the Nazis, were banned and leaders like Werner Naumann, who sought to rally ex-soldiers into new versions of the Freikorps, were arrested. In 1956, the Communist Party was also banned. Adenauer's methods were sometimes autocratic but they helped to establish the political system of the new republic.

Adenauer also built up the republic's strength with the help of Erhard as Minister of Economic Affairs. The Federal Republic smoothly resettled a flood of refugees into the country, overcame the problem of unemployment and embarked on an *Economic Miracle*. Recovery and expansion in the early 1950s were remarkably rapid although Adenauer's commitment to rearmament and the introduction of conscription in 1957 antagonized the trade union movement, which had been moderate and co-operative. West Germany was fortunate in possessing vital raw materials but economic growth was also due to a combination of circumstance, effort and policy. Wartime devastation forced German industry to re-equip with modern plant and Marshall Aid gave the country a helpful start. The Germans made a vigorous national effort and, with official encouragement, invested for the future. Erhard interfered little with capitalist forces, concentrating on flexible policies to encourage enterprise. West Germany was a founder-member of the ECSC and EEC (see Section 14.5(c)) and benefited extensively from these Communities. At the same time Adenauer's government was attentive to popular welfare. It pioneered an extension of welfare pensions, linking them not only to the cost of living but also to the growth of national wealth. West Germany, therefore, combined a strong emphasis on economic private enterprise with a traditional German concern for social welfare. It proved a winning combination: annual growth rates were impressive and the Federal Republic had healthy trade surpluses. Until the economic strains of the late 1970s West Germany raced ahead to ever increasing wealth. A small part of the country's wealth was used to compensate the Jews of Israel as some reparation for the atrocities of the Nazis.

Partly because of constitutional safeguards against the representation of small parties, only three parties were elected to the Bundestag (the Republic's lower house of parliament) in the election of 1961. These were the CDU–CSU alliance, the Social Democrats and the Free Democrats. Adenauer now had to make an alliance with the Free Democrats in order to remain in office. He was also criticized for clinging to power in spite of his advancing age, and opponents referred scornfully to 'Chancellor Dictatorship' as the old man grew closer to de Gaulle, and became arbitrary in his ways. He finally retired in 1963, at last allowing Erhard to take over the Chancellorship.

Fig. 14.2 Adenauer steps down at last. A West German cartoon – the old man advises Erhard: 'I see personal changes ahead . . . an old friend can be very useful to you . . . a bad time for high-flying plans . . . mind the red carpet'

(b) Erhard and Kiesinger

Erhard governed from 1963 to 1966. At last the republic's economic progress began to slow down. Unemployment rose and a neo-Nazi Party, the National Democratic Party (NDP), was set up. Erhard was forced to resign when the Free Democrats withdrew their support from his government.

The new Chancellor was Kiesinger who managed to make a coalition between the CDU and the Social Democrats. The Social Democrats' abandonment of a commitment to Marxism in 1959 and adoption of a policy based on 'as much freedom as possible and as much planning as necessary' made the coalition possible. Kiesinger overcame the unemployment problem, but the NDP continued to cause alarm and, like France, the republic encountered student protest against crowded universities and the nature of Western society. In the general election of 1969 the Social Democrats took office for the first time under Chancellor Willy Brandt.

(c) Brandt and Schmidt

With only a tiny majority in the Bundestag, Brandt courageously committed himself to his *Ostpolitik* (a policy of seeking a new friendly relationship between West Germany and Eastern Europe). He also took advantage of de Gaulle's retirement to encourage new admissions to the EEC, and recognized the great strength of the mark in relation to other currencies by revaluing it upwards. This encouraged people who wished to sell to the Federal Republic, and made German exports more expensive. These were promising beginnings which helped to build up Brandt's reputation as a statesman, but his position in the Bundestag was insecure, a handicap in readjusting West Germany's relations with Eastern Europe. A more decisive victory in the general election of 1972 strengthened Brandt's authority. Two years later, however, he resigned, taking personal responsibility when an East German spy was discovered on his staff. He was perhaps ready enough to step down in any case. His Ostpolitik had proved fruitful, earning him the Nobel Peace Prize; the Social Democrats had proved their ability to govern with continuing economic advances; and Brandt himself was perhaps tired of domestic office which had begun as Mayor of West Berlin in 1957. He was succeeded as Chancellor by Helmut Schmidt who remained in office until 1982. Schmidt had to face difficult economic problems and a disturbing increase in the activities of terrorists within the Republic.

The Federal Republic fared better than most capitalist states in resisting inflation and unemployment and in continuing to market its output. Even so, when Schmidt was re-elected in 1980, the economic miracle seemed to have ended. In 1982, unemployment reached 1.8 million. Prosperity had in any case not brought tranquillity. From the late 1960s there had been much youthful protest against West German society's emphasis on enrichment and consumer goods, and against the Republic's ties with the USA. The most notorious among those who turned to terrorism was the Baader–Meinhof Group whose activities were similar to those of Italian Red Brigades. Ulrike Meinhof died in 1976 and Andreas Baader died a year later. Both deaths occurred in prison and were allegedly suicides. But violence and disorder remained a problem both in West Germany and West Berlin, sometimes fuelled by the Nazi-like activities of the extreme right. Schmidt's government dealt fiercely with suspected enemies of the Republic and such firmness proved an electoral asset in 1980. Schmidt was not an exciting Chancellor but his calmness and firmness in office inspired confidence in the face of crises. He wearied of the struggle, however. Two years after the election of 1980, exasperated by divisions among the Social Democrats and deserted by the

Free Democrats, Schmidt resigned in favour of a government headed by the Christian Democrat, Helmut Kohl.

(d) West Germany and the German Problem

The division of Germany which produced the German Problem (see Section 11.2) had already begun to seem permanent rather than temporary when Adenauer came to power. The Federal Republic was allowed to establish a foreign office in 1951 and from then until 1955, Adenauer had personal charge of West Germany's foreign policy. It was in this period that West Germany settled firmly into the Western capitalist bloc. Soon after the outbreak of the Korean War, the West agreed that the Federal Republic should rearm. It took time to find a way of doing this which would be acceptable to the French but the Western European Union provided a solution to the problem, and West Germany joined both the Union and NATO in 1955. Adenauer undertook to provide NATO with fourteen military divisions. That decision taken, Adenauer visited Moscow.

Adenauer has been criticized for being inflexible on the German problem. He believed that Germany should be reunited as one nation, but he also believed in capitalism, Western democracy and close links with the USA. West German membership of NATO ruled out the possibility of major concessions in Moscow. He nevertheless traded normal diplomatic relations with the USSR for the return of some 10 000 German prisoners-of-war (only a small proportion of those Germans who disappeared in the Soviet Union up to and including 1945). At the same time Adenauer proclaimed the *Hallstein Doctrine*, refusing to recognize East Germany or to have diplomatic relations with any state other than the Soviet Union which did recognize East Germany, since such recognition would be an 'unfriendly act'. West Germany therefore rejected diplomatic relations with all the client states in the East European communist bloc. It is unlikely that Adenauer was ever in a position to alter the division of Germany which had taken place, but his hard-line attitude was not helpful in lessening the Cold War. The two Germanies kept their differing allegiances. The Hallstein Doctrine made it impossible for the West to recognize East Germany and therefore, for the present, both Germanies were shut out from the United Nations Organization.

Adenauer helped to found the EEC and cultivated better relations with France. Having been in French hands since 1945, the Saar was returned to West Germany in 1957 after a new plebiscite and, despite occasional tension, Adenauer drew close to de Gaulle. Towards the West, the Chancellor was constructive. To the East he offered little, insisting on the basic principle of 'no concessions without concessions in return'. He rejected the Rapacki Plan for a nuclear-free zone in Central Europe (see Section 12.3). He feared that this would be a concession to communism, but he accepted a trade agreement with the Soviet Union in 1958 since this was to West Germany's advantage. Erhard and Kiesinger made few changes in Adenauer's policy after 1963 though, in need of parliamentary support, Kiesinger made Brandt his Foreign Minister from 1966 to 1969 and Brandt introduced more liberal ideas. The result was a policy of 'small steps' away from the Hallstein Doctrine: West Germany established diplomatic relations with Rumania and Jugoslavia.

When he became Chancellor, Brandt was ready to go further. Responding to an approach from Gierek, the Polish leader, Brandt's Ostpolitik aimed to reach a series of constructive agreements between East and West. He was prepared to accept the Nuclear Non-Proliferation Treaty and to recognize as final Poland's possession of lands east of the Oder–Neisse Line. From Brandt's negotiations with Poland, there began to develop hopeful prospects for the whole of Europe. In the Soviet Union, Brezhnev also seemed anxious for a general improvement in relations. Brandt reached agreements in Warsaw and Moscow for easier relations between West Germany and the communist bloc, and a four-power agreement relaxed the tension surrounding Berlin. Brandt's treaties linked up with the general movement towards East–West detente, leading to successes at the Conference on Security and Co-operation in Europe in 1975 (see Section 17.2(c)). In the meantime both West Germany and East Germany were admitted to UNO in 1973, and Schmidt inherited from Brandt not only the Federal Chancellorship but the new attitudes towards Eastern Europe of the Ostpolitik.

14.4   The Lesser Powers

Most of Western Europe shared in the spread of prosperity in the 1950s and 1960s and in the economic difficulties which developed in the 1970s. The *Benelux* countries (Belgium, the Netherlands and Luxemburg) were founder-members of the European Communities which helped them to thrive. Others prospered outside the Communities, perhaps none more so than *Austria* which entered the 1980s still comparatively little affected by the general recession. Democracy took firm root in Austria after the Second World War and the country was remarkable in electing in 1971 a Socialist government which had no need for the support of other parties in a coalition. It was led by Bruno Kreisky, who remained in office with increasing votes of confidence until 1983. By the settlement of 1955 Austria was not allowed to join military alliances nor even the EEC, and Austria was able to flourish, like *Switzerland* and *Sweden*, in a neutral role where spending on arms was comparatively low. Fig. 14.3 shows that most of the countries of Western Europe, in contrast, were members of NATO.

It was also a characteristic of the countries of Western Europe that, almost without exception, they practised democracy in the Western sense of the term. It took time, however, for the countries of the Iberian peninsula to come into line. When Salazar retired in *Portugal* in 1968, Caetano preserved much of his system for a further six years. Caetano was overthrown in 1974 by a military coup. There was then rapid movement towards democracy and free elections were held in 1976. Democratic government inevitably encountered difficulties since Salazar and Caetano left a legacy of problems, not least in Portugal's overseas Empire (see Section 16.5). Portugal was also economically behind most of Western Europe, but in the 1980s the country was beginning to seem more a part of Europe than in the days of isolation under Salazar. *Spain* was changing too. Franco's death in 1975 led to the restoration of the monarchy and the revival of democracy. King Juan Carlos was the grandson of Alfonso XIII. He supervised the transition which led to free elections in 1977 and he stood firm on the side of constitutional government, resisting an attempted military coup in 1981 by those who looked back nostalgically to the authoritarian rule of Franco. Apart from general problems of modernization, Spain continued to face separatism, especially in the Basque region. Basque nationalists were not pacified by promises of self-government and their acts of terrorism, countered by vigorous police action, gave Spain her share of the violence which plagued much of Western Europe.

Greece, meanwhile, moved uncertainly towards democracy. There was civil war from 1946 to 1949 (see Section 17.1(*a*)). The monarchy, like parliamentary government, then had a stormy history. The 'Greek Colonels' seized power in 1967 and King Constantine II went into exile, the monarchy finally being abolished in 1973. By that time the Colonels had been charged before the European Commission for Human Rights, though they maintained their authoritarian and anti-communist regime until Greece was again on the edge of civil war in 1974. The country then made another attempt to set up a workable system of democracy, this time with sufficient success for Greece to be admitted to the European Community in 1981. Almost at once, however, elections returned the first Greek Socialist government under Andreas Papandreou, whose policy threatened to be hostile to the EEC, to NATO and to the US bases which were situated on Greek soil.

Turkey, Greece's bitter enemy over the question of Cyprus (see Section 20.4), also had to struggle for democracy. Inönü inherited Kemal's dictatorship in 1938 (see Section 5.3); he moved towards a more liberal system after 1945 and surrendered office when defeated in the election of 1950. Turkish democracy then worked fitfully, the army from time to time intervening to overthrow governments. Inönü held office again from 1961 to 1965 and he at least remained an active supporter of democracy until his death in 1974. But economic problems, left-wing and right-wing extremism and outbreaks of disorder continued to produce alternating periods of martial law and liberalism. About a thousand Turks were killed in political clashes in 1978 alone, by which time the Turkish Republic had economic problems greater than those of almost any other state in Europe. The resurgence of Islam, particularly marked by the overthrow of the Shah in Iran (see Section 19.4), simply added to the divisions in Turkish society.

14.5 Co-operation in Western Europe

Early co-operation in Western Europe was mainly economic and military.

The USA was closely involved in both, at least in the early years after 1945. Inevitably, co-operation in Western Europe became intertwined with the German Problem and the Cold War between capitalism and communism (see Unit Seventeen).

(a) Economic Recovery

Although there was co-operative action to deal with refugees and reconstruction in Europe when the war ended in 1945 (see Section 10.6), it was not until 1947 that George Marshall, American Secretary of State, put forward his Plan 'against hunger, poverty, desperation and chaos'. He called on Europeans to produce a joint programme for recovery, and on the USA to give her assistance. Bevin, the British Foreign Secretary, was quick to welcome this initiative and, within a few months, sixteen European nations drew up the *European Recovery Programme* for action in the period 1948–51. The ERP was accepted in the USA and when the Programme was completed, 12 500 million dollars had been advanced to assist it. To administer and co-ordinate the Programme, the *Organization for European Economic Co-operation* was set up (OEEC), and so successful was this Organization that it continued after the original Programme was completed and, in 1961, was given yet a further lease of life in the *Organization for Economic Co-operation and Development* (OECD). The broad aims of both OEEC and OECD were economic development, co-operation and co-ordination and the promotion of trade. The latter was further assisted by the creation of a *General Agreement on Tariffs and Trade* (GATT) in 1947, to prevent further increases in tariffs and to secure agreed reductions.

The Marshall Plan was in theory designed to assist the whole of Europe, but the USA was neither surprised nor displeased when the communist bloc boycotted the Plan. The OEEC was founded by West Europeans, who later joined NATO, and a few neutral countries such as Sweden and Austria. West Germany also gained benefits and was admitted to membership in 1955. Spain joined a few years later. The USA and Canada were associate members of OEEC and both continued to assist the Organization after 1951, becoming full members of OECD in 1961. Japan joined OECD in 1963.

In 1950 OEEC set up the *European Payments Union* to encourage trade by making possible payments in any of the members' currencies. This in turn gave way to rather more sophisticated machinery in the *European Monetary Agreement* which replaced the Union in 1958. But in spite of all the USA's efforts and immense American spending in Europe in connection with defence and NATO, Europe was still often handicapped by a shortage of dollars. Nevertheless, American aid was remarkably generous and recovery in Europe was much swifter as a result of it.

(b) The Defence of Western Europe

Three months before Marshall put forward his Plan, President Truman asked

COUNTRY	ECONOMIC CO-OPERATION		MOVEMENT TOWARDS UNITY		DEFENCE		POPULATION est. 1972 (millions)	MAIN EXPORT (% OF WHOLE) (1970)	EXPORTS MAINLY TO (% OF WHOLE) (1970)		IMPORTS MAINLY FROM (% OF WHOLE) (1970)	
	OEEC 1948	EFTA 1960	COUNCIL OF EUROPE 1949	ECSC 1952 EEC 1958	WEU 1955	NATO						
USA	☐					✓	208	Machinery 27%	Canada 21%	Japan 11%	Canada 28%	Japan 15%
CANADA	☐					✓	22	Vehicles 20%	USA 65%	Britain 9%	USA 71%	EEC 6%
BRITAIN	✓	☒	✓	✱	✓	✓	56	Machinery 28%	EEC 22%	USA 12%	EEC 20%	USA 13%
FRANCE	✓		✓	✓	✓	✓ ◉	51	Machinery 19%	EEC 48%	USA 5%	EEC 48%	USA 10%
BELGIUM	✓		✓	✓	✓	✓	10	Iron/Steel 17%	EEC 69%	USA 6%	EEC 59%	USA 9%
HOLLAND	✓		✓	✓	✓	✓	13	Chemicals 14%	EEC 62%	Britain 7%	EEC 56%	USA 10%
LUXEMBURG	✓		✓	✓	✓	✓	0·4	(see Belgium – Economic Union, 1970)				
ITALY	✱		✓	✓	✓	✓	57	Machinery 25%	EEC 43%	USA 10%	EEC 41%	USA 10%
WEST GERMANY	✱	✓/☒	✱	✓	✓	✱	64	Machinery 29%	EEC 40%	USA 9%	EEC 44%	USA 11%
DENMARK	✓	☒	✓	✱		✓	5	Machinery 21%	EEC 23%	Britain 19%	EEC 30%	Sweden 16%
ICELAND	✱	✓/☒	✱				0·2	Fish 78%	USA 30%	Britain 13%	W.Germany 15%	Britain 14%
SWEDEN	✓	✓	✓				8	Machinery 25%	Britain 12%	W.Germany 12%	W.Germany 19%	Britain 14%
NORWAY	✓	✓	✓			✓	4	Ships 12%	Britain 18%	W.Germany 18%	Sweden 20%	W.Germany 14%
IRISH REPUBLIC	✓		✓	✱			3	Meat/Livestock 30%	Britain 66%	USA 10%	Britain 53%	W.Germany 7% / USA 7%
SWITZERLAND	✓	✓	✱				6	Machinery 30%	EEC 37%	Switzerland 9%	EEC 58%	USA 9%
AUSTRIA	✓	✓	✱				8	Machinery 20%	EEC 39%	Switzerland 10%	EEC 56%	Switzerland 7% / Britain 7%
PORTUGAL	✓	✓				✓?	9	Textiles 24%	Britain 20%	Angola 15%	W.Germany 15%	Britain 14%
SPAIN	✱					✱✱	35	Machinery 20%	EEC 36%	USA 14%	EEC 33%	USA 19%
GREECE	✓		✱	✱ 1981		✗	9	Tobacco 14%	EEC 46%	USA 8%	EEC 40%	Japan 13%
TURKEY	✓		✱			✗	37	Nuts 21%, Cotton 21%	W.Germany 20%	USA 10%	USA 19%	W.Germany 19%

♦ Became OECD 1961 + USA, CANADA, FINLAND, JAPAN

✓ – Founder Members
✱ – Later Members
✱✱ – Member, 1982
☐ – Associate Members
☒ – Withdrew 1972
◉ – Withdrew from military side 1966

Brussels Treaty Powers

Fig. 14.3 The USA and the European capitalist bloc

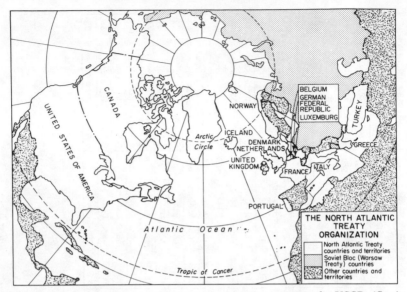

Fig. 14.4   How NATO saw the defence of freedom against the USSR. (Spain became another member of NATO in 1982)

Congress for 400 million dollars to give emergency aid to Greece and Turkey. The President's main aim was to preserve these countries from communism. Thus the Truman Doctrine (of resisting communism) and Marshall Aid (to assist recovery) became linked, at least in the minds of communists. Economics and politics became inescapably mixed and, in 1949, the *North Atlantic Treaty Organization* (NATO) was set up for 'military and other aid and assistance' (see Fig. 14.4).

West Europeans were, however, already organizing their joint defence before the USA joined them in NATO. Bevin drew them together in the *Brussels Treaty Organization* of March 1948. Britain, France and the Benelux countries undertook mutual aid in the case of an armed attack, and agreed on co-ordinated foreign policies and economic co-operation. This Organization was expanded in 1955 to include West Germany and Italy, its name being changed then to the *Western European Union* (WEU).

The Brussels Treaty Organization states readily joined NATO which originally included twelve nations (see Fig. 14.3). Its membership later grew to include Greece, Turkey and West Germany. The Organization was administered by the North Atlantic Council and it established military headquarters, SHAPE (Supreme Headquarters Allied Powers Europe), first in Paris and later, under pressure from de Gaulle, in Brussels.

The Brussels Treaty Organization and NATO clearly existed to preserve their members against communist expansion. Yet the Brussels Treaty grew out of an earlier agreement between Britain and France mainly for mutual aid against future German aggression (signed at Dunkirk in 1947). Events moved swiftly and, in 1952, France, West Germany, Italy and the Benelux countries felt sufficient confidence in one another and sufficient fear of communism to draft a treaty to set up a *European Defence Community* (EDC) with a common army. In fact, the common army did not come into being, for France had second thoughts and refused to ratify the treaty. Thus the defence of Western Europe came to rest solely in NATO and the Brussels Treaty Organization (later the WEU).

(c) The Movement Towards the Unity of Western Europe

Both the USA and the USSR are unions of states in large and powerful units. Even before the Second World War ended there was feeling that the states of Europe should be similarly united. The first step in 1944 was only a tiny one: the exiled governments of Belgium, the Netherlands and Luxemburg agreed on a customs union, *Benelux*, which came into existence in 1947. From an agreement on tariffs, the Benelux states moved towards closer economic integration so that in 1960 they set up an Economic Union with free movement of people, capital and goods between the three states. By that time, however, a larger unit was in the making, the European Economic Community (EEC), often referred to in Britain as the Common Market.

In August 1949, the first meeting took place of the *Council of Europe*, representing foreign ministers and the parliaments of many of the states of Western Europe. It served mainly as a forum for discussion, although it eventually established a Commission for Human Rights and a Court to protect individuals against unjust treatment.

Robert Schuman, the French Foreign Minister, wished to go further than the Council of Europe. He proposed a common market in coal and steel, anticipating that close collaboration in these areas could then be broadened into a movement towards economic and even political unity. France, Italy, West Germany and the Benelux countries agreed to create the *European Coal and Steel Community* (ECSC), which came into being in 1952. ECSC was controlled by a High Authority to which all members had to surrender some of their independence and it was this kind of authority, reducing the individual sovereignty of member-states, which Britain and other nations were unwilling to accept. They therefore remained outside. But ECSC was very successful in boosting European steel production and, in 1957, its six members signed the Rome Treaties to set up the *European Atomic Energy Community* (Euratom) and the *European Economic Community* a year later. This step towards economic unity was also a step in the direction of a political federation, a united states of the six countries.

Sceptics argued that such integration would not work. Indeed de Gaulle's attempts to dominate the Communities caused strains which seemed likely to prove the sceptics right. Certainly, little progress was made in the 1960s towards political unity. On the other hand, the Communities were of great economic advantage to their members, so much so that Britain came round to applying for membership, first under Macmillan and then under Wilson. They made no progress in the face of resistance from de Gaulle, who regarded Britain as a rival to his own authority; he also claimed that Britain had too many economic problems in the 1960s to be a useful member. It took the retirement and death of de Gaulle and the dogged determination of Heath, apparently bent on admission at almost any price, to get Britain into the EEC. Britain joined the Community on 1 January 1973 along with Denmark and the Irish Republic. They joined amidst controversy. The people of Norway had rejected membership in a referendum and many in Britain had misgivings about the loss of a certain amount of national sovereignty and the acceptance of an enormous quantity of economic regulations whose effects upon prices, jobs, overall prosperity and regional development were not really calculable.

Having joined the European Community (the single name adopted in 1967 for the ECSC, EEC and Euratom), the British showed little enthusiasm for membership. Wilson's government went through the motions of renegotiating the transitional arrangements under which Britain had joined. Only minor changes were won but, in a referendum in June 1975, 67 per cent of the British who voted elected to stay in the Community. The Community produced no dramatic solutions to the economic problems of the 1970s and the British in particular felt little benefit, so much so that the debate was soon reopened as to whether Britain should resign after all. European goods flooded into Britain without much increase in the flow of British exports to the continent. On top of that, the British paid higher contributions to the Community budget than did their richer fellow-members. This was partly due to the EEC Common Agricultural Policy (CAP) which from the outset had been designed to benefit European farmers, especially those of France and West Germany. The CAP also led to over-production so that butter mountains and wine lakes accumulated, subsidized by consumers and taxpayers to the profit of European producers. The Community was slow to change such unsatisfactory practices, and slow to tackle other urgent problems such as that of Europe's fisheries. Already in depression, British fishermen bitterly resented continental competition in what they regarded as their traditional waters. Many in the British Labour Party wanted to withdraw from the Community. The Conservatives remained more pro-European, but Thatcher nevertheless pressed for a reduction in Britain's payments to the Community, winning some concessions in 1980 and subsequent years but at the price of some ill-feeling and continuing doubts about Britain's commitment. A referendum in 1982 left no doubts about the attitude of the people of Greenland to the Community. Greenland had joined the association as a dependency of Denmark, but, with increasing independence, now voted to withdraw.

Meanwhile, some changes were made in Community institutions. In 1967 a single Commission was established to exercise executive power. There was criticism that the officials of the Commission were too powerful, ever inclined to clog the machinery with mountains of regulations. A Council of Ministers existed to make decisions on behalf of member-states and in 1974 a European Council was added for summit meetings between heads of government. There were also a Court of Justice, dating from the formation of ECSC in 1952, and an Investment Bank. The whole apparatus seemed remote from the people of Europe, however. A European Parliament had also existed since the early days of co-operation but that too was remote, its members nominated by national parliaments. In an effort to make the Community less remote, elections were held in 1979 so that the people could themselves choose European members of parliament. It was also hoped that this might strengthen the European Parliament and enable it better to control the European Commission. It was a measure of British disillusionment that the turnout of voters in this election was derisory. Voters elsewhere showed more interest, but it would take time for the elected MPs to learn to work together, overcome language differences and build political groupings on European rather than national lines. In the 1980s it remained to be seen whether the European Parliament could inject new life into the Community and tackle deep-rooted problems such as the CAP. There was still little evidence that Europeans as a whole thought in terms of a united Europe rather than in terms of their own individual nationalities.

The European Community was in any case only a Western European association. Eastern Europe had its own organizations (see Section 12.3). There were also critics of the European Community who argued that its interests were narrow, that it was essentially a club for the rich. Member-states, especially France, were quick to defend their own interests. They showed no great sympathy for Britain's problems, and haggling about financial details was often acrimonious. Similarly, the Community showed only limited sympathy for the poorer nations of the world whose exports, for example of sugar and fruit, suffered from the Europeans' eagerness to produce their own supplies within the Community. The Lomé Convention of 1975 went some way towards a more liberal policy: the Community undertook to help forty-six Third-World countries with investment-aid, guarantees of commodity prices and trade preferences in European markets. But this was only a beginning and the Brandt Report of 1980 showed that far more was needed to bridge the wealth gap between North and South (see Section 18.1).

For the poorer areas of Europe, if not for Britain, membership of the Community nevertheless remained attractive. The Republic of Ireland seemed well satisfied with membership, especially the Republic's farmers. Greece took up membership at the beginning of 1981. Both Portugal and Spain applied for membership as soon as they moved towards democracy though negotiations were lengthy. Increased membership seemed itself likely to change the Community quite radically and there was a good deal of new thinking about the Community's role and future in the 1980s. Whether the movement would be towards closer unity or a looser framework had still to be decided.

Shortly before the EEC came into existence in 1958, non-members held talks which resulted in the setting up of the *European Free Trade Association* (EFTA) in 1960. Fig. 14.3 shows the original seven members of EFTA who agreed to reduce tariffs, and to develop their trade without the integration and surrender of sovereignty the EEC required. But there was inevitably some rivalry between the two trading blocs, each maintaining tariffs against the other. When Britain and Denmark decided to switch from one bloc to the other and join the European Community, a new mini-EFTA came into being with an agreement with the Community for free trade in manufactured goods. The original EFTA members had been joined by Iceland in 1970, so that they were now six with Finland an associate member.

Fig. 14.5   UK stamp with the flags of the seven founder members of EFTA, 1967

Further Reading

Ayling, S.E.: *Portraits of Power*. Harrap (London, 1965) – de Gaulle.
Childs, D.: *Germany since 1918*. Batsford (London, 1980).
Elliott, B.J.: *Western Europe after Hitler*. Longman (Harlow, 1968).
Farr, W.: *Daily Telegraph Guide to the Common Market*. Collins (London, 1972).
Hanley, D.L., Kerr, A.P. and Waites, N.H.: *Contemporary France, Politics and Society since 1945*. Routledge & Kegan Paul (London, 1980).
Jamieson, A.: *Leaders of the Twentieth Century*. Bell (London, 1970) – de Gaulle.
Knapp, W.: *Unity and Nationalism in Europe since 1945*. Pergamon (Oxford, 1969).
Mowat, R.C.: *Creating the European Community*. Blandford (Poole, 1973).
Pickles, D.: *France*. Oxford University Press (London, 1971).
Salvadori, M.: *NATO*. Anvil (London, 1957).
Urwin, D.W.: *Western Europe since 1945*. Longman (Harlow, 1981).
Watson, J.B.: *Western Europe 1945–81*. Harrap (London, 1982).

Documentary and Miscellaneous

Absalom, R.: *France, the May Events 1968*. Longman (Harlow, 1971).
Breach, R.W.: *Documents and Descriptions, the World since 1914*. Oxford University Press (London, 1966) – Sections 8–9, 15a.
Vaughan, R.: *Post-War Integration in Europe*. Arnold (London, 1976).
The European Community in Maps. European Commission Wallet (Brussels, 1974).

Exercises
1. Show how far Sections 14.1, 14.2, 14.3 and 14.4 support the argument that Western Europe since 1945 has been (*a*) democratic and (*b*) capitalist.
2. 'Most governments in the democracies leaned a little towards socialism' (page 221). Explain the meaning of this statement and illustrate the truth of it by reference to any *two* countries in Europe since 1945, referred to in Units Thirteen and Fourteen.
3. How far do Unit Thirteen and Sections 14.1 and 14.2 show that democracy based mainly on two parties (in the USA and Britain) has produced more stable government than democracy based on more numerous parties (in France and Italy)?
4. With reference to the Further Reading (above) or a modern encyclopedia, investigate the career of Charles de Gaulle to explain (*a*) why he was popular in France in 1945; (*b*) why he retired from politics in 1951; (*c*) why he became President in 1958; and (*d*) why he resigned in 1969. Add a summary of his main achievements within France and in international affairs.
5. Write *two* views of the Chancellorship of Konrad Adenauer such as might have been written at the time of his retirement in 1963, the *first* from the point of view of a West German Christian Democrat, the *second* from the point of view of an East German Communist.
6. What can you learn about co-operation in Western Europe from Fig. 14.3?
7. Trace the main steps by which Western Europe after 1945 moved towards (*a*) military co-operation and (*b*) economic co-operation.
8. Why was Britain slow to join the European Economic Community and why, having joined, did Britain show 'little enthusiasm for membership' (page 270)?
9. Use Units Twelve and Fourteen, including Figs. 12.3 and 14.3, to explain why Western Europe and Eastern Europe created, after 1945, similar but separate international organizations.
10. Study these extracts from a treaty signed in March 1957, and then answer the questions which follow:

> 1. By this Treaty, the High Contracting Parties establish among themselves a European Economic Community. . . .
>
> 3. . . . The activities of the Community shall include . . .
> (*b*) the establishment of a common customs tariff and of a common commercial policy towards third countries;
> (*c*) the abolition, as between Member States, of obstacles to freedom of movement for persons, services and capital;
> (*d*) the adoption of a common policy in the sphere of agriculture. . . .
>
> 4. The tasks entrusted to the Community shall be carried out by the following institutions; an Assembly, a Council, a Commission, a Court of Justice. . . .

> (*a*) In what city was this Treaty signed, and which six governments were the *High Contracting Parties*?
> (*b*)(*i*) What name and initials are used in this Unit for the *common policy* described in Article 3(*d*)?
> (*ii*) What name is used in this Unit for the *Assembly* mentioned in Article 4,

and what important change took place in 1979 concerning this institution?

(*c*) Explain the meaning and importance of *a common customs tariff*.

(*d*) Briefly describe the role in the EEC of *each* of the *last three* institutions named in Article 4.

(*e*) Explain how these extracts from the Treaty of 1957 would affect the lives of people in EEC *Member States*.

Unit Fifteen

The Expansion of Communism Outside Europe

Only the Soviet Union and the Mongolian People's Republic established lasting communist government before the Second World War. Outer Mongolia had been a province of China until the Chinese (Manchu) Empire fell in 1911. The area then claimed independence and the Mongolian People's Republic was set up in 1924 on the Soviet pattern and under Russian protection. China recognized the Republic's independence in 1946.

With the ending of the Second World War, communism spread further but only in North Korea was it closely connected, as in Eastern Europe, with occupation by the forces of the USSR. In North Vietnam, communism grew with the Viet Minh, a nationalist movement which, like Tito's partisans in Jugoslavia, achieved popularity for resisting foreign invasion. China became communist in 1949, the outcome of a civil war in which the followers of Mao Tse-tung overthrew the inefficient and unpopular Kuomintang. In Cuba, successful rebellion against corruption and exploitation hardened into communism partly in self-defence against the inept policies of Eisenhower and Kennedy, who put the weight of the USA behind the system the Cubans had rejected and drove the new government into dependence on the USSR. In Chile there was a strong movement towards some sort of Marxism simply by way of elections, but right-wing forces, backed by the CIA (see Glossary), ensured that Chilean communism did not survive.

Section 12.2(*h*) has already raised the question of whether even the Soviet Union can properly be called 'communist'. The states the West called 'communist' preferred to describe themselves as 'socialist' and, by the end of the 1970s, 'socialist' was a term which could be applied to numerous countries. Some, such as Ethiopia and Angola in Africa, and Afghanistan in Asia, had close ties with the Soviet Union. Others, like Mozambique and Tanzania, were more independent. Moreover, changes went on occurring. Individual leaders like Nkrumah of Ghana saw merits in 'communism' and borrowed at least some ideas from the communist world, but Nkrumah was overthrown. The end of the war in Vietnam brought 'communism' to the whole of Indochina but it took various forms in Laos, Cambodia and Vietnam herself.

'Communist' as used in the West seemed to mean not only influenced by Marxist ideas but, perhaps more specifically, influenced by the Soviet Union, i.e. linked with the rival power bloc. The Eurocommunism of the Communist Parties of Italy and other Western European countries aimed to create a different image. 'Socialist' was also a term whose meaning was vague. Such terms may be handy but they are less than perfect. Even using 'communist' for the power bloc which rivalled the USA and its allies became less satis-factory at the end of the 1950s when the Soviet Union and China became divided, seeming to create two different communist blocs. 'Communist', 'socialist', 'capitalist' and 'democratic' belong above all to the language of the Cold War and they seem less and less adequate to label countries as the twentieth century goes on. Not all communist states were subservient to the USSR, just as by no means all of the states protected by the USA were democratic.

The countries considered in this Unit are nevertheless those which most alarmed the USA when in the years from 1945 to the 1970s they seemed to have 'gone communist'.

15.1   North Korea

Korea was seized by Japan in 1910 and remained in Japanese hands until their defeat in 1945. The USSR declared war on Japan just in time to put Soviet forces into North Korea before the Second World War ended. Like Germany, the country as a whole was then temporarily partitioned with the Russians occupying the area north of the 38th parallel and the USA the area south of it. North Korea adopted a constitution similar to that of the USSR and the Democratic People's Republic of Korea came into existence in 1948. Power in this North Korean state lay with the leadership of the Workers' Party and particularly with Kim Il-sung, a Marxist trained in the USSR.

Kim remained in power into the 1980s, building up a personal control which many called Stalinist, and an economic structure similar to that of the Soviet Union. The Russians provided assistance. North Korea had useful mineral resources and the Japanese had already built industrial plant. Indus-trialization continued and agriculture was collectivized into co-operatives. Trade with other communist states helped the Republic's development. But Kim did not intend to be merely a Soviet puppet. His first aim was to continue his own regime in North Korea. Russian troops were withdrawn in 1948 and in later years Kim tried to avoid entanglement in the ideological disputes which broke out between the USSR and China. But North Korea was only half of what had once been a distinctive kingdom. Kim would have liked to rule the whole of the country but Syngman Rhee, a right-wing client of the USA, ruled in South Korea and he too had ambitions to take over the whole. It became clear in the Korean War of 1950–3 that neither could succeed in enlarging his territory (see Section 17.1(c)). Syngman Rhee alienated the South Koreans and was overthrown in 1960 and, though elections continued to be held, South Korea went on with rule as authoritarian as that of Kim in the North. There was talk in the 1970s of reuniting Korea by peaceful agree-ment but little progress was made. South Korea had greater resources than North Korea and made faster economic progress, but South Korea also seemed the more turbulent. Having held office since 1962, President Park was assassinated in 1979. Kim meanwhile became the veteran communist leader whose years in office were much longer than those of any other except Hoxha in Albania.

15.2   China – the Years of Conflict

(a) The Revolution of 1911

The 'Save China League' which Sun Yat-sen set up in 1894 was just one of a variety of revolutionary movements which looked for the salvation of China in the end of the Manchu Empire. A few years later, Sun proclaimed his 'Three Principles' – Nationalism to rid China of interference and exploitation by foreigners, Democracy to create a more modern system of government and Socialism to bring about reforms and a better life, especially for the millions of Chinese peasants. The Manchu Empire, like Tsarism in Russia, was unfitted to make these advances, although a flood of reforms in the first decade of the twentieth century, including the abolition of slavery and the calling of a parliament, indicated a belated willingness to try. The effort came too late. China faced problems of backwardness, under-development, poverty and feebleness as vast as its size. Its size and the diversity of its peoples rendered it almost impossible for the Emperor to create one nation. When Pu Yi inherited the throne in 1908 at the age of two, the moment seemed ripe for the revolution which had long been brewing.

In fact, there were two revolutions, both towards the end of 1911. At Peking, as hostility to the Manchu Empire came to the surface throughout China, Yuan Shih-kai took the office of Prime Minister, intent on strong personal rule with or without the imperial dynasty. At Nanking, Sun Yat-sen was proclaimed President by revolutionaries intent on a republic. In February 1912, Pu Yi, now aged six, was persuaded to abdicate, while Sun stood down to allow Yuan to become President of the new Chinese republic. Civil war was avoided; and the Manchu Empire had fallen as easily as Tsarism was to fall in Russia in 1917.

(b) Yuan, War Lords and the Kuomintang

Yuan soon found himself in conflict with the followers of Sun in the *Kuomintang* (a nationalist party which dated from 1891). The Kuomintang wanted a democracy based on a majority in parliament. They themselves won a majority when the first parliament met under the new constitution in 1913. They argued that the President should be only a figure-head but Yuan meant to rule. He outlawed the Kuomintang, chased Sun into exile and dismissed what was left of the parliament. The Kuomintang regrouped in Canton where they set up a rival government. Yuan toyed with the idea of declaring himself Emperor but his authority was disputed in many areas and China seemed to be on the verge of anarchy.

Yuan's death in 1916 led to even greater confusion. Although an attempt was made to restore some sort of democratic government in Peking and the

Kuomintang kept a precarious hold on Canton, China as a whole fell prey to the war lords (quarrelsome militarists who fought against one another like medieval barons, conscripting the peasants and ravaging the countryside in pursuit of personal power). The official government in Peking was unstable and weak, unable to gain much profit or prestige even from joining the First World War on the side of the victorious Allies.

In their disillusionment, a handful of Chinese turned to Marxism and Russia for guidance. In 1921, they formed the Chinese Communist Party. In 1922, they persuaded Sun Yat-sen to accept Russian help and within a year the Kuomintang and the Communists made an entente: Borodin came to Canton to advise Sun on transforming his party into an effective organization. They created a nationalist army which began to consolidate the authority of the Kuomintang in the area around Canton. Borodin brought from Russia advisers, money and equipment and, when Sun died in 1925, the Kuomintang had a new popular appeal, based on a programme of helping the poor and resisting foreign exploitation of the Chinese.

Chiang Kai-shek emerged as the successor to Sun. In 1926, he led the Kuomintang forces northwards and the following year occupied Nanking. The nationalist troops seized the properties of foreigners as they advanced, especially those of the British and the Americans, as well as routing the war lords, whose power had already begun to decline.

(c) Chiang and Mao

Chiang Kai-shek was a nationalist, a military man, trained in Japan before 1911. He had studied Russian military organization in Moscow in 1923 but he had no liking for communism and was disturbed by the activities of Chinese communists against businessmen and landlords. In 1927, when the nationalist army took Shanghai, Chiang turned against the communists and their supporters in the Kuomintang. In a bloody purge, many were killed and others fled; Chiang's example was followed by other military leaders in the Kuomintang. The communists were forced to retire to the south while Chiang pushed northwards, finally entering Peking in June 1928.

Insofar as China now had a single government, it was that of Chiang and the Kuomintang. They chose to make their new capital in Nanking but their authority was still confined largely to the east of China. The communists were steadily reorganizing in the rice-growing south, in the provinces of Hunan and Kiangsi. The Japanese were entrenched in Manchuria, which they were soon to turn into a puppet-state, and the vast areas of central and west China acknowledged no common authority. China seemed about to dissolve into fragments as had always seemed possible.

Chiang decided that his first priority must be to eliminate the communists completely. By the end of the 1920s, the latter had made steady progress in winning peasant support and in setting up soviets in Hupeh, Hunan, Kiangsi and Fukien. This gave them control of an area almost as large as that won by

Chiang, in which their authority was based on a peasant rebellion against their landlords. Among the communists were Chu Teh, a trained soldier, and Mao Tse-tung, once a librarian. Together they created the Kiangsi Red Army and Mao initiated extensive land reforms in the province. He was deeply aware of the importance of the peasants in China. He likened them to the sea in which the communists would swim as fish. On another occasion he wrote, 'We communists are like seeds and the people are like the soil. Wherever we go, we must unite with the people, take root and blossom among them.' But in 1930 Chiang determined to uproot the communists and in a series of campaigns they were forced to abandon the soviets and finally to quit their last base in Kiangsi.

Fig. 15.1 Mao Tse-tung (standing, third from the left) *with other Chinese communists in 1927*

(d) The Long March

In October 1934, Mao led the retreat out of Kiangsi and across the River Yangtse. About 100 000 began the Long March. Their trek covered over 2 000 miles and took them a year before they arrived in Shensi. During the migration, Mao's wife died and their numbers dwindled, but they set up new headquarters at Yenan, in Shensi province, under the now undisputed leadership of Mao Tse-tung. The Long March was an ordeal but it demonstrated Chiang's inability to exterminate the communists and it brought them contact with more of China's peasants, among whom seeds could be planted. It also brought them nearer to the Japanese, whose conquest of Manchuria in 1931 (see Section 8.1) Chiang seemed content to ignore. When Chiang sent the northern militarist, Chang Hsueh-liang, to try to drive Mao's forces from Shensi, many of his troops responded to communist appeals that they should unite against the Japanese, rather than persist in civil war. Chang himself took Chiang Kai-shek prisoner late in 1936, to force him to alter his priorities. Chiang gave way and an uneasy alliance was made between nationalists and communists to resist the invader. The alliance was soon to be needed for in 1937 Japan embarked on all-out war (see Section 8.1(b)).

(e) World War and Civil War

The *Chinese-Japanese War*, one theatre in the Second World War, went on until 1945 and both nationalists and communists fought the invader. But rivalry between them was never far below the surface and long before the war ended their alliance had broken down. Chiang was forced by the Japanese to withdraw to Chungking where his rule became increasingly authoritarian. The strength of the Kuomintang had always been in the towns but many of them had fallen to the Japanese and Chiang made few new friends. Mao used guerilla tactics against the Japanese and continued to spread communist propaganda in the villages. Neither he nor Chiang could dislodge the Japanese from most of eastern China and each accused the other of making too little effort. Chiang was anxious to prevent supplies reaching the communists and Mao was anxious to preserve the strength of the Red Army. Any pretence of co-operation broke down and a renewal of the civil war seemed inevitable.

In the late stages of the Second World War, supplies from the USA began to reach China. Chiang, whose government was still recognized as the official one, began to hope for American support against the communists, but when the Japanese began to withdraw troops to fight elsewhere the communists were first into the areas they left. Chiang seemed to be obsessed with the hunting down of rivals and he stubbornly resisted the efforts of the USA to bring about a coalition of Chinese moderates based on the Democratic League of middle-of-the-road politicians. General Marshall, later the author of the Marshall Plan, could obtain no compromise and, in 1946, the civil war broke out again.

At first, it was the nationalists who were successful. The Soviet Union had advanced into Manchuria in the closing stages of the war against Japan, but the Russians showed little interest in the civil war and actually returned Manchuria to the nationalists. Chiang had half-hearted American support, but the Kuomintang was torn with internal quarrels and American arms often found their way to the communists. From 1947, the latter also received supplies from the USSR. The peasants were strongly pro-communist and, in 1948, the nationalists suffered a major defeat in Manchuria. Other defeats quickly followed. At the beginning of 1949, Peking fell to the communists and in April they took Nanking. Chiang could hold neither Chungking nor Canton and, in December 1949, he set up his last headquarters on the island of Formosa (Taiwan). Formosa had been in Japanese hands from 1895 to

1945 but was confidently expected to be returned to China when the Japanese peace treaty was signed. Before that treaty was signed, at San Francisco in 1951, Chiang was in possession and, spurred on by the Korean War, the USA had undertaken his defence. The Treaty of San Francisco, therefore, ignored Formosa, which was to remain the final stronghold of Nationalist China for decades. In 1954, the USA signed a Mutual Security Pact with Chiang and until 1971 continued to maintain him as one of the Big Five with the right of the veto in the UN Security Council. Chiang ruled Taiwan and the tiny islands of Quemoy and Matsu until his death in 1975, when Nationalist government continued under his son, Chiang Ching-kuo. A developing industrial base and economic links with the USA and Japan brought some prosperity to Taiwan but, in the late 1970s, with changed US relations with China, the island became something of an embarrassment to the Americans. Carter adopted an ambiguous attitude, asserting Taiwan's right to remain independent but reducing the USA's commitment to defend her. The Security Pact of 1954 was allowed to lapse in 1980. Reagan, however, only agreed to phase out military supplies to Taiwan under considerable pressure from Peking. Mainland China showed no immediate intention of claiming possession, but the claim that Taiwan was historically part of China had never been abandoned.

Meanwhile, in October 1949, China herself had become the People's Republic of China led by Mao Tse-tung, its Chairman and the leader of the Chinese Communist Party.

(f) Why did Chiang Kai-shek Fail?

The rout of the nationalists was due primarily to two factors. One was the arrogance, corruption and incompetence of the nationalists themselves. The other was the determination and widespread popularity of the communists. In the final stages of the civil war, the nationalists were totally demoralized. Inflation was rampant and in spite of some reforms in the 1930s, the Kuomintang had little to show for its long period as the official government of China. Of course, it had been constantly handicapped by the struggles against the war lords, the communists and the Japanese. But even as a patriotic force, its record was unconvincing, too often marred by a concern to keep itself in power and by the self-interest of its supporters. Chiang's methods were often brutal and authoritarian. Nationalist China was a one-party state and, when Chiang showed a readiness in 1947 to accept an elected parliament and go some way towards a return to Sun Yat-sen's 'Three Principles', it was already too late. His government had done far too little for the Chinese people. It was the regime of businessmen, landlords and vested interests and, above all, of Chiang Kai-shek himself, now quite discredited.

The success of the Chinese communists owed very little to the USSR. From about 1927 to the very last stages of the civil war, they had received little assistance from Moscow though deserters from Chiang brought them a steady supply of American weapons. 'Political power,' declared Mao Tse-tung, 'grows out of the barrel of a gun' and the Red Army became an efficient fighting unit. But, more important, the communists won the support of the masses. In their soviets, land was redistributed among the peasants, social reforms were made and the poor looked forward to a better life. The peasants were mobilized in a class struggle against landlordism. In 1957, Mao expressed the aims of the communists as being 'to ensure a better life for the several hundred million people of China and to build our economically and culturally backward country into a prosperous and powerful one with a high level of culture'. In 1949, it had seemed far more likely that this could be done by Mao's communists than by Chiang's nationalists.

15.3   China Under Communism

(a) The Political System

Like Lenin, Mao believed that a period of dictatorship was necessary in order

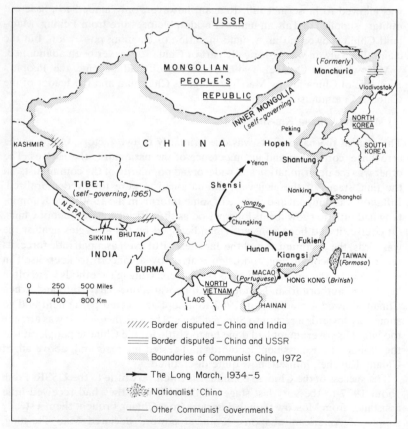

Fig. 15.2 Communist China in the 1970s

to lead the people to communism. After 1949, real power in China lay within the Communist Party, with Mao as its Chairman. In theory, he led a coalition government but it was subject to rigid communist control. Within this framework, the Chinese people had far more opportunity to take part in government and administration than ever before, but the system left little room for dissent from Marxism. Propaganda was intensive and censorship strict but China rapidly achieved a new degree of unity. There was little victimization of those willing to conform, even former members of the Kuomintang, but landlords and implacable opponents were ruthlessly rooted out.

Not until 1954 was a detailed constitution worked out. Like that of the USSR, the Chinese system of government was based entirely on the Chinese Communist Party (CCP), to which all candidates for office had to belong. A system of elected congresses corresponded to Russian soviets, so that China's parliament was known as the National People's Congress. Its work, in practice, was mostly carried on by a Standing Committee. The State Council provided the governing body (executive) whose leader, and in effect Prime Minister until his death in 1976, was Chou En-lai, an early recruit to the CCP and long-time associate of Mao Tse-tung. There were new constitutions in 1975 and 1978, but they made no basic changes in the system. What did change from time to time, however, was the balance of power within the CCP leadership.

Chou En-lai was in general a moderate, Mao Tse-tung a radical. In 1959, Mao stepped down as Chairman of the Republic though he remained Chairman of the CCP. This change followed the upheaval and disappointing results of the Great Leap Forward (see Section (b) below) and, for a time, Mao was less influential. Liu Shao-chi, a moderate, was Chairman of the Republic from 1959 to 1969, but the radicals derided him as a 'capitalist roader' and denounced his henchmen as 'Chinese Khrushchevs'. When Mao launched the Cultural Revolution in 1966 (see Section (c) below) and the radicals made a comeback, Liu fell into disfavour. Lin Piao, on the other hand, a survivor of the Long March, veteran of the People's Liberation Army and Chou En-lai's deputy, supported Mao in the Cultural Revolution, editing and circulating the *Thoughts of Chairman Mao Tse-tung*. But Lin too lost favour. After involvement in a plot to seize power, he died in an air crash in 1971 in Mongolia.

At issue in these and other changes were not only a struggle for power, but arguments about China's road to communism. Mao preached 'permanent revolution' and constant struggle: the radicals who supported him were deeply suspicious of anything that might seem capitalist. They were suspicious, for example, of elitist education (as practised in the Soviet Union) on the grounds that it created 'bourgeois' intellectuals. They rejected the Soviet model of development as too much concerned with industrialization and the exaltation of 'experts' as in the West. With its vast population of peasants, China, they argued, needed a different model. The moderates, on the other hand, were generally less narrow in their outlook, more ready to follow Soviet and even Western examples in pursuit of economic development. At intervals, therefore, China was shaken by fierce disputes about the interpretation of Marxist ideas and about the policies to be adopted. Mao remained the founding-father of the People's Republic, and the constitution of 1975 reaffirmed support for his guiding philosophy. But it also allowed Chinese peasants to pursue some small-scale free enterprise, of which Mao was inclined to disapprove. Only at times was Mao all-powerful, however. When he died in 1976, he seemed to be planning a second Cultural Revolution, to try once again to restore China to the radical path. Shortly after his death, while still praising his many services to China, new leaders asserted that Mao had not always been right.

(b) The Economy

Mao's first priority was the redistribution of land. The Agrarian Law of 1950 struck a mortal blow at landlords who were rooted out, often violently, in 'speak-bitterness' meetings, at which they were put on public trial and their former tenants were encouraged to testify to the cruelty and greed of the landlords. Their property was shared among the poor peasants. The tiny peasant holdings were then grouped into collective farms, although not without some resistance from those peasants who preferred private ownership. By the end of the 1950s, almost all the land had been collectivized, much of it in communes which originated in 1958 and which grouped the collective farms into larger units for more thoroughgoing economic organization, linking agriculture and industry and, at the same time, providing units for local government, education and Marxist indoctrination.

From the outset, communist control was extended to all aspects of the economy. One of Mao's first actions was to bring banking and trade under communist control and to halt the inflation which had set in under Chiang. Capitalists were no longer tolerated and, in 1953, the First Five-Year Plan set out to develop industry with extensive nationalization. Mineral deposits were developed and a considerable emphasis was placed on heavy industry and the production of capital goods, such as tractors and ships. Like Russia in the 1930s China paid little attention to consumer goods. The emphasis was on building for the future with industrialization and collectivization, and on attacking basic problems such as hunger and illiteracy. But Mao was already questioning whether China should follow closely in the USSR's footsteps.

The Second Plan of 1958, the *Great Leap Forward*, was a radical experiment which attracted the derision of Khrushchev. It aimed to double industrial output and increase that of agriculture by 35 per cent. The communes were among the new ideas, however, and, alongside ambitious plans for power stations and similar large enterprises, there was the Campaign for Little Steel in village furnaces. Unlike the Plan of 1953, personal incentives gave way to regimented communal effort and there was an attempt to remove distinctions between industrial and agricultural workers and between intellectuals and the masses. The result was upheaval. Village furnaces and similar small-scale workings in coal-mining, for example, produced very little but took peasants from the land so that food production fell. The Leap fell short of its targets and a succession of bad harvests led to food rationing. During the confusion, Soviet advisers and technicians were withdrawn. The Leap perhaps did something to create a sense of unity and purpose among the Chinese people, but it could not be carried on without modifications. The communes were not abandoned but were developed in less of a headlong rush, some private plots being allowed to reappear. For the moment the moderates reasserted their authority and the new Plan in 1962 was less ambitious.

Nevertheless, development went on. In 1964 China successfully exploded a nuclear weapon and by 1967 she had developed a hydrogen bomb, some evidence of industrial sophistication. Power supplies developed rapidly and industrial complexes grew in the 1960s in several parts of the country. The emphasis was still on capital goods rather than consumer goods and in many ways China remained underdeveloped. In the UNCTAD Conference of 1972 she was, therefore, able to appear in a strangely double role, identifying on the one hand with the world's poor nations (agricultural like herself) but on the other hand sufficiently advanced to be able to offer aid and technical assistance to many of them. Chinese help to Zambia and Tanzania in Africa seemed to be offered more in the spirit of co-operation among the poor than in the form of a charity poured out by the rich, who perhaps expected economic profit in return.

But China seemed less concerned than Stalin in Russia had been to pursue economic development and industrial wealth with ruthless single-mindedness. Progress was not measured only in factory output and railway mileages. A great expansion of cultural activity was encouraged. Much thought was given to how the individual could make his contribution in such a huge state. Communist goals remained but experiments were common. The communes, for example, were reduced in size and made less comprehensive in their functions so that by 1964 there were 74 000 compared with 26 000 in 1958 and, instead of about 5 000 families in each, there were now only about 2 000. The vast majority of Chinese continued to work on the land and modified communes went on spreading, but organization was more flexible than envisaged in the Great Leap Forward. Above all China had to develop a system which could absorb a massive increase in population. The census of 1953 counted just under 600 million inhabitants of mainland China. At the end of the 1970s, the population was around 1 000 million.

(c) Society and Ideology

Mao continued his search for a way to revolutionize society and to create a 'new socialist man'. The Great Leap Forward had been preceded by certain essential reforms but also by an experiment in free expression. The reforms included the granting of equality to women, with equal rights to share in such provisions as health insurance and in political affairs and ownership. Child marriages were made illegal and women were as free to choose their marriage-partners as men were. A start was made on achieving mass literacy. Free expression was encouraged in 1956 when Mao called for a *Hundred Flowers* to bloom with opinions and criticism of the regime. The 'flowers' bloomed only slowly but the CCP found 'weeds' among them: in 1957, the experiment was called off and censorship was restored. Some of those who had responded to Mao's invitation were banished, and intellectuals generally were subjected to tighter control. These were years of ferment. The Great Leap was launched in 1958 and the developing quarrel with the USSR came into the open.

Since 1949 the Russians had given substantial aid to China under the Sino-Soviet Treaty of Friendship, signed in 1950 when Mao had made his first visit to the Soviet Union. But Mao questioned whether the Soviet Union's was the right path to communism. His respect for Soviet leaders diminished after Stalin's death, and he was dismayed by the speech Khrushchev made in 1956 (see Section 12.2(*b*)). He accused the Russians of 'revisionism' (revising the true teachings of Marxism–Leninism). The Russians retorted that Mao was a 'dogmatist', too rigid in his ideas. But the Chinese suspected that the USSR was paying more attention to Russia's interests as a great power than to the fundamental objectives of Marxism. The Russian leaders, especially Khrushchev, were suspicious of the soundness of Chinese economic planning, and Chinese revolutionary enthusiasm seemed likely to unsettle the balance of power, slowly developing between East and West. Moreover, China had a border dispute with India whom the USSR did not wish to antagonize. Even the Chinese-Russian border was not beyond dispute and as the population of China grew rapidly to well over 600 million in the 1950s, the Soviet Union became anxious about the sparsely-populated expanses of eastern Russia. Clashes occurred on the Russian-Chinese borders and, with the development of Chinese nuclear weapons, relations became particularly tense in the late 1960s, revealing the hollowness of the arguments of those who had once alleged that the quarrel was mainly a personal feud between Khrushchev and Mao.

From their beginnings, there had been differences between the communism of Russia and that of China. The Bolshevik Revolution in Russia had, to a large extent, been a revolution of industrial workers. That in China sprang from the peasants and the villages. But their rivalry was also that of two very large countries, both potentially extremely powerful and rivals for the leadership of world communism.

Mao and Lin Piao launched the *Cultural Revolution* in the mid-1960s, attacking both Soviet revisionism and its alleged supporters within China. This was a further round in the ideological struggle between radicals and moderates. Intellectuals and 'experts', who inclined to the supposedly-Russian ideas that there should be more emphasis on consumer goods and more cordial relations with the West, were attacked as fiercely as those who wished to preserve a small measure of private enterprise. Gangs of Red Guards, many of them youths, roamed the country. Schools and places of learning were closed for a time in 1967–8 to allow a complete rethinking of the educational curriculum and its purposes. In a period of great turbulence, the only anchor seemed to be in the little red books which appeared everywhere and which contained the *Thoughts of Chairman Mao Tse-tung*. Supporters of Chinese traditions as well as of all kinds of westernization were rooted out and deprived of authority at all levels. The Communist Party was reorganized and men like Liu Shao-chi expelled from it. Like Lenin in his final years, Mao was anxious that the party should keep in touch with the masses. Above all, he wished to maintain contact with the young, the future upholders of communism. The party had too many bureaucrats who were losing that contact. But to the West it seemed that the hero-worship went beyond even Stalinist proportions as the land was filled with the rapturous retelling of the *Thoughts* of Mao.

Outsiders found it strange and frightening as countless millions of soberly and uniformly-dressed Chinese apparently abandoned themselves to a frenzy of revolutionary enthusiasm. It seemed even stranger that, apparently refreshed by the Cultural Revolution, the people could then settle down to work again and enter the 1970s with an amazing stability.

(d) China since Chairman Mao

1976 saw the deaths, first, of Chou En-lai, then of Chu Teh and then of Mao himself. Chou and Chu had been moderates, the latter a military leader, and both, along with Mao, veterans of the CCP. China would now be under new management and a new generation of CCP leaders: the first question was whether moderates or radicals would get the upper hand. The quarrel with the USSR and fast-improving relations with the West had already brought changes (see Section (e) below), and China had now to decide the direction in which to travel during the remaining years of the twentieth century. Jiang Qing, Mao's widow, aimed to keep alive her husband's radicalism. But she was outmanoeuvred, arrested with three of her supporters and charged with political offences. This speedy routing of the 'Gang of Four' suggested that it was the moderates who had taken control of China. Hua Guofeng had first succeeded Chou as Prime Minister and he then succeeded Mao as Chairman of the CCP. Like Khrushchev after the death of Stalin, Hua travelled to foreign capitals, reinforcing the impression that it was he who had inherited Mao's mantle. That the Chinese leadership was growing more liberal also seemed to be reflected in the new constitution of 1978 with its references to individual freedom and legal rights for the Chinese people.

Hua Guofeng had a rival, however. Deng Xiaoping had been attacked during the Cultural Revolution and had again been thought too right-wing in 1976, when he was linked with the 'April Fifth Movement' which called for liberal reform and condemned dictatorship. In the early 1970s, Deng had been groomed by Chou En-lai as the likely next Prime Minister and his setback in 1976 proved only temporary. His influence grew, especially in support for a policy of Four Modernizations, which would advance Chinese technology, liberalize society and increase links with the West. Hua on the other hand was accused of 'leftist errors' (leaning towards radicalism) and of encouraging a new 'personality cult'. Liu Shao-chi was among the former enemies of Mao who were rehabilitated, and Hua was criticised for being less ready than others to denounce the mistakes that had been made by Mao. For the moment the agreed verdict on Mao was that his 'merits were primary and his errors were secondary' and China stopped short of the weightier criticisms which Khrushchev had heaped on Stalin. Hua Guofeng was, nevertheless, forced to resign the CCP Chairmanship in 1981 in favour of Hu Yaobang who was widely considered a nominee of Deng. At the same time there was also criticism of, and some drawing back from, China's dependence on Western technology and trade, and the period of readjustment after Mao Tse-tung was continuing.

(e) Chinese Foreign Policy

From 1949, Mao Tse-tung loudly preached revolutionary communism and had welcomed 'people's wars' against their oppressors. The Western powers feared Chinese aggression and were sometimes puzzled when China did not match words with actions. Although other countries were less hostile, the USA stubbornly refused to recognize the new regime, maintained a fleet to patrol China's shores, supported Chiang in Taiwan and obstructed the admission of Red China to the United Nations. To the Americans, it was proof of Mao's aggressive intentions that he gave active support to North Korea in the Korean War (see Section 17.1(c)) and encouragement to North Vietnam at a later date; and it was the Korean War which prompted the USA rapidly to rebuild the strength of Japan and to set up SEATO in 1954. In practice, however, China has proved a remarkably peaceful power.

It may be argued that China attacked Tibet in 1950, occupying the east of that country and forcing the Dalai Lama to flee after an unsuccessful rebellion in 1959. In 1965, Tibet was given the status of a self-governing region of China. Tibet, however, was part of the Manchu Empire until 1911 and was regarded as part of China by the Kuomintang as well as by the communists.

In 1962, China briefly went to war with India, mainly over Ladakh and minor disputed areas on the ill-defined Indo-Chinese border. But, having won military success, the Chinese made no attempt to follow up their advantage and mildly withdrew from territory where they considered they had no legitimate claims. Nor did they seek to drive the British from Hong Kong or the Portuguese from Macao, although there was sometimes tension around these remnants of European empires.

Nevertheless, Mao's government kept up violent propaganda against the West and particularly the USA and it deplored the attempts of the USSR to

Fig. 15.3 Chia-Chia and Ching-Ching – China's gift of rare pandas to the London Zoo – whose arrival in the West was evidence of developing goodwill in the 1970s

improve relations with the capitalist world. It was, therefore, surprising that 1971 brought an apparent change of attitude both in Peking and Washington. Through the improbable medium of table-tennis matches, China showed a willingness to make contact with the West. It was a game in which the Chinese excelled and such was their new friendliness, it was suspected that they even, on occasions, deliberately allowed the West to win. The change of climate brought speedy results. The USA abandoned obstruction and China was admitted into the United Nations, shouldering aside the absurd pretensions of Chiang Kai-shek. President Nixon was courteously received in Peking, the first of many Western visits to China which Deng and Hua were later to reciprocate. As well as diplomatic missions there were trade delegations and China became less isolated. In 1978 China at last signed a peace treaty with Japan, more than thirty years after the Second World War had ended: Japan too now scrambled for the new markets which were opening in China for those able to offer modern technology. In 1979 President Carter at last gave full US recognition to the CCP government of China.

Sino-Soviet relations on the other hand remained cool in spite of intermittent, cautious attempts to improve them. China fought a brief war with Vietnam in 1979, regarding Vietnam by this time as a Soviet satellite (see Section 17.1(*d*)). At the end of that year, China was loud in condemning the Soviet invasion of Afghanistan, claiming it as further evidence of the Russian aim of 'hegemony'. Such anti-Soviet postures delighted the Americans and Margaret Thatcher, though there were those in the West who warned of the danger of putting too much trust in the 'China card' in the poker game of great-power relations. The development of China as a major international force, perhaps even a superpower with her nuclear arsenal and vast population, had made great-power relations triangular – the USA, the USSR and China at the three vertices. In the early 1980s the West had drawn closer to China than to the Soviet Union. But the history of the postwar world suggested that there could be no certainty that cordial relations between any two of them would be long-lasting, and there were already ominous rumblings in 1982 when Peking responded angrily to President Reagan's renewed military support for Taiwan.

15.4 North Vietnam

Ho Chi Minh served a long apprenticeship as a communist, much of it at some distance from North Vietnam where he eventually became ruler. His father was a nationalist who lost his job for opposing French colonialism, and Ho spent some time in Britain, Western Europe and at sea, before arriving in Moscow in 1922. He left Russia with Borodin to assist the Chinese Communist Party and then returned to Vietnam to encourage rebellion against French colonial power. The whole of Indochina was at that time under French control (see Fig. 16.1). Ho's plotting led to his flight to China in 1940, where he was imprisoned by Chiang Kai-shek. He returned to Indochina in 1943, however, to lead resistance to the Japanese, who by then had taken over from the French. In the meantime he had helped to organize a Vietnamese resistance movement known as the *Viet Minh*, the first units of which were set up in China by Indochinese exiles.

The defeat of Japan in 1945 did not lead to freedom for Indochina. The French came back and the Viet Minh went on with its nationalist struggles (see Section 16.3(*a*)). Ho declared the independence of the Democratic Republic of Vietnam of which he himself was President but the French were prepared to yield little, except perhaps Tonkin, though even they recognized that Ho's politics and patriotism had a large popular following. The Viet Minh therefore fought a war of independence, and it was not until they were routed at Dien Bien Phu in 1954 that the French were persuaded to give up their claims in Indochina.

Like Mao in China, Ho and the Viet Minh had the support of the peasants. After 1950, the year in which China and the USSR recognized the Democratic Republic of Vietnam, they also received Chinese military supplies to ensure their survival. In 1951, the Viet Minh was reorganized into the Fatherland, or Lien Viet, Front, a popular and communist-based coalition which in due course became the undisputed government of North Vietnam. But, anxious to prevent communist expansion, the USA gave assistance to the French, spending over 1 000 million dollars in 1954 alone. Such spending failed to preserve the French Empire in Indochina, but, when the French withdrew, Vietnam was temporarily divided into two parts, at the 17th parallel. From this division developed the most prolonged confrontation and bloodiest conflict to have occurred so far between the USA and 'communism' (see Section 17.1(*d*)).

The USA took it upon itself to keep communism out of South Vietnam. In North Vietnam, the Fatherland Front was already firmly established under the leadership of Ho Chi Minh, Pham Van Dong (Prime Minister) and General Giap (Minister of Defence in charge of the armed forces), all of them veterans of the struggle for liberation and Marxism. A new constitution in 1960 made little difference to either the North Vietnamese system or the personnel of the government. Ho Chi Minh was re-elected President and the Communist Party continued to direct the development of the state. In spite of some peasant resistance and a crisis in 1956, when the government tried to effect social change too quickly, agriculture was organized into co-operatives. Industries were nationalized, although only Hanoi and Haiphong had extensive industrial areas. A thorough-going attempt was made to eliminate illiteracy and to develop education. But in spite of extensive aid from other communist countries, North Vietnam was still far from being a rich country and development was handicapped severely by the strain of the struggle for South Vietnam, particularly when, after 1964, the USA resorted to the bombing of the North. It seemed an unequal contest as the world's most powerful air force blasted the rail links, ports and industries of an underdeveloped state of less than 20 million people. But the bombing had no marked effect on the loyalties and determination of the North Vietnamese.

Ho Chi Minh died in September 1969, but Pham Van Dong and others continued with his policies. Their government had arisen from the wishes of the people of Vietnam for independence and social reform, and these aims still commanded great support. It was an American delusion that opposition to the USA and to the puppet governments which US troops upheld in South Vietnam was part of a Soviet or Chinese plot to spread Marxism into lands reluctant to receive it. The USSR and China, of course, supplied North Vietnam with invaluable aid, but it was Vietnamese determination which finally sapped the will of the USA to go on with the struggle. Deprived of US support, President Thieu of South Vietnam resigned. Communists took over the whole of South Vietnam during 1975 and arranged nationwide Vietnamese elections in which only their supporters were allowed to stand. A

National Assembly was thus elected and the Socialist Republic of Vietnam was proclaimed in 1976. Vietnam was one country again for the first time since 1859, with a single government led by Pham Van Dong.

It was a devastated land, blasted by years of savage conflict with the USA, its soil polluted by US chemical weapons, and the people of Saigon and other South Vietnamese towns scarred by exposure to the seamiest aspects of the American way of life: drugs, prostitution and a profusion of dollars. A vast problem of reconstruction lay ahead. Not surprisingly there were further upheavals. There was an exodus of refugees, most leaving by sea and attracting the sympathy of the Western press as 'the boat people'. Many were Chinese who had no wish to live under a Vietnamese nationalist government; many fled for political or religious reasons, hostile to or fearful of Marxist government. Reconstruction for Pham Van Dong's government meant social reorganization and the sweeping away of the legacy of colonialism and Americanism. After some opposition from the USA, Vietnam joined the United Nations in 1977. A year later, she joined Comecon, her membership sponsored by the Soviet Union but not wholly welcomed by East European members.

The Soviet Union had won the competition with China to secure the allegiance of the new Vietnam, and Soviet aid was poured in to help with reconstruction. The whole of Indochina had 'gone communist' after the US retreat, and China supported the vicious regime of Pol Pot in Cambodia. Conflict developed between Vietnam and Pol Pot's government, and China briefly invaded Vietnam in 1979 as some sort of warning. Indochina remained turbulent (see Section 17.1(d)). But the roots of its many problems lay in a century of French colonialism whose legacy was made worse by twenty years of US interference.

15.5   Cuba

The Caribbean island of Cuba was liberated by the USA from the hands of Spain in a brief war in 1898. The island became a republic but American troops were needed until 1902, and again from 1906 to 1909, to create stability; American aid was necessary at frequent intervals to ensure solvency. Cuban presidents produced little but revolts and charges of corruption, and the election of General Machado in 1925 degenerated inevitably into dictatorship. A combination of Machado's terrorism and the Great Depression led to further unrest and, in 1933, the year that Hitler came to power in Germany, Cuba fell into the hands of Batista, an enterprising sergeant who secured control of the Cuban army.

Batista became a kingmaker. In the 1930s, he lurked behind a variety of incompetent presidents, pulling the political strings; he emerged in 1940, now with the rank of colonel, to secure his own election as President of Cuba until 1944. His regime had some of the trappings of fascism, although he introduced a constitution in 1940 modelled on that of the USA and declared war

Table 15.1   Communist powers outside Europe in the 1970s

Country	Population (est.1979) millions	Main export (% of whole)	Exports mainly to (% of whole)	Imports mainly from (% of whole)
Mongolian P.R.	1.6	Livestock and meat 46% (1975)	USSR 81% (1976)	USSR 93% (1976)
China	1 000.0	Foodstuffs 30%, textiles 25% (1978)	Hong Kong 20% Japan 19% (1978)	Japan 30% West Germany 10% (1978)
North Korea	17.5	Ores and metals 75% (1975)	China 40% USSR 25% (1978)	China 50% USSR 18% (1978)
Vietnam	51.9	Clothing 10%, fish 10%, rubber 10% (1974)	USSR 46% Japan 10% (1978)	USSR 30% Japan 16% (1978)
Cuba	9.7	Sugar 87% (1976)	USSR 54% (1977)	USSR 71% (1977)
Chile*	10.9	Copper 80% (1972) Copper 50% (1977)	Japan 17% West Germany 14% (1972) West Germany 14% Brazil 13% (1977)	USA 17% Argentina 15% (1972) USA 20% Argentina 12% (1977)

* Chile's Marxist rule under Allende lasted only from 1970 to 1973.

on the Axis powers. 1944 brought Batista temporary eclipse but, in 1952, he seized power again and for a time ruled by decree, securing election as President in 1955 as the only candidate. To mark his success, Batista issued an amnesty to political prisoners. One of those released was Fidel Castro.

Castro wasted little time in resuming the revolutionary activities which had taken him to prison in the first place. At the end of 1956, he led an invasion of Cuba from Mexico, appealing to all those discontented with the rule of Batista. The invasion reduced the Castro faction to a dozen but guerilla headquarters were established in the mountains of the Sierra Maestra and support began to grow. Cuba came close to civil war. Batista fled on 1 January 1959 and Castro's guerillas easily entered Havana to set up a government of the Popular Socialist Party.

Ernesto 'Che' Guevara, an Argentinian, was among Castro's followers. Like Castro, he was a revolutionary, inflamed by hostility to the USA whose influence, he believed, had much to do with the poverty and inequality so widespread in Latin America and the Caribbean. Guevara was also a Marxist who shared Mao Tse-tung's faith in a revolutionary peasantry. He stayed in Cuba only until 1965, organizing agricultural co-operatives among Cuba's peasants and becoming Minister for Industries in 1961. He found administration dull and moved on to South America to promote new revolutions. Two years later, in 1967, he was ambushed and executed in Bolivia. Guevara's was a brand of communism which turned its back on the power politics of the USSR, identifying with poor peasants and downtrodden workers such as the Bolivian tin-miners. Castro shared many of his ideas, but Castro was a Cuban of Spanish descent who now saw it as his mission to rule and reform his own island. Only in 1961 did he declare his support for Marxism–Leninism, though his anti-Americanism had been clear from the start.

The rule of the Popular Socialist Party quickly hardened into a dictatorship and remained one, in spite of new constitutions and changes of name. The United Party of Socialist Revolution was renamed the Cuban Communist Party in 1965, holding all the seats in parliament, since the Republic was a one-party state. Fidel Castro was Prime Minister (President of the Council of State) and his brother Raoul emerged as his right-hand man. From the outset the new Cuban government came into conflict with the USA. US business interests were well established in Cuba, one of the causes in Castro's view of the island's inequalities and extensive poverty and of its vice and corruption, especially in Havana with its casinos and army of prostitutes. An energetic start was made on nationalizing US enterprises and cleaning up the capital. About 1 000 million dollars worth of American investments were seized. The USA hit back with a boycott of Cuban sugar – the island's main export most of which was marketed in the United States. In January 1961 the USA broke off diplomatic relations, expecting quickly to bring Castro to his knees. Castro produced a trump card, however. The Soviet Union stepped in to buy Cuba's sugar and to supply necessities, such as oil, as a result of which, in 1972, Cuba became a member of Comecon.

Meanwhile, US-Cuban relations deteriorated still further. In April 1961, Cuban exiles under Cardona launched an invasion of southern Cuba in the Bay of Pigs. The exploit had been supported by Eisenhower and was inherited by President Kennedy. The invasion was a fiasco. The exiles were routed and the United States government was quite unable convincingly to dissociate itself from the plot. An attempt to impose an economic blockade on Cuba only drove the island into even closer ties with the communist world. But when the USA detected Soviet rocket sites on Cuba in 1962, Kennedy acted vigorously and this time it was Russia who was humiliated: the missiles were dismantled and withdrawn (see Section 17.1(e)).

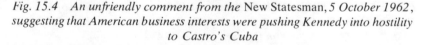

But those behind cried 'forward!'
And those before cried 'back!'
And backward now and forward
Wavers the deep array

Fig. 15.4   An unfriendly comment from the New Statesman, *5 October 1962, suggesting that American business interests were pushing Kennedy into hostility to Castro's Cuba*

Thus Castro's Cuba became steadily communist, much dependent on the USSR although more in sympathy perhaps with the Chinese and Guevara's interpretation of communism. In 1962, Cuba was suspended from the Organization of American States, an association for inter-American co-operation (see Section 18.3(a)). Castro's reply was to found, in 1966, the Latin American Solidarity Organization, to promote guerilla activities to undermine capitalism and the influence of the USA. Cuba became a constant thorn in the flesh of the United States, all the more aggravating for being less than a hundred miles off the coast of Florida. At the end of the 1960s, it became a favourite terminus for hijacked aircraft and a symbol of defiance for all who hated the USA. Castro, meanwhile, went on to confiscate the remaining American property in the island, nearly 3 000 million dollars worth in all.

Fig. 15.5 Fidel Castro: a basketball game in Bulgaria during a tour of Eastern Europe, 1964. The bearded sportsman-politician became a symbol of defiance in the eyes of the USA

Although her leaders would have wished otherwise, Cuba continued to rely heavily on exports of sugar (see Table 15.1). Efforts were made to expand industry and to diversify the economy but it proved difficult to escape from the dependence on sugar which Castro's government had inherited. Indeed, an ultimate goal of 10 million tons of sugar per year was fixed, though output had still not reached 8 million tons by 1977, in spite of modernization and expansion of the industry. Output in general grew comparatively slowly and Soviet assistance to the Cuban economy continued to be necessary. On the other hand, Castro's government was busy in carrying out a social revolution, part of which was to ensure fair shares (where necessary by rationing) and low prices (by controls) of essentials. By the 1980s Cuba was operating a mixed system of centralized planning and some free enterprise to encourage the production of 'extras'. Most of the economy was controlled, however. The collectivization of agriculture had been promoted by the National Institute of Agrarian Reform. Public utilities had been nationalized and most businesses taken over by the state in 1968.

Communist government brought stability to an island accustomed to political intrigue. It also brought more independence than Cuba had ever known in the past, in spite of economic dependence on the USSR. Western critics complained that few democratic freedoms existed and, as from other parts of the communist world, there were refugees from Cuba who disapproved of Castro's government. But for the masses, the government worked hard to bring improvement, developing transport systems, providing better housing and expanding social services. Priority was given to improved health services and to education. Illiteracy was wiped out by the 1970s. The regime befriended the poor, including the negroes who made up about an eighth of Cuba's population. It raised the status of women and vigorously attacked the vice which was deep-rooted in the island. The regime was authoritarian and sometimes inefficient but it brought an honesty to Cuban politics which many found refreshing.

Cuban government was based more on a collective leadership than the outside world popularly imagined. It nevertheless owed a good deal to Fidel Castro himself, and *Castroism* was a distinctive and not always orthodox form of communism. It was rooted in the history of the Caribbean and in the area's anti-Americanism, and Castro was at least as much a Cuban nationalist as a Marxist. Even he could not get rid of the US military base at Guantanamo in the south-east of Cuba, however. Nor had he much success in spreading Castroism to other Caribbean islands, though his influence continued to worry Washington. The USA readily blamed Cuba and, through Cuba, the USSR for all upheavals that occurred in the Caribbean and Central America, though most of them sprang from poverty and injustice. The brutality and self-interest of the Somoza family in Nicaragua led to the overthrow of their regime in 1979 by the Sandanista National Liberation Front, an organization US politicians promptly labelled 'communist'. Two years later, Castro and communists were alleged to be behind the discontent in El Salvador, where the military offered few of the reforms the people had long demanded. In the meantime, in the tiny island of Grenada, the right-wing regime of Eric Gairy was toppled in 1979 by Maurice Bishop, and Bishop too was alleged to be an agent of Castro.

But the USA had not been able to keep Cuba in isolation. Guyana and the English-speaking islands of the Caribbean took the lead in the mid-1970s in resuming economic and diplomatic relations with Castro, and the Organization of American States lifted its boycott of Cuban trade. Some patchy improvement also occurred in US-Cuban relations. US senators and businessmen visited Havana and US tourists were allowed to follow in 1977. Cuba freed political prisoners the following year as a gesture of goodwill. American financiers and the IMF nevertheless frowned on all those suspected of Castroism, as Michael Manley, Prime Minister of Jamaica from 1972 to 1980, found to his cost. In spite of Cuba's own problems, Castro continued to pledge aid to less prosperous countries, helping Jamaica with housing and with work-teams in the later 1970s. He also continued to challenge established conventions, producing his own definition of non-alignment (see Section 11.3(*a*)) and intervening in Africa to the further embarrassment of the USA (see Sections 16.5(*b*) and 19.3).

15.6   Chile

Castro and Che Guevara firmly believed in the emergence of some kind of peasant communism in the states of South America through the revolutionary activities of guerillas. The results were frequently disappointing and Cuba remained for years the sole outpost of communism in the West. Many of the states of Central and South America were politically unstable. Most of them had large populations of poor people. But in some Latin and South American countries there was a tradition of army intervention to ensure the success of governments acceptable to the military; the poor themselves were often apathetic in matters of politics. Dictatorships were more common than democratically-elected governments and although some of them, from time to time, adopted socialist policies, poverty and illiteracy seemed likely long to remain. Although encouraged by the USSR and China, as well as by Castro, revolution made little headway. It was typical of South America that, in 1964, the army removed the President from power in Brazil to make way for a strongly anti-communist dictatorship and that, in 1966, the Argentinian President was similarly overthrown by an army coup prior to an attack on trade unions and the banning of strikes.

One country in South America, however, preserved some attachment to democracy and it was this country, Chile, which in 1970, by a narrow margin, elected a Marxist government under President Salvador Allende. All previous communist governments in the world had arisen out of upheaval – revolution, civil war or wartime dislocation. Chile did the unexpected, legally and peacefully electing to power a coalition of left-wing groups as a Popular Unity Government. Allende himself was a thorough-going Marxist, strongly supported by the Chilean working class. His first cabinet was a bizarre and fragile collection of representatives of the Communist Party, the Socialist Party (which in Chile was more extreme than the communists), the Social Democrats, the Action Movement of Popular Unity, Radicals and others. In opposition were the Christian Democrats who had formed an earlier government, in 1964, under Eduardo Frei, but who unlike the Christian Democrats of Europe were strongly committed to economic planning and development by non-capitalist means. To Europeans, Chilean politics were, therefore, rather strange. Almost all the parties seemed to lean to the left and the Communists were less extreme than the Socialists who tended to support Castroism. Chile could even find room for Independent Marxists, one of whom found a place in Allende's first government.

To South Americans also, Chilean politics were rather strange. Military and other dictatorships seemed to have been left behind in favour of a democratic power struggle between supporters of the working classes and reforming supporters of the middle classes. After 1964, Frei made a start on the setting up of peasant co-operatives and on confiscating the estates of large land-owners, though he was careful not to move too quickly lest he annoy the USA, whose nationals owned much of Chile's vital copper-mining industry. For all their reforming zeal the Christian Democrats in any case remained a mainly middle-class party. Allende belonged to the Socialist Party, which demanded faster change. When he came to power, he quickly nationalized the banks, copper and textiles and speeded up the transfer of land to poor peasants. In 1972 the powerful International Telegraph and Telephone Company (ITT) was dispossessed, and reported to the United Nations for allegedly plotting to overthrow Allende's government.

Capitalist plots and US hostility, including intrigue by the CIA, were only part of the problems the Popular Unity government faced. Allende's policies scared away private investment and made it difficult to sustain the rapid development which was essential for Chile to overcome poverty and illiteracy and to improve housing and the social services. At the same time, the government was an awkward coalition unable to rely on a firm democratic majority. Free speech and a free press remained and there was no reason, in 1972, to believe that the President's Marxism was likely to lead to a dictatorship. On the other hand, progress towards really revolutionary change was less rapid than the extreme left desired, and Allende found himself frustrated by middle-class opposition and threatened by revolutionary extremism. The latter began to express itself in the activities of the Movement of the Revolutionary Left (MIR), whereas the forces of conservatism seemed prepared to bide their time in the hope that Allende would lose the next elections and re-admit Frei to power. In spite of Chile's traditions of democracy and tolerance, civil war began to appear possible. The government survived, however, in the general election of 1973. Meanwhile, although Chile possessed valuable mineral deposits as a basis for industrial development and wealth, grave social problems remained. Allende told the UNCTAD Conference of 1972, which met in his country, that Chile still had '600 000 children who, for want of proteins in the first eight months of life, will never attain their full mental vigour'. It was about their future and about the future of unborn children that the political arguments raged.

In 1970, Allende had demonstrated that, at least in Chile, a communist-inclined government could come to power through the normal democratic processes which were so much prized in the West. The event provided food for thought among capitalists and communists. It seemed to strengthen the arguments of those revisionists who claimed that communism could succeed by methods other than violent revolution. But Allende's experiment was shortlived. In September 1973, his government was destroyed by the violent intervention of the armed forces and Allende himself died either by murder or suicide. There were plenty of arguments to excuse the action of the military although many of them were exaggerated. It was certainly true that inflation was rampant in Chile and that boycotts by small businessmen and transport-owners had done much to paralyse the country. But it could not be denied that, albeit on a minority vote, Allende had been elected and re-elected to power and that his supporters among Chileans were numbered in millions. He had also tried hard to appease the military leaders and even to admit them to a share in power. In the end, however, right-wing forces could simply not accept government by a Marxist and they wiped it out in a blood-bath.

Che Guevara believed that, in South America, communism could only be established by revolution. Allende believed that it could be established by peaceful means. Both died for their beliefs. The death of Allende was a serious setback not only for the revisionists: it was a disaster for the Chilean people. All political parties were banned and the military set up a dictatorship brutal even by South American standards. Its leader was General Pinochet who continued to rule with an iron fist into the 1980s, apparently uninter-ested in any sort of social reform or in restoring civilian government. He eventually brought Chile's roaring inflation down to double figures and by the end of the 1970s to about an annual 25 per cent, and there was some develop-ment of the economy with help from the USA. The USA approved of Pinochet's support for capitalism, but the Chilean regime remained highly unpopular. Only similar right-wing dictatorships had close dealings with it. In moderate and left-wing circles it was detested. Pinochet made some conces-sions to trade unionism in 1979 to ease Chile's problems in overseas trade, but many countries continued to boycott his regime. Dealings with Chile were always likely to spark off fierce controversy in countries like Britain where there was dismay when the Thatcher government reversed previous policy and lifted the ban on the sale of arms.

Further Reading

Ayling, S.E.: *Portraits of Power.* Harrap (London, 1965) – Mao.

Bown, C.: *China 1949–1976.* Heinemann (London, 1980).

Bown, C.: *Revolution in China 1911–1949.* Heinemann Broadsheets (London, 1974).

Bruce, R.: *Sun Yat-sen.* Oxford University Press (London, 1969).

Crankshaw, E.: *Moscow v. Peking, A New Cold War.* Penguin (Harmondsworth, 1963).

Dures, A. and K.: *Mao Tse-tung.* Batsford (London, 1980).

Kennett, J.: *The Rise of Communist China.* Blackie (Glasgow, 1970).

Kuo, Ping-Chia: *China.* Oxford University Press (London, 1971).

Lacouture, J.: *Ho Chi Minh.* Allen Lane (London, 1968).

Purcell, V.: *The Rise of Modern China.* Historical Association (London, 1962).

Robottom, J.: *Modern China.* Longman (Harlow, 1967).

Tregear, T.R.: *The Chinese: How They Live and Work.* David & Charles (Newton Abbot, 1973).

Watson, J.B.: *The West Indian Heritage.* John Murray (London, 2nd edn, 1982) – Cuba.

Documentary

Breach, R.W.: *Documents and Descriptions, the World since 1914*. Oxford University Press (London, 1966) – Sections 18, 42.

Rowe, D.N.: *Modern China*. Anvil (London, 1959).

Tarling, N.: *Mao and the Transformation of China*. Heinemann (London, 1977).

Quotations from Chairman Mao Tse-tung. Foreign Languages Press (Peking, 1966); i.e. the *Thoughts of Chairman Mao*.

Exercises

1. What elements are common to the communist states described in this Unit? What reservations do you have about using the word 'communist' to describe *either* China *or* Cuba?

2. Show how *each* of the following has been important in the history of China: Sun Yat-sen; Chiang Kai-shek; Mao Tse-tung; Chou En-lai.

3. 'To ensure a better life for the several hundred million people of China and to build our economically and culturally backward country into a prosperous and powerful one' (page 282). How far had communist government achieved this aim before the death of Mao Tse-tung in 1976?

4. Using Unit Twelve as well as this Unit, list in two columns the main characteristics since 1950 of the *Soviet Union* and *China* under the following headings: system of government; agricultural organization; industrial development; international supporters; attitudes to Marxism–Leninism. What similarities and what differences between the two powers can you find?

5. How and why did *two* of the following states become communist: North Korea; North Vietnam; Cuba?

6. Account for the popularity with their peoples of Ho Chi Minh and Fidel Castro.

7. How did Chile become a Marxist state and why did she not remain one?

8. Making use of this Unit, the references provided and the Index to this book, trace the history of Chinese foreign policy in the years since 1949. How far does this history support the view that 'China has proved a remarkably peaceful power' (page 288)?

9. Study Fig. 12.3 (page 211) and Table 15.1 (page 293), and then answer these questions:

   (*a*) Identify in the 1970s (*i*) the *two* largest communist powers, (*ii*) the *two* smallest in terms of population, and (*iii*) the European state which had for a time sided with China in the Sino-Soviet quarrel.

   (*b*) How do Fig. 12.3 and Table 15.1 suggest that communist states in Europe were more industrialized than communist states outside Europe?

   (*c*) Explain what you understand by *Comecon* (Fig. 12.3).

   (*d*) What evidence do Fig. 12.3 and Table 15.1 provide that the USSR and China were not on good terms in the 1960s and 1970s? Which state do they suggest sought to maintain good relations with both the USSR and China?

   (*e*) Which *two* capitalist states had by 1978 achieved considerable success in selling their goods to China?

   (*f*) Does Table 15.1 show much evidence to support the argument that a Marxist government in Chile affected the country's overseas trade? Suggest reasons for the changes that *are* shown in the Table.

   (*g*) Explain what you can learn from Table 15.1 about Cuba in the mid-1970s. In what ways would the data in this Table for Cuba in the mid-1950s have been (*i*) similar and (*ii*) different?

Unit Sixteen

The End of Overseas Empires

16.1 Empires at the End of the Second World War

Italy's overseas Empire had been over-run and lost in the Second World War, just as Germany's was in the First (see Section 11.1). But the effects of the Second World War were much wider-ranging (see Section 10.5). States captured by Japan and then liberated were reluctant to return to European control. The Netherlands and France both met fierce resistance in South-East Asia, and, in Singapore and Malaya, Britain could only regain possession for a time. Colonialism was now unfashionable, bitterly attacked in communist propaganda and widely resented throughout the world. Almost everywhere nationalists were impatient for freedom.

The Dutch Empire in the East Indies collapsed with startling ease. The French floundered in Indochina and elsewhere and then tried in vain to construct a French Community. Britain abandoned her Empire rather more gracefully, constructing the Commonwealth instead. But by the end of the 1960s, almost all European overseas possessions had been surrendered; Portugal alone managed to continue for some time longer to hold on to extensive territories in Africa, virtually as if nothing had happened.

16.2 The Dutch Empire

(a) Indonesia

Dr Sukarno declared Indonesia independent of the Dutch only two days after the surrender of Japan. His supporters were well-armed with weapons left behind by the Japanese. The Dutch government had problems in the Netherlands, now liberated from the Nazis, and was in no position to recover the East Indies by force.

Sukarno was proclaimed President of the Republic of Indonesia in 1945 and, when the Dutch tried to bargain, he refused to settle for anything short of total independence. Dutch troops arrived in 1946 but they were quite unable to topple the rebel regime. The Netherlands could only accept the independence of Indonesia at the end of 1949, under pressure from the USA and through the mediation of a United Nations commission. Sukarno agreed to a rather meaningless 'union' with the Netherlands but it was dissolved in 1954. The Dutch also kept possession of West Irian, a part of New Guinea, but their possession was hotly disputed and, in 1962, West Irian was placed under a United Nations administration and transferred to Indonesia in the following year. Meanwhile, in 1957, all Dutch citizens were expelled from

Indonesia and their property confiscated, an ignominious end to an Empire which had lasted for well over three hundred years.

Indonesia remained under the leadership of Sukarno until 1967. He followed his confrontation with the Dutch by quarrelling with Malaysia in 1963. He had for some time resented the British possession of Sarawak and Sabah on the northern coast of Borneo, claiming that the entire island should belong to Indonesia. Britain had already agreed to the independence of Malaya and it now seemed sensible to link these countries with Malaya to create the Federation of Malaysia under the leadership of the Malayan Prime Minister, the football-loving Tunku Abdul Rahman. Sukarno regarded this as a British plot, to deprive him for ever of the total control of Borneo. He used guerillas to try to free Sarawak and Sabah and even sent parachutists into Malaya, in an effort to break up the Federation, but he was condemned in the United Nations and the world was unimpressed when he withdrew from UNO in protest in 1965. Malaysia had support from other members of the Commonwealth and from the USA and, in 1966, Sukarno abandoned the feud.

Meanwhile, Sukarno had become increasingly dictatorial. Indonesia consisted of some three thousand islands, many of which were resentful of domination by Java and the Javanese. Problems also arose from the activities of pro-Chinese communists and, in 1965, there were clashes between the

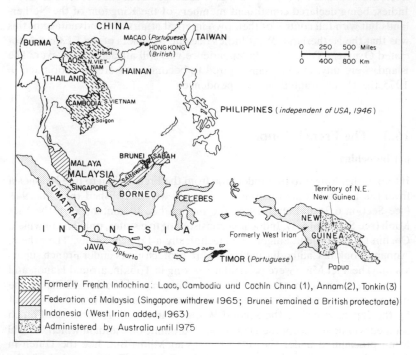

Fig. 16.1 South-East Asia in 1973

communists and the army. Sukarno's authority dwindled. The army alleged that he himself encouraged the communists and, in 1967, he was forced to resign in favour of General Suharto. President Suharto began a purge of both communists, unpopular among devout Indonesians for their atheism, and those of Chinese descent. Some fled and tens of thousands were imprisoned, deported or killed.

There were substantial Chinese minorities in many countries of South-East Asia where they were chiefly involved in commerce and business, sometimes dubbed 'the Jews of the East'. Those who gained wealth were obvious targets for working-class wrath. Those who remained peasants, on the other hand, were suspected of being communist infiltrators. Like anti-Semitic outbreaks in the western world, anti-Chinese outbreaks occurred in South-East Asia. When Vietnam was unified in the mid-1970s, the Vietnamese wasted no time in encouraging resident Chinese to leave the country (see Section 15.4).

(b) The Netherlands West Indies

Nationalism in Surinam and the Dutch islands of the Caribbean was less advanced than in Indonesia and the Dutch had more time after 1945 to plan for the future. Self-government was conceded to Surinam in 1950. Four years later, Surinam and the islands were grouped together as the Netherlands West Indies, being declared constituent members of the Kingdom of the Netherlands but with full control of their own internal affairs. One advantage of this was that the Netherlands West Indies became members of the EEC as Associated Overseas Territories. Independence was still attractive, however. The islands were tiny, but Surinam aspired to become a sovereign nation and in 1975 the Dutch granted her independence.

16.3   The French Empire

(a) Indochina

It took rather longer to free Indochina from the French than to free Indonesia from the Dutch but nationalism was already well-established there in 1941 (see Section 6.3) and after 1945, the French had to contend with the Viet Minh (see Section 15.4). Indochina consisted of five states, only one of which, Cochin China, around Saigon, was technically a French colony. The others, Annam, Tonkin, Cambodia and Laos were protectorates under French supervision. The Viet Minh were particularly strong in Tonkin, around Hanoi, and it was their ambition to unite Tonkin, Annam and Cochin China in the independent state of Vietnam, a union already brought about to some extent by the Japanese before the Second World War ended. At first, the French seemed willing to accept the Democratic Republic of Vietnam which Ho Chi Minh proclaimed under the rule of the Viet Minh. But, like the Dutch in Indonesia, they wanted some continuing links with the area which the nationalists would not permit. Neither side would give way and, at the end of 1946, fighting began.

By 1950, France was ready to concede self-government and to reduce the five states to three, Vietnam, Laos and Cambodia, provided that they remained in the *French Union*, which had been set up in 1946 to advise the French government on the management of the French overseas Empire. The French also now intended to make Vietnam subject to the Emperor, Bao Dai, formerly a puppet ruler in Annam. It took another four years of war to persuade them that such stop-gap measures were useless and that they must totally abandon Indochina. On 7 May 1954, the French army was forced to surrender to the Viet Minh after being besieged for many weeks in Dien Bien Phu. In France, the government was defeated and in July the new Prime Minister, Mendès-France, agreed to the independence of Vietnam, Laos and Cambodia.

All three states thus left the French Union. Cambodia, for a time, continued under the comparatively stable rule of Norodom Sihanouk who had inherited the throne in 1941. Laos had rather more difficulty, with a power struggle between the Pathet Lao, a communist-inclined group led by Souphanou Vong, and the nationalists of Souvanna Phouma. France agreed to withdraw under a settlement made at the Geneva Conference of 1954, which temporarily divided Vietnam between the communist North under Ho Chi Minh and the South under Bao Dai. Thus the stage was set for a new Vietnamese War which was to continue furiously in the 1960s with increasing American involvement (see Section 17.1(*d*)).

(*b*) Algeria

Algeria took up the struggle against French colonialism as soon as independence had been won by the nationalists in Indochina. In November 1954, the *Front de la Libération Nationale* (FLN), under Ben Bella, declared war on France. The FLN was handicapped by a lack of unity among the Arabs but above all it was opposed by the *colons* (French settlers in North Africa), who looked to the French government for effective assistance. A massive French army seemed unable to suppress the FLN: the military blamed the politicians and, in 1958, the army under General Salan rejected the authority of the French government. This helped to bring the Fourth Republic to an end. With the Fifth Republic led by de Gaulle (see Section 14.1) the colons looked forward to strong measures to put down the FLN.

In 1955 the United Nations had called for independence for Algeria, and de Gaulle showed no sign of using force to prevent this. In fury, the colons set up *L'Organisation de L'Armée Secrète* (OAS) to fight against Arab nationalism, demonstrating their anger with atrocities both in Algeria and France. But de Gaulle was intent on a settlement and agreement was reached with the FLN in March 1962. Algeria became independent a few months later, subject only to agreements for economic co-operation and to allow France the use of a naval base and weapon-testing sites.

The OAS continued for a time to splutter in protest but eventually they had to accept the inevitable. The struggle for liberation had been costly in human lives but the tide of nationalism was running with the FLN, not with the OAS.

(c) Morocco and Tunisia

France abandoned Morocco and Tunisia more readily than Algeria. French roots were less deep in these colonies and there was less opposition to independence from the colons. Independence was granted in 1956. In Tunisia, Bourguiba came to power, a veteran nationalist who, like Ben Bella, had been imprisoned in French jails. Such imprisonment was commonplace treatment for nationalists in both the French and British Empires and came to be regarded as an almost essential qualification for future leadership.

The French retreat from Morocco led Spain almost immediately to leave Spanish Morocco (see Section 6.5). But Spain kept possession of the coastal province of Ifni until 1969 and remained even longer in the Spanish Sahara. Saharan nationalists set up a new Liberation Front to speed Spain's departure in 1972, but the colony was rich in phosphates and Franco held on to this remnant of Spain's Empire. Franco's death brought change but not the independence the nationalists demanded. In 1976 Spain ceded the territory to Morocco and Mauritania, leaving the nationalists to continue their struggle for freedom. They organized themselves in the Polisario Front and fought a bitter guerilla war in which the world took little interest, though Algeria showed some sympathy. The plight of the Saharans was just one of the many problems Europeans left to their former African subjects.

(d) The French Union and the French Community

The Viet Minh and the FLN broke the spirit of French colonialism. The Fourth Republic had set up the French Union in 1946 to provide a framework within which the dependencies could move towards self-government while retaining connections with France. The Union was rejected in Indochina. The Fifth Republic in 1958 envisaged instead the French Community which was not very different: dependencies would have internal self-government while the Community would control such matters as defence and foreign policy. France, therefore, would retain considerable influence. De Gaulle was not inclined to insist on the Community, however. He was realist enough to recognize that by 1960 most of the remaining French colonies wanted complete independence and that, in Africa, it would be difficult to deny it.

(e) Other French Possessions in Africa

De Gaulle moved quickly. By the end of 1960, independence was granted to some fifteen new African states, the whole of what had been French

Equatorial and French West Africa. France kept possession only of French Somaliland, renaming it in 1967 the French Territory of Afars and Issas (see Fig. 16.2). It remained a French Territory until 1977 when the French withdrew and the independent state of Djibouti was born.

The divisions which European colonization had imposed on Africa were frequently artificial. After independence, experiments with unions such as the Mali Federation (of the Soudanese Republic and Senegal) made little headway, but looser groupings among African states became commonplace. Many of the former French states came to be known as the *Monrovia Powers* when they met with Ethiopia and other African states at Monrovia, in Liberia, in 1961. Eventually they created an Organization of Inter-African and Malagasy States as some sort of successor to the French Community. This gave rise to the *Organization of African Unity* (OAU), set up at Addis Ababa in 1963 to promote unity and solidarity throughout Africa (see Section 18.3(*b*)). They put emphasis on the end of colonialism, especially in southern Africa where white domination remained, but real political unity remained distant. It was nevertheless a goal at which some African leaders like Nkrumah of Ghana aimed with enthusiasm.

(*f*) The Rest of the French Empire

Comparatively little of the French Empire remained after 1960. Some areas, such as French Guiana and Martinique, had become overseas departments of France in 1946. Pondicherry and other French outposts in India were smoothly transferred to the latter in the 1950s. The EEC had given France new interests and partners in Europe in the late 1950s and, after the final struggle in Algeria, France accepted that the age of huge overseas empires was past. In the end, France parted almost casually with her enormous possessions in Africa, the majority prepared for independence with only two years of self-government, a less careful preparation for the futures of former colonies than that undertaken by Britain. The ex-French states retained, nevertheless, a curious affection for France which the British sometimes thought undeserved. Many retained close economic links with France and gained advantage from Associated membership of the European Community. For their part, though no longer colonial masters, the French did not scruple to meddle extensively in the affairs of their former colonies nor even in Zaire, the former Belgian Congo (see Section 20.2).

16.4   The Belgian Congo

In contrast to the vast and sprawling French Empire, Belgium ruled little but the Congo (see Section 6.5). Until 1957, no inhabitant of the Congo was allowed to vote and even then only municipal elections were held, to appoint councils in the large towns. There was an almost total lack of preparation for future independence and no attempt was made to train the Congolese for future government. The Belgians were content to pursue economic development in the Congo and in particular to exploit its mineral resources. Yet with 150 tribes and a wide variety of languages, the Belgian Congo was likely, after independence, to be one of the most difficult states to govern in the entire African continent.

In the late 1950s, the Congo was caught up in the clamour for independence which was going on all around it, in French and British dependencies. African nationalist parties emerged, among them the Congolese National Movement led by Patrice Lumumba. In 1959, there were outbreaks of rioting, partly due to unemployment in the towns. The Belgian response was fast and foolish. At the beginning of 1960, a conference of African leaders was summoned and Belgium agreed to grant immediate independence, setting the date for the end of June.* Kasavubu became President of the new Democratic Republic of the Congo, Lumumba its Prime Minister. Almost nothing was done to anticipate the problems of those tribes and areas in the vastness of the Congo, which might wish for separate government. The first parliament had over fifty different factions and the rulers lacked experience. By the end of the year, the Congo was in chaos, having already experienced the dismissal of the Prime Minister, declarations of secession, an army coup and United Nations intervention.

The ending of the Belgian Empire in the Congo was thus the beginning of civil war (see Section 20.2).

16.5   The Portuguese Empire

(a) The Overseas Provinces

Salazar learned nothing from the experience of other Europeans. He had no intention of granting independence to Portugal's colonies (see Sections 6.5 and 14.4). Instead, the Portuguese denied that they were colonies at all, calling them overseas territories and ruling them as provinces of Portugal herself. Tiring of their stubbornness, Nehru's government in 1961 used force to expel the Portuguese from Goa and other outposts on Indian soil. Even then the Portuguese went on believing in a Portuguese India though it no longer existed. Outside Africa in fact Portugal's Empire hardly existed at all. All that was left of once extensive possessions was a couple of tiny provinces – Macao on the coast of China and a half-share of the island of Timor in the South Pacific. Communist China showed no urgent interest in recovering Macao whose population was less than 200 000 and which had been greatly overshadowed by the rapid development of neighbouring Hong Kong. But when Dutch Timor became part of Indonesia it seemed only a matter of time before the Indonesians took over the whole of the island.

There were five Portuguese provinces in Africa. Angola and Mozambique each dwarfed Portugal herself. The others – São Tomé, Portuguese Guinea

* Ruanda-Urundi, a Belgian mandate and trusteeship territory, was separated from the Congo and became independent in 1962.

and the Cape Verde Islands – were mere fragments. Despite growing pressure from African nationalists, Salazar's only response was to reinforce Portuguese garrisons. Caetano, his successor in 1968, made too few concessions and, by the early 1970s, African colonial wars had become a serious burden on Portugal's modest resources. But, until Caetano was overthrown by a coup inside Portugal, the Portuguese Empire remained as a decaying memorial of a bygone age. Caetano's successors hastened to catch up with modern developments and by the end of the 1970s nothing was left of the Empire except Macao. The Portuguese half of Timor was among the provinces which were given independence but that led to an Indonesian invasion and yet another post-colonial conflict.

(b) Nationalism and Independence in the African Provinces

Angola and Mozambique in the 1960s were not only old-fashioned colonies which had been by-passed when most of Africa moved on to independence. They were also bastions of white supremacy which helped to shield the white-minority regimes in South Africa and Rhodesia (see Sections 21.1 and 21.3). Geography made them important in the struggle which was developing throughout all of southern Africa around the question of white privilege and black frustration. Portugal signed an agreement for economic co-operation with South Africa in 1964. Portuguese goodwill towards Ian Smith's regime in Rhodesia greatly weakened international sanctions against that country in the late 1960s and early 1970s. With Portuguese Angola to the north, South Africa remained secure in possession of Namibia (see Section 11.3(b)). For black Africans it was therefore vital to remove the Portuguese as fast as possible.

Resistance to Portuguese rule led to civil war in Angola as early as 1961, though the nationalists were handicapped by divisions among themselves. Within a year the disturbances spread to Portuguese Guinea and in 1964 the Front for the Liberation of Mozambique (*Frelimo*), a Marxist movement, was founded under Mondlane, formerly a professor of anthropology. The scale of operations was not that of the Viet Minh in Indochina, but they tied down thousands of Portuguese troops, won support from the Organization of African Unity and grew more menacing. Frelimo operated from bases in Tanzania and by the 1970s began effectively to offer an alternative government for Mozambique. Portugal resisted stubbornly, supported by white mercenaries from countries such as South Africa, West Germany and the USA. Meanwhile the United Nations sent observers to look into the affairs of Mozambique and Angola, and, in the latter, a commission of the ILO reported breaches in the international agreement on the abolition of forced labour.

The Portuguese authorities still insisted that their African provinces were part of Portugal. Progress of any sort was slow. Both Mozambique and Angola were still primarily agricultural, with populations similar to that of

Portugal herself. Angola had important mineral and diamond deposits and industry was growing, but again the pace was leisurely. The Portuguese claimed that their rule benefited the provinces and that there was no mass support for the nationalist movements. It was a claim increasingly difficult to sustain, but Western powers generally hesitated to disturb the *status quo* and to put pressure on Portugal. Change in Angola and Mozambique might well endanger the balance of power throughout all of southern Africa. There seemed no alternative for Africans but a long and bitter war for liberation.

In fact change came suddenly. After Caetano, Antonio de Spinola was briefly in power in Portugal in 1974. He promised freedom to all the African provinces, and other new Portuguese leaders accepted the sense of his judgment: it was the burden of colonial wars which had helped to provoke the disorder inside Portugal. Portuguese Guinea got independence immediately, with the new name of Guinea-Bissau. Mozambique achieved independence in 1975 under the presidency of Samora Machel, the long struggle by Frelimo culminating naturally in a Frelimo government. About the same time, the Liberation Movement came to power in São Tomé and the African Party took control of the Cape Verde Republic. Angola, too, got independence in November 1975 but, like the Congo in 1960, Angola plunged into civil war. The Portuguese had done little to prepare their provinces for independence and the tribal differences which had handicapped the nationalist struggle in Angola remained unresolved.

Three factions competed for the control of independent Angola – the FNLA (National Front for the Liberation of Angola), UNITA (National Union for the Total Independence of Angola) and the MPLA (Popular Movement for the Liberation of Angola), a Marxist movement with similarities to Frelimo in Mozambique. The strategic position of Angola attracted foreign powers like a magnet and Angolans were not left simply to settle their own problems. The superpowers took sides, the USSR backing the MPLA, the USA backing the FNLA. Even China showed interest, encouraging UNITA. The only non-African troops involved in the fighting came from Cuba, despatched by Castro to assist the MPLA and its leader Agostinho Neto, perhaps further to carry on Cuba's conflict with the USA (see Section 15.5). White mercenaries helped Neto's enemies, however, and Zaire too sent support against the MPLA. South Africa became involved, partly to stop the conflict spreading southwards to add to the disturbances in Namibia, partly to protect refugees, some of them Portuguese, who fled southwards from the conflict, and partly in the hope that Neto and communism would be defeated. Though the FNLA and UNITA joined hands against the MPLA they were nevertheless unsuccessful. Neto emerged as Angola's President with a government of the MPLA. Sporadic disturbances continued and Angola was further unsettled when Neto died in 1979 following surgery in Moscow. He had struggled for almost twenty-five years for Angola's independence before becoming her President and, like Machel in Mozambique, had already by 1979 begun to chart a course for his country which suggested decreasing dependence on the USSR and Cuba. Like Machel, however, he was a bitter opponent of white supremacy.

The collapse of the Portuguese Empire transformed the map of southern Africa. There was now increased pressure on the minority white governments which ruled Rhodesia and South Africa, and there was a new urgency about the future of Namibia (see Sections 21.2 and 21.3).

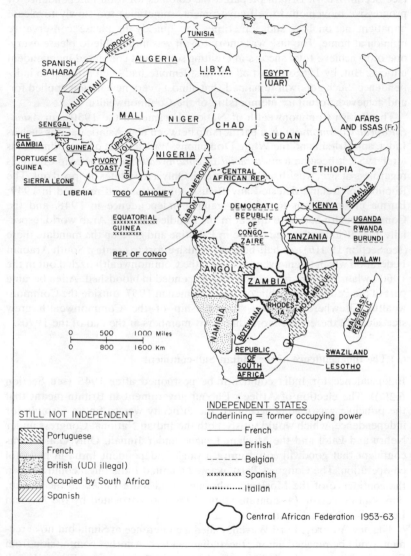

Fig. 16.2 Africa in 1973

16.6   Britain and the Commonwealth

By 1939 Britain had already made the British Commonwealth of Nations a 'white man's club', created from former colonies now known as *Dominions* (see Section 6.2(*a*)). The Commonwealth stood the test of the Second World War and provided, in 1945, the foundations on which to build for the future (see Section 10.4). Britain prepared the colonies for total independence by progressive movement to self-government, sometimes too slowly to please impatient nationalists and sometimes too quickly to please conservative opinion at home. The task was enormous; it was impossible to please everyone or to achieve total success in creating sound and contented independent nations. But, by 1966, almost all the vast Empire had been brought to independence. Such goodwill remained that almost every new nation applied for, and achieved, voluntary membership of the Commonwealth.

The British Commonwealth of Nations became, in the 1950s, an *Asian-European Commonwealth*, a partnership between new Asiatic nations such as India, and Britain and the White Dominions. With a flood of new admissions after 1957, it became a *multi-racial Commonwealth*, a partnership of equals regardless of size, wealth, colour or creed. Only a few states dropped out. The Republic of Ireland detested any British connection and resigned in 1949; Burma preferred not to join on gaining independence in 1948, and the Commonwealth had little appeal in the Middle East and Arab world, especially after Britain admitted failure in Palestine and gave up the mandate there (see Section 19.1(*b*)). A half-hearted British effort to create a South Arabian Federation which might eventually join the Commonwealth fizzled out in the 1960s, when Britain's possession of Aden ended in bloodshed. Aden became part of the People's Republic of South Yemen in 1967, outside the Commonwealth. Elsewhere, however, membership of the Commonwealth grew steadily until there were more than forty members at the end of the 1970s.

(*a*) The Independence of the Indian Sub-continent

Independence for India could not be postponed after 1945 (see Section 6.2(*c*)). The election of Attlee's Labour government in Britain meant that the principle was readily accepted: the difficulty was to find a formula for independence, which would satisfy both the Indian National Congress under Nehru and Patel and the Moslem League under Jinnah. Only Gandhi was confident that goodwill could unite a single independent India in peaceful co-operation. The Congress Party wanted a united India but it could not win the confidence of the Moslems, who more and more rallied to the slogan, 'Pakistan or Perish' (a separate state of the sort advocated by the Moslem League for their religion).

The new Viceroy, Lord Wavell, called a conference at Simla but no agreement could be reached among the Indian leaders. Another commission from England sent by Attlee failed to find an acceptable solution. When Wavell invited Nehru to form a government in August 1946, as a prelude to independence, the Moslem League hit back, calling for demonstrations which quickly degenerated into violence and bloodshed, atrocities and reprisals. Only the British army and the peace-making of Gandhi prevented widespread civil war in the sub-continent. When Attlee called the Indian leaders to London, neither he nor they could produce an acceptable formula.

But Attlee could see no virtue in further delay. In March 1947, Lord Mountbatten, the last Viceroy of India, arrived in Delhi. He had been carefully chosen for his wartime popularity in the country and his task was to find a solution but, in any case, to bring British rule to an end in June 1948. Partition seemed the best answer: it would pacify the Moslem League and Mountbatten persuaded Nehru and the Congress Party to accept it. The final movement to independence was speeded up. In Britain, Attlee pushed the Indian Independence Act quickly through parliament and, on 15 August 1947, India and Pakistan became free nations. Both were admitted to membership of the Commonwealth at their own request.

The separation of Hindus into India and Moslems into Pakistan, however, was no easy matter. Violence flared up between the two as mass migrations began. In *The Times*, in September, it was estimated that 4 million people were already on the move. People were driven by religious frenzy to mass murder, both in the villages and in cities such as Delhi and Calcutta. Gandhi and Nehru both tried to halt the butchery but, in the Punjab alone (divided, like Bengal, when the boundaries between India and Pakistan were drawn), over a quarter of a million lost their lives and nearly 14 million became refugees. Neither Hindus nor Moslems felt that they could be safe if they remained on the 'wrong' side of the boundaries. The killing went on and, in the end, it even claimed the life of Gandhi, assassinated by a Punjabi refugee, a Hindu fanatic, who could not accept the preaching of tolerance to Moslems. Gandhi died in 1948. His death caused a great sense of shock, which at last helped to curb the bloodshed.

Fig. 16.3 Mohandas Karamchand Gandhi, 1869–1948

The new nations had problems enough to achieve economic development and social progress. India had nearly 400 million people, many of them desperately poor and often hungry. Pakistan had only a quarter of India's population but the state had been made in two parts, West and East Pakistan, a thousand miles apart. They were difficult to unite and the East, in particular, was never far from poverty. India speedily established a democratic system of government to which the prestige of the Congress Party gave some stability, and Nehru remained Prime Minister until his death in 1964. He was much respected both for his international statesmanship and for his reforming, socialist-inclined policies within India. Pakistan, on the other hand, experienced almost endless difficulties, searching for stable government. Jinnah, leader of the Moslem League, became Governor-General but lived only until 1948. The first Prime Minister, Liaquat Ali Khan, was assassinated in 1951, leaving the country with no one who could rule effectively. Inevitably, in 1958, democracy was suspended while General Ayub Khan tried to achieve a workable governing system. The turmoil was checked only temporarily and in 1971, Pakistan fell apart (see Section 20.5).

India, meanwhile, became a republic in 1950, an example followed by Pakistan in 1956. In the past the British Crown had always been Head of State in the Dominions, but the Commonwealth took the new development in its stride and many future members preferred republicanism to monarchy. Some took their time over making the change, however. Ceylon gained independence in 1948 but only became a republic in 1972 when the island's name was also changed, to Sri Lanka. But Ceylon created another precedent, being the first member of the Commonwealth – indeed, the first state in the world – to elect a woman prime minister when Mrs Bandaranaike came to office in 1960. That was an example India followed (see Section 22.2).

(*b*) Experiments in Federation

The South Arabian Federation was only one of several federations with which the British experimented. The idea behind a federation was to group various colonial possessions in a single unit, rather like a 'united states' with a central government, in the hope that this might provide a more secure basis for independence. The federations provided evidence of British thought about the future of their colonies but except in Malaysia the experiments ended in failure.

(*i*) **Malaysia.** Malaya gained independence in 1957, under the able Prime Ministership of Tunku Abdul Rahman, who ruled until his retirement in 1970. Britain was so impressed by his leadership that she agreed to transfer her remaining colonies in Borneo to a Federation under the Tunku in 1963. Brunei opted out, preferring to remain under British protection, but Sarawak and Sabah accepted membership of the Federation, as did Singapore. Abdul Rahman successfully resisted a long and bitter struggle with communist guerillas in the north of Malaya, against whom he received Commonwealth assistance from states such as New Zealand. He held the Federation of Malaysia together against the challenge of Indonesia (see Section 16.2) and he made considerable progress towards economic development, though he was unable to keep Singapore in the Federation.

The population of Singapore was mainly Chinese and although Lee Kuan Yew, Singapore's dynamic leader, readily protected the Malays there, as a minority, he was apprehensive of Malayan domination within the Federation. Singapore also favoured free trade but Abdul Rahman insisted on tariffs to protect new industries. Thus they parted company in 1965 and Singapore became an independent republic. The main British Empire in South-East Asia thus came to an end with the minimum of dislocation and gave way to the remarkably successful and stable rule of Abdul Rahman and Lee Kuan Yew.

(*ii*) **The Central African Federation.** In 1953, Britain created a Federation of the colonies of Northern Rhodesia, Southern Rhodesia and Nyasaland, to prepare them for independence as one unit, which would have many economic advantages. This Central African Federation, however, was caught up in the conflict of interests which developed between white settlers and non-white Africans. The first Prime Minister of the Federation was Godfrey Huggins, a Southern Rhodesian with a firm belief in white rule. Black Africans had little opportunity for political activity in Southern Rhodesia (see Section 6.2(*d*)) but there were fewer whites in Northern Rhodesia and Nyasaland; there, National Congresses* were set up, to prepare for independence. In Northern Rhodesia (which the Africans called Zambia) the Congress was led by Kenneth Kaunda. In Nyasaland (which the Africans called Malawi), the Congress was led by Hastings Banda. Both were imprisoned.

Huggins retired and was replaced by Roy Welensky, but neither Zambia nor Malawi was prepared to accept the permanent rule of a white minority. Unrest among both African nationalists and whites – the latter rioted in the copper belt when an attempt was made to forbid racial discrimination in cafes – doomed the Federation. The British government sent two commissions, the Devlin Commission and the Monckton Commission, and their reports were gloomy. Macmillan, the British Prime Minister, was not prepared to hold the Federation together by force, so the Africans were allowed to set up parliaments in Malawi and Zambia. It was clear that there was overwhelming support for Banda and Kaunda, and the Federation was dissolved, in 1963.

Malawi became independent in July 1964, Zambia a few months later, both under governments which represented the will of the people. Southern Rhodesia, now known simply as Rhodesia, remained a British dependency. The whites were firmly in power there, denying political authority to the non-whites who heavily outnumbered them and, in these circumstances, Britain was unwilling to grant independence. When the whites seized it, with a unilateral declaration of independence (UDI) in 1965, Rhodesia became a problem for the whole world (see Section 21.3).

* Similar to the Indian National Congress.

(*iii*) **The Federation of the West Indies.** The problem of the West Indian islands which Britain possessed was partly one of size. Few seemed large enough to stand alone, so in 1958 Britain brought about the Federation of ten of these islands. Britain was hopeful that the Federation could soon achieve independence as a unit. The larger islands in the Federation had doubts. There were arguments about the degree of central control and Jamaica and Trinidad feared that Britain was trying to saddle them with small and backward islands which could become a drain on their own limited resources. Jamaica voted to withdraw, Trinidad was unwilling to remain without Jamaica, and the Federation was abandoned in 1962.

Almost at once, Britain granted independence to both Jamaica and Trinidad which seemed large enough to survive alone. Although by no means free from economic and racial problems, they succeeded in establishing stable and democratic governments similar to that in Britain. Trinidad had long been linked with the neighbouring island of Tobago, and Trinidad–Tobago continued to elect Eric Williams, historian, sociologist and nationalist, as the country's Prime Minister until his death in 1981. In Jamaica, on the other hand, elections produced governments of differing political allegiances. Barbados, a smaller island, became independent in 1966, but other British West Indian islands were smaller still. For some years their future remained uncertain once the West Indies Federation had failed. Many became known as *Associated States*, enjoying internal self-government and the freedom to claim independence when they so wished but, in the meantime, remaining under British authority and protection. Eventually Grenada led the movement of the smaller islands to independence, taking the plunge in 1974. Grenada had a population of only about 100 000. Dominica, independent in 1978, had only some 75 000 and a rush of tiny new West Indian nations now followed. But Britain still held the tiniest islands in the early 1980s. Those like Montserrat, with little more than 10 000 people, could not yet think of a better future than to remain British.

The manoeuvring went on, however. The British had linked St Kitts, Nevis and Anguilla as a single Associated State but Anguilla, little more than an island village, rebelled in 1969 against domination by St Kitts. Britain thought it useful to send troops and forty-five policeman, who restored peace and, in the true spirit of the Commonwealth, encouraged Anguillan children to play cricket. Anguilla's rebellion nevertheless illustrated a Caribbean problem. Individual islands were jealous of their own identities and the area's colonial history had encouraged division rather than unity. It was this separatism which had doomed the West Indies Federation. But West Indian governments tried again. In 1968 they created the Caribbean Free Trade Area (*Carifta*), which was also joined by Guyana, the mainland state of British Guiana to which Britain granted independence in 1966 (see Section 22.4). Free trade led on to the founding of the Caribbean Community and Common Market (*Caricom*) in 1973 to forge closer links between the English-speaking states of the Caribbean. The early progress of the Community was promising, but West Indian economies were hard hit by rising oil prices. Dissension between its members erupted, reminiscent of the ill-fated Federation. Only Trinidad, herself an oil-producer, managed to maintain a reasonably healthy economy into the 1980s. The West Indies, like all the areas of the world where colonial rule had existed, still faced vast problems in the wake of foreign empires. The English-speaking West Indies, on the other hand, during their early years of independence, avoided much of the turbulence which had overtaken Cuba in the early twentieth century and which continued to afflict Haiti and the Dominican Republic.

(c) The End of the Empire

1957, the year of Ghana's independence, was almost as important in the history of the Commonwealth as 1947, the year of India's independence. Ghana, under the leadership of Nkrumah (see Section 22.3(a)), was the first British colony in Africa to become free under a non-white government. It was followed, in 1960, by Nigeria and then by a steady stream of African admissions to the Commonwealth, until only Rhodesia remained. In 1961, it was the turn of Sierra Leone. Then, in the same year, Britain wound up her mandate and trusteeship in Tanganyika which united shortly afterwards with Zanzibar to form Tanzania under the leadership of Julius Nyerere, one of the most remarkable leaders in Africa (see Section 22.3(c)). In the years 1962 to 1964, independence was granted to Uganda, Kenya, Malawi and Zambia (see Fig. 16.2). Britain firmly accepted the principle of majority rule and government in all of them by Africans. Some African nationalists complained that independence was too long delayed and, in Kenya, Britain was involved in a particularly bitter struggle with the *Mau Mau* (a ferocious secret society sworn to mutilating and murdering in the 1950s). But the bitterness seldom lasted once independence was achieved.

The story was a similar one in other parts of the world and Britain steadily withdrew. Equally steadily, the new states joined the Commonwealth – Cyprus in 1960, Malta in 1964, and later Mauritius, Tonga, Fiji and a host of others in the 1960s, 1970s and 1980s, when membership approached fifty. Some dependencies, however, preferred to remain under British control. Brunei had not wished to join Malaysia. Gibraltar welcomed Britain's continuing protection against Spain. Hong Kong seemed to thrive under the British, throbbing with vitality and pouring her exports into the British Isles. Other bits and pieces of the Empire seemed too small for independence, and Britain encouraged self-government while continuing aid and protection. Even Tristan da Cunha with a population of a few hundred had its representative council. When a local volcano erupted in 1961 the entire population was temporarily evacuated to Britain. Tristan da Cunha and other such fragments were all that was left in the 1980s of an Empire which once covered a quarter of the world; but there was now the Commonwealth instead.

*Fig. 16.4   Another new member of the Commonwealth: Milton Obote photo-
graphed at the transfer of power and Uganda's independence ceremony, 1962*

(d) What is the Commonwealth?

The Commonwealth has hardly any machinery except for a Secretariat set up
in 1965. Member Prime Ministers meet regularly to exchange ideas. There are
innumerable contacts at other levels, both professional and amateur, between
educationists, defence experts, finance ministers, parliamentarians, journ-
alists and technicians. But the organization is essentially one for voluntary
co-operation. The Commonwealth is as reluctant as the United Nations to
interfere in internal affairs and often as powerless to settle disputes, even
between members. At the head of the Commonwealth is the British
monarchy, still the symbol of association as laid down in the 1920s. Royal

tours, therefore, often symbolize the Commonwealth connection.

Attlee regarded the meetings of Commonwealth Prime Ministers as 'talk round a table between friends'. As the Commonwealth expanded, the numbers round the table grew and the talk was by no means always friendly. Britain was heavily criticized for her attack upon Egypt in 1956. Criticism of apartheid eventually drove South Africa from the Commonwealth altogether (see Section 21.2(c)).

Each member was almost invariably careful to preserve its national interests, and it was a weakness, as in UNO, that hardly any member was prepared to place the common good first. Nevertheless, the Commonwealth was founded on mutual respect, and in spite of often enormous problems – political disunity, economic difficulties, poverty, and fierce internal pressures, resulting perhaps from racial tensions or tribalism – hardly any member abandoned a fundamental attachment to the values once thought British. Countries struggled to achieve workable democracy although for some, like Pakistan, it often seemed a distant goal. Nevertheless, they persevered. Sometimes the picture was grossly distorted and nowhere more so than in Uganda where the ineffectiveness of the Commonwealth was also in evidence. The high hopes at the time of independence in 1962 were disappointed. Obote became authoritarian and was overthrown in 1971 by a coup in which Idi Amin seized power. Amin ruled with a grotesque and brutal dictatorship which lasted until rebellion and the intervention of Tanzania toppled him in 1979 (see Section 22.3(c)). Amin had ruled in the narrow interests of his own northern Ugandan tribe and of the Moslems, leaving behind him disruption and a legacy of hatred which would take years to overcome. Self-seeking, corruption and even civil war plagued members of the Commonwealth as they plagued many emergent nations, but the ultimate appeal of freedom and justice proved persistent throughout the association. The Commonwealth had more than its share of countries in which elections offered the voters a choice of more than a single governing party.

Much of the work of the Commonwealth greatly expands that done by the specialized agencies of UNO. Commonwealth scholarships and training schemes help the less-developed in education. Teachers, doctors, engineers and experts of all kinds provide varied help and strengthen international ties. It is easy to undervalue their achievements because it is impossible precisely to measure them. Prosperous nations sometimes see the poor only as a drain on their wealth and there are those who argue that the Commonwealth is little but a sham, but it is by no means uncommon for the poor members to help the even poorer. By 1964, India and Pakistan were able to give help on a small scale in Africa; Ghana helped the Gambia and Nigeria helped Tanzania. But, of course, it is the rich countries such as Canada and Britain who can offer the greatest assistance.

In 1967, the average annual income per head of the population was £692 in Canada and £536 in Britain; in India it was £18, in Malawi £17. This was a gap which grew wider in the last quarter of the twentieth century. By 1978, all were suffering inflation but while Canadian and British incomes had risen respectively to £3 906 and £2 883, India's was not quite £80 and Malawi's similarly had not progressed much. Technological development made the rich richer in spite of their economic problems, but the poor simply fell further behind. Members of the Commonwealth played a major part in launching the Colombo Plan in 1950 to promote development in Asia. The Commonwealth also set up the Commonwealth Development Corporation (CDC) and the Special Commonwealth African Assistance Plan (SCAAP), but needs went on galloping ahead of what the association was able to supply.

Britain's admission to the EEC in 1973 brought further changes to the Commonwealth. Twenty developing members of the association got Associated membership of the European Community. On the other hand, Britain had now to abide by Community regulations and this resulted in some weakening of Commonwealth trading links. Britain's attitude to the Commonwealth tended to fluctuate, and in the early 1980s it was still unclear whether joining Europe had produced any lasting change in Britain's Commonwealth loyalties. But Britain's immigration policy and questions of race relations in Britain sometimes created tension between the former mother country and the non-white Commonwealth (see Section 21.4). The suspicion remained that the British had not entirely abandoned the attitudes of empire and that the multi-racial Commonwealth of equals sometimes strained Britain's patience. Queen Elizabeth II had nevertheless made a statement of the Commonwealth ideal as early as 1953, declaring that 'the Commonwealth bears no resemblance to the empires of the past. It is an entirely new conception, built on the highest qualities of the spirit of man: friendship, loyalty and the desire for freedom and peace.' It was certainly a unique institution. No other overseas empire left anything to compare with it. Its aims were to try, however imperfectly, to create something of benefit to millions and, in spite of its weaknesses, uncertainties and lack of machinery, almost all the former dependencies of Britain still wished in the 1980s to belong to it.

Further Reading

Caldwell, M.: *Indonesia*. Oxford University Press (London, 1968).
Hatch, J.: *Africa: the Rebirth of Self-rule*. Oxford University Press (London, 1967).
Hodder, B.W.: *Africa Today*. Methuen (London, 1978).
Hollings, J.: *African Nationalism*. Hart-Davis (London, 1971).
Jamieson, A.: *Leaders of the Twentieth Century*. Bell (London, 1970) – Gandhi, Nehru.
Pandey, B.N.: *The Break-up of British India*. Macmillan (London, 1969).
Roberts, E.: *Gandhi, Nehru and Modern India*. Methuen (London, 1973).
Sithole, N.: *African Nationalism*. Oxford University Press (London, 1969).
Wallerstein, I.: *Africa, the Politics of Independence*. Knopf (New York, 1961).
Watson, J.B.: *Empire to Commonwealth, 1919 to 1970*. Dent (London, 1971).
Watson, J.B.: *The West Indian Heritage*. John Murray (London, 2nd edn. 1982).
Williams, B.: *Modern Africa*. Longman (Harlow, 1970).

Documentary and Maps

Kohn, H. and Sokolsky, W.: *African Nationalism in the Twentieth Century*. Anvil (London, 1965).

The Commonwealth Today. Commonwealth Institute (London).

Wallbank, T.W.: *Documents on Modern Africa*. Anvil (London, 1964).

Wilson, D.: *A Student's Atlas of African Affairs*. Oxford University Press (London, 1971).

Exercises

1. Why did European overseas empires come to an end so quickly after 1945?
2. Why did the people of Indonesia and Indochina have to fight in order to gain independence from European colonial powers? Referring to Section 6.2(c) as well as this Unit, explain how British policy in India differed from that of the colonial rulers of Indonesia and Indochina.
3. Why did bloodshed occur immediately after independence (a) in the Indian sub-continent and (b) in the Congo?
4. Make use of Fig. 16.1 to trace the history of the ending of European empires in South-East Asia, listing at appropriate intervals the dependencies which still existed (a) in 1945, (b) in 1960 and (c) in 1980.
5. Making use of Section 14.1 as well as of this Unit, explain the connections between developments inside France and the winding-up of the French Empire. Repeat the exercise for Portugal and the Portuguese Empire, using Section 14.4 and this Unit.
6. 'Britain abandoned her Empire rather more gracefully, constructing the Common-wealth instead' (page 302). Explain the meaning of this statement and illustrate the truth of it.
7. Write a description of the *Commonwealth* suitable for inclusion in a historical dictionary (c. 500 words). Compare what you have written with an entry in a modern encyclopedia or with the Appendix (*The Commonwealth*) in *The West Indian Heritage* (see Further Reading).
8. Study the map of Africa, Fig. 16.2 on page 311, and then answer these questions:
    (a) Which *two* European countries had before 1950 controlled the largest empires in Africa?
    (b) Why does the key to this map make no mention of 'German'?
    (c) Write the names of *three* African states which had changed their names after independence, stating *in each case* the name by which the state had been known when a colony.
    (d) Select *three* of the states which are shaded on this map and *in each case* give the date at which it would have been appropriate to remove the shading.
    (e) Write a brief account of the Federation mentioned in the key to this map.
    (f) Why did Portuguese and Spanish colonies remain in Africa at the time to which this map refers? Were there different reasons why Rhodesia was also at this time a colony?
    (g) What similarities were there in the problems posed for their European mother countries before the granting of independence between Algeria and Rhodesia?
    (h) 'The collapse of the Portuguese Empire transformed the map of southern Africa' (page 311). Explain the significance of this statement.

Unit Seventeen

International Relations: the Great Powers After 1945

17.1 The Cold War and Containment

(a) Europe

The emergence of the USA and the USSR as superpowers, each with a faithful bloc of European supporters, quickly produced tension in Europe (see Units Twelve, Thirteen and Fourteen). The rivalry between West and East became a *Cold War*, fought mainly with economic weapons and with propaganda. The frontiers between West and East were uneasy, but no territories changed hands, and few lives were lost in the US–Soviet confrontation. Each 'contained' the other until there gradually developed something of a mutual understanding. The basis of this coexistence was an unwritten but apparent acceptance that, in Europe at least, neither side would trespass on the territories of the other. This balance of power was achieved partly through fear, both sides well aware of the destructive powers of nuclear weapons. From time to time there were crises but one or other of the superpowers always showed restraint and, as time passed, it seemed that the possibility of a third world war became less likely. In May 1972 an American President finally set foot on Russian soil in the first such friendly visit since the Yalta Conference of 1945 (see Section 10.2(*a*)).

The West argued that the Cold War began when Stalin imposed Soviet ideological and economic control in Eastern Europe (see Section 12.1). When Britain and the USA tried to consolidate capitalism and democracy in Western Europe, Stalin accused them of creating an anti-Soviet bloc. The two blocs met in Germany, and the German Problem (see Section 11.2) became one of the main bones of contention between them. Almost everything that happened became subject to different interpretations on the two sides of the Iron Curtain until it became almost automatic that West and East bickered about every point at issue. Their quarrel flared dangerously at the time of the Blockade of Berlin and Air-Lift of 1948–9, but by then other disputes had already arisen and the USA had proclaimed and begun to implement the Truman Doctrine, and, alongside it, the Marshall Plan (see Section 14.5(*a*)).

The Truman Doctrine owed a good deal to the turbulent state of affairs in Greece. By 1944, as the Germans retreated, Greece was near to civil war. There were rival partisan organizations, one communist, the other monarchist, which had developed out of the resistance to the Nazi invasion. Churchill sent British troops to assist an orderly return to normality, in effect to support the monarchists and arrange free elections. In 1946 the Soviet Union protested to the UN Security Council against the British presence. She alleged that the troops endangered Greece's 'national and internal situation'. Bevin heatedly declared that the charges involved 'the honour of my country and of the Commonwealth' and the Security Council took no action. The result was civil war as Greek communists tried to take control of the country by force.

The intervention in Greece was a financial burden which Britain, after 1945, was ill-equipped to bear. An appeal to the USA brought American dollars and the Truman Doctrine of March 1947. Truman undertook to 'support free peoples' against 'attempted subjugation by armed minorities or outside pressure' – in effect, to contain communism and prevent its further expansion. With American help, the British army remained in Greece until 1950, by which time something had been saved from communism although it was not necessarily democracy. By 1951, Greece had produced more than a dozen feeble governments and further incompetence and corruption culminated, in 1967, in a military coup. 'The Colonels' suspended the constitution, imprisoned political leaders, purged the universities and ruled by decree (see Section 14.4).

In 1951, meanwhile, Greece joined NATO and the Greek frontier came to mark the limit of communist expansion in the Balkans. The line of demarcation between East and West in Europe was to remain at least into the 1980s. Only when the Soviet Union evacuated eastern Austria in 1955 (see Section 11.1(*b*)), did any change occur in the territories held by communists and non-communists.

With NATO (see Section 14.5(*b*)) and the Warsaw Pact (see Section 12.3), each side consolidated its grip. The German Problem remained unsolved, but central Europe was disturbed by only occasional flurries of activity. Content to have saved Greece, the West made no attempt to intervene in the affairs of the Russian satellite states or even to prevent the building of the Berlin Wall. The communist wall only emphasized the division of the city which, like the division of the whole of Europe, began to seem irrevocable but, at the same time, stable.

(*b*) The Middle East

A similar stability descended on East–West relations in the Middle East. In north-western Persia (Iran), the USSR tried to establish a communist regime under the Tudeh Party but withdrew after the matter was referred to the United Nations in 1946. Persia went on to suppress the Tudeh Party in 1949 but gave less satisfaction to Britain when, in 1951, Dr Mussadiq nationalized the oil industry. It was a costly blow to the Anglo-Persian Oil Company and to Britain's prestige. Mussadiq became the spokesman of hysterical anti-Europeanism. He was later arrested by his own countrymen and a compromise solution in 1954 allowed an international consortium in which British Petroleum had a 40 per cent share to operate alongside the National Iranian

Oil Company. The arrangement lasted only until Iranian nationalism and Moslem anti-Western fervour reasserted themselves in 1979 (see Section 19.4).

For a time after 1945, the Soviet Union also brought pressure to bear on Turkey and endeavoured to set up joint Russo-Turkish control of the Dardanelles. But here, too, Russia was barred from making progress. Further south, in the disturbed area of Palestine, the USSR showed little interest at first but eventually responded to Western support for Israel by wooing the Arabs (see Section 19.1). Such links could be of advantage to the Russians: the West depended heavily on Middle-East oil, Arab successes against Israel would embarrass the USA and the Arab states might provide a bridge between the USSR and Africa. The Arabs had few successes, however, and by the 1970s both the Arab states and the Soviet Union had found little profit in their association. Their relations grew cool.

In 1959, the *Central Treaty Organization* (CENTO) came into existence for joint security and defence between Britain, Persia, Turkey and Pakistan. It was built on the foundations of the Baghdad Pact of 1955, which had also included Iraq. The USA had taken part in some of the committees of the Baghdad Pact and, in 1959, made separate defence agreements with Persia, Turkey and Pakistan but without actually joining CENTO. CENTO was thus seen both in the West and the East as another barrier against communism, not fundamentally very different from NATO and SEATO.

(c) The Far East

(*i*) **ANZUS and SEATO.** The West soon discovered, however, that Russian communism was not the only communism against which to build barriers. The success of the communists in China and the downfall of Chiang Kai-shek caused considerable anxiety to the USA. The communists were also successful in North Korea and North Vietnam (see Unit Fifteen). From 1948, communist guerillas were active in Malaya, where a communist party had been banned since 1926 but where communism had gained popularity in resistance to the Japanese. Jungle warfare in Malaya caused a state of emergency which lasted until 1960 and, even after that, the communists were able to exploit both racial and economic discontents. Britain and members of the Commonwealth assisted in holding back communism in Malaya, but, elsewhere, the USA took on the main burden of resistance. Vigorous efforts were made to rebuild Japan in the image of the USA and to ring China with American bases and an American fleet. Chiang was protected in Taiwan and, in the *ANZUS Pact* of 1951, the USA gave guarantees to Australia and New Zealand. In 1954, the ANZUS Powers, together with Britain, France, Pakistan, the Philippines and Thailand joined together in the *South-East Asia Treaty Organization* (SEATO), for collective action against aggression and subversion. Even so, the USA thought it necessary to resort to force both in Korea and Vietnam.

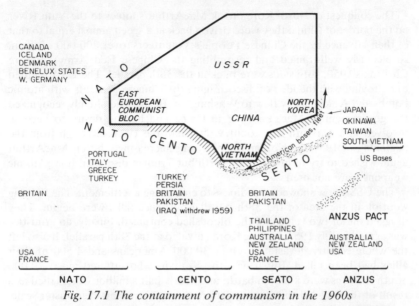

Fig. 17.1 The containment of communism in the 1960s

(*ii*) **The Korean War (1950–3).** After the expulsion of the Japanese in 1945, Korea was divided into two: communist north of the 38th parallel, non-communist south of it (see Section 15.1). South Korea had a considerably larger population than that of the North. The Americans hoped, by establishing a democratic constitution in the South, that free elections could eventually be held for the whole country and that the communists would be outvoted.

Both the USA and the USSR withdrew from Korea in 1948, leaving separate governments behind them in South and North. The National Assembly in the South left 100 seats vacant (out of 303) for representatives from the North. Kim Il-sung, the Northern leader, had no intention of filling them. While wrangling continued about the border between them, communists in the North trained an army of 130 000 men and launched an attack in June 1950. The South was unprepared and total defeat seemed imminent.

However, Kim had timed the invasion badly (suggesting a lack of that close association between Moscow and other communist governments which the USA always assumed to exist). The USSR was temporarily absent from UNO, in protest against the representation there of Chiang Kai-shek, and the United Nations were therefore able to brand North Korea as an aggressor and sanction the use of force against her. The United Nations forces were mainly American with some troops from Britain and fourteen other friendly countries. They were commanded by the American, General MacArthur. By September 1950, he had driven the communists back to the 38th parallel; but he continued to advance and the Anglo-American objective became the liberation and unification of the whole of Korea.

The conquest of North Korea took MacArthur's forces to the Yalu River on the border of China: they were driven back at a speed almost equal to that of their advance by the Chinese People's Volunteers (over 200 000 of them, suspiciously well-trained and resembling the Chinese Red Army). Before Christmas 1950, both sides were back at the 38th parallel. The USA seemed to be toying with the idea of discouraging the Chinese peasants with atomic bombs and Attlee hastily flew to Washington. Britain had already recognized the government of Mao Tse-tung in China and had no desire to become involved in a war with that country. Nor had the USA, although from the beginning of 1951 the Korean War became increasingly bitter. MacArthur again wished to try to invade the North but Truman dismissed him. Atomic weapons were not used.

The USSR now showed a readiness to encourage a settlement. The fighting went on in the area of the 38th parallel but truce talks were begun. They dragged on for two years and the bloodshed continued. Finally, an armistice was agreed in July 1953, leaving Korea divided at the 38th parallel. It also left the whole country devastated. Over 30 000 Americans and 4 500 of their allies had been killed. But it was the Koreans who suffered most. 70 000 South Koreans were killed in battle and nearly half a million others died as a result of the war. North Koreans suffered casualties on an even vaster scale, perhaps 4 million in all.

Neither North nor South Korea knew much of freedom after 1953. The communists remained in power in the North, in possession of much of the country's mineral resources and heavy industry, and Kim developed a regime almost Stalinist in its hero-worship of the leader. In the South, Syngman Rhee's regime fell in 1960 amidst complaints of repression and corruption. His successor, President Park, gave every indication of intending to be president for life. He was assassinated in 1979 (see Section 15.1).

The two Koreas were now separated by a demilitarized zone, an area abounding in disputes, with frequent charges by both sides about illegal fortifications. From time to time, armed clashes occurred. As in Germany, however, time brought a certain stability to Korea. Each side remained heavily-armed, a serious burden on peoples far from rich. In 1972, following the example of more prominent leaders in the world who were seeking improved relationships, Kim proposed a reduction of these forces and at last it began to seem possible that the two parts of Korea could draw together again. Unification would bring economic advantages. Koreans were, moreover, conscious of the growing strength of Japan and ideological differences began to seem less important in the face of the possible danger of more foreign domination. In any case, both parts of Korea seemed now to be ruled in similarly authoritarian ways.

(*d*) **Vietnam and Indochina**

(*i*) **War in Vietnam: the American protection of South Vietnam.** Unfortunately, few of the lessons learned in Korea were applied in Vietnam where the

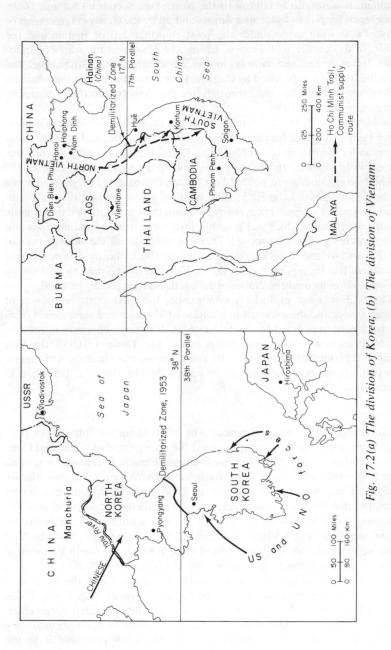

Fig. 17.2(a) The division of Korea; (b) The division of Vietnam

communists were also in control of the North (see Sections 15.4 and 16.3). The French Empire in Indochina was wound up by the *Geneva Agreements* of 1954. These were made under the joint chairmanship of Britain and the USSR, in conference with France, China, the USA and the states of Indochina. It was agreed, temporarily, to divide Vietnam at the 17th parallel, the ceasefire line to be supervised by Canada, Poland and India. The reunification of Vietnam was to take place, through free elections (which the communists expected to win), in 1956.

In January 1955, the USA undertook the protection of South Vietnam, which became a refuge for those fleeing from communism, and a republic was set up under the Presidency of Ngo Dinh Diem. He introduced a few reforms but did little to satisfy the peasants and stirred up considerable unrest.

The free elections were not held on the appointed date. Diem, who was a Catholic, antagonized the Buddhists, some of whom burned themselves to death in protest against his tyranny and corruption. South Vietnam badly needed government which was firm but just, for extremist organizations and vested interests were deep-rooted. Diem, in the end, lost the support even of the Americans and they abandoned him in 1963, shortly before he was murdered. But his regime had set South Vietnam on the road to civil war as the opposition formed the National Liberation Front (NLF) in 1960.

The NLF was not exclusively communist. It aimed at the expulsion of foreign troops and the eventual unification of Vietnam and was, almost from the beginning, supported by North Vietnam. It became common to refer to the NLF, especially its military wing, as the Viet Cong. In 1963, the Viet Cong had about 25 000 soldiers. In 1966, the number had risen to nearly 300 000, about the same number of troops that by then the USA had in Vietnam.

(*ii*) **Increasing American involvement.** The fall of Diem was followed by political confusion and military coups against the background of rising Viet Cong activity and increasing American involvement. President Kennedy first of all poured American 'advisers' into South Vietnam. With them came military equipment and then helicopters but, in 1964, an official American report estimated that the Viet Cong nevertheless controlled over 40 per cent of the villages of South Vietnam. Early in 1965, President Johnson began the bombing of targets in North Vietnam, assuming, perhaps wrongly, that the Viet Cong were actually under the control of Ho Chi Minh, the North Vietnamese leader, who could thus be persuaded to call off their rebellion.

Also in 1965, the government of South Vietnam fell into the hands of a National Leadership Committee led by General Nguyen Van Thieu. Thieu became President by disqualifying all likely rivals and appointed the air chief, Nguyen Cao Ky, as Prime Minister. The Thieu regime was an unconvincing advertisement for Western democracy, but the USA preferred it to the success of the Viet Cong. The USA also secured support from Australia, New

Fig. 17.3   American engineers check a road near Ca Lu in South Vietnam for Viet Cong mines in a regular morning routine before traffic may use the road

Zealand and South Korea and the war in Vietnam escalated steadily. It was, however, a war which neither side seemed capable of winning. The North was blasted by American bombs but that appeared to make little difference to the Viet Cong or to the North Vietnamese forces, perhaps about 70 000 in 1968, who reinforced them. In 1968, in fact, the Viet Cong took the offensive and captured, for a time, 75 per cent of the main towns of South Vietnam and even parts of Saigon. This was in spite of opposition by three-quarters of a million men in the South Vietnamese army, half a million Americans and 50 000 of their allies. The South Vietnamese army suffered extensively from desertion but, even so, it was surprising that the vast military resources of the USA made so little impact, especially as supplies to the Viet Cong from the USSR, China and other communist countries were on a much smaller scale.

(*iii*) **Nixon and Vietnamization.** Johnson came under heavy criticism for the escalation of the war and the USA's failure to win it. In his memoirs, he later stubbornly defended his policies and persistence, almost glorying that 'the American people . . . knew Lyndon Johnson was not going to pull up stakes'. He had much less to say on the awkward leaks of Pentagon papers which cast doubts on the official reasons given by the US government for resorting to the bombing of North Vietnam in 1965. Before the Presidential election of 1968, however, Johnson agreed to stop the bombing of the North in return for the opening of peace talks in Paris. But the war went on and Richard Nixon, the new US President, found that the talks made little progress. Thieu

Fig. 17.4 'If this boy of yours is real, how come we gotta wind him up all the time?' Doubts about Nixon's policy of Vietnamization – the Guardian, 3 May 1972

and the NLF could not agree on a formula for fair elections in South Vietnam; the USA and North Vietnam could not agree on a formula for the withdrawal of foreign troops. Even the death of Ho Chi Minh, the founding father of North Vietnam, brought no change in the deadlock. Seeking desperately for a way out, Nixon announced a new policy towards the end of 1969 – *Vietnamization*.

The central feature of Vietnamization was attractive: the South Vietnamese would take over the defence of South Vietnam. This would permit the withdrawal of American troops and, by the end of 1970, their numbers had been reduced by half. On the other hand, Nixon was reluctant to see the Viet Cong victorious, something which became increasingly difficult to prevent as American troops continued to leave. He thought the solution to this particular problem lay in cutting off the communists' supplies, so he resumed the bombing of North Vietnam (although this had not achieved much when Johnson was President).

The North Vietnamese had not scrupled to use neutral territory in Laos and Cambodia to supply the Viet Cong, any more than the USA had scrupled to bomb it to try to interrupt the supplies. Both Laos and Cambodia in any case had their own Marxist movements aspiring to take over the government – the Pathet Lao and the Khmer Rouge respectively. An army coup in Cambodia in 1970 overthrew Prince Sihanouk (see Section 16.3(*a*)). Sihanouk had tried to keep Cambodia neutral in the war raging in neighbouring Vietnam but the new ruler, General Lon Nol, gave more satisfaction to the Americans by declaring his intention of rooting out the Khmer Rouge and all communist bases in the country. It seemed more likely that he himself might be driven out. In April 1970 Nixon announced a new US campaign to help Lon Nol against communism in Cambodia. Communist bases proved hard to find and the campaign was brief, but Nixon nevertheless persisted for several years in supporting and supplying Lon Nol.

The Viet Cong seemed in no way to have been weakened by the events in Cambodia. They launched a new offensive early in 1972 and threatened Thieu's government on three fronts, around Hué, around Kontum and, in the south, around Saigon (see Fig. 17.2(b)). Many of Thieu's troops showed more talent for rape and chicken-stealing than for defeating communists and Vietnamization was proving no more than a cloak under which US troops could slip away. Thieu could nevertheless still rely on massive American supplies, the ferocity of the US Air Force and the eloquent optimistic smoke-screen of US military advisers. Nixon still hoped that supplies might be the key to the problem. As it was not apparently possible to block them by bombing the North and the Ho Chi Minh Trail through Laos and Cambodia, the US Air Force now dropped mines, to seal the ports of North Vietnam through which many of the supplies arrived from the communist world. It was a strange prelude to Nixon's long-heralded visit to Moscow (which took place in May 1972), at which it was hoped that East and West would reach a better understanding.

(*iv*) **The ceasefire and communist takeover in Indochina.** The fighting in South Vietnam, the US bombing of the North and, with interruptions, the peace talks in Paris all dragged on. For the Americans the main aim now was to get away from Indochina while making a despairing attempt to save face. The US and world press buzzed with revelations and embarrassments. There were investigations from 1969 to 1971 into an incident at My Lai early in 1968. My Lai was a village where US troops had run amok, murdering more than a hundred Vietnamese including women and children; and many suspected that this was no isolated occurrence. There was savage brutality on both sides in the war but it sometimes seemed that the US authorities could not control even their own forces. There was a new scandal in 1972 when the Senate heard evidence of bombing raids by the US Seventh Air Force which seemed to continue unofficially when the government wanted to curtail the bombing to advance the peace talks.

It was also a grave embarrassment to the USA that a superpower could not defeat a small developing nation. North Vietnam showed a remarkable ability and will to survive. The Americans dropped a tonnage of bombs far exceeding what was dropped on Germany in the Second World War, adding horrifying quantities of napalm, and anti-personnel bombs which exploded into lethal splinters to add to the carnage and misery. It was said of Nam Dinh, North Vietnam's third largest community, that Johnson's bombing destroyed 60 per cent of the city and that, after rebuilding, Nixon's destroyed 70 per cent. But the North Vietnamese dispersed what they could of their factories, hospitals and population, worked furiously to repair the damage, adapted to the hardship and went on supporting the Viet Cong.

After yet more devastating bombing at the end of 1972 a ceasefire was at last arranged for the end of January 1973. The US Air Force ceased its operations, prisoners-of-war were exchanged and a hesitant start was made on sorting out the problems left by the longest major war of the twentieth century. All remaining US combat troops left Vietnam in February 1973 while, without enthusiasm, Canada, Hungary, Poland and Indonesia agreed to send a thousand truce supervisors. These four powers and seven others, including the permanent members of the UN Security Council, also undertook to try to bring about a permanent settlement in Vietnam. There was also a new urgency now in trying to resolve the problems of Laos and Cambodia. It was no more than realistic, however, when Douglas-Home, Britain's Foreign Secretary, observed that 'the history of Indochina gives little scope for easy optimism'.

The ceasefire in practice had little meaning. Skirmishing went on throughout Indochina. US advisers remained in Saigon and President Ford, succeeding Nixon, continued to supply Thieu's government in South Vietnam. But Vietnamization had been a total failure. Thieu resigned in April 1975 and the last Americans left. Saigon fell to the communists that same month and the unified Socialist Republic of Vietnam was proclaimed soon afterwards (see Section 15.4). The Khmer Rouge had entered Phnom Penh even before the fall of Saigon, and Cambodia, too, was fast turning to communism. Lon Nol had grown steadily more unpopular. One of Nixon's last decisions concerning Indochina had been that US bombers should pound Cambodia in the summer of 1973, until Congress had insisted that they stop. Either way, Lon Nol could not survive. Nor could a right-wing regime in Laos and there too, by the end of 1975, the communists of the Pathet Lao had taken control. In 1973 US politicians had asserted that the ceasefire had given Americans 'peace with honour'. More realistically, the North Vietnamese claimed 'a socialist victory'.

(*v*) **The cost.** It was estimated that the military casualties of the war in Vietnam included a million dead on the communist side, about 180 000 of the forces of South Vietnam and nearly 50 000 Americans. Over 400 000 South Vietnamese civilians also perished and an untold number of North Vietnamese civilians, undoubtedly many under the weight of US bombing. Vast numbers were maimed, some of them with hideous injuries caused by napalm, a clinging and highly inflammable jelly which turned victims into human torches. That was not the full cost of the war, however. Chemical weapons ravaged the countryside and left it polluted. The war seriously depleted Vietnam's resources. The spending power of the Americans had also played havoc with the South Vietnamese economy, and the passion of some American

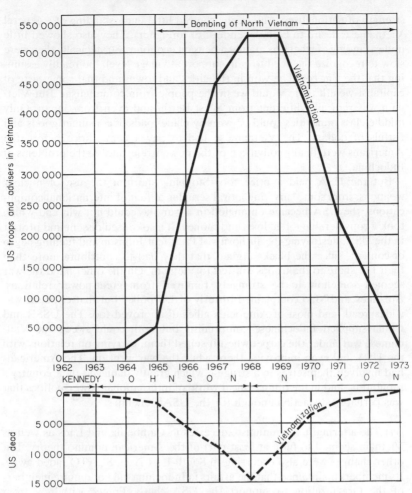

Fig. 17.5 *US involvement in Vietnam, from 1962 to 1973*

servicemen for drugs and women left a trail of demoralization and corruption. The USA had imported into South Vietnam mainly the worst of American civilization rather than the best and it was partly for this reason that Vietnamization had failed. US interference had gone a long way to undermine the very country the Americans were trying to protect.

The USA had first taken up arms in Vietnam with a belief in the 'domino theory': if South Vietnam turned to the communists, other states in Indochina and South-East Asia would follow, falling like a row of soldierly dominoes. For the Americans the issue was simple – the defence of a capitalist system against communism. Not for the first time, the West underestimated the strength of nationalism: Americans showed little understanding of a general Vietnamese desire to be independent of foreigners. They also showed little understanding of what was mainly a peasant economy. Strategically they were slow to recognize the need to gain support at village level, too readily assuming that the war could be won in the cities and towns and that some taste of capitalist wealth there would wean the people from communism. But Vietnam was radically different from West Berlin and even from Japan. Only middle-class minorities could be won by plane-loads of consumer goods and fistfuls of dollars. The Vietnamese had to pay a heavy price before the Americans were finally convinced of their own irrelevance to the problems of Indochina.

But the USA paid a price too. Stopping short of the use of nuclear weapons, from some surviving moral scruples or fear of international complications, the USA became entangled in a war she could not win and which took a considerable toll in lives and money. It also caused dissent and protest in the USA, destroying the authority of President Johnson and fuelling negro discontent, since the blacks argued that they had to contribute more than their fair share to the troops drafted to Vietnam. On the other hand the war seemed somehow to be strangely removed from great-power relations. Brezhnev and Mao complained bitterly of US policy but that criticism was widespread, and most of America's allies disapproved too. The USSR and China supplied Indochinese communists but both could sweep the Vietnamese war under the carpet when it suited them, carrying on relations with the USA and even improving them while the war went on. The Americans had involved themselves in a struggle which greatly damaged their country's reputation, and in the often cynical world of international power-politics that was perhaps satisfaction enough for the USA's enemies.

(*vi*) **The aftermath.** Communist successes in Cambodia and Laos as well as Vietnam seemed to fulfil at least part of the American domino theory. But other changes were also occurring in South-East Asia. SEATO faded away. Its members maintained that the affairs in Indochina did not require members of the Organization to support the USA there. France withdrew from SEATO in 1974 and the alliance was wound up in the late 1970s. To some extent its place had been taken by the Association of South-East Asian Nations (ASEAN), within which Indonesia, Malaysia, the Philippines, Singapore and Thailand in the late 1960s began to develop their own regional system of co-operation. ASEAN included neither the USA nor Europeans. It was not primarily an anti-communist alliance like SEATO, though China remained suspicious of it until the mid-1970s and the USSR longer than that. But for the moment, at least, ASEAN helped to prevent more dominoes falling, while making some effort to establish friendly relations with the new governments in Indochina.

The affairs of Indochina remained turbulent, however. A power-struggle developed between the USSR and China to influence the new communist governments. Vietnam preferred the USSR. Cambodia preferred China. Laos looked for help to Vietnam, and, through Vietnam, to Moscow. All three had great problems of reconstruction, however, with an urgent need for peace and stability. For some time that was delayed particularly in *Cambodia.* When the Khmer Rouge seized Phnom Penh in 1975, Sihanouk was restored. The Khmer Rouge came under the authority of Pol Pot, however, and Sihanouk was ousted. Cambodia was renamed Kampuchea, and Pol Pot presided over a fanatical and savage attempt to build a communist republic so primitive that efforts were made, not only to purge it of anything capitalist or bourgeois, but of almost everything (except weapons) which belonged to the twentieth century. City dwellers were driven off to work on the land in a more extreme version of the radical experiments which had sometimes been made in China. Phnom Penh was depopulated and fell into decay. One result was that relations between Kampuchea and Vietnam deteriorated rapidly. Border conflicts and ideological argument escalated and the Vietnamese invaded Kampuchea towards the end of 1978. Pol Pot and his forces retreated, and only then were the full horrors of his regime exposed. Its vast cruelties seemed at least to match those of the Nazis in Germany. The Vietnamese set up a new communist government in Phnom Penh under Heng Samrin, but Pol Pot continued to wage guerilla war against the invaders.

Heng Samrin promised more liberal and more sensible rule, but China quickly denounced his government. There was a general uneasiness about what smacked of Vietnamese expansionism, and the 'boat people' had already brought the new Vietnam unpopularity (see Section 15.4). China maintained that Vietnam was a puppet of the Soviet Union, however, and that the invasion of Kampuchea was part of the Russian plan to secure 'hegemony'. In 1979 China launched a short punitive war against Vietnam which the Vietnamese endured without changing course. Kampuchea meanwhile plumbed the depths of misery, made worse by Pol Pot's resistance. The people were starving, and it took time to plant and grow new crops even where the Vietnamese could maintain stability. The USSR poured in aid and the West too, albeit hesitantly, sent relief supplies. But many governments in the West and elsewhere continued to assert that, in spite of his atrocities, Pol Pot was Kampuchea's rightful ruler.

Laos proceeded more quietly under the presidency of Souphanou Vong and the Pathet Lao. The USA and other countries sent food supplies when starvation threatened in 1978, but Laos relied most on Vietnam and the USSR for development aid. Like the whole of Indochina, Laos faced a long haul before prosperity could be achieved. In the early 1980s, over a quarter of a century had already passed since the withdrawal of the French but the many upheavals in Indochina had gone on retarding progress. The future of the area was still not entirely settled and all the Indochinese states were now engaged in carrying out economic reorganization and a social revolution. One possible outcome was that an Indochinese Federation might eventually be established, linking the communist states of Vietnam, Laos and Kampuchea.

Such a communist bloc caused unease among the ASEAN states and alarm lest Thailand might turn out to be the next domino.

(e) The Caribbean

It came as a shock to the USA – intent on containing communism in the neighbourhoods of the USSR and China – when Castro seized control of Cuba (see Section 15.5). The shock gave way to angry alarm when, in October 1962, an American spy-plane discovered that Russian missiles were being positioned on the island. President Kennedy demanded their instant removal and imposed a blockade of Cuba to prevent further landings. Khrushchev tried to bargain, demanding the withdrawal of American missiles from Turkey as part of a package deal. The tension lasted almost a week before the Soviet Union gave way. Missile-carrying ships from the USSR turned back and Khrushchev ordered the missiles in Cuba to be crated and returned.

The Cuban Missiles Crisis was, perhaps, the moment when the USA and the USSR were closest to war. It ended in a complete victory for Kennedy and the humiliation of Khrushchev, helping to undermine his position in Russia. But Khrushchev had won a victory for common sense. Peace was preserved and a new telephone link was established to hold out the hope of the peaceful solution of future emergencies, the 'hot line' between Washington and Moscow. Both sides now placed the emphasis almost entirely on defence, and the will to war, if it had ever existed at all, became more remote. Even Castro followed up the Missiles Crisis with an agreement with the USA whereby he released the prisoners taken in the Bay of Pigs in exchange for food and medicine. Ten years later, he joined in the general involvement towards improved relations, by reaching a limited agreement with Nixon on hijacked aircraft.

17.2   Coexistence

(a) The Thaw

It is difficult to identify the exact moment at which the Cold War began to thaw. There was general relief at Stalin's death in 1953, but Khrushchev blew hot and cold, and deep suspicions of communism remained in the West. In the USA, suspicion of China went particularly deep and much bitterness was left on both sides by the Korean War. Events in Vietnam intensified the bitterness and not until the end of the 1960s did relations ease between the USA and China.

But in the meantime, Americans and Russians had apparently become content to coexist. The propaganda war was not much interrupted, but it was significant that the USA did nothing to assist the Hungarian rebels in 1956 and that in 1962 the USSR accepted that the USA had special interests in the Caribbean which must be respected. The superpowers, though armed to the teeth, were beginning to behave with great caution although caution was not entirely new. Neither Stalin nor Truman had been a reckless man.

One of the first visible signs of a slightly less cold relationship between East and West came in the form of personal contacts. In 1955, Russia's leaders emerged from the Kremlin. Khrushchev and Bulganin talked to Tito in Belgrade and then travelled to Geneva for a summit conference with Eisenhower, Eden and Faure, the French Prime Minister. They talked about disarmament, but no major decisions were made and Eden's suggestion that Germany should be reunified was wildly optimistic. In the following year, Khrushchev and Bulganin spent over a week in Britain and, in 1959, Khrushchev went to America and met Eisenhower near Gettysburg. In spite of continued bickering about Berlin and other problems, it seemed an appropriate time to call a second summit conference. After long discussions, it was arranged for May 1960, in Paris.

The summit ended in chaos even before it really began. Khrushchev arrived, determined to get an apology from Eisenhower for the activities of U-2 spy-planes which, although armed only with cameras, had for some time been flying over the USSR. One of them had been shot down over the Urals just before the summit conference was to open. Eisenhower had already stopped the flights but he refused to give the Russians the public declarations they required. Macmillan and de Gaulle were helpless spectators while Khrushchev called the summit off and cancelled Eisenhower's invitation to Moscow.

Before the end of 1960, Khrushchev had made a stormy appearance in the UN General Assembly. The thaw seemed to have come to an end. Nothing was gained when Khrushchev met Kennedy, the new American President, in Vienna in 1961, and the Cuban Missiles Crisis in 1962 was yet another ungracious confrontation. Curiously, however, it suddenly helped to clear the air.

Although the 1960s opened inauspiciously with the summit fiasco in Paris and went on unpromisingly with the escalation of the war in Vietnam, the decade overall saw a considerable improvement in East–West relations. The thaw grew stronger with significant agreements about nuclear weapons (see below). The antagonism between Russia and China (see Section 15.3(c)) served to make international relations more complicated but, for a time at least, less dangerous. The USSR and the USA grew even more cautious, although they continued to elbow each other and struggle for position wherever there was instability. The USSR showed interest in Africa and Latin America and then developed links with the Arab world, especially Egypt in her long feud with Israel. At the beginning of the 1970s, Russia was also making progress in wooing India. But such connections were inclined to fluctuate and many countries in the Third World were not anxious to tie themselves to either of the superpowers. Many African states took offence at the manner of Russia's repression of Czechoslovakia in 1968, and the USA found that even such a well-established ally as Japan could sometimes be a highly-critical one. Both Russian and American embassies were often the targets for hostile demonstrations all over the world, providing them with some sort of common bond in unpopularity.

Moreover, China became increasingly outward-looking, forging links with Pakistan and, as the friend of the poor and a champion against white supremacy, gaining a foothold in Africa. Russia had helped Egypt to finance the Aswan Dam. China helped Tanzania with the Friendship Textile Mill and, in 1970, provided an interest-free loan and skilled assistance to build the Zam-Tan Railway, to enable Zambia and Tanzania to be more self-reliant in the face of racial divisions in southern Africa. China also had the advantage of appearing to ask little in return. The Chinese brought quantities of small red books with the *Thoughts of Chairman Mao* but they came to work, learning the local languages and asking for no special comforts or privileges. Neither of the superpowers could create the same image and both of them found the Chinese activities worrying. This too gave them a new bond.

(b) Disarmament

No subject was debated more earnestly after 1945 than disarmament but nothing whatever was achieved until 1963. There were endless wrangles and, while they went on, the great powers conducted an arms race, especially in nuclear weapons. The USSR tried to catch up with the USA and, in 1952, Britain became the third nuclear power, successfully exploding an atomic device.

Neither the USA nor the USSR wished to sacrifice its own interests. Russia wanted to keep large ground forces but proposed a total ban on nuclear weapons and criticized American air and naval power. In this context, the Rapacki Plan for a nuclear-free zone in central Europe (see Section 12.3) was regarded by the West as part of a Soviet plot to tilt the balance in favour of the East, and it came to nothing. Eisenhower's proposal for 'open skies' was rejected by the USSR, in 1956, with the argument that it was an excuse for the West to spy on Russia from the air, under the pretence of inspecting the size of military forces. Scores of ideas for some reduction of armaments were lost amid these suspicions of the major powers.

Like the League of Nations, the United Nations began optimistically. The Security Council hoped to achieve some disarmament through its Military Staff Committee. In 1946, UNO set up an Atomic Energy Commission and, in 1947, a Conventional Armaments Commission but, in 1950, Russia withdrew from both. A new Disarmaments Commission was set up in 1952 and reconstituted in both 1959 and 1962, but none of this machinery could obtain results.

The first agreement, the *Test Ban Treaty* of 1963, was reached by the three nuclear powers at a meeting in Moscow. They agreed to cease testing nuclear weapons in the atmosphere or underwater, with a view to limiting 'radioactive debris'. Other powers could sign the Treaty if they so wished and about a hundred quickly did so, but they did not include France and China who had joined the nuclear powers by exploding atomic bombs in 1963 and 1964 respectively. The original nuclear powers continued to test weapons underground.

Further progress was delayed by an argument about an American plan to create a single nuclear force for NATO which, the USSR objected, could lead to nuclear weapons in West German hands. The USA abandoned the plan and further lengthy discussion in the UN General Assembly, in the Disarmament Commission and between Johnson and Kosygin in America led to the *Non-Proliferation Treaty* of 1968. Its aim was to prevent the further spread of nuclear weapons. The USA, the USSR and Britain undertook not to transfer such weapons to other states and an attempt was made to offer greater security to non-nuclear countries against the nuclear powers, to discourage them from embarking on the manufacture of atomic bombs. It was a major weakness of the Treaty that, once again, France and China did not sign it.

In themselves, the Treaties of 1963 and 1968 accomplished little, but any agreement on restraint, however small, could become the foundation for further agreements. At the end of the 1960s, discussions began to try to find a way to cut back the development of missiles. These *Strategic Arms Limitation Talks* (SALT) took place in Vienna and Helsinki. Even the superpowers were now beginning to feel the strain of the arms race. Intercontinental ballistic missiles and anti-missiles systems developed to the point of being staggeringly expensive, as well as terrifyingly destructive with their nuclear warheads. Technological changes also brought changed attitudes: arguments about U-2s and 'open skies' became irrelevant with the conquest of space and the use of satellites in orbit to observe rival countries.

By 1964, five nations possessed nuclear weapons and there were others for whom their manufacture was becoming a possibility. This again gave the superpowers reason to pause. In their frenzied struggle, the one to outstrip the other, they were not only using their resources in an extremely costly rivalry but they were leading the world towards possible destruction. The Treaties of 1963 and 1968 and the SALT were the first, rather hesitant attempts to put on the brakes. It was still too soon to think in terms of a reduction of armaments, but at least an attempt was now being made to limit their future growth.

(c) Travelling Hopefully: Detente

The diplomatic travelling of Khrushchev and Eisenhower had opened the way for new contacts between East and West. The superpowers edged towards *detente*, the term the West seemed to prefer for what Khrushchev had called 'peaceful coexistence' (see Glossary). New impetus was added to the movement when Willy Brandt became the Chancellor of West Germany in 1969 and enthusiastically pursued his *Ostpolitik* (eastern policy: see Section 14.3(*d*)). Brandt's aim was to establish more normal relations across the Iron

Curtain, gradually to lead Germany and Europe away from the crisis atmosphere which had existed since 1945. To achieve this aim he was willing to make concessions, the first of which was to accept the Oder–Neisse Line as the permanent boundary between Germany and Poland. This was vital in easing relations between West Germany and Eastern Europe. In 1970, West Germany signed non-aggression treaties with the USSR (the Treaty of Moscow) and with Poland (the Treaty of Warsaw), the latter including recognition of the Oder–Neisse Line. The Treaties were ratified in 1972 when West Germany made another concession, accepting the existence of East Germany, though stopping short of recognizing her permanence. Full diplomatic relations were not established between the two Germanies but there was now contact between them and a measure of co-operation. In the meantime, in 1971, the major powers, building on Brandt's initiative, agreed on a Four-Power Pact on Berlin which eased communications within the city, confirmed links between West Berlin and West Germany (though reaffirming that West Berlin was not part of West Germany), and left the four powers with their garrisons in the city. From West Germany's point of view this was a safeguard against any East German takeover of the city. From East Germany's point of view, it was a setback to the Democratic Republic's ambitions – for which East Germans tended to blame the USSR.

East–West relations were now improving markedly, not only between the Soviet bloc and the West but also between China and the West. Communist China was admitted to the UN in October 1971 (see Section 15.3(e)). Nixon visited Peking in February 1972 and Moscow in the following May, adding to the growing goodwill by seeking at the same time to bring to an end the war in Vietnam. There was little goodwill between the USSR and China, however, and for the moment Nixon seemed to be on surer ground in dealing with the Russians than in dealing with the Chinese. Both the USSR and the USA had powerful positions to defend and saw agreements as the best way to defend them. Brezhnev and the Soviet leaders wished to divert money from weaponry to the production of consumer goods. Nixon was seeking re-election as US President and could benefit from the growing array of treaties.

Brezhnev, Nixon and their ministers therefore scribbled their signatures enthusiastically, piling up agreements and apparently burying past differences under expressions of goodwill. The most important was the SALT agreement, fixing limits on missiles and their locations and anticipating further Talks, though each side kept more than enough weapons to destroy the other several times over. Other agreements dealt with space research, trade and pollution. Above all, however, provision was made for continuing co-operation and for further building on the initiatives of Brandt, Gierek, and Nixon and Brezhnev themselves. Preparations began in 1973 for a general settlement of European problems and Nixon helped them along by giving US recognition to East Germany in 1974. The US–Soviet commission set up to discuss trade produced many new commercial exchanges, and co-operation in space led to the Apollo–Soyuz link-up in 1975.

The European negotiations bore fruit in 1975 when the USA, Canada and thirty-three European nations met in Helsinki in the *Conference on Security and Co-operation in Europe* (CSCE). The Conference agreed that the existing frontiers should be 'inviolable'. It also agreed on ways by which to reduce the risks of accidental conflict in Europe. There were further agreements on extending economic and cultural links throughout the continent and on respecting certain fundamental human rights. The CSCE finally agreed to meet again in 1978 to seek further progress towards 'security' and 'co-operation'. Detente, it seemed, had been achieved – but had it?

(d) New Uncertainties

New Strategic Arms Limitation Talks began in Vladivostok in 1974. The new CSCE met in Belgrade in 1977–8. But the Belgrade Conference was promptly soured by wrangling about human rights. President Carter, and the West generally, persistently alleged that the pledges of 1975 on human rights were not being honoured in the Soviet Union and Eastern Europe. In reply Brezhnev accused the West of trying to interfere in the East's internal affairs. The CSCE achieved little except an agreement to meet again, and many of the same arguments were therefore heard in Madrid in 1980–3. SALT had seemed to make better progress, but the agreement the Talks produced was frustrated when the US Senate defied President Carter and refused to ratify it. By the end of the 1970s the old distrust and suspicions had surfaced again.

As early as 1975 the USA had tried to force the Soviet leaders to allow free emigration from the USSR in exchange for supplies of American grain. After that, Carter often tried to use grain supplies to extort concessions from Moscow. He had little success, but relations deteriorated with allegations about human rights and about the Soviet pursuit of 'hegemony'. The USA had watched with dismay the spread of communism in Indochina after the US withdrawal (see Section 17.1(*d*)). Events in Angola caused similar dismay (see Section 16.5(*b*)), and there was concern about Soviet influence in Ethiopia (see Section 19.3). American fears of some grand Soviet design to spread Marxism were revived. They were encouraged by the Chinese, who loudly alleged not so much a desire to spread Marxism (from which, in Chinese eyes, the USSR had already deviated) as one to spread Soviet power, to achieve 'hegemony'. Certainly it seemed in the later 1970s that Brezhnev was winning more foreign-policy 'successes' than was Jimmy Carter (see Section 13.2(*h*))

The great powers lurched nearer to a new Cold War in 1979–80. At the end of 1979, Soviet forces invaded Afghanistan. China, the West and some Third-World countries were bitter in their condemnation. Even Castro found the Soviet action something of an embarrassment, difficult to defend to the non-aligned movement. Brezhnev argued that the Soviet intervention resulted from Western efforts to destabilize Afghanistan, a country which bordered the USSR and in which the Soviets had for some time had considerable influence. Afghanistan also borders Iran where militant Moslems had recently overthrown the Shah. It was suggested that Moslem militancy alarmed the Soviet Union, giving rise to fears that it might spread not only to Afghanistan but to the USSR's own Moslem population. Whatever the reasons for the Soviet invasion, however, there was some resistance within Afghanistan as well as condemnation in the world at large: the Soviet Union became involved in a guerilla conflict which dragged on into the 1980s.

Meanwhile the Soviet action further enraged Mrs Thatcher who had come to power in Britain earlier in 1979 and was already strongly hostile to the USSR. It also contributed something to Reagan's success in winning the US Presidency in 1980, since Reagan, like Thatcher, made political capital out of the 'need' to take a tough line towards Moscow. It therefore seemed that the progress towards detente in the early 1970s had, after all, been illusory. Even so, for all his election talk, Reagan in 1981 lifted the ban on grain exports to the USSR which Carter had imposed before leaving office – there had been too many protests from American producers whose profits had suffered. In 1982, however, he provoked protests in Western Europe when he tried to halt progress on a pipeline planned to bring natural gas from Soviet Siberia to members of the EEC.

There was uncertainty therefore in the early 1980s. The West's relations with the Soviet Union were uneasy. Sino-Soviet relations remained strained. When the decade opened, China's distrust of the USSR was providing cement for her improved relations with the West, but the latter suffered a setback when Reagan for a time gave renewed US support to Taiwan, thus angering Peking. Ford had followed in Nixon's footsteps, visiting China in 1975, and along with Kissinger, the Republicans' – and perhaps the world's – most industrious negotiator, had laid foundations for American-Chinese accord on which Carter and Vance were able to build. Both in Washington and Peking there was now some faltering, and Brezhnev seized the opportunity to examine what scope there was for healing the rift between Moscow and Peking, an initiative followed up by Andropov.

Meanwhile the world had another nagging worry. India exploded an atomic bomb in 1974. The Indian government denied any intention of building a stockpile of nuclear weapons, but it was now obvious that the manufacture of such weapons was within the reach of a growing number of governments. The superpowers themselves went on amassing weapons of destruction, including not only nuclear arms but also chemical devices, though they had signed an agreement in 1972 to outlaw germ warfare. The SALT achievements and earlier agreements such as the Non-Proliferation Treaty provided only flimsy safeguards against the further spread of armaments which could one day destroy the human race. A revival of earlier anti-nuclear protest movements therefore accompanied what seemed in the early 1980s to be a revival of great-power rivalries and of the icy climate of the East–West Cold War.

Further Reading

Ambrose, S.E.: *Rise to Globalism: American Foreign Policy, 1938–1980.* Penguin (Harmondsworth, 1980).

Bown, C. and Mooney, P.: *Cold War to Detente 1945–1980.* Heinemann (London, 1981).

Buttinger, J.: *Dragon Defiant, Short History of Vietnam.* David & Charles (Newton Abbot, 1973).

Hastings, P.: *The Cold War.* Benn (London, 1969).

Higgins, H.: *Vietnam.* Heinemann (London, 1975).

LaFeber, W.: *America, Russia and the Cold War 1945–1975.* Wiley (New York, 1976).

Maclear, M.: *Vietnam: The Ten Thousand Day War.* Thames Methuen (London, 1981).

Wint, G.: *Asia Handbook.* Penguin (Harmondsworth, 1969) – Korea, Cambodia, Laos, Vietnam.

Documentary

Beggs, R.: *The Cuban Missiles Crisis.* Longman (Harlow, 1971).

Breach, R.W.: *Documents and Descriptions, the World since 1914.* Oxford University Press (London, 1966).

Graebner, N.A.: *Cold War Diplomacy.* Anvil (London, 1962).

Lancaster, A.B.: *From Containment to Co-existence.* Arnold (London, 1976).

Lawrence, A.: *China's Foreign Relations since 1949.* Routledge & Kegan Paul (London, 1975).

Morgan, R.: *The Unsettled Peace.* British Broadcasting Corporation (London, 1974).

Exercises

1. Briefly explain the meaning of *each* of the following terms: Cold War; Containment; Coexistence; Detente; Confrontation; Crisis; Hegemony.

2. Explain why and how the Cold War between East and West developed. What events of importance in the history, of the relationships of the great powers occurred (*a*) in 1953 and (*b*) in 1955?

3. Trace the origins, events and results of the Korean War, 1950–3.

4. Why did the USA become involved in war in Vietnam? Why did President Nixon adopt the policy of Vietnamization and why was it not more successful?

5. 'The history of Indochina gives little scope for easy optimism' (page 332). What reasons were there for this assertion in 1973? How far have more recent events shown reasons for 'optimism' about the future of Indochina?

6. What evidence is there to support the argument that there was a *thaw* in relations between the West and the Soviet bloc in the 1960s and early 1970s? Why is it not possible accurately to date its beginning?

7. Outline the history of attempts to achieve disarmament after 1945 and account for (*a*) the absence of progress before 1963 and (*b*) the limited progress during the twenty years which followed.

8. Making use of this Unit and the Index to this book, trace the history since 1949 of China's relations (*a*) with the West and (*b*) with the Soviet Union. In what ways has China's foreign policy influenced US–Soviet relations?

9. 'It seemed in the later 1970s that Brezhnev was winning more foreign-policy

'successes" than was Jimmy Carter' (page 341). What evidence can you find in
this book to support this statement?
10. Sketch out a plan for a history of Vietnam from 1954 to 1973. Indicate the places
in this history at which you would make use of *each* of the following Figures in
this Unit, *in each case* summarizing the main points you would make in referring to
the Figure: Figs. 17.1; 17.2(*b*); 17.3; 17.4; 17.5.

Unit Eighteen

International Relations After 1945: Construction Outside Europe

18.1 International Trade

(a) Rich and Poor

Not even the rich countries could be complacent about trade after 1945. Essential imports could be paid for only by export earnings, a fact of economic life as important to Britain and the developed nations as to the developing. It was generally recognized that the high tariffs of the 1930s had hindered recovery from the Depression and were undesirable. Soon after the war, tariff reductions followed from GATT, accelerating in the 1960s with the Kennedy Round (see Section 13.2(e)). There was a more general movement too towards other forms of international economic co-operation, the OEEC being expanded in 1961 into the OECD (see Section 14.5(a)). Such institutions were helpful to the economies of the advanced capitalist nations, and the communist world also built its co-operative machinery (see Section 12.3).

Meanwhile, the world recognized that increased exports offered the best means of obtaining wealth with which poor nations could finance their development. This led to the establishment, in 1964, of the *United Nations Conference on Trade and Development* (UNCTAD) and an *International Trade Centre*. Three years later, the United Nations set up an *Industrial Development Organization* (UNIDO) to promote industrialization. Such organizations were willing to discuss the problems of the poor, but it soon became clear that wealthy nations would not give them effective help if it meant subordinating their own interests.

One unfulfilled need was for international agreements on commodity prices (guaranteed minimum prices for the commodities on whose export poor nations often depended heavily): too often the poor were still at the mercy of the rich. Sometimes, they had to compete with synthetics, manufactured by the developed nations, and prices for commodities produced by poorer countries, such as tea, cocoa, copper and rubber, often fell alarmingly. Richer nations showed little inclination to do much about this, for they profited in such a situation. On the other hand, oil-producing countries such as Libya and Iraq were beginning to exploit the enormous needs of the wealthy for their produce, and to force up the price. OPEC (the Organization of Petroleum Exporting Countries), founded in 1961, was highly successful in protecting the interests of its members. They provided a lead and coffee-producing states, such as Brazil and the Ivory Coast, began to think about holding back their produce to bring about a fairer price. Similarly, the copper-producing countries – Chile, Zambia, Zaire and Peru – began to discuss joint policies when, in 1972, the USA tried to seize Chilean copper shipments in protest at the nationalization of that nation's copper production.

Rich nations were inclined to howl in protest at such practices. Britain had already clashed with Persia over oil rights (see Section 17.1(b)) and a new conflict brewed with Iraq in 1972 on a similar issue. But Lady Jackson, a British speaker at UNCTAD III, pronounced a verdict which was perhaps not unfair on the relations between the rich and the poor, when she said: 'The profound, even heart-rending difficulties of the rich . . . are their excuse for doing next to nothing about the infinitely more real and heart-rending problems of the poor.'

(b) New Economic Rocks

Unit Four showed how the world ran into serious economic difficulties in the inter-war years. Economies were wrecked on new economic rocks in the 1970s. The rich nations had on the whole grown steadily richer after the Second World War, though vast areas of the world to the south of them had hardly shared in their growing prosperity. In the mid-1970s, however, the rich began to falter, until by the end of the decade even West Germany and Japan, who had previously been highly successful, had their problems.

The problems for most countries centred on a puzzling combination of inflation and recession. It appeared that the crisis had been triggered off by sudden increases in the price of oil in 1974, partly because OPEC insisted on higher rewards for the producing nations and partly because there was a growing awareness that oil reserves were fast being used up. At the same time Arab oil producers hit back at the West for the support given to Israel in the Yom Kippur War of 1973, withholding the supplies of fuel on which the West depended (see Section 19.1(f)). What the actions of the oil producers showed, however, was that the world economic order was already precariously balanced. Prices rose generally, forcing rich and poor alike to pay more not only for oil but for foodstuffs, raw materials and manufactures. Purchasing power declined so that sales fell, production slowed and unemployment grew. The well-to-do nations who had thought the unemployment of the 1930s a thing of the past had now to grapple with it yet again. There was a slight recovery in the late 1970s but the 1980s opened with the recession deepening.

Both rich and poor searched desperately for solutions to these problems. The leaders of the USA, Britain, West Germany, France, Italy and Japan held an economic summit meeting towards the end of 1975. They met again in 1978, this time with Canadian representation. Such summits seemed likely to become regular but their early impact was limited. The leaders agreed readily enough on pious expressions of good intentions, for example, that the wasteful use of oil and other fuels should be reduced. In general, however, it was left to individual nations to decide what action to take. The energy crisis produced some action but the problems of inflation and unemployment produced little.

One result of the energy crisis was a frenzied search for new supplies of oil. Britain and neighbouring countries intensified their drilling operations in the North Sea. In 1975 work was begun on an Alaskan pipeline to bring oil from the Arctic to the rest of the USA. The Soviet Union also stepped up production. Such activity went some way to ensuring adequate supplies of oil for the present though there was little agreement on the length of time before supplies would run out. Access to oil also helped the producing states to sustain their economies, and piecemeal action was taken to assist the survival of those consuming states that were already desperately poor. A UN emergency fund was set up, supported by the IMF and some of the oil-producing states. Some of the latter also gave more direct help to their neighbours. The Islamic world issued the Declaration of Lahore in 1974 and set up a committee to help the poorer Moslem countries. But obtaining and paying for oil was only one aspect of the crisis in the world economic order. Inflation and unemployment remained widespread. Their impact varied from one country to another. In the developed capitalist world West Germany fared better than did the USA and, in spite of North Sea oil, Britain. In the Third World, oil producers such as Nigeria and Trinidad fared better than most of their neighbours. Even the oil producers, however, had their problems. The industry itself provided only limited employment and could easily unbalance economies which were not already stable and healthy. Moreover, by 1982, there was an over-supply of oil, demand having fallen. Even members of OPEC suffered economic hardship, not least Nigeria.

Such economic upheaval helped to focus attention on the still widening gap between rich and poor nations, broadly between the North (northern hemisphere, mainly north of the Tropic of Cancer) and South (broadly, south of the Tropic of Cancer). Though individual states still struggled to solve their own problems, there was growing awareness that such problems were interdependent and that what was needed was a common assault on a world economic order in serious disarray. Most statesmen flinched in the face of such an enormous challenge, preferring to busy themselves with their own national economies. Spokesmen were nevertheless emerging. Michael Manley of Jamaica was one. Willy Brandt and Edward Heath were others. By the end of the 1970s the debate was well under way, but with little prospect that radical international action would be quick to follow (see Section 18.2(c)).

18.2 The World Economic Order

(a) The Problems of Development

Marshall Aid and similar assistance had gone a long way after 1945 towards overcoming the problems of war-torn Europe, and improvements were soon evident on both sides of the Iron Curtain. It was a far greater problem to develop the economies and societies of most of the non-European world. The developing nations lacked capital, expertise and, many of them, even the basic natural resources for industrialization and the creation of wealth. While the developed countries moved into the age of computers and space techno-

Table 18.1   Average income per head of the population (£s p.a.)*

	1958	1970	1976	Main exports c. 1976 (% of whole)
Developed countries				
West Germany	330	975	4 620	Machinery 29%
USA	880	1 630	4 600	Machinery 27%
Canada	620	1 075	4 300	Vehicles 22%
Australia	460	890	3 100	Wool 12%
Japan	120	630	3 100	Machinery 25%
Britain	425	700	2 200	Machinery 28%
Israel	260	610	1 500	Diamonds 33%
Developing (Third-World) countries				
Jamaica	130	190	600†	Metals 66%
Syria	65	90	430	Crude oil 62%
Peru	70	100	320	Metals 44%
Zambia	47	98	250	Copper 91%
Sri Lanka (Ceylon)	50	56	120	Tea 44%
Kenya	29	43	120	Coffee 37%
Ghana	58	88	110	Cocoa 59%
Tanzania	20	25	85	Cotton 16%
India	27	30	80	Sugar 12%

* Figures based on *Encyclopaedia Britannica* (converted from dollars etc.).
† 1975

Income for 1976 reflects the effects of inflation, and a gap between the rich and poor which is tending to widen.

Average income (approx.) per head of the population (£s p.a.): Regions, 1970

North America	1 600
Europe	880
Latin America	220
Middle East	160
Africa	80
Asia, other than Japan	50

logy, the poor continued to struggle with almost insuperable problems of famine, disease and grinding poverty. Table 18.1 shows that the average income per head of population rose almost everywhere from the 1950s to 1970s, but for many of the poor the rise represented little more than the paper figures of inflation: the rise in real standards was negligible in a great many Third-World countries.

There was little difficulty in identifying Third-World needs. In times of crisis (and natural disasters such as drought, floods, plagues and earthquakes were all too common in the areas least equipped to cope with them), the need was for relief to deal with emergency problems. UNO and other international organizations established a good deal of machinery which was helpful at such times. But the more deep-rooted problem was that of breaking away from persistent poverty: and here the needs seemed bottomless. There was a need for capital and equipment with which to set up industry and power stations, through which to produce future profits; expertise with which to modernize agriculture and transport; schools in which to develop the skills essential to more advanced societies and to wipe out widespread illiteracy, and hospitals in which to conquer disease.

But the problem was not simply one of money, equipment and expertise. The rapid development of communications made the underprivileged societies aware of their disadvantages and eager for improvement. This imposed heavy burdens on national leaders, creating instability in some states but bringing leaders of outstanding quality to the fore in others. Nyerere in Tanzania and Mrs Gandhi in India remained in power for many years carrying on the struggle against underdevelopment. In Asia, problems were often made worse by over-large populations, with more human beings to be fed than primitive agriculture and a hostile climate could manage to satisfy. Such states often possessed no mineral resources and they had to produce something which they could export and sell in exchange for much-needed machinery, vehicles and railway stock. Too often, however, the prices they could get for their commodities were desperately low. Those dependent mainly on one export, as Ghana was dependent on cocoa, Ceylon on tea and Zambia on copper, found it impossible to rely on consistent prices or even on fair ones (see Section 18.1).

Such a situation required a more generous response than the rich powers were usually prepared to make. In the 1960s, the United Nations called upon the prosperous to provide 1 per cent of their national incomes. By the end of the 1960s, only Switzerland, France and West Germany were able to claim that they had exceeded this target. Britain fell a little below it, many other rich nations far short of it. But some progress had been made. Loans to the poor were usually free of interest, a step forward from earlier lending at interest rates which often entangled the poor in debts. Ghana, for example, entered the 1970s with an almost impossible load of debts, the result of earlier commitments to repay money at interest to the profit of the rich. Aid was now devoted to projects such as power stations, irrigation schemes, railways and factories which would create future wealth, rather than to prestige projects such as public buildings and little-used airports. The more enlightened countries had also ceased to attach strings to their aid, no longer seeking special privileges for themselves or compelling the poor to buy in certain markets. Even so, the rich were quick to complain of ingratitude when poor nations acted, for example in foreign policy, in ways that displeased them. They complained also when the poor appeared to waste their small resources in quarrels, military display and even conflict. For some reason, the developed powers appeared to expect a higher standard of conduct among the underdeveloped than they took for granted among themselves.

But in the 1970s, the gulf between the rich and poor continued to widen. States like Kenya and Tanzania, with desperately little to export, and others like India, with large populations, struggled almost in vain to catch up. Moreover, many were feeling the distorting effects of their contacts with the wealthier world. Development was not simply about the problem of obtaining sufficient international aid: it also concerned the transforming of society and the economy. In Ceylon and Ghana, unemployment among the better-educated became a difficulty in the early 1970s. In the West Indies, the attempt to boost income from tourism led to social strains, with those still condemned to live in slums resentful of luxury hotels. In many parts of Africa, a gulf grew between urban and rural communities, a conflict between a Europeanized way of life and an African one. The transition from poor communities to the prosperity of industrialization called for the highest qualities of leadership as well as for generous assistance from the highly-developed.

(b) Aid

The assistance took many forms, from gifts and loans to the skilled advice of teachers, engineers and agriculturalists. Most of the developed nations set up aid programmes, although those involved in the Cold War found it difficult to dissociate aid from foreign policy. When the USA withdrew support from the building of the Aswan Dam in Egypt, the Soviet Union eagerly stepped in, hoping to win a new friend and influence the Arab world. It was easier for neutral countries like Sweden to approach international aid in a more impartial and humanitarian sense. This was also the objective of the UN specialized agencies to which all members of UNO were expected to contribute (see Section 11.3(b)).

Some countries had special interests. The former colonizing powers often went on showing interest in the developing countries they had once ruled. Much of the assistance given by the European Community as a result of the Lomé Convention of 1975 went to countries formerly ruled by France and Britain (see Section 14.5(c)). Britain directed most of her aid to the poorer members of the Commonwealth, itself an association for mutual assistance (see Section 16.6(d) and Table 18.2). Canada, partly through the Commonwealth connection, took a special interest in the Caribbean. West Germany felt a

Fig. 18.1 Contrasting ways of life in Karachi, Pakistan. Acceptable housing for all the nation's people was just one of the amenities totally beyond the reach of governments throughout the Third World. Few cities were without their hideous slums and shanty towns even in the 1980s

special obligation to Israel as some small atonement for the Nazi crimes against the Jews. Aid programmes fluctuated, sometimes dependent on the supposed ideological leanings of the governments in power in the various developed nations. But it remained a true generalization that almost all fell short of UN targets for most of the time. In 1964, the British government managed only about 0.5 per cent of the country's national income – and the figure then fell, standing at not much more than 0.3 per cent in 1973. By 1978, it had again topped 0.4 per cent, but the Thatcher government maintained that cuts had to be made at the beginning of the 1980s, because of Britain's own difficulties. At that moment, however, Japan announced a new aid programme which for the first time would represent a serious effort on her part to come near the international target. Long before then, however, the UN had lowered the target to only 0.7 per cent of national incomes.

But it was not only governments who were grappling with the problems of the underdeveloped nations. In Britain organizations such as *OXFAM, War on Want* and *Christian Aid* provided help. *Voluntary Service Overseas*, the *Peace Corps* in the USA and the specialized agencies of UNO provided an outlet for many individuals who wished to help. But governments inevitably bore the principal burden.

A few examples will illustrate the varieties of aid which were given. In 1950, the Foreign Ministers of the Commonwealth devised the *Colombo Plan* to assist the development of South and South-East Asia; a Council was established to organize training, research, economic development and better health services. In addition to the developed states of the Commonwealth, such as Britain, Australia and Canada, the members of the organization came to include the USA and Asian states from Afghanistan to Japan, all engaged in co-operative development through the Council in Colombo, sometimes with the assistance of experts provided by UNO.

Less ambitious but vitally important was the *Indus Waters Project*. The partitioning of India in 1947 left disputes between India and Pakistan about the

Table 18.2 Examples of international aid: the Commonwealth

In 1969 Britain made grants to members of the Commonwealth of almost £54 million (including spending on technical assistance) and loans of almost £69 million.

The Commonwealth Development Corporation had in hand over 170 projects, mainly in Africa, involving investment of over £150 million.

Commonwealth countries contributing aid through the Colombo Plan included Britain, Canada, Australia, New Zealand, India, Pakistan, Ceylon and Malaysia. Much of this aid took the form of technical assistance.

British Aid to Members of the Commonwealth 1964–9 (£s million)

Total Grants: 835
Total Loans: 862

Some receiving countries:

	Grants	Loans
Pakistan	9	91
India	11	345
Ceylon	4	16
Singapore	8	4
Ghana	9	14
Kenya	96	78
Tanzania	48	23
Zambia	34	8
Jamaica	23	13
Guyana	18	23

Indus basin waters. The International Bank came to mediate. The division of the waters between the two nations was agreed by a treaty in 1960 after which the Bank, with certain countries such as Britain, undertook to give financial help for irrigation works.

In 1958, a Conference at Montreal, in Canada, extended the ideas behind the Colombo Plan by introducing *Commonwealth Assistance Loans*. At the same time, an Education Conference was arranged to meet in Oxford in 1959, out of which *Commonwealth Scholarships* developed. Some years later, another Conference in Montreal brought together Commonwealth nurses and yet another at Toronto established a *Commonwealth Veterinary Bureau* which owed a good deal to the enthusiasm and professional interests of Jawara, the Prime Minister of the Gambia. These exchanges of expertise were just as important to the developing nations as Assistance Loans.

(c) North–South and the Brandt Report

Aid was not in itself an answer to the problems of the Third World. Even if made available on a far greater scale, it could never be sufficient. More far-reaching changes were needed in the world economic order if the gap between North and South were ever to narrow. Firstly, the poorer nations needed to be able to keep more of the wealth they were able to produce. This necessitated stable and substantial commodity prices, a demand for which came regularly from the meetings of UNCTAD. The producers of most commodities had had little of the success of OPEC by the 1980s however. Commodity prices continued to fluctuate, often falling to perilously low levels whenever supplies were plentiful on world markets. Multinational companies also continued to cause anxieties. As had often been alleged against the international oil companies, multinationals concerned with a wide range of production from foodstuffs to minerals, and from radios to vehicles, aimed first to boost company profits, rather than to serve the interests of the countries in which they operated. Though they brought some employment and amenities to the parts of the Third World in which they operated, they also claimed as their price a substantial share of whatever wealth was produced.

The 1970s saw a growing awareness of the complexities of the problem. Institutions such as UNCTAD made possible a North–South dialogue and ensured that Third-World opinion was at least heard. Effective action was slow to follow, but the Brandt Report of 1980 made a major contribution to the debate. It resulted from the work of a commission headed by Willy Brandt and of which Edward Heath was a member. It recommended 'a Programme for Survival'. It also based its findings not simply on justice and humanitarianism but on the interests of peoples everywhere, emphasizing that customers in the Third World offered the best guarantee of the prosperity of the developed nations themselves. In 1980, men and machines in the North stood idle for want of markets for their output. That output was needed in the South but the developing nations lacked the purchasing power to buy. So the problems of

North and South at last came together in a general sickness of the world economic order. The Brandt Report outlined a strategy both for immediate action and for the longer term. The thoroughness with which the commission worked was unprecedented, drawing into the discussion the communist powers as well as the West and the South. It challenged the world's statesmen to turn words into deeds and drew their attention to the ill effects on the whole human race of the vast spending by governments on armaments. The faltering of national economies almost everywhere in the early 1980s underlined the urgency of the international crisis, but at a North–South meeting at Cancun in Mexico in 1981, the North preferred excuses to action.

18.3   Regional Organizations

As old empires crumbled and many new nations emerged, the mutual assistance which it was possible to provide through United Nations agencies, the Commonwealth and organizations such as the Colombo Plan, was also extended through regional groupings. Groupings of European states, in the EEC, EFTA and Comecon, for example, were matched by similar organizations elsewhere. They had a variety of aims, but common to almost all was the furtherance of economic development.

(a) The Americas

The *Organization of American States* (OAS) dated from 1948 but its roots went back to the late nineteenth century. Its members included most of the states of South and Central America and certain islands in the Caribbean, in addition to the USA, inevitably influential in the Americas. Ex-British islands also became members – Trinidad and Tobago, in 1967, and Barbados, in 1968. The aim was to achieve some unity of action in various fields, and to promote inter-American co-operation. In some ways, the OAS was like a regional United Nations Organization; its members set up machinery for arbitration and the peaceful settlement of disputes. But the Organization was also an instrument of US foreign policy. Under pressure from Washington, the OAS boycotted Cuba in 1962 when Castro deeply offended the USA (see Section 15.5). The boycott was not lifted until the mid-1970s when other members of the OAS grew strong enough to bring their own pressure to bear on Washington.

President Kennedy had meanwhile launched the *Alliance for Progress* in 1961, the USA providing much of the finance for a programme of economic co-operation among many Latin American nations. A target was set for annual growth. Though beneficial, the Alliance was again not unrelated to US foreign policy, one objective being to prevent the spread of communism. But few organizations could completely divorce economics from politics, and it was a weakness of Third-World states that they were too poor to stand completely apart from the major powers.

The *Organization of Central American States* (OCAS) was, however, more independent. It was set up in 1951 for economic and social co-operation between Guatemala and her neighbours. In 1960 the same states created the *Central American Common Market*, aiming at a common tariff and free trade. Less successful was the *Latin American Free Trade Association* (LAFTA) of many South American states and Mexico, replaced in 1980 by the *Latin American Integration Association* (LAIA). The *Caribbean Free Trade Association* (CARIFTA) dated from 1968 and this, in its turn, paved the way for the English-speaking *Caribbean Community* (CARICOM) five years later (see Section 16.6(*b*)).

(*b*) Africa

Groupings in Africa began with the *Monrovia Powers* (see Section 16.3(*e*)) and the *Casablanca Powers*, both associations founded in 1961 for co-operation between developing nations. The Casablanca Powers, as one aim, envisaged a common market between Algeria, Ghana, Guinea, Mali and the United Arab Republic. A more ambitious and more comprehensive organization quickly followed when the Monrovia Powers, Casablanca Powers and others such as Tanganyika, Uganda and Libya set up the *Organization of African Unity* (OAU) in 1963. The OAU's first aim was to end colonialism where it still survived in Africa. Beyond that it aimed to develop co-operation and a sense of unity throughout the African continent. The size and diversity of the continent meant that this was a bold venture and inevitably the OAU became caught up in the racial problems of southern Africa which caused further disunity. Nevertheless it was an attempt by Africans to manage African affairs, independent of the influence of richer and longer-established powers.

Britain had once considered an East African Federation. After independence, the three ex-British states in East Africa – Kenya, Tanzania* and Uganda – returned to the idea and, in 1967, set up the *East African Community*. Their aims were mutual economic assistance and a common tariff. In effect, much of the assistance in the early stages was likely to be from the more-advanced Kenya to her less-developed partners but the organization held out hope for the future. Kenya under Kenyatta and Tanzania under Nyerere were among the best-governed states in Africa but this Community too ran into problems. A coup in Uganda in 1971 deposed Obote in favour of General Amin and Amin's vicious dictatorship quickly embittered relationships with Kenya and Tanzania. The Community was well nigh paralysed throughout the 1970s and, even when Tanzanian troops helped to overthrow Amin in 1979, Ugandan affairs remained turbulent. In West Africa, however, the *Economic Community of West African States* (ECOWAS) was founded in 1976, linking some sixteen states, of which oil-rich Nigeria was the cornerstone. ECOWAS entered the 1980s with constructive ideas and good hopes of success. The East African Community, on the other hand, had collapsed and

---

* Formerly Tanganyika and Zanzibar.

there was little immediate prospect of its revival. The OAU struggled on, unable to make spectacular progress in creating real unity between its many diverse members. In January 1982, the OAU sent a peace-keeping force to Chad, the first such all-African venture. The early results were disappointing, however, and the internal strife in Chad dragged on.

(c) The Arab World

The Arab world struggled too. When the *Arab League* was founded in 1945, economic co-operation was only one of several objectives. Arabs wished to free their lands from foreign intrusions. The League loosely linked Egypt and other Middle-East states (see Fig. 18.2). They hoped to put pressure on the French to speed their departure from Syria, Algeria and Tunisia, and to uphold the interests of Arabs in Palestine (see Section 19.1). The British, however, encouraged the foundation of the Arab League, because they saw it as a contribution to stability in the Middle East and a bulwark against communism. The French eventually gave up all their Arab possessions, but the Jews created the state of Israel and resisted the League's championship of Palestinian Arabs. In the face of such resistance the Arab League often proved divided and ineffective. The League survived as an organization for economic co-operation but it was severely handicapped by repeated disputes among its members.

Other Arab unions were even less successful. In 1958, Egypt joined Syria in the *United Arab Republic*, of which Nasser became President. The union was dissolved, at Syria's request, in 1961, largely because Syrians resented Egypt's

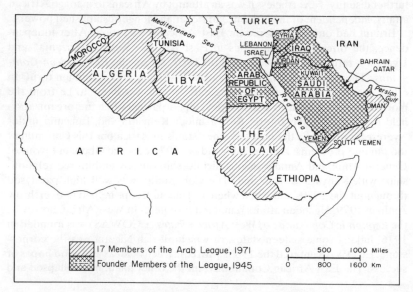

Fig. 18.2 The Arab League in 1971

Table 18.3 The Arab world in 1975

Country	Est. population (millions)	Main export (% of whole)	Exports mainly to (% of whole)	Imports mainly from (% of whole)
Morocco	17.3	Phosphates 55%	France 21%	France 30%
Algeria	16.8	Crude oil 86%	USA 27%	France 34%
Libya	2.4	Crude oil 100%	Italy 22% USA 22%	Italy 26%
Egypt	37.0	Cotton 37%	USSR 43%	USA 19% France 11%
Lebanon	2.6	Machinery 14% Fruit/veg 12%	Saudi Arabia 25%	Rumania 10% USA 7%
Syria	7.3	Crude oil 70%	Italy 18%	West Germany 13% Italy 9%
Jordan	2.7	Phosphates 39%	Saudi Arabia 10% Iran 9%	West Germany 12% USA 11% Saudi Arabia 11%
Iraq	11.1	Crude oil 98%	Italy 17%	Japan 18% West Germany 18%
Saudi Arabia	7.2	Crude oil 93%	Japan 16% France 12%	USA 17% Japan 16%

assumption of a dominant role in the partnership. The UAR also tried, in 1958, to create a federation with Yemen under the title *United Arab States* – but in 1961 that union also collapsed. Even more brief was the union of Jordan and Iraq who tried to create a federation known as the *Arab Union*. It lasted for only two months, from May to July 1968.

Disunity presented many difficulties in the Arab world and though some of the Arab states were rich in oil, economic underdevelopment, political instability and the ever-present problem of Israel made for troubled waters in northern Africa and the Middle East, in which other nations inevitably came to fish. The sudden death of Nasser in 1970, in many ways the most outstanding leader of the Arab world, left little hope for the rapid solution of the many outstanding problems. Nevertheless, the Arabs persevered with the idea of unions. In 1971, a *Federation of Arab Republics* was set up, loosely linking Libya, Syria and Egypt, the latter abandoning its former name of the United Arab Republic in favour of the Arab Republic of Egypt. A year later, Nasser's successor in Egypt, President Sadat, reached agreement with Colonel Gadafy, the Libyan Head of State, for merging Egypt and Libya into a single Arab state.

The plan was destroyed almost at once by bitter arguments and Gadafy became one of the most outspoken critics of Sadat's attempts to heal the divisions between Egypt and Israel (see Section 19.1(g)).

(d) Asia

States in the Far East showed less interest than Arabs and Africans in creating regional organizations. The first major development was the founding of the Association of South-East Asian Nations (ASEAN – see Section 17.1(d), page 334).

18.4   A Special Case: the Reconstruction of Japan

(a) The American Occupation

The USA assumed almost exclusive responsibility for Japan's future after 1945, imposing an army of occupation under MacArthur and fashioning the Treaty of San Francisco (see Section 11.1(b)) without a formal peace conference. The USA intended to plant genuine democracy in Japan and to demilitarize the country. Efforts to break up the *zaibatsu* (huge industrial combines whose businessmen, like the militarists, had often disrupted Japanese political life before 1939) were less successful. By the early 1950s, the zaibatsu had recovered and the army, too, made a comeback when the USA grew worried at the growth of communism in Asia.

Under the new constitution of 1946 Hirohito remained Emperor but he was no longer treated as divine. A parliament of two houses, both elected, and the principle of ministerial responsibility (the government being responsible to parliament rather than to the Emperor) established a more effective form of democracy than Japan had previously known. At first, it was intended that Japan would have no military forces but, in 1950, MacArthur introduced a constabulary which, like the people's police forces of Eastern Europe, soon came to possess tanks and grew into an army.

The occupation of the Japanese mainland ended after the signing of the Treaty of San Francisco but the USA retained Okinawa until 1972. The Americans continued to take a close interest in Japan and in 1960 signed a Security Treaty, guaranteeing her defence. American influence also set Japan on the road to economic recovery and considerable prosperity.

Nevertheless, resentment of the USA was not uncommon in Japan, frequently erupting among the country's turbulent student population. Sometimes it was a protest against too much Americanization, sometimes against the capitalist system and the pursuit of profit, and sometimes against nuclear weapons which had left terrible scars in Hiroshima and Nagasaki. The USA's insistence on keeping bases in Okinawa after 1972 was unpopular in many quarters and there were frequent protests against American involvement in Vietnam. In some ways, the results of American occupation in Japan were impressive but the occupation also left a degree of turbulence in its wake. Japan's cultural heritage was very different from that of the USA and American influence in the country could sometimes seem alien.

(b) Japanese Politics

Political life in Japan seemed to operate on two levels after the US withdrawal. The constitution worked successfully to combine democracy with stable governments. From 1955, governments were based on a union of Liberal–Democrats which continued to win re-election into the 1980s, the Socialists providing the main Opposition. As part of the US legacy, there was widespread enthusiasm in Japan for the pursuit of personal wealth, and rapid economic development seemed to satisfy the majority of Japanese giving the system a built-in bias towards conservatism. Outside parliament, however, there was often turmoil. Violent street battles between formidable riot police and determined demonstrators were by no means uncommon. From the end of the 1960s a Japanese 'Red Army' existed, more than matching the terrorism and violence common to many developed countries. In the 1970s there was furious resistance to Tokyo's new airport, though it was eventually opened in 1978. Western democracy and many of the values Japan seemed to have imported from the USA found little favour with a substantial minority of the population, especially Japan's youth.

(c) The Economy

What made Japan something of a special case was the country's 'economic miracle'. As late as 1958, the average income per head of population in Japan was only about £120 a year, similar to that in Jamaica (see Table 18.1). But the economy achieved spectacular growth rates and average income grew rapidly: £240 in 1963, £630 in 1970, £3 100 in 1976 and about £4 000 at the end of the 1970s. Growth rates for the economy as a whole were over eight per cent a year in the years 1953 to 1962 compared with some five-and-a-half per cent in West Germany and two per cent in Britain. Japan had, of course, already acquired an industrial base before the Second World War and was the leading state in Asia, but her progress was remarkable nevertheless. It was achieved in spite of very limited natural resources. What made the country so successful was the Japanese ability to produce and sell exports. Her achievements in fields such as shipbuilding, electronics, vehicle-building and general engineering produced competition in world markets which few other countries could match. Table 18.4 shows something of Japan's success.

The success could partly be explained in terms of dedicated hard work, linked with enterprising modernization and heavy investment programmes. At the same time, Japan avoided costly foreign-policy commitments and spending on arms, so that resources were directed into economic development. But the high level of average incomes did not mean that all the Japanese people were prosperous. Fewer resources were directed towards social welfare than was common in postwar Europe. Improvements in living standards were comparatively modest. A rapid rise in population imposed severe strains, especially in housing, and environmental problems in Japanese cities remained among the worst in the developed world. By Western standards, wages were generally low and poverty was by no means eliminated. The startling economic progress of postwar Japan was therefore achieved at some social cost. Heavy investment in capital goods ran well ahead of social investment. This was one factor in the social unrest which plagued Japan. Trade unions were hardly effective enough to provide an outlet for dissatisfaction and the security benefits dispensed by the country's large industrial organizations provided only limited compensation for the low level of state services.

(d) Japan's Place in the World

Japan's geographical position also created difficulties. Trade with China fell dramatically after the Second World War and, in general, Japan's relationships with the communist world remained uneasy. Unlike states in Europe, however, Japan had no other neighbours with whom to make economic unions. Aid from the USA was for some time essential to her survival and recovery and American markets continued to be vital.

Close connexions with the USA made it difficult to have close ties with communist powers. Nevertheless, relations with the USSR were restored in the mid-1950s and Japan took care to avoid damaging involvement in either SEATO or the struggle in Vietnam. Admission to UNO was secured in 1956, but there was little to suggest that Japan wished to seek the pre-eminence in world affairs she had enjoyed before 1945. Her principal interests were now economic ones. In 1966, she took a leading part in planning an Asian Development Bank and, four years later, staged the international trade fair, EXPO 70, and seemed content with these peaceful pursuits. The country was no longer dominated by the militarists who had once dreamed of conquest and the Co-Prosperity Sphere.

Nevertheless, the startling economic progress of Japan caused misgivings. Her giant trading companies, the *sogo shosha*, so skilfully cultivated world markets that the effects were felt in many ways. Apprehension about Japan's strength helped to drive North and South Koreans in the 1970s to consider Korean reunification (see Section 17.1(c)). The strength of the Japanese yen and Japan's all-pervasive exports even caused anxiety in Britain and the USA, and international pressures led to the upward revaluation of the yen by almost 17 per cent at the end of 1971. Before the decade was out, however, even the EEC was becoming alarmed at the inflow of Japanese goods. Such was the momentum of Japan's economic upsurge that Japan turned also to communist China, seeking a new friendship with an eye to recovering old markets. The state of war between Japan and China, dating from 1937, was at last officially ended by a peace treaty in 1978. Japan recognized the government of Peking and abandoned support for the Chinese Nationalists in Taiwan. Thus a major

Table 18.4   The Japanese economy

Year	Estimated population (millions)	Main exports (% of whole)	Exports mainly to (%of whole)	Imports mainly from (% of whole)	Trade surplus (million yen)*
1970	104	Machinery 23% Iron/steel 15% Vehicles 10% Textiles 9% Ships 7%	USA 31% South Korea 4%	USA 29% Australia 8%	157 000
1978	115	Machinery 27% Vehicles 21% Iron/steel 14% Ships 7%	USA 26% South Korea 6%	USA 19% Saudi Arabia 11%	3 844 000

* In 1978, 374 yen = £1.

obstacle was removed and it began to seem likely that the Japanese would make deep inroads into Chinese markets too, and that China would benefit from Japanese investment in her development. Even before the treaty, Japan was supplying almost a third of China's imports.

Japan was by no means unaffected by the economic crisis of the 1970s and early 1980s, however. There was a brief panic about obtaining the vast supplies of oil the country needed, and the soaring cost of fuel created wild fluctuations in Japan's trade figures. The vast surplus of 1978 (see Table 18.4) turned into a deficit on visible trade in 1979, though the surpluses then returned as quickly as they had melted away. But inflation caused difficulties, and rising unemployment added to the conflicts in Japanese society. The sogo shosha nevertheless generally continued to flourish, adding to their profits. In 1971 alone the largest of them, the Mitsubishi Corporation, increased its profits by over eleven per cent. It was partly the drive of these companies which had lifted Japan from a comparatively poor country after the Second World War to a commercial giant – a special case whose example developing nations could admire but one which hardly any could ever hope to match. The US occupation, the boost given to Japan's output by the Korean War, continuing US support as a safeguard against communism, and the talents of the Japanese themselves – these provided a unique combination of factors which made possible Japan's economic miracle.

Further Reading

Cameron, N.: *From Bondage to Liberation, East Asia 1860–1952*. Oxford University Press (London, 1978).

Jones, D.: *The Arab World*. Hamish Hamilton (London, 1965).
O'Callaghan, B.: *History Five: In Your Century*. Longman Developing World Series (Harlow, 1981).
Sims, R.: *Modern Japan*. Bodley Head (London, 1973).
Storry, R.: *Japan*. Oxford University Press (London, 1965).
Watson, J.B.: *Empire to Commonwealth, 1919 to 1970*. Dent (London, 1971).
'*What is British Aid?*' Foreign and Commonwealth Office (London, 1967).
Williams, B.: *Modern Japan*. Longman (Harlow, 1969).

Documentary and Miscellaneous

Brandt, W. et al.: *North–South: A Programme for Survival*. Pan (London, 1980).
Gibson, M.: *The Rise of Japan*. Wayland (London, 1972).
Tiedemann, A.C.: *Modern Japan*. Anvil (London, 1963).
Zepke, N.: *The Hundred Year Miracle (Japan)*. Heinemann (London, 1977).
Trade/Aid/Rich World and Poor World. (VCOAD publications – Voluntary Committee on Overseas Aid and Development).
Third World File. Third World First Group (Watlington, Oxfordshire).

Exercises

1. What do Tables 18.1 and 18.2 show about the problems of developing nations and their relationships with the rich?
2. Why have Arab states tried to form unions since 1945? How similar to their attempts have been the movements towards unity in Africa and in the Americas?
3. In what senses is it possible to regard Japan as *a special case*?
4. How would you define poverty (*a*) in Britain and (*b*) in the underdeveloped world?
5. Explain why trade is important to (*a*) Britain, (*b*) Japan and (*c*) the underdeveloped nations. What efforts have been made since 1945 to promote international trade?
6. Making use of this Unit and the Index, describe what has been done by the richer nations to assist the development of poor nations. What criticisms may be made of the richer nations in this field?
7. Outline the history of the attempts to create regional organizations since 1945 in *two* of the following areas: Europe; Africa; the Middle East.
8. Make a list of Japanese-made articles which you possess and which you can see in the shops. What points made in this Unit are illustrated by such a list?
9. What is the attitude of your present government towards aid to underdeveloped nations?
10. Describe and explain the problems which in the mid-1970s caused economies to be 'wrecked on new economic rocks' (page 346). Explain what is meant by 'a general sickness of the world economic order' (page 354).
11. Study Fig. 18.2 (page 356) and Table 18.3 (page 357), and then answer the questions which follow:
    (*a*) Name (*i*) *two* original members of the Arab League, (*ii*) *two* more recent members, and (*iii*) the Arab state with the largest population.
    (*b*) By what name was the Arab Republic of Egypt known during the decade before it took this title? Name the Egyptian leader who died in 1970.
    (*c*) Not all Arab states are oil producers. Use Table 18.3 to illustrate the truth of this statement, and explain how the lack of oil affects the economies of the non-producers.

(*d*) In what important respect did Egypt's trading partners differ in 1975 from those of other Arab states. Use the Index to this book to find out why this was so and whether you would expect this difference to continue.

(*e*) How far does Table 18.3 support the generalization that developing nations often retained strong trading links with their former mother countries?

(*f*) Draw a new map of the states shown in Fig. 18.2 and mark on it *four* Arab unions (other than the Arab League) which have been attempted during the last thirty years.

Unit Nineteen

Confrontations Among the Lesser Powers

19.1 The Middle East

(a) The Independence of the Arab World

The Turkish Empire had been decaying for more than a century before 1918. Europeans moved in to take possession of Arab states such as Algeria and Tunisia, to build the Suez Canal and to establish control over Egypt. When the Turks were defeated in 1918, Iraq, Transjordan, Palestine and Syria were taken over by Britain and France as mandated territories. But Europeans could not hold these lands indefinitely in the face of Arab nationalism. By the end of 1946 Palestine was the last remaining mandate, but it posed a major problem.

Arabs thought that Palestine was an Arab state, destined to secure independence under an Arab government as Egypt had secured independence before the Second World War and Transjordan* immediately after it. All the Arab states faced problems. Egypt, for instance, went through a period of political upheaval in the 1950s, rejecting the monarchy of King Farouk in favour of a military regime under General Neguib, which set up a republic of which Nasser became President in 1956. The Egyptians resented the continuing presence of British troops in the Canal Zone and finally persuaded them to withdraw in 1955. A year later, Nasser nationalized the Suez Canal Company, claiming that a property in Egypt should rightly belong to the Egyptians. The Palestinian Arabs, however, found that their hopes of controlling Palestine constantly diminished rather than increased. For many years after the Second World War they had the support of other Arab states in their struggle, but the years brought them only disappointments until, by the 1980s, their prospects seemed bleak.

(b) The Palestinian Problem

Britain took over the mandate of Palestine in 1920, already faced with the problem of reconciling the interests of Arabs and Jews there. During the First World War, Arabs had been encouraged to fight against Turkey in return for a promise of eventual independence; but in 1917 Arthur Balfour had announced Britain's support for a 'national home for the Jewish people' in Palestine. For religious and historical reasons Palestine had a strong appeal to the Jews,

---

* Thenceforward known as Jordan.

whose World Zionist Organization rejected alternative suggestions. But Palestine had a religious significance for Arabs too, and they hoped to rule it independently of foreign control one day.

In the mid-1920s Jews were arriving in Palestine at the rate of 10 000 a year, encouraged by the British and the terms of the League of Nations mandate (see Fig. 19.1). This influx of Jewish settlers disturbed the Palestinian Arabs. Churchill, Britain's Colonial Secretary in 1922, tried to reassure them by declaring that 'a national home' for the Jews did not mean 'a national state'. Britain already seemed confused about her objectives and there was serious Arab rioting in 1929. A British attempt to restrict immigration led to Jewish rioting in 1933. But 1933 was the year in which Hitler came to power in Germany, and vicious Nazi persecution inevitably drove yet more Jews to seek

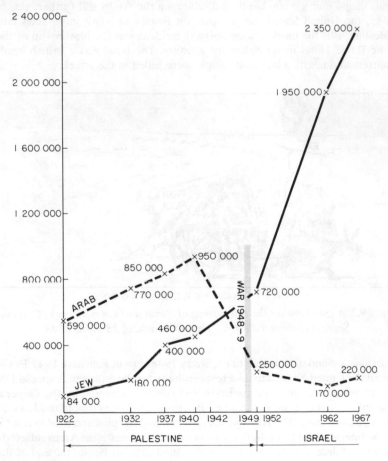

Fig. 19.1 The population of Palestine/Israel

refuge in Palestine. By 1937, Jews in Palestine numbered about 400 000; many of them were far more prosperous than the Palestinian Arabs and they bought up land, thus depriving the Arabs of what they considered to be their heritage. In 1936, the Arabs maintained a general strike for six months and in the following year, Arab guerillas took to the hills in what became known as the Arab Revolt. A pessimistic Report by the Peel Commission declared that the mandate was unworkable and recommended partition. The recommendation was rejected and warfare became more or less open, principally as an Arab rebellion against both the Jews and the British.

When the Second World War broke out, further attempts to solve the Palestinian problem were postponed. Nazi persecution and the war only increased the pressure of Jewish refugees and, meanwhile, the Zionists organized terrorist groups, among them the Stern Gang, and prepared for a confrontation. Illegal immigration continued, alarming the Arabs still further; yet, in 1945, the United States put pressure on Britain to admit more Jews into Palestine. But the most serious postwar incident was the blowing-up of the King David Hotel in Jerusalem by Zionists. The hotel was a British headquarters and nearly a hundred people were killed in the attack.

THE   UNCOVERED   WAGON

Fig. 19.2 A comment on the sad retreat of Bevin and Creech Jones (Colonial Secretary) from Palestine, News Chronicle, *28 April 1948*

Britain's mandate was due to expire in 1948, but in February 1947 Bevin asked the United Nations to take responsibility for the problem. A special UN Commission recommended partition and this was accepted by the General Assembly. Rather more than half of Palestine was to be given to the Jews, to form a Jewish state. The Arab powers condemned the plan and tried to refer it to the International Court but they were outvoted. Palestinian Arabs suffered a number of defeats at the hands of well-armed Zionists before the end of the British mandate, and then Egypt, Syria, Jordan and Iraq declared war on Israel, the newly-proclaimed Jewish state. Britain had managed to extricate herself from the Palestinian problem but, as had long been threatened, war flared up between Arabs and Jews in the Middle East.

(c) The First Confrontation

The struggle lasted from May 1948 to February 1949. The Arabs were defeated partly because their armies were badly co-ordinated, and partly because their leaders quarrelled among themselves about who should lead the Arab world. As a result Israel not only survived but actually increased her share of Palestinian territory (see Fig. 19.3). United Nations mediators brought an end to the war but not before Count Bernadotte had lost his life, murdered by Jewish terrorists in September 1948. His job as mediator was taken over by his deputy, Ralph Bunche. Almost a million Arabs fled from Israel, homeless refugees. Neither side regarded the war as having settled anything; further fighting seemed unavoidable.

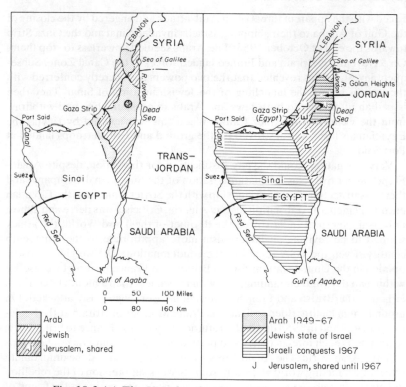

Fig. 19.3 (a) The UN plan for the partition of Palestine;
(b) Israel after the war of 1948–9 and later expansion

A UN Truce Supervisory Commission was still needed to police the frontiers. The city of Jerusalem was divided between Israel and Jordan. Israel claimed possession of the Gaza Strip, tolerating Egypt's presence there only as temporary, and frequent incidents occurred all round the borders of the Jewish state, which the Arabs refused even to recognize. In 1950, Britain, France and the USA issued a Tripartite Declaration, guaranteeing to preserve the existing frontiers and to prevent either side gaining an advantage in armaments, but such a Declaration did nothing to solve the basic problem. A permanent settlement was not possible. Neither side was interested in constructive agreements and while the refugees rotted in temporary camps, both sides looked for a suitable opportunity to obtain a settlement through military success.

In 1955, Egypt secured arms from Czechoslovakia and the Soviet Union. This gave Nasser the confidence to step up the anti-Israeli propaganda and at the same time to nationalize the Suez Canal Company in July 1956. The stage was set for a renewal of the conflict.

(d) The Second Confrontation

Faced with the apparent threat of an Arab attack and angered by the closing of the Gulf of Aqaba to their shipping, Israelis invaded Sinai and the Gaza Strip towards the end of October 1956. The Arabs seemed powerless to stop them. On 5 November, Britain and France landed forces in the Canal Zone. Subsequent investigations revealed that the two powers had secretly conferred with the Israelis before the launching of the Jewish invasion of Sinai. They then issued an ultimatum to both Jews and Arabs to cease fighting and withdraw from the vicinity of the Suez Canal. When this was ignored by Egypt, the Egyptian air force was destroyed on the ground and British troops landed at Port Said.

Very few nations could see any justification for this action, despite Anglo-French anger over Nasser's nationalization of the Suez Canal Company, and their dissatisfaction over his friendship with the Soviet Union and the Egyptian encouragement of Arab nationalists in Algeria. Criticism was fierce and almost universal. Nehru of India voiced the disquiet of the Third World; the attack seemed to be reviving an imperialism more appropriate to the nineteenth century. Even the USA joined in the condemnation. The weight of hostile opinion in the United Nations forced Britain and France to accept a ceasefire within two days of their landing, and withdrawal less than a month later. Even at home, the British and French governments were vigorously attacked. On grounds of ill health, Eden resigned as Prime Minister of Britain at the beginning of 1957 and in 1958 de Gaulle returned to power in France to bring a new realism to French foreign policy and particularly to the country's relationships with the Arab world. The Anglo-French intervention also had the unfortunate effect of distracting world attention from Russia's suppression of the rebellion in Hungary which was going on simultaneously. Russia, posing as the friend of the Arabs and threatening retribution to the aggressors at a timely moment, was able to strengthen her position in the Middle East as a consequence of the ill-judged European action.

Anglo-French aims in the attack were threefold: to preserve oil supplies, to maintain freedom of navigation through the Canal, and to humiliate Nasser. Predictably, the reverse happened. The oil taps were turned off, block ships were sunk in the Canal, while Nasser was able to pose as the aggrieved underdog. United Nations troops quickly replaced the British and French, and once again an uneasy peace was restored in the Middle East.

It was clear that the Arabs were still no match for the Israelis but the confrontation settled nothing. A permanent solution to the Palestinian problem remained as distant as ever, and the United Nations forces continued to police Sinai, the Gaza Strip and the Israeli frontiers. They also removed the obstructions and reopened the Canal. By 1959 there were new quarrels, leading again to border incidents, with raids by Arab guerillas and reprisals by Israeli forces. The situation became particularly tense on the Israeli-Syrian border where the Syrians were able to shell the Jewish settlements from the Golan Heights.

(e) The Third Confrontation

Early in 1967, Syria stepped up the shelling and clashes in the air followed. In May, Nasser moved Egyptian troops to the Sinai frontier. Hussein of Jordan hurriedly patched up his disputes with Nasser, healing one of the splits which so often undermined Arab unity. Nasser requested the removal of United Nations peace-keeping forces from Sinai and the Gaza Strip, leaving U Thant no choice but to comply. Israeli shipping was again obstructed in the Gulf of Aqaba. Rashly, the Arabs again prophesied the imminent destruction of Israel and a third confrontation appeared to be at hand.

The Israelis appointed Moshe Dayan, their hero of the 1956 war, as Minister of Defence. He believed that attack was the best form of defence and on 5 June 1967, devastating raids were made on Arab airfields. Almost at once, Israeli troops tore into the Arab forces, driving the Egyptians back across Sinai, advancing to the Jordan River against the Jordanians and routing the Syrians on the Golan Heights (see Fig. 19.3). King Hussein capitulated on the third day; Syria and Egypt struggled until the sixth.

This time, the United Nations could not persuade the Israelis to give up their conquests. The Israelis now occupied Egypt as far as the east bank of the Suez Canal, and that part of Syria which included the Golan Heights. They intended to hold these territories until the Arabs accepted their permanent title to Palestine. The United Nations sent a new mission, this time to police the Suez Canal, but the Canal itself remained closed. Blocked by the debris of the Six-Day War, it had also become an uneasy frontier, but incidents continued on most fronts. The United Nations had to arrange a new ceasefire in 1970, and now Gunnar Jarring tried to find the basis for a settlement of the problem. But all parties to the dispute remained as adamant as ever (with the possible exception of Jordan), and even the death of Nasser, long the outstanding leader of the Arab world, made little difference to the entrenched attitudes. The major powers could do nothing to bring about a permanent solution.

(f) The Fourth Confrontation

Searching desperately for some way to injure Israel, Arab guerillas began to hi-jack aircraft. This gave them publicity but nothing more. In 1970, the Popular Front for the Liberation of Palestine hi-jacked four aircraft, including a British VC 10, taking them to Jordan where they were blown up. The world was horrified by this wanton destruction of property but showed little concern for the dispossessed Palestinian Arabs. Other outrages followed: in 1972, a suicide squad gunned down a hundred people at Lydda Airport, Tel Aviv, to prove the guerillas' absolute determination to continue their struggle. A few months later, the Black September group (a section of the Liberation movement) seized hostages among Israeli athletes at the Olympic Games in Munich. An ill-timed gun battle with the West German police resulted in the deaths of the hostages and five of the eight guerillas.

These desperate actions aimed to draw attention to the Palestinians'

Fig. 19.4 'Young man! I am warning you.' A shrill protest from Douglas-Home, Britain's Foreign Secretary, as Moshe Dayan retaliates against the Arabs. Brezhnev (centre) turns away, perhaps in boredom. Nixon (next to the coach) shows ineffectual alarm. Brandt and Pompidou (extreme left). The Guardian, *15 September 1972*

dilemma, but they were condemned almost universally. Nothing seemed to bring the problem of Palestine nearer to a solution, and the world in general seemed only to wish that the problem would somehow go away. The Israelis now determined to hit back at the terrorists. Israeli jets struck at refugee camps and suspected guerilla bases, causing casualties far in excess of those at Munich. The intention was to discourage Arab governments from giving support and shelter to the Palestinians.

Meanwhile, in Jordan, Hussein had turned on the Palestinian guerillas, regarding Al Fatah, the Palestinian Liberation Organization, as a threat to his own authority and to his country's security. As time passed, Israel grew even stronger and the future of the Palestinian refugees became bleaker. Egypt showed little inclination to abandon their cause, however, in spite of new leadership after Nasser's death. But a rift developed between President Sadat and Egypt's Soviet supporters. Sadat sent home the Russian military personnel in 1972, pleasing Gadafy of Libya, who was fiercely anti-Soviet, but less popular with Syria, the other member of the Federation of Arab Republics (see Section 18.3(c)). Yet again there was dissension in the Arab world. The Arabs could still unite against Israel, however. In October 1973, soon after the meeting of Third-World states in Algiers, Egyptian and Syrian forces started the fourth Arab-Israeli War, attacking on the day that was holy to the Jews for the observance of Yom Kippur.

The Yom Kippur War produced only momentary Arab successes. Within a fortnight, the Israelis were advancing further into both Egypt and Syria. The Arabs were armed mostly with Soviet weapons, the Israelis with American, but the superpowers had no wish for the conflict to continue and possibly undermine their movement towards detente. A truce was arranged less than three weeks after the fighting began and UN forces again set about establishing demilitarized zones to keep the enemies apart. Western backing for Israel had nevertheless deeply angered the Arabs, and consequences of the Yom Kippur War were the withholding of oil supplies from Western states singled out for disapproval, and steep increases in the price of oil. Here was a powerful new weapon in Arab hands: its effects on national economies were soon felt (see Section 18.1(b)).

(g) Peace Initiatives and Further Confusion

Problems over oil supplies provided a strong incentive for the West to look again at the Arab-Israeli problem. Henry Kissinger, Nixon's Secretary of State, began a vigorous effort to reconcile Arabs and Israelis, busily practising his shuttle-diplomacy (see Glossary). It was therefore possible in 1975 to reach agreement at Geneva on new lines of demarcation between Egyptians and Israelis in the area of the Suez Canal, with the USA offering American civilians to monitor an early-warning system in Sinai to calm fears on both sides. In the same year, normal traffic again flowed through the Canal when wartime debris had been cleared. It took rather longer to bring about disengagement in the

Golan Heights, but there too demarcation was eventually arranged. But almost nothing had been done to resolve the underlying problems and the peace was again little more than a truce.

North of Israel there was little peace at all in the Lebanon. The Palestinian Liberation Organization (PLO) made southern Lebanon its main base after the PLO's expulsion from Jordan in 1970. This automatically made the area a target for Israeli counter-attacks, often ferocious in 1974 and 1975. The Lebanon was in any case unstable and was reduced to civil war in 1975. A tangled conflict between Palestinians and Christians became a battle for control between the left and a Christian (Falangist) right, and a religious war between Moslems and Christians. Syria intervened in 1976 and eventually Arab League forces arrived to try to restore peace. Truces seldom lasted long, however, and the Lebanese economy was seriously disrupted. The Syrians came into conflict with Christian militias and were sometimes regarded as allies of the Moslems as well as of the PLO. The Israelis therefore felt entitled to intervene, from time to time making raids to protect the Christians, as well as continuing to strike at the PLO camps. Another UN force was raised as a result of such upheaval, only to become enmeshed in the early 1980s in a confused but violent struggle in southern Lebanon which was both an offshoot of the Arab-Israeli conflict and a Lebanese civil war. There were spasmodic Israeli-Syrian clashes and Israeli aircraft made strikes far to the north of the turbulent border areas. Several times the Lebanese troubles threatened to produce yet another Syrian-Israeli war.

Meanwhile there was a dramatic shift in Egyptian policy. The Soviet-Egyptian friendship had ended in mutual recriminations and President Sadat had turned to the West. Nixon visited the Middle East and Sadat himself visited the USA in 1975. Two years later Sadat launched a bold new initiative, visiting Jerusalem in November 1977 to talk peace with the Israelis, a lonely figure quickly reviled by many of his Arab neighbours. To Gadafy and President Assad of Syria it was a sort of treachery even to admit the existence of an Israeli government. There had already been skirmishing on the Libyan-Egyptian border, but it was not only Arab disfavour which Sadat risked. Hardline Israelis (the Hawks, see Fig. 19.5) were unlikely to welcome his visit, and the PLO was deeply suspicious of a sell-out. Menachem Begin, the Israeli Prime Minister who came to power in 1977 when the right-wing Likud ousted the Labour Party, himself had the reputation of being an ardent Zionist who in the past had been a 'Hawk'. Begin nevertheless gave Sadat a cautious welcome.

Begin returned Sadat's visit and was welcomed in Cairo. While the two men bargained, both came under criticism from those who feared compromise. In 1978 the initiative seemed to be running out of steam, until President Carter of the USA took a hand. He invited Sadat and Begin to Camp David, and the framework of an Egyptian-Israeli peace treaty was mapped out. In spite of widespread Arab disapproval, Sadat offered full recognition to Israel, the first by any Arab state. In return, the Israelis were to evacuate Sinai, part of their conquests in 1967. That much Sadat and Begin were likely to be able to deliver.

Fig. 19.5 November 1977, a dramatic new initiative by President Sadat of Egypt with an offer of peace in the Arab-Israeli conflict that seemed to many to be a modern miracle. The Guardian

But Sadat felt unable totally to abandon the cause of the Palestinians, and that meant negotiating a homeland for them – in the Gaza Strip and on the West Bank of the Jordan (see Fig. 19.3(*a*)). For the PLO that was hardly enough. For many Israelis it was far too much. Begin and Dayan, his Foreign Minister, gave ground only slowly though, with Carter keeping up the pressure, the Treaty was signed in March 1979. A remarkable diplomatic turnabout had thus been achieved and, for their part in it, Sadat and Begin were awarded the Nobel Peace Prize in 1978.

There were doubts when the Treaty was signed about the extent to which the Israelis would in practice withdraw from 'Arab' lands. They went on planting new Jewish settlements on the West Bank, embarrassing Carter as well as Sadat. On the other hand, a start was made on evacuating Sinai and this was eventually returned to Egypt on schedule in April 1982. By then, holding on to a wafer-thin majority in the Israeli parliament, Begin alone remained of the original peace-makers. Carter had lost office. Dayan, frustrated by Israeli hardliners who resisted every concession to the Arabs, had resigned, and died in October 1981. Dayan's death was only a few days after that of President Sadat, assassinated at a review of Egypt's armed forces. Sadat had been killed, perhaps by Moslem fundamentalists, in protest against his strong links with the West and 'the plastic invasion' of Egypt by Western values. Sadat had given shelter to the Shah of Iran during the final weeks of the Shah's life. He had gloried in his commitment to the West while at the same time turning to authoritarian methods at home. Nor had he wavered in his pursuit of agreements with Israel despite his awareness that many Arabs continued to feel a burning sense of injustice, convinced that the West had created Israel to atone for Europe's crimes against the Jews, but creating it, not at the West's own expense, but at that of the Palestinians. Every new outrage added fuel to the flames and, for many of those involved in the struggle, Sadat's quiet reasonableness had seemed quite unreasonably detached.

Sadat was succeeded by Egypt's Vice-President, Hosni Mubarak, who went on with the peace initiative. But Begin seemed now to be less restrained, in failing health, and seemingly convinced of the urgency of his mission to make Israel more secure. In December 1981, the Israelis declared that the Golan Heights would not be returned to Syria but were now the property of Israel. In 1982, ferocious new strikes were launched against PLO bases in the Lebanon. Paying little heed to UN peace-keeping forces, Israeli troops drove northwards, eventually trapping many members of the PLO in the western half of the city of Beirut. Vast amounts of damage were done to the city and great suffering brought to much of its population before international pressures brought about a truce and the evacuation of the Palestinian guerillas. Though at some cost to its reputation for civilized behaviour, Begin's government had won a major victory: the PLO forces were now dispersed throughout the Arab world and less able, at least in the short term, to launch further anti-Israeli raids. But Middle-Eastern ill-will was again inflamed, and the unhappy Lebanon was again brought to the brink of civil war between Syrian-backed Moslems and Israeli-backed Christians, a bitter disunity which hampered the urgent work of reconstruction in a land where much had been devastated. In spite of the Egyptian-Israeli Treaty, therefore, Arab-Israeli problems remained – the bitter product of a conflict between underprivileged peoples in which emotions were readily fired by religion and race.

19.2　India and Pakistan: the Indian Sub-continent

(a) The Foreign Policies of India and Pakistan

The division of the Indian sub-continent was accomplished in haste (see Section 16.6(a)). It was unavoidable that there were points of detail still to be settled after the partition. The division of the waters of the Indus has already been mentioned (see Section 18.2(b)). Another point concerned the sum of £44 million which Pakistan claimed from India as part of the independence settlement. Gandhi fasted and forced the Indian leaders to settle the debt but, shortly afterwards, he was killed and, although India and Pakistan had become fellow-members of the Commonwealth, there was now no one who could develop that friendship between them which had been one of the Mahatma's last desires.

Under Nehru, India was inclined to follow a neutral foreign policy, steering clear of commitment either to the West or to the communist powers. Pakistan joined SEATO and CENTO and, until well into the 1960s, leaned to the non-communist world. Pakistan would have liked to create a league of Moslem states and had strong sympathies with her co-religionists which extended to a refusal to recognize Israel. Nehru, on the other hand, carried into foreign policy something of the moral teachings of Gandhi, even when this involved strong criticism of India's friends. He angered the British by condemning their attack on Egypt in 1956, for he detested all forms of colonialism as much as he detested racialism and he never regarded the Commonwealth as anything but a partnership in which all members should speak as equals. At the same time, he sought to be constructive. He helped to mediate in the Korean War and in Vietnam in 1954, and he put Indian troops at the service of UNO to help to bring peace to Palestine, Cyprus and the Congo. He warmly supported the Afro-Asian Conference held at Bandung in 1955, but less progress was made than Nehru would have wished towards establishing a united Third World, non-aligned and aloof from the great powers' Cold War.

In 1961, Nehru threw the Portuguese out of Goa, no longer willing to tolerate a European colony on Indian soil. Portugal refused to recognize the legality of his action but it was a comparatively trivial matter which did little to blacken Nehru's reputation as a statesman. A border dispute with China leading to a minor war in 1962 (see Section 15.3(e)) brought India some sympathy, especially from Britain and the USA, and tarnished Indo-Chinese relations which had previously been cordial. But India was never a belligerent state and her involvement in wars, especially with Pakistan, seemed oddly out of keeping with her role in international affairs since independence.

Yet Pakistan long regarded India as her principal enemy. Eventually the rivalry of India and Pakistan distorted the foreign policies of both. The Indo-Chinese border clashes helped Pakistan to see the possibilities of friendship with China, in spite of her earlier commitments to the West, and by the end of the 1960s, India was beginning to lean towards the USSR who showed more understanding of her problems, such as the emergence of Bangladesh, than did the USA. Pakistan and India thus began to line up on different sides in the Sino-Soviet dispute. Neither wished to get deeply involved in that dispute nor in the Cold War, and their own rivalry continued to seem more important. Only when the Soviet Union invaded Afghanistan in 1979 did Pakistan revive her earlier enthusiasm for Western protection and, once again, India then adopted a somewhat different stance, less critical of the Russians than the West would have wished. In the meantime, Indo-Pakistani antagonism centred for many years after 1947 on the disputed state of Kashmir.

(b) Kashmir

In theory at least, the princes of the Indian sub-continent were free, after independence, to join either India or Pakistan. Sir Hari Singh, the Maharajah of Kashmir, had a freer choice than many of them for his state bordered both

India and West Pakistan (see Fig. 20.5). Being Hindu, the Maharajah wished to join India but some 80 per cent of his people were Moslems whom tribesmen from Pakistan undertook to rescue. The disturbances brought troops from both Pakistan and India and, at the beginning of 1948, Nehru referred the dispute to the United Nations. A United Nations Commission arranged a ceasefire and prepared to settle the future of Kashmir through a plebiscite but at that point deadlock set in.

Kashmir had only about 800 000 Hindus in a population of over 4 million. There could be little doubt that the Hindus would be outvoted heavily. India, therefore, obstructed the plebiscite, frustrating even the attempts of Gunnar Jarring to mediate. Members of the Commonwealth were equally unsuccessful in resolving the deadlock and direct talks between India and Pakistan made no progress. Kashmir remained divided along the line where the ceasefire had been agreed.

Nehru died in 1964. Incidents multiplied in Kashmir until Pakistani forces crossed the ceasefire line and a brief war erupted in 1965 which the United Nations again quickly quenched. This time, the Soviet Union tried to mediate, calling Shastri (Nehru's successor) and Ayub Khan, the President of Pakistan, to a meeting with Kosygin in Tashkent. They met in January 1966, agreeing to withdraw their forces to the earlier line of division and to renounce force in the future settlement of the Kashmiri problem. Within hours of signing the agreement, Shastri was dead from a heart attack, but the agreement was honoured. Kashmir returned to its disruptive and economically damaging 'temporary' division, and the fundamental problem remained unsolved, as stubborn as that of Palestine.

Fig. 19.6 Pakistani stamp showing the areas disputed with India, 1960

(c) Bangladesh

The sub-divisions within the Indian sub-continent which seemed to offer a solution to the problems of 1947 turned out, in time, only to have created new problems. Pakistan always suffered from existing in two, widely-spaced parts, West Pakistan and the poorer East Pakistan. In the making of East Pakistan, however, the province of Bengal was divided so that Bengalis were to be found both on the Indian and East Pakistani sides of the frontier. This division took on a new importance when, in 1970, the often unstable political situation in Pakistan led to an open breach between the Western and Eastern parts of the state (see Section 20.5(c)). With a desperation bordering on the insane, President Yahya Khan, who had replaced Ayub in 1969, tried to preserve the unity of the nation by savagely suppressing the separatism of the East. Fleeing in terror from the armies of West Pakistan, millions of refugees poured into India to seek shelter among their fellow-Bengalis. In East Pakistan the butchery was almost unbridled. Bengalis committed atrocities against Punjabis from the West but they themselves suffered the most bloody vindictiveness.

The economic and social problems created by the stream of refugees threatened to overwhelm the Indian administration. The world was full of pious sympathy but the pleas of Mrs Gandhi, who had followed Shastri as Prime Minister of India, brought only a limited response. In any case, Indians and especially Bengalis were enraged by the ill-treatment of the East Pakistanis and, as the killing went on and the flood of refugees continued, Mrs Gandhi felt obliged to intervene. In December 1971, Indian forces invaded East Pakistan. Their objectives were clear-cut and they moved with speed and efficiency. The West Pakistani forces were no match for them. But India was not fighting a war of aggression. Mrs Gandhi's aims were to liberate East Pakistan from the forces of Yahya Khan, to restore law and order and facilitate the refugees' return to their shattered homes. The aims were accomplished and, although there were tremors in Kashmir and some disturbances on the Indian frontier with West Pakistan, fighting ceased when East Pakistan was free.

India's intervention was not universally popular. Nixon committed the USA to particularly fierce criticism, but China limited her encouragement of West Pakistan to little more than sympathy and the Soviet Union gave diplomatic support to Mrs Gandhi. There was now no hope that Pakistan could survive as a united nation and a separate government was established in East Pakistan, a new state known henceforth as Bangladesh (see Fig. 20.5). There were enormous problems of reconstruction and, for a time, violence continued to erupt between the Bengalis and a minority group of Biharis in Bangladesh, who were alleged to have collaborated with the West Pakistanis. West Pakistan, in addition to economic and political difficulties, had to overcome the shock of defeat, especially defeat by India, Pakistan's traditional enemy.

(d) The Simla Conference

There was, however, room for hope that a new harmony in the Indian subcontinent could eventually be built from the conflict. It could be argued that the action of the Indian army had cut short the killing. Mrs Gandhi now showed no great desire to exploit India's victory and in July 1972, Pakistan and India appeared to reach a promising agreement in conference at Simla, looking forward to the complete withdrawal of troops from occupied territory, the return of about 90 000 Pakistani prisoners-of-war, the acceptance of the *status quo* in Kashmir and the abandonment of the propaganda on both sides which had helped prolong hostility since 1947. A further difficulty developed, however, when President Bhutto of Pakistan refused to recognize Bangladesh. Bangladesh was admitted to the Commonwealth and Pakistan consequently resigned from that association in 1972.

The division of Kashmir, like that of Germany, had now begun to seem permanent. The Indians had invested in the economic development of their part of the state and seemed unlikely ever to surrender it. In the later 1970s, each of the three countries – India, Pakistan and Bangladesh – had in any case other problems to contend with and their rivalries were submerged in political upheavals. Pakistan and Bangladesh succumbed to military dictatorships (see Section 20.5(*d*)). In Pakistan, Bhutto was not only deposed but hanged. In India Mrs Gandhi was driven from office in 1977, ending the long years of rule by the Congress Party, though she soon made a spectacular comeback (see Section 22.2(*d*)).

19.3   The Horn of Africa

Turbulence in Africa was by no means uncommon in the wake of the withdrawal of the Europeans, and it was undoubtedly made worse by the availability of arms, which the great powers were ever ready to sell, and by the intrigues of foreign powers in African affairs. This was nowhere more clear than in the Horn of Africa where conflicts grew into serious warfare during 1977. For some time, the Soviet Union had cultivated the friendship of Somalia, strategically placed at the entrance to the Red Sea and near to the Middle-East oilfields about which the West was sensitive. But the Russians transferred their interest to Ethiopia when a coup in that country deposed Haile Selassie in 1974 (see Fig. 16.2). The fall of Haile Selassie opened the way for modernization and radical change after years of authoritarian rule and economic stagnation. The socialist-inclined Colonel Mengistu came to power in 1977 and Soviet advisers were welcomed. So too were Cubans.

The changes in Ethiopia encouraged those who wanted further changes in the Horn of Africa. Secessionist forces sought to liberate from the Ethiopian government the Ogaden Province, an area in the south of the country bordering Somalia. The latter backed the rebels and invaded, at the same time confirming the breach between Somalia and the Soviet Union. The Ogaden war was fought fiercely. Both sides made extensive use of Russian weapons, but the Somalis could not hope to prevail against the tanks and aircraft with which Russians and Cubans assisted Ethiopia and they had little option but to sue for peace in 1978. Ethiopia faced another struggle, however, against Eritreans who resented government from Addis Ababa. A former Italian colony, Eritrea had been linked with Ethiopia in 1952 by the recommendation of the UN General Assembly. At first, Eritrea had been allowed self-government but that had been revoked by Haile Selassie in favour of direct Ethiopian rule. Like the secessionists in the Ogaden, Eritreans now clamoured for independence. But they too could not prevail against Soviet- and Cuban-backed government forces.

Successful Ethiopian resistance did not solve the problems and unrest continued to smoulder into the 1980s both in the Ogaden and in Eritrea. Skirmishing went on, making worse the famine which followed drought in the area of the Ogaden at the end of the 1970s. Relief agencies became involved in trying to alleviate a disaster of considerable proportions. The USA meanwhile, having lost influence to the Russians in Addis Ababa, began cautiously to look for some counter-balancing influence in Mogadishu, the capital of Somalia. Here again threads were intertwined, adding to the complications of the modern world. The West resented Soviet involvement in Ethiopia, noting that the USSR also had influence in the Yemen at the other side of the mouth to the Red Sea and suspecting hostile designs against the West's supplies of oil (see Fig. 18.2). Africans were by no means free to settle their own problems, either in Eritrea or the Ogaden, but grave internal difficulties afflicted Somalia in 1981 and for the moment the Ogaden dispute died down.

19.4 Iran and Iraq

Change in Iran also unleashed a new Iraqi-Iranian war. The Moslem and anti-Western uprising which overthrew the Shah led to the establishment of an Islamic Republic and confrontation with the USA (see Section 13.2(*h*)). Moslem militancy had for some time caused unrest in states where power and influence seemed to rest mainly with westernized middle classes, and where governments had eroded the influence of the Islamic authorities, as Kemal had done in Turkey in the inter-war years. Nasser and Sadat in Egypt and Ayub Khan in Pakistan had all run into problems with religious leaders critical of their secular government, but Iran was the first state fully to feel the effects of resurgent Islam. With the fall of the Shah in 1979, Iranian nationalism and Moslem intolerance produced a new ferment in the Middle East. Western economic interests in Iran were attacked vigorously, and some observers suggested that here were the beginnings of the North–South confrontation which might develop from great differences of wealth (see Section 18.2). Strict new laws in Iran similarly attacked the lax moral codes alleged to have been imported from the developed world. Under the guidance of the Ayatollah Khomeini, Iran embarked on a revolutionary path to effect a social transformation.

The upheaval caused various tremors. Within Iran the traditional unrest of minority peoples increased. The powerful army with which the Shah had been able to impose his authority was weakened, and the new government found it difficult to suppress the Kurds, who launched guerilla attacks in favour of an independent Kurdistan in the north-west of Iran. The vast majority of Iranians were Moslem but only about half of the country's population was of a common Persian stock. The Kurds numbered about four million in a total population of some thirty-five million. Some thirteen million others were Azerbaijani Turks. There were fears that the new Republic would slide deeper into conflicts between the government and ethnic minorities. Iran's neighbours, including the Soviet Union, also feared that the problems might spread, either unsettling minorities or inspiring Moslem assaults on secular government. The Soviet occupation of Moslem Afghanistan seemed to result at least partly from such fears. The upheaval in Iran also added to uncertainties about oil supplies since Iran was one of the major oil producers.

War broke out in 1980 between Iran and another Moslem and oil-producing neighbour, Iraq. Iraq had a left-wing Arab government which distrusted Moslem militancy and had little sympathy with Iranians. The ferment in Iran unsettled minorities in Iraq, especially the Kurds. Both Iran and Iraq were fellow-members of OPEC but they had little else in common and the Iraqi-Iranian border effectively marked the eastern boundary of the Arab world (see Fig. 18.2). Disputes about the border, and general bickering, led to the Iraqi-Iranian War which lasted longer than many had expected, dragging on into 1983. Each side attacked the other's oil installations and oil shipments from the northern end of the Persian Gulf, causing further disruption to fuel supplies. During 1981 the Israelis also took the opportunity to bomb a nuclear reactor in Iraq, allegedly to delay the Arab manufacture of an atomic bomb. Iraq had certainly been a confirmed enemy of the Israelis and a supporter of the Syrians. Indeed at the end of the 1970s Iraq and Syria were considering yet another Arab union (see Section 18.3(c)). Now, while Iraq fought Iran, Syria was deeply involved in conflicts in the Lebanon, and only very limited progress was made towards repairing relations with Egypt after the assassination of Sadat. The upheaval in Iran, producing a strict Moslem morality which Gadafy of Libya already encouraged, simply added to the many stresses which existed in the Middle East.

19.5   Argentina and Britain

Section 16.6 showed how most of Britain's overseas possessions were decolonized after the Second World War. Among the colonies Britain retained at the beginning of the 1980s were the Falkland Islands, with a population of fewer than 2 000 people. These inhabitants were descended from British settlers, Britain having occupied the islands in 1832, at that time expelling an Argentine garrison and repudiating Spanish claims there. In 1982, after 150 years of British rule, the Argentines invaded and declared the Falklands (the Malvinas, their Spanish name) under Argentine sovereignty. Discussions had long been going on about the future of the Islands which were some 8 000 miles away from Britain but only about 300 miles from the coast of Argentina. The main problem had been that, though Britain had no strong desire to cling to possession, the Falkland islanders had no wish to exchange their British way of life for Argentine citizenship. Given the facts of geography, the defence of the Falklands by Britain was likely to be difficult and expensive, but, even so, that defence seemed to have been neglected after 1979 and there was almost nothing to prevent the Argentine takeover.

Britain's response was furious. Armed with condemnation of the Argentines by the UN Security Council, the Thatcher government despatched a huge task force to the South Atlantic (see Section 13.3(i)). It was quickly asserted that the liberation of the Falklands was necessary not only to defend the interests of the inhabitants, but to uphold the rule of law, to deter aggression and to preserve democracy. The rule of Argentina was in the hands of a military junta which was denounced as a fascist dictatorship, though the British and others in the West had until recently eagerly sold armaments to this same government and the USSR had bought Argentine grain. Critics questioned the likely costs of the British operation in terms of lives and money, and some uneasy memories stirred of Britain's part in the Suez War of 1956. The financial costs of the task force seemed sure far to exceed what would have been needed to resettle the Falkland Islanders in comfort elsewhere under British government. But the expedition stirred deep emotions among the British people, and much of the country was swept by a wave of patriotism. When victory was achieved and the Falklands were regained, there was self-congratulation too.

Though war had not formally been declared, the conflict cost the lives of almost 1 800 Argentines and 255 British. Attempts to mediate by the US Secretary of State and Perez de Cuellar, the UN Secretary-General, had not succeeded. The early international support for Britain had nevertheless begun to evaporate. The Spanish-speaking world generally upheld the Argentine cause. In Europe, Britain had support for economic sanctions against Argentina from most of the members of the EEC. The USA, while expressing considerable sympathy with Britain, was nevertheless torn between its American and European alliances. The suspicion lingered, however, that perhaps what was really at stake was rather old-fashioned prestige, both of countries and governments. When Britain had recovered possession of the Falklands, their future still remained to be settled by the renewal of negotiations. The islands were far from Britain and, though for the moment their population was heavily outnumbered by an armed British garrison, discouraging any further Argentine attack, the initial problem remained.

Further Reading

Dodd, C.H.: *Israel and the Arab World*. Routledge & Kegan Paul (London, 1970).
Jamieson, A.: *Leaders of the Twentieth Century*. Bell (London, 1970) – Nasser.
Lloyd, M.: *The Middle East*. Harrap (London, 1983).
Watson, J.B.: *Empire to Commonwealth, 1919 to 1970*. Dent (London, 1971).

Documentary

Breach, R.W.: *Documents and Descriptions, the World since 1914*. Oxford University Press (London, 1966) Sections 35, 37, 40.
Browne, H.: *Suez and Sinai*. Longman (Harlow, 1971).

Fraser, T.G.: *The Middle East 1914–1979*. Arnold (London, 1980).
Janowsky, O.I.: *Foundations of Israel*. Anvil (London, 1960).

Exercises

1. What information can you gather about the history of Palestine/Israel from Figs. 19.1 and 19.3?

2. How would (*a*) an Arab and (*b*) a Zionist have argued in 1948 that his people were entitled to the possession of Palestine?

3. How does Fig. 18.2 (page 356) suggest that Israel might find it difficult to survive? How do you account for Israel's ability to survive?

4. Describe the policies towards Israel of (*a*) Nasser and (*b*) Sadat. How does a comparison of these policies explain the differing attitudes towards these leaders of Arab states other than Egypt?

5. Show what problems still existed at the end of the 1970s concerning (*a*) Israel and her Arab neighbours, and (*b*) Kashmir.

6. What part has been played by UNO in the affairs of the Middle East and those of Kashmir? Why has it proved difficult to find a lasting solution to any of the problems involved?

7. Summarize the policies of *each* of the superpowers towards the events described in each of Sections 19.1, 19.2, 19.3 and 19.4.

8. What events have occurred since this book was written which make it possible to add a further paragraph to *each* of the Sections listed in Question 7?

9. Using this Unit and Section 22.2 make a list of problems India has found difficult to solve since independence. Explain the difficulties in any *three* of these problems.

10. Summarize the *international* problems which existed at the beginning of the 1980s concerning the states named on the map at Fig. 18.2, page 356. Explain why any *one* of these problems should be of concern to Europeans.

11. Explain to what events *each* of the cartoons in this Unit (Figs. 19.2, 19.4 and 19.5) refers. Which of these cartoons do you consider made the most forceful comment on contemporary affairs? Explain the reasons for your selection.

12. Bearing in mind the subject matter of this Unit and the author's criteria for selecting what is included in it, suggest another 'Confrontation among the Lesser Powers' since 1945 which might also have been included. Write an account of this additional confrontation.

Civil Wars – the Problem of Minorities

20.1 Minorities

The essence of the nation state, so much admired by the peace-makers of 1919–20, was that its inhabitants should think of themselves as one people: they were likely to share a common language, culture and sense of nationality. Yet, even in Europe, the nation state was usually something of a myth. After 1945, national boundaries were quite closely related to what Europeans wanted but, nevertheless, most states were held together by a mutual tolerance between majorities and minorities. The latter might differ from the majority of their fellow-countrymen by reason of religion, language, culture or even race, and such differences sometimes caused stresses. Sensible governments sought to reduce such stresses by even-handed administration and by paying attention to minority grievances, and very few European countries faced the imminent threat of civil war. The Basques campaigned furiously against government from Madrid, especially when the tight control of Franco was removed. Corsican nationalists demanded independence from France. Croatians were restless in Jugoslavia, and extremists among minorities in many countries added to the terrorism and violence which grew in the 1960s and 1970s. But most European minorities seemed reasonably content with the continent's national divisions. Belgium, which on the whole successfully accommodated the divisions among the country's people, was more typical of Europe than were Northern Ireland and Cyprus where violent conflicts raged.

There was no room for complacency, however. Most politicians realized the importance of trying to ensure that minorities of whatever sort should not be treated as second-class citizens, since discrimination and adversity could inflame smouldering discontents. In Britain, Scots and Welsh produced Nationalist Parties, complaining of too much ascendancy over the country's affairs by the English and for a time, in the 1970s, the question of constitutional change was debated with some urgency. By that time there was also growing anxiety in Britain about the difficulties faced in British society by ethnic minorities from the Commonwealth and elsewhere (see Section 21.4). The emotional questions of colour and of race relations often added new dimensions to the problem of balancing the interests of minorities and majorities. In Europe and most of the developed world, national leaders sought to solve all such problems by conciliation. Years of stability helped to provide a framework in which adjustments could be made with a minimum of violent confrontation, and prosperity also helped, when all could at least hope to share in it. Reforms were therefore possible in order to safeguard cultures, educational opportunities, civil rights and even languages, though not all minorities were wholly satisfied with the results, and in some cases stubborn problems persisted. Canada wrestled with the discontent of the country's French-speaking regions and in Canada, the USA, Australia and New Zealand there was lingering concern about the rights of the small minorities of indigenous peoples such as Eskimos, Amerindians, Aborigines and Maoris. Both the USA and USSR were vast countries which included many minorities, both national and religious, but even such a tiny country as Mauritius also had ethnic diversities. Everywhere there was need for vigilance and for fostering mutual respect, and hardly any countries after 1945 continued to believe in the theories of racial purity and superiority which Hitler had upheld in *Mein Kampf*. Those that did, as the ruling parties in South Africa seemed to do, attracted universal scorn (see Section 21.2). They also invited internal disorders.

It was easier for long-established nations than for new nations to cope with stresses which developed from conflicting interests between majorities and minorities. From time to time, however, race riots in US cities showed that, even in the USA, tranquillity had not yet been achieved. Among the emerging nations there were even graver problems. National boundaries were often artificial, little more than the legacy of European rule, especially in Africa. They had originally been drawn by the colonizing powers, for their own convenience, and with little regard for local considerations such as African tribal divisions. Newly independent states like the Congo and Nigeria therefore inherited tribal rivalries difficult to contain, and in such circumstances the demand of minorities was often for *secession*, breaking away in order to set up separate states. This Unit examines how such demands led to civil war in both the *Congo* and *Nigeria*. Section 20.5 examines a similar development in the Indian sub-continent where *Bangladesh*, formerly East Pakistan, broke away from West Pakistan, violently renouncing a Pakistani government which was alleged constantly to have favoured the West at the expense of the East. In *Cyprus* (see Section 20.4), civil war resulted from fierce national and religious rivalry between Greek Cypriots and Turkish Cypriots, the latter again alleging discrimination and injustice. In *Northern Ireland* (see Section 20.6) the Catholic minority erupted in protest against the allegedly unfair rule of the Protestants, while the Protestants complained furiously of Catholic intrigue to make Northern Ireland part of the Republic of Ireland in which Protestants would then be in the minority.

Extensive bloodshed followed in all of these countries, a warning of what could occur when minorities were driven to despair. Even so there were many other similar conflicts in addition to those described in this Unit. In the early 1970s, fierce conflict occurred in Burundi between the Hutu and the Tutsi, many Hutu being massacred. Civil war raged in the Sudan until about 1972. Amin's vicious rule in Uganda unleashed tribal killing. In the late 1970s there was conflict in parts of what had been the French Saharan Empire, while Section 19.3 has already referred to Eritrean and Somali separatism and

Section 19.4, outside Africa, to Kurdish wars for secession in Iran and Iraq. Many Third-World countries faced such secessionist and tribal problems, adding to their already formidable difficulties in building new nations. What was remarkable was not that some plunged into civil war. Through good sense and able leadership many avoided such conflict or, where it occurred – in Nigeria for example – quickly made remarkable progress towards healing the wounds when the fighting ended. Scores of new nations gradually took shape in the wake of the colonial empires, each of them distinctive, but all engaged in the common task of nation-building. Each was likely to have its own special difficulties. India, for example, embarked on independence with no common language except English, the language of the elites but not of the common people, so that Hindi had gradually to be spread throughout the whole country. But, in some form or other, almost all had to tackle the problem of reconciling within the national boundaries the interests of majorities and minorities.

20.2 The Congo

The granting of independence to the Belgian Congo in 1960 (see Section 16.4) instantly led to civil war. The Congo contained a population of about fifteen million, divided into some 150 tribes: there seemed to be every likelihood of fragmentation. Areas such as Katanga, which were rich in copper and other minerals, were unwilling to share their wealth with the poorer parts of the country. The separatism of Katanga was encouraged by the Belgians, especially the *Union Minière*, who viewed with dismay the first Congolese government of Patrice Lumumba whose National Movement inclined to socialism.

Lumumba was of the Batatele tribe and other tribes, such as the Baluba of Kasai Province, had little enthusiasm for his rule. In July 1960, within two weeks of the declaration of independence, there was a mutiny in the Congolese army and Katanga and Kasai broke away (see Fig. 20.2). Belgium sent troops to protect Europeans and Belgian mining interests, and Lumumba appealed to the United Nations. The Security Council did not wish the Congo to be broken up, for many other African states might follow suit. An emergency force was sent, but the UN troops had no authority to intervene in internal affairs. Their aim was simply to try to stop the killing while officials tried to mediate. There was already much foreign meddling, however, and Lumumba asked for Soviet help against the Western-backed Katangese. He was overthrown in a military coup, fell into Katangese hands, and was murdered early in 1961.

The Congo now had various rival leaders: Kasavubu and Colonel Mobutu in Leopoldville, Tshombe in Katanga and Kalonji in South Kasai. Dag Hammarskjöld, the UN Secretary-General, was killed in an aeroplane crash in September 1961 while trying to bring them together. U Thant, his successor, continued the effort, but things came to a head when, having been attacked by Katangese troops, UN forces defeated Tshombe's forces. Tshombe fled and, at last, progress was made towards working out an acceptable system of govern ment for a reunited state. UN troops were withdrawn during 1963 but

Fig. 20.1 United Nations peace-keeping in the Congo. The aim of the UN forces was to keep the peace but they were themselves dragged into conflict with the Katangese

considerable confusion continued. In July 1964, Tshombe changed sides and accepted Kasavubu's invitation to become Prime Minister of the whole of the Congo. He remained in power for little more than a year, faced with numerous rebellions against which he had assistance from Belgium, the USA and white mercenaries. The rebels lost ground but crops were destroyed in the fighting and there was a shortage of food. Tshombe was not popular in the rest of Africa where he appeared to be the tool of Western capitalists, and he was dismissed in October 1965. Having led the military coup against Lumumba, Mobutu now led another which removed Kasavubu. Tshombe went into exile, was condemned to death in his absence and, in 1967, imprisoned in Algeria after his aircraft had been hi-jacked. He died two years later.

The government of the Congo was again reorganized under Mobutu. Katangese resistance was once again put down and, in 1968, with the assistance of the Organization of African Unity, Mobutu was able to clear his country of the white mercenaries who had helped to promote dissent and rebellion. European mines were nationalized, and with the restoration of order the Congo embarked on an economic recovery. In 1970, Mobutu was confirmed in office as President, and, a year later, the state was renamed Zaire, the original name of the Congo River. The first decade of independence had been a chaotic one but with the assistance of the United Nations and the intervention of the army, Zaire had survived intact.

Mobutu remained in power into the 1980s but satisfaction with his rule was not universal. He kept a substantial army and his methods were authoritarian. Zaire's copper, zinc, diamonds and coffee were exported to the West and Mobutu retained close ties with the capitalist powers. When neighbouring Angola became independent, he gave support to the FNLA (see Section 16.5(b)). The new Angolan government replied in 1977, tit for tat against Zaire's President. At that time there was a new secessionist uprising in Katanga, now called Shaba since European names had been abolished throughout Zaire. It was suspected that the rebellion was encouraged by Cuba and perhaps also by the USSR, as well as being supported by Angola. What caused alarm among Mobutu's Western sympathizers was that, for all its size, the President's army proved ineffective and he had to call for help from Morocco and Sadat's Egypt. A new anti-Mobutu invasion was launched from Angola in 1978 and this time whites were killed in Kolwezi. The French and Belgians rushed troops to the area, forcing the rebels to retreat and restoring an uneasy calm. Again Zaire remained intact but Shaba's loyalty to Mobutu and a united Zaire had hardly been strengthened.

Both in the early 1960s and late 1970s such events illustrated not only the tribal problems of a new African nation but also the difficulties Africans faced in settling their own problems without foreign meddling. Mineral deposits attracted foreign powers and it was difficult for emerging nations to escape entanglement in Cold-War rivalries. At the end of the 1970s the French began to talk about mounting some sort of military 'fire-brigade' to deal with African crises and, almost at once, the French were involved again in Chad and other former French territories north of Zaire. Such intervention dismayed the Organization of African Unity. The OAU was embarrassed by the frequency with which Europeans and superpowers went on meddling in African affairs and by the limited influence of the Organization itself (see Section 18.3(b)).

20.3   Nigeria and Biafra

Nigeria was one of the largest British colonies in Africa. It was also one of the most advanced, being granted independence in 1960, second only to Ghana which had gained independence and admission to the Commonwealth in 1957. With a population of over 50 million and valuable minerals and oil in the

Eastern Region its future seemed promising. Moreover Balewa, the first Prime Minister of independent Nigeria, soon established a reputation in the Commonwealth for being both capable and statesmanlike. But six years after independence, Balewa was murdered, and a year later, in 1967, the Eastern Region attempted to break away as the independent state of Biafra. A savage conflict developed between Nigerians and Biafrans which excited almost universal horror and gravely weakened the Nigerian economy.

Like most African states, Nigeria was made up of a mixture of tribes. The constitution was a federal one, like India's, allowing regional governments in addition to the central one. But from the outset there was widespread dissatisfaction with the system, especially among the Yorubas of the Western Region and the Ibos of the Eastern Region (see Fig. 20.2). They alleged that the central government was too much dominated by the Hausas who dominated the Northern Region. The Yorubas, in particular, disliked the system under which Balewa was able to interfere in the Western Region, deposing and arresting the Region's Prime Minister, Awolowo, who had founded the Action Group to represent Yoruba interests. After that incident, the West was in almost constant disorder. Charges of corruption against the federal government became commonplace.

In January 1966, Balewa's government was overthrown in a military coup led mainly by Ibo officers. Balewa was killed, along with the Prime Ministers of the Western and Northern Regions. A military government under Aguiyi Ironsi was short-lived. Ironsi was assassinated and a new coup brought to power Gowon, an officer from the Northern Region.

Gowon hoped to secure agreement on a new constitution, but he could do little to stem the killings of Ibos, especially in the North where they were far from their tribal lands in search of work. The Ibos retaliated against Hausas in the Eastern Region and obstructed Gowon's attempts to produce a new system of government. They also found a leader in Colonel Ojukwu who, after a dispute about the oil revenues of the Eastern Region, declared that Region independent in May 1967. The Ibos rallied to the new Republic of Biafra and war with the federal government of Nigeria began a few weeks later.

Biafra resisted for over two years but it was a state with few friends. In Africa, it was recognized by Nyerere of Tanzania and Kaunda of Zambia. Some arms were provided by France and Portugal, but the USSR favoured the Nigerian government and Britain followed suit with the argument that Britain could not allow the Russians to gain too much influence in Nigeria. The Organization of African Unity did its best to mediate between the two sides and the world frequently expressed its horror at the sufferings the conflict caused, but the United Nations limited intervention to relief work. Civilian casualties in Biafra were even greater than military casualties, for starvation and disease took a dreadful toll of the Ibos. Biafra was surrounded and squeezed but still its supporters resisted stubbornly, convinced that defeat would bring annihilation. The Biafrans did not surrender until January 1970. Ojukwu escaped by air and his successor, Major-General Effiong, capitulated.

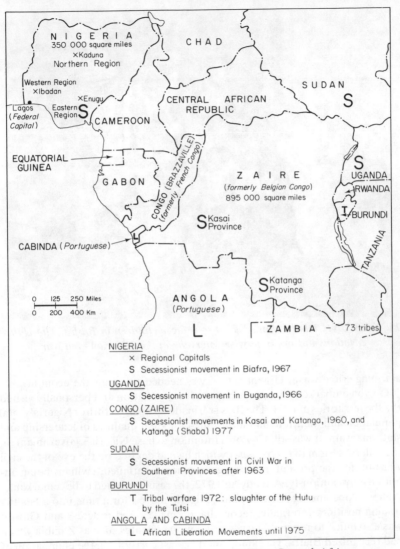

Fig. 20.2 Secessionist movements in West-Central Africa

Only then could the massive relief which the Ibos desperately needed be brought to them.

The crushing of Biafra by the far superior forces at the disposal of General Gowon preserved the territories of Nigeria but it left a legacy of hatred and scars, of tribal warfare and separatism, which could scarcely be expected to heal quickly. In addition, Nigeria faced serious problems of unemployment and an

Fig. 20.3 UNICEF distributed food to refugee children in Biafra. The United
Nations did not otherwise intervene in the Nigerian civil war

alarming crime wave. Urgent action was needed to repair the economy.

Gowon embarked on a programme of reconciliation and personally visited
the Ibo territories in 1971. The Ibos still made up nearly a fifth of Nigeria's total
population and their rehabilitation called for great qualities of leadership and
statesmanship. It was still Gowon's intention to base Nigeria's government on
the federal system of *twelve states* which he had devised on the eve of the civil
war but, for the present, military government continued, civilians being admitted only cautiously. Already, in 1972, the results seemed to be remarkable.
Almost alone among African states, Nigeria moved for a time into a healthy
trading position. Internally, reconciliation made rapid progress and Gowon
was also quick to repair Nigeria's relations with states such as Zambia which
had recognized Biafra. He campaigned against corruption, the elimination of
which was essential before civilian rule could be restored. In spite of useful
progress, there was a new military coup in 1975. Murtala Mohammed ousted
Gowon, but he too was overthrown only a year later. Unlike Gowon, who
retired to Britain to study, Murtala Mohammed was murdered. Control of the
military government now passed to Olusegun Obasanjo whose main aim was to
bring back parliamentary rule. Murtala Mohammed had already introduced
nineteen states within the federal system. A new constitution was worked out
during 1978 and elections were held in the following year. Obasanjo stood

down and President Shagari, the civilian leader of the successful National Party, now led Nigeria. The National Party also won the governorships of seven of the nineteen states, urging policies directed towards national unity rather than sectional divisions. Nigeria had thus returned to civilian and democratic government after thirteen years of military rule.

Fig. 20.4 Nigerian wedding stamp. Gowon successfully resisted the Biafran secessionists but he was deposed from Nigeria's Presidency in 1975

The elections of 1979 had not been free from voting on ethnic lines and it still remained to make a success of combining democracy with national unity. But the military had worked hard to lay firm foundations, and memories of the horrors of the Biafran War provided an impetus towards moderation and agreement. Moreover, Nigeria was the most prosperous country in black Africa. Oil reserves and membership of OPEC brought wealth to the country, though at the same time challenging governments to manage the economy successfully and ensure that a share of the wealth reached the people and the various regions in order to reduce internal stresses. Nigeria's population was growing rapidly, probably over 80 million at the beginning of the 1980s and the country was in social ferment. Oil wealth, industrialization and the growth of towns tended to draw people from the land, causing anxiety about Nigeria's ability to feed herself. In cities like Lagos there was overcrowding and a high crime rate. Traffic accidents took an alarming toll of life. Any Nigerian government faced a massive array of problems in building the new nation but the importance of Nigeria in African and international affairs was already widely recognized. Her importance grew with the founding of ECOWAS (see Section 18.3(*b*)) and the 1980s began with high hopes of prosperity and stability, as well as with pressing difficulties. After twenty years of independence, Nigeria had preserved her national boundaries and struggled through considerable upheavals. Tribalism (see Glossary) had by no means been eliminated but, nevertheless, Nigerians were steadily building national consciousness, trusting never again to have to endure secessionism and civil war.

20.4   Cyprus

Britain granted Cyprus her independence in August 1960. Most of the island's people were Greek-speaking but slightly less than 20 per cent were of Turkish descent. There had already been much conflict between the races, in some ways a continuation of the earlier struggle in the Balkans between Greek Orthodox Christians and Turkish Moslems which had been a feature of the *Eastern Question*; and from 1955 to 1959 Cyprus was in a state of emergency. British troops were trapped in a situation similar to that which had occurred earlier in Palestine: while trying to keep the peace between Turks and Greeks, they were also resented as a barrier to independence. Independence was granted when Sir Hugh Foot concluded successful negotiations with Archbishop Makarios, at a time when the island seemed to be comparatively quiet.

The way for independence was well-prepared. Makarios gave up his support for *Enosis*, a movement for the union of Greece and Cyprus which had always alarmed the Turks, and the new constitution provided for generous Turkish representation in the Cypriot government, police and civil service, and for the appointment of the Turkish leader, Dr Kutchuk, as deputy to President Makarios. Each race also retained the right to veto laws of which it disapproved. Unlike the Belgians in the Congo, the British only abandoned Cyprus when every effort had been made to give the island a stable future. Britain also allocated £12 million to help its future development, and Cyprus was admitted to the Commonwealth.

Cyprus also had the advantage of authoritative leadership. There was no doubt that Makarios alone had the authority to rule. He was always a distinctive figure at Commonwealth Conferences and throughout the 1960s he retained a considerable personal following.

Nevertheless, civil war broke out in Cyprus in 1963. The signal for its beginning was the attempt by Makarios to amend the constitution which so safeguarded both Greeks and Turks that it proved almost unworkable. A United Nations Peace-Keeping Force intervened in March 1964, and mediators tried to work out a new constitution. Incidents still occurred even after the ceasefire and in 1967 the situation was serious enough to bring about the threat of open war between Greece and Turkey. The danger was averted by U Thant and other UN mediators.

A year later, however, Turkish Cypriots elected their own provisional government, in effect partitioning the island. It seemed to be impossible to agree on a new constitution for the whole of Cyprus and the negotiations dragged on into the 1970s. Makarios was troubled by a revival of Enosis among Greeks. He obtained arms from Czechoslovakia with which to resist the pressure for a union with Greece, which could only antagonize Turkish Cypriots still further. But Makarios's own authority was challenged when General Grivas, once the leader of a pro-Greek terrorist movement, resumed his campaigning in 1971. The upshot was the overthrow of Makarios in July 1974. Nikos Sampson emerged from the confusion as the island's new President but by then the problems had multiplied.

Sampson made a brief and unsuccessful attempt to achieve the aims of Enosis, to link Cyprus with Greece. The Turks in Cyprus offered fierce resistance. They seized much of the north of the island with the help of troops from Turkey, and put to flight almost a quarter of a million Greek Cypriot refugees. British and UN troops helped to check the fighting but there now existed in effect two Cypruses. Turkish Cypriots held about a third of the island where there would be no more talk of Enosis, and immigrants from Turkey strengthened this Turkish sector. The Greeks recalled Makarios but he could do nothing to heal the breach. When Makarios died, in 1977, Spyros Kyprianou became President but negotiations to reunite the island made little progress. Turkish Cypriots looked to the leadership of Rauf Denktash and to the protection of Turkey. The mediation of Kurt Waldheim, UN Secretary-General, came up against the stubborn determination of the Turks not to abandon their position, and the island entered the 1980s still deeply divided. Time and again the United Nations Organization extended the stay of its peace-keeping forces in Cyprus, hoping that prolonged peace might eventually heal the division. In the meantime Cypriots learned to live with the partitioning of their island. Progress was made towards restoring the economy of the Greek sector though it remained rather precarious, heavily dependent on tourism which the troubles seemed not much to have damaged. But the Turkish sector had more serious problems and relied heavily on economic support from Turkey.

The upheaval of 1974 not only divided Cyprus: it also weakened NATO. Greece and Turkey had for a time hovered on the brink of war over the island. The USA blamed Turkey more than Greece for the crisis, and suspended arms supplies; and in the late 1970s Turkey began to explore better relations with the Soviet Union, giving rise to doubts about the effectiveness of NATO at the eastern end of the Mediterranean. But Turkey herself had problems with a tottering economy and internal turbulence. Turkish involvement in Cyprus was perhaps a useful diversion from the difficulties at home. Some 3 000 UN troops therefore remained in Cyprus, keeping apart a Turkish minority and the Greek majority from whom the Turks differed in race, religion, language and culture. To build a single Cypriot nation could not be achieved quickly. While any Greeks remained with ideas for uniting the island with Greece, the Turkish Cypriots were unlikely to lower their defences, and the mediators tried in vain to find a way out of the deadlock.

20.5 Pakistan and Bangladesh

(a) Pakistan 1947–58

When the British abandoned their Indian Empire in 1947, Pakistan was created as a country whose future was always in doubt (see Section 16.6(a)). A thousand miles of Indian territory separated West Pakistan from East Pakistan and the two parts had little in common but the Moslem religion. In the West, Urdu was the principal spoken language and wheat the main food crop. East Pakistan spoke Bengali and depended on rice, producing jute for export. East Pakistan was itself created by dividing the Province of Bengal and even on a map the state of Pakistan looked unconvincing (see Fig. 20.5).

It took nearly ten years to devise a system of government for Pakistan. In the meantime, Pakistan made do with that inherited from the British and attempted to practise democracy. The first Prime Minister, Liaquat Ali Khan, the deputy leader of the Moslem League, was assassinated, however. Fanatics killed him in 1951 for his refusal to wage war on India. Since Jinnah was already dead, there was no one now with sufficient standing to rule unchallenged as a democratic leader, and the result was an unsavoury scramble for power among members of the Moslem League. Six prime ministers were appointed during the years 1951 to 1956 and then, when the new constitution of the Islamic Republic of Pakistan at last came into effect, five more in the next two years. Corruption, the power struggle and incompetence threatened to tear the state apart. It survived largely through the efforts of Major-General Mirza as head of state. In 1958 Mirza thought more drastic action was needed: he suspended the constitution and proclaimed martial law. Only the army now had the authority to hold Pakistan together.

(b) Ayub Khan

In October 1958, the Commander-in-Chief of the army, Mohammed Ayub Khan, took control as President. The squabbling politicians were pushed into enforced retirement for six years, while Ayub set himself to 'clear away the mess'. Like de Gaulle in France and, earlier, Kemal in Turkey, the new President intended to rescue his country from indignity and establish an effective system of government. He hoped that eventually there could be a return to democracy, but for the moment Pakistan was governed by a military dictatorship.

Ayub undertook an impressive programme of economic development, with Five-Year Plans for expansion and a vigorous attack on corruption and inefficiency. Pakistan soon saw the benefits of his rule in improved communications, the expansion of house-building, hydro-electric schemes and progress in the production of jute, carpets and leather goods. Agreement with India was reached on the waters of the Indus, although the problem of Kashmir remained and war briefly erupted in 1965 (see Section 19.2).

In that year, Ayub held a presidential election. He won a sweeping success in West Pakistan but did less well in East Pakistan, although even there he got a majority of the votes. It was impossible for him quickly to overcome the problems of flooding and famine which frequently affected Pakistan (especially East Pakistan) and in the later 1960s his popularity began to decline sharply. He intended to prepare the people for a return to democracy by a system of *Basic Democracy*, providing first for the election of local councils and then for

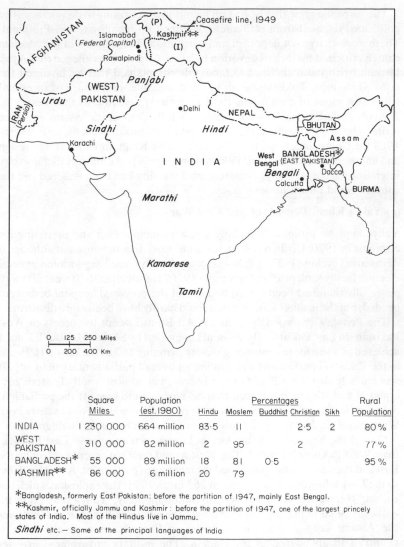

	Square Miles	Population (est.1980)	Percentages					Rural Population
			Hindu	Moslem	Buddhist	Christian	Sikh	
INDIA	1 230 000	664 million	83·5	11		2·5	2	80%
WEST PAKISTAN	310 000	82 million	2	95		2		77%
BANGLADESH*	55 000	89 million	18	81	0·5			95%
KASHMIR**	86 000	6 million	20	79				

*Bangladesh, formerly East Pakistan: before the partition of 1947, mainly East Bengal.

**Kashmir, officially Jammu and Kashmir: before the partition of 1947, one of the largest princely states of India. Most of the Hindus live in Jammu.

Sindhi etc. – Some of the principal languages of India

Fig. 20.5 The Indian sub-continent: the difficulties of unification

the councils to send representatives to a central parliament. He would keep control of the country's government until Pakistan and its politicians developed experience. But by the end of 1968 discontent was widespread, particularly in East Pakistan whose governor was despised as Ayub's puppet, given to referring to the President as 'celestial light'. Ayub was now cultivating hero-worship among his subjects as Nkrumah had done in Ghana.

The suspicion grew that he had no intention of returning to democracy. The politicans, released from retirement, whipped up hostility to the President. There were charges of nepotism and corruption. The mullahs of the Moslem church criticized his lack of devotion to Islam. Communists alleged that Ayub favoured rich industrialists and landlords complained that he favoured the poor. Once more Pakistan began to seem unstable, its mixture of races and tribes suspicious of each other, the East bitterly resentful of the West.

Ayub declared that he would restore a fully democratic system and then retire. The army suspected that this would only produce chaos, so in March 1969 the Commander-in-Chief, General Yahya Khan, forced Ayub to resign and imposed martial law. Thus Pakistan once again had a military dictatorship, intending to rule, so Yahya declared, until stability had been restored and the country could return to democracy.

(c) Yahya Khan, Democracy and Civil War

Yahya kept his promise, launching a new economic Plan and preparing for elections in 1970. Civilian politicians set to work to win votes and although a devastating cyclone in East Pakistan caused delays, the long-awaited general election finally took place in December 1970. The election itself went off more peacefully than had been feared and few of the prepared hospital beds were needed, but the results of the election could hardly have been more disastrous.

The People's Party led by Zulfikar Ali Bhutto swept to success in West Pakistan. In East Pakistan, the Awami League led by Sheikh Mujibur Rahman achieved an even more convincing victory, winning 167 of the East's 169 seats in the Pakistani parliament and gaining an overall parliamentary majority. It was unlikely that West Pakistan would accept an almost wholly Eastern government and Bhutto announced that his party would boycott the parliament unless some formula for government were reached which would satisfy both West and East. Yahya's good intentions had merely created a dilemma.

One of the objectives of the Awami League was to remove East Pakistan from West Pakistan's control. The West would now not accept control by the East and President Yahya postponed the meeting of parliament. A visit by Yahya to the East achieved nothing and, on 26 March 1971, the explosion which had so long threatened occurred. Almost simultaneously, Yahya reasserted the authority of his military government over the whole of Pakistan and outlawed the Awami League, while rebel forces in East Pakistan proclaimed that country's independence as *Bangladesh.* The military government arrested Mujibur Rahman but civil war was now unavoidable.

Bengali refugees fled from the savage vengeance of West Pakistani troops. An estimated eight million poured into India, imposing severe strains on the resources of the Indian government. Frontier incidents occurred, and stories of slaughter and atrocities in East Pakistan increased tension between the Indian and Pakistani governments and led to unrest in Kashmir. In December 1971 India and Pakistan were at war (see Section 19.2(c)). It took only two weeks for the Indian army and the *Mukti Bahini* (the freedom fighters of Bangladesh), to complete the rout of West Pakistan's forces. Tens of thousands of West Pakistani prisoners were taken and before the end of the year Yahya Khan had been forced to resign. His place as President of Pakistan was taken by Bhutto while Mujibur Rahman was released from prison to take control of Bangladesh.

(d) Division and Reconstruction

India's dramatic intervention thus ensured the separation of Bangladesh from Pakistan. Bengalis were no longer threatened with the domination of Punjabis from the West, though the latter stubbornly refused to accept the division of Pakistan as permanent. International bodies were more realistic. Bangladesh was admitted to the United Nations and to the Commonwealth, Pakistan resigning from the latter in angry protest.

In itself the creation of Bangladesh solved little. New tensions quickly developed in the country, between Moslems and Hindus and between Bengalis and Biharis. Both Hindus and Biharis were minorities in Bangladesh and feared discrimination and persecution. But more general problems were pressing. Bangladesh initially had a serious shortage of food, with soaring prices and massive problems of underdevelopment and poverty. The government urgently needed to settle millions of landless peasants and to create an economic structure which would protect millions more from the ever-present threat of starvation. On top of this, the wreckage of war had to be cleared away. Mujibur Rahman hoped to combine an assault on these formidable problems with democratic government, but that was wildly optimistic. He had to resort to emergency powers, but was murdered in 1975. Further assassinations followed and, by the end of 1975, General Ziaur Rahman had seized control of Bangladesh and set up a military government.

Like earlier military leaders in Pakistan, General Ziaur aimed to restore stability as the prelude to restoring democracy. 1978 brought new strains, however, when there was a sudden influx of Moslem refugees from Burma, allegedly fleeing from persecution by Burma's Buddhist majority. Ziaur negotiated for their safety and many were eventually repatriated. With international help, including that of Arab oil producers, Ziaur also began to contain some of Bangladesh's economic problems, concentrating on massive schemes to increase food production. In 1979 it was possible to hold elections. The Awami League, divided into factions, fared badly, and the successes of his Nationalist Party enabled General Ziaur to remain in power as a constitutional President. But assassins struck yet again: Ziaur was murdered in May 1981. Almost a year later, there was a new military coup led by Mohammed Ershad who brought back martial law.

The war of 1971 had also left formidable problems in West Pakistan. Bhutto began work on a new constitution, but his People's Party lacked the great authority the Awami League had seemed to have in Bangladesh. West Pakistani pride had been hurt in the recent war and the country now faced difficult problems of readjustment. There were threats of further dangerous secessionist movements in areas such as Baluchistan. Externally, China's friendship had proved of little use in the war over Bangladesh and there had been no effective help from anywhere else either. Now only a tenth of the size of India, Pakistan seemed to have suffered humiliation at the hands of her old enemy (see Section 19.2). Further disaster struck in 1973 when there were floods in the Indus Valley bringing destruction on a scale vast even by Asian standards. Bhutto remained in office until 1977 and made some progress towards improving the economy and containing minority grievances. Part of his policy was a programme of industrial nationalization. Early in 1977 he won an impressive electoral victory, but there were noisy complaints of corruption, malpractices and fraud, and serious civil disorders followed. In July 1977, Bhutto was overthrown by a military coup. General Zia-ul-Haq seized power, arresting many civilian politicians and declaring himself President in 1978. Bhutto was one of those arrested and in April 1979 he was tried and hanged for alleged crimes against the Pakistani people.

Democracy had therefore collapsed once more in Pakistan. Zia talked of restoring it but his rule was authoritarian. It was also influenced by the Moslem militancy which swept through Iran (see Section 19.4), and the President proclaimed his support for Islamic principles. His regime seemed to be unpopular, resting on force rather than on any widespread support. But Zia vigorously condemned the Soviet invasion of neighbouring Afghanistan and that brought him the favour of the USA and its allies. Bhutto's former supporters on the other hand brooded on Zia's ruthlessness and, by 1981, had begun to organize resistance. Zia offered refuge and encouragement to Afghan rebels resisting Soviet authority in Afghanistan. The USA offered support to Pakistan if it were needed to resist a Soviet attack. But it seemed possible that what Zia might most need was support to keep down his own people.

20.6   Northern Ireland

(a) The Irish Problem continued

Lloyd George's efforts to solve the Irish problem (see Section 6.2(b)) left Ireland divided between the Free State, which later became the Republic, and Northern Ireland. The latter remained within the United Kingdom, with a measure of Home Rule. About a third of the population of Northern Ireland was Roman Catholic; the majority was Protestant. When the Irish Republic withdrew from the Commonwealth in 1949, Britain passed the Ireland Act, asserting that 'in no event will Northern Ireland or any part thereof cease to be part of . . . the United Kingdom without the consent of the Parliament of Northern Ireland'. This Parliament, dominated by Protestants, was unlikely ever to consent to the reunification of all Ireland which many Roman Catholics desired. The Catholic minority in Northern Ireland also considered that they were treated as second-class citizens by Protestants. They were powerless to alter this situation by constitutional means. Such a situation was always potentially an explosive one, especially in a land accustomed to violence.

From 1923 to 1954, however, Ireland was comparatively peaceful. The Irish Republic refused to recognize the legality or the permanence of the arrangements made for Northern Ireland, and when De Valera became Prime Minister in 1932, he reaffirmed his hostility to the partitioning of the country. But Southern governments had problems enough, first in breaking completely with the British monarchy and the Commonwealth and then in establishing a degree of prosperity. In the North, the Protestant majority regularly confirmed its loyalty to the United Kingdom (and to the Conservatives and Unionists) in general elections.

It was the IRA (Irish Republican Army) which, in 1954, revived the issue with a series of outrages which continued for the rest of that decade. Extremists on both sides had never allowed old hatreds to die. Both in the Republic and in Northern Ireland, history was nourished with passionate care. Anti-Popery thrived in the Orange Lodges of the North where decorated walls and frequent processions commemorated triumphs of Protestant over Catholic long forgotten elsewhere. The outspoken sermons of Protestant preachers, ever fearful of the influence of Rome, also helped to turn the Protestant North into a stronghold of bigotry and narrow-mindedness, possessed of a *laager* mentality as stubborn as that of the Boers of South Africa (see Section 21.2). Genuine attempts at reconciliation between the two parts of Ireland and between Protestants and Catholics, undertaken from time to time by less-blinkered politicians such as O'Neill, Prime Minister of Northern Ireland in the mid-1960s, had little hope of success in such an over-heated atmosphere.

(b) Civil Rights and Near-Civil War

It was the concern for *Civil Rights*, which became fashionable in the USA in the 1960s and spread rapidly across the world, which served to plunge Northern Ireland into a state of near-civil war. In 1968, Catholics in Northern Ireland complained bitterly of injustice, taking their case to the European Human Rights Commission. They made allegations of unfairness in the allocation of jobs and houses and in the arrangements for voting. They were embittered by their own inability, as a minority, effectively to alter the system, infuriated by the endless Protestant posturing and reminders about King Billy and the Battle of the Boyne* and also inspired, no doubt, by those who still wished to bring about a united and republican Ireland. In March 1969, their protests developed into severe rioting. In the summer, petrol bombs and gunfire became commonplace in Northern Ireland's cities. The buses of Belfast became popular targets for hi-jackers, eager to convert them into prefabricated barricades and, with civil war threatening, the British government rushed troops to Northern Ireland. Although the British army had some initial success in quietening the rebellion, it soon entered a new phase and the Heath government

---

* William III (Protestant) defeated James II (Catholic) on the Banks of the Boyne in 1690.

Fig. 20.6 A burnt-out bus used as a barricade during street fighting between Catholics and Protestants in Belfast, 1969

found it necessary to suspend the government of Northern Ireland and the parliament at Stormont.

The British army found itself involved in another triangular struggle. Catholics fought Protestants and, in trying to keep them apart, the army found itself under attack as the symbol of the connection with Britain which republicans hated. By early 1972, the toll of dead included over a hundred British soldiers. The Catholic resistance movement was supported by the IRA and another terrorist group, the IRA Provisionals. The Protestants, as the struggle went on, formed similar paramilitary forces. The government used the army, the police and the Ulster Defence Regiment, a well-armed supplementary police force. Although priority was given to re-establishing order and to halting the extensive toll of lives and property, the ferocity of the conflict continued to escalate until well into 1972 when an all-out drive by the British army to destroy the Catholic strongholds brought a measure of relief. The drift towards full-scale civil war, developing from the urban guerilla warfare, was checked for a time. The emergence of new and more violent Protestant organizations such as the Ulster Defence Association (UDA) soon suggested, however, that the respite was to be short-lived.

(c) Political Efforts

Brian Faulkner's government in Northern Ireland had made a last-ditch effort to broaden its support by including some Opposition members and by making reforms before Heath suspended it in 1972. It accepted the principles of equal opportunity in employment and one-man one-vote in local government. A new system for allocating local-authority housing was worked out, and an Incitement to Hatred Act tackled the problem of provocation. But it was too late. The Catholics had a deep distrust of a system of government so long dominated by Protestants and Unionists. The belated changes did little to check the disorders. It was hoped that direct rule from London would provide time for further thought about Northern Ireland's future. Heath sent William Whitelaw to the province to try to devise a system of government more generally acceptable to Northern Ireland's people than that provided by the parliament at Stormont. Many similar missions were to follow. The dilemma that Whitelaw and his successors faced was that which had confronted Lloyd George. The only acceptable solution in the eyes of many Catholics was one which united the whole of Ireland under one Irish government at Dublin. For Protestants this was no solution at all since it would make *them* a minority in a predominantly Catholic country. It was to avoid this that Northern Ireland had originally been created.

In 1974, an attempt was made to set up a new government for Northern Ireland bringing together Protestants and Catholics for an experiment in power-sharing. It lasted only until May, when the economy of the province was paralysed by a widespread strike brought about by Protestant extremists. The new British Prime Minister, Wilson, saw no alternative but to call off the experiment and reimpose direct rule. There seemed little genuine enthusiasm among the majority to make power-sharing work and the bombings and killings went on. British troops continued with their thankless task of trying to keep order. Not all parts of Northern Ireland were much affected by the conflict, and the level of violence tended to rise and fall, but, nevertheless, scenes such as that shown in Fig. 20.6 were all too common, and the toll of casualties mounted. Something like a hopeless stalemate developed. Politicians groped in vain for some political compromise which would provide foundations for a stable future, but too many on both sides, both Protestant and Catholic, found compromise of any sort unacceptable. 'No Surrender' was an old slogan among Northern Ireland's Protestants which inflexible demagogues like Ian Paisley bellowed with an unremitting fury.

A women's peace movement tried in 1976 to bring some sanity to the affairs of the province, protesting at what was then almost daily barbarism, but with little effect on the hardliners on either side. Protestant leaders seemed to have no solution except to return to that which had failed, the simple restoration of Protestant power. Catholic extremists still thought to achieve union with the Republic of Ireland through terrorism. Moderates could not recruit sufficient strength to control affairs, and the difficulties increased when power struggles and personal clashes developed within the Unionist and Protestant movement. The mass of Northern Ireland's people gave little support to the call in 1977 for another massive strike, this time to protest against the alleged weakness of the British government in dealing with the IRA. Nevertheless, they continued to vote in great numbers for men like Paisley when elections were held to the

Westminster House of Commons. They elected Paisley to the European Parliament too, giving him a new stage on which to thunder. Wilson's and Callaghan's governments had been unable to find a way forward so that Thatcher's government inherited the stalemate, and the death toll went on into the 1980s.

Northern Ireland proved that bloody upheaval and 'tribalism' were not confined to the developing countries of the Third World. But it was part of the price the province paid that it remained the poorest area of the United Kingdom, with the highest levels of unemployment. At the same time, it was the area on which British governments spent the most money per head of population. But money could not buy peace. Direct rule had begun in 1972 as a holding action. Ten years later it seemed to have achieved little except to hold, and the dilemma remained. Hardliners on both sides obstructed every effort to devise a system of self-government for Northern Ireland in which minorities could adequately be protected from self-interested Ulster Unionist and Protestant bigotry. To some, it seemed that, like problems in the Third World, the problem was a legacy of colonialism, and that the Irish nation was still divided by British policy. But to Northern Ireland's Protestants, the union of all Ireland would be a 'Surrender' of their avowed determination to remain citizens of the United Kingdom. For British governments, it would also be a surrender to the gunmen and bombers of the terrorist organizations they were determined to resist, a policy in which they were encouraged by other European governments which faced the general threat of terrorism of one sort or another in the 1970s and 1980s. Nor was the Republican government in Dublin quite as anxious to acquire responsibility for the North as its official position on the point seemed to suggest. Most of the pressures on the problem of Northern Ireland were therefore negative ones, prolonging the agony and intensifying the deadlock.

20.7   Solution through Tolerance

The world's mixtures of races and religions cannot easily be unscrambled. The boundaries of many states and the mixing of peoples are a result of the past and each generation must live with the problems it inherits. The consequences of these problems have already proved terrible for the Congo, Nigeria, Cyprus, Pakistan and Ireland. It is far from easy to find solutions to such problems. Unit Nineteen shows, in the case of the Jews, that the creation of new states for minorities offers no trouble-free way out. Nor is it easy to partition an island as small as Cyprus or to unite one the size of Ireland. Reconciliation between minority and majority can offer the only lasting solution to problems such as these. Events have already made reconciliation difficult to achieve for many of the states mentioned in this Unit. But it is worth noting that other states faced with similar problems have so far avoided such outright confrontations, among them African states such as Kenya and Zambia, Trinidad and Guyana in the Caribbean, Malaysia and Singapore in South-East Asia and, most remarkable of all, India whose population of some 700 million includes scores of minorities. Sensible leadership has played its part in many of these states but they have also relied on the restraint and tolerance of their peoples.

Where bloodshed has occurred, religion alone has seldom been the deter-mining factor in the twentieth century, in sharp contrast to earlier centuries when a man's conscience was often not his private property. Economic and political problems seem now to have become more important. Katangese and Ibo separatism were closely related to deposits of copper and oil. East Pakistan believed that West Pakistan was exploiting what wealth the Bengalis had. Catholics in Northern Ireland believed that Protestants were monopolizing jobs and housing. At the same time, the aggrieved minorities wanted more say in how they were governed and their struggle was for political power as the key to economic development and social reform. But fear and distrust tend to be irrational forces and for that reason all the more difficult to control. Though the influence of religion began to decline in the twentieth century as a spur to hatred and conflict, the importance of race and colour increased. Here too strong emotions were aroused, not all of them rational, and yet again they were entangled in stubborn economic and political problems which provoked bitter conflicts (see Unit Twenty-One).

Further Reading

Elliott, F. and Summerskill, M.: *Dictionary of Politics*. Penguin (Harmondsworth, 1970).
Hodder, B.W.: *Africa Today*. Methuen (London, 1978).
Stephens, I.: *The Pakistanis*. Oxford University Press (London, 1968).
Watson, J.B.: *Empire to Commonwealth, 1919 to 1970*. Dent (London, 1971).
Watson, J.B.: *Success in British History since 1914*. John Murray (London, 1983).
Williams, B.: *Modern Africa*. Longman (Harlow, 1970).

Documentary

Breach, R.W.: *Documents and Descriptions, the World since 1914*. Oxford University Press (London, 1966) – Sections 30, 41.
Dures, A.: *Modern Ireland*. Wayland (Hove, 1973).
Magee, J.: *Northern Ireland, Crisis and Conflict*. Routledge & Kegan Paul (London, 1974).
Wallbank, T.W.: *Contemporary Africa*. Anvil (London, 1964).

Exercises

1. What do you understand by the term *minority*? What minorities can you identify in your own community?
2. What do you understand by *tribalism* in Africa? Can it be argued that events in Northern Ireland showed that 'tribalism' was 'not confined to the developing countries of the Third World' (page 402)?
3. Explain why and how independence led to civil war (*a*) in the Congo, and (*b*) in Nigeria.
4. List the main periods in the history of Pakistan from 1947 to 1971 and show how in *each* period the country faced problems difficult to solve. Why did rebellion occur in Bangladesh at the end of this period?

5. Why and how did both Pakistan and Bangladesh come under military rule in the later 1970s?

6. How far can events since 1960 be explained simply in terms of religious intolerance (*a*) in Cyprus, and (*b*) in Northern Ireland?

7. 'The dilemma that Whitelaw and his successors faced was that which had confronted Lloyd George' (page 401). Explain and illustrate this statement.

8. Why have minority problems given rise in recent years to violent conflict in some countries but not in other countries which also include minorities?

9. (*a*) Find out what minority problems exist in any *three* of the following: Australia; Canada; New Zealand; Belgium; Jugoslavia.

   (*b*) Identify *two* distinctive minorities in *each* of the USA and the USSR and consider how far these minorities have reason to be satisfied or to feel aggrieved with their national government.

10. Study the map at Fig. 20.2 on page 389, and then answer the following questions:

    (*a*) Which other large state in southern Africa, not shown on the map, was ruled by the Portuguese in the early 1970s? What do you understand by the letter L on the map in relation to Portugal's African territories?

    (*b*) Explain the phrase which is attached to Lagos on this map.

    (*c*) Explain how secessionist movements developed in 1960 in the Congo (Zaire). Why did they not succeed?

    (*d*) By what name is Katanga now known? What events occurred there in the late 1970s and how did these events illustrate the meddling in African affairs of non-African states?

    (*e*) Name the main tribe which inhabits the Eastern Region of Nigeria. Why and with what results did this tribe rebel in the late 1960s?

    (*f*) By what name was Zambia earlier known? Why does this map refer to '73 tribes'? Why does it not link Zambia with any of the letters L, S or T? What can you assume about Zambia from the absence of this detail?

    (*g*) Use this map to write an account of the problems of West-Central Africa in the 1960s and 1970s making special mention of state boundaries.

Unit Twenty-One

Race Relations

21.1 The Question of Colour

The problems of relationships between different races of the world have become prominent since 1945. The question is often bound up with that of minorities (see Unit Twenty). Many newly-independent states have populations mixed in race and colour: it requires a measure of tolerance for them to live together in harmony.

Many states have worked towards harmonious relations based on tolerance. In the Commonwealth alone, African states such as Kenya under Kenyatta, Tanzania under Nyerere and Zambia under Kaunda, have all made progress in reconciling the interests of different races. The same is true of the multi-racial West Indian islands such as Jamaica and Trinidad and the mainland state of Guyana; of tiny states such as Mauritius and Fiji and of Singapore under Lee Kuan Yew. Sometimes the rulers of these states have been accused of using authoritarian methods, but they have given their countries sound government and, so far, have succeeded in avoiding racial confrontations such as those which will be considered later in this Unit. The racial mixture of each state varies, of course, and it is impossible in a book such as this to examine each in detail.

Perhaps the most important development in the twentieth century has been the unwillingness of traditionally-exploited races to continue to accept their lower status. In its simplest form, this has often involved a readjustment in the relationships of white and non-white. In Kenya, for example, European settlers have had to accept the independence of the state under a black African government and a change in the status of the African from servant to equal. Such adjustments have often been made fairly smoothly and the Commonwealth itself was founded on the basis of this new respect of one race for another (see Section 16.6).

In states still dominated by white men, non-whites have begun to demand a similar equality, some taking their inspiration from Marcus Garvey who founded the Universal Negro Improvement Association and was deported from the USA in 1927. Garvey went to Jamaica where he continued his struggle to persuade those of African and slave descent to take a pride in their race and their culture and to throw off the habit of subservience. A popular slogan of the 1960s was 'Black is Beautiful', which extremists impatiently made aggressive in the *Black Power* movement, while others, such as Martin Luther King, campaigned peacefully for *Civil Rights* and equality.

Few countries with mixed populations were unaffected by these changes of attitude, even those like Australia, which tried to keep out non-white settlers. Others, like the USA, with a large black population found race relations becoming a central political issue (see Section 13.2(*d*)). Eisenhower, Kennedy and Johnson made greater efforts than earlier Presidents to ensure the more equal treatment of American blacks. Much of what was done was hardly more than cosmetic, and millions of non-whites in the USA still endured underemployment, poor incomes and dreadful housing. But a handful of blacks gained a growing number of official appointments and more began to prosper in the professions. It was a popular choice when President Carter, partly with an eye on the black vote, made Andrew Young the US Ambassador to UNO. Fig. 21.1 presents a cartoonist's view of Young's not always tactful exuberance, and Carter felt obliged to dismiss him in 1979. The President was careful to appoint another black ambassador, but the dismissal of the popular Young, together with other disappointments, lost Carter black votes in the election of 1980. Almost anything which involved colour was now a sensitive issue. Progressive white governments made earnest efforts to improve the conditions and prospects for their non-white citizens as exemplified by Castro in Cuba. But even non-white governments sometimes had problems when they could not quickly redress past inequalities and fulfil rising expectations. Jamaica had a black government from the time of independence in 1962 but poverty and unemployment could not be banished overnight. To the supporters of Black Power there was something obscene in the contrast between the luxury hotels of the tourists and the hovels of the poor. Thus in

Table 21.1 South and East African populations in the early 1970s

	Estimated 1971 (millions)*
Black African Governments	
Lesotho	1.0
Swaziland	0.4
Botswana	0.7
Zambia	4.0
Malawi	4.5
Tanzania	13.5
Uganda	10.0
Kenya	12.0 (African 97.5%, Asian 1.7%, White 0.5%)
White Supremacist Governments	
South Africa	22.0 (African 70%, White 17.5%, Coloured 9.5%, Asian 3%)
Namibia	0.6 (African 84%, White 16%)
Rhodesia	5.5 (African 94%, White 5%)
Mozambique	8.5 (African 98%, White 1%)
Angola	5.5 (African 96%, White 3%)

* 99% or more African unless otherwise stated.

Jamaica, as well as elsewhere, distinctions in colour also raised the problems of distinctions in wealth and opportunity. This underlined the importance of economic development as well as of race relations.

In many countries, governments saw the need for urgent action. The problem of colour and racial equality could seldom be isolated if it were to be tackled sensibly. But insofar as the world identified central issues of colour it did so, in the late twentieth century, mainly in relation to South Africa and to southern Africa generally.

Fig. 21.1 The diplomatic progress of Andrew Young. Vorster of South Africa (S.A.) and Smith of Rhodesia, defenders of white privilege, were two of those on whose toes the exuberant Ambassador trod before Carter eventually dismissed him

21.2   South Africa

(a) From Dominion Status to Apartheid

By the South Africa Act of 1909, Britain linked Cape Colony, Natal, the Orange Free State and the Transvaal in the Union of South Africa, to which was granted Dominion Status. The white settlers of Cape Colony and Natal were mainly of British descent but they were outnumbered by about two to one in the rest of the Union by Boers of Dutch descent. The whites formed only about a fifth of South Africa's total population, the great majority being of African descent, mainly Bantu of different tribes. But Britain transferred power to the whites and the first government took office in 1910 with Louis Botha as Prime Minister.

Botha was succeeded by another Boer, Jan Smuts, in 1919. Botha and Smuts successively led the South African Party, the main opposition being that of the nationalists who were critical of South Africa's continued connections with the British monarchy and the Commonwealth. Nevertheless, when the nationalists came to power under James Hertzog in 1924 the connection was not discontinued. Britain was a valuable trading partner and a source of useful investment.

It was clear that the majority of Hertzog's white supporters had abandoned none of their traditional contempt for the non-whites when the Representation of Natives Act of 1936 removed the African voters of Cape Province from the common electoral roll and provided only a tiny representation in parliament for the non-whites, even then requiring that they must elect white representatives. No major party in South African politics believed in racial equality. Smuts was sometimes, quite wrongly, alleged by the nationalists to be 'soft on the *kaffirs*'* and when Hertzog joined forces with him in the United Party in 1933, diehard nationalists promptly formed a new right-wing party, the Afrikaaner Nationalists, under Dr Malan. Malan, even more than Hertzog and Smuts, was committed to the preservation of white privileges and supremacy. Indeed, the three leaders differed in their attitudes to the natives only in degree.

Hertzog resigned as Prime Minister in 1939, when parliament voted by a narrow majority to join Britain in war against Germany. Smuts took over and remained in office until 1948, but throughout the war there had been some sympathy in South Africa for the Nazis and Fascists, and white opinion moved steadily against Smuts when it ended. Smuts had always been an internationalist, an enthusiastic supporter of the Commonwealth and the League of Nations. Hertzog and other South African leaders had few interests outside their own country. This was the *laager* mentality, dating from pioneering days when white men sometimes found themselves surrounded by angry natives and were forced to rely on their own resources and toughness. The world was changing after 1945 with new theories of racial equality, demonstrated by the British when independence was granted to India. In South Africa, such theories were alarming and, in the elections of 1948, Malan conjured up a vision of the 'Black Menace', and held out a lifeline to white voters. Their privileges and status could be preserved by *apartheid*. Malan was returned as Prime Minister by a small majority which the Nationalists then proceeded to consolidate.

Apartheid, the basis of which was the *segregation of the races* in South Africa, was not entirely new. There had long been separation with reserves for the Africans, but African communities had also developed in the towns, where their cheap labour was invaluable. Apartheid was intended to strengthen the separation of non-white from white and to reinforce *baaskap*, white supremacy. How it would do so was probably not understood by many who voted for Malan in 1948 and, indeed, without black labour the South African economy could hardly prosper. Nevertheless, Malan seemed to offer a surer safeguard against the 'Black Menace' than did Smuts.

* A dismissive term for native Africans, mainly Bantu.

Fig. 21.2   South African Prime Ministers, 1910–60: Botha, Smuts, Hertzog, Malan, Strijdom, Verwoerd, all of them Boers

(b) Apartheid in Practice

The Nationalists brought a vigour to the segregating of the races which undoubtedly pleased the white voters. In 1956, coloured electors (of mixed race) were removed from the common register and the parliamentary system further purified in favour of the whites. Successive elections strengthened the Nationalists and weakened the opposition of the United Party, giving ever greater authority to Nationalist prime ministers. Malan retired in 1954 in favour of Strijdom. He died in 1958 and was succeeded by Dr Verwoerd, who was shot by a white farmer in 1960. The farmer opposed apartheid but was declared mentally deranged. Verwoerd recovered only to be stabbed to death in 1966, and his successor was Johannes Vorster. Each of these Prime Ministers zealously applied and polished the principles of apartheid until white supremacy seemed invincible.

The pre-war *pass laws* were tightened and extended so that movement without authority became almost impossible for non-whites. Identity cards recorded the owner's racial group and almost everywhere the races were ruthlessly segregated. African children were educated separately from white children and at a lower level. African housing was apart from white housing. Where possible, jobs, especially those which carried responsibility, were transferred to whites and every effort made, as long as it did not damage the white man's prosperity, to move the non-whites into the reserves under the Group Areas Act. Asians, about 3 per cent of the South African population, were encouraged to return to India while the Nationalist government shrugged off the protests of the Indian government. An earlier Immorality Act was reinforced to prevent marriage and all sexual relations between the races. All resistance was dealt with ruthlessly, not least under the far-reaching Suppression of Communism Act, and when the Nationalists found the courts uncooperative they over-ruled them, creating a new and reliable High Court of Parliament.

The Nationalists took no account of the indignities suffered by non-whites, segregated even when visiting a post office. They asserted that the standard of living of Africans in South Africa was higher than that in other African states and that apartheid was of benefit to blacks. A central feature of apartheid was the creation of *bantustans* by Verwoerd: eight regions which would eventually become self-governing were set aside for the Africans. The first of them was the Transkei, where Chief Kaiser Mantanzima became Prime Minister, but he was less of a puppet than the Nationalists had hoped. He soon demanded that all whites should leave the Transkei and went on, in the early 1970s, to assert his intention to secure just and equal treatment for his people, for the original allocation of land was unrelated to the population of South Africa and the bantustans were to occupy only 14 per cent of the Union. The whites called Mantanzima's claim for more land 'ill-judged' and threatened to delay the Transkei's movement towards self-government if he persisted in it.

Effective resistance to the Nationalists was, however, almost impossible. In 1953, it was made a crime for native workers to strike. Political organizations like the African National Congress were powerless. When Chief Luthuli, a moderate and much-respected leader, tried to organize defiance of the segregation laws in 1952 he was deprived of his chieftaincy and a new law was introduced to impose flogging on those who wilfully broke existing laws. Yet the Africans were unwilling to resort to violence, even though all constitutional forms of protest were closed to them. They still sought to secure relief from oppressive laws by the tactics of Gandhi and, in March 1960, several thousand Africans assembled at Sharpeville to demonstrate against the pass laws and to invite arrest. The authorities sought to terrify them with low-flying jets and eventually the police opened fire, killing sixty-seven as the Africans tried to escape and demonstrating to the world the ruthlessness of the South African system. The further shooting of eleven African miners in 1973 in the course of a violent clash between workers and police at the Western Deep Levels mine in the Transvaal emphasized the tensions in the system.

The collapse of the Portuguese Empire to the north of South Africa brought the Republic a step nearer to crisis. The Nationalists were returned to power in the election of 1974 but there were unprecedented protests by black South Africans two years later, when many African townships, especially Soweto near Johannesburg, flared in revolt. The police hit back with violence far in excess of that used at Sharpeville. Official casualty figures put non-white deaths at Soweto and elsewhere well above two hundred. The authorities meanwhile continued to deal harshly with moderate black leaders. Luthuli had died in 1967. Nelson Mandela, who had tried to found an African Nationalist Congress, had been imprisoned in 1962 and remained in detention. Steven Biko founded a new Black Consciousness movement, still emphasizing peaceful resistance to apartheid, but died of brain injuries while in police custody. Government investigators alleged that nobody was criminally responsible for his death, but this did little to persuade those who alleged that he had been murdered. Though guerilla action against the Nationalists was still only in its infancy at the end of the 1970s, for growing numbers of blacks it seemed to be the only way in which the system could be changed.

Vorster had meanwhile resigned as Prime Minister in 1978. Pieter Botha replaced him and went on to win the election of 1981. Botha claimed that his government was making some progress towards softening the rigidities of apartheid, at least removing some of the petty restrictions. The result of such 'liberalism' was that he was opposed in the election by hardliners whose electoral support served as a warning that there were many whites who wanted no relaxations at all. A formidable group of 'Cappy' white females emerged to campaign for tough policies, adopting the caps worn in the days of the moving frontier. There was also a small increase in the votes of more liberal whites who were unimpressed by Botha's claims to be a reformer.

Fig 21.3 'Apartheid is better described as a policy of good neighbourliness' – Dr Verwoerd. A not-untypical external comment on the system of apartheid, Daily Mirror, 6 March 1961

Much of the Nationalist vote remained solid, but the challenge from the right suggested that Botha would not readily risk further loss of support to hardliners, and that apartheid would remain intact in its essentials. The blacks continued to suffer indignities and hardships and exclusion from political influence. Their complaints, about inadequate educational opportunity for example, brought only trivial concessions, though they were at last allowed to join trade unions.

(c) South Africa's External Relations

Almost the whole of the non-white world condemned apartheid, with the exception of a few black African states such as Malawi, ruled by Dr Banda, who was well aware of his country's economic dependence on South Africa. South Africa's membership of the Commonwealth became increasingly embarrassing as that association grew more multi-racial. When the Nationalists made the Union a Republic in 1960 and broke off the connexion with the British monarchy, it was decided that South Africa must apply to members of the Commonwealth for its own continued membership. Verwoerd made his first journey overseas for over thirty years in 1961 to address the Commonwealth leaders in London. His arguments in support of apartheid made little impression but he refused all requests that he should moderate his policies. No other Commonwealth state expressed approval of apartheid, although Verwoerd undoubtedly had some sympathy from Australia and Britain. It was clear, however, that there could be no place for South Africa in a multi-racial association such as the developing Commonwealth, and Verwoerd finally withdrew his application. South Africa resigned, but was in effect expelled, from the Commonwealth.

Apartheid was frequently condemned elsewhere along with South Africa's continued occupation of Namibia (see Section 11.3(*b*)), where South Africa continued to rule, although making vague preparations for self-government. The Organization of African Unity, the communist powers and the United Nations Organization all deplored South Africa's apparent indifference to criticism. In 1962, the UN General Assembly voted in favour of a resolution to sever diplomatic relations and impose an economic boycott, but although some countries took the necessary action it was ineffective. South Africa was not without friends, at least among certain white capitalist powers. Portugal, with colonies in Angola and Mozambique (see Section 16.5), had a vested interest in white supremacy in southern Africa. The USA, Britain and France condemned apartheid with words but stopped short of taking action. South Africa was well-armed and strategically-situated, perhaps a useful ally in a confrontation with communism, and the capitalist powers were willing to tarnish their own reputations rather than break openly with a blatantly racialist state run by whites of European descent. It was argued that South Africa was stable, with deposits of gold and diamonds more prosperous than other African states, and that apartheid would eventually be modified. Harold Wilson's government refused to supply arms to South Africa and some unofficial bodies in Britain tried to boycott South African goods, but the controversy at this time raged mainly around sporting fixtures, resulting in cancelled cricket tours and South Africa's expulsion from the Olympic Games.

Fig. 21.4 shows that until 1975 South Africa was shielded from all of black Africa, except thinly-populated Botswana, by white-ruled Rhodesia and the overseas territories of the Portuguese. Portugal's territories gained independence in 1975 (see Section 16.5(*b*)). Rhodesia became independent with a

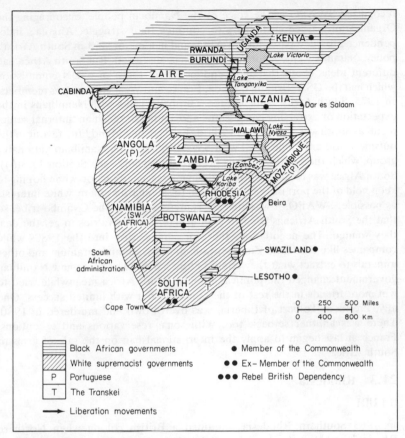

Fig. 21.4 South and East Africa: racial mixture and control in the early 1970s

black government in 1980 (see Section 21.3(d)). The South African *laager* was shrinking. Meanwhile there was no relaxation of external pressures on the Republic. In 1974 the UN General Assembly voted temporarily to suspend South Africa's membership, and UN criticism of the Republic mounted as Afro-Asian and Third-World representation in UNO continued to grow. Many countries boycotted the Olympic Games of 1976 in protest against New Zealand's participation, the New Zealand rugby authorities having insisted on playing matches against South African whites. The world also ignored the 'independence' of the Transkei in 1976, of Bophuthatswana, a collection of six scattered units, in 1977, and of Venda in 1979. These were the first of the bantustans to be given their freedom, but outside opinion refused to accept that they were anything more than puppet-states, set up to suit the convenience of South African whites.

International attention focused more sharply on Namibia. In 1971 UNO recognized SWAPO as the voice of the Namibian people, encouraging the Organization's freedom fighters to continue their struggle. Angola's independence provided bases for SWAPO, and in a major shift in South Africa's policy, Namibia's independence began to be discussed. But South Africa had different ideas about that independence from those of a UN commission which had the USA, Britain, Canada, France and West Germany as members. In 1975, South Africa launched the Turnhalle Talks with Namibians in the expectation of extracting concessions and aiming to reach an 'internal settlement' as Smith was soon to do in Rhodesia. The idea found little favour in the outside world and none at all with SWAPO, the main Namibian nationalist group, which the South Africans preferred to ignore (see Section 11.3(b)). South Africa was clearly fighting a delaying rearguard action while hoping to keep hold of the port of Walvis Bay and to safeguard as many white interests as possible. SWAPO, it was alleged, represented only the Ovambo tribe, so that the South Africans tried to exploit inter-tribal rivalries to get the deal they wanted. The negotiations therefore dragged on into the 1980s while companies like Rio Tinto Zinc went on mining Namibia's uranium and other minerals to extract what they could before SWAPO or some new Namibian government changed the political climate. South Africa meanwhile tried to win more friends in the rest of the continent but with limited success. One ally, President Tolbert of Liberia, was overthrown and murdered in 1980. There was another setback too: with some reservations and exceptions, France at last began to apply the international ban on the sale of arms to South Africa.

21.3   Rhodesia

(a) UDI

In 1963 Southern Rhodesia remained a British colony when Northern Rhodesia and Nyasaland gained independence (see Section 16.6(b)). Britain could not transfer power in Rhodesia* to an African government because of the strength of the white settlers. On the other hand it was unthinkable that power could be transferred to a minority of whites in the 1960s, as had been done in South Africa in 1909. Although the whites were outnumbered by some sixteen to one, they had in effect ruled Rhodesia since the 1920s. Power in Rhodesia had been shifting steadily to the right. The liberal Garfield Todd lost office as Prime Minister in 1958 after legalizing trade unions and increasing the number of Africans entitled to vote. His successor, Sir Edgar Whitehead, displeased the electors when he condemned racial discrimination. He was replaced by Winston Field, the leader of the right-wing Rhodesian Front, in the election of 1962. Field now demanded independence, rightly claiming that his country was in a more advanced state of development than either Northern Rhodesia or Nyasaland. Britain could see no alternative but to

---

* Southern Rhodesia, known henceforth simply as Rhodesia.

delay, for it was now accepted that power should be transferred only to the representatives of the majority. In the Rhodesian parliament, however, Africans were allowed, in effect, only 15 out of 65 seats and their political organizations, such as the African Congress Party, the National Democratic Party and the Zimbabwe African People's Union, had been banned. Field was forced to make way for Ian Smith, the new champion of the Rhodesian Front, in 1964. The whites expected that Smith would be tough enough to force the British to give way.

The principal difficulty in the way of independence was that under the existing constitution the African majority had no power to bring about any change in the system of government. Fewer than 250 000 whites, less than the population of Leicester, could retain supremacy in Rhodesia for ever. Douglas-Home, the British Prime Minister, made it clear that independence could not be granted without constitutional changes. Smith would not accept constitutional changes. The result was deadlock. The new British government elected later in 1964 made it clear that there would be no change in Britain's policy, although Wilson hoped that Smith would find a way to compromise. Instead, Smith talked of UDI.

UDI (a *Unilateral Declaration of Independence*) simply meant that if Britain was not prepared to grant independence, the Rhodesian Front would seize it, following in the footsteps of the Americans who had issued their Declaration of Independence in 1776, and the Irish when they set up their own illegal parliament in 1918. Britain had resisted with force on both occasions. This time, Wilson said that force would be used only if law and order were to break down in Rhodesia. The white police were unlikely to allow that to happen and Smith now saw little to deter him. On 11 November 1965, he declared the state independent, striking a blow, he said, for 'justice, civilization and Christianity'. It would be as independent as, say, Canada or Australia. But unlike Canada and Australia, Rhodesia's independence was illegal.

(b) The Struggle for Rhodesia's Soul

Smith's government set out to reinforce the white man's supremacy, imposing censorship and banning meetings. Sir Humphrey Gibbs, Britain's Governor in Rhodesia, was isolated and powerless. African leaders such as Nkomo were put under arrest. There was uproar: the non-white world, already sensitive about apartheid in South Africa, clamoured for Britain to take action.

Economic sanctions were imposed on Rhodesia. Wilson maintained that the country was still a British colony and that it was therefore only a British problem. Outside interference would not be permitted, although the United Nations Organization helped with the boycotting of Rhodesian trade. Quick results were expected, but although Rhodesia suffered inconvenience and difficulties in disposing of her tobacco crops, Smith's government showed no signs of weakening. It seems likely that the economic sanctions did far more damage to the economy of Zambia, Rhodesia's neighbour (formerly Northern Rhodesia), which tried honestly to implement Britain's policy, than to Rhodesia itself. Rhodesia found supporters in South Africa and Portugal, and in the scores of businessmen, in countries such as France, who preferred profit to moral conflicts about race and exploitation. Oil sanctions proved especially ineffective although the British navy mounted a patrol off Beira to close Rhodesia's pipe-line. This supply route was also Zambia's, heavily dependent on the Rhodesian railway system, and Zambia had to resort to obtaining fuel and other supplies by means of motor vehicles, bumping along ill-made roads through Tanzania.

Recriminations were commonplace. It was suspected that Britain was doing little more than play-acting although sanctions were annually renewed with great solemnity in the British parliament. Zambia and Tanzania, in due course, turned to China who offered to build for them a new railway, the ZamTan Railway, which was begun in the early 1970s. There was renewed pressure for economic sanctions against South Africa who was obviously helping Rhodesia, but capitalist powers declared these impracticable. Several times, the foundations of the Commonwealth were shaken by storms about the ineffectiveness of Britain's responses to UDI. Some African states declared their readiness to take part in an invasion of Rhodesia and in the late 1960s there were numerous clashes in northern Rhodesia between security forces, assisted by South Africans, and African freedom fighters. The whites of southern Africa came to regard the River Zambezi as their frontier against black Africa (see Fig. 21.4) and, inevitably, south of that line, Rhodesia drew closer to South Africa.

From time to time, new diplomatic initiatives were undertaken to try to reach a settlement of the dispute. The British government still argued that independence could be granted legally and sanctions lifted if the Rhodesian constitution were modified to permit, at least eventually, rule by the majority. Wilson met Smith in 1966 on *HMS Tiger* in the Mediterranean. Smith apparently agreed to terms but when he got back to Rhodesia, his government rejected them. In 1968, they met again at Gibraltar, on *HMS Fearless*. The terms offered by Wilson were considered to come near to a sell-out by many supporters of the African majority, but once again the Rhodesians rejected them. The Conservative government of Britain, elected in 1970, tried yet again. This time, Douglas-Home went to Rhodesia, producing yet another formula for settlement. Once again, there were charges of a sell-out, especially when the Rhodesian Front seemed willing to accept the deal. It was decided, therefore, that African opinion in Rhodesia should be consulted to determine whether the settlement was really acceptable. This task was undertaken by the Pearce Commission which could only report that black Rhodesians emphatically rejected the settlement, asserting a complete lack of confidence that the whites would ever be willing to admit them to power.

(c) Rhodesian Front Government

Since UDI, the Rhodesian Front had given them little reason to believe otherwise. Provisions for land tenure remained in force, a similar amount of land being allotted to over four million blacks as to less than a quarter of a million whites. Africans on 'white' land, such as the unfortunate Tangwena tribe, were driven from it, although the Tangwena for years stubbornly refused to be moved to the area allocated to them and Chief Rekayi declined to yield, in spite of the burning of their homes and the kidnapping of over a hundred of their children. In education, the gulf was widened between whites and non-whites and African primary schools were tribalized to promote disunity among the latter. In 1970, Rhodesia was declared a republic and the constitution revised. Whites and non-whites were completely separated on the voting lists, thus taking steps towards apartheid. A so-called Declaration of Rights strengthened the powers of the authorities to deal with resistance. Like South Africa, Rhodesia was subjected to a storm of criticism from outside and sometimes, especially from the churches, from inside; but the Rhodesian Front remained in control, apparently in no mood to authorize Smith to make concessions to British liberalism. They boasted of the figures of increasing white immigration, proof that many whites still looked eagerly for a privileged position in the world. But, like the white mercenaries who had plagued the Congo, many of the newcomers were unscrupulous fortune-hunters who would bring little credit to Rhodesia.

Rhodesia's African population also grew steadily, all the more embittered by white supremacy because of the high level of black unemployment. The security forces kept order, however, and the colony's economy showed no signs of imminent collapse under the impact of sanctions. White morale was boosted by the extensive sanction-busting which went on, and by such dubious manoeuvres as that of the Nixon government in the USA, which lifted the embargo on Rhodesian chrome in order to obtain supplies cheaply. As with the arguments about attitudes to South African apartheid, disputes about how to deal with Rhodesia caused international ill-will and soured race relations elsewhere. Relations became strained between Britain and Nigeria for example, and non-whites in Britain were dismayed by a scattering of car-stickers recommending 'Support Ian Smith'. For ten years or so, Smith seemed as immovable as he seemed uncompromising. But change came suddenly. Mozambique became independent and a Frelimo government was established there under the presidency of Samora Machel. This left Rhodesia almost completely surrounded by states who considered white supremacy to be outdated nonsense (see Fig. 21.4 and Section 16.5(b)).

(d) The Settlement

Economic sanctions had not induced Smith to change course and in the late 1970s the Bingham Report revealed something of the extent to which they had been broken, even by the British. Guerilla warfare now began to have more effect. Rhodesia was penetrated from Mozambique, attacks were stepped up from Zambia, and weapons were supplied by sympathizers, especially the Soviet Union and China. The death toll began to mount and with it white Rhodesian anxiety. International pressure began to increase too. The USA reimposed her embargo on chrome and Dr Kissinger arrived in Africa to try to conjure up a settlement.

Only one settlement was possible: that power in Rhodesia should be transferred from the whites to the overwhelming majority of blacks. This was demanded by the Front-Line Presidents, Rhodesia's black neighbours – Kaunda, Nyerere, Neto, Machel, and Seretse Khama of Botswana. It was the resolute aim of the guerilla leaders – Joshua Nkomo, the veteran leader of Rhodesian nationalism, whose forces operated from Zambia, and Robert Mugabe who, it was alleged, was a Marxist and whose forces operated from Mozambique. Both Nkomo and Mugabe had suffered detention and hardship at the hands of Rhodesian whites and they came together in the Patriotic Front (PF) to fight for the liberation of Zimbabwe (the African name for Rhodesia). Kissinger extracted a declaration of intent from Smith, but all the details of the transfer of power remained to be worked out and the guerillas made sure that the pressures on the whites were not reduced.

A conference at Geneva under British chairmanship towards the end of 1976 made little progress. Smith played for time, cashing in on divisions between Rhodesia's black leaders. Apart from Nkomo and Mugabe there were others who claimed to speak for the Zimbabweans, among them Bishop Abel Muzorewa and Ndabaningi Sithole. Smith argued that it was far from clear to whom power should be transferred. He aimed, however, to ensure the exclusion of the PF, just as the South Africans aimed to exclude SWAPO in Namibia. He therefore tried to by-pass opinion outside Rhodesia by setting up an 'internal settlement'. By early 1978 he was introducing a transitional period with a form of apprenticeship for black ministers under the guidance of ministers of the Rhodesian Front. Muzorewa, Sithole and Chief Chirau co-operated, hoping that they might win power in the elections which were to follow. The PF would have nothing to do with the arrangements, and the Front-Line Presidents condemned them too. Nevertheless, Rhodesia moved on to elections, as a result of which Bishop Muzorewa became Prime Minister in what was now called Rhodesia–Zimbabwe.

The outside world remained highly sceptical. Muzorewa demanded independence but Britain still refused it. The guerila war and negotiations went on. In the USA, Cyrus Vance replaced Kissinger when the Republicans lost the presidential election of 1976. In Britain, Anthony Crosland died suddenly and was followed as Foreign Secretary by David Owen. Vance and Owen, with the enthusiastic support of Andrew Young, insisted on further concessions, including a role in Zimbabwean politics for the PF. Not much progress had been made when the Labour Party lost the British general election of 1979 and Lord Carrington became Foreign Secretary, but things seemed about to come to a head at the Commonwealth Conference of that year which was scheduled to meet in Lusaka, Zambia.

Zimbabwe was at the top of the agenda at Lusaka. Margaret Thatcher attended as well as Carrington. The Commonwealth leaders among the Front-Line Presidents demanded action and the result was the Lancaster House Conference in London later in the year. Carrington worked hard to produce a real settlement, and months of tough negotiation, which involved the PF, Smith and Zimbabwe's internal black leaders, produced a breakthrough. A new constitution was agreed and the PF agreed to stop the fighting. Muzorewa surrendered power to a British governor and new elections were held in Zimbabwe early in 1980 under British supervision and with help from the Commonwealth.

Twenty seats were reserved for whites in the new Zimbabwean parliament. African parties contested the remaining eighty. Lord Soames proved an effective governor and in a country so recently torn by civil war the elections went off remarkably well. But Zimbabweans recognized the contribution the guerillas had made to bringing about the elections. The internal leaders were routed and the voters gave a substantial overall majority to Mugabe who thus became Zimbabwe's Prime Minister, the British making haste to grant legal independence to the country in April 1980. Mugabe's partner in the PF had contested the elections separately, however. While Mugabe won a clear majority, Nkomo won all the seats among the Ndbele people. Fears of inter-tribal rivalries were therefore reinforced. Mugabe had massive support among the Shona but all too little among the Ndbele. Here was a menacing division which would need bridging as a matter of urgency by those building the new nation.

Mugabe began his premiership in a statesmanlike way. Nkomo was given a seat in his Cabinet, and ministries were also found for representatives of moderate white opinion. The Prime Minister preached co-operation, and the whites who had long feared that his rule would lead to some sort of Marxist purge or to anarchy found themselves having to re-examine the prejudices which had for so long sustained Smith and the Rhodesian Front. Nevertheless, the problems were daunting. Not only had past bitterness to be set aside and racial harmony built, but the country's economy had to be revived and the expectations of the under-privileged fulfilled. Land redistribution was one of the urgent problems, to provide black Zimbabweans with more equal shares, and a cautious start was made on this. But another pressing problem was the rehabilitation of the guerillas. Large numbers of armed men with uncertain futures, especially the Ndbele followers of Nkomo, suspicious of the Shona, seemed sure to be a source of unrest. At the same time it would not be easy to resettle these men and to find jobs for them in the short term.

Much would depend on the leadership of Mugabe and the moderation of Nkomo. The latter, 'Big Josh', had given a lifetime's service to the struggle for an independent Zimbabwe, and it was a bitter blow when he failed to win election as the new nation's leader. Nevertheless, Zimbabwe's first year proceeded more smoothly than most had dared hope. Mugabe's intellectual stature appeared equal to that of almost any leader in Africa and he applied himself to reconciliation and nation-building. Though outrages occurred, fewer whites left Zimbabwe than many had predicted. There was still a worrying exodus, however, and, among those who remained, support for the Republican Front (formerly Rhodesian Front) and other right-wing groupings continued strong. In February 1982, Mugabe dismissed Nkomo from the cabinet and at the same time expressed disquiet about the reluctance of some of Zimbabwe's whites to co-operate. Urgent problems of resettlement and reorganization remained and Britain's gift of £75 million, payable in instalments, was little more than a fragment of the capital Zimbabwe desperately required. But much more than money was needed. Tolerance and goodwill helped the country through its first years but by 1983 there was unrest and talk of a one-party state; Nkomo left Zimbabwe for a time.

21.4 Britain: Immigration and Race Relations

(a) Immigration Controls

Easier and faster travel, and a greater knowledge and awareness of other parts of the world have had the effect, particularly since the Second World War, of increasing the rates of migration. Britain, as the mother country of the Commonwealth, became increasingly aware of this in the late 1950s when non-white immigrants were arriving at a rate of about 30 000 a year. This mass immigration of non-whites was almost totally unexpected. The possibility that the traditional British habit of going out to settle in Africa or to administer India could suddenly be reversed did not occur to the authorities in Britain. At first, immigrants were not even counted. But when some 57 000 arrived in 1960 and an alleged 136 000 in 1961, many of whom had little knowledge of the English language, something like panic resulted.

The British economy needed the immigrants, to work in the transport services, the hospitals and on night shifts in textile factories. But Britain already had a shortage of adequate housing and problems soon arose over education, especially when immigrant children knew little English. Moreover, the government had no plans to disperse the immigrants and inevitably they crowded into the areas where they could find work and where they could find fellow-countrymen. The textile towns of Lancashire and Yorkshire and parts of the Midlands and London soon began to notice the substantial number of immigrants, if only because of the colour of their skins. Many of the British were shocked to realize that multi-racialism could also involve a mixture of colours.

The 1961 census showed that there were about two million people in Britain who had been born outside the United Kingdom. Only a third of them were from the Commonwealth, perhaps only a sixth members of the Commonwealth who intended to settle permanently. The population of Britain had increased by about two and a quarter million since 1951, but this was due less to migration (immigration was largely matched by substantial emigration) than to other factors, such as the lengthening of life. But there were howls of protest, based mainly on the fear that members of the Commonwealth, often faced with poverty and unemployment in their own countries, would find Britain increasingly attractive as a land which offered hope, opportunity and stability.

In 1962, the Commonwealth Immigrants Act was passed which, for the first time, placed restrictions on the entry of immigrants into Britain from the Commonwealth. The Act was fiercely criticized both in Britain and elsewhere as being based mainly on prejudice against non-whites. Immigration restrictions are by no means uncommon in the world. Australia, Canada and New Zealand have imposed limitations principally against Asians and negro peoples. The USA has immigration restrictions, and South Africa also controls immigration, especially in relation to the occupations and skills of those seeking entry. It had long been Britain's boast that political refugees were always welcomed and members of the Commonwealth, who could afford to come, had received similar hospitality. However, in 1962 members of the Commonwealth were put into a special category.

They would only be allowed into Britain if they could obtain work vouchers from the Ministry of Labour or if they were closely related to earlier immigrants. In 1965, the annual ceiling for work vouchers was fixed at 8 500 although the actual number issued usually fell short of this figure. It meant that non-white immigration fell to about 50 000 a year, mostly the wives and children of earlier arrivals. Contrary to myths in common circulation, the immigrants were hard-working and made comparatively small demands on the resources of the British welfare state. Hardly any were old enough to qualify for old age pensions, although they often had need of the maternity services. It was in housing that immigration caused real difficulties, simply in adding pressure in an already unsatisfactory situation.

(b) East African Asians

Britain soon blundered into a new problem which involved immigration from the Commonwealth. During the colonial occupation of East Africa, Britain had introduced into that area tens of thousands of Asians, most of them from India. When independence was granted to Uganda and Kenya in 1962 and 1963, the British government allowed these Asians, if they wished, to retain British citizenship. Many of them did so, suspecting that they might not be able to preserve their comparatively prosperous positions in the African states, for African governments were known to favour a policy of *Africanization* (extending the opportunities of native Africans). The Asians felt that, one day, it might be better for them to move to Britain or even to return to India.

Not unnaturally, there was dissatisfaction in Kenya and Uganda that thousands of the countries' inhabitants were able to combine foreign citizenship with comparatively privileged positions. The Asians, moreover, tended to remain apart from the Africans, discouraging intermarriage for example. General Amin, who overthrew Obote in Uganda in 1971, especially disliked their refusal to mix with other Ugandans. He claimed to have a great belief in intermarriage to unite tribes and races, and himself produced children through wives from six different tribes. In vain, he encouraged Afro-Asian marriages.

First in Kenya and then in Uganda, efforts were made to dispossess those Asians who had refused African citizenship. The aim was that Africans should take over their appointments and their businesses. By 1966, many of the Asians were clamouring for admission to Britain. It was now the turn of Wilson's Labour government to panic. Although it accepted Britain's responsibility in the matter, it was thought essential to control the flow of these new immigrants. In the first half of 1968, about 50 000 arrived from Kenya. There were perhaps as many again still in Kenya and almost as many in Uganda. It was decided to impose an annual quota for admissions in a new Immigration Act, in 1968. East African Asians could now not freely enter Britain even if they held British passports. The flow was to be limited to about 5 000 a year.

The situation reflected little credit on any of the governments concerned. In East Africa, the Asians were squeezed to hasten their departure. Those who arrived in Britain with passports but without the necessary authority under the quota system were promptly expelled or, in some cases, imprisoned. Once they had left East Africa, they were refused readmission. Complaints against Britain were made to the European Human Rights Commission and stateless Asians were shuttled about all over Europe. Some sought to return to India, involving the Indian government in the problem. Almost a hundred made an unlikely appearance in Jugoslavia. The change of government in Britain in 1970 made no difference to their plight.

The good sense of the leaders of Kenya, Tanzania and other African states with large minorities of Asians, took much of the heat out of the problem in the early 1970s; they allowed time for things to work themselves out under the quota system. But in 1972, a new crisis suddenly exploded in Uganda. General Amin made an apparently snap decision to expel all those without Ugandan citizenship from his country within ninety days. Britain seemed likely to face the sudden influx of perhaps another 50 000 non-white immigrants within three months (see Table 21.2).

In the event, other members of the Commonwealth came forward with offers of places for thousands of the refugees, among them India, Canada, New Zealand, Australia and Malawi. States outside the Commonwealth offered to help, including Sweden and Iran. And Amin's harsh policies were widely condemned. Not only did other African leaders who faced problems similar to those of Uganda refuse to follow Amin's example, some gave new assurances to their Asian populations that they were under no threat and both

Kaunda of Zambia and Nyerere of Tanzania roundly condemned the inhumanity of the Ugandan actions. The number of immigrants actually entering Britain proved to be not much more than about 20 000 although that total was enough to start new alarms in the country and to reawaken a

Table 21.2 Migration

(a) *Commonwealth Citizens* probably in a position to qualify for British passports, 1972 – mainly Asians. Except in Uganda, there was little to suggest that applications would be made and that immigration into Britain would result. (Foreign and Commonwealth Office Statistics)

Uganda	c.	50 000 – About 20 000 sought entry to Britain, autumn 1972
Malaysia	c.	110 000
Kenya	c.	50 000
Singapore	c.	30 000
India	c.	25 000
Tanzania	c.	20 000
Malawi	c.	6 000
Zambia	c.	6 000
Pakistan*	c.	3 000
Total	c.	300 000

* including Bangladesh

(b) *The British Census, 1971*
Population: 53 828 000
6% of the population in 1971 foreign-born, of which 2.3% were born in the new countries of the Commonwealth (including 0.6 West Indian and 0.6 Indian) and 1.3% were born in the Republic of Ireland.

(c) *Foreign Workers in Europe, 1972*

	millions	*% of active population*
West Germany	2.2	10.3
United Kingdom	1.5	6.0
France	1.3	6.3
Switzerland	0.8	28.0
Sweden	0.2	5.0
Belgium	0.2	5.0
Luxemburg	0.03	21.0
Holland	0.08	2.2

These figures did not include immigrants who had become citizens for permanent settlement, for example Holland took in c. 300 000 refugees from Indonesia.

measure of white hostility towards non-white newcomers. Once again it was clear that racial problems required careful handling. It was, however, significant of the growing care with which statesmen were treating racial problems that Amin found hardly any supporters and that a large number of countries rallied to help tackle the difficulties caused by the expulsion, even though many understood the justice of Africanization when such policies were carried out more sensibly.

Nevertheless, British Conservatives continued to believe that more immigration laws were needed. Heath's government produced the Immigration Act of 1971, creating a unified system of controls for Commonwealth and foreign immigrants, a probationary period before permanent settlement was allowed, and special concessions for those with a parent or grandparent born in the United Kingdom. Few work vouchers were issued during the 1970s and most of those admitted were now the dependants of earlier immigrants, honouring promises already given. The Thatcher government looked more closely at what was meant by 'dependants' and further trivial regulation followed at the beginning of the 1980s. This was then followed by a new Nationality Act making yet more anxious adjustments, perhaps appeasing some of the government's supporters, but scarcely contributing to the improvement of race relations.

(c) Race Relations

Net Commonwealth immigration into Britain was only 19 000 in 1969 and 7 000 in 1970. The non-white population was only about 2 per cent of Britain's total population, rising to about 3 per cent ten years later. Table 21.2(c) shows that other European countries had higher percentages of foreign-born workers although the majority of these migrants had lighter skins and many were only temporary admissions (guest-workers) who were sent home in times of unemployment or other inconvenience. Most British people accepted that many Commonwealth newcomers had settled permanently in Britain. Constructive thinking therefore turned to the building of harmonious race relations which might be helped by legislation to point the way. Race Relations Acts in 1965 and 1968 forbade incitement to violence and discrimination on the grounds of colour, first in public places such as hotels and then in education, employment and transactions involving property and finance. The Acts legislated for a Race Relations Board to investigate complaints, seek reconciliation and, if necessary, take offenders to court. A later Labour government added a further Race Relations Act in 1976, strengthening the law and replacing the Race Relations Board with the Commission for Racial Equality.

Laws alone could not create racial harmony, however. In the end such harmony could only depend on people's attitudes. Occasionally prophets of doom were to be heard, one of whom was Enoch Powell, a fiercely right-wing MP who thought that great dangers existed in the presence of a million or so

Fig. 21.5 Support for Enoch Powell: a demonstration in Britain against immigration in the early 1970s

non-whites. Certainly, atrocious housing and other social problems occasionally led to disturbances between white and non-white, for example in Notting Hill, London, and in Leeds. Hooligans sometimes resorted to 'Paki-bashing' (the mindless persecution of Pakistanis), attacking them with the same demented enthusiasm that they brought to the wrecking of British Rail's special football trains. Such incidents were isolated and untypical but served as a constant reminder that good race relations needed to be cultivated. In the 1970s, the conflict between workmen and employers in industry was often more bitter than that between the races; and no racial disturbances in England approached the savagery of the conflict in Northern Ireland. At the same time, however, non-white school leavers often had special difficulties in finding worthwhile employment and the housing problem continued to cause deep anxiety: there was certainly no room for complacency.

Fig. 21.5 provides a glimpse of the passions sometimes aroused by Powell. But more sinister forces emerged. A National Front developed in Britain in the late 1960s, reviving memories of intolerant pre-war Nazism. It attracted little electoral support but became a noisy rabble in the 1970s, ever ready to inflame opinion against immigrant minorities. In some British cities, tension grew in the non-white communities, especially those in which West Indian youngsters suffered grievously from unemployment, deprivation and anxiety about their futures. There was a violent but brief outburst of protest in Bristol early in 1980, and another a year later in Brixton, London, followed by rioting elsewhere in such places as Toxteth, Liverpool, and Moss Side, Manchester. Blacks complained bitterly of what they claimed was a current of racism in British society, and of police hostility towards non-whites. Violent confrontations were still rare and people of all races in Britain continued to work hard for harmony, but, nevertheless, there was unease from which only the bigots of the National Front could derive any satisfaction.

It may be argued that no problem is of greater importance in the closing years of the twentieth century than that of race relations, especially between white and non-white. The struggle for racial harmony in Britain is only a tiny part of a worldwide struggle. The greatest danger is that racial conflict, though readily inflamed by inequality and deprivation, often has no rational basis. It is also inflamed by those who look for simple solutions to difficult problems merely by finding scapegoats, blaming minorities for difficulties which in reality have quite different causes. Statesmen the world over have recognized that an assault must be made on discrimination. British Race Relations Acts have their counterparts elsewhere, for example in the Civil Rights legislation of the USA. The Act of 1976 in Britain followed quickly on the Sex Discrimination Act which had aimed to reduce the disadvantages from which women had long suffered. In the 1980s, however, the Ku Klux Klan in the USA and the National Front and its counterparts in Britain lived on, some measure of how, even in developed and educated societies, irrational hatred and ignorance are difficult to eradicate. Discrimination, based as it is on prejudice and intolerance, can be eliminated only by the exercise of patient, tactful vigilance.

Further Reading

Brookes, E.: *Apartheid*. Routledge & Kegan Paul (London, 1968).
Cornwall, B.: *The Bush Rebels*. Deutsch (London, 1972).
Davenport, T.R.H.: *South Africa, A Modern History*. Macmillan (London, 1977).
Hiro, D.: *Black British, White British*. Penguin (Harmondsworth, 1973).
Loney, M.: *Rhodesia*. Penguin (Harmondsworth, 1975).
Troup, F.: *South Africa*. Penguin (Harmondsworth, 1975).
Watson, J.B.: *Empire to Commonwealth, 1919 to 1970*. Dent (London, 1971).
Watson, J.B.: *Success in British History since 1914*. John Murray (London, 1983).

Documentary

Breach, R.W.: *Documents and Descriptions, the World since 1914*. Oxford University Press (London, 1966) – Sections 31–2.
Windrich, E.: *The Rhodesian Problem*. Routledge & Kegan Paul (London, 1974).

Exercises

1. What is the meaning of each of the following terms: white supremacy; apartheid; racial discrimination; integration; the quota system?
2. What do you understand by *economic sanctions*? Making use of the Index to this book, explain how economic sanctions came to be imposed on (*a*) Mussolini's Italy, and (*b*) Smith's Rhodesia. Why, in *each* case, were sanctions not more effective?
3. Summarize the arguments which might have been put forward in the 1970s concerning apartheid (*a*) by a supporter of the Nationalist government in South Africa, and (*b*) by a black South African.
4. Identify the states which make up southern Africa, and explain what problems involving race relations existed in *three* of these states in the years after 1950.
5. Making use of this Unit and Section 16.5, explain the importance to southern Africa of the collapse of the Portuguese Empire in the mid-1970s.
6. Why did the British become concerned about immigration during the years after 1945 and to what legislation did this concern give rise?
7. 'Laws alone (can) not create racial harmony' (page 424). What laws have been passed since 1945 which have tried to create racial harmony (*a*) in Britain, and (*b*) in the USA? Why have these laws had only limited success in both of these countries?
8. What parts are played by immigrants in the life and economy of your local community? What would be the effects of their withdrawal from the area?
9. Write accounts of life at the present time from the points of view of *two* different ethnic groups in any local community with which you are familiar and which includes substantial ethnic minorities.
10. Making use of this Unit and, where necessary, of the Index to this book, explain the importance in the history of southern Africa of *each* of the following years: 1948 (South Africa); 1961 (South Africa); 1963 (Central African Federation); 1965 (Rhodesia); 1975 (Mozambique); 1976 (South Africa); 1980 (Zimbabwe). Select, giving your reasons, two further years which were important in the history of Namibia.

Unit Twenty-Two

The Struggle of the Emergent Nations

22.1   The Balance of Prudence

In his annual report to the United Nations General Assembly in 1972, Dr Waldheim, the Secretary-General, welcomed the 'balance of prudence' which now made the world's great powers cautious in their dealings with other great powers. At the same time, however, he felt it necessary to warn them that it was outdated to believe that a concert of great powers could keep peace in the world while ignoring the 'wisdom and importance' of the smaller states. In the early 1970s, few states outside Europe could approach even half of the annual income per head of the population of the United Kingdom or a quarter of that of the USA. But what these states lacked in wealth they made up in numbers. Since 1945, almost all of the great overseas empires of the past had been wound up (see Unit Sixteen) and, as a result, scores of newly-independent nations had been created, sometimes referred to as the *emergent nations*.

The leaders of many of these nations met in Algiers in 1973. The meeting was similar to that at Bandung in 1955 but, by 1973, emergent nations had greatly increased in number. Resentment of the arrogance of the great powers, who so often ignored the lesser nations, had grown too. They were aware that the recent improvements in American-Russian relations and the recent enlargement of the EEC were mainly for the benefit of the wealthy and had been undertaken with little regard for the rest of the world. Most of the emergent nations still feared exploitation and domination by the powerful and they felt keenly their own lack of influence. The ideas for a united Third World, once put forward by Nehru, were increasingly attractive. If the Third World could agree on programmes of united action, it would be less easy to ignore the new nations, despite the poverty of many of them. The driving-force for the meeting in Algiers came from India, Egypt and Jugoslavia and the leaders of the Third World assembled in large numbers.

The conference ended with an agreement to meet again, in 1976, in Sri Lanka (Ceylon), but there were few other hard-and-fast agreements. The Arab states had no difficulty in persuading the meeting roundly to condemn Israel, against whom economic sanctions were proposed and against whom there was a great bitterness born of sympathy with the Palestinian Arabs (see Section 19.1). But there were also plenty of disputes. There was general support for non-alignment and for standing aloof from great-power quarrels. On the other hand Castro of Cuba argued that a non-aligned Third World should automatically be hostile to Western capitalism, with its far-flung financial interests, while friendly to the USSR, an interpretation fiercely rejected by Gadafy of Libia. On this basic question of definition the non-aligned movement was to remain divided into the 1980s. All of the emergent nations shared a deep hatred of imperialism and colonialism but there was no precise agreement on what these terms meant, and no complete agreement on which great powers were most to be blamed. Nor were they able to reach many agreements on how the Third World might best co-operate. In some ways, therefore, the Algiers meeting was a disappointment. But, at the same time, the new nations gained confidence from the size of their conference and from the realization that some of their members possessed oil and raw materials badly needed by the great powers. Almost at once the oil states increased prices. Third-World nations generally left the meeting determined to continue their struggle for genuine independence, though aware that a united Third World was still a pipe-dream.

The Algiers meeting and Dr Waldheim's warnings were shots across the bows of the great powers. Small states no doubt made mistakes. Many of them were unstable and some of their leaders seemed, at times, to act emotionally, and in ways which exasperated others. In 1972, General Amin suddenly brought to a head the question of Ugandan citizenship and adopted harsh policies towards his country's Asians (see Section 21.4(*b*)). There was widespread condemnation of his actions and they caused particular annoyance to Britain where demands were heard that Uganda should be punished and aid suspended. Few indeed were prepared to defend Amin but the Third World had little sympathy in the matter with Britain. Heath's government had shown little sensitivity to the feelings of the new African nations. On taking office in 1970, it had lifted, in part, the ban on the sale of arms to South Africa in defiance of a UN resolution, and Britain, like other Western powers, regularly caused offence to non-white states by her compromising attitude towards such issues as white supremacy in southern Africa, about which many Third-World states felt deeply.

In spite of Waldheim's warning, great-power attitudes to the Third World showed little fundamental change during the next ten years. Issues were debated, especially that of the world economic order (see Section 18.2). Here and there, for example in Zimbabwe, old knots were untied, but by self-help rather than through great-power initiatives. Self-interested meddling by the great powers went on much as before. For all emergent nations the message was clear – that there were no short cuts to successful nationhood and prosperity, and that the first need was for self-reliance. This Unit considers the history of just a few developing nations during their early years of independence.

22.2   India

(*a*) Nehru

After securing independence from Britain in 1947 (see Section 16.6(*a*)), India was fortunate to have Nehru's uninterrupted leadership for seventeen years. The long struggle to achieve independence had strengthened the authority of the Indian National Congress, and Nehru's authority was unquestioned after the death of Patel, the leader of the party's right wing, in 1950.

He faced daunting problems. India was a vast state, with one of the lowest standards of living in the world. Although the average expectation of life was only thirty-two years in the early 1950s, its population of some 400 millions was rising fast. Many were illiterate and the country was difficult to unite, lacking even a common language. There were many minority groups and the partition of the Indian sub-continent left huge refugee camps, adding to the squalor of the slums in India's cities. Communications were often erratic and, if the state was to be modernized, the government would have to overcome deep-rooted religious traditions such as the socially-divisive caste system (see Glossary) and the age-old veneration of cows. In the short term, Nehru also faced the problem of establishing a new constitution and integrating into India areas formerly ruled by about 500 princes. The adoption of a democratic system in such a country seemed wildly optimistic. That India operated such a system with a great deal of success for more than a quarter of a century was a remarkable tribute to her statesmen and people. India became a repub-

Fig. 22.1 Sikhs in traditional dress with traditional instruments photographed at Delhi. The Sikhs, about two per cent of the total population, are one of India's many minorities

lic in 1950. At the first election under the new constitution there were 176 million voters. The election was a gigantic undertaking but it confirmed Nehru and the Indian National Congress in power.

Nehru brought progressive socialist ideas to the task of government. He wished to unite and develop his state, to establish Western-style democracy combined with socialist economic planning, and to use his voice in international affairs in support of morality and an independent, unaligned Third World. He hated both imperialism and racialism and condemned them without hesitation whenever the occasion arose. He was thus distressed when Britain attacked Egypt in 1956 and by the intensification of apartheid in South Africa. At the same time, he welcomed the development of the Commonwealth as a multi-racial association and as a partnership of equals.

Fig. 22.2 Jawaharlal Nehru, Prime Minister of independent India from 1947 to 1964 and father of Indira Gandhi, Prime Minister from 1966

Armed with a new Planning Commission, Nehru embarked on policies which he hoped would eventually effect economic and social revolution in India. By 1961, industrial output had almost doubled but industry still provided jobs for only about one per cent of the population. Thousands of villages gained the benefits of electricity. Co-operatives improved agricultural yields and irrigation schemes helped in many areas to provide more reliable food supplies. But the end results remained disappointing for millions of Indians. Table 18.1 shows that the benefits of increased production were cancelled out by the continuing rise in the country's population and, although an intensive campaign was begun in 1956 to encourage birth control, its success was limited. Other goals would also take many years to achieve, though Nehru made a start. Women were given equal rights to property. Discrimination against untouchables was made an offence. One of the objectives of the constitution was free compulsory education for all children to the age of fourteen, but this and other targets had not been reached when Nehru died in 1964. The level of illiteracy remained alarmingly high. Discrimination could not be wiped out until attitudes changed and in this, as in methods of production in agriculture, change came more slowly than Nehru would have wished. India continued to face other formidable problems too. The country suffered many natural disasters with which it was ill-equipped to cope and which drained resources already severely strained. Even with foreign aid India had not the wealth with which to provide more than a fraction of the schools, hospitals and homes the people needed. There was a similar lack of capital for industrialization and modernization in farming. Most of the foreign aid at this time, moreover, was in the form of loans which had to be repaid, often at considerable rates of interest which imposed a further burden.

Nehru won acclaim for his role in international affairs in spite of confrontation with Portugal over Goa, a brief war with China and a nagging rivalry with Pakistan (see Section 19.2). He sought to mediate in the Korean War in 1951 and in Vietnam in 1954. Indians were quick to respond to the call of the United Nations for troops to intervene in Palestine, the Congo and Cyprus. Nehru's death was therefore mourned not only by millions in India but throughout the world. In many ways the founder of his country, he was also a statesman of great standing. He did much to establish the claims of the underdeveloped nations to be taken seriously in a world dominated by the superpowers and the rich.

(b) Shastri

So firmly had democracy taken root under Nehru that India peacefully appointed a new Prime Minister on his death. The choice fell on the mild and unassuming Lal Bahadur Shastri who, like Nehru, had devoted much of his life to the service of India, spending nine years in prison for civil disobedience against British rule. He had held a variety of appointments under Nehru with particular responsibility for the laws against discrimination which were part of India's social revolution. Members of the right wing of the Indian National Congress resisted his appointment as Prime Minister and, although he went to war with Pakistan over Kashmir in 1965 (see Section 19.2), they continued to deplore his willingness to seek reconciliation and criticized his decision not to make India a nuclear power.

Shastri, however, died suddenly in January 1966 and once again India had to choose a new Prime Minister.

(c) Mrs Gandhi

Many found the choice of Mrs Gandhi surprising. No country in the world faced greater problems than India whose government required strength and abilities far above the average. But Congress chose Nehru's daughter, Mrs Indira Gandhi, who would have to face male prejudice in addition to other problems. Ceylon had created a precedent by appointing Mrs Bandaranaike as Prime Minister in 1960, and Mrs Golda Meir later became the Prime Minister of Israel in 1969; but no woman in the world faced responsibilities as enormous as those of Mrs Gandhi. Nevertheless, her government was so competent that she was re-elected both in 1967 and 1971. Between these elections, she smashed the powers of the *Syndicate*, the group of party bosses who had long dominated the Indian National Congress. Many of them were professional manipulators who did not share Nehru's idealism and they tended to discredit politics in India. For some time it had been thought that the only unity in Indian politics was the predominance of the Indian National Congress in the face of a disunited opposition. By winning re-election in 1971, after the split in Congress between the Syndicate and herself, Mrs Gandhi underlined both the strength of Indian democracy and her own personal authority.

She had been active in Indian politics since 1938 and had been elected President of the Indian National Congress in 1959. By 1964, when she took office in Shastri's cabinet, she was a widow. A woman of tremendous energies and outstanding abilities, she was well-prepared by her father for the strains of the Prime Ministership.

Apart from the struggle with the Syndicate and India's deep-rooted social and economic problems, Mrs Gandhi faced many disturbances. Communism had already taken root in several parts of India. In 1967, West Bengal returned a communist-dominated government and violent rioting there led to a period of presidential rule. Such disturbances always threatened the unity of India and at the beginning of the 1970s there was a new threat from a group of communist agitators known as Naxalites, who spread into India from Nepal armed with the *Thoughts of Chairman Mao*. Disorders were inevitable as long as India struggled even for bare subsistence. Reforms continued to yield results only slowly.

Hindi was being developed as a common language to promote national unity. Economic planning continued but not without setbacks. The fourth Development Plan aimed to increase India's wealth at the rate of 6 per cent per year, provide an additional 19 million jobs and raise average incomes over five years by about 25 per cent. Even if the aims were achieved, India would still be desperately poor but, in 1966, it was necessary to devalue the currency and, a year later, there was a grave food shortage with famine in Bihar. Natural disasters also continued to plague India. In 1971, the coast of Orissa was struck by a huge tidal wave and thousands were killed in this one storm alone.

Many of Mrs Gandhi's policies were socialist. She nationalized the banks and, after the election of 1971, took over the management of general insurance. She wished to rule the country for the benefit of the people as a whole and not in the interests of privileged groups. Her government aimed to achieve ambitious but realistic targets such as that in education, where it was intended to give all Indian children five years' schooling by 1975. People expressed approval of these policies in the election of 1971. Mrs Gandhi's supporters now held nearly 350 seats, having won more than 100. The opposition was hopelessly divided and two bickering communist parties had the next largest representation, with some 25 seats each.

In 1971, a flood of refugees from the war in Bangladesh added new burdens for India (see Section 19.2(*c*)). The soaring price of oil and the economic dislocation of the mid-1970s added yet more (see Section 18.1(*b*)). Disorders continued in India and Mrs Gandhi became more authoritarian. Her opponents alleged malpracice during the election of 1971, and in 1975 she was found guilty in the courts. She resorted to emergency rule, imprisoning critics and suspending the workings of democracy. At the same time, her son Sanjay launched a new drive to check India's ever-rising population which in some areas included compulsory sterilization. The outcry was considerable though the Gandhi government argued that stern action was necessary to stop the country drifting into anarchy. 1976 was a tense year but there was some return to normality at the beginning of 1977 and a new general election was arranged. The result was a massive defeat for Mrs Gandhi and for what some were beginning to call the 'Nehru dynasty'.

(*d*) Janata and Another Swing

The new Prime Minister in 1977 was Morarji Desai whose Janata Party and anti-Gandhi coalition won sweeping victories in the election. Desai was an old opponent of Mrs Gandhi. He had sought leadership of the Congress Party when she was preferred in 1966 and he had been one of the leaders of the Syndicate. New proceedings were started against the ex-Prime Minister but, warned perhaps by the example of Bhutto in Pakistan, Indians began to have second thoughts. Desai's government seemed to flounder amidst the country's problems and was internally divided. It was one thing to charge the Nehru family with corruption and harshness but another to rule India successfully. Desai slowed Gandhi's ambitious development plans and stopped compulsory sterilization but he could not be expected to produce instant results, and Mrs Gandhi's popular appeal proved too strong for him. Another election was held in 1979 and Gandhi swept back to power.

The electoral changes showed India's determination to persevere with democracy. Having rebuffed Nehru's daughter in 1977 for her emergency rule, the voters restored her only two years later. She suffered a grievous personal blow when her son Sanjay was soon afterwards killed in an accident. Her opponents had alleged that Sanjay was being prepared to continue the Nehru premiership. There were also allegations at the beginning of the 1980s that the Prime Minister was again reverting to undemocratic practices. But since independence, India had been almost a model democracy compared with most new nations, despite the enormous problems of government in so vast and so poor a country. Janata had provided no effective solutions to the difficulties, and the majority of Indians still hoped that the Congress (Indira) Party would successfully manage to combine democratic freedoms with real economic and social achievement.

Indira Gandhi's foreign policy still aimed to combine international influence with aloofness from the struggle of the superpowers. India remained one of the most important states in the Commonwealth, though friendship grew with the Soviet Union. Nuclear capability was shown when India exploded an atomic bomb in 1974 but there was no further evidence of any intention to produce and stockpile such weapons.

22.3   Africa

The retreat of the Europeans from Africa in the years after 1945 led to the emergence of about three dozen newly-independent states in the continent. Even the comparatively prosperous ones, such as Ghana, were in fact wretchedly poor. Tribalism also plagued many of the new African states, threatened to tear them apart, and helped to bring about civil war in the Congo and Nigeria (see Unit Twenty). The problems of southern Africa (see Unit Twenty-One) and the presence of Asians in East Africa were further complications. The problems which confronted a group of African states, formerly in the British Empire, during their first years of independence will now be considered.

(a) Ghana

Ghana was the first British state in Africa to achieve independence, in 1957. It was created mainly from the former Gold Coast Colony and the one-time mandated territory of Togoland. The country's first Prime Minister was Dr *Nkrumah* who also became its President when Ghana was declared a republic in 1960. Nkrumah was a socialist, eager to develop Ghana as a model for independent African states and also to advance the pan-African movement (creating links among African states to speed their development and increase their influence in the world). He was an enthusiastic supporter of the Organization of African Unity and, like Nasser in Egypt, was not unwilling to experiment in unions between his state and others. He formed, for example, a short-lived economic union with the former French colonies of Guinea and Mali.

Nkrumah, however, was a man in a hurry. Ghana embarked on a headlong programme of improvement which, although it had many beneficial results, plunged the country deeply into debt. His government, moreover, became increasingly dictatorial, built around a degree of hero worship which finally reached absurd proportions. He was removed from power by a military coup in 1966.

Ghana was unhealthily dependent on the exporting of cocoa, the production of which Nkrumah almost doubled. But the earnings from cocoa and other exports were not large and Ghana had few monetary reserves to fall back on. Nkrumah wished to give his people schools and hospitals and the higher standard of living which was common in Europe but this could be produced only by an industrial revolution. Industrialization, however, itself required vast sums of capital. This was Nkrumah's dilemma as it is the dilemma of all underdeveloped states. Rashly, he borrowed far more than Ghana could hope quickly to repay, until the country's debts amounted to almost £250 million, all the more embarrassing when the world price of cocoa fell steeply in the mid-1960s.

Some of Nkrumah's projects were nevertheless useful and sensible. The Volta River Project of 1961 would produce electricity and irrigate the land; linked to this scheme was an aluminium-smelting plant, begun in 1964. Nkrumah did much to justify his self-elected title of 'Founder of the Nation', with impressive developments in cattle-rearing, forest industries and fishing, in promoting village projects to improve water supplies and the environment, and in extending the social services. But there were also less creditable achievements. Money which Ghana could not afford was spent on prestige projects such as government buildings in Accra and a little-used motorway from Accra to Tema, and Nkrumah himself was soon being widely accused of extravagance.

He dealt harshly with his critics. In 1959, a Preventive Detention Act allowed the imprisonment of opponents without trial and, shortly afterwards, almost a thousand were lodged in jail. Even the President's own party, the Convention People's Party, was purged of dissent. In 1964, Ghana became a one-party state and all parties other than the CPP were disbanded. Although Ghanaians approved of the changes in a referendum and gave Nkrumah a personal vote of confidence, dictatorship and censorship were not what they had hoped for when Ghana became independent.

Nkrumah also had ambitions to play a major role in international affairs. He worked for improvements throughout Africa and took a keen interest in the affairs of the Commonwealth, deploring apartheid in South Africa but statesman enough to wish to persuade the South African government to moderate its policies rather than simply to drive that government from the Commonwealth. He also wished to develop Ghana's contacts both with the USA and the communist world and he travelled extensively. In February 1966, while Nkrumah was visiting China, his regime was overthrown. He was not allowed to return to Ghana and he died in exile in 1972.

The coup which deposed the President was carried out by the army and the police who imposed the military dictatorship of the *National Liberation Council* led by Major-General Ankrah. Overnight, Nkrumah's supporters melted away. The CPP was outlawed but the Council declared its intention to return to democracy as soon as possible and meanwhile (like Ayub Khan in Pakistan) to build the foundations for stable, civilian government. Ghana also intended to pay her debts. Some independence was restored to the courts and many of Nkrumah's political prisoners released from prison, but reorganization was not without its difficulties and, in 1969, Ankrah resigned after charges of corruption and was replaced by Brigadier Afrifa. Nevertheless, a new constitution was painstakingly worked out and, in August 1969, elections were held which brought to power the Progressive Party led by Dr *Busia*. The National Liberation Council was dissolved a month later.

The restoration of democracy reflected considerable credit on Ghana's military leaders but many of the country's basic problems remained. There

Fig. 22.3 President Nkrumah (second from the right) with Russian technicians at a Soviet Trade Fair in Accra, Ghana

was almost no tradition of genuine parliamentary government. Nkrumah had argued, with some justice, that strong rule was essential in the face of tribalism and violence by those in opposition. Now Busia not only faced the problem of paying Ghana's debts but also a high level of unemployment and sharply rising prices. In 1971, he was forced to devalue the currency and impose restrictions on imports. Labour troubles led to the abolition of the Ghanaian Trades Union Congress and it became clear that parliamentary government was in difficulties. The end was not long delayed. In January 1972, a military coup led by Colonel *Acheampong* removed Busia's government from power. Although the World Bank had renegotiated the terms under which Ghana's debts should be paid, the burden remained crippling, eating up a third of the country's export earnings and, with heavy interest payments, showed few signs of diminishing. Like the National Liberation Council, Busia had honestly sought to repay the money but, with a population of only eight million and an economy geared mainly to the production of cocoa, Ghana faced an almost impossible task. It was to some extent the responsibility of these richer nations who were insisting on their pound of flesh, that parliamentary government again collapsed in the country.

Acheampong ruled with a military council, hoping to restore civilian government towards the end of the 1970s. But this time it was military rule which ended in confusion. Acheampong stepped down in 1978 amidst charges of mismanagement. The new military leader was Fred *Akuffo* but preparations for the return to democracy were interrupted when a new coup overthrew Akuffo in 1979. Control of events seemed to pass to a new group of more youthful Ghanaians led by Jerry *Rawlings*. Afrifa, Acheampong and Akuffo were executed, but that produced a backlash, not least a Nigerian threat to cut off Ghana's oil supplies. Events continued to move rapidly and a general election was held in June 1979. Ghana thus embarked on another attempt to make democracy work and the new civilian government insisted that Rawlings retire. Its leader, Hilla *Limann*, was a comparative newcomer to politics though a distinguished scholar. Economic difficulties, corruption and tribal rivalries proved too much for him and, at the end of 1981, *Rawlings* seized power again, intent this time on a thorough cleansing of Ghanaian politics.

(b) Kenya

Independence was granted to Kenya in 1963 and the state was declared a republic a year later. The economy was basically agricultural, heavily dependent on the exporting of produce such as tea, coffee and sisal, and the country possessed little industry and few mineral resources. There were racial problems to be faced, for in addition to Arabs, Asians and Europeans, Kenya contained a variety of African ethnic groups and many tribes with strong intertribal rivalries. The dominant tribe was that of the Kikuyu to which Jomo Kenyatta, the first Prime Minister and President, belonged and which in the 1950s had been closely associated with the *Mau Mau*, a terrorist society which had sought to speed independence.

Kenyatta recognized the country's need for firm and continuous government. He was unwilling to resort to the more extreme authoritarian methods of Nkrumah but he aimed to give Kenya stability and to develop racial harmony. One-party rule proved necessary, that of KANU, the Kenya African National Union. Kenyatta also thought it necessary to imprison his former supporter, Oginga Odinga, lest a parliamentary opposition should encourage separatism. In 1969, Kenyatta's hopes of building one nation received a major setback when Tom Mboya, one of the government's most gifted ministers, was assassinated. Mboya was a Luo, one of the few non-Kikuyu to have a share in power.

Kenyatta also faced problems with Asians who, at independence, had retained non-Kenyan citizenship. The President was determined that there should be opportunities for all who were Kenyan citizens regardless of race and tribe, and Europeans who had accepted Kenyan citizenship were favourably impressed with the fairness and competence of his government. On the other hand, his policies of Africanization, although stopping far short of Amin's in Uganda, made it clear that those who refused Kenyan citizenship could not hope to retain their privileges.

Kenya's stability was a tribute to Kenyatta's leadership. Economic targets were steadily achieved and, in 1972, the President was returned to power in elections, although not all of his supporters were successful. At that time, Kenya had avoided both the financial anarchy of Ghana and the separatist troubles of Nigeria and the Congo. Much progress had been made towards racial harmony. Kenyans had certain restrictions on their freedom but the nation had survived with the minimum of bloodshed and progress was steady. Nevertheless, there was anxiety in the 1970s. Kenyatta entered his eighties and it remained to be seen whether he had built a system which could survive his death. It did so with hardly a tremor. When Kenyatta died in 1978, the Vice-President, Daniel Arap Moi, succeeded him. New elections were held in 1979 and Kenya continued along the moderate and mainly capitalist course which Kenyatta had charted. Moi, however, again thought it necessary to debar Oginga Odinga from politics in 1982, and the President's increasing authoritarianism led later in the year to an attempted coup which Moi survived.

(c) Tanzania

Tanganyika achieved independence from Britain in 1961, uniting with Zanzibar in 1964 to form Tanzania. One of the poorest states in Africa, Tanzania had one great asset, the distinctive rule of Nyerere, much younger than Kenyatta and one of the twenty-six children of an African chief.

Tanzania faced similar problems to Kenya, with added strains which arose from being closer to the racial problems of southern Africa and bordering on Mozambique. Government was in the hands of TANU, the Tanzania African National Union. Nyerere ruled as President, providing for many years an administration which was stable, competent and idealistic. He was uncompromising in his condemnation of racialism and bold in his defiance of European vested interests. Whereas Kenya pursued broadly capitalist policies, Nyerere favoured socialism. It was not, however, the socialism of industrialized Russia; in many ways it was closer to that of Mao, as was perhaps inevitable in a country so dependent on agriculture. Underlying Nyerere's philosophy was a passionate belief in equality. His *Arusha Declaration* committed Tanzania to extreme austerity in which all, including members of the government, would share. There was to be no room in the country for nepotism and corruption. Progress would be made largely by the efforts of Tanzanians themselves. Village projects such as those of Nkrumah in Ghana were encouraged. Nationalization was extensively practised and much of the economy was managed by the National Development Corporation.

Progress was slow, for hardly any countries in the world were poorer than Tanzania. Nyerere's goal was not, however, simply a matter of economic prosperity. He intended to develop new attitudes, a sort of African socialism far removed from the competitiveness of European and colonial society. Tanzania became a haven for socialists from all over the world, observing and in some cases contributing to one of Africa's most exciting experiments. The nation had little help from outside, for Nyerere's uncompromising hostility to capitalists, financiers and the pursuit of profit frequently exasperated the richer powers. But perhaps no country could claim with greater justification to be attempting to build a new society. Without doubt, the driving force behind this remarkable undertaking was to be found in the cheerful but thoughtful Nyerere, once a schoolteacher but, from 1955, the dedicated leader of his people.

Fig. 22.4 Julius Nyerere, a stamp of 1962 when Tanganyika became a republic. Self-help and co-operative villages were a distinctive part of the President's vision of the African socialism he aimed to encourage

Nyerere played an important part in helping both Frelimo to win control of Mozambique and the Zimbabweans to wrest their country from the minority whites. He also helped Ugandans to get rid of Amin. Border disputes between Uganda and Tanzania escalated until Nyerere finally sent troops into Uganda at the beginning of 1979 to assist Ugandan rebels. There were pious complaints that Tanzanians were interfering in the affairs of another state. But it was a comment on the disunity of African and other international bodies that it was left to one of the world's poorest nations to liberate Ugandans from a regime whose bombast and butchery were universally despised and condemned. Nyerere, at least, would not allow his ideals for Africa to be compromised any longer by the grotesque image of the continent projected by Amin. The intervention strained Tanzania's modest resources but Nyerere's troops remained in Uganda until 1981, helping in the enormous tasks of reconstruction. Obote returned to power, though by no means to a universal welcome, and Uganda balanced precariously on the verge of anarchy. Amin left a legacy of economic chaos and tribal hatreds. Civil war threatened and Obote's government was almost bankrupt. But the Tanzanians had their own problems and it was for the Ugandans to sort out the mess that Amin had left. At the beginning of the 1980s Tanzania was herself in grave economic difficulty as the costs of essential imports soared. She was desperately short of capital and had disappointing results to show for her co-operative village projects.

(d) Zambia

One of Nyerere's closest friends was Kenneth Kaunda, who led Northern Rhodesia to independence in 1964 as the new nation of Zambia and became President of the Zambian Republic. Kaunda shared at least some of Nyerere's ideals as well as his detestation of racialism.

Kaunda hoped to build a state free from racial discord but, in addition to a multiplicity of tribes, he faced the problem of being Southern Rhodesia's neighbour, in the front line of the conflict between black Africa and the white supremacists in the south of the continent. Zambia was also much dependent on copper-mining and on the world price of copper, which accounted for more than 90 per cent of the country's exports. Table 22.1 shows that, in 1970, when the price of copper was high, Zambia had a healthy balance-of-payments surplus. But it was a difficulty of developing nations that the prices of commodities, such as copper, fluctuated widely. The surplus in 1978 was much smaller and at other times, for example in 1975 and 1976, there were deficits. Such fluctuations meant that sometimes imports had to be cut back fiercely and that advance planning was always difficult because it was subject to price changes over which Third-World governments had little control.

Unemployment, crime and violence added to Kaunda's problems although for years he struggled, like Kenyatta, to keep his nation united and to restrain intertribal rivalries. Like Kenyatta, he was also faced with the difficulties created by a breakaway supporter. In the late 1960s, there was a suspicion that Kapwepwe, the Vice-President of Zambia, was aiming to set up a breakaway group in favour of the Bemba tribe of the north. The President was forced to become increasingly authoritarian and, in 1973, he reluctantly turned Zambia into a one-party state, perhaps the best safeguard against separatism among the country's seventy-three tribes. The 1970s proved difficult nevertheless. The ZamTan Railway provided an essential link, given Zambia's strained relations with white Rhodesia and Kaunda's conscientious efforts to enforce the international sanctions against his neighbour. But Zambia suffered from the economic disruption in southern Africa and shortages of maize brought further difficulties at the end of the 1970s. Kaunda, like Nyerere, worked hard to bring about a solution to the Rhodesian problem and, before a settlement was reached, Zambia suffered from Rhodesian counter-attacks against the bases of Nkomo and his guerillas north of the Zambezi. The birth of Zimbabwe in 1980 at last produced more normal conditions in the area. Kaunda had weathered the storm and Zambia could perhaps now look forward to making more substantial progress in the 1980s than had been possible previously.

Kaunda's aim was humane government which would put Zambia on the 'road to unity, peace and freedom'. At the height of the Rhodesian crisis he was often abused by a hostile press in Britain, misleadingly seen as hostile to African whites. But, like many other leaders in black Africa, Kaunda's aim was simply an end to racial discrimination and the privileges which in the past, in the Northern Rhodesian copper-belt as well as elsewhere in Africa, had gone along with being white. Zambia still had a need for white expertise in copper-production, and what the Zambian authorities wanted was racial harmony. Nation-building was never achieved overnight, however, and although the conflicts within southern Africa generally added to the stresses within Zambia, Kaunda remained as both a stabilizing and civilizing force.

22.4   Guyana

After considerable delay, when there seemed to be a danger that leadership in British Guiana would rest with the Marxist, Cheddi Jagan, Britain finally granted independence to the colony in 1966. The new nation was established with the name of Guyana and under the government of Forbes Burnham and the People's National Congress, which could now outvote in parliament Jagan's People's Party. At that time the British assumed that Burnham was more kindly disposed towards capitalism than Jagan was, but a more important difference between the parties in Guyana was that of race. History had left Guyana with a population about half of which was Asian, mainly of Indian descent. Another third were Africans, the rest being Amerindian or of mixed race. It had been Guyana's misfortune that the earliest political parties had been founded mainly on the basis of race, creating problems similar to those which developed in Africa when political parties largely represented tribes. Jagan was of Indian descent, Burnham of African descent. Burnham tended to attract the votes of those of mixed race. Other areas of the West Indies had similar racial mixtures but, in Trinidad, Dr Williams had founded the ruling People's National Movement on a broader base. In the struggle of emergent nations to establish unity it was a grave handicap when political parties were closely identified with the interests of racial or tribal groups, a problem seen at its worst in the general election in Pakistan in 1971.

In Guyana, Burnham was returned to power in the 1968 election in spite of protests by Jagan about vote-rigging. Two years later, the state was declared a republic. The nationalization of the Demerara Bauxite Company in 1971 and the increasing concentration of financial control in the hands of Guyanese showed that the government was increasingly favouring the socialist policies to which many emergent nations turned. Guyana also sought closer relationships with the USSR and China, in some ways seeming to adopt policies Jagan advocated. In 1972, Guyana joined Trinidad, Jamaica and Barbados in defying the wishes of the USA by establishing diplomatic links with Castro's Cuba. Burnham also joined the English-speaking Caribbean Free Trade Area and then the Caribbean Community and Common Market. He was prepared to pursue any economic ties that were in the interests of Guyana and, like many Third-World leaders, was little interested in the rivalries of the superpowers. In 1978, Guyana became an associate member of Comecon.

Guyana had a stronger economic base than many African states. Exports, mainly bauxite and sugar, largely financed imports. There was progress in electrification, land settlement and improving communications. Efforts were made, as in most emergent nations, to extend education and to develop social services. But the 1970s brought acute economic problems and Guyana like most other countries had to wrestle with inflation, unemployment and disappointed expectations. Guyana's problems were all the greater because of racial tension which hindered the growth of real national unity. Elections were postponed in the late 1970s while a new constitution was discussed, and Asians grew restless under what seemed to have become permanent government by Burnham and the People's National Congress. They complained of inequalities and of the Prime Minister's growing authoritarianism. The problem was to change the rigid political–racial divisions which had developed during the years of British rule and to admit Guyana's Asian population to a more effective part in government. Guyana therefore entered the 1980s balanced uneasily between a system that on paper appeared democratic and a government which relied heavily on security forces.

22.5   Israel

The development of Israel had to take place against the background of disturbed relationships with the neighbouring Arab world (see Section 19.1). The government's aim was to make the state self-supporting but a high level of imports, unmatched by exports, called for considerable skills in management. On the other hand, Israel had an advantage over many emergent nations. Financial assistance came from Jews in many parts of the world and reparations were paid by West Germany, at about £14 million a year up to 1965.

Israel needed both capital and imagination to develop into a modern state, prosperous and powerful enough to resist hostile neighbours. A large part of the country was infertile desert and, although a profitable export trade in diamonds developed, Israel had to depend to a large extent on producing fruit and textiles and on developing the production of oil, discovered in the Negev. About a thousand co-operative villages (*kibbutzim*) were among the imaginative experiments of the Israelis, developing the lands of Palestine like pioneers. Water was supplied to the western Negev from the River Yarkon with a pipeline almost six feet in diameter.

Israel continued to have a small minority of Palestinian Arabs but the state was overwhelmingly Jewish and national unity was encouraged by the hostility of Arab neighbours. It was also encouraged by the government of David Ben-Gurion who gave Israel a solid start as the first Prime Minister. Ben-Gurion was born in Poland, founded Israel's Labour Party (the Mapai), but ruled for many of the years until he resigned in 1963 as head of a coalition government. No man did more than he to found and establish the Jewish state.

Table 22.1   The trading position of some emergent nations in the 1970s

Country	Estimated population (millions)		Main exports % of whole (1970)	Exports mainly to % of whole (1970)	Imports mainly from % of whole (1970)	Trade balance Exports as % of imports	
	1971	1978				1970	1978
India	547.0	638.4	Jute manufactures 13% Tea 8%	USA 16% Japan 12%	USA 27% Britain 8%	93%	87%
Ghana	8.5	10.8	Cocoa 64% Timber 8%	Britain 23% USA 18%	Britain 24% USA 18%	110%*	94%**
Kenya	11.7	14.9	Coffee 29% Tea 16%	Britain 21% West Germany 10%	Britain 29% Japan 11%	54%	60%
Tanzania	13.3	16.3	Coffee 18% Cotton 14%	Britain 22% USA 10%	Britain 21% China 14%	89%	41%
Zambia	4.1	5.5	Copper 95%	Britain 26% Japan 24%	Britain 23% South Africa 23%	199%*	108%*
Guyana	0.8	0.8	Bauxite 34% Sugar 27%	USA 29% Britain 19%	Britain 31% USA 23%	99%	106%*
Israel	3.0	3.7	Diamonds 32% Fruit 16%	USA 19% Britain 10%	USA 22% Britain 16%	54%†	53%†

* Trade surplus ** 1977
† Israel's trade balance distorted because of the heavy importing of armaments.
(See also Table 18.1: income per head of the population.)

Ben-Gurion was succeeded by Eshkol, who had been born in Russia and, when Eshkol died, two years later, Mrs Golda Meir became Prime Minister. She had also been born in Russia. For a time she had served as Secretary of the Mapai and thus she continued the mildly left-wing government traditional in Israel since the state was founded. She also had to continue the delicate work of governing in such a way as to balance the demands for social improvement and economic development against the need to maintain strong military power for defence. In 1971, there was growing criticism that too little was being done for Israel's underprivileged, especially the oriental Jews, and that too much emphasis was being placed on foreign policy and defence. Such complaints were silenced when Israel was attacked by the Arabs in the Yom Kippur War of 1973 but after the war there were new charges alleging unreadiness for battle. Golda Meir resigned in 1974. The Labour Party now suffered from internal wrangling and Yitzhak Rabin, Israel's new Prime Minister, soon lost popularity, partly because of the imposition of heavy taxes. The general election of 1977 resulted in a victory for the more rightwing Likud and Menachem Begin came to power. Few voters could have expected that, with his record of fervent nationalism, Begin would soon be responding to Sadat's peace initiative, but such was the case. Not all of his supporters approved and there was perhaps more enthusiasm in Israel for the punitive raids which Begin continued to launch against Palestinians in the Lebanon. Begin became even more belligerent as the election of 1981 approached. His government survived that election by the narrowest of margins and much of Begin's energies were required in 1982 simply to remain in office. The Prime Minister nevertheless kept faith with Egypt by restoring Sinai in April that year, though he went on to escalate Israeli action in the Lebanon (see Section 19.1(g)). He also caused widespread dismay by continuing into 1983 to plant new Jewish settlements on the West Bank of the Jordan – land provisionally earmarked for the Palestinians.

22.6 The Tight-rope

Almost every government in the emergent nations is walking on a tight-rope. From this brief consideration of a small selection of states in Asia, Africa, the West Indies and the Middle East, one can see that the emergent nations face formidable though varied problems. Their fundamental needs are to establish a working and stable system of government and to use whatever resources may be available to push forward social and economic development as quickly as possible. But they work under intimidating difficulties. They must try to satisfy the expectations of subjects to whom independence offered both excitement and promise. Often they must work with tiny resources, a serious lack of capital and a shortage of personnel experienced in administration, business, industry and almost every other field. Far more perhaps than in long-established countries, the quality of leadership is of outstanding importance in the emergent nations. This Unit shows that at least some of these nations have been fortunate in the choices they have made. Yet there are limits to what even the most able leaders can achieve and in the 1980s it seemed to grow ever more urgent that the world as a whole should begin some reform of the world economic order (see Section 18.2). Without such reform, scores of emergent nations had little hope of escaping from the poverty trap in which they were caught.

Further Reading

Ayling, S.E.: *Portraits of Power*. Harrap (London, 1965) – Nehru.
Buah, F.K.: *A History of Ghana*. Macmillan (London, 1980).
Busia, K.: *Africa in Search of Democracy*. Routledge & Kegan Paul (London, 1969).
Davidson, B.: *Black Star, Kwame Nkrumah*. Penguin (Harmondsworth, 1973).
Edwardes, M.: *Nehru, A Political Biography*. Penguin (Harmondsworth, 1973).
Hodder, B.W.: *Africa Today*. Methuen (London, 1978).
Jones, P.: *Kwame Nkrumah and Africa*. Hamish Hamilton (London, 1965).
Nussbaum, E.: *Israel*. Oxford University Press (London, 1968).
Watson, J.B.: *The West Indian Heritage*. John Murray (London, 2nd edn. 1982).

Documentary

Breach, R.W.: *Documents and Descriptions, the World since 1914*. Oxford University Press (London, 1966) – Sections 27, 28, 33, 39, 57.
Nyerere, Julius: *Ujamaa, Essays on Socialism*. Oxford University Press (Dar es Salaam, 1968).

Exercises

1. Why is the progress of economic development slow in the nations mentioned in this Unit? Which of them may be expected to develop most quickly?
2. What does Table 22.1 reveal about the problems of emergent nations?
3. How do Fig. 14.3 and Table 22.1 illustrate differences between the economies of developed and developing nations? Explain why the wealth gap between rich and poor nations has recently widened and may be expected to widen further.
4. Select *two* of the nations mentioned in this Unit and *in each case* explain the importance to the nation of stable commodity prices.
5. Outline the history of India since independence paying particular attention to (a) political leadership, (b) economic problems and (c) social problems. Account for the limited change in relation to India shown in Table 18.1 on page 348.
6. Why, since independence, has the history of Ghana been apparently more turbulent than the histories of Kenya, Tanzania and Zambia?
7. What problems common to many emergent nations can be illustrated by reference to the history of Israel and Guyana? What less typical problems have *each* of these countries faced since independence?
8. Select from the following list those countries which in recent years have faced problems of development similar to the countries considered in this Unit: Canada; Indonesia; Jamaica; Malawi; Malaysia; New Zealand; Sri Lanka; Sweden. Find out more about *one* of the countries you have named and write an account of its history since independence similar to the accounts in this Unit.
9. Without reform of the world economic order 'scores of emergent nations (have)

little hope of escaping from the poverty trap in which they (are) caught' (page 446)
After re-reading Sections 18.1 and 18.2, explain and illustrate this statement.

10. Study this extract from the writings of Julius Nyerere, and then answer the questions which follow:

> The Arusha Declaration talks of men, and their beliefs. It talks of socialism and capitalism, of socialists and capitalists. It does not talk about racial groups or nationalities. On the contrary, it says that all those who stand for the interests of the workers and peasants, anywhere in the world, are our friends. . . . For if the actions taken under the Arusha Declaration are to mean anything to our people, then we must accept the basic oneness of man. . . . The colour or origin of the man who is working to that end does not matter in the very least. And each one of us must fight, in himself, the racialist habits of thought which were part of our inheritance from colonialism. . . . The equality of man is the first item in the TANU Creed. . . . Socialism and racialism are incompatible.

(a) Of which country was the author of this extract the ruler? What European countries had ruled this country during the years of *colonialism*?

(b) Find out more about and explain what is meant by *The Arusha Declaration*.

(c) What is *TANU*?

(d) Choose *one* of the following adjectives which seems best to describe this extract, and argue in support of your choice: authoritarian; communist; idealistic; revolutionary.

(e) What do you understand by *racialism*? What does the writer mean by *racialist habits of thought which were part of our inheritance from colonialism*?

(f) Suggest examples of how TANU tried to introduce *socialism* in the country you have named in (a).

(g) Making use of the Index to this book, show in what ways the author of this extract tried in his foreign policy to combat *racialism*.

Unit Twenty-Three
The Contemporary World

23.1 Into the 1980s

The cartoon with which the *Guardian* cartoonist Les Gibbard greeted the year 1980 caught much of the uncertainty and anxiety with which the world looked forward to another new decade (see Fig. 23.1). As the twentieth century went on, changes seemed to occur at an ever accelerating speed, producing one crisis after another, in rapid succession. In addition to two world wars the century had already witnessed unprecedented technological change with its accompanying social upheaval. Moreover, the international state system had been torn apart not merely by the emergence of the super-powers but by the collapse of the vast overseas empires which had earlier been a unifying force. It was therefore not surprising that the 1970s had seen a large number of storms and crises from which no continent had escaped unscathed. Indeed, it can be argued that what was more remarkable was that the world had absorbed so many shocks during the twentieth century without even more conflict and misery. There were nevertheless good reasons for the common fear in 1980 that the world's 'Destination' was now 'Unknown'.

An economic crisis was already almost universal (see Unit Eighteen). The 'Energy Crunch' had brought greatly increased prices for oil which were beginning to reflect the fact that oil reserves would not last for ever. Inflation was widespread, and it was now often linked with recession and soaring unemployment. Late in 1982 the latter afflicted over thirteen per cent of Britain's labour force, some ten per cent of that in the USA and around eight per cent of West German workers. All three countries faced formidable economic difficulties and West Germany's remarkable economic progress had come almost to a standstill. The communist world was no longer divorced from the world's economic problems, and the plight of many Third-World nations was desperate.

Gibbard filled the downstairs of his bus with British politicians – on the front seat, Margaret Thatcher, the Prime Minister, and Geoffrey Howe, Chancellor of the Exchequer. The upstairs passengers represented statesmen from various nations. At the front sat the two superpowers, whose vast nuclear arsenals were just one of the dangers the world faced. An anxious Jimmy Carter at this time faced a new election campaign at the end of which he was to be defeated heavily, not by Edward Kennedy his fellow-passenger and rival for the Democratic nomination, but by Ronald Reagan, the Republican (see Section 13.2(*h*)). Brezhnev was well into his seventies in 1980 and in failing health. The influence of Moscow both in Eastern Europe and further afield was perhaps now less than it had been when he came to power in 1964, and there was no shortage of those who argued that the Soviet system was yet another god that had failed during the twentieth century. The Soviet invasion of Afghanistan had just sparked off a new international crisis, seeming almost to confirm that the goodwill and detente between East and West in the mid-1970s had turned towards a new Cold War by the end of the decade (see Section 17.2).

The Ayatollah Khomeini was a comparative newcomer on the international stage, but a turbulent one (see Section 19.4). President Giscard of France, behind him, was soon to leave the stage, defeated in the French presidential election of 1981. Begin, Sadat and a disconsolate Palestinian represented the now old and deep-rooted problems of the Middle East (see Section 19.1) – Sadat soon to be assassinated, and the Palestinian guerillas to be evicted in 1982 from the Lebanon as they had earlier been evicted from Jordan. By that time, Begin's popularity was rapidly diminishing under fierce criticism of his aggressively interventionist tactics in the Lebanon and allegations of Israeli blunders in allowing the massacre of Palestinian civilians in Beirut.

The bus was full, but its passengers represented only a few of the problems

'*Good luck Kid – and by the way, there don't seem to be any brakes!*'

Fig. 23.1   New Year's Day 1980. An apprehensive start to the 1980s

the 1970s had left unsolved and which have been considered in earlier Units. No one imagined that there would not be new problems to add to them in the 1980s, and some of these too have already been glimpsed.

23.2   The Shifting Balance of Power

President Nixon referred to the early 1970s as an 'age of negotiation'. Many remarkable changes resulted from it. Communist China and the two Germanies were admitted to UNO. A flurry of treaties greatly relaxed East–West tensions in Europe and also increased contacts across the Iron Curtain. The urgency with which detente was now being pursued was seemingly symbolized in a new hot-line telephone link between East and West Germany. US–Soviet and US–Chinese relations seemed to improve steadily with the US withdrawal from Vietnam helping in the general thaw of Cold-War attitudes. Even in the Caribbean there was a thaw when small English-speaking nations and others, like Mexico, began to dismantle the diplomatic and commercial barriers which for more than ten years had isolated Cuba. But there was less change in other directions. Virtually no improvement took place in relations between the Soviet Union and China: indeed they soon seemed to deteriorate further, with rivalry for influence in Indochina after the ending of the Vietnam War. And countries the world over continued to spend money on armaments at rates which were economically ruinous and morally bankrupt. The early 1970s talks in Europe which made *least* headway were those in Vienna about the reduction of forces and weaponry in the centre of the continent.

The awesome accumulation of the weaponry of the USA and the Soviet Union, still the only real superpowers in the early 1980s, went on growing with fast developing technology and new devices such as the neutron bomb, capable of killing people while leaving property intact. In 1981 it was estimated that the Soviet Union had some $3\frac{1}{2}$ million men under arms, the USA some 2 million. France and West Germany each had almost half a million – the largest forces in Europe except for those of the USSR. China's forces seemed to exceed 4 million, though that was not excessive in a population of now over 1 000 million and by the yardstick of proportions elsewhere. China commanded growing attention not least for her sheer size. But despite her nuclear arsenal, China still lagged well behind in the technological race of the superpowers. Nevertheless, China's emergence during the 1960s and 1970s had fundamentally altered the balance of power. What after 1945 had seemed to be a simple East–West confrontation had become a three-cornered contest involving the USA, the USSR and China in which, at the start of the 1980s, it seemed to be the USSR which was being isolated by the other two (see Unit Seventeen).

There was therefore anxiety in the early 1980s lest the movement towards detente between the US and Soviet blocs should turn out after all to be no more than an illusion. Europe was no longer the main bone of contention between the superpowers and their allies, and the new Cold War, if such it was, centred elsewhere. The West insisted on regarding Soviet policy in Afghanistan as an outrage, suspicions heightened by the West's great anxieties about the security of its oil supplies from the Middle East. It was by no means clear that the USSR intended to threaten those supplies and, like the interventions in Hungary in 1956 and Czechoslovakia in 1968, the invasion of Afghanistan could be seen as a question of Soviet security (see Section 17.1(*d*)). Nevertheless, it was this invasion and the outcry it provoked that brought the phrase 'Cold War' back into fashion (see Fig. 23.2). It was an invasion which also angered many Third-World nations who saw it as yet another example of great-power 'imperialism'.

Fig. 23.2 The return of the Cold War? A speculative comment in 1980. President Carter viewed the Soviet invasion of Afghanistan with dismay and the new coldness between the superpowers threatened to put Detente to flight. The 1980s had still to show whether the Cold War Yeti was real

Decolonization since 1945 had all but ended the once vast colonial empires (see Unit Sixteen). But it did not end imperialism: the developed world continued to interfere unashamedly in the affairs of former colonies, manipulating economies and political systems to the advantage of Americans, Europeans and Russians. Economic weakness and Third-World disunity left the emergent nations vulnerable to such manipulation. Yet there were already indications that change was afoot. The overthrow of the Shah of Iran and expulsion of US influence ended the 1970s with a major rebuff to one of the superpowers. In 1982, Argentina and Britain confronted one another over the Falkland Islands. The great powers already found it increasingly difficult to get their own way in the UN General Assembly in face of the votes of Third-World nations, and it seemed more than likely that the 1980s would see further evidence that the balance of power was shifting along the lines forecast in 1972 by Dr Waldheim (see Section 22.1). International relations, it seemed, were growing ever more complicated: the US–Soviet rivalry being complicated first by China, and the affairs of all the major powers becoming further complicated by a growing determination to be heard on the part of the scores of emergent nations of the South.

Section 18.2 has shown that this was an economic problem as well as a political one. What was in fact becoming increasingly clear in the 1970s and 1980s was the world's inter-dependence. Not only were problems intertwined: the well-being of nations was intertwined. The near-breakdown of the world economic order and the state of flux of the world's political and diplomatic order seemed to guarantee that the 1980s would be a Decade of Confusion. Fast growing population, the consumption of the earth's resources, greater awareness of inequalities and the existence of vast armouries in a world brutalized by almost uncountable twentieth-century wars – all these made the outlook daunting and constructive action urgent. But what was certain was that the pace of change would not slow down, and that alone was enough to alarm the passengers travelling on Gibbard's bus (Fig. 23.1) – a bus which did not appear to have 'any brakes'.

23.3   An Age of Violence

The 1960s and 1970s each set new standards as a decade of violence. The terrible atrocities of the war in Vietnam added new dimensions to the history of man's inhumanity to man, all the more degrading as the world's richest nation used its airpower mercilessly to pulverize the towns of North Vietnam. Alongside the raids of the B–52s, the world's other atrocities sometimes seemed almost insignificant, but they were all part of a dismal picture of intolerance and barbarism which showed no signs of lessening in the 1980s. The US withdrawal from Vietnam had not halted the killing in Indochina. In Pol Pot's Kampuchea, by speeding up change, it seemed only to have unleashed more killing and the country was engulfed in an orgy of genocide. Conflict between Kampuchea and Vietnam and between Vietnam and China brought yet more bloodshed and devastation to the area.

Units Nineteen, Twenty and Twenty-One considered some of the areas in which there was killing in the years after 1945. In some of them, like the Middle East and Northern Ireland, peoples seemed to have become trapped in regular outbreaks of bloody confrontation from which it seemed impossible to escape. Each successive year produced only some new horrific variation on the monotonous basic theme. It was a characteristic of the postwar world that wars were no longer ordinarily confined to armies and to formal engagements. Between the Arab-Israeli wars fought by the armies there occurred numerous commando raids, terrorist attacks and deadly 'incidents'. In the prelude to the Yom Kippur War, the Jews raided neighbouring territories to kill guerillas and destroy their bases, and shot down an Arab airliner, killing nearly all its passengers. Arabs too made raids, and sent letter-bombs by post, hardly discriminating among the victims they killed. Atrocities and reprisals merged into a grim pattern of cruelty, revolving murderously around the Palestinian problem and scores of other problems involving nationalist rivalries throughout the world. In the Arab-Israeli confrontation, the Yom Kippur War was no more than an interlude. Israeli-Egyptian relations improved but there was little change elsewhere and, as has been seen, the Lebanon became the setting for new vicious conflict.

Whether the origins of a problem were international or national made little difference to the violence and ferocity with which causes were promoted. Hi-jacking aircraft, seizing embassies and diplomats, taking and sometimes murdering hostages, planting bombs and assassinating were activities which seemed in the 1960s, 1970s and 1980s to spread like some modern plague. Individual countries like Uganda which suffered first the butchery of Amin, and then the frenzied killing in the confusion which followed Amin's overthrow, endured their own horrors, ever hopeful that some sort of peace might eventually be restored as it had been in other new nations such as Nigeria and Bangladesh. But the high level of violence was by no means confined to the world's emergent nations. In most of the countries of the developed world the urban terrorist became a familiar figure during the 1970s. Organizations such as the IRA, the Italian Red Brigades, and the anarchists of West Germany known as the Baader–Meinhof Group were only some of those who stained the 1970s with blood, and the broken bodies and corpses of their victims bore regular witness to the savagery of the modern world. Few countries escaped the activities of assassins, arsonists, bombers and the ruthless bully-boys who, with or without official approval, preferred force to argument in pursuit of their aims. The safety of public figures everywhere became just one of the matters for concern. Within weeks in 1981, President Reagan of the USA and Pope John Paul II were both wounded by the bullets of would-be assassins.

At that time El Salvador was developing as a comparatively new theatre of armed conflict, the military government there adopting many of the tactics towards dissent that Pinochet had used in Chile. In Afghanistan, the Soviet Union seemed to be becoming trapped in a conflict which had already begun to show similarities to that in which the USA had been involved in Vietnam. The Lebanon and Uganda continued in their anguish. Liberation forces in Africa – SWAPO in Namibia, the Polisario Front and the Eritreans – carried on their struggles. Basques in Spain continued to do battle with the government, and the level of violence in Northern Ireland went on unabated. Violence itself hardened attitudes and made ever more difficult the solution of the genuine problems from which the violence stemmed.

The terrorists (or freedom fighters in the eyes of their friends) argued that there was no alternative course of action since governments neglected to tackle injustice and inequalities. It was another feature of the modern world that people generally were less willing to suffer injustice quietly. Almost everywhere the underprivileged raised their voices in protest. Red Indians as well as blacks protested in the USA. Jews and dissidents protested in the USSR. The aborigines protested in Australia. Students remained turbulent in Japan, and aggrieved labour forces made industrial relations stormy in innumerable countries. For those in authority and those accustomed to take their own comforts for granted, such unrest was disquieting, challenging it seemed the very fabric of existing societies.

Equally disquieting in the 1970s and 1980s were the violent crime and hooliganism which afflicted many societies. Cities generally, especially those in the USA, were plagued by criminals, particularly 'muggers' – thugs, many of them youngsters, who practised robbery with violence. Wanton vandalism was widespread too, especially in the West, where public and sometimes private property seemed to attract growing malice from the disaffected. The twentieth century had certainly not invented violence, but never had violence seemed so widespread and never had it shown itself more frequently in the form of apparently senseless cruelty and destructiveness.

23.4   The Human Environment

Not only was man doing violence to man: there was growing awareness that he was also doing violence to his environment. The world's population at the beginning of the 1970s was nearing 3 750 million. The Brandt Report of 1980 put the then total at 4 300 million, forecasting that by the end of the century it would reach 6 000 million or more. Such figures are difficult to comprehend, but the Report dramatized 'the present staggering growth' by adding that in 1980 the world's population was increasing by over a million every five days. Along with concern about this upsurge went concern about the ways in which human beings were using up the earth's resources and polluting the environment.

(a) Population

90 per cent of the increase in population occurs in Third-World countries, much of it in Asia. In the 1970s already over half of the world's people were Asians, living on about a fifth of the world's land surface. Such was the rate of increase that from about 2 000 million in the early 1970s the population of Asia was likely to rise to around 3 000 million by the end of the 1980s. Almost half these Asians lived in China. About a quarter lived in India. China's government claimed that policy kept pace with the needs of the rising population, though by the early 1980s the outside world had glimpses of food shortages in China. The effects of population growth could be seen more clearly in India, however. In the early 1970s the annual birth rate in India was around 4.2 per cent, the death rate around 1.7 per cent, and the country's population increased at an annual rate of about 2.5 per cent. That was by no means the fastest in the world. It was higher than that of any country in Europe but lower than that of many states in the Middle East and some states

in Africa. Nevertheless, it was a grave threat to India's future development and efforts to break free from poverty. In the 1970s some 200 million Indians lived in dire poverty and the situation changed hardly at all from one year to the next.

Fig. 23.3 A stamp of 1966, part of India's campaign to reduce the country's birth rate. Such campaigns achieved only limited success

1974 was designated World Population Year and the World Population Conference met in Bucharest. 'The urgency of the global crisis' produced declarations of anxiety but the Conference could hardly be expected to do much more than publicize the problem. For the moment the problem varied from one part of the world to another. The populations of countries already wealthy grew more slowly than those elsewhere though hardly anywhere was population actually diminishing. The annual growth in the USA and the USSR was around one per cent a year. In Britain and many parts of Europe it was below one per cent. Increasing wealth in these countries more than matched population increases and what problems resulted from the latter had more to do with crowded urban living than with feeding the starving. There was little overcrowding in Africa. Some states like Botswana and Namibia were indeed thinly populated with plenty of space for expansion. Growth rates were such that the population of Africa seemed likely for the first time to outstrip that of Europe some time during the 1980s. Like emergent nations generally, however, most African states were engaged in a desperate struggle to match increases in population with increases in wealth. Even then they would not improve their living standards: to raise the latter, economic growth needed to run ahead of population growth. But in India, other parts of Asia and parts of Latin America, all the various problems combined. Cities such as Calcutta were already dreadfully overcrowded; reserves of land were dangerously low, and the economic difficulties were such that the production of extra wealth could at best barely keep pace with the growing number of human beings to be supported. Feeding, housing, educating, employing and sustaining the population, even at modest levels, already taxed many emergent nations to their limits. This was the dilemma to which there were no ready solutions to be had either in World Population Year or in the years which followed.

The growth of population in countries such as India, Pakistan, Bangladesh and Indonesia threatened to combine with economic and social discontent to undermine political stability. There were also fears that, just as population pressures increased Japan's aggressiveness in the 1930s, the changing balance of the world's population might cause international problems in the future. The USSR suspected that the thinly-populated lands beyond the Urals might eventually prove a great temptation to a more densely-populated China. Africa and Latin America were obviously about to outstrip Europe and North America in manpower. Non-whites already outnumbered whites, and the gap was certain to go on growing – all the more so since, while life expectancy throughout the northern hemisphere was already over 65, this was not yet true anywhere in the southern hemisphere with the exception of Argentina and Australasia. The implications of these changes were yet only dimly perceived as the twentieth century moved towards its close.

(b) Resources and Pollution

The wealthy nations sometimes regarded the rapid growth of population as a problem mainly for the poor, about which they would prefer to remain ignorant. Nevertheless, it was a fact in the 1970s that a child born in the USA was likely to consume during his lifetime twenty times as much as a child born in India; he would also contribute about fifty times as much to the pollution of the environment. A conference of over a hundred nations met in Stockholm in 1972 to discuss environmental problems, a belated recognition of problems already urgent: man was steadily destroying the 'air, water, land, flora and fauna' around him and was rapidly consuming some of the earth's most important resources.

(i) **The problems**. Technological development was much to blame for the damage to the environment. Industrial plant consumed large quantities of fuel and raw materials. Industry also produced suffocating smoke and poisonous gases and gave rise to dangerous and unsightly waste which was deposited on land, in rivers and in the sea. Developments in nuclear power not only produced deadly radioactive fall-out when weapons were tested, but such dangerous by-products that nuclear power stations were introduced more slowly than had been expected. Resistance movements grew up protesting against such power stations, and in Austria so effectively that, at the beginning of the 1980s, plant which had been built remained unused. Governments and experts blandly asserted that nuclear power stations were 'safe', but, nevertheless, accidents and leakages occurred in the USA and elsewhere.

The relentless march of technology caused a disquiet that produced a variety of pressure groups in the developed world. They had plenty about which to campaign. Poisonous discharges into rivers upset the balance of nature and killed fish. Dangerous deposits on land, for example of cyanide, threatened immeasurable hazards to future generations. The use of pesticides on crops gave rise to anxiety about their effects on human and animal life. Even the seas became ever more contaminated, a dump for all manner of waste products, regularly fouled by oil spillages. There was concern at holiday resorts as oil, sewage and miscellaneous rubbish floated onto their beaches, but the greatest danger lay in the likelihood that the seas would grow ever more hostile to life, until the oceans became as dead as many of the rivers in the industrialized countries.

For millions in the cities, smog (a suffocating mixture of smoke, fumes and fog) was already another hazard. The exhaust gases of motor vehicles added to the fumes produced by industry. Diseases such as bronchitis and lung cancer took a heavy toll of city dwellers and, in some places, drove people to wearing masks and even to seeking to survive with refreshing breaths of oxygen. Tokyo and Los Angeles in the 1970s presented a bleak picture of the fate in store for cities everywhere if steps were not urgently taken to restore fresh air to their peoples. By the end of the 1970s another danger was being identified. The lead in petrol seemed a likely cause of brain damage to children forced to live in close proximity to heavy traffic. The motor car and the aeroplane were twin symbols of the twentieth century but both had their drawbacks. Along with industry they depleted the world's oil supplies until, in spite of the discovery of new oilfields such as those under the North Sea, petroleum products seemed by no means certain to outlast the twentieth century. Utterly dependent on their motor vehicles, the citizens of the developed world viewed the prospect with alarm. Oil became dearer too, one consequence of which was to raise doubts about the viability of the Anglo-French Concorde. Concorde successfully demonstrated technological skill in supersonic passenger flight in the 1970s, but its costs of production were enormous and it consumed vast quantities of expensive fuel. It also aroused the furious opposition of those who objected to its noise since here was another sort of pollution. The roar of traffic, aircraft and all kinds of machinery, and the spread of transistor radios made people sensitive to new sources of disturbance. Supersonic flight was therefore banned over many areas, and, even where non-supersonic flight was the issue, the siting of airports became a matter for fierce controversies. It seemed that attitudes were changing, and that growing numbers of people by the 1980s were concerned more with the protection of their environment than with the onward march of ever more sophisticated technology.

(*ii*) **The search for solutions**. Many countries, Britain, for example, brought in laws to tackle specific environmental problems, improving the atmosphere with Clean Air Acts and making a start on cleaning up the waters of rivers like the Thames. Individual countries searched for new supplies of fuel and experimented with new sources of power, such as wave-power and solar power. African states were among those which made earnest efforts to preserve wild life, so often threatened since the invention of the gun and the growth of markets among the wealthy and insensitive for ivory, skins and furs. The well-to-do consuming nations had an appetite not only for oil and what they regarded as essentials, but for luxuries and trinkets – a passion for fur coats and ivory chessmen, for example, which showed scant regard for a natural heritage that might not survive for future generations. Individuals and nations were slow to curb their own greed but it was a feature of the 1970s and 1980s that the greedy came in for growing criticism. Japan and the Soviet Union, insensitive, it seemed, to the need to conserve the world's shrinking whale population, were condemned almost annually; and the Canadian enthusiasm for killing seal pups, partly for their skins and partly it was claimed to protect the livelihood of fishermen, produced widespread disgust.

The United Nations Conference on the Human Environment which met in Stockholm in 1972 provided a forum for the discussion of environmental problems at an international level. The British representative stated the general principle with which there was agreement: 'We believe that the pressing need is to create more of the right kind of wealth and to use it much more wisely: to clean up rivers, to quieten engines, and above all, on a global scale, to get rid of poverty, illiteracy and disease.' There could be no retreat from technology, no abandonment of development. The Third-World nations at Stockholm insisted on their right to pursue industrialization as the likeliest key to raising their living standards. But all were aware of the problems that uncontrolled development had already created, polluting the North and the oceans, and plundering the South for resources. The aim of the Conference was to lay down guidelines for future co-operative effort in which there would also be protection for man's environment.

No master-plan could be agreed. The problems were too big for immediate solution and the nations were inclined to disagree on detail. China wanted to place the blame for pollution on 'the plunder and aggression of imperialism and colonialism', and suggested the total abolition of nuclear weapons. When neither proposal was accepted, the Chinese refused to sign the rather vague Declaration in which members of the Conference expressed their intention to protect and improve the environment and guard against the exhaustion of 'the non-renewable resources of the earth'. Neither China nor France was willing to stop testing nuclear weapons in the atmosphere. Japan insisted on reserving the right to hunt whales. Other countries too safeguarded what they considered their special interests. But the Conference was not a failure. There was recognition of problems which the world could no longer ignore. There were a number of specific agreements on the protection of plants and animals, on monitoring the atmosphere and the seas and on surveying the earth's remaining resources. Much was left to individual governments to carry out but the UN was expected to promote further action. A Council was soon afterwards set up to monitor what became the UN Environmental Programme (UNEP).

Even before the end of 1972 more than fifty nations had agreed not to dump in the sea certain categories of waste and gradually such agreements multiplied. The Law of the Sea was debated at Caracas in 1974, though with limited results concerning such difficult problems as oil pollution and the preservation of fish stocks. Here too foundations had been laid when the UN Conference on the Law of the Sea (UNCLOS) became another regular institution in which to seek solutions and the betterment of the lives of millions. It was encouraging that, at Stockholm and now elsewhere, mankind had begun to recognize that there existed 'only one earth'. By 1982, UNCLOS drew up a wide-ranging Law-of-the-Sea Treaty dealing with conservation, rights of passage and the mining of the seabed. Outside of twelve miles of territorial waters and an economic zone extending two hundred miles from national coastlines, the Treaty declared the seas 'the common heritage of mankind'. It was warmly welcomed, especially in the Third World; but seabed-mining nations in the North had reservations about the restrictions which might now be imposed on their operations. The Soviet Union, France and Canada signed the Treaty at a meeting of UNCLOS in Jamaica towards the end of 1982. The USA, Britain and West Germany declined to sign though support for the Treaty came from well over a hundred other nations. It was not surprising that in many developed states ecology parties were now growing, seeking to put political pressure on governments to widen their horizons and to serve peoples rather than narrow sectional interests. Such an Ecology Party played a prominent part in the general election in West Germany early in 1983 after the retirement of Helmut Schmidt.

Despite the world's violence and troubles, there was greater awareness of man's problems in the 1980s than at any time in history. It was also true that, in spite of the world's many miseries, countless millions now enjoyed a standard of living and quality of life undreamed of by earlier generations. Armies of people were at work to bring about the further betterment of the human race. In international organizations such as the United Nations and the Commonwealth, in regional organizations such as the Alliance for Progress, the OAU and ASEAN, in countless voluntary organizations such as Oxfam, War on Want and the Save the Children Fund, unnumbered people devoted themselves to constructive effort to spread prosperity and tranquillity. But all too easily the history of the contemporary world can seem to be no more than a journey through chaos leading only to disaster. Constructive work seldom captures the headlines, and newspapers and the rest of the media seem drawn more readily to disruption and confrontation than to construction and co-operation. Only occasionally does the quiet service to mankind which constantly goes on receive much publicity – for example, for some splendid achievement such as the near-eradication of smallpox, some dramatic initiative such as Sadat's pursuit of peace with Israel, or some especially heroic devotion to relief work such as that of the Red Cross and other agencies in West Beirut, when that city was under attack by the Israelis in the summer of 1982. To dwell only on the gloom of a world beset with problems is to neglect the array of people and institutions whose services to mankind have already more than matched the activities of the power-seekers, the bombers and the thugs.

Further Reading

Hayes, D.: *Terrorists and Freedom Fighters*. Wayland (Hove, 1980).
Jenkins, I.M.L.: *Science and Technology*. Hamish Hamilton (London, 1966).
Jones, C., Gadler, S.J. and Engstrom, P.H.: *Pollution: The Population Explosion*. Dent (London, 1972).
Population Growth. (Folder) VCOAD Education Unit.
Richardson, R. (ed): *Learning for Change in World Society*. World Studies Project (London, 1976).

Exercises

1. Write an account of the uncertainties with which the world entered the 1980s. What particular problems faced any *two* of the 'upstairs passengers' shown in the cartoon at Fig. 23.1?

2. Define *each* of the terms *Cold War* and *detente*. Explain what progress there had been towards detente during the 1970s in the relations of the USA and the USSR. Which term has better described US–Soviet relations since the 1970s?

3. What has been meant in recent years by *hegemony*? What arguments would have been put forward in the early 1980s by those who alleged that the USSR was seeking hegemony? What arguments would have been put forward by those who denied that this was so?

4. 'The 1960s and 1970s each set new standards as a decade of violence' (page 452). Identify *two* episodes in *each* of these decades which would support this statement. What were those responsible for the violence of the episodes you have selected hoping to achieve?

5. Select *one* place of conflict during the last twenty years or so and explain how those involved might be depicted by their enemies as 'terrorists' but by their friends as 'freedom fighters' (page 453).

6. Account for, and examine the consequences of, what the Brandt Report called 'the present staggering growth' of the world's population (page 454).

7. Making use of the Index to this book, show how the supply and price of oil have resulted in crises during the 1970s and 1980s.

8. What activities for the benefit of mankind do you associate with (*a*) UNEP, and (*b*) UNCLOS? Suggest and describe *one* further example of a UN institution which works for the good of the human race. Why is the progress made by all these institutions not more rapid?

9. List the environmental problems which exist in your own community. What action has been and is being taken to deal with them?

10. List *ten* major technological achievements of the years since 1945. Alongside *each* set down the ways in which the achievement may be considered (*a*) to have benefited the human race, and (*b*) to have had less desirable effects for the human race. What conclusions can you draw from this exercise about the benefits or otherwise of 'the onward march of ever more sophisticated technology' (page 457)?

Glossary

Amnesty The granting of forgiveness, a pardon, usually to political offenders.

Apartheid South African system for separating the races.

Appeasement Reaching agreement by negotiation and conciliation. In the late 1930s it came to be identified with giving way to aggressive powers.

Arbitration The settlement of disputes through the verdict of a third party.

Autarky A plan for economic self-sufficiency in Nazi Germany. Germany would not be economically dependent on other nations.

Authoritarian Not liberal; usually applied to a government which imposes strict discipline and represses its opponents.

Autocracy Absolute rule by one man, a dictatorship.

Bolshevik Party Part of the Russian Socialist Democratic Party which believed in working as a dedicated organization to bring about a Marxist revolution; followers of Lenin. Members of the party were known as *Bolsheviks*. The party later changed its name to the Russian Communist Party.

Bourgeoisie The middle classes.

Caste Hereditary class in India, its members socially equal and united in religion. Usually linked with occupation and the means of livelihood. Exclusive, having little contact with those outside the caste. The term is often applied to the over 2 000 divisions of Hindu society. The four main divisions are into priests, rulers and warriors, traders and farmers, and artisans. Those outside these divisions are *untouchables* (see below).

Centre Middle-of-the-road, usually of political parties. Neither extreme socialists nor extreme conservatives.

CIA Central Intelligence Agency. A national security body of the United States Federal Government operating secretly for the gathering of strategical and political information and in the pursuit of US policy. Much suspicion attaches to its operations, e.g. concerning the overthrow of Allende in Chile.

Coexistence A state of international relations in which rivals tolerate one another and exist side by side despite continuing dislike and differences. Compare *detente* (see below).

Cold War A war fought with propaganda and economic weapons, stopping short of military confrontation, as between the USA and the USSR after 1945.

Containment The building of alliances to prevent expansion by a rival power.

Coup d'état   A sudden and illegal change of government; a seizure of power.

Curzon Line   The proposed Polish-Russian frontier put forward by the British in 1920.

Democracy   Rule by the people: a system of government which permits some effective control to the masses.

Desegregation   The ending of *segregation* (see below).

Detente   The easing of strained relations, the relaxation of tension between states. A state of international relations rather less negative than that of *coexistence* (see above).

Dictatorship   Rule by a dictator, similar to *autocracy* (see above).

Dominion   Term used to describe the first independent members of the British Commonwealth of Nations, e.g. Canada. *Dominion status* was defined in 1926. The Dominions were free from British control but retained a connection with the British monarchy.

Franchise   The right to vote.

Guerilla   A fighter engaged in irregular warfare, often as a member of fairly small bodies resisting authority. *Guerilla warfare* is often associated with resistance movements using hit-and-run tactics and resorting to sabotage. *Urban guerillas* operate in towns.

Hegemony   Leadership and influence. It was an allegation commonly made by the Chinese after c.1960 that the Soviet Union's ambition was hegemony – to exert influence and authority over other countries.

Holocaust   Sweeping destruction, purging: a term applied to the Nazi slaughter of the Jews.

Impeachment   A charge before a court or tribunal, usually in connection with the misuse of official authority.

Indemnity   Often used for a sum of money, a sort of fine, required by one country from another after war. See *reparations*.

Independence   Freedom. The freedom granted to former colonies when the mother country gives up control of them.

Integration   Merging together; the merging together of peoples of different race into one society.

KGB   Soviet Committee for State Security, set up in 1954 after the downfall of Leonid Beria. In addition to supervising the secret police and maintaining internal security, the KGB became involved in espionage and counter-espionage. Compare the United States *CIA*.

Ku Klux Klan   An American secret society and terrorist organization with bigoted right-wing views. The Klan originated in 1866 soon after slavery ended in the USA. Anti-black, anti-Catholic, anti-communist, Klan activities are murky, pseudo-religious and vicious.

Lebensraum Living-space, elbow room. The areas which N̶ claimed were necessary for Germany's development. Such areas we̶ rich in economic resources.

Mafia Robber bands which originated in Sicily – a criminal organization.

Mandates Mandated territories. Areas placed under the control of selected powers by the League of Nations, so that they could be prepared for *independence*. Some of them remained to become UN Trust Territories at the end of the Second World War, e.g. Tanganyika.

Ministerial responsibility The responsibility of government ministers to parliament. Ministers must answer to parliament for their actions. This is regarded in many countries as an essential part of a system which is democratic.

Monetarism A belief that national economies can be controlled by managing the money supply; made fashionable at the end of the 1970s by the work of economists such as Milton Friedman.

Nation Loosely, an independent country.

Nationalism Pride in one's country, enthusiasm for the country's success. Nationalism may take various forms, e.g. a campaign to free one's country from foreign control; a campaign to make one's nation united and strong; a campaign to make one's country supreme over others.

Nationality Belonging to a nation. The citizens of France have French nationality.

Nation state An independent country populated to a large extent by people of common stock united by language and culture.

Nationalization Converting into national property, placing under state ownership, i.e. the nationalization of railways, making railways the property of the nation instead of the property of private owners.

Oder–Neisse Line The Polish-East German boundary since 1945 (see Fig. 11.2). The effect of this boundary was to remove from Germany lands to the east of the Line.

Pact An agreement, a treaty.

Partisans Fighters for freedom, freedom fighters: see *guerilla*. A term used during the Second World War, e.g. in Jugoslavia.

Plebiscite A vote by people in a given area on a particular question, e.g. the inhabitants of the Saar on the future of that region.

Proletariat The working masses.

Protection A system of *tariffs* (see below) to protect home industries against foreign competition. The opposite of free trade.

Race A group of persons of common descent, of distinctive ethnic stock. Strictly, mankind is divided into five races, e.g. Caucasoids, Negroids.

Europeans are Caucasoids, but can be sub-divided, e.g. Nordic, Mediter-ranean. *Race* is used not uncommonly (though strictly speaking not accurately) for further sub-divisions similar to nationalities (see *nationality*).

Radical Enthusiastic for major change, for reform.

Reactionary Backward-looking, desiring to put back the clock; opposed to change.

Referendum Direct consultation of the people, similar to a *plebiscite* (see above).

Reparations Compensation for injury and damage. Similar to an *indemnity* (see above) but compensation rather than a fine.

Republic A state without a monarchy.

Reserves (gold/foreign currency) Gold and foreign currency available within a state to pay for its imports and to support its own currency. For example, if Britain possesses large reserves of gold and US dollars, there is likely to be more confidence in the value of the pound.

Revisionism Theories which depart from the teachings of Karl Marx and seek to 'revise' (amend) them. Commonly used by the Chinese of the policy of the Soviet Union under Khrushchev and later leaders, and intended as a term of abuse. 'Revisionism' can take many forms: Marx's ideas have often been adapted, e.g. by Lenin (Marxism–Leninism) and by Mao (Maoism). Mao used the term to denounce those who argued that communism might be achieved by non-violent means, though Marx himself had not ruled this out.

Sanctions Penalties, methods with which to put pressure on nations which commit unpopular acts. *Economic sanctions* (e.g. against Rhodesia in the 1960s) involve restrictions on trade. *Military sanctions* (e.g. against North Korea in 1950) involve armed action.

Secession Separation, breaking-away: within any union (of states, tribes or nationalities) one part may wish to break away, to secede.

Segregation Separation, usually imposed. The authorities may wish to seg-regate different groups of people. See *apartheid, desegregation*.

Separatism A movement in favour of breaking away, usually of *secession*.

Shuttle-Diplomacy Diplomacy conducted by one mediator 'shuttling' between the various parties to a dispute. A style of mediation favoured by Henry Kissinger, American Secretary of State 1971–7, in the Middle East, southern Africa and elsewhere.

Soviet A council, committee. Often thought of as being revolutionary as a result of the development of soviets in Russia in 1917.

Status quo 'The state in which', i.e. the unchanged position. To restore the *status quo* is to return to the previous state of affairs before change occurred.

Suffrage The right to vote.

Tariffs   Taxes on imports. See *protection*.

Third World   Those parts of the world outside the superpowers (USA and USSR) and the economically developed (i.e. advanced) countries (e.g. Canada, Britain, Czechoslovakia). The phrase is usually taken to include all developing and emergent nations (e.g. Guyana, Nigeria, Indonesia).

Totalitarian   Permitting no rival parties, involving total control by the authorities.

Tribalism   Loyalty to the tribe often in preference to loyalty to the nation.

UDI   Unilateral Declaration of Independence. The declaration of *independence* without the permission of the mother country.

Untouchables   Those outside the main divisions of the Indian caste system. (See *caste*.) Usually associated with menial tasks and under-privilege.

Welfare state   A state with comprehensive social services (e.g. in health) and social security (e.g. insurance against unemployment, old age).

Zionist   A supporter of the colonization of Palestine by the Jews. The World Zionist Organization was founded in 1897.

Bibliography

Further Reading has been suggested at the end of each Unit. The following books will be found useful on the period as a whole.

Purnell's *History of the Twentieth Century* (originally issued in weekly parts).
Keesing's Contemporary Archives.

Documentary Collections
Bettey, J.H.: *English Historical Documents, 1906–39*. Routledge & Kegan Paul (London, 1967).
Breach, R.W.: *Documents and Descriptions, the World since 1914*. Oxford University Press (London, 1966).
Grenville, J.A.S.: *The Major International Treaties 1914–1973*. Methuen (London, 1974).
Lane, P.: *Documents on British Economic and Social History*, Books 2 and 3, 1870–1939 and 1945–1967. Macmillan (London, 1968).
Lane, P.: *Documents and Questions, British History 1914–1980*. John Murray (London, 1981).
Morgan, R.: *The Unsettled Peace*. British Broadcasting Corporation (London, 1974).
Snyder, L.L.: *Fifty Major Documents of the Twentieth Century*. Anvil (London, 1955).
Wallbank, T.W.: *Documents on Modern Africa*. Anvil (London, 1964).
Wroughton, J.: *Documents on British Political History, 1914–1970*. Macmillan (London, 1972).
Wroughton, J. and Cook, D.: *Documents on World History, 1919 to the Present Day*. Macmillan (London, 1976).

Sketch Map Books
Catchpole, B.: *A Map History of the Modern World, 1890 to the Present Day*. Heinemann (London, 1968).
Perry, D.G. and Seaman, R.D.H.: *Sketch Maps in Modern History, 1789–1970*. John Murray (London, 1971).
Richards, I., Goodson, J.B. and Morris, J.A.: *A Sketch Map History of the Great Wars and After*. Harrap (London, 1965).
Sellman, R.R.: *A Student's Atlas of Modern History, 1485–1971*. Arnold (London, 1972).

Collected Biographies
Ayling, S.E.: *Portraits of Power*. Harrap (London, 1965).
Jamieson, A.: *Leaders of the Twentieth Century*. Bell (London, 1970).

Some National and International Histories
Ambrose, S.E.: *Rise to Globalism: American Foreign Policy 1938–80*. Penguin (Harmondsworth, 1980).

Bown, C.: *China 1949–1976*. Heinemann (London, 1980).

Charlesworth, M.: *Revolution in Perspective*. Lowe (London, 1972).

Childs, D.: *Germany since 1918*. Batsford (London, 1980).

Cobban, A.: *A History of Modern France, 1871–1962*. Penguin (Harmondsworth, 1965).

Craig, G.: *Germany 1866–1945*. Oxford University Press (London, 1981).

Dukes, P.: *The Emergence of the Super Powers*. Macmillan (London, 1970).

Fetjö, F.: *A History of the People's Democracies of Eastern Europe*. Penguin (Harmondsworth, 1975).

Garraty, J.A.: *The American Nation since 1865*. Harper & Row (New York, 1979).

Hill, C.P.: *British Economic and Social History, 1700–1975*. Arnold (London, 1977).

Hodder, B.W.: *Africa Today*. Methuen (London, 1978).

Jones, R.B.: *The Making of Contemporary Europe*. Hodder & Stoughton (London, 1980).

Nove, A.: *An Economic History of the USSR*. Penguin (Harmondsworth, 1972).

Rodney, W.: *How Europe Underdeveloped Africa*. Bogle-L'Ouverture Publications (London, 1976).

Rundle, R.N.: *International Affairs, 1890–1939*. Hodder & Stoughton (London, 1979).

Rundle, R.N.: *International Affairs, 1939–1979*. Hodder & Stoughton (London, 1981).

Seaman, L.C.B.: *Post-Victorian Britain*. Methuen (London, 1966).

Spear, P.: *A History of India, Vol. 2*. Penguin (Harmondsworth, 1965).

Walters, F.P.: *History of the League of Nations*. Oxford University Press (London, 1960).

Waterlow, C.: *Superpowers and Victims, Outlook for the World Community*. Prentice-Hall (Englewood Cliffs, New Jersey, 1974).

Watson, J.B.: *Success in British History since 1914*. John Murray (London, 1983).

Watson, J.B.: *Success in European History, 1815–1941*. John Murray (London, 1981).

Watson, J.B.: *The West Indian Heritage*. John Murray (London, 2nd edn. 1982).

Westwood, J.N.: *Endurance and Endeavour, Russian History 1812–1980*. Oxford University Press (London, 1981).

Wiskemann, E.: *Europe of the Dictators, 1919–1945*. Fontana (London, 1970).

Wiskemann, E.: *History of Italy since 1945*. Macmillan (London, 1971).

Reference and Self-Testing

Clarke, E.: *Objective Tests in O Level History, Europe and the Modern World 1870–1970*. John Murray (London, 1975).

Moore, W.G.: *The Penguin Encyclopaedia of Places*. Penguin (Harmondsworth, 1971).

Palmer, A.W.: *A Dictionary of Modern History, 1789–1945*. Penguin (Harmondsworth, 1964).

Palmer, A.W.: *The Penguin Dictionary of Twentieth Century History, 1900–1978*. Penguin (Harmondsworth, 1979).

Rayner, E.G., Stapley, R.F. and Watson, J.B.: *New Objective Tests in Twentieth Century History*. Hodder & Stoughton (London, 1974).

Rayner, E.G., Stapley, R.F. and Watson, J.B.: *Evidence in Question: Twentieth-Century World Affairs*. Oxford University Press (London, 1980).

Watson, J.B., Rayner, E.G. and Stapley, R.F.: *Evidence in Question: European History, 1815–1949*. Oxford University Press (London, 1980).
Williams, N.: *A Chronology of the Modern World*. Penguin (Harmondsworth, 1975).

Index